Best of

The ACT Assessment®

COPYRIGHT © 2002 Peterson's, a division of Thomson Learning, Inc.

ISBN 0-7689-1326-8

Printed in the United States of America

10 9 8 7 6 5 4 3 2 1   03 02

Contents

The Insider's Declaration of Independence

The ACT has become one of the crucial hurdles in the lives of most Americans. Your performance on the ACT plays a major role in determining whether or not you'll be able to attend the college of your choice.

Taking the test is also a major rite of passage for American teenagers. Every year, close to a million students (along with their parents, friends, and families) invest countless days and nights in the anxiety-, hope-, and fear-inducing rituals centered on the exam: cramming beforehand, sweating through the four-hour testing ordeal, nervously comparing notes afterward, and checking the mailbox daily looking for that oh-so-slow-in-coming envelope containing the fateful scores. It all feels nerve-wracking and more than a little unfair.

To survive the process—and to make it work for you—you need help.

YOU CAN'T DEPEND ON THE TEST-MAKERS

Unfortunately, it seems that almost everyone involved in the standardized testing industry (and make no mistake, it *is* an industry—a big one) has some kind of ax to grind.

The test-makers themselves—specifically, the employees of an organization called American College Testing, which writes and administers the test—have a huge vested interest in the survival and credibility of their exam. ACT is a not-for-profit organization. That doesn't make the ACT people immune to the pressures felt by every organization in a competitive industry. The people at ACT make their living by producing the ACT for use by colleges as part of the student admission process. The salaries and offices enjoyed by the executives at ACT are dependent on having college admission officers, and the general public continue to believe that the ACT is a useful, accurate, and basically fair tool for measuring student abilities. If that belief were to vanish, colleges would stop asking students to take the ACT, and the people who work at ACT would have to find new jobs.

Therefore, everything the test-makers say publicly about the ACT must serve the purpose of bolstering public confidence in the accuracy and fairness of the exam. They must be careful to avoid any suggestion that the ACT, or any part of the ACT, can be successfully negotiated by mastering a handful of relatively simple techniques. If students can score higher on the ACT by using a few easy-to-learn "tricks," then the exam begins to appear more like a gimmick than a serious educational tool. From the test-makers' point of view, that would never do.

Thus, the test-makers have a vested interest in stressing how difficult, time-consuming, and intellectually challenging it is to prepare for the ACT. They desperately want to bolster the image of the ACT as an "unbeatable" exam. It's understandable. In their shoes, most of us would feel—and behave—the same way.

Don't misunderstand. We don't consider the ACT people crass, unprofessional, or venal. They are highly competent specialists in test design and administration, and undoubtedly they sincerely believe in the value of their work. But the nature of that work makes it impossible for them to offer you the kind of disinterested, unbiased, and completely honest advice you need about the best and easiest ways to prepare for the ACT.

TEST-PREP SCHOOLS HAVE THEIR OWN AGENDA

What about the other sources of test-taking advice and information? Aren't they immune to these biases?

Yes, but most of them have their own biases. For example, over the last two decades, several nationwide chains of test-preparation schools have sprung up. They offer classroom courses, supplemented with printed and electronic study material—all to help students prepare for the ACT and other exams. Some of these have become big businesses in their own right, owned by or affiliated with major media conglomerates. You can buy books and software bearing the names of these schools and containing some of the techniques and strategies taught in their classroom programs.

Naturally, like any business people, the executives who manage these schools are interested in keeping profits high. To do this, they must funnel as many students as possible through their classroom programs. Given a choice, they'd much rather have you buy one of their ambitious, multi-week courses than a book or even a piece of software. (The profit on a book that costs $15 to $20 can't begin to compare with the profit on an $800 course.) Thus, they must view their books primarily as promotional vehicles for their schools. They hope that some of the students who buy their books will be sufficiently impressed—and perhaps sufficiently intimidated—to sign up for a class.

In their case, the vested interest lies in making the ACT appear scary enough to drive you into an $800 classroom program—and in making the test-taking strategies and techniques you need to learn appear complicated and arcane enough to demand weeks of work with a teacher or tutor.

Again, don't misunderstand. Some test-preparation schools offer fine programs. And some of the books and software they produce can be quite helpful in preparing for an exam. But, just as with the test-makers themselves, we think the inherent self-interest in how the test-prep schools do business inevitably colors the kind of advice they give you and the kinds of preparation they recommend.

OUR PLEDGE

We have no such bias. We have no vested interest in the reputation or image of the ACT, and we are not selling classroom courses for any exam. Our only concern is to offer you the most efficient, accurate, and useful guidance for earning your highest possible score on the ACT. If a particular type of math question can be solved without performing any calculations, or a certain kind of English question can be answered even if you don't recognize some of the words, or some parts of a reading passage can be safely ignored, we're free to say so, thus letting you focus your time and energy in more effective ways—and earn a higher score in the process.

Authorized and controlled by no one, we serve only one master: you, our reader. Thanks for making this book part of your preparation program for the ACT. We hope you'll enjoy using it to boost your test scores and help you gain admission to the college of your dreams.

How This Guide Was Researched and Written

The authors of this book are specialists in test-preparation, teaching, and the writing of educational materials. We've followed the development of the ACT for 20 years, tracking and analyzing the changes in the kinds of questions used and the skills tested. We've also worked with students (and teachers) in various settings, helping them to develop the test-taking abilities and self-confidence needed to do well on the exam.

Based on these years of experience, we've developed a keen awareness of what the ACT is like and what techniques the test-makers use to measure the strengths and weaknesses of individual students. Equally important, we've developed a strong sense as to what kinds of test-taking strategies most students find really beneficial and which ones, frankly, are more complicated or confusing than helpful. This expertise has helped to shape both the content and style of this guide.

All the test-taking advice in this book is based on extensive analysis of actual ACT exams. Take, for example, "The Insider's ACT Word List." Rather than simply create a vocabulary list based on instinct or on the recommendations of high school English teachers, we started by compiling a list of all vocabulary words actually tested on recent ACT exams, including difficult words used in answer choices, vocabulary questions related to reading passages, and sentence completion and analogy questions. We then selected the words that turned up most frequently on the exam, eliminating some that would have made the list only through the quirk of appearing in a particular reading passage and are unlikely to recur any time soon.

To increase the value of the list as a learning tool, we then added not only clear, accurate definitions and sample sentences illustrating the meanings of the words, but also word root explanations—we call them Tracers—that will help you to connect these words to others that have appeared on the ACT. This will make it easy for you to learn two, three, or four new words rather than one at a time. The result, we believe, is the most up-to-date, complete, and truly useful ACT vocabulary list currently available. And we've applied a similar approach to every topic on the exam.

SPECIAL FEATURES

To help you get the most out of this book quickly and easily, the text is enhanced with special sidebars that provide guidance and practical information.

We also recognize you need to have quick information at your fingertips and thus have provided the following helpful sections at the back of the book:

1. The Insider's Word List for the ACT

2. The Insider's Math Review for the ACT

3. The Insider's Writer's Manual for the ACT

4. The Insider's Science Review for the ACT

5. The Insider's Stress-Buster's Guide

6. College Admissions Calendar and Checklist

7. College Application Log

8. Financial Aid Glossary

9. State Student Financial Aid Offices

Part I

First Things First

Chapter 1

An Insider's Look at the ACT

INSTRUCTIONS

The following ACT Diagnostic Exam will provide your first look at the format, contents, and difficulty levels of the ACT. It will also allow you to diagnose your strengths and weaknesses and help you focus on the skills and test areas where you have the greatest opportunity to boost your ACT score.

This exam is about half the length of the real ACT. Take it under true testing conditions. Complete the entire test in a single sitting. Eliminate distractions (TV, music) and clear away notes and reference materials. You may use a calculator only where indicated in the directions for a particular test.

Time each test separately with a stopwatch or kitchen timer, or have someone else time you. If you run out of time before answering all the questions, stop and draw a line under the last question you finished. Then go on to the next test. When you are done, score yourself based only on the questions you finished in the allotted time. Later, for practice purposes, you should answer the questions you were unable to complete in time.

Enter your responses on the answer sheets provided. The answer key, explanatory answers, and information about interpreting your test results appear at the end of the exam.

The ACT Diagnostic Test

Answer Sheet

Section 1

1. Ⓐ Ⓑ Ⓒ Ⓓ	10. Ⓕ Ⓖ Ⓗ Ⓙ	19. Ⓐ Ⓑ Ⓒ Ⓓ	28. Ⓕ Ⓖ Ⓗ Ⓙ
2. Ⓕ Ⓖ Ⓗ Ⓙ	11. Ⓐ Ⓑ Ⓒ Ⓓ	20. Ⓕ Ⓖ Ⓗ Ⓙ	29. Ⓐ Ⓑ Ⓒ Ⓓ
3. Ⓐ Ⓑ Ⓒ Ⓓ	12. Ⓕ Ⓖ Ⓗ Ⓙ	21. Ⓐ Ⓑ Ⓒ Ⓓ	30. Ⓕ Ⓖ Ⓗ Ⓙ
4. Ⓕ Ⓖ Ⓗ Ⓙ	13. Ⓐ Ⓑ Ⓒ Ⓓ	22. Ⓕ Ⓖ Ⓗ Ⓙ	31. Ⓐ Ⓑ Ⓒ Ⓓ
5. Ⓐ Ⓑ Ⓒ Ⓓ	14. Ⓕ Ⓖ Ⓗ Ⓙ	23. Ⓐ Ⓑ Ⓒ Ⓓ	32. Ⓕ Ⓖ Ⓗ Ⓙ
6. Ⓕ Ⓖ Ⓗ Ⓙ	15. Ⓐ Ⓑ Ⓒ Ⓓ	24. Ⓕ Ⓖ Ⓗ Ⓙ	33. Ⓐ Ⓑ Ⓒ Ⓓ
7. Ⓐ Ⓑ Ⓒ Ⓓ	16. Ⓕ Ⓖ Ⓗ Ⓙ	25. Ⓐ Ⓑ Ⓒ Ⓓ	34. Ⓕ Ⓖ Ⓗ Ⓙ
8. Ⓕ Ⓖ Ⓗ Ⓙ	17. Ⓐ Ⓑ Ⓒ Ⓓ	26. Ⓕ Ⓖ Ⓗ Ⓙ	35. Ⓐ Ⓑ Ⓒ Ⓓ
9. Ⓐ Ⓑ Ⓒ Ⓓ	18. Ⓕ Ⓖ Ⓗ Ⓙ	27. Ⓐ Ⓑ Ⓒ Ⓓ	36. Ⓕ Ⓖ Ⓗ Ⓙ

Section 2

1. Ⓐ Ⓑ Ⓒ Ⓓ Ⓔ	9. Ⓐ Ⓑ Ⓒ Ⓓ Ⓔ	17. Ⓐ Ⓑ Ⓒ Ⓓ Ⓔ	24. Ⓕ Ⓖ Ⓗ Ⓙ Ⓚ
2. Ⓕ Ⓖ Ⓗ Ⓙ Ⓚ	10. Ⓕ Ⓖ Ⓗ Ⓙ Ⓚ	18. Ⓕ Ⓖ Ⓗ Ⓙ Ⓚ	25. Ⓐ Ⓑ Ⓒ Ⓓ Ⓔ
3. Ⓐ Ⓑ Ⓒ Ⓓ Ⓔ	11. Ⓐ Ⓑ Ⓒ Ⓓ Ⓔ	19. Ⓐ Ⓑ Ⓒ Ⓓ Ⓔ	26. Ⓕ Ⓖ Ⓗ Ⓙ Ⓚ
4. Ⓕ Ⓖ Ⓗ Ⓙ Ⓚ	12. Ⓕ Ⓖ Ⓗ Ⓙ Ⓚ	20. Ⓕ Ⓖ Ⓗ Ⓙ Ⓚ	27. Ⓐ Ⓑ Ⓒ Ⓓ Ⓔ
5. Ⓐ Ⓑ Ⓒ Ⓓ Ⓔ	13. Ⓐ Ⓑ Ⓒ Ⓓ Ⓔ	21. Ⓐ Ⓑ Ⓒ Ⓓ Ⓔ	28. Ⓕ Ⓖ Ⓗ Ⓙ Ⓚ
6. Ⓕ Ⓖ Ⓗ Ⓙ Ⓚ	14. Ⓕ Ⓖ Ⓗ Ⓙ Ⓚ	22. Ⓕ Ⓖ Ⓗ Ⓙ Ⓚ	29. Ⓐ Ⓑ Ⓒ Ⓓ Ⓔ
7. Ⓐ Ⓑ Ⓒ Ⓓ Ⓔ	15. Ⓐ Ⓑ Ⓒ Ⓓ Ⓔ	23. Ⓐ Ⓑ Ⓒ Ⓓ Ⓔ	30. Ⓕ Ⓖ Ⓗ Ⓙ Ⓚ
8. Ⓕ Ⓖ Ⓗ Ⓙ Ⓚ	16. Ⓕ Ⓖ Ⓗ Ⓙ Ⓚ		

Section 3

1. Ⓐ Ⓑ Ⓒ Ⓓ	6. Ⓕ Ⓖ Ⓗ Ⓙ	11. Ⓐ Ⓑ Ⓒ Ⓓ	16. Ⓕ Ⓖ Ⓗ Ⓙ
2. Ⓕ Ⓖ Ⓗ Ⓙ	7. Ⓐ Ⓑ Ⓒ Ⓓ	12. Ⓕ Ⓖ Ⓗ Ⓙ	17. Ⓐ Ⓑ Ⓒ Ⓓ
3. Ⓐ Ⓑ Ⓒ Ⓓ	8. Ⓕ Ⓖ Ⓗ Ⓙ	13. Ⓐ Ⓑ Ⓒ Ⓓ	18. Ⓕ Ⓖ Ⓗ Ⓙ
4. Ⓕ Ⓖ Ⓗ Ⓙ	9. Ⓐ Ⓑ Ⓒ Ⓓ	14. Ⓕ Ⓖ Ⓗ Ⓙ	19. Ⓐ Ⓑ Ⓒ Ⓓ
5. Ⓐ Ⓑ Ⓒ Ⓓ	10. Ⓕ Ⓖ Ⓗ Ⓙ	15. Ⓐ Ⓑ Ⓒ Ⓓ	20. Ⓕ Ⓖ Ⓗ Ⓙ

Section 4

1. Ⓐ Ⓑ Ⓒ Ⓓ	6. Ⓕ Ⓖ Ⓗ Ⓙ	11. Ⓐ Ⓑ Ⓒ Ⓓ	16. Ⓕ Ⓖ Ⓗ Ⓙ
2. Ⓕ Ⓖ Ⓗ Ⓙ	7. Ⓐ Ⓑ Ⓒ Ⓓ	12. Ⓕ Ⓖ Ⓗ Ⓙ	17. Ⓐ Ⓑ Ⓒ Ⓓ
3. Ⓐ Ⓑ Ⓒ Ⓓ	8. Ⓕ Ⓖ Ⓗ Ⓙ	13. Ⓐ Ⓑ Ⓒ Ⓓ	18. Ⓕ Ⓖ Ⓗ Ⓙ
4. Ⓕ Ⓖ Ⓗ Ⓙ	9. Ⓐ Ⓑ Ⓒ Ⓓ	14. Ⓕ Ⓖ Ⓗ Ⓙ	19. Ⓐ Ⓑ Ⓒ Ⓓ
5. Ⓐ Ⓑ Ⓒ Ⓓ	10. Ⓕ Ⓖ Ⓗ Ⓙ	15. Ⓐ Ⓑ Ⓒ Ⓓ	20. Ⓕ Ⓖ Ⓗ Ⓙ

SECTION 1

ENGLISH

36 Questions

Time—23 Minutes

Directions: This test consists of three passages in which particular words or phrases are underlined and numbered. Alongside the passage, you will see alternative words and phrases that could be substituted for the underlined part. You must select the alternative that expresses the idea most clearly and correctly or that best fits the style and tone of the entire passage. If the original version is best, select "No Change."

The test also includes questions about entire paragraphs and the passage as a whole. These questions are identified by a number in a box.

After you select the correct answer for each question, mark the oval representing the correct answer on your answer sheet.

Passage I

Toni Morrison

[1]

Now that Toni Morrison has, as a writer, clearly
become a star in the world of literature, it has
1
become commonplace for critics to deracialize
her by saying that Morrison is not just a "black
2
woman writer," that she has moved beyond the
limiting confines of race and gender to larger
"universal" issues. And Morrison, a Nobel
3
laureate with six highly acclaimed novels, scoffs
at the idea of choosing between being a writer
and being a black woman writer. 4

[2]

[1] One example is the role of the supernatural in her work: many of her characters treat their dreams as "real," are nonplussed by visitations from dead ancestors, and experience intimate connections generally with beings whose exist-
5
ence isn't empirically verifiable. [2] To call her simply a writer denies the key roles that Morrison's African-American roots and her black female perspective has played in her
6
work. [3] While critics might see Morrisons use
7
of the supernatural as purely a literary device,

GO ON TO THE NEXT PAGE ➤

Morrison herself explains, "That's simply the way the world was for me and the black people I knew." [4] Morrison's work has given voice to this little-remarked facet of African-American culture. [8]

[3]

[9] Morrison contends that the range of emotion and perception she has had access to as a black person and a woman is greater than people who are neither. "My world did not shrink because I was a black female writer. It just got bigger."
10

1. (A) NO CHANGE
   (B) Given the fact that the writer Toni Morrison has risen to the point of being a literary star,
   (C) In view of Toni Morrison's elevation to the heights of stardom among writers of literature,
   (D) With the ascendance of Toni Morrison's literary star,

2. (F) NO CHANGE
   (G) in stating that
   (H) through saying, that
   (J) as they say

3. (A) NO CHANGE
   (B) Yet
   (C) So
   (D) While

4. Which of the following sentences, if added here, would most clearly and succinctly summarize the point of the first paragraph?
   (F) She willingly accepts classification as the latter.
   (G) She wants to be recognized as a writer who is both black and a woman, both of which are important elements in her personality.
   (H) She is not just a writer, she insists; she is very agreeable to being considered as a black woman writer above all.
   (J) She resents the idea that she should write only about black themes and subjects.

5. (A) NO CHANGE
   (B) (Place after *and*)
   (C) (Place after *experience*)
   (D) (Place after *verifiable*)

6. (F) NO CHANGE
   (G) is playing
   (H) have played
   (J) are to play

7. (A) NO CHANGE
   (B) Morrison's use
   (C) Morrisons' use
   (D) Morrison's using

8. Which of the following sequences of sentences will make Paragraph 2 most logical?
   (F) NO CHANGE
   (G) 2, 1, 3, 4
   (H) 3, 1, 4, 2
   (J) 4, 1, 2, 3

9. Which of the following sentences, if inserted at this point, would provide the most effective transition to the third paragraph?
   (A) Since she won the Nobel Prize, sales of Morrison's books have grown enormously.
   (B) Morrison's use of the supernatural in her work does not imply that she believes in the supernatural herself.
   (C) Her work has also affirmed the unique vantage point of the black woman.
   (D) Morrison acknowledges that she has been influenced by great writers of every race.

10. (F) NO CHANGE
    (G) than those for
    (H) than that of
    (J) in comparison to

Passage II

Ratifying the Constitution

[1]

The delegates to the Constitutional Convention were realists, they knew that the greatest
                                    11
battles would follow the convention itself. The delegates had overstepped their bounds. Instead of amending the Articles of Confederation by which the American states have previously been governed, they had
                                    12
proposed an entirely new government. Under these circumstances, the convention was understandably reluctant to submit it's work to the
                                    13
Congress for approval.

[2]

Instead, the delegates decided to pursue what
        14
amounted to a revolutionary course. They declared that ratification of the new Constitution by nine states would be all that would be
                                    15
necessary to establish the new government. In
        15
other words, the Constitution was directly being
                                    16
submitted to the people. [17]

[3]

The leaders of the convention shrewdly wished to bypass the state legislatures, which were
                                    18
attached to states' rights and which required in most cases the agreement of two houses. For speedy ratification of the Constitution, the single-chambered, specially elected state ratifying conventions offered the greatest promise of agreement.

[4]

[19] The Federalists, as the supporters of the Constitution were called, had one solid advantage: they came with a concrete proposal.

GO ON TO THE NEXT PAGE

Unlike their opponents, the Antifederalists. Since
_____
                    20
the Antifederalists were opposing something with

nothing, their objections, though, sincere were
            _____
                              21
basically negative. They stood for a policy of

drift while the Federalists were providing clear

leadership.

[5]

Nonetheless, although the Antifederalists claimed
_____
    22
to be the democratic group, their opposition to

the Constitution did not necessarily spring from

a more democratic view of government. Many of

the Antifederalists were as distrustful of the

common people as their opponents. In New

York, for example, Governor George Clinton

criticized the people for their fickleness and

their tendency to "vibrate from one extreme to

another." Elbridge Gerry, who refused
                         _____
                               23
to sign the Constitution, he asserted that "the
_____
          23
evils we experience flow from the excess of

democracy," and John F. Mercer of Maryland

professed little faith in his neighbors as voters

when he said that "the people cannot know and

judge the character of candidates." 24

11. (A) NO CHANGE
    (B) realists. Knowing
    (C) realists. They knew
    (D) realists; knowing

12. (F) NO CHANGE
    (G) were being governed previously
    (H) previously were governed
    (J) had previously been governed

13. (A) NO CHANGE
    (B) to submit its work
    (C) for submitting it's work
    (D) about submitting its work

14. (F) NO CHANGE
    (G) (Do NOT begin new paragraph)
         Furthermore,
    (H) (Begin new paragraph) However,
    (J) (Begin new paragraph) Neverthe-
         less,

15. (A) NO CHANGE
    (B) would suffice
    (C) was required
    (D) would do the trick

16. (F) NO CHANGE
    (G) (Place after *submitted*)
    (H) (Place after *people*)
    (J) OMIT the underlined portion

17. At this point, the writer is considering the addition of the following sentence:

    > Not even the Congress, which had called the convention, would be asked to approve its work.

    Would this be a logical and relevant addition to the essay?

    (A) Yes, because it suggests why many in Congress opposed the adoption of the new Constitution.
    (B) Yes, because it emphasizes the revolutionary nature of the plan pursued by the delegates.
    (C) No, because it refers to the original establishment of the convention, which predates the events discussed in the essay.
    (D) No, because the idea it states is obvious from the rest of the paragraph.

18. (F) NO CHANGE
    (G) legislatures, that were
    (H) legislatures. Which were
    (J) legislatures

19. Which of the following sentences would provide the best transition to the topic of Paragraph 4?

    (A) The state legislators were understandably angered.
    (B) Many Americans were reluctant to approve the new Constitution.
    (C) The results were dramatic.
    (D) Battle lines were quickly drawn.

20. (F) NO CHANGE
    (G) Their opponents, the Antifederalists, came with none.
    (H) The Antifederalists, who opposed them, did not have such a proposal to offer.
    (J) Not so their opponents—the Antifederalists.

21. (A) NO CHANGE
    (B) objections—though, sincere, were
    (C) objections, though sincere, were
    (D) objections; though sincere, were

22. (F) NO CHANGE
    (G) However,
    (H) Furthermore,
    (J) Yet

23. (A) NO CHANGE
    (B) who refused to sign the Constitution,
    (C) refusing to sign the Constitution, he
    (D) while he refused to sign the Constitution,

24. The writer wants to conclude the essay with a sentence that suggests the outcome of the battle over ratifying the Constitution in a way that is logically connected to Paragraph 5. Which of the alternatives best accomplishes this purpose?

    (F) The ultimate ratification of the Constitution demonstrated that the Federalists' strategy of bypassing the state legislatures was a wise one.
    (G) Many of the Antifederalists actually advocated a less democratic and more autocratic form of government.
    (H) However, the Federalists themselves professed a strictly limited faith in the power of the average citizen to govern wisely.
    (J) In the end, the Antifederalists' lack of faith in the people contributed significantly to the Federalists' victory.

GO ON TO THE NEXT PAGE

Passage III

Reflections on My Disability

[1]

I enjoyed the use of my legs for 44 years until a simple misstep on a hiking trail rendered them useless, paralyzed. Now, years after the initial shock, I can reflect more calmly on my fate, and the thing it is that surprises me is that my own
<u>25</u>
reactions to becoming disabled have been easier to live with <u>and in adaptation to</u> than
<u>26</u>
able-bodied society's responses.

[2]

My responses are what I think of as "pure": grief, rage, self-pity, depression, pride, anger. 27 Yet society's responses to me and to my disabled peers are less <u>direct; akin</u> to the averted gaze
<u>28</u>
<u>and sidelong look</u> with which most people look
<u>29</u>
not at us, but somewhere to the left of us. In nine encounters out of ten, an able-bodied person will be responding not to me, the reality of who I am and what I am, but to <u>one's</u> own supreme dis-
<u>30</u>
comfort with "the handicapped." In a culture which <u>glorifies</u> the body beautiful, a disabled per-
<u>31</u>
son is overturning an American ideal.

[3]

[1] Today, <u>like the normal cannot get over their</u>
<u>32</u>
own guilt at being normal, we have the optimistic terms "differently abled" or "physically challenged"—labels so vague as to describe anyone and no one. [2] One way that normal society manages <u>its</u> own discomfort
<u>33</u>
with the abnormal is to classify us. [3] First <u>their</u> was the word "cripple": a bald statement
<u>34</u>
of the truth of our situation, yet one suggestive of deviance. [4] Then came the less loaded terms, which are still, however, euphemisms: "handicapped" and "disabled." 35

25. (A) NO CHANGE
    (B) the thing that surprises
    (C) I find that the thing that surprises
    (D) what surprises

26. (F) NO CHANGE
    (G) and adapt to
    (H) or adopt
    (J) as well as adapt

27. At this point, the writer is considering the addition of the following sentence:

> In recent years, researchers have discovered that many of these psychological afflictions have chemical causes.

Would this be a logical and relevant addition to the essay?

(A) Yes, because it shows that the writer has done research into his own mental state.

(B) Yes, because the essay focuses largely on the relationship between the body and the mind.

(C) No, because the writer's disability is not a chemical condition.

(D) No, because it is unrelated to the issue of how society treats the disabled.

28. (F) NO CHANGE
    (G) direct, akin
    (H) direct, they are akin
    (J) direct. Akin

29. (A) NO CHANGE
    (B) or the sidelong look
    (C) and look from sidelong
    (D) OMIT the underlined portion.

30. (F) NO CHANGE
    (G) their
    (H) your
    (J) his

31. (A) NO CHANGE
    (B) of glorifying
    (C) that glorify
    (D) for glorification of

32. (F) NO CHANGE
    (G) as if
    (H) like as
    (J) being that

33. (A) NO CHANGE
    (B) our
    (C) it's
    (D) their

34. (F) NO CHANGE
    (G) they're
    (H) it
    (J) there

35. For the sake of logic and coherence, Sentence 1 should be placed:

(A) where it is now.
(B) after sentence 2.
(C) after sentence 3.
(D) after sentence 4.

Item 36 poses a question about the essay as a whole.

36. The writer wishes to include the following sentence in the essay:

A disabled person is also a constant reminder of a terrible possibility: "This could happen to me."

That sentence will fit most smoothly and logically into Paragraph:

(F) 1, after the last sentence.
(G) 2, after the second sentence.
(H) 2, after the last sentence.
(J) 3, after the last sentence.

STOP   End of Section 1. If you have any time left, go over your work in this section only. Do not work in any other section of the test.

SECTION 2: MATHEMATICS

30 Questions

Time—30 Minutes

> **Directions:** Solve each problem below and mark the oval representing the correct answer on your answer sheet.
>
> Be careful not to spend too much time on any one question. Instead, solve as many questions as possible, and then use any remaining time to return to those questions you were unable to answer at first.
>
> You may use a calculator on any problem in this test; however, not every problem requires the use of a calculator.
>
> Diagrams that accompany problems may or may not be drawn to scale. Unless otherwise indicated, you may assume that all figures shown lie in a plane and that lines that appear straight are straight.

1. If the fraction $\dfrac{60}{N}$ has been simplified to simplest form, which of the following numbers can be a factor of N?

   (A) 25
   (B) 27
   (C) 49
   (D) 110
   (E) 213

2. The original price of a computer was $1,200. What was the price of the computer after two 10% markdowns?

   (F) $960
   (G) $972
   (H) $980
   (J) $1,000
   (K) $1,072

3. Margaret has an average of 88 on her first four calculus exams. To get an A, she must have a 90 average. What grade must she get on the next exam to bring her average to 90?

   (A) 90
   (B) 92
   (C) 94
   (D) 96
   (E) 98

4. If $3y - 6 = 2 - y$, then the value of $y^2 + 2y = ?$

   (F) 0
   (G) 2
   (H) 4
   (J) 6
   (K) 8

5. The ratio of passing to failing students in a class is 5:2. Which of the following could be the number of students in the class?

    (A) 12
    (B) 15
    (C) 21
    (D) 30
    (E) 34

6. Three consecutive integers are written in increasing order. If the sum of the first and second and twice the third is 93, what is the second number?

    (F) 22
    (G) 23
    (H) 24
    (J) 34
    (K) 37

7. Arlene has a block of wood in the form of a rectangular solid 14 inches long with a square base, which is 6" on a side. A right circular cylinder is drilled out of the block, as shown below. What is the volume of the wood remaining, to the nearest cubic inch?

    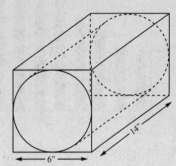

    (A) 54
    (B) 108
    (C) 396
    (D) 485
    (E) 495

8. In a group of 20 singers and 40 dancers, 20% of the singers are under 25 years old and 40% of the entire group are under 25 years old. What percent of the dancers are under 25 years old?

    (F) 20%
    (G) 30%
    (H) 40%
    (J) 50%
    (K) 60%

Questions 9 and 10 refer to the graphs below.

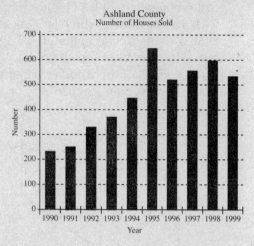

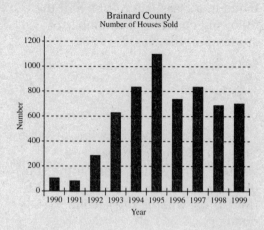

9. What was the total number of houses sold in the two counties combined in 1994?

    (A) 820
    (B) 1,010
    (C) 1,070
    (D) 1,280
    (E) 1,720

10. What was the approximate percent decrease in number of houses sold in Brainard County from 1995 to 1996?

    (F) 10%
    (G) 15%
    (H) 20%
    (J) 25%
    (K) 35%

11. The cost of 4 rolls, 6 muffins, and 3 loaves of bread is $9.10. The cost of 2 rolls, 3 muffins, and a loaf of bread is $3.90. What is the cost of a loaf of bread?

    (A) $1.05
    (B) $1.10
    (C) $1.20
    (D) $1.25
    (E) $1.30

12. In the diagram shown below, $AB = 3$, $AD = 4$, and $BC = 12$. What is the perimeter of the quadrilateral $ABCD$?

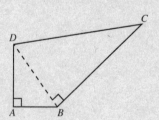

    (F) 32
    (G) 30
    (H) 28
    (J) 26
    (K) 24

13. If x and y are positive integers, and $2x + y = 7$, which of the following is the value of $4x^2 - y^2$?

    (A) 0
    (B) 6
    (C) 14
    (D) 15
    (E) 35

14. The point $(a,5)$ lies on a line of slope $\frac{1}{3}$ that passes through $(2,-3)$. What is the value of a?

    (F) -26
    (G) -3
    (H) 3
    (J) 26
    (K) 35

15. If a is chosen from $A = \{-1,-6,3\}$ and b is chosen from $B = \{-4,4,5\}$, then what is the largest possible value of $\frac{a}{b}$?

    (A) 0.25
    (B) 0.75
    (C) 1.5
    (D) 1.6
    (E) 1.75

16. If five more than twice a number n is 17, then 2 less than $\frac{1}{2}n = ?$

    (F) -2
    (G) -1
    (H) 0
    (J) 1
    (K) 2

17. Given that ℓ_1 is parallel to ℓ_2 in the figure below, then the value of $x + y + z = ?$

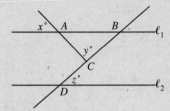

    (A) 90
    (B) 120
    (C) 180
    (D) 210
    (E) 270

18. One side of a rectangle with an area of 18 square inches is the diameter of a circle. The opposite side is tangent to the circle. What is the circumference of the circle?

    (F) 2π
    (G) 6π
    (H) 9π
    (J) 12π
    (K) 18π

19. What is the difference in sales price between a coat that cost $200 wholesale sold at 40% markup and a coat listed at $300 on sale for 10% off?

    (A) $0
    (B) $10
    (C) $20
    (D) $30
    (E) $40

GO ON TO THE NEXT PAGE

20. $\dfrac{n}{6} - \dfrac{6}{n} = ?$

(F) $\dfrac{(n-6)}{(6-n)}$

(G) $\dfrac{(n-6)(n+6)}{6n}$

(H) $\dfrac{(n-6)}{6n}$

(J) $\dfrac{(n^2-6)}{n}$

(K) $\dfrac{(n-36)}{6n}$

21. If $x = \log 2$, $y = \log 3$, and $z = \log 5$, then $\log \dfrac{5}{12} = ?$

(A) $z - x - 2y$
(B) $z + x - 2y$
(C) $z + x + 2y$

(D) $\dfrac{z}{2xy}$

(E) $z - 2x - y$

22. Simplified to simplest form, $\dfrac{3x^2y^3 + 6xy^4}{(6x^2y + 12xy^2)} = ?$

(F) $\dfrac{y^2}{2x}$

(G) $\dfrac{y^2}{2}$

(H) $\dfrac{xy^2}{(2x^2y + 4xy^2)}$

(J) $\dfrac{(x^2 + y^4)}{18x^2y^2}$

(K) $\dfrac{3x^2y^4}{(2x^2y + 4xy^2)}$

23. One x-intercept for the parabola $y = x^2 + 4x - 13$ is in which of the following intervals?

(A)   [0,1]
(B)   [1,2]
(C)   [2,3]
(D)   [3,4]
(E)   [4,5]

24. In an arithmetic progression, the third term is 13 and the tenth term is 55. What is the first term?

(F)   1
(G)   3
(H)   5
(J)   7
(K)   9

25. If $f(x) = \dfrac{x}{(2+x)}$ and $g(x) = \dfrac{1}{x}$, then $f(g(x)) = ?$

(A) $\dfrac{(x+2)}{x}$

(B) $2x + 1$

(C) $\dfrac{1}{(2x+1)}$

(D) $\dfrac{2}{(1+x)}$

(E) $\dfrac{1}{(2+x)}$

26. Given $A = \begin{bmatrix} 1 & 4 \\ -1 & 3 \end{bmatrix}$ and

$B = \begin{bmatrix} -1 & 2 \\ 1 & 0 \end{bmatrix}$, then $2A - B = ?$

(F) $\begin{bmatrix} 3 & -3 \\ 2 & 6 \end{bmatrix}$

(G) $\begin{bmatrix} 3 & 6 \\ 3 & 6 \end{bmatrix}$

(H) $\begin{bmatrix} -3 & 0 \\ 3 & 6 \end{bmatrix}$

(J) $\begin{bmatrix} 3 & 6 \\ -3 & -6 \end{bmatrix}$

(K) $\begin{bmatrix} 3 & 6 \\ -3 & 6 \end{bmatrix}$

27. Which of the following expressions is the equation of a line parallel to $y = 3x - 2$ that has x-intercept -4?

(A) $y = 3x - 4$
(B) $y = 3x - 12$
(C) $y = -4x - 2$
(D) $y = 3x + 12$
(E) $y = -2x + 4$

28. An isosceles triangle has two legs that are 3 feet long and the angle between them is 32°. What is the length of the third side?

(F) $3 \cos 32°$
(G) $3 \sin 32°$
(H) $3 \sin 16°$
(J) $6 \tan 16°$
(K) $6 \sin 16°$

29. If $12^{2x} = 4$, then $x = ?$

(A) $\dfrac{\log 4}{2\log 12}$

(B) $\dfrac{(\log 4 = \log 12)}{2}$

(C) $\dfrac{1}{2} \log \dfrac{1}{3}$

(D) $\dfrac{2}{\log 12}$

(E) $\log \dfrac{1}{6}$

30. The parabola $y = x^2 - 5$ and the circle $x^2 + y^2 = 25$ intersect in how many points?

(F) 0
(G) 1
(H) 2
(J) 3
(K) 4

STOP   End of Section 2. If you have any time left, go over your work in this section only. Do not work in any other section of the test.

SECTION 3: READING

20 Questions

Time—18 Minutes

> **Directions:** This test consists of two passages, each followed by several questions. Read each passage, select the correct answer for each question, and mark the oval representing the correct answer on your answer sheet.

Passage I—Social Science

Line In the summer of 1904, the great Russian Empire was, unlike most of the countries of Europe by that time, still under the control of one man, the 36-year-old Tsar
(5) Nicholas II, who had ruled since the death of his father, Alexander III, ten years before. By many accounts a kind man with a genuine love for his country, Nicholas was nevertheless beginning to
(10) be pictured as a ruthless dictator by those who wished to see the empire democratized, and the complaints of his people were very much in the Tsar's thoughts that summer. One event,
(15) however, took Nicholas' mind away from his political difficulties. On August 12, he wrote in his diary "A great, never-to-be-forgotten day when the mercy of God has visited us so clearly. Alix gave birth to a
(20) son at one o'clock. The child has been called Alexis."

Married to Nicholas since 1894, the former Princess Alix of Hesse-Darmstadt and one of Queen Victoria's numerous
(25) grandchildren, the Tsarina (called Alexandra after her marriage), had given birth to four daughters—Olga, Tatiana, Marie and Anastasia—between 1897 and 1901. But the laws of succession decreed
(30) that only a male could succeed the Tsar, so the birth of Alexis, which assured the continuation of the three hundred year old Romanov dynasty, was a cause of great rejoicing for his parents as well as
(35) throughout the vast empire.

But within a few months it became clear that the apparently healthy child was not healthy at all—he had hemophilia, a disease he had inherited

(40) through his mother from his great grandmother, Queen Victoria, many of whose other descendants also had the disease. Hemophilia is a blood disorder in which the blood not does clot prop-
(45) erly. A small, external scratch or cut presents no real problem as the bleeding can be stopped relatively quickly, but bumps and bruises, such as children are prone to, create internal bleeding. This
(50) blood, in turn, gathers in knee and elbow joints, causing excruciating pain and, sometimes, permanent injury. Once Alexis' diagnosis was confirmed, however, it was decided that, for the good of
(55) the dynasty and the country, the boy's illness would remain a family secret. That decision may have changed history.

Despite his joy at the birth of an heir, Nicholas' political problems continued.
(60) Just a few months later, in January, 1905, government troops fired on a crowd of unarmed petitioners at the Winter Palace in St. Petersburg, killing over one hundred and wounding hundreds more. This
(65) in turn, set off country-wide demonstrations against the government. Despite halfhearted efforts on Nicholas' part to satisfy the dissidents, notably the October Manifesto of 1905, which
(70) converted Russia into a constitutional monarchy with an elected parliament called the *Duma*, these problems would plague him for another dozen years.

In the meantime, in her anguish over
(75) her son's illness, Alexandra turned to religion, and to a newcomer to the Russian court, for help. Grigory Rasputin, born in Siberia in 1871, was an Eastern Orthodox mystic who had been intro-

(80) duced to the court by one of the Tsar's numerous relatives. Although it was well known that he led a dissolute life, he had mesmerizing eyes that captivated many of the Tsar's courtiers. More important, (85) he was able—although to this day no one knows how—to calm the young Alexis when he had hurt himself and, apparently, to ease his pain considerably. For the Tsarovich's distraught mother, this (90) was sufficient, and for the rest of their lives Alexandra heeded Rasputin's advice, both personal and, more important, political. For nearly a decade after Alexis' birth, the political situation in (95) Russia grew worse. Even the great patriotic fervor which greeted the empire's entry into the First World War took a downturn when the nation's early victories gave way to progressively (100) greater defeats and the loss of hundreds of thousands of Russian lives. In an effort to stem the tide, Nicholas decided it was his duty to lead the army himself, and in 1915 left St. Petersburg and took up (105) residence at Army Headquarters, in effect leaving Alexandra to rule the country with Grigory Rasputin at her side.

The increasingly dire situation at the (110) front resulted in a repudiation of the war by many in Russia, which led to even more demonstrations at home by dissidents, most importantly the Bolsheviks, who wanted not a constitutional (115) monarchy but, rather, a fully democratic state answering only to the people. The Tsar and Tsarina came increasingly under personal attack, as did Rasputin. The Russian people, not knowing of the (120) Tsarovich's hemophilia, could not understand why the mystic seemed to have so much power over the imperial family, and both he and Alexandra were much reviled in the press. Rasputin had (125) also made important enemies at court. On December 16, 1916, he was assassinated by three courtiers.

Three months later, on March 15, 1917, the Tsar abdicated his throne, and (130) on November 7th the Bolshevik Revolution brought the communists to power. Less than a year later, on July 29, 1918, Nicholas and his family, including Alexis, who would have been the next Tsar, were (135) executed on orders of Bolshevik authorities at Ekaterinburg in the Ural Mountains, ending the three-hundred-year-old Romanov dynasty.

1. The passage implies that those who in 1904 regarded Nicholas II as a "ruthless dictator" (line 10) primarily objected to:
   (A) the excessive influence of Rasputin over court affairs.
   (B) his refusal to consider establishment of an elected parliament for Russia.
   (C) his maintenance of an autocratic form of government in Russia.
   (D) the failure of the Tsar and his wife to produce a male heir to the throne.

2. According to the passage, political power could not devolve onto the daughters of the Tsar and Tsarina because of:
   (F) legal restrictions.
   (G) Nicholas's insistence on a male heir.
   (H) popular sentiment.
   (J) custom and tradition.

GO ON TO THE NEXT PAGE

3. The passage quoted by the author from Nicholas' diary (lines 17–21) serves to illustrate all of the following EXCEPT:

    (A) the depth of his desire for a son.
    (B) the sincerity of his religious faith.
    (C) his hope that the birth of Alexis might save the Romanov dynasty.
    (D) his preoccupation with his people's demands for democratization.

4. The author implies that the decision of the Romanovs not to disclose the fact that Alexis suffered from hemophilia:

    (F) delayed but could not prevent the collapse of the Russian monarchy.
    (G) contributed to the ultimate downfall of the Romanov dynasty.
    (H) strengthened the public revulsion against the monarchy when the truth was revealed.
    (J) was a significant motivating factor in the Bolsheviks' decision to execute the Tsar and his family.

5. The author implies that the October Manifesto of 1905 failed to placate those who advocated reform of the Russian government because it was:

    (A) unaccompanied by religious, economic, and social changes.
    (B) undermined by the continuing dictatorial behavior of Nicholas.
    (C) unable to prevent the onset of the First World War.
    (D) only a partial step toward the establishment of full democracy.

6. The author implies that the decision of Nicholas to assume personal leadership of the Russian army stemmed mainly from his:

    (F) sense of responsibility.
    (G) political desperation.
    (H) inability to trust other leaders.
    (J) fear of popular revolt.

7. The "downturn" mentioned in line 98 refers most directly to:

    (A) personal attacks on the Tsar and Tsarina in the Russian press.
    (B) national disaffection with Russia's undemocratic form of government.
    (C) the Tsar's distraction from civic duties by his son's illness.
    (D) public dismay over Russian military failures.

8. The passage implies that Nicholas' attempts to exercise military leadership were basically:

    (F) symbolic.
    (G) unsuccessful.
    (H) unpopular.
    (J) halfhearted.

9. The author implies that, if the Russian people had known of Rasputin's ability to ease the symptoms of the Tsarovich, they would have:

    (A) insisted that the Romanov dynasty abdicate in favor of a more democratic regime.
    (B) sympathized with the motives of the Tsarina in relying on Rasputin.
    (C) renewed their support of the Tsar and the war effort he was leading.
    (D) been won over to the religious and mystical views Rasputin advocated.

10. The passage suggests that the murder of Rasputin was motivated primarily by:

(F) the growing demand among the Russian populace for true democracy.

(G) hostility in the popular press against both Rasputin and the imperial couple.

(H) intrigues and jealousies among the Tsar's retinue.

(J) increasing disaffection with the war among many Russians.

Passage II—Natural Science

Line For years, the contents of a child's sandbox have confounded some of the nation's top physicists. Sand and other granular materials such as powders,
(5) seeds, nuts, soil, and detergent, behave in ways that seem to undermine natural laws and cost industries ranging from pharmaceuticals to agribusiness and mining billions of dollars.
(10) Just shaking a can of mixed nuts can show you how problematic granular material can be. The nuts don't "mix"; they "unmix" and sort themselves out, with the larger Brazil nuts on top and the
(15) smaller peanuts on the bottom. In this activity and others, granular matter's behavior apparently goes counter to the second law of thermodynamics, which states that entropy, or disorder, tends to
(20) increase in any natural system.
Mimicking the mixed-nut conundrum with a jar containing many small beads and one large bead, one group of physicists claimed that vibrations causing the
(25) beads to percolate open up small gaps rather than larger ones. Thus, when a Brazil nut becomes slightly airborne, the peanuts rush in underneath and gradually nudge it to the top. Another group of
(30) physicists color-coded layers of beads to track their circulation in the container and achieved a different result. Vibrations, they found, drive the beads in circles up the center and down the sides

(35) of the container. Yet downward currents, similar to convection currents in air or water, are too narrow to accommodate the larger bead, stranding it on top.
One industrial engineer who has
(40) studied the problem says that both the "percolation" and "convection current" theories can be right, depending upon the material, and that percolation is the major factor with nuts. Given the inabil-
(45) ity of scientists to come up with a single equation explaining unmixing, you can see why industrial engineers who must manage granular materials go a little, well, "nuts." Take pharmaceuticals, for
(50) instance. There may be six types of powders with different-sized grains in a single medicine tablet. Mixing them at some speeds might sort them, while mixing at other speeds will make them
(55) thoroughly amalgamated. One aspirin company still relies on an experienced employee wearing a latex glove who pinches some powder in the giant mixing drum to see if it "feels right."
(60) Granular material at rest can be equally frustrating to physicists and engineers. Take a tall cylinder of sand. Unlike a liquid, in which pressure exerted at the bottom increases in direct propor-
(65) tion to the liquid's height, pressure at the base of the sand cylinder doesn't increase indefinitely. Instead it reaches a maximum value and stays there. This quality allows sand to trickle at a nearly
(70) constant rate through the narrow opening separating the two glass bulbs of an hourglass, thus measuring the passage of time.
Physicists have also found that forces
(75) are not distributed evenly throughout granular material. It is this characteristic that may account for the frequent rupturing of silos in which grain is stored. In a silo, for instance, the col-
(80) umn's weight is carried from grain to grain along jagged chains. As a result, the container's walls carry more of the weight than its base, and the force is significantly larger at some points of

GO ON TO THE NEXT PAGE

(85)   contact than at others. Coming up with equations to explain, much less, predict, the distribution of these force chains is extremely difficult. Again, using beads, physicists developed a simple theoretical

(90)   model in which they assume that a given bead transmits the load it bears un-equally and randomly onto the three beads on which it rests. While the model agrees well with experimental results, it

(95)   doesn't take into account all of the mechanisms of force transmission between grains of sand or wheat.

In the struggle to understand granular materials, sand-studying physicists have

(100)   at least one thing in their favor. Unlike particle physicists who must secure billions of dollars in government funding for the building of supercolliders in which to accelerate and view infinitesi-

(105)   mal particles, they can conduct experiments using such low-cost, low-tech materials such as sand, beads, marbles, and seeds. It is hoped that more low-tech experiments and computer simulations

(110)   will lead to equations that explain the unwieldy stuff and reduce some of the wastage, guesswork, and accidents that occur in the various industries that handle it.

11. Which of the following titles most accurately describes the above passage?

(A)   New Theories About the Physical Properties of Sand

(B)   The Behavior of Granular Matter in Motion and at Rest

(C)   Theoretical and Practical Problems in Handling Granular Matter

(D)   How Physicists Are Helping to Solve Industrial Riddles

12. The passage suggests that a can of mixed nuts seems to disobey the second law of thermodynamics because it:

(F)   fails to mix when shaken.

(G)   becomes increasingly disordered over time.

(H)   sorts smaller nuts to the bottom rather than the top of the can.

(J)   does not readily separate into different kinds of nuts.

13. The percolation theory of unmixing is best illustrated by which of the following examples?

(A)   Larger rocks rising to the surface in a garden after a period of frost

(B)   Contents settling in a bag of potato chips so that the package appears less full after handling

(C)   Large nuts blocking the upward movement of small nuts in a shaken container

(D)   A can of multi-sized beads sorting into layers of large and small beads upon shaking

14. In saying that the percolation and convection current theories may both be right (lines 40–42), the industrial engineer means that:

(F) both theories are still unproven, since they have not been tested on a variety of material.

(G) though the theories have different names, they describe the same physical mechanisms.

(H) the mechanism causing unmixing varies depending upon the type of granular material.

(J) both mechanisms are involved in all instances of unmixing.

15. As it is used in line 21, the word "conundrum" most nearly means:

(A) hypothesis

(B) enigma

(C) paradox

(D) phenomenon

16. Which of the following appears to be the best solution for combatting the "unmixing" problem faced by pharmaceutical manufacturers which must prepare large quantities of powders?

(F) To craft powders so that all the grains have similar sizes and shapes

(G) To craft powders in which every grain weighs the same amount

(H) To mix all the powders together at the same speed

(J) To hire only engineers who have years of experience in powder mixing

17. The passage implies that, if the top bulb of an hourglass were filled with water instead of sand, the pressure pushing the water through the opening would:

(A) increase as water trickles through the opening.

(B) decrease as water trickles through the opening.

(C) remain constant as water trickles through the opening.

(D) make the water trickle down in drops rather than a stream.

18. According to the passage, why do silos in which grain is stored frequently rupture?

(F) Because the walls of a silo are often less strong than its base

(G) Because the smaller particles of grain tend to settle toward the bottom of the silo

(H) Because the weight of the grain is unequally and unpredictably distributed

(J) Because the pressure at the base of the silo is the same as the pressure at the top

GO ON TO THE NEXT PAGE

19. According to the passage, physicists studying granular material:

    (A) are grappling with issues that are less complicated than those confronting particle physicists.

    (B) are fortunate in having available a selection of relatively easy means of crafting experiments.

    (C) are less likely to receive government funding than are particle physicists.

    (D) know less about grains of sand than particle physicists know about infinitesimal forms of matter.

20. According to the passage, scientists are studying granular matter in the hope of improving industrial handling of:

    (I)   medicines
    (II)   grain
    (III) beads
    (IV)   nuts

    (F) I and II only
    (G) I, II, and IV only
    (H) II and III only
    (J) III and IV only

STOP   End of section 3. If you hve any time left, go over your work in this section only. Do not work in any other section of the test.

SECTION 4: SCIENCE REASONING

20 Questions

Time—18 Minutes

Directions: This test consists of three passages, each followed by several questions. Read each passage, select the correct answer for each question, and mark the oval representing the correct answer on your answer sheet. You may NOT use a calculator on this test.

Passage I

Researchers are interested in optimizing methods for cooling electronic components such as *semiconductors* (a type of computer chip). Semiconductors generate heat as they operate, but excess levels of heat cause such components to malfunction or may shorten their lifespan. However, cold objects cannot be applied directly to these components, because they are too sensitive.

One cooling method that has been used is the placement of foam material between the semiconductors and a cooling plate. Foam acts as a *heat conductor*. Heat from the computer chip flows through the foam, towards the cooling plate. As heat is conducted through the foam in this manner, the semiconductor is cooled, and the temperature difference between the cooling plate and the semiconductor becomes smaller. Various experiments were performed to determine more about the heat conduction properties of foam.

Experiment 1

Foam pads that all had a surface area of 1 inch^2 but were of various thicknesses were inserted between a semiconductor and a cooling plate. The temperature of the cooling plate was kept constant. The semiconductor was generating 1 watt of heat. The researchers measured the difference in temperature between the semiconductor and the cooling plate. Results appear in Table 1.1.

Table 1.1

Trial #	Thickness of Foam (mm)	Measured Temperature Difference Between Computer Chip and Plate (°C)
1	1	2.2
2	2	3.9
3	4	7.2
4	6	11.0
5	8	14.2
6	10	16.3

Experiment 2

Researchers placed a foam pad between a semiconductor and a cooling plate, but in this experiment the thickness of the pad was 6 mm in all cases, while the surface area of the pad varied. The heat generated by the semiconductor remained at 1 watt. Results appear in Table 1.2.

Table 1.2

Trial #	Foam Surface Area (inches^2)	Measured Temperature Difference Between Computer Chip and Plate (°C)
1	0.2	17.4
2	0.4	13.3
3	0.6	11.0
4	0.8	8.3
5	1.0	7.1
6	1.5	5.3

GO ON TO THE NEXT PAGE

Experiment 3

The researchers were interested in seeing the performance of the foam cooling system when the heat dissipated (released) by the semiconductor was varied. To vary the heat dissipation, they varied the wattage generated by the semiconductors. A foam pad that had a surface area of 1 inch^2 and a thickness of 6 mm was used in all of the tests. The results appear in Table 1.3.

Table 1.3

Trial #	Heat Dissipation (watts)	Measured Temperature Difference Between Computer Chip and Plate (°C)
1	.25	4.2
2	.5	6.3
3	1.0	11.3
4	2.0	17.6
5	3.0	22.5
6	5.0	24.0

1. Which of the following are differences between Experiments 1 and 3?

   (A) Heat was dissipated in Experiment 3, but not in Experiment 1.

   (B) The semiconductor used in Experiment 3 was generating heat, while the semiconductor used in Experiment 1 remained cool.

   (C) Experiment 1 was designed to measure conduction properties, while Experiment 3 was designed to measure heat dissipation.

   (D) Heat dissipation was varied in Experiment 3, while the thickness of the foam pad was varied in Experiment 1.

2. Which of the following pairs of trials demonstrate inconsistencies in the experimental data?

   (F) Experiment 1, trial 1 and Experiment 2, trial 5

   (G) Experiment 1, trial 1 and Experiment 3, trial 3

   (H) Experiment 2, trial 5 and Experiment 3, trial 3

   (J) Experiment 1, trial 3 and Experiment 2, trial 5

3. Which of the following statements is supported by the data from Experiments 1 and 2?

   (A) Thicker foam pads are better heat conductors.

   (B) Heat conduction is favored by a thin foam pad with a large surface area.

   (C) Heat dissipation was greatest when the surface area of the foam was 0.2 inches^2.

   (D) Using a piece of foam with a surface area of 0.8 inch^2 and a thickness of 0.6 mm appears to be equivalent to using a piece with a surface area of 1 inch^2 and a thickness of 4 mm.

4. Under which of the following conditions would you predict the lowest temperature difference between the semiconductor and the cooling plate?

(F) A foam pad 1 mm thick and 1.5 inches^2 is used to cool a conductor producing 0.25 watts.

(G) A foam pad 1 mm thick and 1.0 inch^2 surface area is used to cool a semiconductor producing 1 watt.

(H) A foam pad 10 mm thick and 0.2 inch^2 surface area is used to cool a semiconductor producing 5 watts.

(J) A foam pad 1 mm thick and 1.5 inch^2 surface area is used to cool a semiconductor producing 1 watt.

5. If a foam pad with a surface area of 1 inch^2 and an unknown thickness were used with a semiconductor generating 1 watt of heat, and the measured difference between the semiconductor and the cooling plate was found to be 15.0°C, which of the following is probably closest to the thickness of the pad?

(A) 3 mm
(B) 5 mm
(C) 9 mm
(D) 12 mm

6. A foam pad 6 mm thick with a surface area of 1 inch^2 is used to cool a semiconductor generating 1 watt of heat. Which of the following steps, by itself, would produce the greatest decrease in the measured temperature difference between the chip and the cooling plate?

(F) Reducing the wattage generated by 50%

(G) Decreasing the thickness of the foam by one third

(H) Increasing the surface area of the foam by 50%

(J) It cannot be determined from the information provided.

GO ON TO THE NEXT PAGE

7. Which of the following graphs best represents the relationships between foam thickness, foam surface area, and heat conduction seen in experiments 1 and 2? (In the following graphs, Td = Temperature difference between semiconductor and cooling plate.)

Figure 1

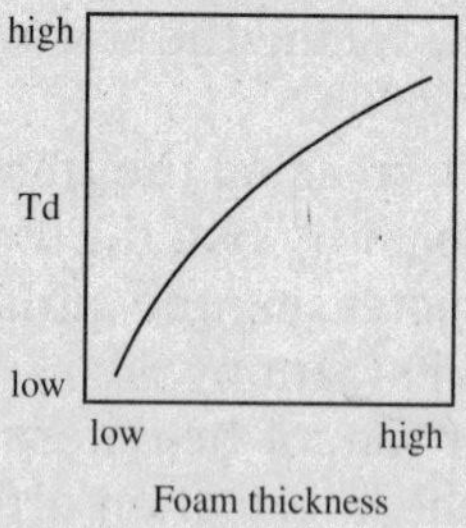

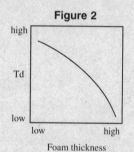

Foam thickness

Figure 2

Foam thickness

Figure 3

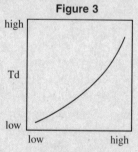

Foam surface area

Figure 4

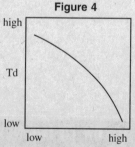

Foam surface area

(A) Figures 1 and 4
(B) Figures 1 and 3
(C) Figures 2 and 4
(D) Figures 2 and 3

8. Experiment 3 indicates that the foam seems to be a better conductor at higher temperatures (the difference in temperature between the semiconductor and the cooling plate rises more slowly as the semiconductor wattage goes higher). Which of the following statements could be a practical explanation for this observation?

(I) At higher temperatures, the foam expands, which gives it a larger surface area for conduction.

(II) At higher temperatures, more of the heat is conducted through the air, giving the appearance that the foam is a better conductor.

(III) At higher temperatures, the molecular structure of the foam may be altered slightly to allow greater conduction.

(F) I and II only
(G) I and III only
(H) II and III only
(J) I, II, and III

Passage II

Biologists have discovered certain *genes* (the basic unit of genetic material found on the chromosomes) that behave very differently depending on whether they are passed down to offspring from the father or the mother. These genes, called *imprinted genes*, are chemically altered in cells that give rise to eggs and sperm. These alterations result in dramatically different properties. In the imprinted genes that have been most fully studied, the female alters the gene so that certain proteins are not produced. The protein remains active in the father's genes. Researchers have posed numerous theories to explain the evolution of imprinted genes. Three of the theories are presented below.

Competing Parental Interest Theory

Some biologists think that imprinted genes evolved in a battle between the sexes to determine the size of offspring. It is to the genetic advantage of the female to rear a number of offspring, all of which will pass along her genetic material. Consequently, while she wants each offspring to be healthy, she does not want them to be so large that the strain of feeding and/or delivering them would jeopardize her ability to bear future babies.

Conversely, it is to the genetic advantage of males in *nonmonogamous species* (species that do not always mate for life) to have the mother expend as much of her resources as possible to ensure the health of his offspring. He is not concerned with her ability to bear future offspring, since these will not necessarily be fathered by him (and, therefore, will not be transmitting his genetic material.) Hence, imprinted genes have developed in this parental tug-of-war. Normally, each offspring receives one copy of an imprinted gene from the father and one from the mother. The changes that the parents make in their genes result in an offspring that is smaller than the male would like and larger than the female would like.

Anti-Cancer Theory

This theory holds that imprinted genes evolved to prevent cancer. The genes have been found in the *placenta* (an organ that develops to nourish a growing fetus). Placental tissue grows and burrows into the uterus, where the fetus develops. The ability to grow and invade tissues is also seen in aggressive cancers. Imprinted genes might have developed to ensure that the potentially dangerous placenta will not develop if there is no fetus to nourish. The female might inactivate certain growth genes in her eggs, while the sperm kept them turned on. If no fertilization took place, the growth would not occur. If a sperm did join the egg, the male's gene would ensure that the protein developed.

Protein Control Theory

A third group of biologists holds that imprinted genes developed to ensure the precise regulation of certain proteins. Genes do their work by initiating the production of different proteins. Some proteins involved in the growth of embryos may need to be regulated with great precision to ensure the healthy development of the offspring. Proponents of the protein control theory suggest that this careful regulation might be easier if only one parent is involved. Thus, one parent might turn off such genes, leaving the regulation to the other.

9. Which of the following experimental findings poses the most serious difficulties for proponents of the anti-cancer theory?

   (A) When a mouse was genetically engineered so that it contained two copies of every gene from its mother only, the embryo was unable to develop.

   (B) Research in animals that lay eggs has never turned up an imprinted gene.

   (C) Imprinted genes have been found in plants, which have no placentas.

   (D) Research has shown that imprinted genes have not evolved rapidly as they usually do in competitive situations.

GO ON TO THE NEXT PAGE

10. Supporters of the protein control theory believe that:
    (F) imprinted genes are used to regulate crucial proteins.
    (G) imprinted genes are active only in females.
    (H) imprinted genes should not be found in monogamous species (ones that mate for life).
    (J) only the male passes down imprinted genes to the offspring.

11. Supporters of the competing parental interest theory assume that:
    (A) only females have an interest in regulating the size of their offspring.
    (B) only males have an interest in ensuring the health and survival of their offspring.
    (C) both males and females have an interest in producing as many offspring of their own sex as possible.
    (D) both males and females have an interest in transmitting their genetic material to as many offspring as possible.

12. Supporters of all three theories would agree that:
    (F) Imprinted genes should be absent in *nonplacental animals* (animals whose offspring develop without a placenta).
    (G) If an embryo is formed without female-imprinted genes, the future ability of the mother to bear offspring will be jeopardized.
    (H) Imprinted genes should always be turned off in the mother.
    (J) Imprinted genes evolved as a means of regulating reproduction-related events.

13. Which of the following findings is best explained by the competing parental interest theory?
    (A) An imprinted gene has been discovered in humans that appears to influence a child's social skills.
    (B) In the imprinted genes that have been most fully studied, the female turns the gene off, while the male's gene remains active.
    (C) Studies with a monogamous mouse species indicate that imprinted genes are not active.
    (D) One of the imprinted genes studied is known to control a growth-stimulating hormone.

14. In a rare pregnancy disorder called *hydatidiform mole*, an abnormal cluster of cells grows in place of the placenta. This cluster grows so large that there is no room for the development of the fetus. The embryo in such pregnancies has been found to carry only the father's genes. This fact could be used to support:
    (I)   The competing parental interest theory
    (II) The anti-cancer theory
    (III) The protein control theory

    (F) I only
    (G) II only
    (H) II and III only
    (J) I, II, and III

15. Researchers conducted breeding studies with two species of mice. Species A was monogamous, while Species B was not. Supporters of the competing parental interest theory hypothesized that the monogamous species was unlikely to have active imprinted genes (since the fathers would have the same genetic stake in all the offspring born). Which of the following experimental results would they expect?

(A) When females from Species A were bred with males from Species B, the resulting offspring were extremely small.

(B) When females from Species A were bred with males from Species B, the resulting offspring were extremely large.

(C) When females from Species B were bred with males from Species A, the resulting offspring were extremely large.

(D) The offspring of Species B mice were consistently smaller than the offspring of Species A mice.

Passage III

The periodic table is a listing of each element along with its *atomic number* (the number of protons in the *nucleus* or center of the atom) and its *atomic mass* (the combined weight of protons and neutrons in the nucleus). The atomic mass is approximately equal to the number of protons and neutrons that an element has.

The table is arranged into *periods* vertically and *groups* (indicated with roman numerals) horizontally. Similar chemical properties are exhibited by elements that are in the same group. Moving across a period from group I to group VII, chemical similarities decrease. Part of the table is reproduced in the following figure.

GO ON TO THE NEXT PAGE

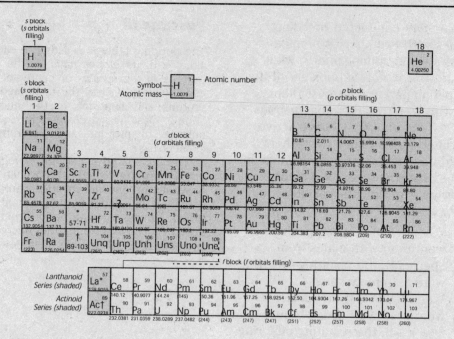

16. Based on the information in the figure, which of the following statements is true?

    (F) Atomic number decreases as period number increases.

    (G) Atomic number increases across a period as group number increases.

    (H) Increasing period numbers correspond to decreasing atomic masses.

    (J) Atomic mass decreases as atomic number increases.

17. Which of the following pairs of elements could be expected to be most similar chemically?

    (A) Ca and Sr
    (B) Ca and Ti
    (C) Sr and Zr
    (D) Sr and Y

18. Which of the following elements has the greatest number of neutrons?

    (F) Li
    (G) Cu
    (H) Sn
    (J) Si

19. When the periodic table was first created by Mendeleyev, there were some blank spots. He predicted that these spots would be filled by undiscovered elements, and he was able to accurately predict a number of the characteristics these elements would have. A blank spot (marked with a question mark) has also been left in the figure. Which of the following properties can be predicted for this element?

(I)   An atomic mass between 90 and 96
(II)   An atomic number of 35
(III)   Chemical similarities with Ta

(A)   I only
(B)   I and III only
(C)   II only
(D)   I, II, and III

20. Elements may exist as different *isotopes*. Isotopes of an element have the same number of protons, but vary in their number of neutrons and, therefore, their atomic masses. A carbon isotope with an atomic mass of 12 is represented as C(12). It has six protons and six neutrons. Another example of a carbon isotope is C(13), which has six protons and seven neutrons and an atomic mass of 13. Based on this information and the information in the figure, which one of the following statements is true?

(F)   Ca(40) has the same number of neutrons as K(40).
(G)   Be(10) has an equal number of neutrons and protons.
(H)   Ca(40) has 3 fewer neutrons than Sc(45).
(J)   V(51) has the same number of neutrons as Cr(52).

STOP   End of Section 4. If you have any time left, go over your work in this section only. Do not work in any other section of the test.

Answer Key

Section 1: English	Section 2: Mathematics	Section 3: Reading	Section 4: Science Reasoning
1. D	1. C	1. C	1. D
2. F	2. G	2. F	2. H
3. B	3. E	3. D	3. B
4. F	4. K	4. G	4. F
5. B	5. C	5. D	5. C
6. H	6. G	6. F	6. H
7. B	7. B	7. D	7. A
8. G	8. J	8. G	8. J
9. C	9. D	9. B	9. C
10. H	10. K	10. H	10. F
11. C	11. E	11. C	11. D
12. J	12. F	12. F	12. J
13. B	13. E	13. D	13. C
14. F	14. J	14. H	14. J
15. B	15. C	15. B	15. B
16. G	16. J	16. F	16. G
17. B	17. C	17. B	17. A
18. F	18. G	18. H	18. H
19. D	19. B	19. B	19. B
20. G	20. G	20. F	20. J
21. C	21. E		
22. H	22. G		
23. B	23. C		
24. J	24. F		
25. D	25. C		
26. G	26. K		
27. D	27. D		
28. G	28. K		
29. D	29. A		
30. J	30. J		
31. A			
32. G			
33. A			
34. J			
35. D			
36. H			

Scoring Guide

COMPUTING YOUR SCALED SCORES

Test 1—English: Count the number of correct answers you chose for the questions in Test 1. Write the total here: _____. This is your English Raw Score.

Look up your English Raw Score on the Score Conversion Table. Find the corresponding English Scaled Score and write it here: _____.

Test 2—Mathematics: Count the number of correct answers you chose for the questions in Test 2. Write the total here: _____. This is your Mathematics Raw Score.

Look up your Mathematics Raw Score on the Score Conversion Table. Find the corresponding Mathematics Scaled Score and write it here: _____.

Test 3—Reading: Count the number of correct answers you chose for the questions in Test 3. Write the total here: _____. This is your Reading Raw Score.

Look up your Reading Raw Score on the Score Conversion Table. Find the corresponding Reading Scaled Score and write it here: _____.

Test 4—Science Reasoning: Count the number of correct answers you chose for the questions in Test 4. Write the total here: _____. This is your Science Reasoning Raw Score.

Look up your Science Reasoning Raw Score on the Score Conversion Table. Find the corresponding Science Reasoning Scaled Score and write it here: _____.

Your Composite Score: Total your four scaled scores and divide the sum by 4. (Round a fraction to the nearest whole number; round $\frac{1}{2}$ up.) This is your Composite Score. Write it here: _____.

Score Conversion Table

Table 4.4
Insider's ACT Diagnostic Test

Raw Score	English Scaled Score	Math Scaled Score	Reading Scaled Score	Science Scaled Score
36	36			
35	34			
34	32			
33	30			
32	29			
31	28			
30	27	36		
29	26	35		
28	25	33		
27	24	31		
26	23	30		
25	22	29		
24	21	28		
23	20	27		
22	20	26		
21	19	25		
20	18	24	36	36
19	17	23	33	33
18	17	22	30	30
17	16	21	92	29
16	15	20	27	27
15	15	19	25	25
14	14	18	24	24
13	13	17	23	23
12	13	17	21	21
11	12	16	20	20
10	11	15	19	19
9	10	15	17	18
8	10	14	15	17
7	9	13	14	16
6	8	12	12	15
5	7	12	11	14
4	6	11	10	12
3	5	10	7	10
2	4	7	5	7
1	2	5	3	5
0	1	1	1	1

Explanatory Answers

SECTION 1: ENGLISH

1. **The correct answer is (D).** Each of the alternative phrasings is quite verbose and awkward, whereas choice (D) states the same idea more clearly using fewer words.

2. **The correct answer is (F).** The preposition "by" describes the relationship most clearly: the critics "deracialize" Morrison *by* what they say about her, not *in* or *through* what they say about her. Choice (J), using the conjunction "as," makes the relationship very vague.

3. **The correct answer is (B).** This sentence describes Morrison's reaction to the critics' comments about her. Since she strongly disagrees with what they say, it seems logical to use the conjunction "But" to connect the two sentences.

4. **The correct answer is (F).** If Morrison "bristles" at having to choose between being "just" a writer and being a black woman writer, this means that she is happy to accept her blackness and her femaleness as part of her identity. Choices (F), (G), and (H) all make this point, but choice (F) makes it most succinctly and pointedly.

5. **The correct answer is (B).** The adverb "generally" modifies the verb "experience," since it gives information about how Morrison's characters experience supernatural connections. Therefore, it should be as close as possible to the word "experience," which is where choice (B) places it.

6. **The correct answer is (H).** The subject of the verb "has played" is the plural noun "roles." Therefore, the verb should also be plural: "have played."

7. **The correct answer is (B).** To make "Morrison" into a possessive, add apostrophe s at the end: "Morrison's." Choice (D) is wrong because "Morrison's using of the supernatural" is awkward and non-idiomatic (that is, not the normal way of saying it).

8. **The correct answer is (G).** Sentence 2 is the best way to start the paragraph, since it makes a clear connection to the discussion of Morrison's identity as a black woman writer in the first paragraph.

9. **The correct answer is (C).** The third paragraph summarizes Morrison's proud affirmation of the richness of experience she has enjoyed as a black woman writer. Choice (C) makes this point clearly.

10. **The correct answer is (H).** To be logical, the sentence must compare "the range of emotion and perception she has had access to" with the range of those things experienced by other writers. As originally written, the sentence is wrong because it seems to compare "the range" with "people who are neither"—a case of apples and oranges, which are not directly comparable. In choice (H), the pronoun "that" stands for "the range," and is a shorthand, concise way of stating the necessary comparison.

11. **The correct answer is (C).** The original sentence is a run-on; two separate sentences have been jammed together with a comma between them. Choice (C) fixes this by making the two sentences independent, as they should be.

12. **The correct answer is (J).** Since this verb phrase is referring to something in the past *prior to* another past event, it should be in the past perfect tense: "had been governed" rather than "have been governed."

13. **The correct answer is (B).** "To submit" is perfectly correct and idiomatic, but "its" should be spelled without an apostrophe. (Use "it's" only to mean "it is.")

14. **The correct answer is (F).** It's correct to start a new paragraph here, since the essay is moving on to a new topic: the method of ratification chosen by the delegates to the convention. Also, "Instead" is the appropriate word to link the two paragraphs; Paragraph 1 tells what the delegates did *not* want to do, while Paragraph 2 tells what they chose to do instead.

15. **The correct answer is (B).** This is the most succinct and appropriate phrasing among the alternatives. Choice (C) is wrong because the verb phrase "declared that" should be followed by the helping verb "would" rather than "was." Choice (D) is too informal (slangy) to fit the tone of the rest of the essay.

16. **The correct answer is (G).** The adverb "directly" describes how the Constitution was being "submitted"; therefore, it should follow that word immediately.

17. **The correct answer is (B).** The proposed sentence makes a good addition to the paragraph because it emphasizes the radical break being made by the delegates: they were turning their back on the very Congress which had called them into being. This neatly echoes the point made in the first sentence of the paragraph.

18. **The correct answer is (F).** The original phrasing is perfectly correct. Choice (G) is less good, because the pronoun "that" inaccurately suggests that only *certain* legislatures—the ones "attached to states' rights"—were being bypassed. (Choice J seems to imply the same thing.) In choice (H), the second sentence is a fragment rather than a complete sentence.

19. **The correct answer is (D).** The fourth paragraph begins the discussion of the positions taken by the opposing groups. The sentence given in choice D states this emphatically and concisely.

20. **The correct answer is (G).** The original wording lacks a verb and therefore is a sentence fragment. So is choice (J). Choice (H) is grammatically correct, but it's wordy by comparison with choice (G).

21. **The correct answer is (C).** The parenthetical phrase "though sincere" should be set off by commas on either side. Choice C does that correctly.

22. **The correct answer is (H).** Paragraph 4 described one political weakness of the Antifederalists; Paragraph 5 describes another. Therefore, "Furthermore" seems a logical word to introduce Paragraph 5.

23. **The correct answer is (B).** Both the original wording and choice (C) awkwardly include the word "he," which needlessly restates the subject of the sentence, "Elbridge Gerry." Choice (D) obscures the relationship between Gerry's refusal to sign the Constitution and her opposition to excessive democracy by using the vague connector "while."

24. **The correct answer is (J).** Only choice (J) fulfills the requirements stated in the question: to suggest the outcome of the battle (i.e., that the Federalists succeeded in having the Constitution ratified) and to draw a connection to the main point of the paragraph (i.e., the Antifederalists' lack of faith in democracy).

25. **The correct answer is (D).** All of the alternatives are clear and grammatically correct, but choice (D) is by far the most concise version.

26. **The correct answer is (G).** Two things are being described that should be grammatically parallel (i.e., similar) in form: "to live with and adapt to."

27. **The correct answer is (D).** The theme of the essay is how able-bodied people treat the disabled, and virtually every sentence connects with that theme in some way. The proposed addition does not, however, and therefore it should be omitted.

28. **The correct answer is (G).** A semicolon (;) should generally be used only to connect two independent clauses (two clauses each of which could be a sentence by itself). That's not the case here; what follows the semicolon isn't an independent clause. Choice (G) corrects the error. Choice (H) is wrong because it creates a run-on sentence; what follows the comma in that version *is* an independent clause, and therefore it needs a semicolon (or some other appropriate connector).

29. **The correct answer is (D).** The underlined phrase can be omitted altogether because it's redundant; an "averted gaze" and a "sidelong look" are exactly the same thing, and therefore nothing is gained by including both phrases in the sentence.

30. **The correct answer is (J).** Since the pronoun refers back to "an able-bodied person," the correct pronoun is "his," not "one's."

31. **The correct answer is (A).** The other answer choices are either vague and non-idiomatic (choices B and D) or grammatically incorrect (choice C, which uses the plural verb form "glorify" rather than the correct, singular "glorifies").

32. **The correct answer is (G).** When introducing a clause (a group of words containing both a subject and a verb), the conjunction "as" is needed rather than the preposition "like." In this sentence, since what's being described is a situation contrary to fact, "as if" is the proper phrase.

33. **The correct answer is (A).** Since the antecedent "society" is singular, the singular pronoun "its" is correct (as opposed to the plural pronouns "our" and "their").

34. **The correct answer is (J).** In this context, the correct word is "there," not the pronoun "their" or the contraction "they're" (meaning "they are").

35. **The correct answer is (D).** The paragraph describes how the use of words to describe the disabled has changed over time. It would be logical to arrange the sentences in time sequence: "First" (sentence 3), "Then" (sentence 4), and finally "Today" (sentence 1).

36. **The correct answer is (H).** The end of Paragraph 2, where the writer is explaining why able-bodied people are uncomfortable around the disabled, is the most logical place to insert this sentence, which gives another reason for that discomfort.

SECTION 2: MATHEMATICS

1. **The correct answer is (C).** Since the fraction has been simplified to simplest form, N cannot have as a factor any number whose prime factorization has any numbers in common with the prime factors of 60. But $60 = (2)(2)(3)(5)$. Thus, the answer must be 49 since, in this set, only $49 = (7)(7)$ has a prime factorization lacking the factors 2, 3, and 5.

2. **The correct answer is (G).** Marking down $1,200 by 10% reduces the price by 10% of $1,200 = $120. The new price is $1,200 − 120 = $1,080. Marking that down 10% reduces the price by 10% of $1,080 = 108, so that the final price is $1,080 − 108 = $972.

3. **The correct answer is (E).** If her average is 88 on four exams, she must have a total score of $(4)(88) = 352$. In order to average 90 on five exams, her total must be $(5)(90) = 450$. Therefore, she must score $450 − 352 = 98$ on her last exam.

4. **The correct answer is (K).** Solving the equation: $3y − 6 = 2 − y$; $4y = 8$; $y = 2$.

    If $y = 2$, then $y^2 + 2y = 4 + 4 = 8$.

5. **The correct answer is (C).** Since $P:F = 5:2$, we can let $P = 5k$ and $F = 2k$. But the total number in the class must be $5k + 2k = 7k$. Clearly, choice C, 21, will work (letting $k = 3$). If you try the other possibilities, k will be a fraction, for which neither $5k$ nor $2k$ will be a whole number. Of course, you can't have a fractional number of students, so the answer must be C.

6. **The correct answer is (G).** Calling the smallest number x, the second is $x + 1$, and the third is $x + 2$. Therefore:

$$x + (x + 1) + 2(x + 2) = 93$$
$$x + x + 1 + 2x + 4 = 93$$
$$4x + 5 = 93$$
$$4x = 88$$
$$x = 22$$

Hence, the middle number is $22 + 1 = 23$.

7. **The correct answer is (B).** The original volume of the solid was $V_B = (6)(6)(14) = 504$. Since the circle goes from one side to the other of the square base, it must have a diameter of 6, which means it has a radius of 3. Hence, the volume of the piece drilled out is $V_H = \pi(3)^2(14) = 126\pi$. Using $\pi \approx \frac{22}{7}$, $126\pi \approx 396$. Therefore, the volume of the remaining wood is about $504 - 396 = 108$ in^3.

8. **The correct answer is (J).** Of the whole group of 60, 40% are under 25. 40% of 60 is $(0.4)(60) = 24$. For the singers, 20% of 20 $= (0.2)(20) = 4$ are under 25. Hence, the remaining 25 or unders must be dancers. That is, 20 dancers, or one-half of all the dancers, fall into this category. One-half is 50%.

9. **The correct answer is (D).** Reading the first bar graph, we see that the number of houses sold in Ashland in 1994 was about 450. The number sold in Brainard, where the scale is twice as large, was about 830. The total is 1280.

10. **The correct answer is (K).** The number of houses sold in Brainard in 1995 was 1,100. In 1996, the number was about 720, for a decline of $1,100 - 720 = 380$. The fraction decline was $\frac{380}{1,100} =$ about 0.345 or 34.5%. Clearly, the closest choice is 35%.

11. **The correct answer is (E).** Letting r, m, and b be the prices in cents of rolls, muffins, and bread respectively yields two equations:

$$4r + 6m + 3b = 910$$
$$2r + 3m + b = 390$$

If we multiply the second equation by -2 and add the two equations together, we have:

$$4r + 6m + 3b = 910$$
$$\underline{-4r - 6m - 2b = -780}$$
$$b = 130$$

Hence, the price of a loaf of bread is $1.30.

12. **The correct answer is (F).** This example uses two well-known right triangles. We see that, in triangle ABD, one leg is 3 and one is 4, which makes $BD = 5$ (the famous "Pythagorean triple" 3-4-5). This tells us that triangle BDC is 5-12-13 (another famous Pythagorean triangle). Thus, CD is 13, and the entire perimeter is $3 + 4 + 12 + 13 = 32$.

13. **The correct answer is (E).** Since $4x^2 - y^2 = (2x - y)(2x + y) = 7(2x - y)$, $4x^2 - y^2$ must be divisible by 7. Therefore, 6 and 15 are not possible. If the result is to be zero, $2x - y = 0$, which means $y = 2x$, so that $2x + 2x = 4x = 7$, which is also impossible for any integral values. Hence the result must be 14 or 35. If the result is to be 14, $2x - y = 2$. Adding gives us:

$$2x + y = 7$$
$$2x - y = 2$$
$$4x = 9$$

This has no integer solutions. Hence, 35, which you get when $x = 3$ and $y = 1$, is the only possibility.

14. **The correct answer is (J).** Since $m = \dfrac{y_1 - y_2}{x_1 - x_2}$, we must have $\dfrac{1}{3} = \dfrac{5 - (-3)}{a - 2}$.

This means:

$$\frac{1}{3} = \frac{8}{a - 2}$$

Cross-multiplying,

$$a - 2 = 24$$
$$a = 26.$$

15. **The correct answer is (C).** To find the largest possible value of $\dfrac{a}{b}$, you certainly want a positive number, which you can get in two ways: a positive divided by a positive, or a negative divided by a negative. The largest fraction you can form using positive numbers from A and B is $\dfrac{3}{4}$. However, using the negative possibilities, we have $\dfrac{-6}{-4} = \dfrac{3}{2} = 1.5$.

16. **The correct answer is (J).** Five more than twice n is $2n + 5$. Thus, $2n + 5 = 17$, which we solve to get $n = 6$. Two less than $\dfrac{1}{2}$ of 6 is 2 less than 3, or 1.

17. **The correct answer is (C).** In triangle ABC, the measure of $\angle A = x°$ by the property of vertical angles, and the measure of $\angle B = z°$ by the property of alternate interior angles. Hence, $x + y + z = 180$.

18. **The correct answer is (G).** From the description, the situation must be that shown in the diagram below.

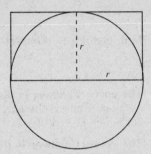

Calling the radius r, we see that the rectangle has a width of r and a length of $2r$. Hence, the area is $2r^2 = 18$. Thus, $r^2 = 9$, and $r = 3$. The circumference of the circle is $2\pi r = 6\pi$.

19. **The correct answer is (B).** 40% of $200 = 0.4(200) = \$80$, so, with the markup, the first coat is sold for $200 + 80 = \$280$. Subtracting 10% of $300 (30 from 300) leaves only $270 for the second coat. The difference is $10.

20. **The correct answer is (G).** The least common denominator is $6n$, so we rewrite:

$$\frac{n}{6} = \frac{n^2}{6n} \text{ and } \frac{6}{n} = \frac{36}{6n}$$

Subtracting:

$$\frac{n^2}{6n} - \frac{36}{6n} - \frac{(n^2 - 36)}{6n} = \frac{(n - 6)(n + 6)}{6n}$$

21. **The correct answer is (E).** Using the laws of logarithms, $\log\dfrac{5}{12} = \dfrac{\log 5}{\log 12} =$

$\dfrac{\log 5}{\log(2^2)(3)} = \log 5 - [\log 2^2 + \log 3] = \log 5 - 2\log 2 - \log 3 = z - 2x - y$.

22. **The correct answer is (G).** Factoring $3xy^3$ in the numerator and $6xy$ in the denominator, we have $\dfrac{(3xy^3[x + 2y])}{(6xy[x + 2y])}$. Then, we can divide out the common factor $3xy(x + 2y)$, leaving $\dfrac{(3xy^3[x + 2y])}{(6xy[x + 2y])} = \dfrac{y^2}{2}$.

23. **The correct answer is (C).** Setting $y = 0$ and solving by the quadratic formula with $a = 1$, $b = 4$ and $c = -13$:

$$x = \frac{-(4) \pm \sqrt{(4)^2 - 4(1)(-13)}}{2(1)} = \frac{-4 \pm \sqrt{68}}{2} = \frac{-4 \pm 2\sqrt{17}}{2} = -2 \pm \sqrt{17}.$$

Since $\sqrt{17}$ is a little greater than 4, choosing the addition sign, $-2 + \sqrt{17}$ is a little greater than 2.

24. **The correct answer is (F).** Since $a_n = a + (n - 1)d$, we have, for $n = 3$, $a + 2d = 13$, and, for $n = 9$, $a + 9d = 55$. Subtracting the first equation from the second gives us: $7d = 42$ and $d = 6$. Therefore, from the first equation, $a + 12 = 13$, and $a = 1$.

25. **The correct answer is (C).** $f(g(x)) = \dfrac{g(x)}{2 + g(x)} = \dfrac{\frac{1}{x}}{2 + \frac{1}{x}}$.

Multiplying the numerator and the denominator by x, we have $f(g(x)) = \dfrac{1}{(2x + 1)}$.

26. **The correct answer is (K).** Each entry in the matrix you seek is 2 times the entry in A minus the entry in B. For example, in row 1, column 1, you have $2(1) - (-1) = 3$.

27. **The correct answer is (D).** Parallel lines have the same slope. Hence, the line you want must be of the form $y = 3x + b$. You can find b by requiring that the x-intercept be -4. That is, when $y = 0$, $x = -4$. Hence, $0 = 3(-4) + b$, or $b = 12$. Thus, $y = 3x + 12$.

28. **The correct answer is (K).** As you can see from the figure below, if we call half the base x, $\sin 16° = \dfrac{x}{3}$; $x = 3 \sin 16°$; and the entire base is thus $6 \sin 16°$.

29. **The correct answer is (A).** Taking logs of both sides of the equation, we have $2x\log 12 = \log 4$. Dividing by 2 log 12 gives us $\dfrac{\log 4}{2\log 12}$.

30. **The correct answer is (J).** If you try to solve simultaneously, you can substitute from $y = x^2 - 5$, $x^2 = y + 5$, into $x^2 + y^2 = 25$ to give $y + 5 + y^2 = 25$. Collecting terms on the lefthand side:

$$y^2 + y - 20 = 0$$
$$(y + 5)(y - 4) = 0$$
$$y = -5$$
or
$$y = 4$$

Of course, $y = -5$ occurs only at the point $(0,5)$ on both curves, while $y = 4$ yields $x^2 = 9$, and you have solutions $x = 3$ and $x = -3$. Hence, there are three points of intersection.

SECTION 3: READING

1. **The correct answer is (C).** The first paragraph attributes the opposition to "those who wished to see the empire democratized," and it has already explained that Russia was, at this time, one of the few countries in Europe still ruled by a single individual—in other words, "an autocratic form of government."

2. **The correct answer is (F).** The second paragraph states clearly, "the laws of succession decreed that only a male could succeed the Tsar."

3. **The correct answer is (D).** The diary excerpt, with its expression of joy over the birth of a son and its fervent thanks to God, clearly illustrates the points named in choice (A), (B), and (C). The political issues Nicholas faced at the time are not reflected at all.

4. **The correct answer is (G).** See the last sentence of the third paragraph and the middle of the seventh paragraph. These statements imply that veiling the child's hemophilia in secrecy may have cost the Tsar's family the sympathy of the Russian people and so contributed to their ultimate downfall.

5. **The correct answer is (D).** The fourth paragraph describes the October Manifesto as one of Nicholas's "halfhearted efforts . . . to satisfy the dissidents." It was an inadequate step toward full democracy.

6. **The correct answer is (F).** See paragraph six: "Nicholas decided it was his duty to lead the army himself."

7. **The correct answer is (D).** The sentence that mentions the "downturn" attributes it specifically to "progressively greater defeats" in the war.

8. **The correct answer is (G).** The seventh paragraph tells us that, *after* the Tsar took personal command of the army, the military situation became "increasingly dire."

9. **The correct answer is (B).** The latter portion of the seventh paragraph makes this clear. It says that Rasputin and Alexandra "were much reviled in the press" because the Russian people did not understand the health concerns that had driven the Tsarina to rely on Rasputin.

10. **The correct answer is (H).** We're told in the last two sentences of the seventh paragraph that Rasputin's murder came about because he "had also made important enemies at court."

11. **The correct answer is (C).** Answer (A) is too narrow; answers (B) and (D) are too broad. Choice (C) is good because it brings out the *practical* slant of the passage, which after all focuses on the industrial use of granular matter and the role played by science in facilitating it.

12. **The correct answer is (F).** According to the passage, the second law of thermodynamics suggests that entropy, or disorder, should tend to increase in any system; and it links this concept of "disorder" with the idea that nuts should mix when shaken. Thus, the failure of the nuts to mix is taken as evidence that the nuts are somehow violating the law.

13. **The correct answer is (D).** Review the first two sentences of the third paragraph. The percolation theory deals with how small and large objects interrelate when a mass of granular material is shaken, as in a can of nuts.

14. **The correct answer is (H).** See the first sentence of the fourth paragraph; the engineer says that both theories can be right, "depending on the material."

15. **The correct answer is (B).** A conundrum is a puzzle, riddle, or mystery. Enigma is a close synonym.

16. **The correct answer is (F).** As the fourth paragraph makes clear, the problem pharmaceutical firms face in dealing with granular materials is based mainly on the fact that different-sized grains are present in a single product. Clearly, it would help matters if all the grains could be made the same size.

17. **The correct answer is (B).** The fifth paragraph explains that, unlike with sand, the pressure in a liquid "increases in direct proportion to the liquid's height." In other words, the higher (or deeper) the mass of liquid, the greater the pressure at the bottom. Therefore, as the water trickled through (getting shallower, of course), the pressure would decrease.

18. **The correct answer is (H).** See the first four sentences of the sixth paragraph, which explain this phenomenon.

19. **The correct answer is (B).** Notice the way the granular scientists' "low-cost, low-tech" experiments are contrasted with the complicated and expensive studies that particle physicists must somehow fund.

20. **The correct answer is (F).** Medicines are mentioned in the fourth paragraph, grains in the sixth. Beads and nuts are only mentioned in connection with the experiments conducted by scientists; they are easy-to-find, easy-to-study experimental substitutes for the granular matter the scientists are really interested in learning to manage.

SECTION 4: SCIENCE REASONING

1. **The correct answer is (D).** As explained in the passage, in Experiment 1, the thickness of the foam pad was varied between 1 and 10 millimeters, while in Experiment 3 the amount of heat dissipated was varied by varying the wattage generated by the semiconductor.

2. **The correct answer is (H).** In the two experimental trials named, the conditions were the same: the surface area of the foam pad was 1.0 square inch, and its thickness was 6 mm. However, the measured temperature difference was not the same, suggesting some sort of inconsistency not explained by any data presented here.

3. **The correct answer is (B).** Experiment 1 shows that heat conduction is favored by the thinnest possible foam pad; Exeriment 2 shows that it is favored by the largest possible surface area. In both instances, the greater heat conduction is indicated by the smaller temperature difference between the semiconductor and the cooling plate.

4. **The correct answer is (F).** Of the four alternatives, this choice gives us the thinnest foam pad, the largest surface area, and the lowest-wattage semiconductor, all conditions chosen to maximize heat conduction and minimize the temperature difference.

5. **The correct answer is (C).** Refer to Table 1.1, which shows the results of trials involving pads one square inch in area with a 1-watt semiconductor. We can see in the third column that a temperature difference of 15.0° would fall right between trials 5 and 6; in other words, between a pad 8 mm thick and one 10 mm thick. Therefore, it seems reasonable to conclude that the pad in the trial described would probably be midway between those two in thickness—9 mm.

6. **The correct answer is (H).** The conditions described in the question match Experiment 1, trial 4 and Experiment 2, trial 3, in both of which the temperature difference was measured at 11.0°. From Experiment 3, trial 2, we can see that reducing the wattage by 50% (to .5 watts) would reduce the temperature difference to 11.3° (choice F). From Experiment 1, trial 4, decreasing the thickness of the foam by one third will make the difference 7.2° (choice G). From Experiment 2, trial 6, increasing the surface area by 50% will make it 5.3° (choice H)—the greatest difference.

7. **The correct answer is (A).** The graphs in the figures match the data given: They show a low temperature difference when the foam thickness is low, a high temperature difference when the thickness is high, a high temperature difference when the area is low, and a low temperature difference when the area is high.

8. **The correct answer is (J).** Any of the three explanations suggested is consistent with the information stated in the question.

9. **The correct answer is (C).** Since the anti-cancer theory is based on the idea that gene imprinting evolved as a reaction to the possibility that the placenta might develop in a cancerous fashion, the theory would be severely undermined if it were true that plants, which have no placentas, had also developed the imprinting mechanism.

10. **The correct answer is (F).** The first sentence of the paragraph defining the protein control theory states this point succinctly.

11. **The correct answer is (D).** The competing parental interest theory assumes that both males and females seek to maximize the chances that their genes will be passed along to the next generation through a large number of healthy offspring. (It then postulates that, because males and females have different reproductive patterns, they have evolved different strategies for pursuing this result.) This assumption is stated in choice (D).

12. **The correct answer is (J).** All three theories relate to reproduction in one way or another: the parental interest theory in regard to the transmission of genetic material through reproduction, the anti-cancer theory in relation to the development of the placenta, in which the fetus grows; and the protein control theory in relation to the healthy development of the embryo.

13. **The correct answer is (C).** Notice that the competing parental interest theory makes sense only if nonmonogamous species are involved (since it is the differing reproductive habits of males and females that drives them to handle their genetic material differently). The finding described in choice (H) fits that theory because it suggests that imprinting is an unnecessary strategy in a monogamous species.

14. **The correct answer is (J).** This disorder supports the competing parental interest theory because the father's genetic material in that theory is associated with excessive growth, as here; it supports the anti-cancer theory because that theory associates imprinting with the need to control excessive growth of the placenta, as here; and it supports the protein control theory because, if the mother's genes are absent when the disorder occurs, this could explain the abnormal development found.

15. **The correct answer is (B).** This result would be consistent with the theory, since the female genes from Species A would not be imprinted for small size, while the male genes from Species B would be imprinted for large size. The combination would produce very large offspring.

16. **The correct answer is (G).** Glance from left to right across any of the periodic rows to confirm that this is accurate.

17. **The correct answer is (A).** The passage states that similar chemical properties are exhibited by elements in the same group—that is, the same vertical column. The elements Ca (calcium) and Sr (strontium) are both in group IIA. (Note: you can't tell the full names of the elements from the passage, nor do you need to; we mention them here just in case you're interested.)

18. **The correct answer is (H).** The number of neutrons would equal approximately the atomic mass minus the number of protons, which is the same as the atomic number. Thus, Li (lithium) would have about $6.94 - 3 =$ about 4 neutrons; Cu (copper) would have about $63.55 - 29 =$ about 25 neutrons; Sn (tin) would have about $118.71 - 50 =$ about 69 neutrons; and Si (silicon) would have about $28.09 - 14 =$ about 14 neutrons.

19. **The correct answer is (B).** Extrapolating from the elements on either side of the question mark, we can figure that the atomic mass of the missing element would be greater than 91 but less than 96; that it would have an atomic number of 41; and that it would be chemically similar to the other elements in group VB, which are V (vanadium) and Ta (tantalum). Thus, I and III are correct. (The missing element is, in fact, Nb, niobium.)

20. **The correct answer is (J).** V(51) would have an atomic mass of 51; since its atomic number is 23, it would have $51 - 23 = 28$ neutrons. That's the same number as Cr(52).

Chapter 2

Making Your Plan

GET THE SCOOP ON . . .

- The three levels of ACT skills and how you can improve all three
- How to develop a personalized study plan focused on your current skill levels and needs
- How to tailor your study plan to the amount of time you have to prepare

HOW TO GET WHERE YOU WANT TO GO

As you know, your scores on standardized tests—especially the ACT Assessment—will play a crucial role in determining whether or not you'll win acceptance to the college or university of your choice. How can you make sure that your ACT scores will be a help rather than a hindrance to you when you apply to colleges? What steps can you take to close the gap that may exist between your current levels of ACT skills and the ones you'll need to earn your highest possible score?

The rest of this book will help you answer those questions.

THE INSIDER'S ROUTE TO TOP SCORES

Three levels of skill can help boost your ACT scores, and each requires a different kind of preparation. Most important, each requires a different time frame to be completely developed. If you want to reach your full potential on the ACT, you'll want to devote time and energy to all three levels of skill.

Here's how the three levels work.

Level One—Testwiseness (2–5 points)

This first level of test-taking skill is the "low-hanging fruit" of test-preparation: skills that are relatively quick and simple to learn and that can rapidly boost your composite ACT score from 2 to 5 points.

Level One includes such skills as:

- Familiarity with the format, structure, and question types found on the exam

- Ability to budget your time wisely as you work on each ACT test

- Understanding of how to maximize your score on each test by tackling the easier questions first

Level One skills are specific to the ACT. A student who'd never seen an ACT exam before and had done no preparatory reading about the test would lack these skills, and therefore would lose points through sheer ignorance of the rules of the game.

Fortunately, Level One skills are easy to learn. Many students pick up some of them just by taking an ACT exam. That's why, as the test-makers admit, most students increase their scores by at least a few points whenever they take the exam a second time, even if they do no studying between the two test dates.

If your preparation for the ACT is condensed into just a couple of weeks, you'll need to focus especially on Level One skills. Chapters 1–3 and 8–10 in this book are particularly focused on Level One.

Level Two—Topic Strategies (5–10 points)

Skills at this level are a bit more complex. They generally take longer to learn but have a correspondingly greater payoff. If you work to improve your Level Two skills (as well as your Level One skills), you can expect to boost your composite ACT score by anywhere from 5 to 10 points.

Level Two includes skills such as:

- Ability to see the points of agreement and disagreement between two alternative theories in the Science Reasoning Test

- Ability to recognize the logical connections between parts of a passage in the Reading Test

- Awareness of how and when to use rounding off, "guesstimating," and "plugging in numbers" when working on problems in the Mathematics Test

- Understanding of how the test-makers evaluate the logical coherence of a prose passage in the English Test

Level Two skills relate specifically to particular question types on the ACT. However, they involve intellectual abilities that can be used in other contexts as well. For instance, if you're good at seeing the logical connections between parts of a reading passage, this will help you not only on the ACT but whenever you do any difficult reading—in a high school textbook, for example.

You've probably developed some Level Two skills already, both in and out of school. However, you probably aren't aware of how to apply these skills directly to answering ACT questions. Because these skills are somewhat complex (and because there are many of them), it'll take you a while to master them. But the rewards can be great.

If you have four weeks or more to prepare for the ACT, you'll have enough time to delve fairly deeply into Level Two skills. Chapters 4–7 of this book explain them in detail.

Level Three—Broad-Based Verbal and Math Abilities (10–20 points)

These are the most general skills, and they take the longest time to fully develop. In a sense, Level Three skills are the ones the test-makers originally intended the ACT to focus on, and certainly your performance on the test will be heavily affected by your Level Three skills. If you devote significant time and effort to improving your Level Three skills (along with Levels One and Two), you can aim for an increase of your composite ACT score from 10 to 20 points.

Level Three includes such skills as:

- Knowledge of the meanings and correct usage of a large number of difficult English words

- Ability to read and understand complex passages dealing with challenging topics from natural science, the humanities, the social sciences, and literature

- Familiarity with the basic facts, principles, and procedures of arithmetic, algebra, geometry, and other math topics

- Understanding of the key principles of scientific reasoning and the ability to evaluate the design of an experiment or the logic of a scientific hypothesis

Level Three skills clearly go well beyond the requirements of the ACT exam. In fact, you've probably been learning and practicing skills like these in every high school class you've ever taken (well, maybe not gym).

You'll continue to develop and improve your Level Three skills in many ways between now and when you take the ACT: through your ongoing high school coursework; through challenging reading that you may do for school or any other purpose; and through the intellectual exercise you get whenever you take a test, including sample ACT exams you use as part of your test-prep program.

The more time you have between now and the exam, the greater your chances are to improve your Level Three skills. In this book, Appendixes A through D specifically address these skills by offering you help in building your word knowledge, sharpening your understanding of mathematics, improving your understanding of the rules of grammar and usage, and reviewing the basic elements of scientific thinking.

In addition, you'll find that you are using and practicing your Level Three skills every time you work on an exercise or sample test from any chapter in this book. Just as regular, disciplined exercise improves your overall muscle tone and strengthens your heart, *mental workouts* are the key to strengthening your Level Three skills.

MAKING THE MOST OF THE TIME YOU HAVE

As with almost any form of learning, preparing for the ACT is an investment of time. The more you have, the better your chances of significantly boosting your score. Next, we'll walk you through three different study plans, each tailored to a specific amount of preparation time. Find the plan that fits your circumstances and adapt it to your needs.

If You Have Two Weeks To Prepare

Obviously, if you plan to take the ACT in two weeks or less and are just beginning your preparation program, your time is at a premium. You'll have to make the most of every available hour between now and the day of the test. As much as you can, cut back or eliminate nonessential activities over the next two weeks (sports, movies, after-school jobs) and focus your energies on the exam.

You can still develop a plan, leaning heavily on Level One skills, that will make a significant difference in your test scores, but you need to make it your highest priority starting *today*. The outline shown in Table 2.1 will help.

If You Have Four to Six Weeks to Prepare

With a month or more to get ready for the ACT, you can make some major improvements in your test-taking skills. You can delve rather deeply into Level Two skills, as well as mastering all the key Level One skills. Of course, it'll take some discipline and hard work. Try to cut back on nonessential activities between now and the day of the exam, and set aside significant blocks of time (evenings, weekends) for reading, study, and practice. If you do this, following the steps we suggest in Table 2.2, and you'll boost your score noticeably.

If You Have Three Months or More To Prepare

Congratulations! Through astute planning, admirable self-discipline, or sheer good luck, you've positioned yourself so that you have ample time

Table 2.1
Your Two-Week Plan—The Steps To Take

1. If you haven't already, take the Insider's ACT Diagnostic Test (chapter 1). Take the exam under true test conditions. Then grade your performance using the Scoring Guide in this book.
2. Based on the results of your Insider's ACT Diagnostic Test, identify the *two* question types in which you need the greatest improvement.
3. Turn to Part II of this book and read chapter 3, Finding Your Way Around the ACT. It will give you an overview of the real ACT and a number of important hints about test-taking strategies that will help boost your scores.
4. Then find the two chapters from chapters 4 through 7 that cover the two question types you identified in Step 2. Study those chapters, and try your hand on at least two of the practice exercises in each one. If you achieve an above-average or excellent score on both practice exercises, move on. Otherwise, reread the chapter and do as many additional practice exercises as you can.
5. Turn to Appendix B, The Insider's Math Review for the ACT. This part of the book covers the fifty math topics most frequently tested on the ACT. Take 15 minutes to skim this appendix with a pencil in hand. Circle the number of any topic you find new or unfamiliar. Then set aside an afternoon or evening to read those topics in detail.
6. If you have time, read the chapters in Part II that you haven't already read.
7. Some time in the week before the ACT, take the Insider's ACT (chapter 8) under true test conditions. Then grade your performance using the Scoring Guide in this book.
8. Compare your performance on the Insider's ACT with your performance on the Insider's ACT Diagnostic Test. Is there any *one* question type where your performance still lags? If you have time, read or reread the chapter in Part II that covers that question type.
9. Two days before the ACT, read chapter 9 and follow its advice about how to approach the weekend of the exam.
10. After taking the ACT, read chapter 10.

to prepare thoroughly for one of the most important challenges of your academic life. With three months or more to prepare, you can improve all three levels of your ACT skills and give yourself an excellent chance of achieving or surpassing your score goals.

Take advantage of your foresight by pacing yourself intelligently. Set aside time every week to pursue your test-prep program, preferably in major chunks—two or three hours at a time on an evening or a weekday. An extended study program spread out over twelve weeks or more will

Table 2.2
Your Four- to Six-Week Plan—The Steps To Take

1. If you haven't already, take the Insider's ACT Diagnostic Test (chapter 1). Take the exam under true test conditions. Then grade your performance using the Scoring Guide in this book.

2. Based on the results of your Insider's ACT Diagnostic Test, identify the *three* question types in which you need the greatest improvement.

3. Turn to Part II of this book and read chapter 3, Finding Your Way Around the ACT. It will give you an overview of the real ACT and a number of important hints about test-taking strategies that will help boost your scores.

4. As soon as possible, begin to set aside 15 minutes each day to study Appendix A, The Insider's ACT Word List. Plan to read the definitions and explanations of fifteen words from the word list each day. At this rate, you'll have been exposed to every word on the list within five weeks.

5. Now, find the three chapters from chapters 4 through 7 that cover the three question types you identified in Step 2. Over the next two weeks, study those chapters, and try your hand on at least two of the practice exercises in each chapter. If you achieve an above-average or excellent score on both practice exercises, move on. Otherwise, reread the chapter and do as many additional practice exercises as you can.

6. Next, turn to Appendix B, The Insider's Math Review for the ACT. This part of the book covers the fifty math topics most frequently tested on the ACT. Over the next week, read this appendix thoroughly. With a pencil, circle the number of any topic you find difficult or confusing. Between now and the date of the exam, review the circled topics from time to time.

7. Read Appendix C, The Insider's Writer's Manual for the ACT, and Appendix D, the Insider's Science Review for the ACT. Note any topics you find difficult or confusing, and review these topics from time to time between now and the date of the exam.

8. If you have time, read any chapter in Part II that you haven't already read.

9. Some time in the week before the ACT, take the Insider's ACT (chapter 8) under true test conditions. Then grade your performance using the Scoring Guide in this book.

10. Compare your performance on the Insider's ACT with your performance on the Insider's ACT Diagnostic Test. Is there any *one* question type where your performance still lags? If you have time, read or reread the chapter in Part II that covers that question type.

11. Two days before the ACT, read chapter 9 and follow its advice about how to approach the weekend of the exam.

12. After taking the ACT, read chapter 10.

Table 2.3
Your Three-Month Plan—The Steps To Take

1. If you haven't already, take the Insider's ACT Diagnostic Test (chapter 1). Take the exam under true test conditions. Then grade your performance using the Scoring Guide in this book.

2. Based on the results of your Insider's ACT Diagnostic Test, rank the four question types in order of priority, from the one in which you need the greatest improvement to the one in which you currently perform the best.

3. Turn to Part II of this book and read chapter 3, Finding Your Way Around the ACT. It will give you an overview of the real ACT and a number of important hints about test-taking strategies that will help boost your scores.

4. As soon as possible, begin to set aside 15 minutes each day to study Appendix A, The Insider's Word List for the ACT. Plan to read the definitions and explanations of fifteen words from the word list each day. At this rate, you'll have been exposed to every word on the list within five weeks. As suggested in the appendix, also start your own vocabulary notebook and add to it frequently.

5. Now, read chapters 4 through 7 in the priority sequence you identified in Step 2. Also try your hand on at least two of the practice exercises in each chapter. If you achieve an above-average or excellent score on both practice exercises, move on. Otherwise, reread the chapter and do as many additional practice exercises as you can.

6. Next, turn to Appendix B, The Insider's ACT Math Review. This part of the book covers the fifty math topics most frequently tested on the ACT. Over the next week, read this appendix thoroughly. With a pencil, circle the number of any topic you find difficult or confusing. Between now and the date of the exam, review the circled topics from time to time.

7. Read Appendix C, The Insider's ACT Writer's Manual, and Appendix D, the Insider's Science Review for the ACT. Note any topics you find difficult or confusing, and review these topics from time to time between now and the date of the exam.

8. Some time in the week before the ACT, take the Insider's ACT (Chapter 8) under true test conditions. Then grade your performance using the Scoring Guide in this book.

9. Compare your performance on the Insider's ACT with your performance on the Insider's ACT Diagnostic Test. Is there any *one* question type where your performance still lags? If you have time, reread the chapter in Part II that covers that question type.

10. Two days before the ACT, read chapter 9 and follow its advice about how to approach the weekend of the exam.

11. After taking the ACT, read chapter 10.

boost your score more than an intensive, high-pressure program with the same number of study hours crammed into fewer weeks.

The steps in Table 2.3 will guide you through the planning process.

After you've sketched your plan, turn to chapter 3. There you'll begin developing your Level One skills by learning what to expect on the real ACT and some of the best test-taking strategies for every part of the exam.

JUST THE FACTS

- Level One skills involve Testwiseness and can be developed quickly.
- Level Two skills involve Topic Strategies and take more time to develop.
- Level Three skills involve Broad-Based Verbal and Math Abilities and take the longest time to develop.
- Skills at all three levels can help boost your ACT scores.
- Depending on your schedule, your personal study program can delve more or less deeply into all three kinds of skills.

Part II

Getting Inside the ACT

Chapter 3

Finding Your Way Around the ACT

Get the Scoop On . . .

- What to expect when you take the ACT
- Why you *don't* have to answer every question
- How to make the most of every minute
- What to do when time runs short

THE OFFICIAL DESCRIPTION

How the Test Is Organized

The ACT Assessment is roughly a three-hour test made up of four separately-timed tests. (Actually, you'll be in the testing room for 4 hours or more on exam day. You'll spend 3 hours answering questions and 1 to 1½ hours filling out forms, listening to instructions, resting briefly between sections, and so on.) The tests range in length from 35 minutes to 60 minutes each.

The four ACT tests are:

- **The English Test,** which lasts 45 minutes and includes 75 questions related to grammar, usage, and other writing skills

- **The Mathematics Test,** which lasts 60 minutes and includes 60 math problems involving arithmetic, algebra, geometry, trigonometry, and other topics from high school math

- **The Reading Test,** which lasts 35 minutes and includes 40 questions testing your ability to understand reading passages in fiction, the humanities, social studies, and the natural sciences

- **The Science Reasoning Test,** which lasts 35 minutes and includes 40 questions based on passages that describe experimental work or research findings from biology, earth science, chemistry, and physics

Two important notes about the structure and contents of the ACT:

- **More than one form of the assessment may be given at any time.** The test-makers refer to different editions of the ACT as "forms." Each form has a different batch of questions (also called "items"). On any given test day, several forms are used, not only across the country but even within the same test room. The person sitting next to you may be working on a completely different exam. (Among other benefits to the test-makers, this discourages cheating!) So don't be alarmed if you notice that your neighbor is working on different test questions than you. It's no mistake.

- **The test-makers may change the test format if they wish.** Don't assume that your ACT will precisely follow the format outlined here (or in the official guides provided by the test-makers). Although variations are rare, they do happen; and from time to time, the test-makers experiment with new formats and new types of questions.

The Map of the ACT (Table 3.1) gives a more detailed listing of the types and quantities of questions you'll probably encounter on the exam.

How You Mark Your Answers

FYI

If something weird comes up on your ACT, don't let it boggle you. It's just the test-makers playing tricks with your mind. Any truly weird questions are probably for experimental purposes, in which case they won't count in your test score.

All of the questions on the ACT are multiple-choice questions. You'll have four answers to choose from, except in the Mathematics Test, where you'll have five. On odd-numbered questions, the answers are labeled (A) through (D); on even-numbered questions, they're labeled

Table 3.1
Map of the ACT

English Test
40 questions on usage and mechanics
35 questions on rhetorical skills

75 QUESTIONS TOTAL

Mathematics Test
14 questions on arithmetic
10 questions on elementary algebra
 9 questions on intermediate algebra
 9 questions on coordinate geometry
14 questions on plane geometry
 4 questions on trigonometry

60 QUESTIONS TOTAL

Reading Test
10 questions on prose fiction
10 questions on a passage about the humanities
10 questions on a passage about social studies
10 questions on a passage about the natural sciences

40 QUESTIONS TOTAL

Science Reasoning Test
15 data representation questions
18 research summaries questions
 7 conflicting viewpoint questions

40 QUESTIONS TOTAL

(F) through (J). (This funny system has the advantage of making it slightly harder for you to lose track of which question you are working on.)

After you pick the best answer, you'll mark your choice on the separate answer sheet by using a pencil to darken the appropriate oval next to the number for that question. This produces an answer sheet that can be scored quickly, accurately, and cheaply by a machine.

How the Test is Scored

FYI

Unlike some other standardized tests, on the ACT, no points are deducted for incorrect answers—the so-called guessing penalty. So it pays to answer every question, even if you have no idea as to the correct answer. It can't hurt, and it might help.

Several steps are involved in taking your ACT answer sheet, covered with blackened ovals, and turning it into the collection of two-digit numbers that will be your answer to the age-old, nosy question, "Whadjaget?"

First, for each of the tests, your *raw score* is calculated. Your raw score is simply the number of questions you answer correctly.

The raw score is then converted into a *scale score*. You'll receive several different scale scores. First, there is a scale score for each test: English, Mathematics, Reading, and Science Reasoning. These are the two-digit scores most people are thinking of when they talk about ACT scores. The lowest possible scale score, for each test, is 1; the highest is 36.

You'll also receive subscores for particular topics on three of the tests. In English, you'll receive subscores in usage/mechanics and rhetorical skills; in Mathematics, you'll receive subscores in pre-algebra/elementary algebra, algebra/coordinate geometry, and plane/geometry/trigonometry; and in Reading, you'll receive subscores in social studies/natural sciences and prose fiction/humanities. (There's no subscore in the Science Reasoning test.) These subscores range from 1 (low) to 18 (high).

You'll also receive a Composite score—one overall number that summarizes how you did on the ACT. It's simply the average of your four test scores.

The system of converting a raw score into a scale score varies slightly from one test battery to another, since the test forms vary slightly in difficulty. If you get a slightly "harder" ACT, the score conversion table for your exam will be a little easier: You'll be able to get a couple more questions wrong while still earning the same scale score. The test-makers have an elaborate system based on statistical theories for figuring out exactly how much they need to compensate for slightly harder or easier test forms. The idea is to make any given score—say, a 21 in English—represent the same level of difficulty no matter when or where the test is given.

The test-makers point out—quite properly—that the scale scores are only approximately accurate, in the following sense. If you took the ACT a hundred times (how's *that* for a fun idea?), the scores you'd earn would obviously vary. On a good day, you might earn a Mathematics score of (let's say) 26. On a bad day, you might score 22. But, your hundred scores should supposedly cluster around some central number which represents your "true" ability. Maybe in your case it's around 24.

Now, of course, it's impractical to expect anyone to take the ACT a hundred times. (*Too bad!* say the test-makers.) So the ACT people have to be satisfied with a single score, which they consider an approximation of your "true" score. Statistical theory suggests that, for the ACT, your scaled score is probably within about 2 points of your "true" score. Therefore, strictly speaking, if you earn a score of 24 on the Math portion of the ACT, you should think of it as representing a range of about 2 points either way—that is, from 22 to 26. And if your best friend scores 23, does that mean you are "better" at math than she is? Maybe, maybe not. The ACT isn't a precise enough measuring tool to say for sure.

FYI

The score conversion formulas for every ACT are a little different—but notice how high you can score if you answer just 65 to 75 percent of the questions right!

Finally, you'll also be given a *percentile score*. This is based on a comparison of your Composite score to the Composite scores of two groups of college-bound students: those in your home state, and those from the entire nation. The percentile score shows what percentage of these students scored lower than you. Obviously, the higher your percentile scores, the better.

Average ACT scale scores vary from time to time, but in recent years, the average score for each of the four tests has ranged between 20 and 21. What is a "good" ACT score? It all depends. It depends on what colleges you hope to be admitted to; it depends on how many students you are competing against for admission, and how high *their* scores are; it depends on your other credentials, and how heavily you want the ACT to weigh in the admission decision. We'll discuss the deeper meanings of ACT scores—and how they may change your life—more thoroughly later in this book.

THE INSIDER'S REPORT

You Don't Need To Answer Every Question

There are many differences between a standardized exam like the ACT and the classroom tests you're used to taking. Here's a crucial difference: To do well on a classroom test, you need to answer correctly 80 to 90 percent of the questions, or more. Not on the ACT. You can earn a high score on the ACT by answering two-thirds to three-quarters of the questions right.

Think about that. On a classroom test, if you get 66 to 75 percent of the questions right, you'll earn a grade of D or (at best) C. On the ACT, the same percentage right yields a grade that's the equivalent of B+! The Sample Score Conversion Table (Table 3.2) gives a few details.

This fact about the ACT has several important implications for you.

■ **You don't have to answer every question.** In truth, most students omit some questions on each test. And that's perfectly okay. Even if you leave two or three questions blank on each test, you can still score well into the 30s (provided you perform well on the questions you *do* answer, of course).

■ **Getting a handful of questions wrong is not fatal.** If you run into a series of tough questions—several questions based on a reading or science passage that you find very hard to understand, for example—don't despair. Give an educated guess for each of the tough questions—get a couple of them right—and

Table 3.2
Sample Score Conversion Tables

English		
Raw Score	**Percentage Right**	**Scaled Score**
75	100	36
67	89	30
56	73	25
44	58	20
Mathematics		
60	100	36
52	87	30
41	68	25
31	52	20
Reading		
40	100	36
32	80	30
26	65	25
20	50	20
Science Reasoning		
40	100	36
35	88	30
29	73	25
21	53	20

then move on. You can still earn a high overall score, as long as you don't let the few "killer questions" get you down.

- **Almost everyone gets some questions wrong.** On a classroom test, if everyone scores 95%, the teacher is usually delighted; it means she has done a great job of teaching. If everyone scored 35 or 36 on the ACT, the test-makers would be depressed. Their job is to create a test that yields a broad *range* of scores. They want a few 35s, a few 10s, and a nice sampling of 18s, 22s, and 25s in between. This proves that they are differentiating among students—sorting the sheep from the goats, and both from the donkeys, cows, and emus—which is what they are paid to do. To accomplish this, they write questions that vary greatly in difficulty: a few very hard, a few very easy, and many others scattered along the range in between. Thus, when you take the ACT, *expect* each test to include a few questions you find very difficult. Answer them the best you can and move on. Almost no one gets every question right.

Every Question Is Worth the Same Amount

Some of the questions will be very hard. You may find that it takes you two or three minutes to solve some of the math problems—an eternity on the ACT. Others will be shockingly easy. The answer may jump out at you as soon as you see the question—you may spend 15 seconds or less on the item. *The easy questions are worth just as much as the hard ones.* The test-makers only look at how many questions you answer right; they couldn't care less which ones they are.

MAKING THE TEST WORK FOR YOU

Budget Your Time

FYI

Don't get bogged down on a few very hard questions. The time you spend wrestling one tough problem into submission could be spent answering three easy questions— and getting three times as much credit.

The ACT isn't a speed test. Most students find they have time to answer all, or nearly all, of the questions in each section. But, you'll have no time to waste. If you aren't efficient in the use of your precious minutes, you may find yourself having to leave some questions blank that you could surely have answered—and losing some valuable points. Here are the best methods for making sure you don't run out of time before you run out of questions:

- **Overview each test before you begin your work.** When the proctor says, "Begin work on Test 1" (or 2, or whatever), don't immediately begin answering questions. Take the first 30 seconds to overview the entire test. Leaf through the test booklet to check the format, contents, and length of the section. How many questions are there? How many reading passages?

How many problems of the type you hate (or like) the most? Overviewing the test will prevent you from having the unpleasant surprise of turning what you thought was the last page of the test to discover one more set of questions—just as the proctor says, "Put down your pencil."

■ **First tackle the question types you find easiest.** Having overviewed the test, you'll know before you begin to work what question types appear and in what order. Now consider: You don't have to work through the questions in the order they're printed. Instead, pick the questions that deal with the topic you find easiest, fastest, even (if possible) the most fun. Start with that batch of questions, no matter where it appears.

This strategy has several benefits. It will allow you to quickly rack up a bunch of easy points at the very start of the test period. It will help you develop a good rhythm and a sense of confidence for the rest of the test. And, it will eliminate the possibility of running out of time just as you begin work on the questions you find easiest. (If you *must* run out of time—and with practice there's no reason why you should—it's better to omit several questions you find very hard and of which you'd probably get only a couple right, rather than several easy questions that represent sure points for you.)

FYI

Remember: If you start work on a question other than question 1, be sure to mark your answers in the right spaces on your answer sheet.

■ **Skip and mark the hardest questions so that you can try them later.** Because every question on the ACT is worth the same amount, it's crucial not to get bogged down on a few very tough questions. (Every test has them.) Instead, once you've discovered that a particular question is a very hard one—a math problem requiring complicated figuring, for example—stop working on it. Put an X mark in the margin of your test booklet next to the question number, and move on. If you have time at the end of that test, you can double back and tackle the three or four toughest questions you'd skipped and marked before. This will ensure that you get to all of the easier questions in the test.

This strategy might help you in another way. Sometimes, when you return to a question several minutes after skipping it, the right answer that eluded you before seems obvious. Why does this happen? No one knows for sure. Maybe your unconscious mind ponders the question while you consciously think about other items. But this effect does occur, and you should take advantage of it.

■ **Practice timing along with test-taking skills.** Between now and the day of the ACT, whenever you work on practice exercises or sample tests, follow the time restrictions given. Set up a kitchen

FYI

Ever notice how, when you watch a TV show, you always "know," without looking at a clock, when it's time for the next commercial? Through your years of TV watching, you've developed an inner clock that's finely tuned to the rhythms of TV. In the same way, practicing the timing of the real ACT will enable you to sense, as you work, when you need to move a little faster or when you have plenty of time and can afford to cruise.

timer while you work, or ask your Mom or your brother to "proctor" you. Not only will this give you practice in working under time pressure, but it will also allow you to develop an inner clock keyed to the timing of the real ACT.

Never Read the Directions

One piece of test-taking advice dispensed by old-fashioned teachers (and some current books, alas) is, "Always read the directions carefully before you start work—preferably twice." The trouble with this advice is that, on the ACT, the precious minutes allotted for each test *include* the time for reading the directions. So if you spend (say) three minutes studying the directions, that's three fewer minutes you have to answer the questions.

The truth is that the test directions don't change from one exam to the next (unless the test-makers are trying out some weird new question type, as explained earlier in this chapter—in which case the questions won't count in your score anyway). So get to know the directions, and the best strategies for answering the questions, thoroughly *before* the day of the exam. Then, when you take the test, all you need to do is verify the question type and immediately begin work.

Using the Answer Sheet

As we've explained, you'll mark your answers on an answer sheet that is separate from the question booklet. How you use the answer sheet *does* matter. Follow the directions provided by the test-makers: Completely fill in the oval for the answer you want and erase all stray marks, lest you confuse the stupid machine that the test-makers have hired to grade your exam. Here are some important additional tips:

FYI

Reset your watch at the start of each test. A small trick but a very helpful one: reset your watch to noon as each test begins. This makes it easy to tell at a glance how many minutes remain. You'd be surprised how tricky it can be, in the midst of a grueling exam, to have to figure out: "Let's see—I started work on this test at 10:47— it's now 11:04— how many minutes does that leave me . . . ?"

- **Check your location on the answer sheet frequently.** Get into the habit of making sure that you are filling in the right answer in the right location at least once every five questions. This will preclude your discovering, as you complete a test, that you've mismarked the answers for the last 20 questions (ouch!).

- **Be extra careful when you skip questions.** It's easy to forget to leave a blank space on the answer sheet when you skip a question. Make a point of remembering.

- **Practice using sample answer sheets.** Most study books (including this one) with practice tests include answer sheets with ovals like those used on the real exam. Don't ignore them, instead, use them when you take practice tests. Filling in the real sheet on the day of the ACT will be second nature to you—and one less thing you have to worry about.

Table 3.3
The Five-Minute Drill

1. When you notice that five minutes remain to work on the test, promptly answer the question you are looking at. Then overview the remaining questions in the test by glancing through them quickly.
2. Decide which of the remaining questions look quickest and easiest. Read and answer them promptly, guessing if necessary.
3. If a reading or science reasoning passage remains, take about 30 seconds to *skim* through it, looking only for the main idea and the author's overall point of view. Then glance at the questions that follow the passage and answer whichever ones you have a hunch about.
4. If a batch of math problems remains, glance at them and pick three to five to answer. Focus on items with math topics you are comfortable with.
5. Guess freely but judiciously. On every item where you feel there is a particular answer that sounds wrong, guess at random from among the other answers. If you have a good feeling about a particular answer choice, pick it and move on.

- **If you do goof up . . . and discover that you have mismarked the last five or ten answer spaces, don't panic!** Raise your hand and get the attention of the proctor. Explain what happened and ask for five minutes *after* the test is over with your answer sheet *only*, so you can (calmly and carefully) correct the misplaced answer choices. She will probably say yes.

What To Do When Crunch Time Comes

Occasionally, despite having practiced and used the best time-budgeting techniques, you might find yourself running out of time before you run out of questions on a particular test. If that happens, don't get upset. Instead, spend the last five minutes extracting the most possible points from the remaining questions. How? By following the procedure described in The Five-Minute Drill (Table 3.3).

JUST THE FACTS

- Preview each test before you start work and budget your time accordingly.

- Remember that every question is worth the same amount—don't sweat the hardest ones.

- Don't waste time reading the directions—they don't change.

- Fill in your answer sheet with care.

- Use the Five-Minute Drill if you're running out of time.

Chapter 4

The English Test

GET THE SCOOP ON . . .

- Quick and accurate ways to tackle English test items
- The kinds of grammar and writing errors often tested on the ACT—and the kinds the test makers ignore
- How to focus on the only possible answer choices within just a few seconds
- How to spot words and sentences that disrupt the unity and logic of a paragraph, and what to do about them
- The test-makers' definition of "good style," and how to recognize it when you see it

THE TEST CAPSULE

What's the Big Idea?

The ACT English Test consists of five passages of nonfiction prose resembling articles from magazines, passages from books, or student essays. Each passage contains 15 questions about how it is written. For some items, part or all of a sentence is underlined, and four answer choices are presented, three of which rephrase or eliminate the underlined portion. You then must decide which of the four alternatives is best from the standpoint of grammatical correctness, proper English usage, clarity, conciseness, and style. For other items, questions are asked about the passage's overall organization or about changing, adding to, or deleting some of the contents of the passage. For these items, you must decide which alternative will add to the overall effectiveness of the passage as a piece of writing.

How Many?

Your ACT English Test will probably have a total of 75 questions based on five passages, 15 items per passage.

How Much Time Should They Take?

You should be able to answer English Test items at a rate of almost two per minute—30 seconds each. That will leave you a little extra time to check your work at the end of the test.

What's the Best Strategy?

On Usage/Mechanics questions, rather than simply reading all four versions of the sentence looking for the one that seems best, you should actively search for the error that has been inserted (75% of the time) in the original sentence. Then, *before looking at the answer choices*, decide how you would correct that error. Finally, *scan* the answer choices, looking only at the part of the sentence in which the original error appeared, and eliminate any answer which does not correct the error. You can usually eliminate one or two answer choices this way, allowing you to focus your attention strictly on the answers that fix the original mistake.

What's the Worst Pitfall?

Getting bogged down in long, complex, hard-to-follow verbiage, much of which may be irrelevant to the grammatical or stylistic issue central to the question. Learn to ignore extraneous phrases and clauses that may complicate a sentence without affecting its basic logical and grammatical structure.

THE OFFICIAL DESCRIPTION

What They Are

The ACT English Test focuses on the stylistic conventions and grammatical rules of "standard written English" and your ability to apply those rules to several sample pieces of writing. They test your ability through what might be called an editing exercise: you are given a passage that contains a number of grammatical mistakes, stylistic weaknesses, errors in punctuation, lapses in logic, and other writing flaws. Your job is to detect those flaws and pick alternative ways of writing and organizing the passage so as to correct the flaws without introducing any new ones.

What They Measure

The test-makers' phrase for the language tested on the ACT is "standard written English." This means the language used in serious, "respectable" publications that feature works of nonfiction prose written in contemporary American English. What does this definition exclude? Slang, colloquialisms, technical jargon, geographic or ethnic dialects, archaic language (like Shakespeare's) and creative or experimental language (like James Joyce's)—all are excluded. To get a fix on ACT English, think of the prose in which publications like *The Atlantic Monthly, National Geographic, Time* Magazine, and *Readers Digest* are written—or the style in which you probably write compositions in English class. This is "standard written English."

What They Cover

The English Test items fall into two broad categories: Usage/Mechanics and Rhetorical Skills. Usage/Mechanics refers to the degree to which a sentence obeys the rules of English grammar and usage, including such specific principles as subject-verb agreement, correct construction of verb tenses, parallel sentence structure, and proper use of punctuation marks. Rhetorical Skills include the overall organization of the passage (Which topic logically belongs first? Which belongs last?), clear transitions from topic to topic, smart decisions about what to include and what to omit from the passage, and avoiding stylistic problems like wordiness, redundancy, and vagueness.

When you take the ACT, you'll encounter passages that are guilty of sins against both correctness and effectiveness, and you'll be expected to know how to correct them without creating any new errors in the process. Very subtle stylistic or esthetic considerations are not tested on the ACT, nor are rules of grammar and usage that are disputed or changing (we'll give examples of these later).

The Directions

The directions for the ACT English Test are similar to the following:

> **Directions:** This test consists of five passages in which particular words or phrases are underlined and numbered. Alongside the passage, you will see alternative words and phrases that could be substituted for the underlined part. You must select the alternative that expresses the idea most clearly and correctly or that best fits the style and tone of the entire passage. If the original version is best, select "No Change."
>
> The test also includes questions about entire paragraphs and the passage as a whole. These questions are identified by a number in a box.
>
> After you select the correct answer for each question, mark the oval representing the correct answer on your answer sheet.

THE INSIDER'S REPORT: STRATEGIES THAT REALLY WORK

Start by Spending 20 Seconds Skimming the Whole Passage

When you tackle the English Test, you're in the position of a writer who is about to revise the rough draft of a piece of work he or she is writing. Although the five passages on the test may not much resemble the kinds of compositions *you* write, you'll have to pretend they do, and project yourself into the process of rewriting them as if they were your own.

Naturally, to do this, it helps to have a general sense before you begin of the overall meaning and purpose of the passage. It's especially important because, as you'll see, some of the test items turn on the *meaning* of a given sentence or paragraph as well as its grammatical form.

Therefore, it's a good strategy to begin work on a particular passage by skimming the whole thing, looking for its general theme, its style and tone, and the basic sequence of ideas. Twenty seconds should be ample time for this. The passages are generally short—300 to 400 words—and the writing is usually not arcane. Just let your eye glide down the columns of type, grasping what you can in 20 seconds, and then return to the top, ready to begin reading and answering questions.

When a Sentence Contains a Test Item, Read the Whole Sentence, *Listening* for the Error

Most of the English test items are based on underlined words or phrases which may or may not contain errors in grammar, word usage, punctuation, or style. (As we'll discuss later, there are some other items not based on underlined portions of the passage. They need a strategy of their own.) Not every sentence contains an underlined portion. But when you read a sentence that does, you should use your "ear" to search for the possible error.

Here's what we mean. There are many ways in which people learn to use a language correctly. If you were raised in a non-English-speaking country, you probably first learned English in the same way most Americans learn Spanish, French, or German—from a teacher in a classroom. You studied grammar, vocabulary, and sentence structure from a textbook, and you practiced English through dialogues, exercises, quizzes, and compositions. At first, English was a collection of rules to be memorized and followed; only later, perhaps after you moved to the United States, did it become for you a living language about which you developed a "feeling," an "instinct."

Most Americans, however—as well as Canadians, Britons, Australians, and many others—learn English "at their mothers' knees," and the *feeling* for English as a living language comes long before any formal study of English grammar or word usage. In fact, nowadays many Americans hardly study grammar at all. Whatever knowledge of grammar "rules" they have is picked up almost by accident. An English teacher notes your error in the use of a verb in the margin of a term paper; a friend corrects you during a conversation ("Not 'If I *was*'; you mean, 'If I *were*' "); you hear some "language maven" on TV discussing "who" versus "whom." That's the full extent of most people's "study" of English grammar these days.

If this describes you, *don't be concerned*. The ACT is designed to be friendly to people like you. Items on the test do test your ability to apply the rules of English grammar and usage correctly. However, the test rewards the writer whose knowledge of the language is a matter of "feeling" or "instinct." On the ACT, you never have to explain or identify a grammar error; no grammar terminology is used or tested; you never have to diagram or otherwise analyze the structure of a sentence. Instead, you just have to pick the version of the sentence that *sounds right* from a collection of versions that sound, and are, wrong.

The first step, then, in tackling most English Test items is simply to read the entire sentence, *listening*, as if you were reading aloud, for any part of the sentence that sounds "odd," "weird," "awkward," or "wrong." In most of the sentences, you'll notice such a part—anything from one word to a whole phrase or clause that doesn't "sound right." It's like tasting a dish in the kitchen before bringing it out to the table, or giving the leg on a chair you're fixing one last shake before sitting on it: if something is wrong, you'll probably know it, whether or not you can name or describe it in words.

Let's consider an example—a sentence something like those you'll encounter in the passages on the ACT, though presented here *without* any answer choices:

> Unlike Eisenstein, whose movies clearly tran-
> scend any ideological purpose, Riefenstahl is
> generally dismissed <u>with merely being a propa-
> gandist</u> for an evil political cause.

Does any part of this sentence sound wrong to you? (Of course, the fact that certain words have been underlined by the test-makers offers a significant clue as to which part of the sentence you should focus on.) The "wobbly" piece of this sentence is the phrase "dismissed with merely being"; it's not the normal wording for the idea being expressed here.

Think about how you've seen the verb "dismissed" used in other sentences. Can you form, in your mind, the normal phrasing of the words that would follow "dismissed?" That's the first and crucial step you'd take in tackling this sentence if it appeared in a real ACT passage.

In a moment, we'll see how the rest of this item might look on the exam. But for now, note that the first step in analyzing the question is simply to read the sentence with care, trying to observe any part of it that "sounds" or "feels" wrong—any part that your instinct for English rebels against. Improving your skill on the English Test is largely a matter of honing this instinct through practice, much as a musician sharpens her ear by listening to good music as often as she can.

Does this mean that it's pointless to study (or review) the rules of grammar? Not at all. Your instinct for correct English can be greatly enhanced by knowing the rules that linguists and grammarians have devised to explain how sentences are normally constructed.

In Appendix C, The Insider's Writer's Manual for the ACT, we've captured the 40 rules of grammar, usage, and punctuation most commonly tested on the ACT. You may want to pause right now in your reading of this chapter and skim the pages of that appendix. Do the contents look somewhat familiar from an English course? Or are the rules explained there completely new to you? If the latter, you should devote some time over the next week to reading the appendix so as to acquaint yourself with the basic principles of English grammar and sentence structure—what verbs and nouns are, how they relate to one another, and so on. We'll refer to these principles—though with a minimum of jargon—as we consider some sample ACT items in the rest of this chapter. You'll find it helpful to have at least a nodding acquaintance with them.

On the assumption that you know at least the rudiments of English grammar, or will pick up whatever knowledge you lack by studying Appendix C, we suggest you look at Table 4.1. It offers four basic principles for error-spotting in ACT sentences. These are techniques that can help you zero in on the grammar and stylistic errors most often

Table 4.1
ACT English Error-Spotting Strategies

When in doubt about where the error is located in a sentence containing an underlined word or phrase, follow these four steps in the sequence indicated. If there is an error, it will probably be uncovered through this process.

- Find the verb, then its subject. Check subject-verb agreement, correct tense, and proper verb formation.

- Examine all pronouns. Make sure each has a clear antecedent with which it agrees in person and number.

- Look for wobbling of the sentence structure. Make sure modifiers are attached to what they modify, parallel ideas are grammatically parallel, and comparisons are clear and logical.

- Listen for awkwardness, verbosity, and incorrect use of idioms.

appearing in ACT passages—a useful supplement and aid to your instinctive "ear" for what's right and wrong in English. If any of the rules mentioned there, or the terms used, seem unfamiliar, you'll find them clearly explained in the appendix.

Once You Spot the Error, Consider How You'd Correct It

When a sentence in an ACT passage has an underlined word or phrase, approximately three times out of four that sentence contains an error in grammar, usage, or style; and, in most cases, you'll be able to "hear" that error by reading the sentence carefully.

Having done that, the next step in tackling the question is to consider how you'd correct the error if you had written the sentence. Do this before looking at any of the answer choices. Try rephrasing the faulty part of the sentence in your mind, figuring out what word or words you'd eliminate, change, move, or add, and imagine how the improved phrase or clause would read.

You may or may not find it easy to do this; it depends on the degree of writing skill you possess, and how tricky the particular test item is. However, as you'll see in a moment, this is an important time-saving step as well as a way of avoiding the confusion and errors that can easily occur if you plunge immediately into the answer choices.

Let's see how this would work, first by referring back to the sample item we saw a moment ago:

> Unlike Eisenstein, whose movies clearly tran-
> scend any ideological purpose, Riefenstahl is
> generally dismissed with merely being a propa-
> gandist for an evil political cause.

As we noticed before, the error here lies in the phrase that follows the verb "dismissed," which is not worded as it would normally be. (The technical term for this error is non-idiomatic usage. It's frequently tested on the ACT.) Can you decide how you'd rephrase it? Having come up with your own version of those words, you're ready to move on to the next step in the process, which is to:

Scan the Second, Third, and Fourth Answers, Looking for Answers That Correct the Error

Each ACT item based on an underlined word or phrase provides you with four versions of the underlined words from the original sentence. These are the four answer choices you'll to have to choose from. Here's how this item might look, complete with answer choices, on the real exam:

Unlike Eisenstein, whose movies clearly transcend any ideological purpose, Riefenstahl is generally dismissed <u>with merely being a propagandist</u> for an evil political cause.

1. (A)   NO CHANGE
    (B)   as being a propagandist merely
    (C)   for being merely a propagandist
    (D)   as a mere propagandist

If you were able to anticipate how the error in the original sentence should be corrected, picking the best answer choice will be fairly easy. Just scan answers (B), (C), and (D), looking for the wording you thought would be correct. If you find that wording in one of the answer choices, you've probably found the correct answer.

In this case, if you knew that the normal English idiom would be "to dismiss [someone] as a" propagandist (or whatever), without using the words "with" or "being," you could zero in quickly on answer choice (D)—which is the best version of the underlined words. Recognizing the error and anticipating how it should be corrected obviates the necessity of reading through all of the answer choices, let alone plugging them into the entire, lengthy sentence to hear how they sound in that context.

Try this method with another example:

Due to current limitations in scientific methods, the age of many inorganic substances, including the minerals that largely constitute the inner layers of the earth, <u>are impossible to determine precisely.</u>

2. (F)   NO CHANGE
    (G)   may precisely not be determined.
    (H)   is impossible to determine precisely.
    (J)   are not able precisely to be determined.

Can you "hear" the error in the original wording? If you're not sure, try using the error checklist from Table 4.1. One of the first "hot spots" to examine in any ACT sentence is the main verb of the sentence; errors often focus on that word or phrase.

In this case, the verb is the first underlined word, "are," and the error associated with it is one of the most common ACT error types: faulty subject-verb agreement. A detailed explanation of this topic, complete with examples, appears in Appendix C, but the gist is that the subject and verb of a sentence must agree in number; a singular subject requires a singular verb, while a plural subject requires a plural verb.

That rule is violated in this sentence. To find the subject of the verb "are," ask yourself: "What are impossible to determine precisely?" The answer is, "The age of many" blah blah blah. (Exactly what doesn't matter. The key word is age, since it's the age that can't be determined, and, therefore, "age" is the subject of the verb. The complex words that follow "the age of many" don't affect the grammar of the sentence, and, therefore, we can safely ignore them, thinking of them merely as "blah blah blah.") Since "age" is a singular subject, a singular verb is needed rather than the plural "are." The verb should be "is" instead.

With that in mind, scan—don't read—the answer choices. Two of them can be eliminated immediately. (F), of course, is wrong; and (J) contains the verb "are," which caused the problem in the first place. However, (H) looks promising; it uses the correct singular verb "is" instead. And (G) is a possibility; it changes the verb altogether, to "may . . . be," which does agree with the subject "age." So now you must choose between two potential answer choices. This requires you to read both in full, and leads to the next step in the process:

Pick an Answer That Corrects the Error Without Introducing Any New Error

Scanning the answer choices to eliminate those that fail to correct the error will usually leave you with one or two possible options. If there are two options to choose from, read them both carefully. Although each corrects the original error, you'll generally find that one introduces some new error. Your job is to "listen" for any new errors and find the answer choice that doesn't contain one.

In this case, answer (G) introduces a new error. It moves the location of the adverb "precisely" into an awkward and unclear spot. (Generally speaking, an adverb should be as close as possible to the word it modifies. In this sentence, "precisely" should be as close as possible to "determine," since that is the word whose meaning it affects.) Thus, (H) is the correct answer.

Try yet another example:

Once almost hidden under centuries of soot and grime, skilled preservationists have now restored Michelangelo's famous frescoes on the ceiling of the Sistine Chapel.

3. (A) NO CHANGE
   (B) the restoration of Michelangelo's famous frescoes on the ceiling of the Sistine Chapel has been done by skilled preservationists.
   (C) skilled preservationists on the ceiling of the Sistine Chapel have now restored Michelangelo's famous frescoes there.
   (D) Michelangelo's famous frescoes on the ceiling of the Sistine Chapel have now been restored by skilled preservationists.

Can you spot the error in the original sentence? The mistake is another common ACT error known as a misplaced modifier. The opening phrase of the sentence, "Once almost hidden" blah blah blah, is a *modifying phrase* because it describes or gives more information about something else in the sentence. The rule is that a modifying phrase should be right next to the word or phrase that names what is being described.

Now, what is being described here?—in other words, what was "Once almost hidden?" The answer is "Michelangelo's famous frescoes." Therefore, in this sentence, the words "Michelangelo's famous frescoes" should follow the modifying phrase immediately, so as to make it clear that the frescoes are being modified or described by the words "Once almost hidden." The way the original sentence is written, it almost sounds as through "the skilled preservationists" were "Once almost hidden"—surely a bizarre image.

Now scan—don't read—the answer choices, looking for any that put "Michelangelo's famous frescoes" right at the start of the underlined portion, next to the modifying phrase. Only one answer qualifies— choice (D). That's the correct answer.

On the ACT, the underlined sentence portions—and the answer choices—will sometimes be quite lengthy, as in this example. Focusing on the few words that need to be changed to correct the original error can save you a lot of time by making it unnecessary to read every answer choice in detail.

Sometimes, as in this next example, the underlined words will straddle two sentences:

> Although my brother was a talented painter, he
> gave up his dream of a life as an <u>artist. Making
> instead</u> a living as an electrical engineer and
> painting on weekends.

4. (F)   NO CHANGE
   (G)   artist, instead making
   (H)   artist. Instead he makes
   (J)   artist—rather, making

Here, the test-makers want to check whether you recognize a problem with the overall structure of the second sentence. It's a sentence fragment—a collection of words that can't stand alone as a sentence since it doesn't contain an independent subject and verb. (The subject is what's missing.)

The problem could be corrected in several ways. One way would be to fix the second sentence by giving it an independent subject and verb. That's what answer (H) tries to do. However, if you read the new version of the sentence using "Instead he makes" as its opening words, you see that a new problem crops up. The phrase at the end, "and painting on weekends," doesn't fit the new sentence, since it doesn't grammatically match "he makes." (If it read, "and paints on weekends," it would be all right.)

The best answer choice is (G). It corrects the fragment by linking it to the preceding sentence. Choice (J) tries the same strategy, but the use of the dash and the word "rather" are both awkward and confusing, making this a poor alternative.

Tackle Questions Related to Overall Structure Last

FYI

When you're struggling to choose the best sequence for a group of sentences or a group of paragraphs, try looking for the sentence or paragraph that should appear first. It will often introduce the overall topic that the rest of the material will talk about. Once you've found the opening element, the others will usually fall easily into place.

As we mentioned earlier, a few ACT English items are not based on underlined portions of the passage. They're marked by boxed item numbers appearing in various places in the passage—between sentences, at the end of paragraphs, or at the end of the entire passage.

The questions based on underlined words are generally what ACT calls Usage/Mechanics items—questions dealing with the rules of grammar, usage, and such "mechanical" details as punctuation. The boxed items, by contrast, are generally Rhetorical Skills items, which deal with larger questions of writing strategy, overall organization, the choice of contents, and style.

One type of Rhetorical Skills item you'll certainly encounter is the overall structure question. This deals with the sequence of ideas in the passage. The question takes two forms. In one form, you're asked to select the best sequence of sentences within a paragraph. In the other, you must select the best sequence of paragraphs for the passage as a whole.

Here's an example of what an overall structure question might look like in the context of a typical ACT passage:

[1] The immigration laws led, ultimately, to a quota system based on the number of individuals of each national origin reported in the 1890 census. [2] The United States, which was founded mainly by people who had emigrated from northern Europe, had an essentially open-door immigration policy for the first 100 years of its existence. [3] But starting in the 1880s and continuing through the 1920s, Congress passed a series of restrictive immigration laws. [4] The door to freedom hadn't been slammed shut, exactly, but it was now open only to the "right" sort of people. [5]

5. Which of the following sequences of sentences will make this paragraph most logical?

   (A) 4, 3, 1, 2
   (B) 2, 3, 1, 4
   (C) 1, 3, 2, 4
   (D) 2, 3, 4, 1

Notice the bracketed numbers preceding each sentence. When you see these in a given paragraph, you can tell that the test-makers will be asking you a question about the sequence of sentences.

Generally, some specific clues will appear that will alert you to the best sequence of ideas for a paragraph or the passage as a whole. Often, a clear time sequence is apparent. In the paragraph above, for example, you can see that the second sentence describes American immigration policy during the early years of the country's history, while the other sentences describe how that policy later changed. Thus, it would make sense to think of putting sentence 2 first.

Having decided that sentence 2 ought to come first in the paragraph, glance at the answer choices. Only answers (B) and (D) are possible. Read the paragraph in both sequences, and you'll probably be able to tell that answer (B) is better. (Sentence 4 makes a better conclusion for the paragraph than sentence 1; it offers a general summation of the theme of the paragraph that ties together the various ideas presented quite neatly.) So (B) is the best choice.

There are some other kinds of Rhetorical Skills items, which we'll discuss later in this chapter.

THE INSIDER'S REPORT: THE BEST TIPS

Expect About One Quarter of the Items To Be Perfectly Correct and in Need of No Change

Generally speaking, the test-makers will give you roughly equal numbers of each answer choice on any given test section. In other words, out of 75 items on the English Test, about one quarter will have the first choice (A or F) as the correct response, one quarter will have the second choice (B or G), and so on.

Therefore, about one quarter of the ACT English items should be answered with choice (A) or (F). This choice usually means that the original sentence contains *no* errors and is better than any of the other variations offered. These are NO CHANGE sentences—perfectly correct as written and in no need of revision.

This simple fact has two consequences for your test-taking strategy.

FYI

Some of the grammar and usage rules most often discussed by teachers and others are not tested on the ACT. This is because, like many aspects of language, they are changing; as a result, some usages once considered wrong are now accepted by many speakers of English. Examples: the split infinitive, ending a sentence with a preposition, and the use of hopefully to mean "it is to be hoped that."

- **If you read a sentence that sounds perfectly okay, it probably is.** Depending on where you are in the test section and on the time constraints you're feeling, you have two choices. If you are near the start of the section and/or have plenty of time to work with, go ahead and read the other answer choices so as to confirm that the original version is the best. If you are near the end of the section and/or running low on time, don't bother: if the original sentence seems fine, simply pick the NO CHANGE answer and move on.

- **Keep count of the number of (A) and (F) answers, and adjust if the count is too high or too low.** When you've completed the first passage with its 15 test items, check how many (A)s and (F)s you've picked. If you've found no (A) or (F) items, you may be overanalyzing the sentences, finding "errors" where none actually exist. If you've found too many—say, six or more—you may be too forgiving, overlooking errors you should be spotting. Adjust accordingly.

All Things Being Equal, Choose the Shortest Answer

Occasionally, you'll find that eliminating all the answers that contain errors does not narrow your options to a single choice. You may find that two (or rarely three) answer choices all appear completely correct and equally clear, graceful, and unambiguous.

When this happens, choose whichever answer is shortest. Generally speaking, the test-makers regard a concise, tightly worded sentence as more stylistically effective than a wordy, loosely-structured one. Therefore, when all other factors appear equal, the shortest sentence is the one that the test- makers are most likely to consider correct.

Expect Each Paragraph To Be Unified Around a Single Idea

Some of the Rhetorical Skills questions on the ACT English Test focus on the clear and logical development of the ideas in the passage. These questions work in various ways. You may be asked to choose a sentence that would make a logical addition to the passage; you may be asked whether it would be a good idea to delete a particular sentence; or you may be asked where in the passage a certain idea would fit best.

Here's a sample of what this kind of question may look like:

FYI

Pay close attention when the question stem is long and detailed, as it is in sample question 6. The test makers are going out of their way to spell out the kind of answer choice they want you to pick. Don't reject their generosity!

Many owners of professional baseball teams are concerned about sagging attendance figures. Various gimmicks have been tried to boost attendance, from ballpark giveaways to special "nights" honoring various ethnic groups. Teams have changed the colors of their uniforms,

played rock music between innings, and set off
fireworks after the game. 6

6. The writer wishes to add another relevant example to this
paragraph without straying from the purpose of illustrating the
gimmicks used by baseball in an effort to improve attendance.
Which of the following sentences does that best?

(F)   It's hard to see what playing Duran
      Duran over the centerfield loudspeak-
      ers adds to the experience of a
      ballgame.

(G)   For many sports fans, baseball is just
      too slow-paced; they prefer the quick,
      constant action of basketball.

(H)   They've even tinkered with the rules
      of the game, introducing the so-called
      designated hitter.

(J)   Some teams claim they are losing
      millions of dollars each year due to
      poor attendance.

The most important principle to apply to question like this is that every
paragraph should be unified around a single idea. No sentence should
appear in a paragraph that doesn't clearly relate to that idea, either by
explaining it, illustrating it, defending it, elaborating on it, or otherwise
supporting it.

Notice that the sample question gives you a broad hint as to the kind of
sentence that should be added to this paragraph: It should be one that
offers "another relevant example to this paragraph without straying
from the purpose of illustrating the gimmicks used by baseball in an
effort to improve attendance." (This is typical of the test-makers.
They're not trying to trick you.) With that in mind, you can scrutinize
the four answer choices, looking for the one that serves the purpose
defined.

Only answer (H) does the trick. It names another way in which the
baseball owners have "tinkered" with their offerings to fans, trying to
make the game more appealing. The other answer choices do different
things altogether. Answer (F) adds a comment about the use of rock
music in stadiums rather than adding another example; and answers (G)
and (J) bring in fundamentally new ideas rather than developing the
main theme of the paragraph, which is the gimmicks used by baseball
owners. If you chose them to insert in the paragraph, you'd violate its
unity and make the onward flow of the passage confusing and unclear.

When tackling a Rhetorical Skills question that deals with adding or deleting material, look for an idea that will develop the theme of the paragraph or the entire passage without disrupting its unity. That's what the test-makers want.

Transitions Call for Linking Words That Logically Connect What Comes Before with What Comes After

Another common type of Rhetorical Skills item focuses on the transition between one idea and the next. Such a question may appear at either the beginning or ending of a sentence or a paragraph, asking you to pick the word or phrase that most logically links what comes before the break with what comes after.

Here's an example:

> Pablo Picasso is generally regarded as the quintessential modern artist. And undoubtedly the most significant revolution in modern art was the invention in the 1930s of the purely abstract painting. Thus, in all of Picasso's long and varied career, he never painted any significant abstract picture.

7. (A)   NO CHANGE
    (B)   Furthermore,
    (C)   So,
    (D)   Nonetheless,

FYI

You can often recognize a Rhetorical Skills items by glancing at the answer choices. When all four answers are grammatically similar, as they are in sample question 7, you can tell that the question focuses not on grammar but on the logical connections between ideas. Thus, you'll want to look for clues related to the meaning of the sentences, not just their grammatical structure.

The difference among the four answer choices for this item lies in their meaning. "Furthermore," in answer (B), suggests that what follows elaborates on or adds to what has been said previously. That's not a logical connection for the sentences in this paragraph, making (B) a wrong answer.

"Thus," the word in the original sentence (and in answer (A), of course), means much the same as "So" in answer (C): both imply that what follows is a logical result of what comes before. ("It is raining outside; thus, the streets are wet.") Unfortunately, this also makes no sense in the context of the paragraph. We've read that Picasso was a revolutionary twentieth century artist, and that abstract painting was the greatest revolution in twentieth century art. Following this, the fact that Picasso never made an abstract painting doesn't follow as a logical result; rather, it's a surprising contradiction.

The right answer, of course, is (D). "Nonetheless" fits the sense of surprise or contradiction we feel when we read the two sentences; it links them appropriately and logically.

You'll have several transition-based questions on your ACT English Test. When you encounter them, consider what comes before and what comes after, and pick the word or phrase that draws the most logical connection.

THE INSIDER'S REPORT: THE MOST IMPORTANT WARNINGS

Don't Get Bogged Down in Mere Verbiage

Occasionally, an ACT English passage contains some complex, convoluted sentences whose ideas may be difficult to follow.

Don't let this throw you off. Remember, these are not reading comprehension passages; you won't be asked to explain the meaning of the sentences or to interpret the ideas they contain. If you focus on the basic grammatical structure of each sentence and the connections among its main grammatical features, you can spot any errors the sentence contains even if you don't understand every detail of the long and convoluted verbiage.

To illustrate, consider this sentence:

> The average person's conception of scientific method is fundamentally flawed insofar as it assumes that theory develops automatically from observations of natural events; which are essentially unaffected by the preconceptions of the observer.

8. (F)   NO CHANGE
    (G)   events, which are
    (H)   events, these being
    (J)   events; themselves

This is a fairly long (33 words) and complicated sentence. It includes phrases like "scientific method" and "the preconceptions of the observer," which most of us don't use every day (and consequently have to stop to think about when we read them). Furthermore, if you're slightly intimi-dated by the topic of science—as many people are—the very theme of the sentence may make you nervous.

Our advice: forget all that. The key things to notice about this sentence are the following:

■ **Only a few words are underlined.** Thus, the problem is localized in a small part of the sentence rather than being a sentence-wide structural problem.

- **The underlined portion is near the end of the sentence.** Thus, the error is likely to involve mainly or exclusively the latter half of the sentence rather than the first half of the sentence.

In combination, these features tell you that you don't need to worry too much about what appears near the start of the sentence. If you understand it, fine. If you don't, don't agonize over it. Read the sentence fairly quickly, make sure you recognize where its key features appear (verb, subject, direct object or subject complement), and feel free almost to ignore phrases or groups of words that don't relate directly to the underlined part of the sentence.

Thus, you might read this sentence as follows:

> The average person's [blah blah blah] assumes that theory develops automatically from observations of natural events; which are essentially unaffected [blah blah blah].

Notice how this simplified version of the sentence makes the grammatical error more obvious. The last part of the sentence, following the semicolon, is a dependent clause, because it starts with the pronoun "which." This makes it wrong to use the semicolon. Only an independent clause—a clause that can stand alone as a sentence—may follow a semicolon. Read what follows the semicolon in this case, and you can probably "hear" that it cannot stand alone as a sentence.

(If you're unfamiliar with this grammatical rule, you'll find it explained in more detail in Appendix C, The Insider's ACT Writer's Manual.)

To correct the sentence, the connection between the final clause and the rest of the sentence needs to be repaired. Changing the semicolon to a comma, as in answer (F), fixes the error. Answer (J) retains the error, and answer (G) introduces a new error by inserting the non-idiomatic "being" construction.

In any case, notice how fundamentally irrelevant most of the first half of the sentence is to the error and its correction. You mustn't let long, complex, hard-to-understand verbiage confuse or slow you down. Instead, mentally replace the toughest phrases with "blah blah blah" and focus on the grammatical connections rather than the overall meaning of the sentence.

Avoid Answers That Repeat Ideas

The test-makers say that the ACT English Test focuses on both the "rules" of grammar and usage and more nebulous qualities such as "style," "verbosity," and "clarity." Fortunately, the way in which the ACT people test these qualities is fairly straightforward, even if the concepts themselves are not.

One basic test of style used by the ACT test-makers is redundancy. This is needless repetition of ideas in a sentence. When the same concept is stated twice or more in a given sentence, the test-makers are sending you a broad hint that this is an ineffective sentence that needs to be simplified. Here's an example:

> The remarkable growth in increased attendance currently being enjoyed by such formerly moribund sports franchises as baseball's Cleveland Indians shows that building a new stadium can have a powerful effect on the popularity of a team.

9. (A) NO CHANGE
   (B) The growth in attendance remarkably being enjoyed currently
   (C) The remarkable growth in increased attendance currently enjoyed
   (D) The remarkable attendance boom currently enjoyed

The original phrasing here contains not one but two examples of redundancy. The words "growth" and "increased" both convey the same idea concerning attendance at Indians games. And the word "being" tells you merely that this phenomenon is happening now—the same idea that the word "currently" expresses.

The best rephrasing is choice (D), which eliminates both redundancies without changing the meaning of the sentence (as answer (B) does by changing "remarkable" to "remarkably").

Listen for redundancy when reading sentence correction items. It's a very straightforward and concrete type of stylistic weakness, which makes it popular with the test-makers.

Avoid Answers That Separate Basic Sentence Elements

Another stylistic flaw to watch for is awkwardness. This, too, can be hard to define precisely. However, one strong clue often used by the ACT test-makers is when basic sentence elements—subject and verb, verb and object, or verb and complement—are needlessly separated in a sentence. When words that appear naturally to belong together are separated by other words, the result is an awkward sentence that the test-makers expect you to reject.

Here's an illustration:

> The Beach Boys, as other rock bands of the 1960s, considered the Beatles as the preeminent innovators whose creativity and style they strove to emulate.

10. (F)   NO CHANGE
    (G)   Like other rock bands of the 1960s,
          the Beach Boys considered the
          Beatles
    (H)   The Beach Boys, as did other rock
          bands of the 1960s, considered the
          Beatles to be
    (J)   The Beatles were considered by the
          Beach Boys, like other rock bands of
          the 1960s,

The original sentence contains two flaws. One is a confusion between "as" and "like." "As" is a conjunction which should be followed by a clause (a group of words containing a subject and a verb), which is not the case here. In this case, the preposition "like" should be used instead.

The second flaw lies in the fact that the sentence needlessly separates the subject—"The Beach Boys"—from the verb "considered." The best answer, choice (G), corrects both flaws (unlike answer (H), for instance).

Like other stylistic matters, the use and abuse of commas is partly a matter of taste and "ear," developed over years of thoughtful reading and writing. However, on the ACT English Test, overused punctuation is generally fairly easy to spot: listen for the sentences that sound patched together rather than flowing smoothly, and find the answer choice that eliminates the unnecessary cobbling.

JUST THE FACTS

- The ACT English Test measures your knowledge of both grammar rules and the principles of stylistic clarity and conciseness.

- Tackle each Usage/Mechanics item by first reading the original sentence, looking for the error it probably contains.

- Anticipate how the error should be corrected and scan answers (B) through (D), looking for answers that fix the error.

- Expect each paragraph to be unified around a single idea; avoid adding ideas that disrupt this unity.

- When organizing a paragraph or the passage, look for the unit that should go first; the others will usually fall into place.

PRACTICE, PRACTICE, PRACTICE: ENGLISH TEST EXERCISES

Instructions

The following exercises will give you a chance to practice the skills and strategies you've just learned for tackling ACT English Test questions. As with all practice exercises, work under true testing conditions. Complete each exercise in a single sitting. Eliminate distractions (TV, music) and clear away notes and reference materials. Time yourself with a stopwatch or kitchen timer, or have someone else time you. If you run out of time before answering all the questions, stop and draw a line under the last question you finished. Then go ahead and tackle the remaining questions. When you are done, score yourself based only on the questions you finished in the allotted time.

Understanding Your Scores

0–7 correct: A poor performance. Study this chapter again, and (if you haven't already), study the rules of grammar, usage, and punctuation taught in Appendix C, The Insider's Writer's Manual for the ACT.

8–13 correct: A below-average score. Study this chapter again, focusing especially on the skills and strategies you've found newest and most challenging.

14–18 correct: An average score. You may want to study this chapter again. Also be sure you are managing your time wisely (as explained in Chapter 3) and avoiding errors due to haste or carelessness.

19–24 correct: An above-average score. Depending on your personal target score and your strength on other question types, you may or may not want to devote additional time to the English Test.

25–30 correct: An excellent score. You are probably ready to perform well on the ACT English Test.

EXERCISE 1

30 Questions

Time—18 Minutes

Directions: This test consists of two passages in which particular words or phrases are underlined and numbered. Alongside the passage, you will see alternative words and phrases that could be substituted for the underlined part. You must select the alternative that expresses the idea most clearly and correctly or that best fits the style and tone of the entire passage. If the original version is best, select "No Change."

The test also includes questions about entire paragraphs and the passage as a whole. These questions are identified by a number in a box.

After you select the correct answer for each question, mark the oval representing the correct answer on your answer sheet.

Passage I

The Magic of Special Effects

The movies are one place where magic can come true. You can see sights you might never <u>under any circumstances</u> hope to see in real
₁
life—ocean liners sinking, earthquakes swallowing cities, planets exploding. You can also see sights that might never exist at <u>all; such as</u>
₂
rampaging monsters, battles in outer space, sky-high cities of the future.

All these are examples of the movie magic known as special effects. <u>Its the work of</u>
₃
amazingly clever and skilled effects artists.

And the real magic lies in how <u>they're able to</u>
₄
make a man in a gorilla suit into King Kong . . . tiny plastic models into huge space ships . . .

and instructions in a computer into images of a world that no one <u>have ever imagined</u> before.
₅

Effects artists have developed many tricks and techniques over the years. Working closely with movie directors, producers, and actors, <u>a growing role in movie making today is played</u>
₆
<u>by them.</u>
₆

[1]   They   can   be   used to <u>save money, some movie scenes</u> would be
₇
impossibly costly to produce using ordinary methods. [2] Special effects techniques are useful to movie makers in several ways. [3] Clever use of special effects can cut those costs dramatically. [4] For example, to show an imaginary city, it would cost millions of dollars to build real buildings, roads, and so on. $\boxed{8}$

[9] Battle or disaster scenes involving explosions, floods, or avalanches can be very dangerous to film. Effects artists can simulate such in ways that give audiences the thrill of
<u>10</u>
witnessing a dangerous event without the exposing of actors to real hazards.
<u>————————</u>
11

Most important, special effects allow movie
<u>————</u>
12
makers to film scenes that would otherwise be impossible. They let movies show non-existent, even impossible worlds. [13] Special effects are a movie makers tool for communicating a
<u>————————————</u>
14
unique imaginative experience. And after all—
<u>————————</u>
15
that's one of the reasons we all go to the
<u>————————</u>
15
movies.

1. (A) NO CHANGE
   (B) normally
   (C) in daily life
   (D) OMIT the underlined portion

2. (F) NO CHANGE
   (G) all, such as
   (H) all. Such as
   (J) all—such as

3. (A) NO CHANGE
   (B) It's the work of
   (C) They're by
   (D) They are the work of

4. (F) NO CHANGE
   (G) Nonetheless,
   (H) Although
   (J) Because

5. (A) NO CHANGE
   (B) could ever imagine
   (C) has ever imagined
   (D) ever had been imagining

6. (F) NO CHANGE
   (G) movie making today requires them to play a growing role.
   (H) they play a growing role in movie making today.
   (J) their role in movie making today is a growing one.

7. (A) NO CHANGE
   (B) to save money. Some movie scenes
   (C) for saving money, some movie scenes
   (D) to save money; since some movie scenes

8. Which of the following sequences of sentences will make the paragraph most logical?
   (F) 2, 1, 4, 3
   (G) 3, 1, 4, 2
   (H) 2, 4, 3, 1
   (J) 1, 4, 3, 2

9. Which of the following sentences would provide the best transition here from the topic of the previous paragraph to the new topic of this paragraph?
   (A) Today's movie makers are highly budget conscious.
   (B) Some of the most exciting special effects involve computer-simulated inmagery.
   (C) There is a long history to the use of special effects in movies.
   (D) Special effects can also make movie making safer.

10. (F)   NO CHANGE
    (G)   these events
    (H)   those
    (J)   it

11. (A)   NO CHANGE
    (B)   exposing actors
    (C)   actors being exposed
    (D)   actors having to be exposed

12. (F)   NO CHANGE
    (G)   To summarize,
    (H)   On the other hand,
    (J)   Nevertheless,

13. At this point, the writer is considering the addition of the following sentence:

> Visions of unknown, unseen worlds have long stimulated the imaginations of human beings the world over.

Would this be a logical and relevant addition to the essay?

    (A)   Yes, because it emphasizes the important role that special effects play in the movies.
    (B)   No, because it does not directly relate to the topic of movie special effects.
    (C)   Yes, because it underscores the universal appeal of works of the imagination.
    (D)   No, because most of the world's most popular movies are produced in the United States, not "the world over."

14. (F)   NO CHANGE
    (G)   movie maker's
    (H)   movie makers'
    (J)   OMIT the underlined portion

15. (A)   NO CHANGE
    (B)   And—after all, that's
    (C)   And, after all, that's
    (D)   And that after all, is

Passage II

Cities on the Sea

[1]

Hunger has long plagued millions of the world's people, especially in the vast cities of the underdeveloped nations of Africa, Asia, and India. The food to feed the world's growing population may come largely from ocean resources. 16

[2]

Three quarter's of the earth's surface is covered
17
with water. Many scientists are now looking at these vast watery regions for solutions to some pressing human dilemmas.

[3]

Minerals such as iron, nickle, copper, aluminum, and tin are in limited supply on the earth. Undersea mines are expected to yield fresh supplies of many of these resources. Oil and gas deposits,
18
have been discovered under the ocean floor. 19
18

[4]

To take advantage of these ocean-based resources, some scientists foresee entire cities on the ocean. At first, it will be built close to the
20
shore. Later, floating cities might be located hundreds of miles at sea. These cities could

serve many functions, playing a variety of roles.
                                    21
Some of the people living there could harvest

fish and sea plants, like farmers of the ocean.

Others could operate oil and gas wells or work

in undersea enclosures mining the ocean floors.

Also the floating cities could serve as terminals
——
22
or stations for international travel, where ships

could stop for refueling or repairs.

[5]

Much of the technology needed to build such

cities have already been developed. Oil drilling
      ———————————————
      23
on a large scale is already conducted at sea.

Rigs as large as small towns built on floating

platforms or on platforms anchored into the

seabed serving as homes to scores of workers
      ——————————————————
      24
for months at a time. The same principles, on a

larger scale, could be used to create ocean-

going cities.

[6]

The cities would have to be virtually self-
——————
25
sufficient, although shipping supplies from the
           ————————
           26
mainland would be costly. Each city would be a

multi-story structure with room for many kinds
                                    ——————
                                    27
of facilities needed by the inhabitants. The
————————————————————————————————
27
ocean itself could provide much of the needed

food and other raw materials; while solar panels
                          ——————————
                          28

and generators running on water power could

provide energy.

[7]

Many thousands of men, women, and children

might inhabit such a city. They would probably

visit the mainland from time to time, but

otherwise would spend their lives at sea as

ocean-dwelling pioneers.

16. Which of the following sentences, if
    added here, would most effectively
    support the assertion made in the
    previous sentence?

    (F) Fish, sea-grown plants, and even
         foodstuffs synthesized from
         algae are all examples.
    (G) If population growth can be
         brought under control, the
         problem of hunger may well be
         alleviated.
    (H) Pollution of the seas has not yet
         reached a level where it endan-
         gers the use of salt-water fish by
         humans.
    (J) For thousands of years, humans
         have drawn nourishment from
         the seas around us.

17. (A) NO CHANGE
    (B) Three quarters
    (C) Three fourth's
    (D) Three-quarter's

18. (F) NO CHANGE
    (G) deposits has
    (H) deposits have
    (J) deposits, has

19. The writer wishes to add another relevant example to Paragraph 3. Which of the following sentences does that best?

    (A) Exploration of the deepest reaches of the ocean floors has only recently begun.

    (B) And the tides and thermal currents—water movements caused by temperature variations—may be future energy sources.

    (C) Solar energy, too, is expected to become a major supplier of the world's future energy needs.

    (D) The sea, after all, is the ultimate source of all life on Earth.

20. (F) NO CHANGE
    (G) they will be built
    (H) they will build them
    (J) it will be

21. (A) NO CHANGE
    (B) and play many roles.
    (C) with a variety of roles to play.
    (D) OMIT the underlined portion.

22. (F) NO CHANGE
    (G) (Place after *could*)
    (H) (Place after *serve*)
    (J) (Place after *travel*)

23. (A) NO CHANGE
    (B) has already been developed.
    (C) have been developed already.
    (D) is already developed.

24. (F) NO CHANGE
    (G) serving for homes
    (H) have served like homes
    (J) serve as homes

25. (A) NO CHANGE
    (B) (Begin new paragraph) The cities, however,
    (C) (Do NOT begin new paragraph) Furthermore, the cities
    (D) (Do NOT begin new paragraph) And these cities

26. (F) NO CHANGE
    (G) since
    (H) when
    (J) whereas

27. (A) NO CHANGE
    (B) apartments, small factories, offices, schools, and stores.
    (C) various living and other quarters to be used by the town's citizens.
    (D) people to live and engage in other activities as in a land-based city.

28. (F) NO CHANGE
    (G) materials. While
    (H) materials, while
    (J) materials,

Items 29 and 30 pose questions about the essay as a whole.

29. The writer wishes to include the following sentence in the essay:

    Tourists might find the floating cities attractive vacation spots for boating, swimming, and fishing.

    That sentence will fit most smoothly and logically into Paragraph:

    (A) 3, after the last sentence.
    (B) 4, before the first sentence.
    (C) 4, after the last sentence.
    (D) 6, after the last sentence.

30. For the sake of the unity and coherence of this essay, Paragraph 1 should be placed:

    (F)   where it is now.
    (G) after Paragraph 2.
    (H) after Paragraph 3.
    (J)   after Paragraph 4.

EXERCISE 2

30 Questions

Time—18 Minutes

> **Directions:** This test consists of two passages in which particular words or phrases are underlined and numbered. Alongside the passage, you will see alternative words and phrases that could be substituted for the underlined part. You must select the alternative that expresses the idea most clearly and correctly or that best fits the style and tone of the entire passage. If the original version is best, select "No Change."
>
> The test also includes questions about entire paragraphs and the passage as a whole. These questions are identified by a number in a box.
>
> After you select the correct answer for each question, mark the oval representing the correct answer on your answer sheet.

Passage I

The Devastation of El Niño

[1]

Throughout 1998, it seemed, whenever anything went wrong, someone could be heard exclaiming, "Blame it on El Niño!" This unusually powerful weather system received so much attention in the news media around the world that El Niño came to seem like a good scapegoat for almost any mishap. [2]

[2]

Every year, in late December—around Christmas time—oceanic winds from the West tend to shift, causing warm water from the western Pacific to move towards South America, heating the waters along its coast. These hot currents and the weather disturbances they cause has been dubbed El Niño—Spanish for "the child"—because of their annual association with the Christmas holiday.

[3]

Usually, the temperature of the water increases for six months, then returns to normal. In 1998 however, the wind shifts occurred around April and didn't peak until January, lasting substantially longer than usual. The resulting storms and other climatic changes produced widespread flooding and erosion. And, among other problems, devastated Peru's population of seals and birds.

[4]

When El Niño hit, vast schools of small fish, such as anchovies and sardines, sought cooler temperatures <u>furthest down in the depths of the</u>
6
Pacific than the levels where they are usually found. While this protected the fish from the unseasonable weather conditions, their predators were unable to reach them at these new, <u>greater depths, thus the predators had no food</u>
7
readily available.

[5]

Aquatic mammals were hit <u>especially hardly.</u>
8
Along one Peruvian beach, the Punta San Juan, a whole season's pup production of fur seals and sea lions died, <u>as well as</u> thousands of juveniles
9
and breeding adults. By May 13, 1998, only 15 fur seals were counted, when there are usually hundreds. <u>On the other hand,</u> only 1,500 sea
10
lions were found in an area that usually houses 8,000.

[6]

The Humboldt penguins also faced population losses due to El Niño. These penguins normally breed twice a <u>year; but</u> in 1998, their second
11
breeding ground was flooded by 52 consecutive

hours of rain. Only 50 of the 3,500 to 5,000 penguins that usually lay eggs were <u>able to do so.</u>
12

[7]

Because Peru is <u>so close in distance</u> to the
13
Pacific regions where the wind shifts and water warming of El Niño originate, it experiences the harshest effects of this unpredictable weather phenomenon. Two or three more such years may spell an end to many species of wildlife that once thrived on Peruvian shores. [14]

1. (A) NO CHANGE
   (B) as a good
   (C) as if it was a good
   (D) as a

2. Which of the choices best introduces a central theme of the essay and provides the most appropriate transition between the first and second paragraphs?
   (F) Yet the underlying meteorological causes of El Niño remain obscure.
   (G) Unfortunately, the problems it really caused for creatures living on the Pacific coast of Peru were all too real.
   (H) All over the United States, people found their lives disrupted by the violent effects of El Niño.
   (J) But the real effects of El Niño proved to be surprisingly mild.

3. (A) NO CHANGE
   (B) have been dubbed
   (C) was dubbed
   (D) is known as

4. (F) NO CHANGE
   (G) However in 1998,
   (H) In 1998, however,
   (J) In 1998—however,

5. (A) NO CHANGE
   (B) erosion; and,
   (C) erosion, and,
   (D) erosion and

6. (F) NO CHANGE
   (G) more far
   (H) farther
   (J) farthest

7. (A) NO CHANGE
   (B) depths: thus
   (C) depths—thus
   (D) depths. Thus,

8. (F) NO CHANGE
   (G) hard, especially.
   (H) especially hard.
   (J) specially hardly.

9. (A) NO CHANGE
   (B) as also
   (C) at the same time as
   (D) so did

10. (F) NO CHANGE
    (G) Yet
    (H) Similarly,
    (J) Likewise,

11. (A) NO CHANGE
    (B) year, but
    (C) year. And
    (D) year, however

12. (F) NO CHANGE
    (G) capable of this.
    (H) able to lay them
    (J) possible.

13. (A) NO CHANGE
    (B) very close in distance
    (C) not distant
    (D) so close

14. Which of the following sentences, if added here, would best conclude the passage and effectively summarize its main idea?

    (F) Two or three more such years may spell an end to many species of wildlife that once thrived on Peruvian shores.
    (G) Fortunately, other countries in South America do not suffer the ill effects of El Niño to the same extent as does Peru.
    (H) Government officials in Peru are currently at work to develop plans for dealing with the problems caused by El Niño the next time it strikes.
    (J) However, aid from foreign countries has helped Peru to save certain of the endangered species whom El Niño has decimated.

15. Suppose the writer were to eliminate Paragraph 4. This omission would cause the essay as a whole to lose primarily:

    (A) relevant details about how Pacific fish are destroyed by the effects of El Niño.
    (B) irrelevant facts about feeding patterns among creatures in the southern Pacific ocean.
    (C) relevant information about how El Niño affects aquatic animals on the shores of Peru.
    (D) irrelevant details about the kinds of fish that live off the shores of Peru.

Passage II

The First Thanksgiving:
Turkey Day and a Whole Lot More

Every autumn, when Thanksgiving rolls around, anxiety and stress levels in millions of American families rise. Hosting friends and relatives from all over the country and then to prepare one of
<u>16</u>
the largest meals of the year is not an easy job. But when the typical Thanksgiving dinner of today is compared with the celebration of the
<u>17</u>
first Thanksgiving, it doesn't seem like quite a feat.
<u>18</u>

First, consider the menu. At a typical
<u>19</u>
modern-day Thanskgiving, there is a roast turkey, baked yams, stuffing, cranberry sauce, gravy, and some sort of dessert—maybe ice cream and some pie or cake. Of course, you can fix everything yourself, from scratch, if you like; but if you prefer, all of the food can be purchased at a local supermarket: just one trip,
<u>20</u>
and you have all you need for your dinner.

Today's menu seems stingy by comparison to the Pilgrims meal enjoyed on the first
<u>21</u>
Thanksgiving in 1621. According to contemporary records, the list of foods included five deer; wild turkeys, geese, and duck; eels, lobsters, clams, and mussels fished from the ocean;

pumpkin; an assortment of biscuits; hoe and ash cakes (whatever those were); popcorn balls,
<u>22</u>
made with corn and maple syrup; pudding; berries of several kinds—gooseberries, cranberries, strawberries—plums, cherries, and bogbeans; beer made from barley; and wine spiked with brandy. Just in case this wasn't enough,
<u>23</u>
you could fill in the corners with "flint corn," a rock-hard corn ground into a mush. 24 And once the dinner was served, the meal didn't last a few hours, but a few days— and with no
<u>25</u>
football on TV to distract the Pilgrims and their friends from the serious business of eating.

The other major difference was the guest list. Nowadays, in many households, the whole family comes for Thanksgiving, this provokes
<u>26</u>
many groans from besieged hosts. Statistics show that the average Thanksgiving dinner boasts 23 total guests—no tiny gathering, at that. 27 At the first Thanksgiving, when Squanto, the Indian-in-residence, decided to invite Massasoit, the leader of the Wampanoags, for a
<u>28</u>
little pot-luck supper, the Pilgrims weren't expecting him to bring along the other 90 Wampanoags. With the Pilgrims, that made a

140-person guest list. I guess <u>they weren't</u>
                                    29
<u>overdoing it, after all.</u>
       29
So, when the next Thanksgiving rolls around,

and <u>your</u> tempted to complain about "all this
        30
cooking—all this food—all these people!"—just

be thankful it isn't 1621 and you aren't hosting

the first Thanksgiving!

16. (F) NO CHANGE
    (G) preparing
    (H) working on preparation of
    (J) doing preparation for

17. (A) NO CHANGE
    (B) is compared against
    (C) is viewed in reference to
    (D) compares with

18. (F) NO CHANGE
    (G) as great a feat.
    (H) all that much of a feat.
    (J) such a feat.

19. (A) NO CHANGE
    (B) Start by thinking about the food
         that was served.
    (C) The menu is the first thing we
         shall discuss.
    (D) The food at the first Thanks-
         giving was incredible.

20. (F) NO CHANGE
    (G) supermarket, just one trip
    (H) supermarket. One trip;
    (J) supermarket; one trip is all,

21. (A) NO CHANGE
    (B) what the Pilgrims'
    (C) the meal that the Pilgrim's
    (D) the dinner the Pilgrims

22. (F) NO CHANGE
    (G) (what they are is unknown to
         me)
    (H) (unheard-of today)
    (J) OMIT the underlined portion.

23. (A) NO CHANGE
    (B) this weren't
    (C) all of the above weren't
    (D) one didn't find this

24. At this point, the writer is considering
    the addition of the following sen-
    tence:

    Everything, of course, was
    prepared by hand; there were no
    food processors, microwave
    ovens, or other appliances to
    help.

    Would this be a logical and
    relevant addition to the essay?

    (F) Yes, because it emphasizes how
         difficult it was to prepare the
         first Thanksgiving dinner.
    (G) Yes, because many readers may
         not be aware that the Pilgrims
         lived in a time when technol-ogy
         was relatively primitive.
    (H) No, because the rest of the
         passage does not focus on
         technological differences
         between 1621 and today.
    (J) No, because it is unconnected to
         the list of foodstuffs that
         occupies most of the rest of the
         paragraph.

25. (A) NO CHANGE
    (B) rather a few days—
    (C) but instead a few days:
    (D) a few days, rather;

26. (F) NO CHANGE
    (G) so as to provoke
    (H) the provocation of
    (J) provoking

27. Which of the following sentences, if inserted here, would provide the best transition between the first half and the second half of the paragraph?

    (A) We rarely have that many guests in my house.

    (B) It could be a lot worse, however.

    (C) Both family and friends are included in this number.

    (D) And all of them show up hungry.

28. (F) NO CHANGE

    (G) the Wampanoag's leader,

    (H) who was leading the Wampanoag's

    (J) Wampanoag leader,

29. (A) NO CHANGE

    (B) the repast served was not, in fact, excessive,

    (C) that dinner menu wasn't overdoing it,

    (D) it wasn't too much,

30. (F) NO CHANGE

    (G) your feeling a temptation

    (H) you're tempted

    (J) there's a temptation

EXERCISE 3

30 Questions

Time—18 Minutes

> **Directions:** This test consists of two passages in which particular words or phrases are underlined and numbered. Alongside the passage, you will see alternative words and phrases that could be substituted for the underlined part. You must select the alternative that expresses the idea most clearly and correctly or that best fits the style and tone of the entire passage. If the original version is best, select "No Change."
>
> The test also includes questions about entire paragraphs and the passage as a whole. These questions are identified by a number in a box.
>
> After you select the correct answer for each question, mark the oval representing the correct answer on your answer sheet.

Passage I

The Girls Choir of Harlem

It is rare to hear of choirs composed of just girls.
<u>   </u>
                    1
In fact, for every girls' choir in the United States, there are four boys' and mixed choirs. But the Girls Choir of Harlem in <u>1977 was founded</u>, to
                                    2
complement the already existing and justly renowned Boys Choir.
<u>   </u>
            3
    <u>To this day</u>, the Boys Choir of Harlem
        4
overshadows the Girls Choir. They have been around longer <u>(1968 was when they were</u>
                                    5
<u>founded)</u>, and have received the attention
    5
needed to gain funding and performance opportunities. The boys have appeared in some of the world's <u>most prestigious</u> musical settings. They
            6
have sung a sunrise concert for the Pope on the Great Lawn in New York's Central Park; <u>they have traveled to Washington, D.C. and seen</u>
                                    7
<u>the Lincoln Memorial.</u>
            7
    Such glorious moments have eluded their female counterparts. During the 1980s, when funds dried up, the Girls Choir temporarily disbanded. However, in 1989, <u>the choir were</u>
                                    8
reassembled, and in November of 1997, they made their debut at Alice Tully Hall at Lincoln Center, performing music by Schumann and Pergolesi before an audience of dignitaries (including <u>the mayors wife</u>) and thousands of
                    9
music lovers.

    [1] The choir members speak confidently of someday becoming lawyers, doctors, and politicians—jobs which once appeared out of reach

to them. [2] Both the Girls Choir and the Boys Choir of Harlem act as havens for inner-city children, giving kids from broken families and
____10
poverty-stricken homes new confidence and hope for their future. [3] The boys and girls in the choirs attend the Choir Academy, a 500-student public school with a strong emphasis on singing. [4] It's a fine learning environment
____11
that has given the girls ambitions most of them never before considered. [12]

Now that the Girls Choir of Harlem is beginning to receive some of the recognition that the boys have long enjoyed, perhaps corporations and wealthy individuals will be motivated for giving generously to support the
____13
choir and ensure it will never again have to shut down for lack of money.
____14

1. (A) NO CHANGE
    (B) just of girls'.
    (C) only of girls.
    (D) of girls, alone.

2. (F) NO CHANGE
    (G) (Place after *But*)
    (H) (Place after *was*)
    (J) OMIT the underlined portion.

3. (A) NO CHANGE
    (B) famous (justly so)
    (C) renowned, justly,
    (D) just renowned

4. (F) NO CHANGE
    (G) As of today,
    (H) On this day,
    (J) At the moment,

5. (A) NO CHANGE
    (B) (having been founded in 1968)
    (C) (their founding dates to 1968)
    (D) (since 1968)

6. (F) NO CHANGE
    (G) more prestigious
    (H) very prestigious
    (J) prestige-filled

7. Which of the alternative clauses would most effectively support the assertion made in the previous sentence about the musical appearances of the Boys Choir?

    (A) NO CHANGE
    (B) they have produced recordings enjoyed by listeners around the world.
    (C) they have sung on the same bill as Luciano Pavarotti, the great Italian tenor.
    (D) they sing a wide variety of music, both classical and popular.

8. (F) NO CHANGE
    (G) it were
    (H) the choir was
    (J) the girls

9. (A) NO CHANGE
    (B) the mayor's wife
    (C) the mayors' wife
    (D) a wife of the mayor

10. (F) NO CHANGE
    (G) they give
    (H) thus giving
    (J) and it gives

11. (A) NO CHANGE
    (B) Its
    (C) They offer
    (D) That is

12. Which of the following sequences of sentences will make the paragraph most logical?
    (F) 1, 4, 3, 2
    (G) 2, 1, 4, 3
    (H) 2, 3, 4, 1
    (J) 3, 4, 1, 2

13. (A) NO CHANGE
    (B) generously for giving
    (C) to give generously
    (D) for generosity in giving

14. (F) NO CHANGE
    (G) because they are lacking money.
    (H) as a result of money being lacking.
    (J) without money.

Item 15 poses a question about the essay as a whole.

15. Suppose the writer had been assigned to write an essay describing the musical achievements of the Girls Choir of Harlem. Would this essay successfully fulfill the assignment?
    (A) Yes, because the concert at Alice Tully Hall is explained in some detail.
    (B) Yes, because the essay makes it clear that the girls in the choir are talented performers.
    (C) No, because the essay discusses the Boys Choir as extensively as it discusses the Girls Choir.
    (D) No, because the music performed by the choir is scarcely discussed in the essay.

Passage II

The Poetry of Economics

"The poetry of economics?" a reader might ask. "How can 'the dismal science' be associated with the subtlety and creativity of poetry?" You're skepticism is understandable, and per-
— 16 —   17
haps a story from an economist's life can sketch the poetry of economics at work.

Shortly after the Second World War, the agricultural economist Theodore Schultz, later to win a Nobel prize, spent a term based at Auburn University in Alabama, he interviewed
— 18 —
farmers in the neighborhood. One day he interviewed an old and poor farm couple. And was struck by how contented they
— 19 —
seemed. Why are you so contented, he asked, though very poor? They answered: You're wrong, Professor. We're not poor. We've used up our farm to educate four children through college, remaking fertile land and well-stocked
— 20 —
pens into knowledge of law and Latin. We are rich.

The parents had told Schultz that the physical capital, which economists think they
— 21 —
understand, is in some sense just like the
— 21 —
human capital of education. The children now

owned it, and so the parents did, too. Once it had been rail fences and hog pens and it was also their mules. Now it was in the
_____
22
children's brains, this human capital. The farm couple was rich. The average economist was
___
23
willing to accept the discovery of human capital as soon as he understood it, which is in fact how many scientific and scholarly discoveries get received. It was an argument in a metaphor
_____
24
(or, if you like, an analogy, a simile, a model). A hog pen, Schultz would say to another economist, is "just like" Latin 101.

The other economist would have to admit that there was something to it. Both the hog
_____
25
pen, and the Latin instruction, are paid for by
_____
25
saving.   Both   are   valuable   assets for the earning of income, understanding "in-
_____
26
come" to mean, as economists put it, "a stream of satisfaction." Year after year, the hog pen and the Latin cause satisfaction to stream out as
_____   __
27   28
water from a dam. Both last a long time, but finally wear out—when the pen falls down and the Latin-learned brain dies.

And the one piece of "capital" can be made into the other. An educated farmer, because of
_____
29
his degree in agriculture from Auburn, can get a
_____
29

bank loan to build a hog pen; and when his children grow up he can sell off the part of the farm with the hog pen to pay for another term for Junior and Sis up at Auburn, too. ☐30

16. (F) NO CHANGE
    (G) Your
    (H) One's
    (J) A reader's

17. (A) NO CHANGE
    (B) but
    (C) therefore
    (D) so

18. (F) NO CHANGE
    (G) Alabama. Where he interviewed
    (H) Alabama, interviewing
    (J) Alabama so as to interview

19. (A) NO CHANGE
    (B) couple, and was struck
    (C) couple; struck
    (D) couple. Struck

20. (F) NO CHANGE
    (G) so remaking
    (H) this remade
    (J) and to remake

21. (A) NO CHANGE
    (B) understood by economists (or so they think),
    (C) that is thought by economists to be understood,
    (D) OMIT the underlined portion.

22. (F) NO CHANGE
    (G) also
    (H) as well
    (J) OMIT the underlined portion.

23. (A) NO CHANGE
    (B) (Begin new paragraph) The
    (C) (Begin new paragraph) So the
    (D) (Do NOT begin new paragraph)
         Yet the

24. (F) NO CHANGE
    (G) are received.
    (H) become received.
    (J) have their reception.

25. (A) NO CHANGE
    (B) Both the hog pen and the Latin
         instruction
    (C) The hog pen, and the Latin
         instruction as well,
    (D) Both the hog pen, and also the
         Latin instruction,

26. (F) NO CHANGE
    (G) for income's earning,
    (H) for earning income,
    (J) with which income may be
         earned,

27. (A) NO CHANGE
    (B) causes
    (C) produce
    (D) makes

28. (F) NO CHANGE
    (G) similarly to
    (H) as with
    (J) like

29. (A) NO CHANGE
    (B) due to having a degree from
         Auburn in agriculture,
    (C) as a result of a degree in
         agriculture from Auburn
    (D) OMIT the underlined portion

30. The writer wants to link the essay's
    opening and conclusion. If inserted at
    the end of the essay, which of the
    following sentencees best achieves
    this effect?
    (F) The wisdom of the farmer is
         greater, in the end, than the
         wisdom of the economics
         professor.
    (G) Human capital is a concept
         based on a metaphor—and
         metaphor is the essential tool of
         poetry.
    (H) Thus, education is the most
         valuable form of human capital,
         even for the farmer.
    (J) Physical capital and human
         capital are ultimately not so
         different after all.

EXERCISE 4

30 Questions

Time—18 Minutes

Directions: This test consists of two passages in which particular words or phrases are underlined and numbered. Alongside the passage, you will see alternative words and phrases that could be substituted for the underlined part. You must select the alternative that expresses the idea most clearly and correctly or that best fits the style and tone of the entire passage. If the original version is best, select "No Change."

The test also includes questions about entire paragraphs and the passage as a whole. These questions are identified by a number in a box.

After you select the correct answer for each question, mark the oval representing the correct answer on your answer sheet.

Passage I

Note: The paragraphs that follow may or may not be in the most appropriate order. Item 15 will ask you to choose the most logical sequence for the paragraphs.

A People's Art, for Good and Ill

[1]

During the early years of movies—say, from 1910 to 1940—the greatness of film as an art form lay in its own ingenuity and invention. And this in every instance originated in cinema's role as entertaining a large and avid public. Between 1920 and 1930, a generation of filmmakers grew up who were not failed novelists or playwrights who'd had no success but moviemakers, through and through. Their essential vision belonged to no other medium with the exception of the cinema, and this made it vital and exciting.

[2]

Furthermore, their public was a universal audience of ordinary people, spread across the world. Comparable to the first dramas of Shakespeare, their art was not a product of the palace, the mansion, or the village square, but rather of the common playhouse where working people sat shoulder to shoulder with the middle class and the well-to-do. This is what gave the early movie makers the strength and freshness we still perceive in their art.

104

[3]

Thus, today, with movies more popular than ever, and with box-office receipts for the great <u>international hit films running into hundreds of</u>
8
<u>millions of dollars</u>, movies are becoming more
8
and more <u>conventional, unimaginative,</u> and
9
stale. The freshness of the early movie makers <u>has been lost.</u>
10

[4]

<u>However,</u> there is a price to be paid for this
11
democratic appeal to the common person. The artist who serves an elite audience has a known patron <u>only,</u> or group of patrons, to satisfy. If he
12
is strong enough, he can, like the painters of the Renaissance, mold <u>their</u> taste in the image
13
<u>of his own.</u> This can also be true of the greater and more resolute artists of the cinema, from Chaplin in the nineteen twenties to, say, Bergman or Antonioni in the sixties. But the larger the audience and the more costly the movies to produce, <u>great become</u> the pressures
14
brought to bear on the less conventional creator to make his work conform to the pattern of the more conventional creator.

1. (A) NO CHANGE
   (B) —say from 1910, to 1940—
   (C) —from 1910, say to 1940—
   (D) —from 1910 to 1940, say;

2. (F) NO CHANGE
   (G) of entertaining
   (H) to entertain
   (J) as entertainers on behalf of

3. (A) NO CHANGE
   (B) playwrights lacking success
   (C) playwrights without any successes
   (D) unsuccessful playwrights

4. (F) NO CHANGE
   (G) than
   (H) aside from
   (J) from

5. (A) NO CHANGE
   (B) As were
   (C) Not dissimilarly to
   (D) Like

6. (F) NO CHANGE
   (G) Shakespeare, some of whose plays have been made into outstanding motion pictures,
   (H) Shakespeare, who also wrote a number of highly-acclaimed narrative and lyric poems,
   (J) Shakespeare, although he lived nearly three centuries before the invention of the movies,

7. Which of the choices is most consistent with the writer's point concerning the style of the early moviemakers?
   (A) NO CHANGE
   (B) the private club,
   (C) the tenements of the poor,
   (D) the athletic arena,

8. Which of the alternative clauses most effectively supports the writer's point concerning the current situation of moviemakers?
   (F) NO CHANGE
   (G) and with movie stars like Harrison Ford known and admired by millions of people around the world,
   (H) and with thriving motion picture industries not only in Hollywood but in many other countries,
   (J) and with more opportunities for talented young filmmakers than ever before,

9. (A) NO CHANGE
   (B) conventional—unimaginative—
   (C) conventionally unimaginative,
   (D) conventional; unimaginative;

10. (F) NO CHANGE
    (G) have been
    (H) are being
    (J) will be

11. (A) NO CHANGE
    (B) Fortunately,
    (C) Surprisingly,
    (D) Therefore,

12. (F) NO CHANGE
    (G) (Move after *has*)
    (H) (Move after *satisfy*)
    (J) OMIT the underlined portion.

13. (A) NO CHANGE
    (B) of his taste.
    (C) like his own.
    (D) of his own personal taste.

14. (F) NO CHANGE
    (G) so much greater become
    (H) greater are
    (J) the greater

Item 15 poses a question about the essay as a whole.

15. For the sake of the unity and coherence of this essay, Paragraph 3 should be placed:
    (A) where it is now.
    (B) before Paragraph 1.
    (C) before Paragraph 2.
    (D) after Paragraph 4.

Passage II

Regeneration, A Natural Miracle

Urodeles, a kind of vertebrate that <u>include</u> such small, lizard-like creatures as newts and salamanders, have an enviable ability <u>few other</u> animals enjoy. They can regenerate arms, legs, tails, heart muscle, jaws, spinal cords, and other organs that are injured or destroyed by accidents or <u>those who prey on them.</u>

[19] <u>Planaria, a kind of simple worm, have</u> their own form of regenerative power. A single worm can be sliced and diced into hundreds of pieces, <u>and each piece giving rise</u> to a completely new animal.

<u>However,</u> while both urodeles and planaria have the capacity to regenerate, they use different means to accomplish this amazing feat.

In effect, urodeles turn back the clock. When injured, the animal <u>first</u> heals the wound at the site of the missing limb. Then various special-

ized cells at the site, such like bone, skin, and
<u>24</u>
blood cells, seem to lose their identity. They

revert into unspecialized cells, like those in the
<u>25</u>
embryo before birth. Ultimate, as the new limb
<u>26</u>
takes shape, the cells take on the specialized

roles they had previously cast off.

By contrast, planaria regenerate using spe-
<u>27</u>
cial cells called neoblasts. Scattered within the

body, these neoblasts remain in an unspecialized

state, this enables them to turn into any cell
<u>28</u>
type that may be needed. Whenever planaria
<u>29</u>
are cut, the neoblasts migrate to the site and

begin to grow and develop. Soon, an entirely

new animal is formed from the broken frag-

ments from an old one.
<u>30</u>

16. (F)   NO CHANGE
    (G)   includes
    (H)   comprise
    (J)   numbers

17. (A)   NO CHANGE
    (B)   only few
    (C)   nearly no
    (D)   scarcely no

18. (F)   NO CHANGE
    (G)   animals who eat them
    (H)   predatory animals
    (J)   predators

19. Which of the following sentences, if added here, would provide the best transition between the first paragraph and the second?
    (A)   Urodeles are not the only creatures with this amazing ability.
    (B)   Scientists have long marveled at the regenerative power of urodeles.
    (C)   Regeneration affords to those creatures that possess it a kind of immortality.
    (D)   There are dozens of different species of urodeles living in North America.

20. (F)   NO CHANGE
    (G)   Planaria—a kind of simple worm,
    (H)   A simple kind of worm, known as planaria,
    (J)   Planaria, simply a kind of worm,

21. (A)   NO CHANGE
    (B)   each piece gives rise
    (C)   with each piece giving rise
    (D)   each one rising

22. (F)   NO CHANGE
    (G)   Furthermore,
    (H)   And
    (J)   Meanwhile,

23. (A)   NO CHANGE
    (B)   (Place after *When*)
    (C)   (Place after *wound*)
    (D)   (Place after *limb*)

24. (F)   NO CHANGE
    (G)   such as
    (H)   namely
    (J)   as

25. (A)   NO CHANGE
    (B)   to the form of
    (C)   to being
    (D)   toward being

26. (F)   NO CHANGE
    (G)   So,
    (H)   Thus,
    (J)   Ultimately,

27. (A)   NO CHANGE
    (B)   Nonetheless,
    (C)   In fact,
    (D)   Otherwise,

28. (F)   NO CHANGE
    (G)   thus able
    (H)   enabling
    (J)   enabled in this way

29. (A)   NO CHANGE
    (B)   which are necessary.
    (C)   for which there is a requirement.
    (D)   one may want.

30. (F)   NO CHANGE
    (G)   that are part of the old.
    (H)   of the old.
    (J)   out of the old one.

EXERCISE 5

30 Questions

Time—18 Minutes

> **Directions:** This test consists of two passages in which particular words or phrases are underlined and numbered. Alongside the passage, you will see alternative words and phrases that could be substituted for the underlined part. You must select the alternative that expresses the idea most clearly and correctly or that best fits the style and tone of the entire passage. If the original version is best, select "No Change."
>
> The test also includes questions about entire paragraphs and the passage as a whole. These questions are identified by a number in a box.
>
> After you select the correct answer for each question, mark the oval representing the correct answer on your answer sheet.

Passage I

Tunnel Vision: The Bane of Business

<u>Businesses don't always get into trouble be-</u> <u>1</u> cause they are badly run or inefficient. Sometimes, well-managed companies fail <u>because their leaders don't understand, simply, how the world is changing around them.</u> <u>2</u> What happened to Wang, the office automation company, is a classic example.

In the early 1980s, Wang represented the preeminent office automation capability in the world—<u>so much so that in many offices the name "Wang" had become a synonym for "office automation."</u> <u>3</u> With a reputation for quality and with proprietary hardware and software that guaranteed the uniqueness of its product, Wang had built a market position <u>seeming unassailable.</u> <u>4</u>

Yet in less than a decade, Wang <u>faded to near</u> <u>5</u> obscurity. <u>Shrinking</u> dramatically and surviving <u>6</u> only by transforming itself to use its software and engineering strengths in completely different ways. In place of Wang's specialized computer systems, versatile personal computers <u>linked together in networks</u> had become the <u>7</u> dominant office tools. The new personal computers first transformed the market for office automation networks <u>then wiping out</u> the old <u>8</u> market.

Wang <u>had saw itself</u> as a specialized kind of <u>9</u> computer company using large machines to serve entire companies. <u>It's</u> excellence and <u>10</u>

109

leadership in innovation was highly respected,
                                    _____
                                            11
and it was important to Wang not to lose that

position. That view led Wang to stick to its

familiar business until it was too late. It failed to

see the opportunity presented by the personal

computer. Eventually, Wang did attempt to

move into personal computers, but by this time

the company's opportunity to move forward

was gone. Wang had been badly outmaneuvered
         _____
                                12
and was left with no market.
_____
            12
     Sometimes a business leader stumbles into

this kind of trap by waiting to see what

develops, trading time for the prospect of more

information and a decrease in uncertainty.
            _____
                        13
Sometimes the leader is simply so afraid to lose

that he or she is incapable of the bold action
                   _____
                              14
required for success. Regardlessly, the leader is
                      _____
                                15
operating with limited vision, and the company

suffers as a result.

1. (A) NO CHANGE
   (B) A business doesn't
   (C) No business
   (D) Businesses may not

2. (F) NO CHANGE
   (G) because, simply, their leaders
        don't understand
   (H) because their leaders fail simply
        at understanding
   (J) because their leaders simply
        don't understand

3. The writer intends to emphasize the
   degree to which Wang dominated its
   marketplace in the early 1980s. If all
   of these statements are true, which
   best accomplishes the writer's goal?
   (A) NO CHANGE
   (B) only IBM had a better reputation
        among corporate leaders around
        the world.
   (C) the company's founder was
        generally regarded as one of the
        world's most successful busi-
        nesspeople.
   (D) with many thousands of employ-
        ees in scores of offices around
        the globe.

4. (F) NO CHANGE
   (G) seemingly unassailable.
   (H) that seemed unassailable.
   (J) that was unassailable, or so it
        seemed.

5. (A) NO CHANGE
   (B) Although
   (C) And
   (D) For

6. (F) NO CHANGE
   (G) obscurity, shrinking
   (H) obscurity. It shrank
   (J) obscurity; shrinking

7. (A) NO CHANGE
   (B) linked, network-style, together
   (C) that were linked together
        forming networks
   (D) linked to form networks together

8. (F) NO CHANGE
   (G) and then wiping out
   (H) wiping out subsequently
   (J) and then wiped out

9. (A) NO CHANGE
   (B) had seen itself
   (C) itself had been seen
   (D) having seen itself

10. (F) NO CHANGE
    (G) Its
    (H) Their
    (J) Wangs'

11. (A) NO CHANGE
    (B) was respected highly
    (C) were highly respected
    (D) had won high respect

12. Which of the following sentences, if added here, would best summarize the point of the paragraph and provide a clear transition to the next paragraph?
    (F) NO CHANGE
    (G) Today, Wang is developing new business niches that it hopes will bring it renewed success in the future.
    (H) Wang's reputation for excellence remained untarnished.
    (J) The market for personal computers continues to grow.

13. (A) NO CHANGE
    (B) and less uncertainty.
    (C) or certainty.
    (D) but a smaller degree of uncertainty.

14. (F) NO CHANGE
    (G) is unable for taking
    (H) finds it impossible to perform
    (J) can not do

15. (A) NO CHANGE
    (B) In either case,
    (C) Anyway,
    (D) Because

Passage II

The Unblinking Eye

Photography is of course a visual art like many
                    ‾‾‾‾‾‾‾‾‾‾‾‾‾
                          16
others, including painting, drawing, and the

various forms of printmaking. But photography

is unique as one of these arts in one respect: the
         ‾‾‾‾‾‾‾‾‾‾‾‾‾‾‾‾‾‾‾‾‾‾‾‾‾‾‾
                    17
person, place, event, or other subject

that have been photographed is always real,
‾‾‾‾‾‾‾‾‾‾‾‾‾‾‾‾‾‾‾‾‾‾‾‾‾‾
          18
captured by a photographer who is an on-the-

spot eyewitness to its reality. A painting may

depict a scene that is partly or in whole
                       ‾‾‾‾‾‾‾‾‾‾‾‾‾‾‾‾‾
                              19
imaginary—a knight battling a dragon, a city

beneath the sea, or the features of a woman who

never existed. But a photograph is a document

reflecting with more or less completeness and
‾‾‾‾‾‾‾‾
   20
accuracy something that was actually happen-

ing as the shutter clicked.

Viewers have an awareness concerning this
       ‾‾‾‾‾‾‾‾‾‾‾‾‾‾‾‾‾‾‾‾‾‾‾‾‾‾‾‾
                     21
feature of photography, of course, which ex-

plains why photos (and, today, film and televi-

sion footage) of world events can have

such a powerful emotional and intellectual
‾‾‾‾‾‾‾‾‾‾‾‾‾‾‾‾‾
         22
impact. The photographed image of a starving

child in Africa or India 23 conveys the reality of

a tragedy halfway around the world with an

immediacy and force <u>shared by no purely verbal</u>

report.
<u>   </u>
24

24

[25] Photos can indeed mislead when the

photographer, either deliberately or inadvert-

ently, exaggerates or omits crucial details of the

real-life scene, or <u>freezing</u> on film a momentary

26

image that distorts or falsifies the flow of reality.

When photography is <u>enrolled in the service of</u>

27

political, social, or commercial causes, such

deceptions are all too common. [28] Nonethe-

less, no conscientious photographer will be

<u>guilty of them.</u> At its best, photography is

29

unequalled as a purveyor of truth, <u>and</u> this is

<u> </u>
30

the goal of every self-respecting camera artist.

16. (F) NO CHANGE
    (G) is, of course, a
    (H) is of course, a
    (J) is—of course, a

17. (A) NO CHANGE
    (B) as a member of these
    (C) compared to other
    (D) among these

18. (F) NO CHANGE
    (G) that has been
    (H) having been
    (J) OMIT the underlined portion.

19. (A) NO CHANGE
    (B) in part or entirely
    (C) partly or wholly
    (D) partly, or in its entirety,

20. (F) NO CHANGE
    (G) to reflect
    (H) that reflect
    (J) for reflecting

21. (A) NO CHANGE
    (B) are wary concerning
    (C) have awareness of
    (D) are aware of

22. (F) NO CHANGE
    (G) so much powerful
    (H) so powerful
    (J) the power of

23. The writer is considering adding the
    following phrase at this point in the
    essay:

    —its belly distended, eyes sunken,
    ribs protruding—

    Would this phrase be a relevant and
    appropriate addition to the essay, and
    why?

    (A) No, because the kind of image it
         conveys is excessively familiar
         from newspapers and television.
    (B) Yes, because it suggests vividly
         the power of a photographic
         image to move the viewer
         emotionally.
    (C) No, because it distracts the
         reader's attention from the
         writer's point about the nature
         of photography.
    (D) Yes, because it encourages the
         reader to take action on behalf
         of children starving in distant
         lands.

24. (F) NO CHANGE
    (G) not shared by any report that is
         purely verbal.
    (H) more than can be had by any
         purely verbal report.
    (J) beyond that of a report which is
         verbal, purely.

25. Which of the following sentences, if added here, would most effectively provide a transition to the new paragraph?

   (A) Words, of course, can be used to deceive.
   (B) Not all photographers are interested in depicting social or political problems.
   (C) This is not to say that the camera never lies.
   (D) It takes true artistry to produce compelling photographs.

26. (F) NO CHANGE
   (G) freezes
   (H) by freezing
   (J) to freeze

27. (A) NO CHANGE
   (B) for the purpose of serving
   (C) so as to promote
   (D) in helping to create interesting in

28. The writer is considering adding the following sentence at this point in the essay:

   > Computer-generated imagery is even more prone to distortion and fabrication than photography.

   Would this sentence be a relevant and appropriate addition to the essay, and why?

   (F) No, because the topic of computer-generated imagery is unrelated to the main theme of the essay.
   (G) Yes, because computer-generated imagery is now widely used in advertisements and other commercial presentations.
   (H) No, because most people are well aware that computer-generated images are often dis-torted.
   (J) Yes, because, like photography, computer-generated imagery is a form of visual art.

29. (A) NO CHANGE
   (B) involved with such.
   (C) a party to these things.
   (D) among those who take part in them.

30. (F) NO CHANGE
   (G) for
   (H) yet
   (J) so

Answer Key

Exercise 1	Exercise 2	Exercise 3	Exercise 4	Exercise 5
1. D	1. A	1. C	1. A	1. A
2. G	2. G	2. G	2. G	2. J
3. B	3. B	3. A	3. D	3. A
4. F	4. H	4. F	4. G	4. H
5. C	5. C	5. D	5. D	5. A
6. H	6. H	6. F	6. F	6. G
7. B	7. D	7. C	7. B	7. A
8. F	8. H	8. H	8. F	8. J
9. D	9. A	9. B	9. A	9. B
10. G	10. H	10. F	10. F	10. G
11. B	11. B	11. A	11. A	11. C
12. F	12. F	12. H	12. G	12. F
13. B	13. D	13. C	13. A	13. B
14. G	14. F	14. F	14. J	14. F
15. C	15. C	15. D	15. D	15. B
16. F	16. G	16. G	16. G	16. G
17. B	17. A	17. B	17. A	17. D
18. H	18. J	18. H	18. J	18. G
19. B	19. A	19. B	19. A	19. C
20. G	20. F	20. F	20. F	20. F
21. D	21. D	21. A	21. C	21. D
22. G	22. F	22. J	22. F	22. F
23. B	23. A	23. B	23. A	23. B
24. J	24. F	24. G	24. G	24. F
25. A	25. A	25. B	25. C	25. C
26. G	26. J	26. H	26. J	26. G
27. B	27. B	27. A	27. A	27. A
28. H	28. F	28. J	28. H	28. F
29. C	29. C	29. A	29. A	29. A
30. G	30. H	30. G	30. H	30. F

Answer Explanations

EXERCISE 1

1. **The correct answer is (D).** The underlined phrase is redundant, since the words "under no circumstances" add nothing to the meaning conveyed by the word "never." It can be omitted with no loss of meaning, making the sentence more concise.

2. **The correct answer is (G).** The semicolon in the underlined portion is wrong, since what follows it cannot stand alone as a sentence. Instead, a comma should be used.

3. **The correct answer is (B).** When the word "its" is used in place of the words "it is," it should be spelled "it's"; the apostrophe stands for the omitted letter "i" in the contraction.

4. **The correct answer is (F).** "And" is the most logical conjunction among the answer choices for connecting this sentence with the previous one. The other answer choices all imply a contraction or some other shift in meaning, which in fact doesn't exist.

5. **The correct answer is (C).** The subject of the verb "have . . . imagined" is the pronoun "no one," which is singular. Therefore, the singular verb "has . . . imagined" is necessary to make the subject and verb agree in number.

6. **The correct answer is (H).** The modifying phrase with which the sentence begins, "Working closely" etc., describes effects artists. In order to keep the modifier from "dangling," what follows the phrase should be a word naming the people being described. Thus, it's correct for the word "they" (meaning, of course, the effects artists) to immediately follow the comma. Answer (H) is also more concise and graceful than the other answer choices.

7. **The correct answer is (B).** As originally written, the sentence is a run-on—two complete sentences jammed together with a comma between them. Choice (B) corrects the error by breaking the two sentences apart at the logical place.

8. **The correct answer is (F).** It makes sense to start with sentence 2, which makes the general point (about the usefulness of special effects) that the rest of the paragraph then explains in more detail. And it makes sense for sentence 3 to follow sentence 4, since it refers to "those costs" described in that sentence.

9. **The correct answer is (D).** This sentence introduces the topic around which the other sentences in the paragraph are organized.

10. **The correct answer is (G).** The pronoun "such" is vague, leaving the reading slightly uncertain what is being referred to. (It also is awkward and non-idiomatic; i.e., "weird sounding.") "These events" refers back to the previous sentence clearly and understandably.

11. **The correct answer is (B).** This wording is the simplest and most concise of the answer choices.

12. **The correct answer is (F).** The words "Most important" introduce the point made in the final paragraph in a logical fashion: the idea that special effects free movie makers to depict impossible words is, arguably, the "most important" or at least most remarkable idea in the passage. The other alternative connecting words or phrases don't make as much sense in the context.

13. **The correct answer is (B).** Since this sentence adds nothing to our understanding of movie special effects or how they are used, it can be omitted without losing anything.

14. **The correct answer is (G).** The word "maker's" is a possessive; the sentence refers to something (the "tool" of special effects) that belongs to the movie makers. Therefore, it should be spelled with an apostrophe s, as possessives generally are.

15. **The correct answer is (C).** The parenthetical phrase "after all" should be surrounded by commas to set it off from the rest of the sentence.

16. **The correct answer is (F).** We're looking for a sentence that will support the idea that the hungry people of the world may be fed from resources in the sea. The sentence in answer F does this by giving several concrete examples of foods derived from the oceans.

17. **The correct answer is (B).** The phrase "three quarters" is neither a possessive nor a contraction; it's a simple plural, and therefore should be spelled without an apostrophe.

18. **The correct answer is (H).** There's no reason to separate the subject ("deposits") from the verb ("have been discovered") with a comma.

19. **The correct answer is (B).** Only the sentence given in answer (B) offers an additional example of important resources that may be provided by the oceans.

20. **The correct answer is (G).** Since the sentence is talking about the "cities on the ocean" mentioned in the previous sentence, the logical pronoun to use is "they" (a plural pronoun to match the plural antecedent). Choice (H) is wrong because it seems to refer to a "they" we can't identify—some unnamed group of people who will build the futuristic cities on the sea.

21. **The correct answer is (D).** The words "playing a variety of roles" mean exactly the same as the words "could serve many functions" which precede them. Since the underlined phrase adds no new information to the sentence, it can and should be eliminated.

22. **The correct answer is (G).** It's generally best for the adverb to be as close as possible to the word it modifies—in this case, the verb "could serve." It should be graceful and natural to insert it in the middle of the verb phrase: "could also serve."

23. **The correct answer is (B).** The subject of the verb "have . . . been developed" is the singular pronoun "much." Therefore, the verb should also be singular: "has been developed."

24. **The correct answer is (J).** As originally written, the sentence is a fragment; it has no independent verb. Answer (J) fixes the problem by turning the gerund "serving" into the verb "serve," whose subject is the word "rigs" way back at the start of the sentence.

25. **The correct answer is (A).** It makes sense to start a new paragraph here. The previous paragraph talks about the existing oil-rig technology that could be used to build cities on the sea; this paragraph talks about what these new cities would be like. The ideas are distinct and deserve separate paragraphs.

26. **The correct answer is (G).** The logical relationship between the two clauses in this sense is best expressed by the word "since"; the fact that shipping supplies from the mainland would be costly is the reason why the cities would have to be self-sufficient. "Since" states this relationship.

27. **The correct answer is (B).** The original phrase is vague, as are choices (C) and (D). Answer (B) names the kinds of facilities to be included in the new cities rather than merely alluding to them.

28. **The correct answer is (H).** Since what follows the semicolon can't stand alone as a sentence, that punctuation mark is incorrect. It must be changed to a comma.

29. **The correct answer is (C).** Paragraph 4 is devoted to describing the various purposes that cities on the sea might serve. The new sentence, which adds an extra example of these purposes, would make sense at the end of that paragraph.

30. **The correct answer is (G).** Paragraph 1 describes an example of the "human dilemmas" introduced in paragraph 2. Therefore, it makes sense to have paragraph 1 follow paragraph 2.

EXERCISE 2

1. **The correct answer is (A).** The conjunction "like" is correct: it's idiomatic to say that something "seems like" something else, rather than "seems as" something else.

2. **The correct answer is (G).** Since the first paragraph talks in a somewhat light-hearted way about how people blamed all kinds of problems on El Niño, while the rest of the passage describes the very serious problems El Niño really caused, a transitional sentence is needed that says to the reader, "All kidding aside—El Niño produced some real headaches." The sentence in answer (G) does that.

3. **The correct answer is (B).** The subject of the verb "has been dubbed" is plural—it's the two things "hot currents" and "weather disturbances" (a compound subject). Therefore, the plural verb "have been dubbed" is needed.

4. **The correct answer is (H).** The parenthetical word "however" needs to be set off from the rest of the sentence by a pair of commas, one before it and one after it.

5. **The correct answer is (C).** The last sentence of the paragraph, as originally written, is a fragment, lacking any real subject. By changing the period before it into a comma, the sentence is merged with the previous one, and "storms and . . . climatic changes" becomes the subject of the verb "devastated."

6. **The correct answer is (H).** Two things are being compared: the greater depths the fish sought during El Niño and the lesser depths at which they normally swim. Since only two things are being compared, the comparative adjective "farther" is wanted rather than the superlative "farthest."

7. **The correct answer is (D).** Break this sentence into two, since it's a run-on as it stands.

8. **The correct answer is (H).** The adverb form of the adjective "hard" looks the same as the adjective: "hard." The usually suffix isn't used in this case.

9. **The correct answer is (A).** The conjunction "as well as" is the most graceful and idiomatic of the answer choices. Note that answer (D) would turn the sentence into a run-on: "So did thousands of juveniles and breeding adults" could and should stand on its own as a complete sentence.

10. **The correct answer is (H).** Logically, the word "similarly" makes the most sense here, since what's being described in the sentence is a phenomenon that resembles the one described in the previous sentence. "Likewise" sounds awkward in this context.

11. **The correct answer is (B).** When two potentially complete sentences are linked in one with a coordinating conjunction (in this case, "but"), it's normally correct to use a comma before the conjunction rather than some other punctuation mark.

12. **The correct answer is (F).** The original wording is the clearest and most concise choice. Answers (G) and (J) are vague and confusing, and answer (H) sounds clumsy.

13. **The correct answer is (D).** The words "in distance" are redundant, since "close" obviously refers to distance; they should be eliminated.

14. **The correct answer is (F).** This sentence neatly ties together the various destructive effects of El Niño on wildlife living on the shores of Peru.

15. **The correct answer is (C).** Paragraph 4 explains the indirect way El Niño affects the Peruvian mammals (by reducing the availability of their food, the schools of anchovies and sardines). It's necessary if we are to understand how El Niño affected the seals and sea lions in Peru.

16. **The correct answer is (G).** Because it is grammatically parallel with "hosting," the present participle "preparing" is better than the infinitive "to prepare."

17. **The correct answer is (A).** The idiomatic phrase is "compared with," not "compared against" or any of the other answer choices.

18. **The correct answer is (J).** In this rather casual, mildly humorous essay, the phrase "such a feat" sounds both idiomatic and appropriate. The other answer choices either sound a bit awkward or are verbose by comparison.

19. **The correct answer is (A).** The original sentence is clear and concise. The alternatives add words without adding anything to the meaning or tone of the essay.

20. **The correct answer is (F).** Note that what follows the colon restates or summarizes what precedes it. This is a good example of the proper use of a colon.

21. **The correct answer is (D).** Choice (D) states the idea most clearly of all the answer choices. The original wording is wrong, among other reasons, because the phrase "Pilgrims meal" would have to be written as the possessive "Pilgrims' meal."

22. **The correct answer is (F).** The parenthetical phrase is appropriate in this light-hearted look back at a long-ago, slightly amazing, and mysterious holiday celebration. Answers (G) and (H) say almost the same thing, but less gracefully and idiomatically.

23. **The correct answer is (A).** The original wording is more concise and clear than the alternatives.

24. **The correct answer is (F).** The proposed addition fits logically into the overall theme of the essay. Note, too, that it picks up on the idea that the original Thanksgiving dinner was much harder to prepare than today's Thanksgiving dinners, which can be purchased ready-made at the supermarket (as mentioned in the second paragraph).

25. **The correct answer is (A).** The original wording is correctly parallel to the phrase it's paired with: not "a few hours, but a few days."

26. **The correct answer is (J).** As written, the sentence is a run-on. By changing the subject-verb pair "this provokes" into the present participate "provoking," the second half of the sentence is tightly and correctly linked with the first half, and the run-on problem is eliminated.

27. **The correct answer is (B).** The first half of the paragraph talks about the many guests who show up at today's Thanksgiving dinners, while the second half talks about how many more guests there were at the first Thanksgiving. The sentence in choice (B) deftly links the two ideas.

28. **The correct answer is (F).** The original word is both perfectly correct and idiomatic.

29. **The correct answer is (C).** As originally worded, the underlined phrase is pretty vague; it's hard to tell what the writer is getting at. Choice (C) clarifies the point: the huge menu described in the previous paragraph makes sense when you consider how many people attended the dinner.

30. **The correct answer is (H).** The contraction "you're" is necessary in this sentence, since what's intended is the same meaning as the two words "you are."

EXERCISE 3

1. **The correct answer is (C).** It's more graceful, idiomatic, and clear to leave the prepositional phrase "of girls" intact, putting the modifying adverb "only" in front of the phrase rather than in the middle of it.

2. **The correct answer is (G).** In most sentences, a modifying phrase like "In 1977," telling when the event described in the sentence takes place, fits best at the beginning. In this case, it would slip in nicely after the introductory conjunction "But."

3. **The correct answer is (A).** The idiomatic phrase "justly renowned" is perfectly clear and correct as used in the original sentence.

4. **The correct answer is (F).** The other answer choices change the meaning of the phrase in a way that isn't logical, given the context. The sentence is explaining how and why the Boys Choice overshadows the Girls Choir, given the history of the two organizations. Thus, it makes sense to introduce the sentence with the phrase "To this day," which says that the Boys Choir still overshadows the younger Girls Choir, even 20 years after the Girls Choir was founded.

5. **The correct answer is (D).** All the answer choices say the same thing; choice (D) does it most concisely.

6. **The correct answer is (F).** Since *all* of the world's musical settings are being compared (at least implicitly), the superlative adjective "most prestigious" is needed, rather than the comparative "more prestigious" or some other form.

7. **The correct answer is (C).** The writer is trying to suggest that the Boys Choir has performed on many "prestigious" occasions. The concert for the Pope is an example; so is performing on the same bill as Pavarotti. The other statements, while interesting, don't describe prestigious occasions for musical performances.

8. **The correct answer is (H).** The collective noun "choir" is normally treated, for grammatical purposes, as a singular word; therefore, it should be paired with the singular verb "was reassembled" rather than the plural "were."

9. **The correct answer is (B).** The correct form of the possessive here would be "the mayor's wife."

10. **The correct answer is (F).** The original wording is grammatically correct and clear. Choice (G) would turn the sentence into a run-on; choice H needlessly adds the word "thus"; and choice (J) uses the pronoun "it," whose antecedent and meaning aren't clear in the context.

11. **The correct answer is (A).** The original "It's" is perfectly correct. In this context, "it's" means "it is," so the form of the word including an apostrophe is right.

12. **The correct answer is (H).** Sentence 1 draws a conclusion based on the rest of the paragraph, so it logically belongs last. Sentence 2 introduces the paragraph's overall topic, so it makes sense to put that one first. And sentences 3 and 4 clearly belong together, in that order.

13. **The correct answer is (C).** The idiomatic expression is, "motivated *to do* something" rather than "motivated *for doing* something."

14. **The correct answer is (F).** The phrase "for lack of money" is an idiomatic and familiar one. Choices (G) and (H) are verbose and awkward by comparison; choice (J) is vague and hard to understand.

15. **The correct answer is (D).** Read the explanation of the assignment carefully: the writer has been asked to "describe the musical achievements" of the choir. The essay we've read explains a bit about the choir's history and its importance in the lives of its inner-city members, but it really doesn't describe their musical achievements.

16. **The correct answer is (G).** In this context, what's needed is the possessive "your" rather than the contraction "you're" (= you are).

17. **The correct answer is (B).** The logical conjunction here is "but," since there is a contrast in meaning between the skepticism referred to in the first half of the sentence and the explanation offered in the second half, which is intended to disarm that skepticism.

18. **The correct answer is (H).** As written, the sentence is a run-on; the second half of the sentence, beginning "he interviewed," could stand alone as a sentence. Choice (H) fixes this by making the last five words into a modifying phrase that explains what Schultz did in Alabama, tacked neatly on to the rest of the sentence.

19. **The correct answer is (B).** It's incorrect to handle this as two sentences, since what follows the period is lacking a subject for the verb "was struck." As shown in choice (B), the two should be unified, so that "he" becomes the subject for both verbs: "interviewed" and "was struck."

20. **The correct answer is (F).** The original word is grammatically correct and logical in meaning.

21. **The correct answer is (A).** The original wording is more clear and idiomatic than either of the two alternatives (choices B and C). It would be wrong to delete the phrase altogether (choice D), since it ties into one of the main ideas of the essay: how Schultz used a poetic metaphor to explain a new economic idea through analogy with an old, familiar idea.

22. **The correct answer is (J).** For the sake of parallelism, eliminate these words. The list should simply read, "rail fences and hog pens and mules."

23. **The correct answer is (B).** It makes sense to begin a new paragraph here, since the main idea has changed. The previous paragraph summarizes the old farm couple's concept of "human capital"; the new paragraph, which begins at this point, discusses how metaphors can help to explain new theoretical concepts.

24. **The correct answer is (G).** The phrase "get received" is very slangy, too much so for the context of this fairly serious, formal essay on economics. "Are received," which means much the same thing, is more appropriate.

25. **The correct answer is (B).** The commas in the original are needless; among other flaws, they separate the subject of the sentence (it's the compound subject "hog pen" and "Latin instruction") from its verb ("are paid for"). The subject and the verb shouldn't be separated by commas unless it's unavoidable.

26. **The correct answer is (H).** This wording is the most concise and graceful of the four alternatives.

27. **The correct answer is (A).** The plural verb "cause" is necessary, since the compound subject "hog pen" and "Latin" is plural.

28. **The correct answer is (J).** What follows the underlined word is the noun phrase "water from a dam." Therefore, the preposition "like" is correct. (The conjunction "as" would be correct only if what followed was a clause, such as "water pours from a dam.")

29. **The correct answer is (A).** All three alternatives mean much the same thing, but the original wording is clearest and most graceful. To omit the underlined words would obscure the point of the sentence, which is that the educated farmer can use his knowledge to produce concrete wealth (a hog pen).

30. **The correct answer is (G).** This sentence serves the stated purpose best because it summarizes the main point of the essay by linking its opening and closing paragraphs, using the concept of "the poetry of economics" as the connecting theme.

EXERCISE 4

1. **The correct answer is (A).** The punctuation in the original is correct. It sets off the entire parenthetical phrase with a pair of dashes (one correct way to do it), and separates the additional interjection, "say," from the rest of the phrase with a comma of its own.

2. **The correct answer is (G).** It's idiomatic to speak of one's "role of doing something," rather than, for example, a "role as doing something" or the other choices.

3. **The correct answer is (D).** The underlined phrase should be grammatically parallel to "failed novelists." "Unsuccessful playwrights" fits.

4. **The correct answer is (G).** The normal idiom is, "no other X than Y."

5. **The correct answer is (D).** The simple preposition "Like" is the clearest and most concise way of expressing the desired meaning.

6. **The correct answer is (F).** Answers (G), (H), and (J) all offer parenthetical clauses that could be inserted after the word "Shakespeare" in the essay. However, in each case, the additional information provided is only marginally relevant to the topic of the essay. The original version, with none of these clauses, is the best.

7. **The correct answer is (B).** The writer is contrasting the humble audiences for the first movies with the elite audience for other forms of art. To fit this notion, "the private club" makes more logical sense than any of the other answer choices.

8. **The correct answer is (F).** The point of the paragraph—and the major point of the essay—is that the large amounts of money involved in modern movie making have taken away some of the freshness and creativity of movies as an art form. To support this point, the original clause is the best.

9. **The correct answer is (A).** The original punctuation is correct. The three adjectives, "conventional, unimaginative, and stale," are being listed in a series, and it's proper to separate the items in the list by commas.

10. **The correct answer is (F).** "Has been" is correct; it's a singular verb, to match the singular subject "freshness."

11. **The correct answer is (A).** The conjunction "However" logically introduces this paragraph, which shifts the topic of the essay from the freshness of the early movies to the conventionality produced by the money pressures felt by today's movie makers. "However" suggests the change in theme.

12. **The correct answer is (G).** The adverb "only" sounds most natural, and its meaning is clearest, when it follows "has": the sequence makes it clear that the writer is implying, "only a known patron, not a vast collection of unknown patrons like those in the movie audience."

13. **The correct answer is (A).** The original wording is understandable, grammatical, and idiomatically correct.

14. **The correct answer is (J).** The proper idiomatic pairing is, "the more costly . . . the greater."

15. **The correct answer is (D).** Since paragraph 3 offers a conclusion based on the existence of financial pressures in today's movie industry, it's logical to put that paragraph after the paragraph in which those pressures are described—paragraph 4.

16. **The correct answer is (G).** The subject of the verb "include" is the pronoun "that," which can be either singular or plural. To tell which it is, refer back to its antecedent, which is "kind." Since "kind" is singular, so is "that"; so the singular verb "includes" is needed.

17. **The correct answer is (A).** The original wording is best. Each of the other answer choices is non-idiomatic and awkward-sounding.

18. **The correct answer is (J).** All four answer choices say much the same thing. Therefore, the concise single-word alternative "predators" is better than the other, more wordy versions.

19. **The correct answer is (A).** This sentence makes for the best transition, since it leads the reader from the topic of urodeles toward the second type of animal being discussed, planaria, which are also capable of regeneration.

20. **The correct answer is (F).** The apposite phrase "a kind of simple worm," which briefly describes "planaria," is appropriately set off from the rest of the sentence by being enclosed within a pair of commas.

21. **The correct answer is (C).** It's incorrect to use the conjunction "and" at the start of this phrase. Instead, the preposition "with" links the phrase to the rest of the sentence in a way that makes it meaning and its relation to the other parts of the sentence clear.

22. **The correct answer is (F).** Up to this point, the essay has described a similarity between urodeles and planaria: both can regenerate. Now, a difference will be discussed: their varying means of accomplishing this. Thus, the connecting word "However," which suggests a change in theme, makes sense.

23. **The correct answer is (A).** This sentence is telling what the animal first does when injured. (Later, we'll learn what the animal does second.) Thus, the adverb "first" most directly modifies the verb "heals," which means it should be placed as close as possible to that verb. The original location, therefore, is the best one.

24. **The correct answer is (G).** "Such like" is not idiomatic; "such as" is.

25. **The correct answer is (C).** The idiomatic expression to use with the verb "revert" is "to being."

26. **The correct answer is (J).** What's needed in this context is the adverb "ultimately" rather than the adjective "ultimate." It modifies the entire sentence by telling when the event described takes place: at the end of the entire regeneration process.

27. **The correct answer is (A).** "By contrast" sets up an appropriate transition from the previous paragraph, which discussed how urodeles regenerate, to this one, which shifts to the topic of how planaria regenerate.

28. **The correct answer is (H).** The sentence as originally worded is a run-on; the second half of the sentence, beginning with "this enables," could stand alone as a sentence. Choice (H) fixes the problem by turning the second half of the sentence into a modifying phrase clearly attached to the first half of the sentence.

29. **The correct answer is (A).** The original wording is the clearest way of stating the idea. Choice (B) is wrong because of the plural verb "are" (it should be singular, to match its subject, "which," referring back to "cell type"); choice (D) is wrong because of the weird use of the pronoun "one." (Whom could it possibly refer to?)

30. **The correct answer is (H).** The idiomatic phrasing "of the old" implies "of the old [animal]," grammatically parallel to the phrase "an entirely new animal" earlier in the sentence.

EXERCISE 5

1. **The correct answer is (A).** The original wording is the best choice. Note that answers (B) and (C) are wrong because they shift to a singular construction ("business" rather than "businesses,"), which doesn't fit with the pronoun "they" later in the sentence.

2. **The correct answer is (J).** Choice (J) is the most concise and graceful alternative. One clue: note that both the original wording and choice (G) include commas around the adverb "simply," which is often a telltale sign of unnecessary awkwardness.

3. **The correct answer is (A).** The clause in the original sentence does the best job of underscoring Wang's preeminent position in the office automation marketplace. The other statements suggest vaguely related ideas, but none clearly states that Wang was number one in its field, as the original clause does.

4. **The correct answer is (H).** Choices (F) and (G) are unclear in their reference; choice (J) is wordy and awkward. Choice (H) makes the point clearly and concisely.

5. **The correct answer is (A).** The dramatic shift in tone between the first paragraph (describing Wang's former greatness) and the second paragraph (describing its later collapse) is appropriately signaled by the "Yet."

6. **The correct answer is (G).** The sentence in the original essay beginning with the word "shrinking" is actually a fragment. Choice (G) fixes this by attacking it to the previous sentence, where it becomes a long phrase modifying "Wang."

7. **The correct answer is (A).** All four answer choices say much the same thing; choice (A) does it most concisely and gracefully.

8. **The correct answer is (J).** The subject of the sentence is "computer"; the writer's intention is to have a compound verb, "transformed" and "wiped out." Choice (J) sets up this structure and makes the relationship between the various parts of the sentence quite clear.

9. **The correct answer is (B).** The correct past participle of the verb "to see" is "seen"; whenever an auxiliary (helping) verb is used, "seen" should be used, not "saw."

10. **The correct answer is (G).** In this sentence, "its" is being used as the possessive form of the pronoun "it." Therefore, no apostrophe should be used. (In this way, of course, "its" and other possessive pronouns, such as "yours" and "hers," differ from other possessives.)

11. **The correct answer is (C).** The plural verb "were" must be used, since the subject is also plural: the compound "excellence and leadership."

12. **The correct answer is (F).** This paragraph describes the missteps that led Wang to ignore the personal computer market until it was too late, severely damaging Wang's business prospects. Only the sentence in choice (F) summarizes this information accurately.

13. **The correct answer is (B).** The hypothetical business leader discussed in this sentence is trading time for two other things: "more information" and "a decrease in uncertainty." Since two similar things are being listed, it would be desirable for them to be described in grammatically parallel terms: "more information and less uncertainty."

14. **The correct answer is (F).** It's perfectly idiomatic to speak of someone being "incapable of [bold] action." Thus, the original wording is correct.

15. **The correct answer is (B).** There's no such word as "regardlessly." The answer choice which best fits the context is (B); the phrase "in either case" refers back to the two causes of business leaders' hesitation to act described in the previous two sentences.

16. **The correct answer is (G).** The parenthetical phrase "of course" should be set off from the rest of the sentence by a pair of matching bookends: two commas, one before the phrase and one after.

17. **The correct answer is (D).** The most concise and graceful wording is choice (D).

18. **The correct answer is (G).** The singular verb "has been" is needed; its subject, "that," is singular, since it refers back to the singular antecedent "subject." Answer (J) is wrong because the sentence becomes a bit confusing when the underlined words are eliminated altogether.

19. **The correct answer is (C).** The two adverbs should be grammatically parallel to one another, as they are in choice (C).

20. **The correct answer is (F).** The alternatives versions are all less idiomatic and "normal-sounding" than the original.

21. **The correct answer is (D).** This version makes the point in fewer, clearer words than either version (A) or (C). Note that answer (B) distorts the meaning of the sentence: "wariness" and "awareness" are two very different things.

22. **The correct answer is (F).** The original version is grammatically correct and idiomatic.

23. **The correct answer is (B).** The point of the paragraph is the emotional impact that a vivid photograph can have. The interjected phrase strengthens this point by calling to mind an image that clearly illustrates this impact.

24. **The correct answer is (F).** This version is the shortest and most concise way of saying what all four answer choices say.

25. **The correct answer is (C).** The topic of the new paragraph is the fact that photos—despite their inherent realism—can be used to mislead. Choice (C) establishes a clear transition to this topic by making it clear that the writer does not want to exaggerate the claims for the realism of photography stated previously in the essay.

26. **The correct answer is (G).** The verb "freezes" should be used in order to maintain grammatical parallelism with the verbs "exaggerates" and "omits" earlier in the sentence.

27. **The correct answer is (A).** The other answer choices are awkward and less idiomatic than this version.

28. **The correct answer is (F).** If this were a more general essay on the topic of truth and falsehood in art, then a digression on the new computer-generated imagery and its capacity for deception might be relevant and interesting. However, this essay deals solely with photography; in this context, a sentence on computer images seems out of place.

29. **The correct answer is (A).** By comparison to this phrasing, the others sound awkward and a little vague.

30. **The correct answer is (F).** The logical connection between the two halves of the sentence is best conveyed by "and." There is no sharp contrast between the two, so "yet" is wrong, nor is there a cause-and-effect relationship, which eliminates "for" and "so."

Chapter 5

The Mathematics Test

Get the Scoop On . . .

- Proven strategies for tackling ACT math problems
- How rounding off and guesstimating can save time and help avoid errors
- How to work backward to untangle challenging questions
- How to find answers in the diagrams provided by the test-makers
- How and when to use your calculator—and when *not* to

THE TEST CAPSULE

What's the Big Idea?

Questions on the ACT Mathematics Test are designed to test your knowledge of the basic facts and skills taught in most high school math programs. You'll be given a varied mixture of problem types, including some word problems, problems that involve reading and interpreting graphs and charts, geometry problems with and without diagrams, some trigonometry problems, and a few straightforward arithmetic and algebra problems. For each question, five answer choices are provided; you just have to pick the right one.

How Many?

Your ACT will probably have a total of 60 math problems.

How Much Time Should They Take?

Plan to answer the ACT math problems at a rate of one per minute. Some items, you'll find, are relatively time-consuming, and may take two or three minutes to solve. To make up for these items, you'll have to answer other questions in just 15 to 30 seconds. As you'll see, this timing is quite possible.

What's the Best Strategy?

When in doubt, try something. The problem itself will often suggest a procedure you've often used in math class. If so, use it, even if you can't see how it will lead to the answer you want. Quite often, this sort of "tinkering with the numbers" will quickly lead you toward the solution.

What's the Worst Pitfall?

Getting bogged down in lengthy or complex calculations. Most ACT math questions are deliberately designed to make complicated calculations unnecessary: The test-makers are more interested in seeing whether you understand the basic structure of the problem than whether you can correctly complete a series of computations. If you find yourself starting a complicated set of calculations, stop—you're probably overlooking a simple shortcut.

THE OFFICIAL DESCRIPTION

What They Are

The math problems on the ACT are designed to test your ability to use knowledge of specific math facts, formulas, techniques, and methods to solve problems. Basic information about the rules and procedures of math is needed, as well as skill in applying those rules to non-routine or real-world situations.

What They Measure

To score high, you must be very comfortable with the basic operations of arithmetic—not only addition, subtraction, multiplication, and division, but also such procedures as working with fractions and decimals, figuring out averages, and the like. You'll also need to be skilled in the basic operations of algebra, including solving equations, using negative numbers and square roots, and factoring. Many of the principles of geometry are tested, including such concepts as the properties of triangles, circles, and quadrilaterals and determining the areas and volumes of simple figures. Finally, the test covers basic principles of trigonometry, including solving trigonometric equations, graphing functions, and understanding the values and properties of functions.

What They Cover

The math areas tested on the ACT, including the multiple-choice items, are those studied by most high school students: arithmetic, basic algebra, and plane and coordinate geometry. Some advanced and specialized math topics are *not* covered on the ACT, including calculus. See Appendix B, The Insider's Math Review for the ACT, for a detailed review of the math concepts most frequently tested on the exam.

The Directions

The directions for the ACT Mathematics Test are similar to the following:

Directions: Solve each problem below and mark the oval representing the correct answer on your answer sheet.

Be careful not to spend too much time on any one question. Instead, solve as many questions as possible, and then use any remaining time to return to those questions you were unable to answer at first.

You may use a calculator on any problem in this test; however, not every problem requires the use of a calculator.

Diagrams that accompany problems may or may not be drawn to scale. Unless otherwise indicated, you may assume that all figures shown lie in a plane and that lines that appear straight are straight.

THE INSIDER'S REPORT: STRATEGIES THAT REALLY WORK

Focus on What's Actually Being Asked

Read the question carefully and make sure you know the answer being sought.

Most ACT math problems will include a series of interrelated facts. The kinds of facts will vary depending on the kind of question.

In a word problem, these facts might include the speed of a train, the distance between two cities, and the time when the train leaves the station.

In a geometry problem, the facts might include the degree measures of two angles in a triangle, the length of one side of the triangle, and the diameter of a circle in which the triangle is inscribed.

In a graph-reading problem, the facts might include an entire series of numbers as depicted in the graph: monthly inches of rainfall in a particular county over a one-year period, for example.

One key to tackling any of these kinds of problems is to make sure you know which fact is being asked about and what form the answer should take. If you read hastily, you may *assume* a particular question when, in fact, the test-makers want to focus on a different one. Rather than asking about when the train will arrive at City B, they may ask when the train will reach the one-third point of the trip. Rather than asking about the area of either the triangle or the circle, they may ask instead about the area of the odd-shaped shaded region that falls between them. And rather than asking about the amount of rainfall in any particular month, they may ask about the *difference* among two of the months—a number that doesn't appear directly on the graph itself.

When in Doubt, Try Something

Occasionally, you'll find yourself staring at a problem without knowing how to begin solving it. If you're at a loss . . . try something. Often the numbers stated in the problem will suggest a starting point—by reminding you of operations and procedures you often used in math class.

If fractions are involved, for example, try simplifying them to the simplest form or multiply them out to rename them as whole numbers. Or rename them as decimals or percentages if they lend themselves easily to that process (for example, $\frac{1}{10} = 10\%$).

If a geometry diagram appears, work from what you know (such as the degree measures of certain angles) to fill in information you don't know: the complementary angle alongside the angle that's marked, for example, or the angle on the other side of the transversal which must be equal to the angle you know.

If you're given a problem involving probability or permutations (varying combinations of things), just start listing all the possibilities.

Quite often, seemingly random experimenting like this will lead you quickly toward the right answer. Why? Because of the peculiar way in which ACT math problems are designed. The test-makers want to test you on a wide array of math topics in a short period of time. That means they want to ask you lots of questions that you can do quickly—in just about a minute each. Therefore, the questions are written so that the numbers themselves are generally "obvious." What's tricky is the underlying connection among the numbers. As soon as you "see" that connection, the math is usually simple.

As a result, ACT math tends to reward students who are willing to "mess around" with the numbers in the problem until an insight into the solution emerges. Once that "Aha!" moment happens, the answer is usually close at hand.

Round Off and "Guesstimate" Freely

It's not always necessary to work with exact numbers in solving the math problems in the ACT. Sometimes the fastest and even the most accurate way to an answer is to guesstimate. Here's an example:

> Juanita earns a weekly salary of $960. She is scheduled to receive a 10% salary increase next year and a 5% increase the year after that. What will her new weekly salary be?

(A) $975.00
(B) $1,104.00
(C) $1,108.80
(D) $1,920.00
(E) $2,064.00

If you understand the logic behind this question, the calculations aren't difficult. You need to figure out the answer in two steps. First, add 10 percent to Juanita's current salary of $960. (This gives a result of $960 + $96 = $1,056.) Then add 5 percent of the larger salary ($1,056 + $52.80 = $1,108.80). Using either your calculator or pencil and paper, the math isn't hard; the right answer, as you see, is choice (C).

However, a situation could arise in which you haven't time to perform the precise calculations. For example, the proctor may have just announced "Five more minutes to go," and you have 10 more math items to complete. Under those circumstances, guesstimating is a useful strategy.

Here's how you'd approach the question. Juanita's starting salary is a little under $1,000. An additional 10 percent will be a little less than $100 (you should be able to figure that out in your head, just by moving the decimal point one space to the left). That brings her salary up to something under $1,100. Another five percent will bring it to a little over $1,100—making either answer B or C clearly correct.

You now have a 50 percent chance of guessing correctly, having spent just a few seconds on the question. (The correct answer is C.)

Here's another example of how rounding off and guesstimating can work:

A radio that normally sells for $59.95 is on sale for 30% off. What is the sale price, to the nearest dollar?

(A) $18
(B) $27
(C) $39
(D) $42
(E) $48

Again, you can take the time to work this out precisely—if you *have* the time. But if you're pressed, it's easy to guesstimate the best answer. Notice that $59.95 is very close to $60—a nice, round number that's simple to work with. You need to deduct 30% from $60. Now, you may be able to figure out, in your head, that 30% of $60 is $18. If not, you may be able to "see" that 30% is a little less than one third. One third of $60 is $20; so the discount offered during the sale is a little less than $20. You might guess $18 or $19. Either way, $42—choice (D)—is clearly the best answer.

Rounding off and guesstimating isn't necessary on most ACT items; in some cases, the numbers used are so few and so simple that you might as well work with them directly. But chances are you'll encounter several problems on every exam that will be made easier and quicker by guesstimating.

If Stymied, Plug In an Answer and Work Backward

On some questions, a quick route to the answer will jump out at you within a few seconds. In other cases, experimenting in some obvious way with the numbers will quickly direct you toward a solution. If neither of these methods works, try grabbing an answer from the five multiple-choice options and plugging it into the question. This will often lead you to the right answer quickly.

Here's an example:

> During the first weekend after the opening of a certain new movie, ticket sales for the movie total $72 million. Each subsequent weekend, ticket sales decline by the same fraction. If ticket sales during the fourth weekend after the opening total $21 million, what is that fraction?
>
> (A) $\frac{1}{4}$
>
> (B) $\frac{1}{3}$
>
> (C) $\frac{1}{2}$
>
> (D) $\frac{2}{3}$
>
> (E) $\frac{3}{4}$

The fastest way to a solution is to plug in an answer. Try choice (C), and see what happens. If ticket sales decline by $\frac{1}{2}$ with each passing weekend, then on the second weekend, sales will be half of $72 million—$36 million.

On the third weekend, sales will be half of $36 million, which is $18 million. *Stop!* The problem says that ticket sales will be $21 million during the *fourth* weekend. Obviously, if the sales are less than that during the *third* weekend, they'll be way too low during the fourth! So choice (C) cannot be the answer.

We can see that the weekly decline in ticket sales is less than $\frac{1}{2}$. The correct answer must then be a smaller fraction, meaning either choice

(A) or choice (B). If you're pressed for time, choose one and move on; you have a 50% chance of being right. If you have time, plug in either and see whether it works. If you do, you'll see that choice (B) is correct.

Would it be possible to develop a formula to answer this question? Probably—some movie executive with an MBA has done it, I'll bet. But it would be crazy to try to devise a formula for the exam. Remember the unique advantage of a test like the ACT: *All the correct answers have been provided.* When it's not obvious which one is correct, pick one and try it. Even if the one you pick first is wrong, this method will usually let you pinpoint the best choice fairly quickly.

THE INSIDER'S REPORT: THE BEST TIPS

For Word Problems, Build an Equation That Will Yield the Answer You Want

For some students, word problems pose the toughest math challenge. You know the kind: They deal with planes traveling at a certain speed, pipes filling vats with liquid at a particular rate, workers painting walls at so many square feet per hour, and so on.

Curiously enough, in most word problems, the math itself is not difficult. You may have a couple fractions to multiply or divide or a simple equation to solve, but the computations will be easy. What's tricky is setting up the math in the first place—in other words, turning the words into numbers and symbols. Here are some pointers that will help.

Let the Unknown Quantity Equal What You Want To Solve For

If the question asks "What fraction of the entire job will be completed after three hours?" begin writing your equation with $J =$, where J represents that fraction of the job. Conversely, if the question asks, "How many hours will it take to do $\frac{3}{7}$ of the entire job?," begin your equation with H, which should equal the hours of work needed. This way, once you've solved the equation, you automatically have your answer, with no further conversions needed.

Break the Problem Down into Phrases, and Translate Each into a Numerical Expression

Word problems can be intimidating because of their length and complexity. Your strategy: Divide and conquer. Break the problem into its component parts, and give each an appropriate number or symbol. Then devise an equation or formula that describes the relationship among these parts, and go ahead with the math.

Here's an example, using one typical kind of word problem—an age problem:

Paul is eight years older than Sarah. Four years ago, Sarah was half the age Paul is now. How old is Sarah now?

FYI

When creating an equation for a word problem, use obvious letter symbols (T for Ted's age, H for hours worked, P for price, and so on) rather than "textbook" letters such as x, y, or z. They're easier to remember and less likely to cause you confusion.

First, notice that what you're looking for is Sarah's age now. So try to set up your equation making S (Sarah's age now) the unknown for which you will solve. The only other letter we'll need is P, which stands for Paul's age now.

Now create a couple simple equations that state in symbols and numbers what the sentences in the problem say.

"Paul is eight years older than Sarah" becomes: $P - 8 = S$.

"Four years ago, Sarah was half the age Paul is now" becomes $S - 4 = \dfrac{P}{2}$.

To get rid of the fraction (usually a good idea), multiply this equation through by 2: $2S - 8 = P$.

Now you can solve for S by substituting the expression $2S - 8$ for P in the first equation:

$$(2S - 8) - 8 = S$$
$$2S - 16 = S$$
$$-16 = -S$$
$$S = 16$$

So Sarah's age today is 16. (Paul is 24.)

Check out Table 5.1, which gives you some of the most common translations of words and phrases into mathematical operations. Learn the list—it'll work as a kind of "foreign phrasebook" for turning English into numbers on the exam.

Table 5.1
Words and Phrases With Mathematical Translations

Equals	*is, amounts to, is the same as*
Addition	*and, with, along with, added to, in addition to, increased by, more than, greater than, larger than*
Subtraction	*less than, fewer than, without, take away, difference, decreased by, reduced by, smaller than*
Multiplication	*times, each, per, by, of, product*
Division	*divided by, part of, fraction, piece, portion*

Rename All Quantities as Units That are Easier To Work With

Don't feel locked into the numbers presented in the problem. If you can see that a different number you can easily get to will be simpler to work with, go for it by renaming the units of measurement.

In particular, when you can, look for opportunities to rename working units as the units in which the answer is wanted. So, for example, if you see that the answers are all stated in terms of square feet, while one of the numbers in the problem is in square yards, rename it as square feet before beginning your work. (One square yard equals nine square feet.)

On Geometry Problems, Mine the Diagram for Clues to the Answer

Most geometry problems on the ACT are accompanied by diagrams. They are set up this way for a reason. You can usually leap from what you know—the facts you are given—to what you need to know simply by using the parts of the diagram as "stepping stones." Here's an example:

> In the figure below, A and B are points on circle O. If the circumference of the circle is 12π, how much longer is arc AB than a straight line connecting the two points?

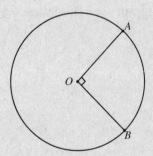

(A) $12\pi - 6$
(B) $6\pi - \sqrt{2}$
(C) $3\pi - 6$
(D) $3\pi - 6\sqrt{2}$
(E) $\pi - \sqrt{2}$

Solving a geometry problem like this one is a matter of working methodically. Just fill in the blank parts of the diagram using what you can deduce from the information you're given. (Use your pencil to mark the new facts right in the question booklet.) After you get to the fact being asked about, you're home free.

Here's how you'd apply the method to this item. First, note what you're being asked: "how much longer" one distance is as compared with another. In other words, what is the difference between the two lengths?

Whenever a question asks about a difference, you should quickly think "subtraction"—and, sure enough, each of the answer choices includes a subtraction sign. To find the difference between the two lengths, you'll need to subtract the shorter length from the longer. Thus, solving the problem means figuring out what each of those lengths equals.

First, the longer of the two. The problem tells you that the circumference of the circle is 12π. The arc AB is a part of this circumference. How can you find its length? Just apply three basic geometric facts you should know: (1) The degree measure of an entire circle is 360; (2) An arc has a degree measure equal to that of the central angle that intercepts it; (3) A right angle has a degree measure of 90 degrees.

Based on these facts, you can see that the degree measure of arc AB is 90 degrees. That makes it one quarter of the entire circle; so its length must be one quarter the circumference of the circle, or 3π. Note that answers (C) and (D) both begin with 3π. You can already tell that one of these is probably correct. If you were running out of time, choose one and move on to the next question.

Now, the shorter length: the straight line from A to B. Draw it in on the diagram (see the following). What new geometric figure is created?

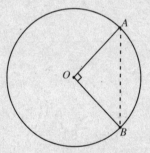

Of course, it's right triangle AOB. Not only that: It's a special kind of right triangle you ought to know, an *isosceles right triangle,* since it has two legs of equal length. In such a triangle, the ratio of lengths of the three sides is $1-1-\sqrt{2}$, with $\sqrt{2}$ representing the hypotenuse. Thus, the length of $\overline{AB}$ will be equal to the length of either leg times $\sqrt{2}$.

What's the length of either leg? It's the same as a radius of the circle. We can figure that out from the formula for the circumference of the circle: $2\pi r$. Since $2\pi r = 12\pi$ (in this case), we can see that $2r = 12$, so the radius must have a length of 6. Therefore, $\overline{AB}$ has a length of $6\sqrt{2}$. When we subtract this from 3π, we get the difference in the two lengths: $3\pi - 6\sqrt{2}$, which is answer choice (D).

In some geometry questions, studying the diagram can make "math" totally unnecessary:

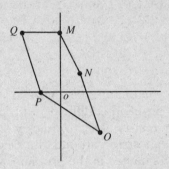

In the figure above, which two sides of polygon *MNOPQ* have the same slope?

(A) $\overline{MN}$ and $\overline{OP}$
(B) $\overline{NO}$ and $\overline{PQ}$
(C) $\overline{NO}$ and $\overline{OP}$
(D) $\overline{OP}$ and $\overline{QM}$
(E) $\overline{PQ}$ and $\overline{QM}$

When you studied coordinate geometry in school, you learned that the slope of a line is often expressed as a fraction. You also learned a formula for calculating the slope of a line from its endpoints. It's possible you may need to use that formula for one question on the ACT. (If you've forgotten it, don't worry; you can refresh your memory of it in Appendix B, The Insider's Math Review for the ACT.)

However, *the formula is totally unnecessary for this problem—and so are any numbers whatsoever.* You can tell which two sides have the same slope just by looking at the diagram and deciding which two sides of the polygon "go in the same direction." It's easy—the only possibility is choice (B), *NO* and *PQ*, which are obviously parallel to one another.

As long as you have even a vague idea as to what the word *slope* means, you can scarcely get this question wrong. The diagram does all the work for you.

If No Diagram is Given, Sketch One

Sometimes, a question without a diagram simply cries out for one. That's what your pencil is for—and that's also why the test-makers kindly leave a generous margin of blank space on most pages of the exam. Draw your own diagram and read the answer right off it.

Here's an example.

In the standard (x,y) coordinate plane, three corners of a square are (2,3), (−1,0), and (2,−3). Where is the square's fourth corner?

(A)   (−1,3)

(B)   (1,−3)

(C)   (2,0)

(D)   (3,−2)

(E)   (5,0)

Can you picture this figure in your head? Me neither. Without a diagram, this problem is difficult; with one, it's very easy. Just use the margin of your test booklet to quickly sketch the (x,y) coordinate plane. Include enough space around the O point—the origin—to fit all of the three points named in the problem, and mark their location as indicated. Your sketch should look something like the following figure.

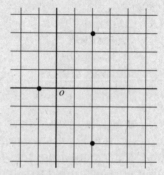

You can see that the square is set diagonally into the grid, with adjacent points separated from one another by three diagonal spaces. The fourth, missing corner is off to the right, at the point designated (5,0) (see the following figure).

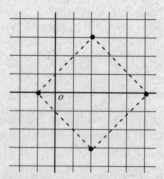

Thus, the answer is choice (E).

On Graph Problems, Spend 30 Seconds Analyzing the Graph(s) Before Tackling the Questions

Your Mathematics Test may include one or more sets of questions designed to test your ability to understand and use information presented in a table or graph. Again, the math involved is usually not hard. The key is knowing how to find the relevant information and separating it from the mass of other information in which it is embedded.

Think of these problem sets as resembling reading questions. Spend 30 seconds "reading" the graph(s) first, noting their structure and basic contents. Then turn to the questions, referring back to the details—the specific data in the graph(s)—as often as necessary.

There are many different types of graphs. Three kinds commonly appear on the ACT: *bar graphs*, *line graphs*, and *circle graphs*.

Bar Graphs
Bar graphs are good for making simple comparisons, such as comparing a single set of statistics (birth rates, for example) for different countries or different years. The following figure shows an example.

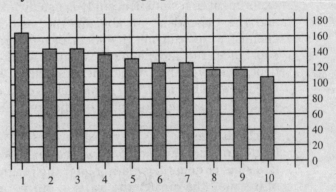

Sales of the Top Ten Industrial Corporations
in the Fortune 500, 1996 (Billions of Dollars)

1. General Motors
2. Ford Motor Company
3. Mitsui
4. Mitsubishi
5. Itochu
6. Royal Dutch/Shell
7. Marubeni
8. Exxon
9. Sumitomo
10. Toyota Motor

In this graph, each bar represents the annual sales of a different major industrial corporation. This type of graph makes the differences in size from one corporation to another very clear. However, if the data were more complex, this graph would be more difficult to look at and understand. (You wouldn't use a bar graph, for example, to show the sales of the entire *Fortune* 500!) A bar graph also has limitations when it comes to spotting trends.

Line Graphs
Line graphs, by contrast, can be both precise and intricate. Large numbers of data points can be shown in one or more lines on a graph,

and trends of increase or decrease can be easily and quickly "read" on a line graph. For this reason, line graphs are the kind of graph most often used by scientists and statisticians.

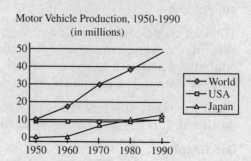

Motor Vehicle Production, 1950-1990
(in millions)

FYI

The structural features of the graph—the labels on the axes, the units of measurement, and any information in the key—are more important than the data presented. If you understand the structure of the graph, you'll understand the kind of information it presents and the nature of the questions that the graph is designed to answer. Once you know these things, the specific details provided by the data—the answers to the questions, in effect—are easy to look up when you need them.

All bar and line graphs have two *axes*, the *horizontal* (or *x*) *axis* and the *vertical* (or *y*) *axis*. By convention, the independent variable in an experiment or a statistical study is usually placed on the horizontal axis, and the dependent variable on the vertical axis. For example, if a chemist were studying the effect of temperature on the solubility of a substance, the independent variable would be temperature, and the dependent variable would be solubility. When the experiment was documented later, a graph of the data would have temperature along the horizontal axis and solubility on the vertical axis.

Circle Graphs

Circle graphs are used to show the breakdown of some large quantity into smaller quantities. The greater the relative size of a particular "slice of the pie," the greater the fraction of the overall quantity represented by that sector of the circle. Typical uses of a circle graph would include the division of the budget of a nation, business, or family into portions representing either different sources of income or different types of spending, and the division of a general population into particular categories (by age, religion, or occupation, for example).

Enlisted Personnel, US Armed Forces,
by Race, 1996 (Total = 419,397)

☒ Black
■ Hispanic
☐ Other
☐ White

All properly-designed graphs are clearly labeled with the names of the variables being studied and the units of measurement (degrees, centimeters, percent, etc.). The divisions along the axes should be clearly numbered. All graphs should also have a title. Many graphs have a *key* providing additional information about the graph or the data. The key is usually found in one corner of the graph, or outside the limits of the graph altogether. A key is most often used when more than one line (or bar, or set of points) is plotted on one graph. Because it would be otherwise impossible for the viewer to know what is meant by the data in such a case, different sets of data are distinguished from each other by using different shadings or patterns for each line, bar, or set of points. The key explains to the viewer what each of the colors or patterns represents. You should always be sure to examine all of these features carefully whenever you encounter a graph on the ACT.

THE INSIDER'S REPORT: THE MOST IMPORTANT WARNINGS

Avoid Lengthy Calculations and Working with Big Numbers

We've already seen examples of how straightforward are the mathematical computations on the ACT. You can count on this format. In fact, if you find yourself getting involved in long, complicated, or tricky calculations—especially ones using big numbers—stop working! You've probably overlooked a shortcut or trick that would make the calculations unnecessary.

Here's an example:

> Students in a chemistry class were asked to rate the teacher on a scale from 1 to 5. 10% of the students gave the teacher a rating of 1; 30% gave a rating of 2; 40% gave a rating of 3; 15% gave a rating of 4, and 5% gave a rating of 5. What was the average of the ratings given?
>
> (A)   1.85
> (B)   2.40
> (C)   2.75
> (D)   3.25
> (E)   3.50

There are several ways you could solve this problem. One way would be to assume a certain number of students in the class and then perform a series of multiplications to figure out the "total rating." If there were 100 students in the class, for example (a nice round number), then 10 would have given a rating of 1 ($10 \times 1 = 10$), 30 would have given a rating of 2 ($30 \times 2 = 60$), and so on. You'd find that the total rating is 275, which, when divided by 100 (the number of students in the class) gives you an average rating of 2.75.

However, none of this figuring is necessary. Instead, look at the pattern of ratings. More ratings of 3 were given than any other, with 2 a close second. The remaining ratings—a relatively low number, at that—were scattered among 1, 4, and 5. Based on these facts alone, and with no actual calculations, you could have concluded that the average rating would fall somewhere between 2.0 and 3.0, and that the average would probably be closer to 3.0 than to 2.0 (since more 3s than 2s were given). Only answer (C) fits those criteria.

Still somewhat unconvinced? Make a simple table of the ratings, like this:

Rating	1	2	3	4	5
Percentage	10	30	40	15	5

Now imagine that this scale is a kind of seesaw, with the middle value, 3, being the fulcrum on which the whole thing balances. It happens that more ratings fall at that middle value than at any other—so the largest "weight" is sitting right at the balancing point. Then, consider: on which end of the seesaw—the lower end or the higher end—is there more weight? Obviously, the lower end; in fact, there are exactly twice as many ratings in the 1/2 region as there are in the 4/5 region. Thus, the seesaw will "tip" toward the lower end—though not completely, since the plurality of ratings still fall smack in the middle. Again, you can see that the average rating will be just a little below 3.0.

The lesson: Avoid long calculations, and especially shun working with big numbers. The test-makers usually don't want you to mess with them. On many ACT items, you can "see" the correct answers without having to do much figuring.

FYI

If you plan to use a calculator on the test, follow these tips: (1) Don't buy a special calculator—a simple machine that can add, subtract, multiply, and divide is all you need. (2) Practice beforehand with the exact calculator you plan to use the day of the exam. (3) Put in fresh batteries the day of the test—or use a solar-powered device that doesn't need batteries.

Use Your Calculator Sparingly

If you're used to working with a calculator, by all means bring your favorite to the test. You'll be happy you did if you blank out in the middle of the exam and forget what 8×7 equals.

If you're smart, however, you'll be very selective in using the calculator. Most students should touch the calculator on only one question out of four—or less. Here are the reasons why.

- Math questions on the ACT are specifically designed *not* to require a calculator. As we've explained, the exam focuses on mathematical reasoning, not on your ability to perform computations.

- It's easy to hit the wrong key, hit the right key twice instead of once, or make other mistakes when using a calculator, especially when you are hurriedly working with big numbers. (Ever get a wrong number on the phone? Everyone has. It's even easier with the small, flimsy buttons on most calculators.)

- You may be lulled into a false sense of security because you rely on the accuracy of the machine. Therefore, you may overlook a math mistake you'd otherwise spot.

- If you *do* suspect a math error when using your calculator, it's impossible to retrace your steps, since there are no notes or figures to check. (Calculators that print on paper are forbidden on the ACT.)

Don't get us wrong; a calculator can be a useful tool. But don't lean on it too heavily. If you find yourself working the calculator on all or even most questions, you're overdoing it. Put it aside, and grab it only when it's really necessary.

Most important: Start work on each question *without* the calculator in hand. The key is to decide what the question is asking, what information you have, and how to get from here to there. Only after you've figured these things out should you start calculating—if you must.

JUST THE FACTS

- On ACT multiple-choice math problems, guesstimate and look for shortcuts; most questions have them.

- Break word problems into simple phrases that you can translate into numbers or symbols.

- Mine geometry diagrams for answer clues—and sketch your own when necessary.

- On problems that require you to read a graph, spend a few seconds analyzing the data before tackling the question.

- Don't overuse your calculator—focus on concepts, not computations.

PRACTICE, PRACTICE, PRACTICE: ACT MATH EXERCISES

Instructions

The following exercises will give you a chance to practice the skills and strategies you've just learned for tackling ACT math problems. As with all practice exercises, work under true testing conditions. Complete each exercise in a single sitting. Eliminate distractions (TV, music) and clear away notes and reference materials. Time yourself with a stopwatch or kitchen timer, or have someone else time you.

If you run out of time before answering all the questions, stop and draw a line under the last question you finished. Then go ahead and tackle the remaining questions. When you are done, score yourself based only on the questions you finished in the allotted time.

Understanding Your Scores

0–3 correct: A poor performance. Study this chapter again, as well as the Insider's Math Review for the ACT (Appendix B).

4–6 correct: A below-average score. Study this chapter again, as well as all portions of the Insider's Math Review for the ACT (Appendix B) that cover topics you find unfamiliar or difficult.

7–8 correct: An average score. You may want to study this chapter again. Also be sure you are managing your time wisely (as explained in Chapter 3) and avoiding errors due to haste or carelessness.

9–10 correct: An above-average score. Depending on your personal target score, you may or may not want to devote additional time to math review practice.

11–12 correct: An excellent score. You are probably ready to perform well on the ACT Mathematics Test.

EXERCISE 1

12 Questions

Time—12 Minutes

Directions: Solve each problem below and mark the oval representing the correct answer on your answer sheet.

Be careful not to spend too much time on any one question. Instead, solve as many questions as possible, and then use any remaining time to return to those questions you were unable to answer at first.

You may use a calculator on any problem in this test; however, not every problem requires the use of a calculator.

Diagrams that accompany problems may or may not be drawn to scale. Unless otherwise indicated, you may assume that all figures shown lie in a plane and that lines that appear straight are straight.

---

1. The advertised price of potatoes is 35¢ per pound. If a bag labeled "3 pounds" actually weighs $3\frac{1}{4}$ pounds, what is the closest approximation in cents to the actual price per pound for that bag?

    (A) 32
    (B) 33
    (C) 34
    (D) 35
    (E) 36

2. If $\left(\dfrac{-2}{5}\right)^3$ is equal to N thousandths, what is N?

    (F) −100
    (G) −64
    (H) −32
    (J) 32
    (K) 64

3. If the larger circle shown below has an area of 36π, what is the circumference of the smaller circle?

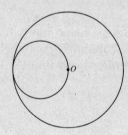

    (A) 2π
    (B) 4π
    (C) 6π
    (D) 8π
    (E) 12π

4. If $r = -2$, then $r^4 + 2r^3 + 3r^2 + r = ?$

    (F) −8
    (G) −4
    (H) 0
    (J) 6
    (K) 10

145

5. How many liters of 50% antifreeze must be mixed with 80 liters of 20% antifreeze to get a mixture that is 40% antifreeze?

(A) 80
(B) 100
(C) 120
(D) 140
(E) 160

6. Horace averaged 70 on his first m exams. After taking n more exams, he had an overall average of 75 for the year. In terms of n and m, what was Horace's average for his last n exams?

(F) $\dfrac{5m + 75}{n}$

(G) $\dfrac{5m}{n} + 75$

(H) $\dfrac{5n}{m} + 75$

(J) $\dfrac{70m + 75n}{m + n}$

(K) 80

7. Shayna rolls a six-sided die twice. What is the probability that she rolls the same number both times?

(A) 0

(B) $\dfrac{1}{36}$

(C) $\dfrac{2}{36}$

(D) $\dfrac{1}{12}$

(E) $\dfrac{1}{6}$

8. Which of the following is a common factor of both $x^2 - 4x - 5$ and $x^2 - 6x - 7$?

(F) $x - 5$
(G) $x - 7$
(H) $x - 1$
(J) $x + 5$
(K) $x + 1$

9. The diagram below shows a cube 3 units on a side with a 1×1 square hole cut through it. How many square units is the total surface area of the cube?

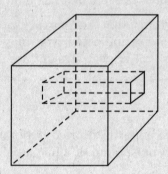

(A) 52
(B) 54
(C) 60
(D) 64
(E) 66

Use the following information to answer questions 10–11.

The bar graph below shows the payments made by XYZ Corporation on contracts to four different suppliers last month. The same information is displayed in the pie chart.

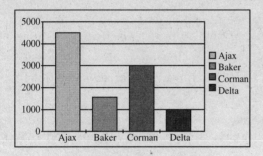

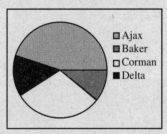

10. How many degrees are there in the angle of the sector of the pie chart representing Corman?

    (F) 36
    (G) 60
    (H) 100
    (J) 108
    (K) 120

11. If Corman goes out of business and XYZ divides up its payments among the three suppliers Ajax, Baker, and Delta in the ratio of 3:2:1, how many degrees in the new pie chart will be in the sector representing Baker?

    (A) 25
    (B) 45
    (C) 60
    (D) 75
    (E) 90

12. Which of the following is a correct factorization of $3x^2y^3 - 6xy^2$?

    (F) $3xy^2(x - 2y)$
    (G) $3xy^2(xy + 2)$
    (H) $3xy^2(xy - 2)$
    (J) $3x^2y(x - 2y)$
    (K) $3x^2y^2(x - 2)$

EXERCISE 2

12 Questions

Time—12 Minutes

> **Directions:** Solve each problem below and mark the oval representing the correct answer on your answer sheet.
>
> Be careful not to spend too much time on any one question. Instead, solve as many questions as possible, and then use any remaining time to return to those questions you were unable to answer at first.
>
> You may use a calculator on any problem in this test; however, not every problem requires the use of a calculator.
>
> Diagrams that accompany problems may or may not be drawn to scale. Unless otherwise indicated, you may assume that all figures shown lie in a plane and that lines that appear straight are straight.

1. For which n is the remainder greatest when 817,380 is divided by n?

   (A) 4
   (B) 5
   (C) 6
   (D) 8
   (E) 9

2. Two rectangles have the same area. One is twice as long as the other. If the longer rectangle has a length of L and a width of W, what is the perimeter of the shorter rectangle?

   (F) $2L + 2W$
   (G) $2L + 4W$
   (H) $L + 4W$
   (J) $2L + W$
   (K) $4L + 2W$

3. If $4x + 2y = 13$ and $4y - x = 8$, what is the value of $x + 2y$?

   (A) -7
   (B) -3
   (C) 0
   (D) 5
   (E) 7

4. If the area of the rectangle in the figure below is equal to the area of the triangle, what is the perimeter of the triangle?

   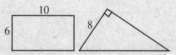

   (F) 17
   (G) $8 + \sqrt{15}$
   (H) $8\sqrt{12}$
   (J) 40
   (K) 42

5. If $2^3 = \sqrt{N}$, what is N?

   (A) 8
   (B) 16
   (C) 32
   (D) 64
   (E) 128

6. Four boys own a total of 150 baseball cards. If the first boy owns 28% of the cards, the second owns 24% of the cards, and the third owns three times as many cards as the fourth, what is the greatest number of cards owned by any one boy?

   (F)   28
   (G)   36
   (H)   42
   (J)   54
   (K)   64

7. If $(x - 2)(x + k) = x^2 + mx - 10$, then $mk = ?$

   (A) -20
   (B) -15
   (C)   12
   (D)   15
   (E)   20

8. A box contains five blocks numbered 1, 2, 3, 4, and 5. John picks a block and replaces it. Lisa then picks a block. What is the probability that the sum of the numbers they picked is even?

   (F) $\dfrac{9}{25}$

   (G) $\dfrac{2}{5}$

   (H) $\dfrac{1}{2}$

   (J) $\dfrac{13}{25}$

   (K) $\dfrac{3}{5}$

9. If a fleet of m buses uses g gallons of gasoline every two days, how many gallons will be needed by four buses every five days?

   (A) $\dfrac{10g}{m}$

   (B) $10gm$

   (C) $\dfrac{10m}{g}$

   (D) $\dfrac{20g}{m}$

   (E) $\dfrac{5g}{4m}$

10. The ratio of the arithmetic mean of two numbers to one of the numbers is 3:5. What is the ratio of the smaller number to the larger?

    (F)   1:5
    (G)   1:4
    (H)   1:3
    (J)   2:5
    (K)   1:2

11. The cost of producing a certain machine is directly proportional to the number of assembly line workers required and inversely proportional to the square of the number of hours of assembly line downtime during production. If the cost was $1,500 when there were 12 workers and only two hours of downtime, how many hours of downtime was there when nine workers were producing machines at the cost of $2,000 per machine?

(A) 1
(B) 1.5
(C) 2
(D) 2.5
(E) 3

12. Which of the following is one root of the equation $x^2 - 4x + 13 = 0$?

(F) -1
(G) 5
(H) $4 + 3i$
(J) $2 - 6i$
(K) $2 + 3i$

EXERCISE 3

12 Questions

Time—12 Minutes

> **Directions:** Solve each problem below and mark the oval representing the correct answer on your answer sheet.
>
> Be careful not to spend too much time on any one question. Instead, solve as many questions as possible, and then use any remaining time to return to those questions you were unable to answer at first.
>
> You may use a calculator on any problem in this test; however, not every problem requires the use of a calculator.
>
> Diagrams that accompany problems may or may not be drawn to scale. Unless otherwise indicated, you may assume that all figures shown lie in a plane and that lines that appear straight are straight.

1. If a fleet of seven taxicabs uses 180 gallons of gasoline every two days, how many gallons will be used by four taxicabs during a seven-day week?

   (A) 180
   (B) 240
   (C) 300
   (D) 360
   (E) 420

2. If $a = -1$ and $b = -2$, what is the value of $(2 - ab^2)^3$?

   (F) 27
   (G) 64
   (H) 125
   (J) 216
   (K) 343

3. If four boxes of books each weighing at least 20 pounds have an average weight of 60 pounds, and if one of the boxes weighs 80 pounds, what is the maximum possible weight of the heaviest box in pounds?

   (A) 90
   (B) 100
   (C) 110
   (D) 120
   (E) 140

4. A quadrilateral has angles in the ratio 1:2:3 and a fourth angle that is 31° larger than the smallest angle. What is the difference in degree measure between the two middle-sized angles in the quadrilateral?

   (F) 16
   (G) 31
   (H) 47
   (J) 51
   (K) 63

5. What is the area of the region shown below, if the curved side is a semi-circle?

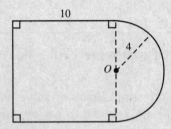

(A) $20 + 4\pi$
(B) $20 + 6\pi$
(C) $40 + 6\pi$
(D) $60 + 8\pi$
(E) $80 + 8\pi$

6. How many gallons of milk that is 2% butterfat must be mixed with milk that is 3.5% butterfat to yield 10 gallons that is 3% butterfat?

(F)   3
(G) $\dfrac{10}{3}$
(H) $\dfrac{7}{2}$
(J) $\dfrac{11}{3}$
(K)   4

Use the following information to answer questions 7–8.

An advertisement for a men's clothing store reads, "Men's shirts $22 each; 3 for $55. Receive a 10% discount on any sale of $100 or more."

7. What is the total cost of eight shirts?

(A) $136.80
(B) $138.60
(C) $154.00
(D) $158.40
(E) $176.00

8. What is the greatest number of shirts you can buy if you have $100 to spend?

(F)   4
(G)   5
(H)   6
(J)   7
(K)   8

9. What is the greater value of x if $x^2 + 6x + 8 = 0$?

(A) -6
(B) -4
(C) -2
(D)   2
(E)   4

10. In the figure below, M is the midpoint of RS. What is the area of triangle MOP?

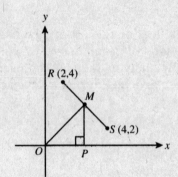

(F) $\sqrt{7}$
(G)   3
(H)   3.5
(J)   4
(K)   4.5

Use the following information to answer questions 11–12.

The maximum speed of airplanes has increased from the 30 miles per hour that the Wright Brothers' first plane flew in 1903 to the much greater speeds possible today. The following graph shows increases in the air speed record from 1903 to 1967.

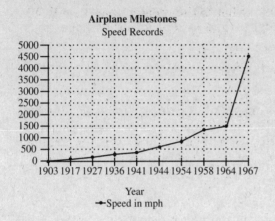

Airplane Milestones
Speed Records

Year
→Speed in mph

11. In approximately what year did a plane first fly over 500 miles per hour?
   (A) 1940
   (B) 1941
   (C) 1943
   (D) 1948
   (E) 1950

12. The air distance from New York to Los Angeles is about 3,000 miles. How much longer (in hours) would it take a plane flying at the 1944 record speed to fly that distance than a plane flying the same distances at the 1964 record speed?
   (F) 2
   (G) 2.5
   (H) 3
   (J) 4
   (K) 6

EXERCISE 4

12 Questions

Time—12 Minutes

Directions: Solve each problem below and mark the oval representing the correct answer on your answer sheet.

Be careful not to spend too much time on any one question. Instead, solve as many questions as possible, and then use any remaining time to return to those questions you were unable to answer at first.

You may use a calculator on any problem in this test; however, not every problem requires the use of a calculator.

Diagrams that accompany problems may or may not be drawn to scale. Unless otherwise indicated, you may assume that all figures shown lie in a plane and that lines that appear straight are straight.

1. If 6 drums of oil will heat 5 identical buildings for 3 days, how many days will 10 drums of oil last when heating 2 of the same buildings?

    (A)   10
    (B)   12
    (C)   12.5
    (D)   14.5
    (E)   18

2. In the figure below, the centers of all three circles lie on the same line. The medium-sized circle has a radius twice the size of the radius of the smallest circle, and the smallest circle has a radius whose length is 2. What is the area of the shaded region?

    (F) 3π
    (G) 4π
    (H) 6π
    (J) 8π
    (K) 10π

3. At a certain bakery, the cost of 4 rolls, 6 muffins, and 3 loaves of bread is \$9.10, and the cost of 2 rolls, 3 muffins, and a loaf of bread is \$3.90. What is the cost of a loaf of bread?

   (A) \$1.05
   (B) \$1.10
   (C) \$1.20
   (D) \$1.25
   (E) \$1.30

4. If x and y are positive integers, and $x - 2y = 5$, which of the following could be the value of $x^2 - 4y^2$?

   (F) -3
   (G) 0
   (H) 14
   (J) 45
   (K) 51

5. What is the perimeter of a rectangle that is three times as long as it is wide and that has the same area as a circle whose circumference has a length of 6?

   (A) $\dfrac{8}{\sqrt{3\pi}}$

   (B) $\dfrac{8\sqrt{3}}{\sqrt{\pi}}$

   (C) $4\sqrt{3\pi}$

   (D) $8\sqrt{\pi}$

   (E) $8\sqrt{3\pi}$

6. A plane is flying from City A to City B at m miles per hour. Another plane flying from City B to City A travels 50 miles per hour faster than the first plane. The cities are R miles apart. If both planes depart at the same time, in terms of R and m, how far are they from City A when they pass?

   (F) $\dfrac{R}{m} + 50$

   (G) $\dfrac{Rm}{2m} - 50$

   (H) $\dfrac{Rm}{2m + 50}$

   (J) $\dfrac{R + 50}{m + 50}$

   (K) $\dfrac{m + 50}{R}$

7. When the units and tens digits of a certain two-digit number are reversed, the sum of the two numbers is 121 and the difference is 9. What is the tens digit of the original number?

   (A) 1
   (B) 3
   (C) 4
   (D) 6
   (E) 7

8. $\sqrt{\dfrac{5}{\sqrt{25}}} = ?$

   (F) $\dfrac{\sqrt{5}}{5}$

   (G) 1

   (H) $\sqrt{5}$

   (J) $2\sqrt{5}$

   (K) $m5\sqrt{5}$

9. If x and y are positive integers, and $x + y = 10$, what is the value of $|x - y|$ when $x^2 + y^2$ is as small as possible?

   (A) 0
   (B) 2
   (C) 4
   (D) 6
   (E) 8

10. If $\log_x(0.001) = 3$, then $x = ?$

   (F) $(.001)^3$
   (G) 0.01
   (H) 0.1
   (J) 10
   (K) 1000

11. Which of the following is the inverse function for $f(x) = \dfrac{2x}{x - 4}$?

   (A) $g(x) = \dfrac{4x}{x - 2}$
   (B) $g(x) = \dfrac{4x}{2 - x}$
   (C) $g(x) = \dfrac{x - 4}{2x}$
   (D) $g(x) = \dfrac{-2x}{x + 4}$
   (E) $g(x) = \dfrac{4x}{x + 2}$

12. Which of the following is an equation of the straight line that has y-intercept 2 and is perpendicular to the line $3x - 5y = 11$?

   (F) $5x - 3y = 2$
   (G) $5x + 3y = 2$
   (H) $3x - 5y = 9$
   (J) $3x - 5y = -10$
   (K) $5x + 3y = 6$

EXERCISE 5

12 Questions

Time—12 Minutes

> **Directions:** Solve each problem below and mark the oval representing the correct answer on your answer sheet.
>
> Be careful not to spend too much time on any one question. Instead, solve as many questions as possible, and then use any remaining time to return to those questions you were unable to answer at first.
>
> You may use a calculator on any problem in this test; however, not every problem requires the use of a calculator.
>
> Diagrams that accompany problems may or may not be drawn to scale. Unless otherwise indicated, you may assume that all figures shown lie in a plane and that lines that appear straight are straight.

1. Andover and Diggstown are 840 miles apart. On a certain map, this distance is represented by 14 inches. Lincoln and Charleston are 630 miles apart. On the same map, what is the distance between them in inches?

   (A) $9\frac{1}{2}$

   (B) 10

   (C) $10\frac{1}{2}$

   (D) 11

   (E) $11\frac{1}{2}$

2. Combined into a single monomial,
   $$10y^2 - \frac{4y^4}{2y^2} = ?$$

   (F) $\dfrac{5y}{2}$

   (G) $\dfrac{6}{y}$

   (H) $6y^2$

   (J) $8y^2$

   (K) $-6y^2$

3. In the (x,y) coordinate plane, what is the distance from $P(-2,8)$ to $Q(3,-4)$?

   (A) $\dfrac{12}{5}$

   (B) $\sqrt{17}$

   (C) $\sqrt{145}$

   (D) 13

   (E) 18

4. In the figure below, what is the area of the region shown?

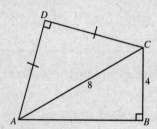

(F) $8\sqrt{3}$

(G) 16

(H) $12 + 4\sqrt{3}$

(J) $8 + 8\sqrt{3}$

(K) $16 + 8\sqrt{3}$

5. The figure below shows a square garden with a 1-yard-wide concrete path around it. If the area of the path is 80 square yards, what is the length of one side of the garden in yards?

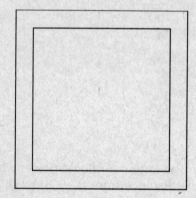

(A) 18

(B) 19

(C) 20

(D) 32

(E) 40

6. If $A < 2 - 4B$, which of the following is true?

(F) $\dfrac{2 - A}{4} > B$

(G) $\dfrac{2 - A}{4} < B$

(H) $B > 4A + 2$

(J) $B < 4A + 2$

(K) None of the above

7. If $9^{2x} = 3^{3x - 4}$, then $x = ?$

(A) -4

(B) $-\dfrac{4}{3}$

(C) 1

(D) $\dfrac{4}{3}$

(E) 4

8. If $x = 4.04$, what is the value of $\dfrac{(x^2 - 16)}{(4x + 16)}$?

(F) 0.01

(G) 0.04

(H) 1.01

(J) 1.04

(K) 4.01

9. If $x < y < -1$, which of the following expressions is greatest?

(A) $\dfrac{x}{y}$

(B) $\dfrac{y}{x}$

(C) $\left(\dfrac{y}{x}\right)^2$

(D) 0

(E) $\left(\dfrac{x}{y}\right)^2$

10. The length of a walk-in closet is 4 feet greater than its width. Its area is 60 square feet. How many feet wide is the closet?

(F) 4
(G) 6
(H) 8
(J) 10
(K) 12

11. If $\dfrac{1}{x} - \dfrac{4}{3} = \dfrac{2}{x}$, what is the value of x?

(A) -3

(B) $-\dfrac{4}{3}$

(C) $-\dfrac{3}{4}$

(D) $\dfrac{3}{4}$

(E) $\dfrac{4}{3}$

12. Simplified to simplest form,
$$\dfrac{4x^2 - 9}{2x^2 + x - 3} = ?$$

(F) $\dfrac{2x + 3}{x - 1}$

(G) $\dfrac{2x - 3}{x + 1}$

(H) $\dfrac{2x + 3}{x + 1}$

(J) $\dfrac{2x - 3}{x - 1}$

(K) $\dfrac{2x^2 - 9}{x^2 + x - 3}$

Answer Key

Exercise 1	Exercise 2	Exercise 3	Exercise 4	Exercise 5
1. A	1. D	1. D	1. C	1. C
2. G	2. H	2. J	2. J	2. J
3. C	3. E	3. D	3. E	3. D
4. K	4. J	4. F	4. J	4. K
5. E	5. D	5. E	5. B	5. B
6. G	6. J	6. G	6. H	6. F
7. E	7. D	7. B	7. D	7. A
8. K	8. J	8. H	8. G	8. F
9. D	9. A	9. C	9. A	9. E
10. J	10. F	10. K	10. H	10. G
11. E	11. B	11. C	11. A	11. C
12. H	12. K	12. J	12. K	12. J

Explanatory Answers

EXERCISE 1

1. **The correct answer is (A).** At 35¢ per pound, the 3-pound bag will be marked $1.05 or 105¢. Dividing this by the weight of the bag, we have $105 \div 3.25 \approx 32.3$. Hence, 32 is the closest answer.

2. **The correct answer is (G).** Cubing, $\left(\dfrac{-2}{5}\right)^3 = \dfrac{-8}{125}$. To rename this fraction as thousandths, multiply the numerator and the denominator by 8 to get $\dfrac{-64}{1000}$. Hence, $N = -64$.

3. **The correct answer is (C).** The larger circle has an area of $A_L = \pi(r)^2 = 36\pi$. This means that $r^2 = 36$ and $r = 6$. The diameter of the smaller circle equals the radius of the larger one, so its radius is $\dfrac{1}{2}(6) = 3$. Therefore, its circumference must be $C_S = 2\pi(3) = 6\pi$.

4. **The correct answer is (K).** Substituting: $(-2)^4 + 2(-2)^3 + 3(-2)^2 = 16 - 16 + 12 - 2 = 10$.

5. **The correct answer is (E).** Let x be the unknown number of liters of 50% antifreeze. The final mixture will have $(x + 80)$ liters, and the amount of antifreeze will be:

$$0.50x + 0.20(80) = 0.40(x + 80)$$
$$0.5x + 16 = 0.4x + 32$$
$$0.1x = 16$$
$$x = 160$$

6. **The correct answer is (G).** Because his average overall was 75, he had a total overall score of $75(m + n) = 75m + 75n$ on $n + m$ exams. Since he averaged 70 on m exams, he had a total of $70m$ on the first m. That means that his total on the last n exams was $75m + 75n - 70m = 5m + 75n$, and his average was $(5m + 75n) \div n = \dfrac{5m}{n} + 75$.

7. **The correct answer is (E).** It really does not matter what number you roll on the first roll; in any case, the chance of matching it the next time you roll is $\dfrac{1}{6}$.

8. **The correct answer is (K).** $x^2 - 4x - 5 = (x - 5)(x + 1)$, and $x^2 - 6x - 7 = (x - 7)(x + 1)$. The common factor is $x + 1$.

9. **The correct answer is (D).** Each side of the square has an area of $3 \times 3 = 9$. Because there are six sides, the original cube had a surface area of 54 square units. Two 1×1 squares are now missing, making the outside area 52. The "hole" has four 3×1 rectangular sides with a total area of 12, giving a grand surface area total of 64.

10. **The correct answer is (J).** Totaling the payments made to all four suppliers, you have $4,500 + $1,500 + $3,000 + $1,000 = $10,000$. Of this total, $3,000 was paid to Corman (that is, 30% of the total). Hence, the sector representing Corman must be 30% of $360° = 108°$.

11. **The correct answer is (E).** Corman was paid $3000. Since this is divided in the ratio 3:2:1, we can write this ratio as $3x:2x:1x$. We know $3x + 2x + 1x = 3000$; $6x = 3000$; $x = 500$. Baker receives $2x$, or $1000 for a total of $2500 (with the initial $1500). This is one-fourth of the total ($10,000). Baker then has one-fourth of the pie chart. The whole chart is $360°$, so Baker's share is $\dfrac{1}{4} \times 360 = 90°$.

12. **The correct answer is (H).** The first term could be thought of as $3xy^2(xy)$, and the second as $3xy^2(-2)$. Hence, we can divide out the common factor $3xy^2$, leaving as the other factor $(xy - 2)$.

EXERCISE 2

1. **The correct answer is (D).** 817,380 is divisible by all the numbers in the list except 8. Hence, 8 must give the greatest remainder, because it is the only remainder that is not zero. To confirm, start with 5; 7,380 is divisible by 5, because its last digit is 0. It is divisible by 2 because it is even, and by 4 because 80 is divisible by 4. However, it is not divisible by 8, because 380 isn't. In addition, the sum of its digits is 27, which is divisible by 3 and by 9. Because it is divisible by both 2 and 3, it is also divisible by 6.

2. **The correct answer is (H).** The perimeter of the longer rectangle is $2L + 2W$. The other rectangle must have a length of $\frac{1}{2}L$ and a width of $2W$, since the area is the same. Thus, the second rectangle has a perimeter of

    $$2\left(\frac{1}{2}L\right) + 2(2W) = L + 4W.$$

3. **The correct answer is (E).** We could solve the two equations simultaneously to find x and y. However, it is easier to proceed as follows: Reorder the terms in the second equation so as to start with the x term. Thus:

    $$-x + 4y = 8$$

    Add to this the second equation:

    $$-x + 4y = 8$$
    $$\underline{4x + 2y = 13}$$
    $$3x + 6y = 21$$

    Divide by 3:

    $$x + 2y = 7$$

4. **The correct answer is (J).** The area of the rectangle is $6(10) = 60$. Using the legs of the right triangle as base and height (with the unknown leg called h), we have $\frac{1}{2}(8)h = 60$; that is, $4h = 60$, and $h = 15$. Hence, the triangle is an 8–15–17 right triangle (one of the famous "Pythagorean triples") with a perimeter of 40.

5. **The correct answer is (D).** $2^3 = 8$, and 8 is the square root of 64.

6. **The correct answer is (J).** 28% of $150 = 0.28(150) = 42$. 24% of $150 = 0.24(150) = 36$. Thus, $150 - 42 - 36 = 72$ cards, which are divided between the other two boys in the ratio of 3:1. That is, one boy owns $\frac{1}{4}$ of the 72 cards (18), and the other owns $\frac{3}{4}$ of them (54).

7. **The correct answer is (D).** Using the FOIL Method: $(x - 2)(x + k) = x^2 + (k - 2)x - 2k$. Because $-2k = -10$, $k = 5$; and since $(k - 2) = m$, $m = 3$. Hence, $km = 15$.

8. **The correct answer is (J).** Because each person had five choices, there are 25 possible pairs of numbers. The only way the sum could be odd is if one person picked an odd number and the other picked an even number. Suppose that John chose the odd number and Lisa the even one. John had three possible even numbers to select from, and for each of these, Lisa had two possible choices, for a total of $(3)(2) = 6$ possibilities. However, you could have had John pick an even number and Lisa pick an odd one, and there are also six ways to do that. Hence, out of 25 possibilities, 12 have an odd total and 13 have an even total. The probability is $\dfrac{13}{25}$.

9. **The correct answer is (A).** Running m buses for two days is the same as running one bus for $2m$ days. If we use g gallons of gasoline, each bus uses $\dfrac{g}{2m}$ gallons each day. So if you multiply the number of gallons per day used by each bus by the number of buses and the number of days, you should get total usage. Thus: $\dfrac{g}{2m} \times 4 \times 5 = \dfrac{10g}{m}$.

10. **The correct answer is (F).** Calling the numbers x and y, $\dfrac{x+y}{2} : x = \dfrac{3}{5}$. That is,

    $\dfrac{x+y}{2x} = \dfrac{3}{5}$. Cross-multiplying: $5x + 5y = 6x$; $5y = x$.

    Hence, one number is five times as large as the other, so their ratio is 1:5.

11. **The correct answer is (B).** Letting C = cost, w = number of workers, and

    t = time in hours, we have the relationship $C = k\dfrac{w}{t^2}$. Therefore, when $w = 12$

    and $t = 2$, we have $1500 = k\dfrac{12}{4} = 3k$; therefore, $k = 500$. Using $k = 500$ and

    substituting $w = 9$ and $C = 2000$, we have:

    $$2000 = \frac{500 \times 9}{t^2} = \frac{4500}{t^2}$$

    Multiplying by t^2 and dividing by 2000, we have:

    $$t^2 = \frac{9}{4}$$

    $$t = \frac{3}{2} = 1.5.$$

12. **The correct answer is (K).** Using the quadratic formula with $a = 1$, $b = -4$, and $c = 13$:

    $$x = \frac{-(-4) \pm \sqrt{(-4)^2 - 4(1)(13)}}{2(1)} = \frac{4 \pm \sqrt{16 - 52}}{2} = \frac{4 \pm \sqrt{-36}}{2}$$

    $$x = \frac{4 \pm 6i}{2} = 2 \pm 3i$$

    Hence, one root is $2 + 3i$.

EXERCISE 3

1. **The correct answer is (D).** Running 7 cabs for 2 days is the same as running one cab for 14 days, while running 4 cabs for 7 days is the same as running one cab for 28 days. Thus, you simply need twice as much gasoline! Here's another way to look at this: The fact that we use 180 gallons of gasoline by running 7 cabs for 2 days means that we use 180 gallons running one cab for 14 days. In other words, each cab uses $\dfrac{180}{14}$ gallons each day. So if you multiply the number of gallons per day used by each cab by the number of cabs and the number of days, you should get total usage. That is:

$$\frac{180}{14} \times 4 \times 7 = 360.$$

2. **The correct answer is (J).** Substituting, $[2 - (-1)(-2)^2]^3 = [2 - (-4)]^3 = 6^3 = 216.$

3. **The correct answer is (D).** If the boxes have an average weight of 60 pounds, then the four must total 240 pounds. Because one weighs 80, the other three total 160. The largest box could weigh 120, with the other two each weighing 20.

4. **The correct answer is (F).** Calling the smallest angle x, the others are $2x$, $3x$, and $(x + 31)$. Because the angles in the quadrilateral must sum to 360, we get:

$$
\begin{aligned}
x + 2x + 3x + (x + 31) &= 360 \\
7x + 31 &= 360 \\
7x &= 329 \\
x &= 47
\end{aligned}
$$

That makes the degree measures of the four angles 47, 94, 141, and 78. The difference between the two in the middle is $94 - 78 = 16$.

5. **The correct answer is (E).** The dotted line divides the region into a rectangle and a semi-circle. Because the radius of the circular arc is 4, the diameter of the circle is 8, and that is the width of the rectangle. The length is 10. Hence, its area is 80. The area of the whole circle would be $\pi r^2 = \pi(4^2) = 16\pi$. Hence, the area of the semi-circle is half of that, or 8π. Therefore, the total area is $80 + 8\pi$.

6. **The correct answer is (G).** Let g be the number of gallons that is 2% butterfat. Then $10 - g$ will be the amount that is 3.5% butterfat. The total amount of butterfat is:

$$
\begin{aligned}
0.02g + 0.035(10 - g) &= 0.03(10) \\
0.02g + 0.35 - 0.035g &= 0.3
\end{aligned}
$$

Now, multiply by 1000 to clear out the decimals:

$$
\begin{aligned}
20g + 350 - 35g &= 300 \\
-15g &= -50 \\
g &= \frac{10}{3}
\end{aligned}
$$

7. **The correct answer is (B).** Eight shirts are two sets of three, plus two singles, which will cost $110 plus $44, or $154. Then you get a $15.40 discount (10%), bringing the final cost to $138.60.

8. **The correct answer is (H).** If you buy five shirts, you get three for $55 plus two more for $22 each, for a total of $99. But if you buy six shirts (two sets of three), you pay $110 less a 10% discount of $11, bringing your cost down to $99. The extra shirt is free!

9. **The correct answer is (C).** Factoring: $x^2 + 6x + 8 = (x + 2)(x + 4) = 0$. Therefore:

$$x + 2 = 0$$
or
$$x + 4 = 0$$

$$x = -2$$
or
$$x = -4$$

The greater root is -2.

10. **The correct answer is (K).** The midpoint has coordinates that are the average of the end points; that is, (3,3). Hence, the triangle is an isosceles right triangle with legs 3 units long and an area equal to $\frac{1}{2}bh = \left(\frac{1}{2}\right)(3)(3) = 4.5$.

11. **The correct answer is (C).** In 1941, the record was under 500 miles per hour, and in 1944, it was over 500 mph. The line graph seems to cross the 500 grid line at about 1943.

12. **The correct answer is (J).** The 1964 record was 1,500 mph. To fly 3,000 miles at this speed would take 2 hours. In 1944, the speed record was 500 mph. To fly 3,000 miles at that speed would take 6 hours, or 4 hours longer.

EXERCISE 4

1. **The correct answer is (C).** Letting x be the unknown number of days, we know that the ratio of "number of drums" to "number of building-days" must be constant; that is, 6:15 = 10:2x. Written as a fractional equation:

$$\frac{6}{15} = \frac{10}{2x}.$$

Thus,

$$\frac{2}{5} = \frac{5}{x}.$$

Cross-multiplying:

$$2x = 25$$
$$x = 12.5.$$

2. **The correct answer is (J).** The smallest circle has a radius of 2, the medium circle has a radius of 4, and the diameter of the large circle must be 12, which makes its radius 6. The area of a semi-circle is half that of the entire circle; that is, $\frac{1}{2}\pi r^2$. The area of the shaded region is the area of the largest semi-circle minus the areas of the two smaller ones; that is, $\frac{1}{2}\pi(36) - \frac{1}{2}\pi(16) - \frac{1}{2}\pi(4) = 8\pi$.

3. **The correct answer is (E).** Letting r, m, and b be the prices in cents of rolls, muffins, and bread respectively yields two equations:

$$4r + 6m + 3b = 910$$
$$2r + 3m + b = 390$$

If we multiply the second equation by -2 and add the two together, we have:

The first equation:	$4r + 6m + 3b = 910$
-2 times the second equation:	$-4r - 6m - 2b = -780$
	$b = 130$

Hence, the price of a loaf of bread is \$1.30.

4. **The correct answer is (J).** Because $x^2 - 4y^2 = (x - 2y)(x + 2y) = 5(x + 2y)$, $x^2 - 4y^2$ must be divisible by 5. Therefore, -3, 14, and 51 are not possible answers (none is divisible by 5). If the result is to be zero, $x + 2y = 0$, which means that $y = -2x$; so both numbers cannot be positive. Hence, the expression must equal 45, which you get if $x = 7$ and $y = 1$.

5. **The correct answer is (B).** If the circle has a circumference of 6, its radius is given by $6 = 2\pi r$, so that $r = \frac{3}{\pi}$. The area of a circle with a radius of $\frac{3}{\pi}$ is $\pi\left(\frac{3}{\pi}\right)^2 = \frac{9}{\pi}$. Now, let the width of the rectangle be w. Its length is $3w$ and its area is $3w^2$, which must equal $\frac{9}{\pi}$. Thus:

$$3w^2 = \frac{9}{\pi}$$
$$w^2 = \frac{3}{\pi}$$
$$w = \sqrt{\frac{3}{\pi}} = \frac{\sqrt{3}}{\sqrt{\pi}}$$

Therefore, the perimeter is $2L + 2W = 6W + 2W = 8W = \frac{8\sqrt{3}}{\sqrt{\pi}}$.

6. **The correct answer is (H).** The planes pass at the moment when the total distance traveled by both equals R. Call this time t. The first plane, going m mph, has traveled mt miles. The second plane, going $(m + 50)$ mph, has traveled $(m + 50)t$. The two sum to R. Thus:

$$R = mt + mt + 50t$$
$$R = (2m + 50)t$$

Thus:

$$t = \frac{R}{2m + 50}$$

Hence, the planes' distance from City A is m times this time:

$$mt = \frac{Rm}{2m + 50}$$

7. **The correct answer is (D).** Calling the number $10t + u$, when we reverse the digits, we get $10u + t$. The sum is then $(10t + u) + (10u + t) = 11t + 11u = 121$. Dividing by 11, we have $t + u = 11$. Taking the difference: $(10t + u) - (10u + t) = 9t - 9u = 9$, and dividing by 9: $t - u = 1$. Finally, adding:

$$t + u = 11$$
$$t - u = 1$$
$$2t = 12$$
$$t = 6$$

8. **The correct answer is (G).** Because $\sqrt{25} = 5$, $\frac{5}{\sqrt{25}} = 1$, and $\sqrt{1} = 1$.

9. **The correct answer is (A).** If $x = 5$ and $y = 5$, $x^2 + y^2 = 50$. For any other choice—say, 6 and 4—the sum is larger. Hence, the value of $x^2 + y^2$ is least when $x = y$ and $|x - y| = 0$.

10. **The correct answer is (H).** The logarithmic equation is equivalent to $x^3 = 0.001$; $x^3 = \frac{1}{1000}$, for which $x = \sqrt[3]{\frac{1}{1000}}$; $x = \frac{1}{10} = 0.1$.

11. **The correct answer is (A).** To find the inverse function, write y for $f(x)$, and then interchange x and y in the original equation and solve for y in terms of x. Thus, $y = \frac{2x}{x - 4} \to x = \frac{24}{y - 4}$. Multiplying by $(y - 4)$, we have $xy - 4x = 2y$. Bringing $2y$ to the left side and $4x$ to the right gives us: $xy - 2y = 4x$; $y(x - 2) = 4x$, and dividing by $(x - 2)$, $y = \frac{4x}{x - 2}$.

12. **The correct answer is (K).** Solving $3x - 5y = 11$ for y, we have $5y = 3x - 11$; $y = \frac{3}{5}x - \frac{11}{5}$. Hence, the slope is $m = \frac{3}{5}$. The slope of the perpendicular line must be $m = -\frac{5}{3}$; combined with the y-intercept $b = 2$, we have the equation $y = -\frac{5}{3}x + 2$. Multiply by 3: $3y = -5x + 6$; add $5x$ to both sides: $5x + 3y = 6$.

EXERCISE 5

1. **The correct answer is (C).** The actual distance and the distance on the map must be in the same proportion. That is: 630:840 = x:14, where x is the unknown distance. In fractions: $\frac{630}{840} = \frac{x}{14}; \frac{3}{4} = \frac{x}{14}$. Cross-multiplying: $4x = 42; x = 10.5$.

2. **The correct answer is (J).** The fraction simplifies to $2y^2$, and $10y^2 - 2y^2 = 8y^2$.

3. **The correct answer is (D).** By the distance formula, $d = \sqrt{(3 - [-2])^2 + (-4 - 8)^2} = \sqrt{25 + 144} = \sqrt{169} = 13$.

4. **The correct answer is (K).** Because $BC = 4$ and $AC = 8$, we know that triangle ABC is a 30°-60°-90° right triangle. Hence, we know that $AB = 4\sqrt{3}$. Taking one-half the product of the legs, the triangle has an area of $\frac{1}{2} \times 4 \times (4\sqrt{3}) = 8\sqrt{3}$. Because triangle ADC is an isosceles right triangle with a hypotenuse of 8, each leg must be $\frac{8}{\sqrt{2}}$. Again, taking one-half the product of the legs, the triangle has an area of $\frac{1}{2} \times \frac{8}{\sqrt{2}} \times \frac{8}{\sqrt{2}} = \frac{64}{4} = 16$. Adding the two areas, we have $16 + 8\sqrt{3}$.

5. **The correct answer is (B).** Calling the side x, then the entire area including the walkway is $(x + 2)^2$. The area of the garden is x^2, and the difference is the area of the walkway. Thus:

    $$(x + 2)^2 - x^2 = 80$$
    $$x^2 + 4x + 4 - x^2 = 80$$
    $$4x + 4 = 80$$
    $$4x = 76$$
    $$x = 19$$

6. **The correct answer is (F).** Add -2 to both sides, thus:

    $$\begin{array}{rcl} A & < & 2 - 4B \\ -2 & = & -2 \\ \hline A - 2 & < & -4B \end{array}$$

    Divide by -4, remembering to reverse the inequality:

    $$\frac{2 - A}{4} > B$$

7. **The correct answer is (A).** In order to equate exponents, the bases must be the same. We can rewrite: $9^{2x} = (3^2)^{2x} = 3^{4x}$, and now we can equate $4x = 3x - 4$, yielding $x = -4$.

8. **The correct answer is (F).** Factoring the numerator and denominator of the fraction, we see that we can divide out the common factor $(x + 4)$ thus:

$$\frac{x^2 - 16}{4x + 16} = \frac{(x - 4)(x + 4)}{4(x + 4)} = \frac{x - 4}{4}$$

Substituting $x = 4.04$ yields $\frac{0.04}{4} = 0.01$.

9. **The correct answer is (E).** Because $x < y < -1$, the ratios $\frac{x}{y}$ and $\frac{y}{x}$ are both positive numbers, but $\frac{y}{x} < 1$, while $\frac{x}{y} > 1$. Therefore, $\left(\frac{x}{y}\right)^2 > \frac{x}{y}$, and must be the greatest.

10. **The correct answer is (G).** Calling the width w, the length is $w + 4$, and the area is $w(w + 4) = 60$. Thus, $w^2 + 4w - 60 = 0$. Factoring, $(w - 6)(w + 10) = 0$ gives us two roots: $w = 6$ and $w = -10$. Of course, we need the positive root, 6 (since there's no such thing as "negative width").

11. **The correct answer is (C).** Clear fractions by multiplying each term in the equation by the least common denominator, $3x$, yielding $3 - 4x = 6$; $-3 = 4x$; $x = \frac{-3}{4}$.

12. **The correct answer is (J).** Factoring numerator and denominator:

$$\frac{4x^2 - 9}{2x^2 + x - 3} = \frac{(2x - 3)(2x + 3)}{(x - 1)(2x + 3)}.$$

Dividing out the common factor $(2x + 3)$ yields $\frac{2x - 3}{x - 1}$.

Chapter 6

The Reading Test

Get the Scoop On . . .

- How the three-stage reading method can help you master ACT reading passages and get more questions right
- How to separate main ideas from supporting details when you read
- How to recognize the vital connections among ideas in the passages
- Why you should read with pencil in hand, and how marking up the passage can earn you extra points
- The kinds of deceptive wrong answers the test-makers love to use—and how to avoid them

THE TEST CAPSULE

What's the Big Idea?

On the ACT Reading Test, you'll be given four passages to read. One will be a fictional narrative; the others will be nonfiction discussions of topics from the natural sciences, social science, and the humanities. You'll then have to answer a group of questions about each passage, testing how well you've understood its content.

How Many?

Your ACT will probably have a total of 40 reading questions based on four passages.

How Much Time Should They Take?

You should spend about eight to nine minutes on each reading passage and the questions that follow. Expect to spend about half of that time on reading, the other half on answering the questions.

What's the Best Strategy?

Use the *three-stage method* when reading passages: previewing, reading, reviewing. With this approach, you'll gather much more information from the passage than with conventional one-step reading, and you'll be able to answer the questions that follow more quickly and more correctly.

What's the Worst Pitfall?

Choosing answers merely because they sound familiar or are factually true. The answers you pick must not only be plausible and true but must also relate directly to the question and be drawn from the most relevant portion of the passage.

THE OFFICIAL DESCRIPTION

What They Are

The Reading Test on the ACT involves two steps. The first step is reading a prose passage, usually between 700 and 900 words long, which may take any of a variety of literary forms and deal with almost any subject. The second step is answering a group of 10 questions dealing with the content, form, and style of the passage.

What They Measure

ACT reading is designed to measure your ability to handle the varied kinds of sophisticated, complex, and subtle reading that college students are called upon to do. In order to answer the questions, it's not enough to understand the basic facts presented in the passage; you also need to notice the more elusive *implications* in the passage (that is, ideas that are suggested rather than directly stated) as well as the *form, structure, and style* of the passage (that is, how the author has chosen to present her ideas).

What They Cover

ACT reading passages consist of edited excerpts from a wide range of materials: scholarly or popular nonfiction books about almost any subject; articles from magazines, newspapers, or journals; and fictional narratives (stories). The ACT does not use passages of poetry or drama on the Reading Test.

The Directions

The directions for the ACT Reading Test are similar to the following:

> **Directions:** This test consists of four passages, each followed by several questions. Read each passage, select the correct answer for each question, and mark the oval representing the correct answer on your answer sheet.

THE INSIDER'S REPORT: STRATEGIES THAT REALLY WORK

Read Each Passage in Three Stages:
Previewing, Reading, Reviewing

Reading on the ACT poses a unique time-management problem. Unlike the other question types, ACT reading requires you to spend a large chunk of time doing something *before* you look at the questions— namely, reading the passage itself. Under the circumstances, with time pressure a real concern for most students, it's easy to get impatient. The temptation to rush through the passage in your haste to start filling in answers may be very great.

Don't do it! Unless you invest some time in getting to know the passage well, your chances of answering most of the questions right are pretty slim. In fact, we'll go further. We'll recommend that you spend *more time* reading the passages than you normally would. Whereas most people ordinarily read anything once and once only, we suggest that you read (or at least scan) each passage on the ACT *three* times before answering a single question.

We have good reasons for this recommendation. The three-stage reading method is a proven technique long taught and used by skilled readers as the best way of getting the most information out of anything in writing. Paradoxically, you'll discover—we can virtually guarantee it—that if you practice the three-stage method, you'll gather more information out of what you read *more quickly than ever before.*

Here's how the three-stage method works:

Previewing

First, preview the passage in one of two ways. You can skim its contents by letting your eyes quickly scroll down the page, picking up as much information as you can. Or you can actually read selected sentences from the passage: specifically, the *first* sentence of each paragraph in the passage and the *last* sentence of the entire passage. Either of these methods works well; we suggest you experiment with both and choose the one you prefer.

What's the point of previewing? It's to give you some idea of what the passage is about and, generally, how it is organized *before* you actually read it. Think about it: When you know, in general, what a teacher will be teaching, don't you find it easier to understand and absorb the lesson? (Educational researchers have proven it's true.) The same idea applies here—if you know generally what the passage is about before reading it, you'll understand it better.

Don't spend long on previewing. On the average ACT reading passage, this stage should take about 30 seconds. Practice with a watch until you get a feel for it.

Reading

Having previewed the passage, go ahead and read it through, more or less in the conventional way. (Actually, we'll be suggesting some special reading techniques for this stage in a moment, but for now, just think of stage two as the familiar reading process you've always done.)

Reviewing

The third stage involves scanning the passage one more time, reminding yourself of its main ideas, most important details, and overall structure. Like previewing, this should be a fast process—spend no more than 30 seconds to review an average ACT passage.

Why bother with reviewing? There are three main reasons. First, by the time you finish reading a complex, subtle, or confusing ACT passage, you may find that you don't really remember how the passage began. Reviewing refreshes your memory for the structure of the entire passage, making it easier for you to "hold it in mind" as a unit.

Second, reviewing can help you to understand the earlier parts of the passage better than you did when you first read them. Quite often, a point made in the first or second paragraph isn't fully explained until the sixth or seventh paragraph. Reviewing the whole thing ties together loose ends that otherwise might have remained slightly confusing.

FYI

If previewing quickly is a problem for you, try this: Sweep your index finger in a single, steady motion down the passage, taking about 30 seconds to scan the whole thing. Let your eyes follow your traveling finger as a guide. This will force you to keep moving as you preview rather than getting stuck with reading a sentence or paragraph that catches your attention.

Third, reviewing helps you remember which topics are discussed in which parts of the passage. This will make it easier when you need a specific detail to answer a question. Rather than scanning the whole passage, you'll probably be able to zero in on the right paragraph quickly.

Here's how the timing of the three-stage method works. Let's say the reading passage is 750-words long (pretty typical for an ACT passage). The average student reads about 250 words per minute. So the three stages would take a total of four minutes:

Stage Number	Stage Name	Time
Stage 1	Previewing	½ minute
Stage 2	Reading	3 minutes
Stage 3	Reviewing	½ minute
Total Time		4 minutes

You'd spend about the same amount of time on the questions that follow the passage, making a total of 8 minutes for the passage and questions. On the exam, you'll find that this kind of timing works well and will leave you with ample time for the other passages in the test.

Focus on Big Ideas, Not Little Details

Almost everything you read—on the ACT or elsewhere—can be broken down into two kinds of information: *main ideas* and *supporting details*. It's important to distinguish between the two when reading for the exam. The main ideas are worth focusing on; the supporting details are usually not.

How can you recognize the main ideas in a passage? There are several clues to look for:

- Main ideas tend to be broad and general; supporting details tend to be narrow and specific.

- Often, each paragraph of a passage is centered on a single main idea, which is explicitly stated somewhere in the paragraph.

- The main idea often appears first or last in the paragraph; supporting details usually appear in the middle of the paragraph.

Consider the following example from a typical social studies reading passage:

> Do women tend to devalue the worth of their work? Do they apply different standards to rewarding their own work than they do to rewarding

FYI

Some students wonder whether they should learn "speed-reading" to improve their ACT performance. For most students, it's unnecessary. If you can read at an average rate of 250 words per minute, as most high school students do, you'll have plenty of time for the passages on the exam. If you're not sure of your current reading speed, test yourself with a sample ACT passage and a watch. Just count the words and divide by the number of minutes spent to determine your words-per-minute rate.

the work of others? These were the questions asked by Michigan State University psychologists Lawrence Messe and Charlene Callahan-Levy. Past experiments had shown that when women were asked to decide how much to pay themselves and other people for the same job, they paid themselves less. Following up on this finding, Messe and Callahan-Levy designed experiments to test several popular explanations of why women tend to shortchange themselves in pay situations.

The first two sentences in this paragraph state broad questions about women and their attitudes toward work. The sentences that follow delve into the nitty-gritty details about the work of two psychologists, Messe and Callahan-Levy, who tried to explore these questions experimentally. (Subsequent paragraphs of the passage describe the experiments in even more specific detail.)

Thus, the first two sentences of this paragraph state the main idea—the topic around which the entire paragraph revolves. The remaining sentences give details: the names of the psychologists, the fact that they were doing follow-up work in the wake of previous experiments dealing with the same subject, and so on. The most important point for you to gather from this paragraph is the fact that Messe and Callahan-Levy were interested in exploring women's attitudes toward work and themselves. If you understand this, you can track down specific details as needed to answer the questions.

FYI

The list of body parts in the sentence about urodeles is a classic example of the kind of specific detail ACT reading passages contain. Don't waste energy trying to remember the items on that list. In the unlikely event there's a question about them, you can find them in a flash.

Here's another example, this one from a natural sciences passage:

Urodeles, a class of vertebrates that includes newts and salamanders, have the enviable ability to regenerate arms, legs, tails, heart muscle, jaws, spinal cords, and other organs when these are damaged or lost. Similarly, planaria, a form of simple worm, can be sliced and diced in hundreds of pieces, with each piece giving rise to a completely new animal. However, while both urodeles and planaria have the capacity to regenerate, they use entirely different means of accomplishing this feat.

Which sentence states the main idea of this paragraph? It's the last sentence, which ties together the details previously stated: Both types of animals being discussed (urodeles and planaria) can regenerate organs, though they do so very differently. (Presumably, the later paragraphs of this passage will explain how.)

In this paragraph, the first sentence, dealing with urodeles, gives many specific facts that you don't need to master, including a list of some of the organs the urodele can regenerate ("arms, legs, tails," and so on). The second sentence gives similar specific facts about planaria. You can easily look up these specific facts if they're asked about. The main idea that gives them their broader significance is the concept of regeneration—the unusual ability that unites urodeles and planaria and which the passage as a whole focuses on.

In both of these paragraphs, the details are interesting; they certainly add to the experience of reading the passage, and they help make the author's point vivid and understandable. *But the details are of secondary importance.* Don't spend a lot of time struggling to understand the details of a passage if they are tricky, and certainly don't try to memorize them. Instead, read them quickly and make a mental note of where they are in case a question is asked about them. *It probably won't happen.*

Look for the Connections among the Parts of the Passage

Think of a reading passage as a *structure of ideas*. Most passages are devoted to conveying a number of ideas that are connected to one another in some way. If you understand these ideas *and* the connections among them, you truly understand the passage as a whole.

Quite often, the structure of ideas will be made very explicit, even obvious. Consider, for example, a reading passage containing five paragraphs that begin with the following five sentences:

(1) Historians have long debated the reasons for the defeat of the Confederacy in the American Civil War.

(2) For decades, the dominant theory held that the North's victory was due primarily to the superior economic resources available to the Union armies.

(3) A second school of historians pointed instead to the geographic advantages enjoyed by the Northern generals.

(4) In recent years, however, more and more historians have begun to claim that, contrary to traditional Southern belief, the Northern generalship was consistently superior.

(5) In the end, perhaps the most likely explanation of the Northern victory is that it was caused by a combination of several factors.

Simply by reading these five sentences you can get a good idea of the content and structure of the whole passage. The passage deals with the issue of why the North won the Civil War. Its structure is clear-cut. Paragraph (1) sets forth the question to be discussed. Paragraphs (2), (3), and (4) each suggest a different answer to the question. And paragraph (5) concludes the passage by suggesting a possible resolution of the disagreement.

Why is it helpful to recognize the logical structure of a reading passage? It helps you in several ways.

- It makes it easy to see the main ideas of the passage. In this case, the main ideas are the three separate theories being presented and discussed.

- It tells you the *purpose* of the supporting details—even when you don't know what those details are. In this passage, for example, we've looked at only the first sentence of paragraph (2). Nonetheless, we can easily imagine what kind of supporting details will be given in the rest of the paragraph. The missing sentences will probably give examples of the superior economic resources enjoyed by the North (coal mines, factories, or railroad lines, for instance).
  If, in reading the complete passage, the actual details turned out to be complex or tricky, that would be okay. We'd still understand their purpose and basic thrust, even if the fine points were elusive. In most cases, that would be enough to answer any questions.

- The logical structure *organizes* all the information in the passage, making it easy to locate any detail that may be asked about. In this passage, if a question focuses on some detail related to the third of the three theories (Northern generalship), you'll be able to find the relevant paragraph quickly.

- The structure explains how the main ideas are related to one another. In this case, the main ideas are three different, conflicting explanations of the same historical event. One or more questions are likely to focus on the relationships among these ideas; for example, how they differ from one another, and why the earlier theories have been superseded by later ones.

ACT passages don't always boast such clear-cut logical structures, but a structure of some kind is usually present. With practice, you can learn to recognize it.

Table 6.1 will help. It lists several of the most common types of logical structures found in ACT reading passages. Either alone or in combination, these structures underlie many of the passages you'll encounter on the exam. Practice looking for them whenever you read.

Table 6.1
Types of Logical Structures Often Used in
ACT Reading Passages

1. Several theories or approaches to a single question or topic (often one theory or approach per paragraph)
2. One theory or idea illustrated with several detailed examples or illustrations (often one example or illustration per paragraph)
3. One theory or idea supported by several arguments (often one argument per paragraph)
4. Pro-and-con arguments presented on both sides of a single issue
5. A comparison or contrast between two events, ideas, phenomena, or people
6. A cause-and-effect sequence showing how one event led to another (presented either in chronological order or via "flash-back," with later events named *before* the earlier ones)

Mark Up the Passage As You Read

FYI

As you practice, you'll find that you quickly develop your own system of signs and symbols. That's fine; no one has to understand your scratches but you, and you only need to under-stand them for the 8 to 10 minutes you'll be working on a given passage. So don't worry about neatness or comprehensibil-ity—the notes are for your benefit only.

When tackling ACT reading passages, read with your pencil in hand. Use it to mark key points and logical connections as you find them by underlining, circling, or starring them in the margin.

This will help you in two ways: the physical act of underlining particular words and phrases will strengthen your memory of the ideas you've highlighted, and the marks themselves will make it easier to find key parts of the passage if you need to locate them later.

Here are some specific suggestions about what to look for and mark as you read:

- Look for the main idea of the passage as a whole. This is one sentence that summarizes the central theme of the passage. Most passages contain such a sentence. It often appears near the beginning of the passage, to introduce the key idea; in other cases, it appears near the end, as a kind of summary or conclusion. When you find it, circle it.

- Look for the main idea of each paragraph. Remember the idea of the "topic sentence"? Your English teacher may have taught you to include one in every paragraph you write. ACT paragraphs often contain such a sentence, which summarizes the central point of the paragraph. When you find one, underline it.

- Look for the logical structure of the passage, and use numbers, symbols, or words to annotate it. For example, if a passage is organized as a pro-and-con presentation of arguments on both sides of an issue, label each argument with the word "pro" or "con" in the margin. If a passage presents a series of historical events, showing how one led to the next, circle the date of each event where it appears in the passage and number the events in sequence in the margin—1, 2, 3, and so on.

- Practice marking up reading passages each time you work on critical reading between now and the day of the test.

Truth is, the *process* of marking the passage is as important as the marks themselves. It encourages an active approach to reading as opposed to a passive one. Using this as part of the three-stage reading method will help you delve more deeply into the meaning of a passage than you ever did with conventional ways of reading.

THE INSIDER'S REPORT: THE BEST TIPS

Always Start with the Passage You Like Best

In each ACT Reading Test, you'll have four separate reading passages to work on. They're likely to be quite different in subject, style, and tone. Glance at all four when you start the test and decide which one appears most interesting or just easiest. Tackle that passage first, even if it comes later in the test section. You'll probably maximize your total score that way. (Just remember to mark your answers in the correct spaces on the answer sheet.)

Try Previewing the Question Stems along with the Passage

Remember, the question stem is the part of the question that precedes the answer choices: "The author of the passage includes the details concerning Picasso's father primarily in order to emphasize . . . " would be an example of a question stem.

By previewing the stems, some students feel they get an advance look at the main themes of the passage and the details the test-makers plan to focus on. Other students, however, find this strategy more time-consuming than useful. Our recommendation: Try this technique a couple of times and decide whether you find it helpful. If you do, use it.

When Answering ACT Reading Questions, Refer Back to the Passage as Often as is Necessary

Most questions will focus on a particular paragraph or sentence of the passage. Many of the questions will contain explicit references to specific line numbers in the passage; others will simply mention particular details and expect you to locate them.

When this happens, you'll usually need to look back at the passage to answer the question correctly. Don't try to answer from memory. Quite often the wrong answer choices will be *subtly* wrong; only a careful review of the specific detail being asked about will enable you to see which answer is correct and why the others are not.

THE INSIDER'S REPORT: THE MOST IMPORTANT WARNINGS

Don't Pick the First Answer Choice That Sounds Good

On all non-math questions, there are *degrees* of right and wrong. (By contrast, on math questions, correctness is much more black and white: if the right answer to a math problem is 16, then the answer 13 isn't "partially right" or "arguably right," it's just plain *wrong*.)

The "grayness" of non-math answer choices is especially noticeable on reading questions. The test-makers are highly skilled at crafting wrong answer choices (distractors) that are plausible and attractive. So if you begin reading the answers to a reading question and find that choice A sounds good, *don't* just select it. Read on. Choice (C) may sound even better, and choice (D) may be best of all. You always have to read all four choices to a reading item before making your choice.

Don't Pick an Answer Just Because It Sounds Familiar

One popular trick used by ACT in crafting distractors is to draw the information for wrong answers from the passage itself. This makes for distractors that are especially tempting because they sound (and are) familiar. Your reaction may be, "Oh, yes, it says that right here in paragraph 2. This must be the right answer."

Such reasoning may be flawed. The correct answer for the particular question may be found in paragraph 4, and paragraph 2 may simply be irrelevant. Don't fall for this.

The best way to avoid this trap is to refer back to the portion of the passage being asked about before you pick an answer. Make sure the answer you choose comes from *there*, not from some other part of the passage.

FYI

If you do preview the question stems, remember these two important don'ts. (1) Don't try to memorize the question stems— it's too much to keep in mind and may distract you when you're trying to read the passage. (2) Don't preview the answer choices. Remember, 75 percent of those choices are wrong! Why clutter your mind with falsehoods, distortions, and inaccuracies? Read the question stems only, and save the answer choices for later.

Don't Pick an Answer Just Because It's True

FYI

Some students have been taught that certain words or phrases mark wrong answers to reading questions. For instance, some teachers say that answer choices with words like "all," "every," "always," "none," and "never" are usually wrong. False! The ACT test-makers are specifically trained not to fall into giveaway patterns like these. There are no such simple rules you can count on— unfortunately.

Most of the passages you'll read on the ACT will be about topics you know only a little about. That's okay. The test-makers don't expect you to have any background knowledge, and none is needed to answer the questions.

Occasionally, however, you may encounter a passage on a topic you're familiar with. It may even be a topic you personally are fascinated by. This can be helpful—reading about something you like and care about is fun, and you'll probably find the passage easy to understand.

However, this situation can also be dangerous. The danger lies in bringing your own outside knowledge and opinions to the questions. You may be tempted to pick an answer choice because you happen to know it's true or because you personally agree with it. Those aren't good reasons. The correct answer must be based specifically on the information in the passage, and it must accurately reflect the opinions and ideas expressed there—even if you happen to disagree with them.

So set aside your own knowledge and beliefs when reading a passage on a topic you care about. Pick answers based solely on what you find in the passage—not on anything else you happen to know.

On Vocabulary Questions, Look for the Meaning That Fits the Word's Context in the Passage

Most ACT Reading Tests will include questions about the vocabulary used in the passages. Always answer these questions by looking back at the sentence referred to; it will generally be cited by line number. You need to pick the right answer based on how the word is used *in that sentence,* not based on your general sense of the word's meaning.

The words tested in this way won't necessarily look "hard." On some real ACTs, vocabulary questions have been based on such words as "engages," "gasps," and "marked." In one sense, these are "easy" words—most grade-school kids know and use them. But they are "tricky" in that each can have several meanings. Consider these sentences containing the "easy" word "impress," for example:

> Tony was eager to impress the college admissions officer with his intelligence and charm.

> During the early 1800s, officers of the British Navy would sometimes impress American citizens into serving as sailors on British ships.

> The king's scribe used a metal seal to impress the hot wax with the royal coat-of-arms.

In the first sentence, "impress" means something like "attract the favorable notice of." In the second sentence, it means "coerce." In the third sentence, it means "stamp." The three meanings are vaguely related (the general idea of "pressing" or "marking" is involved in all three), but they're nonetheless quite different.

The lesson is clear: Always refer back to the word's context in the passage. Only by doing so can you pick the meaning the test-makers are looking for.

JUST THE FACTS

- Use the three-stage method—previewing, reading, reviewing—to get the most out of every passage on the ACT.

- As you read, look for the main ideas in the passage and the connections among them.

- Read with pencil in hand and mark up key ideas in the passage as you find them.

- Learn the most common types of wrong answers used by the test-makers and how to avoid choosing them.

PRACTICE, PRACTICE, PRACTICE: CRITICAL READING EXERCISES

Instructions

The following exercises will give you a chance to practice the skills and strategies you've just learned for tackling ACT reading questions. As with all practice exercises, work under true testing conditions. Complete each exercise in a single sitting. Eliminate distractions (TV, music) and clear away notes and reference materials. Time yourself with a stopwatch or kitchen timer, or have someone else time you. If you run out of time before answering all the questions, stop and draw a line under the last question you finished. Then go ahead and tackle the remaining questions. When you are done, score yourself based only on the questions you finished in the allotted time.

Understanding Your Scores

0–5 correct: A poor performance. Study this chapter again, and (if you haven't already), begin spending time each day in building your vocabulary using the Insider's Word List for the ACT in Appendix A.

6–8 correct: A below-average score. Study this chapter again, focusing especially on the skills and strategies you've found newest and most challenging.

10–12 correct: An average score. You may want to study this chapter again. Also be sure you are managing your time wisely (as explained in Chapter 3) and avoiding errors due to haste or carelessness.

13–15 correct: An above-average score. Depending on your personal target score and your strength on other question types, you may or may not want to devote additional time to the Reading Test.

16–20 correct: An excellent score. You are probably ready to perform well on the ACT Reading Test.

EXERCISE 1

20 Questions

Time—18 Minutes

> **Directions:** This exercise consists of two passages, each followed by several questions. Read each passage, select the correct answer for each question, and mark the oval representing the correct answer on your answer sheet.

Passage I

Prose Fiction

Line Shipwrecks are *a propos* of nothing. If
men could only train for them and have
them occur when they had reached pink
condition, there would be less drowning
(5)   at sea.
    Of the four in the dinghy, none had
slept any time worth mentioning for two
days and two nights previous to embark-
ing in the dingy, and in the excitement of
(10) clambering about the deck of a foundering ship they had also forgotten to eat
heartily.
    For these reasons, and for others,
neither the oiler nor the correspondent
(15) was fond of rowing at this time. The
correspondent wondered how in the
name of all that was sane there could be
people who thought it amusing to row a
boat. It was not an amusement; it was a
(20) diabolical punishment, and even a genius
of mental aberrations could never
conclude that it was anything but a
horror to the muscles and a crime
against the back. He mentioned to the
(25) boat in general how the amusement of
rowing struck him, and the weary-faced
oiler smiled in full sympathy. Previously
to the foundering, by the way, the oiler
had worked double-watch in the engine
(30) room of the ship.
    "Take her easy, now, boys," said the
captain. "Don't spend yourselves. If we
have to run a surf you'll need all your
strength, because we'll sure have to
(35) swim for it. Take your time."
    Slowly the land arose from the sea.
From a black line it became a line of
black and a line of white, trees and sand.

Finally, the captain said that he could
(40) make out a house on the shore.
    "That's the house of refuge, sure,"
said the cook. "They'll see us before long
and come out after us."
    The distant lighthouse reared high.
(45) "The keeper ought to be able to make us
out now, if he's looking through a
spyglass," said the captain. "He'll notify
the lifesaving people."
    "None of those other boats could have
(50) got ashore to give word of the wreck,"
said the oiler, in a low voice. "Else the
lifeboat would be out hunting us."
    Slowly and beautifully the land
loomed out of the sea. The wind came
(55) again. It had veered from the northeast
to the southeast. Finally, a new sound
struck the ears of the men in the boat. It
was the low thunder of the surf on the
shore. All but the oarsman watched the
(60) shore grow. Under the influence of this
expansion, doubt and direful apprehension was leaving the minds of the men.
The management of the boat was still
most absorbing, but it could not prevent
(65) a quiet cheerfulness. In an hour, perhaps,
they would be ashore.
    Their backbones had become thor-
oughly used to balancing in the boat, and
they now rode this wild colt of a dinghy
(70) like circus men. The correspondent
thought that he had been drenched to
the skin, but happening to feel in the top
pocket of his coat, he found therein eight
cigars. Four of them were soaked with
(75) seawater; four were perfectly dry. After a
search, somebody produced three dry
matches, and thereupon the four waifs
rode impudently in their little boat, and
with an assurance of an impending

(80) rescue shining in their eyes, puffed at the big cigars and judged well and ill of all men. Everybody took a drink of water.

But then: "Cook," remarked the captain, "there don't seem to be any
(85) signs of life about your house of refuge."

"No," replied the cook. "Funny they don't see us!"

The surf's roar was dulled, but its tone was, nevertheless, thunderous and
(90) mighty. As the boat swam over the great rollers, the men sat listening to this roar. "We'll swamp sure," said everybody.

It is fair to say here that there was not a lifesaving station within twenty miles in
(95) either direction, but the men did not know this fact, and in consequence they made dark and opprobrious remarks concerning the eyesight of the nation's lifesavers. Four scowling men sat in the
(100) dinghy and surpassed records in the invention of epithets.

"Funny they don't see us."

The lightheartedness of a former time had completely faded. To their sharp-
(105) ened minds it was easy to conjure pictures of all kinds of incompetency and blindness and, indeed, cowardice. There was the shore of the populous land, and it was bitter and bitter to them that from
(110) it came no sign.

"Well," said the captain, ultimately. "I suppose we'll have to make a try for ourselves. If we stay out here too long, we'll none of us have strength left to
(115) swim after the boat swamps."

And so the oiler, who was at the oars, turned the boat straight for the shore. There was a sudden tightening of muscle. There was some thinking.
(120) "If we don't all get ashore—" said the captain. "If we don't all get ashore, I suppose you fellows know where to send news of my finish?" They briefly ex- changed some addresses and admoni-
(125) tions. The shore was still afar.

1. In the first sentence, the narrator wishes to suggest that shipwrecks

   (A) occur all too frequently.
   (B) strike at random.
   (C) reflect the malign nature of the sea.
   (D) usually take place at the worst of times.

2. It can be inferred from the passage that the men in the dinghy are tired because they

   (F) have been rowing the dinghy for the past two days.
   (G) are unaccustomed to physical labor.
   (H) have spent the previous two days on a sinking ship.
   (J) had to swim a long distance to reach the dinghy.

3. In comparing the dinghy to a "wild colt" (line 69), the narrator suggests that it is

   (A) bounding roughly on the waves.
   (B) too small for its four passengers.
   (C) under no human control.
   (D) rapidly filling with water.

4. The men in the dinghy experience a sense of "quiet cheerfulness" (line 65) because they

   (F) know that the storm that sank their ship is past.
   (G) see the shore getting closer and closer.
   (H) believe that the lifeboat is out searching for them.
   (J) think their dinghy will be able to land safely on shore.

5. When the narrator says "the four waifs rode impudently in their little boat" (lines 77–78), he is suggesting that the men

   (A) are enjoying what they know might be their last cigar.
   (B) are rejoicing over their good fortune at having survived the shipwreck.
   (C) believe that their skill at seamanship will save them from disaster.
   (D) feel certain they will soon be rescued.

6. It can be inferred from the passage that the other people who had been aboard the same ship as the four men in the dinghy

   (F) have already perished.
   (G) are now safely on shore.
   (H) are themselves afloat in other dinghies.
   (J) are clinging to the wreckage of the ship.

7. The passage implies that the greatest danger to the men in the dinghy arises from the fact that

   (A) their boat is too small to safely navigate the great waves breaking on the shore.
   (B) their supply of food and drinking water is rapidly being depleted.
   (C) they are unable to steer their boat in the direction of the shore.
   (D) they are too exhausted to row their boat toward the land.

8. As it is used in the passage, the word *dark* (line 97) means most nearly

   (F) obscure.
   (G) harsh.
   (H) muttered.
   (J) unintelligible.

9. The passage implies that the "thinking" being done by the men in the dinghy (line 119) primarily concerns

   (A) what they must do to reach the shore safely.
   (B) how they might signal their plight to those on shore.
   (C) the possibility that they may drown.
   (D) their bitterness over the failure of the lifesavers to rescue them.

10. The passage suggests that the anger felt by the men in the dinghy toward the lifesavers is

   (F) justified.
   (G) excessive.
   (H) ironic.
   (J) misguided.

Passage II

Natural Science

Line   In the early years of the twentieth century, astrophysicists turned their attention to a special category of stars, known as cepheid variables. A variable
(5)   star is one whose apparent brightness changes from time to time. Among some variables, the change in brightness occurs so slowly as to be almost imperceptible; among others, it occurs in
(10)   sudden, brief, violent bursts of energy.

The most impressive form of variable star is the nova, characterized by short-lived, extremely forceful explosions of energy. At its height, a nova may emit
(15)   as much energy as 200,000 suns, and novas, especially those that are relatively close to our planet, are among the most brilliant objects in the night sky. One or two are noted in our own Milky Way
(20)   galaxy each year. A nova typically goes through a number of cycles of extreme brightness followed by quiescence, repeatedly giving off huge amounts of energy and mass, until finally its mass is
(25)   too small to continue the process.

The supernova, an even more spectacular object, is not a variable star but rather an exploding star, which may briefly attain a brightness equivalent to
(30)   10 billion suns before fading away forever. The single powerful burst of a supernova may leave behind a bright gaseous cloud of matter known as a nebula; the Crab nebula, first observed
(35)   as a supernova in A.D. 1054, is a familiar example.

Among the true variable stars, the cepheid variables (which take their name from the constellation Cepheus, where the first such star was discovered) have
(40)   special characteristics that make them an especially useful astronomical tool.

It was Henrietta Leavitt, an astronomer at the Harvard Observatory, who
(45)   first examined the cepheid variables in detail. She found that these stars vary regularly in apparent brightness over a relatively short period of time—from one to three days to a month or more. This
(50)   variation in brightness could be recorded and precisely measured with the help of the camera, then still a new tool in astronomy.

Leavitt also noticed that the periodic-
(55)   ity of each cepheid variable—that is, the period of time it took for the star to vary from its brightest point to its dimmest and back to its brightest again—corresponded to the intrinsic or absolute
(60)   brightness of the star. That is, the greater the star's absolute brightness, the slower its cycle of variation.

Why is this so? The variation in brightness is caused by the interaction
(65)   between the star's gravity and the outward pressure exerted by the flow of light energy from the star. Gravity pulls the outer portions of the star inward, while light pressure pushes them out-
(70)   ward. The result is a pulsating, in-and-out movement that produces increasing and decreasing brightness. The stronger the light pressure, the slower this pulsation. Therefore, the periodicity of the cepheid
(75)   variable is a good indication of its absolute brightness.

Furthermore, it is obvious that the apparent brightness of any source of light decreases the further we are from
(80)   the light. Physicists had long known that this relationship could be described by a simple mathematical formula, known as the inverse square law. If we know the absolute brightness of any object—say, a
(85)   star—as well as our distance from that object, it is possible to use the inverse square law to determine exactly how bright that object will appear to be.

This laid the background for Leavitt's
(90)   most crucial insight. As she had discovered, the absolute brightness of a cepheid variable could be determined by measuring its periodicity. And, of course, the apparent brightness of the star when
(95)   observed from the earth could be determined by simple measurement. Leavitt saw that with these two facts and the help of inverse square law, it would be possible to determine the distance
(100)   from earth of any cepheid variable. If we know the absolute brightness of the star and how bright it appears from the earth, we can tell how far away it must be.

(105)   Thus, if a cepheid variable can be found in any galaxy, it is possible to measure the distance of that galaxy from earth. Thanks to Leavitt's discovery, astronomical distances that could not (110) previously be measured became measurable for the first time.

11. The primary purpose of the passage is to explain

   (A) the background and career of the astronomer Henrietta Leavitt.
   (B) the development of the inverse square law for determining an object's brightness.
   (C) important uses of the camera as an astronomical tool.
   (D) how a particular method of measuring astronomical distances was created.

12. According to the passage, a nova differs from a supernova in all of the following ways EXCEPT that a supernova

   (F) emits its energy in a single powerful burst.
   (G) may leave behind the gaseous cloud of a nebula.
   (H) passes through several cycles of extreme brightness.
   (J) is not a true variable star.

13. According to the passage, the cepheid variables are especially useful to astronomers because of the

   (A) regularity with which they vary in brightness.
   (B) unusually great apparent brightness they exhibit.
   (C) slowness of their average cycle of variation.
   (D) ease with which their absolute brightness may be observed.

14. The passage states that Leavitt's work enabled astronomers to measure the distance from earth of any galaxy containing a

   (F) nebula.
   (G) variable star.
   (H) nova or supernova.
   (J) cepheid variable.

15. According to the passage, the absolute brightness of a cepheid variable

   (A) depends upon its measurable distance from an observer on earth.
   (B) may be determined from the length of its cycle of variation.
   (C) changes from time to time according to a regular and predictable pattern.
   (D) indicates the strength of the gravitation force exerted by the star.

16. The passage states that cepheid variables are so named after

   (F) a variable star first observed by Leavitt.
   (G) the first star whose periodicity was studied by Leavitt.
   (H) the constellation containing the first cepheid variable known.
   (J) the first galaxy whose distance from earth was measured by Leavitt's method.

17. According to the passage, Leavitt's work provided astronomers with the means of determining which of the following?

   I.   The absolute brightness of any observable cepheid variable
   II.   The apparent brightness of any object a given distance from an observer
   III. The distance from earth of any galaxy containing an observable cepheid variable

   (A) III only
   (B) I and II only
   (C) I and III only
   (D) I, II, and III

18. It can be inferred from the passage that a cepheid variable of great absolute brightness would exhibit

   (F) a relatively rapid variation in brightness.
   (G) a correspondingly weak gravitational force.
   (H) slow and almost imperceptible changes in brightness.
   (J) a strong outward flow of light pressure.

19. It can be inferred from the passage that it is possible to observe each of the following with the naked eye EXCEPT the

   (A) explosion of a supernova.
   (B) precise brightness of a variable star.
   (C) period of greatest brightness of a nova.
   (D) existence of a nebula.

20. The passage implies that Leavitt's work on cepheid variables would not have been possible without the availability of

   (F) the camera as a scientific tool.
   (G) techniques for determining the distances between stars.
   (H) an understanding of the chemical properties of stars.
   (J) a single star whose distance from earth was already known.

EXERCISE 2

20 Questions

Time—18 Minutes

> **Directions:** This exercise consists of two passages, each followed by several questions. Read each passage, select the correct answer for each question, and mark the oval representing the correct answer on your answer sheet.

Passage I

Social Science

Line   When the Framers of the Constitution set to work devising the structure of the United States government, it was natural for them to consider the forms already
(5)   existing in the several states. The three most basic patterns may be referred to as the Virginia, Pennsylvania, and Massachusetts models.

The Virginia model borrowed its
(10)   central principal, legislative supremacy, from the thinking of the English philosopher John Locke. Locke had favored making the legislature the dominant focus of government power, and he
(15)   stressed the importance of preventing a monarch, governor, or other executive from usurping that power. In line with Locke's doctrine, Virginia's constitution provided that the governor be chosen by
(20)   the assembly rather than by the people directly, as were the members of a special governor's council. The approval of this council was necessary for any action by the governor.
(25)   Also derived from Locke was Virginia's bicameral legislature, in which both chambers must concur to pass a bill. Thus dividing the legislative power was supposed to prove its domination by any
(30)   single faction—the so-called "division of powers" that later became an important feature of the national constitution.

Pennsylvania's constitution was probably the most democratic of any in
(35)   the former colonies. Pennsylvania extended the right to vote to most adult males. (With the exception of Vermont, the other states allowed only property

owners to vote; New Jersey alone
(40)   extended the privilege to women.) Pennsylvanians elected the members of a single-house legislature, as well as an executive council. These bodies jointly selected the council president, who
(45)   served as the state's chief executive officer; there was no governor. Neither legislators nor council members could remain in office more than four years out of seven.
(50)   The most conservative of the models was found in Massachusetts. The legislature here included two chambers. In the house of representatives, the number of legislators for a given district was based
(55)   on population; in the "aristocratic" senate, representation was based on taxable wealth. The governor could veto legislature, he appointed most state officials, and he was elected indepen-
(60)   dently of the legislature.

As the delegates to the Constitutional Convention began to debate the merits of these varying models, several fault lines began to appear along which the repre-
(65)   sentatives of the former colonies were divided. One such line was geographic. The economic and social differences between the Northern and Southern states, which would lead, three genera-
(70)   tions later, to the cataclysm of the Civil War, were already making themselves felt. Dependent chiefly on the exporting of such raw materials as cotton, tobacco, and rice, the Southern states strongly
(75)   opposed giving Congress the power to regulate international trade, fearing the imposition of onerous taxes or tariffs. Too, the white slaveholders of the South feared federal restrictions on the practice

(80) of slavery, which was already a point of controversy between sections of the new nation.

Another dividing line among the states was based on population. The less *(85)* populous states opposed the notion of allocating political power based on population; they feared having the larger states, especially Virginia, New York, Massachusetts, and Pennsylvania, ride *(90)* roughshod over their interests. This division to some extent echoed the North-South split, since most of the more populous states were in the north.

The debates over governmental *(95)* structure quickly focused on the makeup of the legislative branch. The most populous states favored making representation in Congress proportional to population, while the smaller states *(100)* fought for equality of representation. For a time, it appeared as though the convention might break up over this issue.

The successful resolution was a *(105)* compromise originally proposed by the delegation from Connecticut, and therefore often referred to as the Connecticut Compromise, or the Great Compromise. According to this plan, which remains in *(110)* effect to this day, the Congress is a bicameral legislature like those in Virginia and Massachusetts. In the Senate, each state has two representatives, no matter what its size, while seats *(115)* in the House of Representatives are apportioned by population. Both houses must concur in the passage of legislature, and bills proposing the expenditure of government funds must originate in the *(120)* House—a precaution demanded by the larger states to protect their financial interests.

The Southern states won a series of specific concessions. Although the *(125)* convention refused to include slaves on an equal basis in the population count for Congressional representation—after all, the slaves were neither citizens nor taxpayers nor voters—it was agreed to *(130)* count the slave population, a notorious compromise long regarded as a racist blot on the Constitution. The North also accepted constitutional clauses forbid-

ding export taxes and preventing Con-*(135)* gress from interfering with the slave trade until at least 1808—over twenty years in the future. The sectional differences between the North and South and the simmering issue of slavery were thus *(140)* postponed for future generations to face.

1. The author's primary purpose in writing the passage is to explain

  (A) how various models of state government influenced the debate over the U.S. Constitution.
  (B) the differing roles of the legislature in each of the original American states.
  (C) the contrasting forms of government found in the various original American states.
  (D) the influence of John Locke's philosophy on the Framers of the U.S. Constitution.

2. The state governments described in the passage varied in all of the following respects EXCEPT

  (F) the existence of the office of governor.
  (G) restrictions on tenure in state offices.
  (H) whether the members of the legislature were chosen directly by the people.
  (J) restrictions on the eligibility of citizens to vote.

3. According to the passage, the principle purpose of the "division of powers" in the Virginia model was to

A. allow citizens of every social class to participate fully in government.

(B) prevent any one group from controlling the legislative power.

(C) ensure the independence of the executive from legislative manipulation.

(D) discourage the concentration of power in the hands of the governor.

4. It can be inferred from the passage that those who favored a democratic system of government would most strongly support

(F) apportioning seats in the legislature on the basis of taxable wealth.

(G) limitation on the number of terms in office served by legislators.

(H) establishment of a bicameral legislature.

(J) granting the power to veto legislation to a popularly elected executive.

5. According to the passage, the philosophy of John Locke most strongly influenced the governmental system of

(A) Massachusetts.

(B) New Jersey.

(C) Pennsylvania.

(D) Virginia.

6. According to the passage, the right to vote was limited to property owners in all of the states EXCEPT

   I.   New Jersey.

  II.   Pennsylvania.

 III.   Vermont.

(F) II only

(G) I and II only

(H) II and III only

(J) I, II, and III

7. It can be inferred from the passage that the Southern states most favored which of the following features of the new constitution?

(A) The apportionment of seats in the Senate

(B) The apportionment of seats in the House of Representatives

(C) The requirement that funding bills originate in the House of Representatives

(D) The restriction of voting privileges to white male citizens

8. As it is used in line 131, the word *notorious* most nearly means

(F) remarkable.

(G) infamous.

(H) ingenious.

(J) celebrated.

9. According to the passage, the leaders of the Southern states were concerned with defending the interests of which of the following?

   I.   Slaveholders

  II.   Exporters of raw materials

 III.   The less-populous states

(A) I only

(B) I and II only

(C) II and III only

(D) I, II, and III

10. One of the main ideas of the passage is that

(F) resentment by the South of its treatment during the Constitutional Convention was an underlying cause of the Civil War.

(G) most white Americans at the time of the Constitutional Convention rejected the new constitution's implicit racism.

(H) the Framers of the Constitution devised only temporary solutions for the rift between the Northern and Southern states.

(J) the issue of slavery nearly caused the failure of the Constitutional Convention.

Passage II

Natural Science

Line   Today, the theory of "continental drift," which supposes that the earth's great land masses have moved over time, is a basic premise accepted by most geolo-
(5)   gists. However, this was not always so. In fact, it was not until the mid-twentieth century that this concept won widespread acceptance among scientists.

Although Alfred Wegener was not the
(10)   first to propose the idea that the continents have moved, his 1912 outline of the hypothesis was the first detailed description of the concept and the first to offer a respectable mass of supporting
(15)   evidence for it. It is appropriate, then, that the theory of continental drift was most widely known as "Wegener's hypothesis" during the more than fifty years of debate that preceded its ulti-
(20)   mate acceptance by most earth scientists.

In brief, Wegener's hypothesis stated that, in the late Paleozoic era, all of the present-day continents were part of a
(25)   single giant land mass, Pangaea, that occupied almost half of the earth's surface. About 40 million years ago,

Pangaea began to break into fragments that slowly moved apart, ultimately
(30)   forming the various continents we know today.

Wegener supported his argument with data drawn from geology, paleontology, zoology, climatology, and other fields. He
(35)   pointed, for example, to the fact that continental margins in several regions of the globe appear to closely match one another, as though they had once been united. The fit between the land masses
(40)   on either side of the Atlantic Ocean—Europe and Africa on the east and North and South America on the west—was especially close. Furthermore, Wegener also showed that rock formations in
(45)   Brazil and West Africa, on opposite sides of the Atlantic, are remarkably similar in age, type, and structure. This, too, was consistent with the notion that the continents had once been joined.
(50)   So impressive was Wegener's array of evidence that his hypothesis could not be ignored. However, until the 1960s, most scientists were reluctant to accept Wegener's ideas. There are several
(55)   reasons why this was so.

First, although Wegener showed that continental movement was consistent with much of the geological and other evidence—for example, the apparent
(60)   family relationships among forms of plants and animals now separated by vast expanses of ocean, once geographically united on the hypothetical Pangaea—he failed to suggest any causal
(65)   mechanism for continental drift sufficiently powerful and plausible to be convincing.

Second, while the period during which Wegener's theory was propounded and
(70)   debated saw rapid developments in many branches of geology and an explosion of new knowledge about the nature of the earth and the forces at work in its formation, little of this
(75)   evidence seemed to support Wegener. For example, data drawn from the new science of seismology, including experimental studies of the behavior of rocks under high pressure, suggested that the
(80)   earth has far too much internal strength and rigidity to allow continents to "drift"

across its surface. Measurements of the earth's gravitational field made by some of the early scientific satellites offered (85) further evidence in support of this view as late as the early 1960s.

In fact, this data pointed to a genuine flaw in Wegener's theory. He had assumed that the continental plates floated (90) atop the ocean crust, which was relatively plastic and so would permit the continents to move across its surface. This was false. The true explanation for continental movement was not uncov-(95) ered until the discovery, through seismic studies, of the existence of asthenosphere, a layer of plastic, slowly-moving material that lies under both the continental plates and the ocean crust at (100) depths of 50 to 150 kilometers (30 to 80 miles). The malleability of the athenosphere permits movement of the layers above it.

Third, and perhaps most significant, (105) Wegener's theory seemed to challenge one of the most deeply held philosophical bases of geology—the doctrine of uniformitarianism, which states that earth history must always be explained (110) by the operation of essentially unchanging, continuous forces. Belief in the intervention of unexplained, sporadic, and massive shaping events—known as catastrophism—was considered beyond (115) the pale by mainstream geologists.

Wegener was not, strictly speaking, a catastrophist—he did not suggest that some massive cataclysm had triggered the breakup of Pangaea—but his theory (120) did imply a dramatic change in the face of the earth occurring relatively late in geologic history. Such a belief, viewed as tainted with catastrophism, was abhorrent to most geologists throughout the (125) first half of this century.

11. It can be inferred from the passage that the majority of geologists today

(A) reject the theory of continental drift.
(B) have softened in their opposition to catastrophism.
(C) question the relevance of most of Wegener's geological evidence.
(D) disagree with Wegener's idea that the continents were once united.

12. According to the passage, Wegener believed that Pangaea

(F) was destroyed in a massive cataclysm occurring about 40 million years ago.
(G) consisted of several large land areas separated by vast expanses of ocean.
(H) was ultimately submerged by rising oceans at the end of the Paleozoic era.
(J) contained in a single land mass the basic material of all the continents that exist today.

13. It can be inferred from the passage that, by the end of the Paleozoic era

(A) many forms of plant and animal life existed on earth.
(B) the land mass of Pangaea no longer existed.
(C) a series of unexplained catastrophes had changed the face of the earth.
(D) most of today's land forms had taken their current shape.

14. According to the passage, Wegener supported his hypothesis by pointing to the geological similarities between rock formations in West Africa and

   (F)   Brazil.
   (G)   North America.
   (H)   Europe.
   (J)   the floor of the Atlantic Ocean.

15. The passage provides information to answer which of the following questions?

   I.   What geological forces caused the breakup of Pangaea?
   II.   What evidence discovered in the 1960s lent support to Wegener's hypothesis?
   III. When did Wegener's hypothesis win acceptance by most earth scientists?

   (A)   I only
   (B)   III only
   (C)   I and III only
   (D)   II and III only

16. The phrase "tainted with catastrophism" (line 123) implies that most geologists in the early twentieth century considered catastrophism

   (F)   fascinating but unproven.
   (G)   somewhat questionable.
   (H)   completely incredible.
   (J)   demonstrably true.

17. The passage implies that the most significant reason for the opposition to Wegener's hypothesis on the part of many scientists was its

   (A)   indirect challenge to a fundamental premise of geology.
   (B)   impossibility of being tested by experimental means.
   (C)   conflict with data drawn from the fossil record.
   (D)   failure to provide a comprehensive framework for earth history.

18. According to the passage, Wegener was mistaken in his beliefs concerning the

   (F)   movements of the asthenosphere.
   (G)   former existence of Pangaea.
   (H)   plausibility of movement by the continental plates.
   (J)   malleability of the ocean crust.

19. As used in line 120, the word *dramatic* most nearly means

   (A)   exciting.
   (B)   violent.
   (C)   large-scale.
   (D)   rapid.

20. The author refers to the scientific information gathered by satellites in order to suggest the

   (F)   philosophical changes that ultimately led to the acceptance of Wegener's hypothesis.
   (G)   dramatic advances in earth science during the 1960s.
   (H)   differing directions taken by various earth scientists in the decades following Wegener.
   (J)   nature of the some of the evidence that appeared to refute Wegener.

EXERCISE 3

20 Questions

Time—18 Minutes

> **Directions:** This exercise consists of two passages, each followed by several questions. Read each passage, select the correct answer for each question, and mark the oval representing the correct answer on your answer sheet.

Passage I

Humanities

Line   Often considered the beginning of
        modernism in painting, the French
        impressionists of the late nineteenth
        century—Manet, Degas, Pissarro, Monet,
(5)   and others—had a far-reaching effect on
        artists around the world, as much for the
        philosophy underlying their work as for
        the new painterly esthetic they pio-
        neered. For although the impressionists
(10)   expressly disavowed any interest in
        philosophy, their new approach to art
        had significant philosophical implica-
        tions. The view of matter that the
        impressionists assumed differed pro-
(15)   foundly from the view that had previ-
        ously prevailed among artists. This view
        helped to unify the artistic works created
        in the new style.
            The ancient Greeks had conceived of
(20)   the world in concrete terms, even
        endowing abstract qualities with bodies.
        This Greek view of matter persisted, so
        far as painting was concerned, into the
        nineteenth century. The impressionists,
(25)   on the other hand, viewed light, not
        matter, as the ultimate visual reality.
            The philosopher Taine expressed the
        impressionist view of things when he
        said, "The chief 'person' in a picture is
(30)   the light in which everything is bathed."
        In impressionist painting, solid bodies
        became mere reflectors of light, and
        distinctions between one object and
        another became arbitrary conventions;
(35)   for by light all things were welded
        together. The treatment of both color
        and outline was transformed as well.
        Color, formerly considered a property

inherent in an object, was seen to be
(40)   merely the result of vibrations of light on
        the object's colorless surface. And
        outline, whose function had formerly
        been to indicate the limits of objects,
        now marked instead merely the bound-
(45)   ary between units of pattern, which often
        merged into one another.
            The impressionist world was com-
        posed not of separate objects but of
        many surfaces on which light struck and
(50)   was reflected with varying intensity to
        the eye through the atmosphere, which
        modified it. It was this process that
        produced the mosaic of colors that
        formed an impressionist canvas. "Light
(55)   becomes the sole subject of the picture,"
        writes Mauclair. "The interest of the
        object upon which it plays is secondary.
        Painting this conceived becomes a purely
        optic art."
(60)   From this profoundly revolutionary
        form of art, then, all ideas—religious,
        moral, psychological—were excluded,
        and so were all emotions except certain
        aesthetic ones. The people, places, and
(65)   things depicted in an impressionist
        picture do not tell a story or convey any
        special meaning; they are, instead,
        merely parts of a pattern of light drawn
        from nature and captured on canvas by
(70)   the artist.
            Paradoxically, the impressionists'
        avowed lack of interest in subject matter
        made the subject matter of their work
        particularly important and influential.
(75)   Prior to the impressionist revolution,
        particular themes and subjects had been
        generally deemed more suitable than
        others for treatment in art. Momentous
        historic events; crucial incidents in the

(80)   lives of saints, martyrs, or heroes; the
deeds of the Greek and Roman gods; the
images of the noble, wealthy, and
powerful—these dominated European
painting of the eighteenth and early
(85)   nineteenth centuries.

The impressionists changed all that. If
moral significance is drained from art,
then any subject will serve as well as any
other. The impressionists painted life as
(90)   they found it close to hand. The bustling
boulevards of modern Paris; revelers in
smoky cafes, theatres, and nightclubs;
working-class families picnicking by the
Seine—these are typical of the images
(95)   chosen by the impressionists. It was not
only their formal innovations that
surprised and disturbed the academic
critics of their day. The fact that they
chose to depict the "low life" of contem-
(100)   porary Paris rather than the exalted
themes preferred by their predecessors
made some wonder whether what the
impressionists created was art at all.

In this regard as in so many others,
(105)   the impressionists were true precursors
of twentieth-century painting. Taking
their cue from the impressionists,
modernists from the cubists to the pop
artists have expanded the freedom of the
(110)   creator to make art from anything and
everything. Picasso, Braque, and Juan
Gris filled their still lifes with the ma-
chine-made detritus of a modern city,
even pasting actual printed labels and
(115)   torn sheets of newsprint into their
pictures and so inventing what came to
be called collage. Six decades later, Andy
Warhol carried the theme to its logical
conclusion with his pictures of Camp-
(120)   bell's soup cans, depicted in a style as
grandiose and monumental as any king
or prophet in a neoclassical painting.
Among its other messages, Warhol's work
is proclaiming, "If art is a game of
(125)   surfaces—an experiment in color and
light—then the beauty and importance of
a tin can is equal to that of Helen of
Troy." In this, he was a true kin—if a
distant one—to Degas, Renoir, and
(130)   Pissarro.

1. The author of the passage is primarily
concerned with explaining

(A)   how new scientific ideas concerning light and color have
affected the visual arts.
(B)   the philosophical implications of
the impressionist style of
painting.
(C)   the artistic techniques that the
impressionist painters were the
first to develop.
(D)   the influence of thinkers like
Taine and Mauclair on impressionist painting.

2. The main point of the last paragraph
is that the impressionists deeply
influenced twentieth century painters
in their

(F)   choice of subject matter.
(G)   treatment of light.
(H)   use of art to tell stories.
(J)   application of collage tech-
niques.

3. According to the passage, the impressionist painters differed from the
ancient Greeks in that they

(A)   considered color to be a property inherent in objects.
(B)   regarded art primarily as a
medium for expressing moral
and aesthetic ideas.
(C)   treated the objects depicted in a
painting as isolated, rather than
united in a single pattern.
(D)   treated light, rather than matter,
as the ultimate reality.

4. According to the passage, an impressionist painting is best considered

   (F) a harmonious arrangement of solid physical masses.
   (G) a pattern of lights of varying intensities.
   (H) a mosaic of outlines representing the edges of objects.
   (J) an analysis of the properties of differing geometric forms.

5. The passage suggests that the impressionist painters regarded the distinctions among different kinds of objects to be painted as

   (A) primarily of psychological interest.
   (B) arbitrary and essentially insignificant.
   (C) reflecting social and political realities.
   (D) suggestive of abstract truths.

6. The passage suggests that an impressionist painter would be most likely to depict which of the following scenes?

   (F) A military victory by a Roman general
   (G) A can of Campbell's soup
   (H) Coffee drinkers in a Parisian restaurant
   (J) The death of a Christian martyr

7. It can be inferred from the passage that the impressionist approach to painting was

   (A) highly objective.
   (B) politically motivated.
   (C) profoundly religious.
   (D) ultimately conservative.

8. It can be inferred that the "low life" mentioned by the author in line 99 refers mainly to the

   (F) activities of the criminal underworld in nineteenth-century France.
   (G) everyday existence of middle-class and working-class Parisians.
   (H) exploits of figures from Greek and Roman mythology.
   (J) hand-to-mouth poverty in which most impressionist painters were forced to live.

9. The author refers to Helen of Troy (lines 127–128) as an example of the kind of subject matter preferred by

   (A) many pre-impressionist painters.
   (B) the impressionists.
   (C) Picasso, Braque, and Gris.
   (D) Andy Warhol.

10. It can be inferred from the passage than an impressionist painter would be most likely to agree with which of the following statements?

   (F) A picture is significant primarily as a symbol of the artist's mental state.
   (G) The highest purpose of art is to teach philosophical truths.
   (H) The quality of a picture has nothing to do with the nature of the objects it depicts.
   (J) An artist should strive to recreate on canvas the inner nature of objects from real life.

Passage II

Natural Science

Line Community cancer clusters are localized
patterns of excessive cancer occurrence.
The following passage discusses the
difficulties involved in identifying com-
(5) mon causes for community cancer
clusters.

Community cancer clusters are viewed
quite differently by citizen activists than
by epidemiologists. Environmentalists
(10) and concerned local residents, for
instance, might immediately suspect
environmental radiation as the culprit
when a high incidence of cancer cases
occurs near a nuclear facility. Epidemi-
(15) ologists, in contrast, would be more
likely to say that the incidences were
"inconclusive" or the result of pure
chance. And when a breast cancer
survivor, Lorraine Pace, mapped twenty
(20) breast cancer cases occurring in her
West Islip, Long Island, community, her
rudimentary research efforts were guided
more by hope—that a specific environmental agent could be correlated with
(25) the cancers—than by scientific method.

When epidimiologists study clusters
of cancer cases and other noncontagious
conditions such as birth defects or
miscarriage, they take several variables
(30) into account, such as background rate
(the number of people affected in the
general population), cluster size, and
specificity (any notable characteristics of
the individual affected in each case). If a
(35) cluster is both large and specific, it is
easier for epidemiologists to assign
blame. Not only must each variable be
considered on its own, but it must also
be combined with others. Lung cancer is
(40) very common in the general population.
Yet when a huge number of cases turned
up among World War II shipbuilders who
had all worked with asbestos, the size of
the cluster and the fact that the men had
(45) had similar occupational asbestos
exposures enabled epidemiologists to
assign blame to the fibrous mineral.

Furthermore, even if a cluster seems
too small to be analyzed conclusively, it
(50) may still yield important data if the
background rate of the condition is low

enough. This was the case when a
certain vaginal cancer turned up almost
simultaneously in a half-dozen young
(55) women. While six would seem to be too
small a cluster for meaningful study, the
cancer had been reported only once or
twice before in the entire medical
literature. Researchers eventually found
(60) that the mothers of all the afflicted
women had taken the drug diethylstil-
bestrol (DES) while pregnant.

Although several known carcinogens
have been discovered through these
(65) kinds of occupational or medical clusters, only one community cancer cluster
has ever been traced to an environmental cause. Health officials often discount
a community's suspicion of a common
(70) environmental cause because citizens
tend to include cases that were diagnosed before the afflicted individuals
moved into the neighborhood. Add to
this the problem of cancer's latency.
(75) Unlike an infectious disease like cholera,
which is caused by a recent exposure to
food or water contaminated with the
cholera bacterium, cancer may have its
roots in an exposure that occurred ten to
(80) twenty years earlier. Citizens also
conduct what one epidemiologist calls
"epidemiologic gerrymandering," finding
cancer cases, drawing a boundary
around them, and then mapping this as a
(85) cluster.

Do all these caveats mean that the
hard work of Lorraine Pace and other
community activists is for naught? Not
necessarily. Together with many other
(90) reports of breast cancer clusters on Long
Island, the West Islip situation highlighted by Pace has helped epidemiologists lay the groundwork for a well-
designed scientific study.

11. The "hope" mentioned in line 23 refers specifically to Pace's desire to

    (A) help reduce the incidence of breast cancer in future generations.
    (B) determine the culprit responsible for her own breast cancer case.
    (C) refute the dismissive statements of epidemiologists concerning her research efforts.
    (D) identify a particular cause for the breast cancer cases in West Islip.

12. The case of the World War II shipbuilders with lung cancer (lines 39–47) is an example of

    (F) an occupational cluster.
    (G) a medical cluster.
    (H) a radiation cluster.
    (J) an environmental cluster.

13. The case of six young women with vaginal cancer (lines 53–62) is an example of a cluster that has

    (A) a high background rate and is fairly specific.
    (B) a low background rate and is fairly specific.
    (C) a high background rate and small size.
    (D) a low background rate and is nonspecific.

14. The passage suggests that the fact that "only one community cancer cluster has ever been traced to an environmental cause" (lines 66–68) is most likely due to the

    (F) methodological difficulties in analyzing community cancer clusters.
    (G) reluctance of epidemiologists to investigate environmental factors in cancer.
    (H) lack of credibility of citizen activists in claiming to have identified cancer agents.
    (J) effectiveness of regulations restricting the use of carcinogens in residential areas.

15. As it is used in line 68, the word *discount* most nearly means

    (A) exacerbate.
    (B) doubt.
    (C) ridicule.
    (D) heed.

16. In lines 68–73 ("Health officials . . . into the neighborhood"), the author suggests that activists may mistakenly consider a particular incidence of cancer as part of a community cluster despite the fact that

    (F) the affected individual never worked with any carcinogenic material.
    (G) the cancer was actually caused by a long-ago exposure.
    (H) a high background rate suggests a purely random incidence.
    (J) the cancer actually arose in a different geographic location.

17. The reference to cancer's "latency" in line 74 refers to the tendency of cancer to

   (A) exist in a dormant or hidden form.

   (B) spread through the body at a surprisingly rapid rate.

   (C) pass through phases of apparent cure and recurrence.

   (D) be masked by other, unrelated illnesses.

18. The "epidemiological gerrymandering" that the author describes in lines 80–85 is most closely analogous to

   (F) a toddler's declaring that all the toys in one area of the school playground are now his property.

   (G) a school principal's redistributing students in two classrooms so that each classroom has the same number of gifted students.

   (H) a politician's drawing of election district boundaries so as to give one political party control of a majority of districts.

   (J) a nurse's erasing information on a patient's chart and substituting false data.

19. As it is used in line 86, the word *caveats* refers to the

   (A) incidence of "gerrymandering" by citizens concerned about cancer.

   (B) potential flaws in amateur studies of cancer clusters.

   (C) warnings by activists concerning environmental dangers in their communities.

   (D) tendencies of activists to assume environmental causes for cancer.

20. The author suggests that the work of concerned citizens who map cancer clusters

   (F) has proven the existence of several environmental causes of cancer.

   (G) frequently involves the manipulation of data in order to strengthen a case.

   (H) has sometimes paved the way for further studies by trained epidemiologists.

   (J) is normally of little or no value to the scientific community.

EXERCISE 4

20 Questions

Time—18 Minutes

> **Directions:** This exercise consists of two passages, each followed by several questions. Read each passage, select the correct answer for each question, and mark the oval representing the correct answer on your answer sheet.

Passage I

Prose Fiction

Line   Although Bertha Young was thirty she
still had moments like this when she
wanted to run instead of walk, to take
dancing steps on and off the pavement,
(5)   to bowl a hoop, to throw something up
in the air and catch it again, or to stand
still and laugh at—nothing—at nothing,
simply. What can you do if you are thirty
and, turning the corner of your own
(10)   street, you are overcome, suddenly, by a
feeling of bliss—absolute bliss!—as
though you'd suddenly swallowed a
bright piece of that late afternoon sun
and it burned in your bosom, sending
(15)   out a little shower of sparks into every
particle, into every finger and toe . . . ?

Oh, is there no way you can express it
without being "drunk and disorderly?"
How idiotic civilization is! Why be given
(20)   a body if you have to keep it shut up in a
case like a rare, rare fiddle?

"No, that about the fiddle is not quite
what I mean," she thought, running up
the steps and feeling in her bag for the
(25)   key—she'd forgotten it, as usual—and
rattling the letter-box. "It's not what I
mean, because—Thank you, Mary"—she
went into the hall. "Is Nanny back?"

"Yes, M'm."

(30)   "I'll go upstairs." And she ran upstairs
to the nursery.

Nanny sat at a low table giving Little B
her supper after her bath. The baby had
on a white flannel gown and a blue
(35)   woolen jacket, and her dark, fine hair
was brushed up into a funny little peak.
She looked up when she saw her mother
and began to jump.

"Now, my lovey, eat it up like a good
(40)   girl," said Nanny, setting her lips in a way
that Bertha knew, and that meant she
had come into the nursery at another
wrong moment.

"Has she been good, Nanny?"

(45)   "She's been a little sweet all the
afternoon," whispered Nanny. "We went
to the park and I sat down on a chair
and took her out of the carriage and a
big dog came along and put its head on
(50)   my knee and she clutched its ear, tugged
it. Oh, you should have seen her."

Bertha wanted to ask if it wasn't
rather dangerous to let her clutch at a
strange dog's ear. But she did not dare
(55)   to. She stood watching them, her hands
by her side, like the poor little girl in
front of the rich little girl with the doll.

The baby looked up at her again,
stared, and then smiled so charmingly
(60)   that Bertha couldn't help crying:

"Oh, Nanny, do let me finish giving her
supper while you put the bath things
away."

"Well, M'm, she oughtn't to be
(65)   changed hands while she's eating," said
Nanny, still whispering. "It unsettles her;
it's very likely to upset her."

How absurd it was. Why have a baby
if it has to be kept—not in a case like a
(70)   rare, rare fiddle—but in another woman's
arms?

"Oh, I must!" said she.

Very offended, Nanny handed her
over.

(75)   "Now, don't excite her after her
supper. You know you do, M'm. And I
have such a time with her after!"

Thank heaven! Nanny went out of the
room with the bath towels.

(80)   "Now I've got you to myself, my little precious," said Bertha, as the baby leaned against her.

She ate delightfully, holding up her lips for the spoon and then waving her
(85) hands. Sometimes she wouldn't let the spoon go; and sometimes, just as Bertha had filled it, she waved it away to the four winds.

When the soup was finished Bertha
(90) turned round to the fire.

"You're nice—you're very nice!" said she, kissing her warm baby. "I'm fond of you. I like you."

And, indeed, she loved Little B so
(95) much—her neck as she bent forward, her exquisite toes as they shone transparent in the firelight—that all her feeling of bliss came back again, and again she didn't know how to express it—what to
(100) do with it.

"You're wanted on the telephone," said Nanny, coming back in triumph and seizing *her* Little B.

1. It can be inferred from the passage that Nanny is afraid that Bertha will make the baby

   (A) overly excited.
   (B) unwilling to finish her supper.
   (C) physically ill.
   (D) unwilling to have a bath.

2. Bertha's feelings toward Nanny may best be described as a mixture of

   (F) resentment and despair.
   (G) timidity and jealousy.
   (H) contempt and hostility.
   (J) exasperation and affection.

3. When the narrator compares the body to "a rare, rare fiddle" (line 21), she suggests that Bertha feels

   (A) excessively frail and vulnerable.
   (B) precious yet difficult to handle.
   (C) unable to express her feelings.
   (D) giddy, confused, and anxious.

4. It can be inferred from the (lines 17–21) that Bertha believes that revealing her emotions openly will

   (F) expose her to social disapproval.
   (G) cause people to doubt her sanity.
   (H) hurt the feelings of those she loves.
   (J) make others think she is intoxicated.

5. The comparison of Bertha to "the poor little girl" (line 56) primarily suggests Bertha's

   (A) desire to spend more time with Little B.
   (B) wish that her family had more money.
   (C) emotional and psychological immaturity.
   (D) yearning for some sign of friendship from Nanny.

6. We can infer that what the narrator considers "absurd" (line 68) is

   (F) Nanny's gingerly treatment of Little B.
   (G) the class distinctions that separate Nanny and Bertha.
   (H) the powerful love for Little B that Bertha is feeling.
   (J) Nanny's haughty attitude toward Bertha.

7. The facial expression worn by Nanny in the eighth paragraph (lines 39–43) suggests that she

   (A) does not enjoy feeding Little B.
   (B) is tired of working as a nurse for another woman's child.
   (C) dislikes when Bertha visits the nursery.
   (D) wishes to hide the nature of her relationship with Little B.

8. We can infer from the word "triumph" in line 102 that Nanny

(F) is happy that Little B has finished eating her supper.

(G) feels proud of her ability to control the activities of the household.

(H) wishes she had a baby of her own.

(J) is glad to be able to take Little B out of Bertha's arms.

9. The passage suggests that the "bliss" experienced by Bertha is basically

(A) a form of maternal love.

(B) impossible to fully explain.

(C) a desire to rebel against civilization.

(D) a sign of her immaturity.

10. Given the way she is presented in the passage, Bertha can best be described as

(F) emotional and impulsive.

(G) rigidly self-controlled.

(H) vain and insecure.

(J) arrogant and demanding.

Passage II
Social Science

Line   As the climate in the Middle East changed beginning around 7000 B.C.E., conditions emerged that were conducive to a more complex and advanced form of
(5)   civilization in both Egypt and Mesopotamia. The process began when the swampy valleys of the Nile in Egypt and of the Tigris and Euphrates Rivers in Mesopotamia became drier, producing
(10)   riverine lands that were both habitable and fertile and attracting settlers armed with the newly developed techniques of agriculture. This migration was further encouraged by the gradual transforma-
(15)   tion of the once-hospitable grasslands of these regions into deserts. Human population became increasingly concen-

trated into pockets of settlement scattered along the banks of the great rivers.
(20)   These rivers profoundly shaped the way of life along their banks. In Mesopotamia, the management of water in conditions of unpredictable drought, flood, and storm became the central
(25)   economic and social challenge. Villagers began early to build simple earthworks, dikes, canals, and ditches to control the waters and reduce the opposing dangers of drought during the dry season (usu-
(30)   ally the spring) and flooding at harvest time.
       Such efforts required a degree of cooperation among large numbers of people that had not previously existed.
(35)   The individual village, containing only a dozen or so houses and families, was economically vulnerable; but when several villages, probably under the direction of a council of elders, learned
(40)   to share their human resources in the building of a coordinated network of water-control systems, the safety, stability, and prosperity of all improved. In this new cooperation, the seeds of the
(45)   great Mesopotamian civilizations were being sown.
       Technological and mathematical invention, too, were stimulated by life along the rivers. Such devices as the
(50)   noria (a primitive waterwheel) and the Archimedean screw (a device for raising water from the low riverbanks to the high ground where it was needed), two forerunners of many more varied and
(55)   complex machines, were first developed here for use in irrigation systems.
       Similarly, the earliest methods of measurement and computation and the first developments in geometry were
(60)   stimulated by the need to keep track of land holdings and boundaries in fields that were periodically inundated.
       The rivers served as high roads of the earliest commerce. Traders used boats
(65)   made of bundles of rushes to transport grains, fruits, nuts, fibers, and textiles from one village to another, transforming the rivers into the central spines of nascent commercial kingdoms. Mud from
(70)   the river banks originally served as the region's sole building material, as well as

the source of clay for pottery, sculpture, and writing tablets. With the opening of trade, other materials became available. (75) Building stones such as basalt and sandstone were imported, as was alabaster for sculpture, metals such as bronze, copper, gold, and silver, and precious and semiprecious gemstones for (80) jewelry, art, and decoration.

Eventually, Middle Eastern trade expanded surprisingly widely; we have evidence suggesting that, even before the establishment of the first Egyptian (85) dynasty, goods were being exchanged between villagers in Egypt and others as far away as Iran.

By 3500 B.C.E., Mespotomanian society was flourishing. The major (90) archeological source from which we derive our knowledge of this period is the city of Uruk, site of the modern Al Warka. Two major structures from the time are the so-called Limestone Temple, (95) an immense structure about the size of an American football field (250 x 99 feet), and the White Temple, built on a high platform some 40 feet above the plain. Associated discoveries include several (100) outstanding stone sculptures, beautifully decorated alabaster vases, clay tablets, and many cylinder seals, which were both artistic expressions and symbols of personal identification used by Meso- (105) potamian rulers. Clearly, a complex and advanced civilization was in place by the time these artifacts were created.

Historians have observed that similar developments were occurring at much (110) the same time along the great river valleys in other parts of the world—for example, along the Indus in India and the Hwang Ho in China. The history of early civilization has been shaped to a remark- (115) able degree by the relationship of humans and rivers.

11. The primary purpose of the passage is to explain

(A) how primitive technologies were first developed in the ancient Middle East.

(B) how climatic changes led to the founding of the earliest recorded cities.

(C) the influence of river life on the growth of early Mesopotamian civilization.

(D) some of the recent findings of researchers into early human history.

12. It can be inferred from the passage that, prior to 7000 B.C.E., relatively more of the Mesopotamian population could be found in

(F) grasslands away from the rivers.
(G) mountainous regions.
(H) villages along the riverbanks.
(J) deserts areas far from the rivers.

13. According to the passage, the unpredictability of water supplies in Mesopotamia had which of the following social effects?

I.   It led to warfare over water rights among rival villages.

II. It encouraged cooperation in the creation of water-management systems.

III. It drove farmers to settle in fertile grasslands far from the uncontrollable rivers.

(A) I only
(B) II only
(C) II and III only
(D) Neither I, II, nor III

14. As it is used in line 69, the word *nascent* most nearly means
    (F) powerful.
    (G) emerging.
    (H) crude.
    (J) wealthy.

15. According to the passage, the earliest trade routes in the ancient Middle East
    (A) were those between various centrally ruled commercial kingdoms.
    (B) were those that linked villages in Egypt with others in Iran.
    (C) served to link the inhabitants of small villages with the dynastic kings who ruled them.
    (D) connected villages that were scattered along the banks of the same river.

16. The author states that the trade goods imported into Mesopotamia included
    I.   alabaster.
    II. clay tablets.
    III. semiprecious stones.
    (F) I only
    (G) III only
    (H) I and III only
    (J) II and III only

17. It can be inferred from the passage that the emergence of complex civilizations in the Middle East was dependent upon the previous development of
    (A) basic techniques of agriculture.
    (B) symbolic systems for writing and mathematical computation.
    (C) a system of centralized government.
    (D) a method of storing and transferring wealth.

18. The main purpose of the last two paragraphs (lines 88–116) is to describe the
    (F) recent work of archeologists in studying Mesopotamian society.
    (G) political and social structures that evolved in Mesopotamia.
    (H) artistic styles favored by Mesopotamian craftspeople.
    (J) archeological evidence of high Mesopotamian culture.

19. The passage implies that the size of the Limestone Temple suggests which of the following characteristics of Mesopotamian society?
    (A) Its access to building materials imported from distant regions
    (B) Its fascination with the use of mathematical models in architecture
    (C) Its focus on the priesthood as the source of political and economic power
    (D) Its ability to marshal significant material and human resources for a building project

20. The author refers to emerging civilizations in India and China primarily in order to emphasize the
    (F) importance of water transportation in the growth of early trade.
    (G) relatively advanced position enjoyed by the Middle East in comparison to other regions.
    (H) rapidity with which social systems developed in the Middle East spread to other places.
    (J) crucial role played by rivers in the development of human cultures around the world.

EXERCISE 5

20 Questions

Time—18 Minutes

> **Directions:** This exercise consists of two passages, each followed by several questions. Read each passage, select the correct answer for each question, and mark the oval representing the correct answer on your answer sheet.

Passage I

Humanities

Line It is widely believed that every word has
a correct meaning, that we learn these
meanings principally from teachers and
grammarians (except that most of the
(5) time we don't bother to, so that we
ordinarily speak "sloppy English"), and
that dictionaries and grammars are the
supreme authority in matters of meaning
and usage. Few people ask by what
(10) authority the writers of dictionaries and
grammars say what they say.

I once got into a dispute with an
Englishwoman over the pronunciation of
a word and offered to look it up in the
(15) dictionary. The Englishwoman said
firmly, "What for? I am English. I was
born and brought up in England. The
way I speak *is* English." Such self-
assurance about one's own language is
(20) not uncommon among the English. In the
United States, however, anyone who is
willing to quarrel with the dictionary is
regarded as either eccentric or mad.

Let us see how dictionaries are made
(25) and how the editors arrive at definitions.
What follows applies, incidentally, only to
those dictionary offices where firsthand,
original research goes on—not those in
which editors simply copy existing
(30) dictionaries. The task of writing a
dictionary begins with reading vast
amounts of the literature of the period or
subject that the dictionary is to cover. As
the editors read, they copy on cards
(35) every interesting or rare word, every
unusual or peculiar occurrence of a
common word, a large number of
common words in their ordinary uses,

and also the sentences in which each of
(40) these words appears, thus:
> pail—The dairy *pails* bring home
> increase of milk
> Keats, *Endymion,* I, 44–45

That is to say, the context of each
(45) word is collected, along with the word
itself. For a really big job of dictionary
writing, such as the *Oxford English
Dictionary* (usually bound in about
twenty-five volumes), millions of such
(50) cards are collected, and the task of
editing occupies decades. As the cards
are collected, they are alphabetized and
sorted. When the sorting is completed,
there will be for each word anywhere
(55) from two to three to several hundred
illustrative quotations, each on its card.

To define a word, then, the dictionary
editor places before him the stack of
cards illustrating that word; each of the
(60) cards represents an actual use of the word
by a writer of some literary or historical
importance. He reads the cards carefully,
discards some, rereads the rest, and divides up the stack according to what he
(65) thinks are the several senses of the word.
Finally, he writes his definitions, following
the hard-and-fast rule that each definition
must be based on what the quotations in
front of him reveal about the meaning of
(70) the word. The editor cannot be influenced
by what *he* thinks a given word *ought* to
mean. He must work according to the
cards or not at all.

The writing of a dictionary, therefore,
(75) is not a task of setting up authoritative
statements about the "true meanings" of
words, but a task of *recording,* to the
best of one's ability, what various words
have meant to authors in the distant or

(80) immediate past. *The writer of a dictionary is a historian, not a lawgiver.* If, for example, we had been writing a dictionary in 1890, or even as late as 1919, we could have said that the word "broad-
(85) cast" means "to scatter" (seed and so on), but we could not have decreed that from 1921 on, the commonest meaning of the word should become "to disseminate audible messages, etc., by radio trans-
(90) mission."

To regard the dictionary as an "authority," therefore, is to credit the dictionary writer with gifts of prophecy which neither he nor anyone else
(95) possesses. In choosing our words when we speak or write, we can be *guided* by the historical record afforded us by the dictionary, but we cannot be *bound* by it, because new situations, new experiences,
(100) new inventions, new feelings, are always compelling us to give new uses to old words. Looking under a "hood," we should ordinarily have found, five hundred years ago, a monk; today, we
(105) find a motorcar engine.

The way in which the dictionary writer arrives at his definitions merely systematizes the way in which we all learn the meanings of words, beginning
(110) at infancy, and continuing for the rest of our lives. Let us say that we have never heard the word "oboe" before, and we overhear a conversation in which the following sentences occur:
(115) He used to be the best *oboe* player in town . . . Whenever they came to that *oboe* part in the third movement, he used to get very excited . . . I saw him one day at the music shop, buying a new
(120) reed for his *oboe* . . . He never liked to play the clarinet after he started playing the *oboe* . . . He said it wasn't much fun, because it was too easy.

Although the word may be unfamiliar,
(125) its meaning becomes clear to us as we listen. After hearing the first sentence, we know that an "oboe" is "played," so that it must be either a game or a musical instrument. With the second sentence the possi-
(130) bilities as to what an "oboe" may be are narrowed down until we get a fairly clear idea of what is meant. This is how we learn by verbal context.

1. The author describes the attitude of the Englishwoman (lines 12–18) primarily in order to illustrate the fact that the

(A) English tend to view the language habits of Americans with disdain.

(B) pronunciation of words is not of great importance.

(C) dictionary is not an authority on how language should be used.

(D) English are more careful in their use of language than are Americans.

2. It can be inferred that the author regards the attitude of the typical American toward the dictionary as resulting from

(F) a misunderstanding of the role of the dictionary writer.

(G) an unwarranted self-assurance on the part of most people who speak English.

(H) an excessive sense of respect for those in positions of authority.

(J) a mistaken belief that the meanings of words never change.

3. The author uses the word "context" in line 44 to refer to the

(A) primary meaning of a word.
(B) sentence in which a word appears.
(C) significance of the author who uses a word.
(D) way in which the definition of a word changes through time.

4. The *Oxford English Dictionary* is mentioned in the passage as an example of a dictionary that

(F) is largely copied from the work of previous dictionaries.

(G) attempts to describe how words should be used as well as how they have been used.

(H) reflects the language of England rather than that of the United States.

(J) is based on very extensive firsthand research.

5. As it is used in line 80, the word *immediate* most nearly means

(A) instantaneous.
(B) recent.
(C) ancient.
(D) rapid.

6. As it is used in line 36, the word *peculiar* most nearly means

(F) incorrect.
(G) unintelligible.
(H) specific.
(J) distinctive.

7. The author's explanation in the sixth paragraph (lines 74–90) concerning the meaning of the word "broadcast" illustrates how language may change as a result of

(A) the careless misuse of words.
(B) changes in technology.
(C) the appearance of a new dictionary.
(D) new interpretations of linguistic history.

8. The main idea of the seventh paragraph (lines 91–105) is that

(F) no one can foresee how language will change in the future.

(G) the dictionary is a largely useless tool for most writers.

(H) careful writers are guided by the historical meanings of the words they choose.

(J) most dictionaries are outdated as soon as they are published.

9. The author uses the example of the word "oboe" to illustrate how word meanings are learned

(A) in infancy.
(B) by those who edit dictionaries.
(C) from hearing them used in conversation.
(D) from dictionary definitions.

10. It can be inferred from the passage that the author would most strongly agree with which of the following statements?

(F) Every word has a correct meaning.

(G) The writer of a dictionary is basically a historian.

(H) Anyone willing to quarrel with the dictionary is eccentric or mad.

(J) Grammars are the supreme authority in matters of usage.

Passage II

Natural Science

(The article from which this passage is excerpted was written in 1986.)

Line   Around the turn of the century, two
major innovations in the field of forensic
science were added to the repertoire of
scientific crime-fighting tools. One was
(5)   fingerprinting; the other was blood-
typing. Only in the last ten years,
however, have scientists begun to believe
that genetic markers in blood and other
body fluids may someday prove as useful
(10)   in crime detection as fingerprints.

The standard ABO blood typing
originated in the work of Austrian
pathologist Karl Landsteiner. He found in
1901 that four basic blood types existed
(15)   and that these were transmitted from
generation to generation according to the
recently rediscovered laws of inheritance
developed by Gregor Mendel in the
previous century.

(20)   The four blood types classified by
Landsteiner are known as A, B, AB, and
O. Their names derive from the presence
or absence of two substances, designated A and B, found on the surface of
(25)   some blood cells. Persons with blood
type A have red blood cells with substance A on their surface. Their blood
also contains an antibody that reacts
defensively against blood cells with
(30)   substance B on their surface. Conversely,
persons with blood type B have substance B on the surface of their red
blood cells, as well as an antibody
against substance A.

(35)   When a person of either of these
blood types is transfused with blood of
the opposite type, the antibodies swing
into action, destroying the transfused
cells. (Indeed, it was the failure of many
(40)   blood transfusions that had first led
physicians to suspect the existence of
mutually incompatible blood groups.)

Blood type AB contains both substances and neither antibody; it can
(45)   harmlessly receive a transfusion of any
blood type. Hence its designation as the
"universal recipient." Blood type O
contains neither substance and both
antibodies; it reacts negatively to blood

(50)   types A, B, and AB, and can receive only
type O blood. However, type O blood
may be safely transfused into any
recipient, since it lacks any substance
that could cause a negative reaction;
(55)   therefore, type O is the "universal
donor."

In addition to their obvious importance in medical treatment, the four
basic blood types of the ABO system
(60)   have long been used by police as a form
of negative identification. Testing traces
of blood found in or around a crime
scene could help rule out suspects who
were members of a different blood group.
(65)   Added sophistication came with the
discovery of additional subgroups of
genetic markers in blood (such as Rh
factor, by which an individual's blood
type is generally designated as either
(70)   positive [+] or negative [-], depending
on whether or not the factor is present)
and with the discovery that genetic
markers are present not only in blood
but in other body fluids, such as perspi-
(75)   ration and saliva.

These discoveries were still of limited
use in crime detection, however, because
of the circumstances in which police and
scientists must work. Rather than a
(80)   plentiful sample of blood freshly drawn
from a patient, the crime laboratory is
likely to receive only a tiny fleck of dried
blood of unknown age from an unknown
"donor" on a shirt or a scrap of rag that
(85)   has spent hours or days exposed to air,
high temperature, and other contaminants.

British scientists found a method for
identifying genetic markers more pre-
(90)   cisely in small samples. In this process,
called electrophoresis, a sample is placed
on a tray containing a gel through which
an electrical current is then passed. A
trained analyst reads the resulting
(95)   patterns in the gel to determine the
presence of various chemical markers.

Electrophoresis made it possible to
identify several thousand subgroups of
blood types rather than the twelve
(100)   known before. However, the equipment
and special training required were
expensive. In addition, the process could
lead to the destruction of evidence. For

example, repeated tests of a blood-
(105) flecked shirt—one for each marker—led
to increasing deterioration of the evidence and the cost of a week or more of
laboratory time.

It remained for another British
(110) researcher, Brian Wrexall, to demonstrate
that simultaneous analyses, using
inexpensive equipment, could test for ten
different genetic markers within a
24-hour period. This development made
(115) the study of blood and fluid samples a
truly valuable tool for crime detection.

11. The author of the passage is mainly
concerned with describing

(A) how advances in crime detection
methods have led to new
discoveries in science.

(B) various ways in which crime
detection laboratories assist the
police.

(C) the development of new scientific tools for use in crime
detection.

(D) areas of current research in the
science of crime detection.

12. According to the passage, a person of
blood type AB could safely donate
blood to a person of which blood
type?

I.   Type A
II. Type B
III. Type AB
IV. Type O

(F) III only
(G) I or III only
(H) II or III only
(J) III or IV only

13. According to the passage, a person of
blood type B- would have blood cells
containing which of the following?

I.   Substance A
II. Substance B
III. Antibodies against substance A
IV. Rh factor

(A) I only
(B) II only
(C) II and III only
(D) II and IV only

14. The passage implies that the practice
of transfusing blood from one patient
to another began

(F) prior to the twentieth century.
(G) after the work of Landsteiner.
(H) when electrophoresis became
widely available.
(J) around the middle of the
twentieth century.

15. It can be inferred from the passage
that blood typing is useful to forensic
scientists only in cases where

(A) the crime victim's blood is
readily accessible.

(B) the blood type of every potential
suspect is previously known.

(C) blood from the perpetrator is
found at the crime scene.

(D) a fresh sample of blood from the
suspect is available.

16. At the time this passage was written,
blood-typing as a crime-detection
tool, by comparison with fingerprinting, was

(F) less costly.
(G) more precise.
(H) less effective.
(J) more widely used.

17. It can be inferred from the passage that electrophoresis resembles fingerprinting in that both

   (A) provide a form of negative identification in crime detection.
   (B) may be used to help identify those who were present at the time of a crime.
   (C) were developed by scientists at around the same time.
   (D) must be employed almost immediately after a crime to be effective.

18. The passage implies that electrophoresis may help scientists determine

   (F) whether or not a sample of blood could have come from a particular person.
   (G) the age and condition of a dried specimen of blood or other body fluid.
   (H) the means by which the victim of a violent crime was probably attacked.
   (J) the age, gender, and ethnic background of an unknown criminal suspect.

19. According to the passage, Wrexall's refinement of electrophoresis led to

   (A) more accurate test results.
   (B) easier availability of fluid samples.
   (C) wider applicability of the tests.
   (D) more rapid testing.

20. According to the passage, all of the following may reduce the usefulness of a fluid sample for crime detection EXCEPT

   (F) the passage of time.
   (G) discoloration or staining.
   (H) exposure to heat.
   (J) exposure to contaminants.

Answer Key

Exercise 1	Exercise 2	Exercise 3	Exercise 4	Exercise 5
1. B	1. A	1. B	1. A	1. C
2. H	2. H	2. F	2. G	2. F
3. A	3. B	3. D	3. C	3. B
4. G	4. G	4. G	4. F	4. J
5. D	5. D	5. B	5. A	5. B
6. F	6. H	6. H	6. F	6. J
7. A	7. A	7. A	7. C	7. B
8. G	8. G	8. G	8. J	8. F
9. C	9. D	9. A	9. B	9. C
10. J	10. H	10. H	10. F	10. G
11. D	11. B	11. D	11. C	11. C
12. H	12. J	12. F	12. F	12. F
13. A	13. A	13. B	13. B	13. C
14. J	14. F	14. F	14. G	14. F
15. B	15. B	15. B	15. D	15. C
16. H	16. H	16. J	16. H	16. H
17. C	17. A	17. A	17. A	17. B
18. J	18. J	18. H	18. J	18. F
19. B	19. C	19. B	19. D	19. D
20. A	20. J	20. H	20. J	20. B

Answer Explanations

EXERCISE 1

1. **The correct answer is (B).** You need to read the entire paragraph to fully understand the first sentence. The point is that shipwrecks don't usually take place at convenient times; those on board ship can't prepare and train for them. Instead, they occur at random times—"*a propos* of nothing," as the first sentence says.

2. **The correct answer is (H).** The second paragraph and the last sentence of the third paragraph combine to answer this question. They make it clear that the weariness of the men in the dinghy is a result of the fact that they have spent the last two days "clambering about the deck of a foundering [that is, sinking] ship."

3. **The correct answer is (A).** Look at the rest of the sentence containing this phrase. It says that the men had become "used to balancing in the boat," and it compares them to "circus men." The idea is that the boat is bucking and bouncing on the waves like a bronco in a circus.

4. **The correct answer is (G).** The (temporary) good mood of the men is attributed, in the same paragraph, to "the influence of this expansion"—namely, the growing visibility of the shore as their little boat gets closer and closer to it.

5. **The correct answer is (D).** The description of the men smoking their cigars includes the explanatory phrase, "with an assurance of an impending rescue shining in their eyes."

6. **The correct answer is (F).** See the eighth paragraph, where the oiler says, "None of those other boats could have got ashore to give word of the wreck." It appears from this sentence that several boats were lowered from the sinking ship, of which the dinghy is one, and that none of the others reached safety.

7. **The correct answer is (A).** The growing fear of the men is attributed to their belief that "We'll swamp sure" in the mighty surf whose noise they hear. In other words, the waves breaking on the shore are so large and powerful that it will be impossible for them to land their boat safely. The men *are* exhausted, as choice (D) asserts, but the problem is not that they cannot row toward shore—they can; the problem is that they can't land safely once they get there.

8. **The correct answer is (G).** The word "dark" is used in the phrase "dark and opprobrious remarks," describing the angry comments made by the men in the dinghy toward the lifesavers, who they think are ignoring them. The context makes it clear that the remarks are harshly negative ones—"dark" in that sense only.

9. **The correct answer is (C).** Immediately after the sentence, "There was some thinking," the men in the dinghy exchange addresses so that they can notify one another's next of kin in the event that some of them drown. Obviously, the "thinking" they are doing is about the possibility that they may not survive.

10. **The correct answer is (J).** The fourteenth paragraph states "that there was not a lifesaving station within twenty miles in either direction." Thus, it would have been impossible for any lifesavers to see and rescue the shipwreck victims, and the lifesavers are not to blame for the men's plight.

11. **The correct answer is (D).** The last paragraph of the passage neatly summarizes the significance of Leavitt's work with cepheid variables.

12. **The correct answer is (H).** It is the nova, not the supernova, that "passes through several cycles of extreme brightness." As the third paragraph makes clear, all of the other answer choices accurately describe the supernova.

13. **The correct answer is (A).** Because the cepheid variables change in brightness according to a regular pattern, it is possible to determine their absolute brightness—and, from this, their distance. Thus, it is the regularity of their variation that makes them useful to astronomers.

14. **The correct answer is (J).** See the first sentence of the last paragraph.

15. **The correct answer is (B).** The sixth paragraph describes the important relationship Leavitt discovered: that the cepheid variable's periodicity (its cycle of variation) and its absolute brightness vary together. Thus, each one can be determined from the other.

16. **The correct answer is (H).** The fourth paragraph explains that the cepheid variables are named after the constellation Cepheus, where the first cepheid variable was found.

17. **The correct answer is (C).** As the last sentence of paragraph six makes clear, statement I is true; from its periodicity (which is easily observable), we can determine the absolute brightness of a cepheid variable. Statement III is supported by the last paragraph of the passage. Statement II is false because the passage doesn't suggest that Leavitt developed the method by which astronomers measured stars' apparent brightness; in fact, in paragraphs five and nine, Leavitt appears to take this method for granted and build upon it.

18. **The correct answer is (J).** Paragraph six explains that a star with a great absolute brightness is also a star with relatively stronger light pressure; hence, the slower in-and-out pulsation and the longer periodicity that Leavitt observed.

19. **The correct answer is (B).** We're told in the passage about how brilliant and noticeable both novas and supernovas are; and the existence of the Crab nebula since shortly after 1054 A.D. makes it obvious that it, too, must have been visible without the aid of a telescope. However, the "precise brightness of a variable star" could only be measured with the help of the camera, according to paragraph five.

20. **The correct answer is (A).** See the last sentence of the fifth paragraph. It seems clear that the camera was a necessary tool for Leavitt's work to be possible.

EXERCISE 2

1. **The correct answer is (A).** The first six paragraphs describe the various models of state government available to the Framers of the Constitution; the last five paragraphs discuss the debates among the Framers over how to adapt these models to the needs of the new nation.

2. **The correct answer is (H).** All of the variations mentioned in the other answer choices are noted somewhere in the passage; however, none of the state governments discussed is said to involve a legislature that is not popularly elected.

3. **The correct answer is (B).** The second sentence of the third paragraph makes this point.

4. **The correct answer is (G).** The fourth and fifth paragraphs describe the government of Pennsylvania, which is said to be the "most democratic" among the former colonies. Of the answer choices, only choice (G) describes a feature of this state's government.

5. **The correct answer is (D).** See the first sentence of the second paragraph.

6. **The correct answer is (H).** The fourth paragraph explains that only Pennsylvania and Vermont did not restrict voting to property owners.

7. **The correct answer is (A).** Among other demands, the Southern states, which were mostly small, wanted to protect their interests by having equal representation for states of all sizes rather than making representation proportional to population. Thus, the equal numbers of legislators in the Senate would have appealed to the Southerners at the convention. The passage does not suggest that *any* of the states favored extension of voting privileges to non-white males, so choice (D) is wrong.

8. **The correct answer is (G).** *Notorious* and *infamous* are near-synonyms; both mean "well-known and much-hated or widely despised."

9. **The correct answer is (D).** The seventh paragraph states that the white leaders of the Southern states wanted to protect their interests as exporters and as slaveholders; the last sentence of the eighth paragraph makes the point that the Southern states were, for the most part, less populous than the Northern states.

10. **The correct answer is (H).** The last half of the passage develops this theme, especially in the seventh and eleventh paragraphs. It's clear that the compromises related to slavery were only temporary "band-aids" rather than permanent solutions to the problem.

11. **The correct answer is (B).** Since most geologists today accept Wegener's hypothesis—despite its flirtation with catastrophism—it's clear that the abhorrence of catastrophism must have diminished in recent decades.

12. **The correct answer is (J).** See the first sentence of the third paragraph, which summarizes this point neatly.

13. **The correct answer is (A).** In the sixth paragraph, the passage explains that Wegener used the existence of similar plants and animals on widely separated continents as evidence that all the Earth's land masses were formerly connected in the supercontinent of Pangaea. For this evidence to be valid, it would have to mean that many plants and animals existed prior to the breakup of Pangaea, which paragraph three tells us began late in the Paleozoic era.

14. **The correct answer is (F).** The next-to-last sentence of the sixth paragraph states that rock formations in Brazil are quite similar to those in West Africa.

15. **The correct answer is (B).** The first paragraph tells us that Wegener's hypothesis was accepted some fifty years after it was first proposed in 1912; thus, in the early 1960s. This answers question III. Question I is not answered; the passage only says (end of paragraph 6) that Wegener himself had no answer for this question. Question II is not answered; in fact, paragraph 7 refers to evidence from the 1960s that seemed to undermine, rather than support, Wegener's hypothesis.

16. **The correct answer is (H).** The word "taint" implies that most scientists were so opposed to catastrophism that any theory with even a passing resemblance to catastrophism was considered unacceptable.

17. **The correct answer is (A).** See the first sentence of the ninth paragraph. The "perhaps most significant" reason for many scientists' discomfort with Wegener's hypothesis was that it seemed to challenge their deep-seated belief in uniformitarianism.

18. **The correct answer is (J).** The eighth paragraph explains Wegener's error. He believed that the ocean crust was "relatively plastic" (that is, flexible or malleable) and that this explained how the continents could drift on its surface. In fact, the ocean crust is quite rigid, as the satellite studies mentioned in paragraph seven found. The existence of the asthenosphere, which Wegener did not know about, was the correct alternative explanation.

19. **The correct answer is (C).** As used in this passage, the word *dramatic* refers to changes on a vast scale—changes in the very shape and appearance of the earth's continents, in fact.

20. **The correct answer is (J).** You'll find this stated in the last sentence of the seventh paragraph.

EXERCISE 3

1. **The correct answer is (B).** The first sentence of the passage announces this topic, and the whole passage sticks closely to it.

2. **The correct answer is (F).** The last three paragraphs of the passage discuss the influence of the impressionists on the choices of subject matter made by later artists; and we are told at the start of the last paragraph, "In this regard as in so many others, the impressionists were true precursors of twentieth-century painting."

3. **The correct answer is (D).** The second paragraph of the passage expresses this idea: see the third sentence in particular ("The Impressionists, on the other hand, viewed light, not matter, as the ultimate visual reality").

4. **The correct answer is (G).** The third and fourth paragraphs make this point clear, especially the first sentence of the fourth paragraph, which refers to "light . . . reflected with varying intensity to the eye."

5. **The correct answer is (B).** The first sentence of the third paragraph states this point explicitly.

6. **The correct answer is (H).** This scene is most similar to the typical impressionist scenes listed in the seventh paragraph. Choices (F) and (J) sound like typical subjects of the pre-impressionists (see paragraph six), and the Campbell's soup can, of course, is associated with Andy Warhol, six decades after the impressionists (paragraph eight).

7. **The correct answer is (A).** This summarizes the fifth paragraph, which explains how the impressionists excluded all ideas and most emotions from their art. If virtually all human feelings and thoughts are eliminated, the result is an extreme objectivity.

8. **The correct answer is (G).** This answer seems to best fit the list of typical impressionist subjects given in the fourth sentence of paragraph six.

9. **The correct answer is (A).** Helen of Troy, a heroine of Greek legend, would epitomize the kind of subject European painters in the eighteenth and early nineteenth centuries might have favored (according to paragraph six).

10. **The correct answer is (H).** The fifth paragraph is the key. It tells us that the impressionists were not interested in the "meaning" of the things they painted—only in the pattern of light they created. Hence, the nature of the objects depicted is irrelevant.

11. **The correct answer is (D).** Refer back to the sentence in which the word "hope" appears. It says that Pace wanted to "correlate" something in the environment with the incidence of cancer, which is the same idea paraphrased in choice (D).

12. **The correct answer is (F).** Since the workers were all exposed to asbestos on the job, it seems clear that their cancers were an example of an occupational cluster.

13. **The correct answer is (B).** The story told in the third paragraph involves a "low background rate" because the number of people in the general population who suffer from this kind of cancer is very small; it is a "fairly specific" cluster (according to the definition given in the second paragraph) because of the notable characteristic shared by all the victims—all had taken DES while pregnant.

14. **The correct answer is (F).** Paragraph four, from which this observation is taken, is devoted to describing the difficulties experts have in gathering and interpreting information about cancer clusters with suspected environmental causes.

15. **The correct answer is (B).** We're told that health officials "discount" local suspicions because of the imprecision with which community members gather data. In other words, the officials are dubious about these suspicions.

16. **The correct answer is (J).** As the sentence says, "citizens tend to include cases that were diagnosed before the afflicted individuals moved into the neighborhood."

17. **The correct answer is (A).** Read the sentence *after* the one in which the word "latency" is used; it explains exactly what is meant by this concept.

18. **The correct answer is (H).** The "gerrymandering" described in the passage involves community activists drawing boundaries to fit their preconceived ideas or wishes, just as a politician does when he draws an election district boundary to produce a particular electoral result.

19. **The correct answer is (B).** The sentence in which the word "caveats" appears refers back to the previous paragraph, which describes the doubts the experts have about the work amateurs do in studying cancer clusters.

20. **The correct answer is (H).** This restates the idea found in the very last sentence of the passage.

EXERCISE 4

1. **The correct answer is (A).** The fourteenth and eighteenth paragraphs make this point: "It unsettles her; it's very likely to upset her" and "Now, don't excite her after her supper."

2. **The correct answer is (G).** Paragraph 12 provides good evidence for both points. Bertha "does not dare to" criticize Nanny's handling of the baby, even indirectly; and we're told that she feels "like the poor little girl in front of the rich little girl with the doll" when she sees Nanny with Little B. Later, she expresses unhappiness over the fact that her baby is "in another woman's arms." Clearly, Bertha is both a little jealous of Nanny and a little intimidated by her.

3. **The correct answer is (C).** Reread the third paragraph, which contains the metaphor being asked about. Bertha is frustrated over keeping her body "shut up in a case like a rare, rare fiddle" because she is eager to find some way of expressing the feeling of "bliss" she is experiencing.

4. **The correct answer is (F).** The key sentence is "How idiotic civilization is!" which makes it clear that Bertha restrains her emotions out of concern about the judgment "civilization" (i.e., society) would pass upon her if she expressed them openly.

5. **The correct answer is (A).** Bertha is clearly well-to-do (since she employs a nanny and, apparently, another servant—Mary, from paragraph four). Thus, the literal answer, choice (B), cannot be correct. The rest of the scene between Bertha, Nanny, and Little B makes it clear that Bertha longs for a closer connection to her own child, and that she and Nanny are subtly competing to "own" the baby.

6. **The correct answer is (F).** The exclamation "How absurd it was" is made in response to Nanny's expression of concern that Little B will be "unsettled" or "upset" by Bertha.

7. **The correct answer is (C).** The sentence states that Nanny's pursed lips indicate that Bertha "had come into the nursery at another wrong moment." (Note the word "another," which suggests that she is forever "intruding" into the nursery.) Clearly Bertha is somehow unwelcome in her own child's room.

8. **The correct answer is (J).** Nanny is "triumphant" in the final sentence because she is able to send Bertha away (to answer the telephone) and can reclaim "*her* Little B." As we've already seen, much of the passage deals with the subtle competition between these two women for the attention and love of the baby.

9. **The correct answer is (B).** The first two paragraphs of the passage describe this emotion rather fully. Both make it clear that the "bliss" Bertha feels is caused by no specific event but rather is something that happens "suddenly," "turning the corner of your own street"—with no apparent explanation.

10. **The correct answer is (F).** The passage describes Bertha as overwhelmed by her own feelings, struggling to control her expression of her emotions, unable to refrain from "crying" out her wishes (though somewhat afraid to do so). The words "emotional and impulsive" seem appropriate to summarize Bertha's personality—at least, on the day when this passage takes place.

11. **The correct answer is (C).** The first sentence of the second passage neatly summarizes its main theme. Note how virtually all of the ideas and details in the passage relate to the influence of the rivers on early Mesopotamian civilization.

12. **The correct answer is (F).** See the next-to-last sentence of the first paragraph, which says that people moved to the riverbanks as "the once-hospitable grasslands" turned into deserts.

13. **The correct answer is (B).** The third paragraph of the passage describes how the need for water-management systems encouraged cooperation among large groups of Mesopotamian villagers. Statement I is not supported by the passage, and Statement III is contradicted by the last sentence of the first paragraph.

14. **The correct answer is (G).** *Nascent* means "being born." It is generally used figuratively, as it is here, to mean "newly emerging" or "taking shape."

15. **The correct answer is (D).** See the first sentence of the fifth paragraph.

16. **The correct answer is (H).** See the fifth paragraph, which lists the items that the Mesopotamians imported. Clay tablets, we're told there, were *not* imported goods; rather, they were made out of "mud from the river banks," which of course was available locally.

17. **The correct answer is (A).** In the first paragraph, we're told that the development of great civilizations in the Middle East began when the river valleys attracted "settlers armed with the newly developed techniques of agriculture."

18. **The correct answer is (J).** This paragraph describes the archeological findings from the city of Uruk, from which "we derive our knowledge of this period" (i.e., the high point of Mesopotamian culture).

19. **The correct answer is (D).** The last sentence of the seventh paragraph summarizes the point: "a complex and advanced civilization was in place by the time these artifacts were created." The great size of the Limestone Temple would support this idea because it suggests that the Mesopotamians were able to bring together large amounts of money, raw materials, talent, and power in order to complete so enormous a project.

20. **The correct answer is (J).** The last paragraph, where India and China are mentioned, is used to make the point that life along river valleys has played a crucial role in the development of civilization in many parts of the world.

EXERCISE 5

1. **The correct answer is (C).** The Englishwoman described in the anecdote feels that she has no need to consult the dictionary because *she* is as much of an authority on the proper use of language as any reference book. The author seems to agree with her—hence, choice (C).

2. **The correct answer is (F).** The first paragraph explains the mistaken attitude that most Americans have toward the "authority" of the dictionary, and the rest of the passage is devoted to explaining why it is wrong by showing the reader what the true function of the dictionary writer is.

3. **The correct answer is (B).** As the example (showing how the poet Keats used the word "pail" in a sentence) illustrates, the *context* collected by the dictionary editors is simply the sentence in which the word appears.

4. **The correct answer is (J).** Notice the second sentence of the third paragraph, in which the author mentions that his purpose is to explain what firsthand dictionary research is like. He then alludes to the *Oxford English Dictionary* as an example of a project for which such research was undertaken.

5. **The correct answer is (B).** The author draws a contrast between "the distant past" and "the immediate past." Thus, he is using the word *immediate* to mean the opposite of *distant*—that is, "recent."

6. **The correct answer is (J).** According to the author, dictionary editors strive to collect "every unusual or peculiar occurrence of a common word." The context makes it clear that *peculiar* is being used here to mean "distinctive" or "special."

7. **The correct answer is (B).** As you can see by rereading the last sentence of the sixth paragraph, the new meaning of "broadcast" came about as a result of the invention and popularity of radio. Therefore, the story illustrates how new technology may create the need for a new word meaning. (The example of the word "hood" in the very next paragraph illustrates the same point.)

8. **The correct answer is (F).** As the paragraph states, "new situations, new experiences . . . are always compelling us to give new uses to old words." Therefore, a dictionary writer cannot predict how language will change and shouldn't be expected to do so.

9. **The correct answer is (C).** The author quotes several sentences from an imaginary overheard conversation that illustrate the meaning of the word "oboe." The anecdote shows how one might learn such a word by listening to a similar conversation. Although the author says that we learn words in this way "beginning at infancy," this particular example doesn't relate to infancy, since babies don't normally talk about oboes; thus, choice (A) is wrong.

10. **The correct answer is (G).** The italicized sentence in the sixth paragraph states this very point. The other three answer choices are all stated in the first two paragraphs as elements of the mistaken attitude the author attributes to most Americans.

11. **The correct answer is (C).** The passage deals with the development and use of blood-typing as a crime-fighting tool; other aspects of blood-typing, such as its role in medical treatment, are mentioned only as side issues.

12. **The correct answer is (F).** A person of blood type AB has blood cells with both substance A and substance B on their surface. This, types A, B, and O would all react badly to AB blood, since they all contain some antibodies that would be triggered by it. Only type AB can safely receive an AB blood transfusion.

13. **The correct answer is (C).** Cells of blood type B- (B negative) would contain substance B and antibodies against substance A; they would not contain Rh factor (otherwise, they would be designated B+, as stated in paragraph six).

14. **The correct answer is (F).** The parenthetical sentence in the fourth paragraph says that Landsteiner's investigation into blood types was triggered by the "failure of many blood transfusions." If this is so, then blood transfusion must have been a well-known practice prior to 1901, when Landsteiner made his major discovery.

15. **The correct answer is (C).** Since the object of the forensic scientist is to discover the perpetrator of a crime, blood-typing can only be useful when a sample of blood from the (presumed) criminal is found at the crime scene.

16. **The correct answer is (H).** The last sentence of the first paragraph makes it clear that, at the time the passage was written, fingerprinting was more useful in crime detection than blood-typing.

17. **The correct answer is (B).** Both fingerprinting and electrophoresis can be used as a means of identifying the person who produced a given sample of blood, from which their presence at a crime scene may be inferred. Choice (A) is wrong because only fingerprinting is referred to in the passage as a "negative" form of identification (see the sixth paragraph of the passage).

18. **The correct answer is (F).** The ninth paragraph of the passage suggests this idea. The fact that electrophoresis can identify thousands of blood subgroups suggests that this method is capable of narrowing down the identity of a blood "donor" quite specifically.

19. **The correct answer is (D).** The last paragraph explains that Wrexall showed how "simultaneous analyses" could produce useful results within 24 hours—in other words, "more rapid testing."

20. **The correct answer is (B).** All of the answer choices except choice (B) are explicitly mentioned somewhere in the passage.

Chapter 7

The Science Reasoning Test

Get the Scoop On . . .

- Proven strategies for conquering Science Reasoning passages more quickly and easily
- Key concepts to look for in reading each of the three types of passages
- How to keep from getting bogged down in complex calculations and arcane terminology
- The four types of questions you can expect, with techniques for tackling each

THE TEST CAPSULE

What's the Big Idea?

In the Science Reasoning Test, you'll be given seven passages containing several kinds of science information: data presented in the form of graphs, tables, charts, or diagrams; descriptions of experimental studies and their results; and presentations of differing theories or hypotheses about a particular scientific question. After reading each passage, you'll have to answer several questions that require you to understand and interpret the information presented.

How Many?

Your ACT will probably have a total of 40 Science Reasoning questions based on seven passages.

How Much Time Should They Take?

You should spend about five minutes on each passage and the questions that follow. Expect to spend about half of that time on reading and analyzing the passage itself; spend the rest of the time answering the questions.

What's the Best Strategy?

Learn the three types of Science Reasoning passages and the key elements to look for in each. In Data Representation passages, *trends* in the data are crucial. In Research Summary passages, look for *similarities and differences* among the experiments described. And in Conflicting Viewpoints passages, focus on *hidden assumptions* underlying each of the theories presented. If you can locate these key elements in each passage tape, the questions that follow will not be difficult.

What's the Worst Pitfall?

Getting bogged down in numbers, scientific jargon, and details. Each Science Reasoning passage will contain dozens or even hundreds of details. Only a handful will be asked about. Rather than trying to master (or memorize) the details as you read the passage, just look for the main ideas in the passage and note the location of the details. You can then refer back to the passage to find the few details that are needed to answer questions.

THE OFFICIAL DESCRIPTION

What They Are

Each set of items in the Science Reasoning Test on the ACT involves two steps. The first step is reading and analyzing the information presented in the passage. This information may take several forms: a straightforward prose passage; a graph, table, chart, or diagram; a narrative description of one or more experimental procedures and the results obtained; or a combination of these. The second step is answering a group of (usually) five to seven questions dealing with the information in the passage.

What They Measure

ACT reading is designed to measure your "scientific reasoning skills"—your ability to understand, analyze, dissect, interpret, compare, and evaluate various kinds of scientific information. Some of the skills tested are fairly straightforward: for example, your ability to understand what a number in a table means. Others are more complex or subtle: for example, your ability to recognize the hidden assumptions underlying a scientific theory or to determine whether a particular piece of information strengthens or weakens an unproven hypothesis. As you'll see, the thinking skills tested resemble those you've used in your high school science courses.

What They Cover

The Science Reasoning Test includes passages drawn from four broad disciplines:

- Biology, including cell biology, botany, zoology, microbiology, ecology, genetics, and evolution

- Earth/Space Sciences, including geology, meteorology, oceanography, astronomy, and environmental sciences

- Chemistry, including atomic theory, inorganic chemical reactions, chemical bonding, reaction rates, solutions, equilibriums, gas laws, electrochemistry, organic chemistry, biochemistry, and properties and states of matter

- Physics, including mechanics, energy, thermodynamics, electromagnetism, fluids, solids, and light waves

You may not have taken courses covering all of these topics. You also may not remember many details about the science topics you *have* studied in high school. That's all right. The exam is written so that anyone who has successfully completed two years of high school science should be able to answer the questions.

As you'll see, only the most basic science knowledge is assumed in the passages. Information beyond what's very basic is provided. For example, in a typical ACT passage dealing with the life cycle of bacteria (biology), the test-makers will assume that you know that the cell is the basic building block of life; they *don't* assume that you know specifically how bacteria reproduce.

Nonetheless, you'll feel more comfortable and score higher on the Science Reasoning Test if your background of science knowledge is strong. Appendix D, The Insider's ACT Science Review, covers many of the basic science skills and terms you should know. Reading it will help you determine whether you may need additional review in any particular science topic.

The Directions
The directions for the ACT Reading Test are similar to the following:

> **Directions:** This test consists of seven passages, each followed by several questions. Read each passage, select the correct answer for each question, and mark the oval representing the correct answer on your answer sheet. You may NOT use a calculator on this test.

THE INSIDER'S REPORT: STRATEGIES THAT REALLY WORK
Don't Let the Word "Science" Scare You
British scholar C. P. Snow wrote a famous essay in which he deplored the fact that the world of educated people was becoming divided into "two cultures." One involves "culture" in the traditional sense: People knowledgeable about this culture read (and write) novels, attend concerts, and visit art galleries. Another separate group of people,

according to Snow, is immersed in the new culture of science and math: They know how machines work, are familiar with the latest findings about the structure of the universe, and understand the impact of Einstein's theory on contemporary thinking. Very few people, in Snow's view, are comfortable in both worlds.

There's much truth in Snow's observation—even in American high schools. Many students pigeonhole themselves as either "science nerds" or the opposite. The nerds feel unappreciated and pretend to look down on the kids in the drama club, on the yearbook staff, and on the football team; the others feel intimidated by science and make fun of the nerds' supposed lack of social skills.

The truth is that any intelligent person is quite capable of understanding—and even appreciating—both kinds of "culture." And in today's world, both are equally important. Whether you consider yourself a nerd or an anti-nerd, you need to know how science works. This doesn't mean memorizing a lot of facts; it means understanding how scientists think. That's what the ACT Science Reasoning Test measures: *not* your recall of details from the periodic table, the names of stars, or the sequence of geological eras (which came first, Jurassic, Cretaceous, or Silurian?), but rather your ability to understand the scientific approach to a problem.

Luckily, there's nothing occult about scientific thinking. It's just a special form of common sense. Appendix D, The Insider's Science Review for the ACT, reviews several of the key ideas that make up scientific thinking. You may want to pause and read it now. Then, return to this chapter. We'll focus here on how to apply this kind of thinking to earning a high score on the ACT Science Reasoning Test.

Adapt the Three-Step Reading Method to Science Reasoning Passages

One way to think about Science Reasoning is as a special form of reading comprehension. Some of the language is different, and the information is presented not only in words but visually, in graphs, tables, and diagrams. Nonetheless, the basic challenge is the same: to read and digest a mass of information (the "passage") and answer questions about it.

Therefore, the three-step reading method we taught in chapter 6 is an important foundation for the Science Reasoning Test. (If you haven't already read that chapter, do so now.) Here's how to apply that technique to Science Reasoning.

Preview the Passage

Your first step with each of the seven Science Reasoning passages should be to spend 30 seconds glancing through all of the information provided. Just skim the page, letting your eye move down the columns of type and data, absorbing as much as you can.

In particular, try to determine the format of the passage. Three distinct formats are used in Science Reasoning: (1) Data Representation, (2) Research Summaries, and (3) Conflicting Viewpoints. They're easy to recognize.

In a *Data Representation* passage, there will usually be one or two short paragraphs of prose followed by one to five visual elements: graphs, charts, tables, diagrams, or pictures.

In a *Research Summaries* passage, one or two introductory paragraphs will be followed by two or three sections describing particular scientific research projects, usually headed *Experiment 1, Experiment 2,* and so on, or *Study 1, Study 2,* and so on. Graphs summarizing the results may also appear.

Finally, in a *Conflicting Viewpoints* passage, one or two introductory paragraphs are followed by two or three sections describing differing theories or ideas about a scientific question. They'll be given headings like *The [X] Hypothesis* or *The [Y] Theory*. Again, a graph or two might appear.

The three formats are so different from one another that, with practice, you'll be able to recognize the format of a particular passage within just a few seconds.

Because previewing is a brief process, don't try to absorb a lot of information. You're about to read the passage in more detail, which will draw you much deeper into its contents.

Read the Passage

Next, take between one and two minutes to actually read the passage. Will this be enough time? Surprisingly, yes. Here's why.

First of all, as we mentioned in chapter 6, most high school students can read about 250 words per minute. The amount of ordinary text in most Science Reasoning passages is not very great; on average, between 100 and 300 words. Thus, 1 to 2 minutes is plenty of time, especially since previewing will have given you a head start on understanding the contents of the passage.

Second, you won't literally *read* the contents of the tables, charts, graphs, and diagrams that make up the majority of many Science Reasoning passages; that is, you won't examine each word or number they contain. Instead, you'll "read" them like this:

■ **For graphs (that is, visual depictions of data such as line graphs, scatter graphs, and pie charts):** Read the labels on the

FYI

It's important to know the passage format because, as you'll see later, the kinds of information to be derived from the passage—and the kinds of questions that will be asked—are quite different for the three passage types.

vertical and horizontal axes; read other legends or explanatory notes; and identify both the units of measurement used and the scale of values (grams, degrees, light years, and so on). Notice any obvious trends or groupings in the data (more on this later). *Then move on.*

■ **For tables or charts (that is, grids containing columns of numbers or other data):** Read the names at the tops of the columns, indicating what kind of information is presented; read other legends or labels that may appear. *Skim* the (usually vertical) list of items presented, and the data itself (usually a collection of numbers). *Then move on.*

■ **For diagrams or drawings (that is, images depicting a sequence of steps or relationships):** Read the labels that name the various steps in the sequence. Note how the process begins and ends and what the direction of the sequence is. *Then move on.*

Some passages—especially Conflicting Viewpoints passages—have relatively longer prose passages; and all passages will contain at least a couple of paragraphs of written material. In a few moments, we'll suggest what you need to look for as you read this material. For now, just be aware that the amount of time you spend reading the passage must be brief—again, one to two minutes—if you are to have enough time to answer the questions that follow.

Review the Passage

After reading the passage, spend a final 30 seconds scanning the entire passage one more time. Use this review to solidify in your mind your understanding of how the pieces of the passage fit together. For example, as you review the opening paragraphs of a Research Summary passage, remind yourself of the objective with which the experiments were originally designed; in reviewing a Conflicting Viewpoints passage, refresh your memory of the scientific phenomenon that the differing theories presented are intended to explain.

Reviewing will also help you to recall where within the passage various details can be found, in the event they're asked about in the questions.

Here's how the timing of the three steps in reading the passage ought to work:

Previewing	30 seconds
Reading	1–2 minutes
Reviewing	30 seconds
Total	2–3 minutes

FOCUS ON THE MAIN IDEAS IN EACH PASSAGE

As you learned in chapter 6 on the ACT Reading Test, every ACT passage is made up of two kinds of elements: main ideas and details. The main ideas are "big" concepts—broad, general ideas that are the most important points being made by the author of the passage. If you were the author, the main ideas would be the handful of concepts you'd want people to remember after reading the passage.

The details, by contrast, are "small" concepts—narrow, specific facts that help to explain, illustrate, or support the main ideas. They're not as important to understand or remember as the main ideas.

The same division between main ideas and details applies to Science Reasoning passages. Actually, most Science Reasoning passages include *dozens* of details: the individual data points on each graph; the specific numbers that fill the grid of a table or chart; the readings or values obtained in each experiment described. There's no way you can master or memorize all of them.

And you don't need to—remember, there are only five to seven questions for each passage, and, as you'll see, only a few of them focus on specific details. Therefore, out of the dozens of details that appear in the passage, only a handful will be asked about. You can always look them up as needed. So trying to master them all is a waste of time.

Instead, focus on the main ideas of each passage, and try to get a general sense of *where* the details appear and what *significance* they have in relation to the main ideas. Then, when answering detail questions, you'll easily be able to locate the relevant details you need.

Now, how can you recognize the main ideas in the passages? As usual, the test-makers follow certain formulas. Each of the three Science Reasoning formats is marked by particular types of main ideas that habitually appear. If you know what they are, you'll be able to look for them as you read.

Data Representation Passages

In Data Representation passages, focus on (1) what is being measured, (2) relationships among the variables, and (3) trends in the data.

As you know, a Data Representation passage presents a collection of scientific facts in the form of one or more graphs, tables, charts, or diagrams. In most cases, numbers are involved, shown either straightforwardly, as in a table, or visually, as in a graph. To understand the information in a Data Representation passage, you need to know what the numbers measure, how different factors affect the numbers, and what trends the numbers reveal.

Here's a brief example resembling a real ACT passage:

Sample Passage I

The optimum population density for the survival and growth of a particular species of animal is often an intermediate one. Excessive crowding produces competition for scarce resources, such as water, food, space, and light, and encourages the spread of infectious diseases. On the other hand, a low population density has its own disadvantages, including diminished protection against attacks by predators, inability to modify the environment in a helpful fashion, and greater vulnerability to changes in temperature.

The following figure, depicting the effect of initial population density upon the rate of population growth in the flour beetle, illustrates this principle.

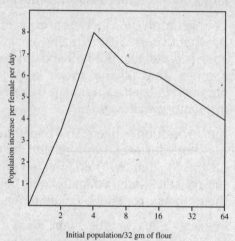

Initial population/32 gm of flour

Let's apply the three key questions to this sample passage.

What is Being Measured?

Reread the first sentence of the passage. It refers to "the optimum population density for the survival and growth of a particular species of animal." Thus, what both the prose text and the graph examine is what level of population density is best ("optimum") for a species's "survival and growth" (that is, for the species to increase in numbers). What is being measured is how the rate of growth in the numbers of a species is affected by the population density.

Since the passage focuses on how population density affects or influences the rate of population growth, population density is the *independent variable*, while rate of growth is the *dependent variable*. (If these scientific terms aren't completely familiar to you, read the explanation in Appendix D. They're important.)

What Are the Relationships Among the Variables?

Here is where the graph is essential. Line graphs like this one are the most common type of graph used on the ACT. As with virtually all line graphs, this one depicts the independent variable (population density) on the *horizontal axis,* and the dependent variable (rate of growth) on the *vertical axis.* As the dependent variable increases and decreases, the line on the graph rises and falls.

Check out the scales on the horizontal and vertical axes. The horizontal scale shows initial numbers of beetles per 32 grams of flour (population density). (By the way, don't buy your flour from the grocery where this study was done!) The further to the right we go on this scale, the more beetles we have to start with. The vertical scale shows how fast the beetle population grew, measured in baby beetles born per female per day. The higher we go on this scale, the faster the population growth.

What Are the Trends in the Data?

Now look at the shape of the line on the graph. It has a couple of bumps and bends, but basically the shape is a rising-and-falling one; its high point is in the middle, where the horizontal scale indicates an initial population density of around five bugs. That's the basic trend to recognize: population growth is greatest not when the initial population density is very low or very high, but in the middle ranges.

Once you've recognized this trend, your analysis of the passage is done. You probably have all the information you need to answer the questions that follow. If a specific detail is asked about (for example, "What is the rate of population increase when the initial beetle population is 32 beetles/32 grams of flour?"), you can simply look back at the graph to find the answer (4 per female per day).

If the information in a Data Representation passage is presented in table form, the same facts will appear not as a line on a graph but as a set of numbers in a chart. In that case, recognizing the trend involves noticing where the highest and lowest numbers fall rather than observing the movement of a line. Nevertheless, the underlying principle is exactly the same.

Research Summary Passages

In Research Summary passages, focus on (1) the question asked, (2) the variables being tested, and (3) similarities and differences in the experimental results.

A Research Summary passage begins with the posing of a scientific question. This is followed by descriptions of two or three experiments or studies conducted in an attempt to answer that question. The results of the experiments are described or presented in the form of graphs or tables. The questions that follow require you to compare the experiments, recognize why they were designed as they were, and draw some basic conclusions as to what the experiments prove or don't prove.

Here's an example that resembles a typical ACT Research Summary passage.

Sample Passage II

It has long been known that different species of flowering plants flower at various times of the year in response to some environmental stimulus. Botanists have found that the duration and timing of light and dark conditions to which a plant is exposed, known as its *photoperiod,* is the crucial factor in flowering. Botanists generally classify flowering plants in three groups: *long-day plants,* which flower when the day length exceeds some critical value, usually in summer; *short-day plants,* which flower when the day length is below some critical value; and *day-neutral plants,* which can bloom during either long or short days.

In an effort to define more precisely the critical element in the photoperiod, scientists conducted the following experiments.

Experiment 1

A greenhouse in which conditions of light and darkness were carefully controlled was stocked with several long-day and short-day plants. These were maintained with a light regime of 14 hours of daylight alternating with 10 hours of darkness. Under these conditions, the long-day plants flowered, while the short-day plants did not.

Experiment 2

A similar greenhouse was stocked with several long-day and short-day plants. These were maintained with a light regime of 12 hours of daylight and 12 hours of darkness. The short-day plants flowered, while the long-day plants did not.

Experiment 3

In a similar greenhouse with the same assortment of plants, 12 hours of daylight and 12 hours of darkness were maintained. However, halfway through the dark period, all the plants were illuminated by a momentary flash of white light. Under these conditions, the long-day plants flowered, while the short-day plants did not.

These results are summarized in the following figure.

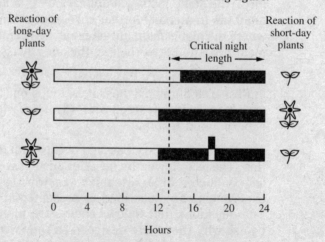

In reading a Research Summary passage like this, you'd focus on the main ideas by asking yourself the following key questions.

What is the Question Being Asked?

The passage tells us that scientists already know that the relative length of day and night affects the flowering of plants. The sentence immediately preceding the experimental results tells us that the purpose of the experiments was "to define more precisely the critical element in the photoperiod"; in other words, to figure out exactly what the plants are responding to when they either flower or fail to flower.

What are the Variables Being Tested?

The experimenters are usually trying to determine what influences what: that is, how differing variables produce differing results or outcomes. To test this, they'll keep certain conditions in their experiments unchanged, while varying the others (hence the name "variables"). You can recognize the variables being tested by noting what is different from one experiment to the next.

In some Research Summary passages, only one condition may change from one experiment to the next; in others, there may be two or more variables. (Naturally, the greater the number of variables, the more complex the experiments.)

In Sample Passage II, you might decide, after reading about Experiments 1 and 2, that the key variable is the number of hours of daylight. (After all, the plants being tested are classified as "long-day" and "long-night" plants, which suggests that hours of daylight is the key factor.) But Experiment 3 should change your thinking. In that experiment, the number of hours of daylight and darkness is the same as in Experiment 2, but the darkness is interrupted by a flash of light—with significantly different results (as we'll see).

Thus, a careful description of what differs among the three experiments is *not* "hours of daylight" but rather "hours of *uninterrupted darkness*." Notice: the passage doesn't tell you this explicitly; it must be inferred from the experimental descriptions—a typical ploy in a Research Summary passage.

FYI

The last sentence *before the description of the experiments is usually where the purpose of the experiments can be found. (What comes before this sentence is general background information.) Focus on this sentence when you read a Research Summary passage.*

What Similarities and Differences Exist in the Experimental Results?

This will tell you what answer the experiments suggest to the scientific question originally posed in the passage. In the sample passage, the results of Experiments 1 and 2 are, perhaps, predictable: the long-day plants flower when daylight is long and darkness is short, while the short-day plants flower when daylight is short and darkness is long. Opposite conditions produce opposite results, as you might expect.

Experiment 3 introduces a new wrinkle. The hours of darkness and light correspond to "short-day" conditions: twelve hours of each. However, the flash of light that interrupts the "nighttime" period apparently has the effect of reversing the expected results: long-day plants flower in Experiment 3, while short-day plants don't.

This suggests, then, that the length of daylight hours isn't the critical factor after all. Instead, it's the length of darkness that makes the crucial difference; and it appears to be essential that this darkness be uninterrupted, since the flash of light in Experiment 3 has the effect of turning "short-day" (or "long-night") conditions into their opposite.

The key to understanding a Research Summary passage, then, lies in comparing the experiments. The ways in which they resemble one another—and, more important, the ways in which they differ—reveal what the scientists are interested in studying and the conclusions their work suggests. Knowing these things, you'll probably find the questions that follow pretty easy.

Conflicting Viewpoints Passages

In Conflicting Viewpoints passages, focus on Three Important Concepts: (1) what must be explained, (2) similarities and differences in the theories presented, and (3) the hidden assumptions that underlie each theory.

A Conflicting Viewpoints passage begins with a paragraph briefly outlining some scientific problem. It's usually a phenomenon that must be explained somehow: a disease whose cause must be determined, a geological process whose workings must be described, or an astronomical observation that doesn't seem to fit with other known facts about the universe and that must be explained. Then, two or three alternative explanations are offered, each under its own heading.

FYI

Don't assume that the terminology used in the passage accurately summarizes the purpose of the experiments. In this case, "long-day" and "short-day" turn out to be misleading descriptions of the plants. Look closely at the experimental set-ups, and infer from them the key variables being examined by the scientists.

Here's a sample resembling those you'll find on the real ACT:

Sample Passage III

The *salmonids* are a family of fishes that includes salmon, trout, and char. Many species of salmonids are capable of navigating great distances, and they use this ability in long-range migrations, often involving thousands of miles of both ocean and fresh-water swimming. Salmon in particular are known for their homing behavior, in which maturing adults return to their parents' spawning (egg-laying) sites with 84 to 98 percent accuracy. Two main theories have been proposed to explain how salmon are able to navigate such great distances so successfully.

Chemoreception Theory

Salmon are one of many species of fish that are sensitive to the presence of particular chemicals in their environment, and they use stimuli provided by these chemicals and detected by the sense of smell as navigational clues. These stimuli are sometimes present over large areas of water. For example, it has been demonstrated that sockeye salmon spawned in the Fraser River in Canada can recognize water from that river in the open sea as much as 300 kilometers from its mouth.

To test the hypothesis that smell is the crucial sense for salmon navigation, scientists blocked the nasal cavities of some migrating coho salmon with absorbent cotton and marked the fish to facilitate tracing. Another group of coho salmon was differently marked and not treated in any other way. When the travels of both groups of salmon were studied, it was found that the untreated group returned accurately to their rivers of origin, while the salmon that were unable to smell selected rivers at random.

Magnetic Direction-Finding Theory

Various species of animals navigate using clues provided by the earth's magnetic field. This field, which generates magnetic lines of force running in a north-south direction, can be used in direction-finding by many birds and, some scientists believe, by some fish, including salmon.

One species of Pacific salmon, the chum, was tested for its sensitivity to magnetism in the following way. An experimental apparatus consisting of two electrical coils was built around a tank housing the salmon. When a current was run through the coils, a magnetic field was generated, capable of intensifying, weakening, or altering the earth's magnetic field, depending on the positioning of the coils. When this field was rotated 90° from the normal north-south orientation, the chum's own orientation also rotated, indicating the fish's ability to directly detect the earth's magnetic field and its responsiveness to that stimulus.

Unlike in some birds, however, whose skulls have been shown to contain particles of *magnetite*, a metal sensitive to magnetism, no mechanism for detecting magnetism has yet been discovered in salmon.

As you'll see, the relationship between the two (or three) theories presented in a Conflicting Viewpoints passage may differ. In some cases, the two theories may flatly contradict one another: if one is true, the other must be false. In other cases, they may be independent of one another or even complementary: either theory, neither, or *both* could be true. As you read a Conflicting Viewpoints passage, look for the answers to the following questions.

What Must Be Explained?

The answer to this question is usually found in the introductory paragraph that precedes the description of the theories. In the sample passage, the key sentence is the last one in that paragraph: "Two main theories have been proposed to explain how salmon are able to navigate such great distances so successfully." This makes it clear that what must be explained is the mechanism whereby salmon can find their way accurately over such long distances. The two theories that follow offer differing explanations for this phenomenon.

What Similarities and Differences Exist in the Theories Presented?

Several of the questions that follow the passage will require you to compare the theories. Thus, as you read the description of each theory, you should mentally note the similarities and differences among them.

To recognize these similarities and differences, you may need to mentally "step outside" the passage, considering not only what is mentioned there but what is *not* included. For example, in the sample passage, note that both theories suggest that the salmon respond to environmental stimuli, as opposed, for example, to some purely internal or instinctive mechanism. This is a significant similarity between the theories, which could be the basis of a question.

On the other hand, the theories differ in the nature of the stimulus that the salmon supposedly rely on. One theory considers the sense of smell to be crucial, the other focuses on magnetism. They differ, too, in that the Chemoreception Theory (the "smell theory") suggests a particular organ in the fish as the site of the phenomenon—the "nasal cavities"—whereas the Magnetic Direction-Finding Theory has no such organ to point to. (It says that scientists have *not* found magnetite particles in the skulls of the fish, as they have in some birds.)

One more difference between the theories lies in how the supposed navigational mechanism might be affected by changes in the environment. It seems logical that the "smell" mechanism—if it exists—could be thrown off by pollution in the salmon's waters, which might change the balance of chemicals in the water. By contrast, the magnetic mechanism would be upset only by some kind of change in the earth's magnetic field (or perhaps by some massive electromagnetic disturbance; could a huge power plant have this effect?). It's quite possible that a question could be asked about this difference.

What Hidden Assumptions Underlie Each Theory?

Hidden assumptions are facts or ideas, *not stated in the passage,* that must be true if a theory is to be considered valid. Hidden assumptions of some kind underlie every theory or hypothesis. This is inevitable because no theory can state explicitly every single fact or idea that's needed to support a particular conclusion. (Life is too short.) However, assumptions are the secret pitfall of many an argument. If they are true, the theory may be sound, valid, and convincing. If they are false, it is likely to break down completely. And since they are unstated—"hidden" in that sense—they are easy to overlook, though crucial.

Since assumptions don't actually appear in the passage, you must "read between the lines" to recognize what is not being said but what *must* be true if the argument is valid.

In the "smell" hypothesis, several assumptions are made:

(1)   Whatever chemical gives the water in the salmon's spawning ground its distinctive "smell" must persist over time. (If the smell changed constantly, the salmon couldn't recognize it when they try to return to their "home" river.)

(2)   The chemicals the salmon smells must be widely dispersed since the salmon's travels often extend thousands of miles, according to the introductory paragraph. (Is this plausible? One would need an expert on ocean currents to decide for sure. But a question could be asked about this.)

The "magnetism" hypothesis is based on other assumptions, including, most crucially, this one:

If not magnetite, then some other substance or organ must exist in the salmon that is sensitive to magnetic fields. (After all, every other sense is located in a specific organ: sight in the eyes, hearing in the ears, etc. If the salmon can sense magnetic fields, there must be "something" in the body of the salmon that is responding to magnetism.)

FYI

Here's another way to think about assumptions: They are often necessary links *between the evidence and the conclusion. If the assumption is sound, then the evidence leads inexorably to the conclusion. If the assumption is weak—like a crumbling footbridge—then there's no real connection between the evidence and the conclusion, and the argument collapses.*

If any of these assumptions could be proven to be false, then the theory associated with it would be in trouble. The questions that followed this passage might include one or two that focus on hidden assumptions like these.

Get into the habit of looking for hidden assumptions when you read a Conflicting Viewpoints passage.

THE INSIDER'S REPORT: THE BEST TIPS

To this point, we've spent our time studying the passage itself. Now we're ready to tackle the questions that follow.

Look for the Four Most Common Question Types

The 40 questions you'll have to tackle in each Science Reasoning test will generally fit into four main categories. Each poses a particular challenge. Here's how they work.

The Main Idea Question

Questions of this kind ask about one of the main ideas you focused on in reading the passage. For example, as we've seen, in a Data Representation passage any important *trend* in the data can be considered a main idea. You're likely to encounter one or more questions on any Data Representation passage that focus on such a trend.

Here's an example, based on Sample Passage I above (the beetles-in-the-flour passage):

1. Based on the data presented in the figure, the flour beetle population will grow most quickly when initial population density is

   (A) below $\frac{2}{32}$ gm of flour.

   (B) around $\frac{4}{32}$ gm of flour.

   (C) between 16 and $\frac{32}{32}$ gm of flour.

   (D) greater than $\frac{64}{32}$ gm of flour.

If you can trace the overall shape of the line on the graph, this question is an easy one to answer: choice (B) is correct.

A main idea question based on Sample Passage II (flowering plants) might be as follows:

2. The results of the experiments suggest that the critical factor in determining when a plant flowers is most likely to be the

(F) overall number of hours of daylight.
(G) number of hours of uninterrupted daylight.
(H) overall number of hours of darkness.
(J) number of hours of uninterrupted darkness.

As we saw when we discussed this passage earlier, the experimental results show that interrupting the period of darkness with a flash of light affects the flowering of plants. Thus, choice (J) is correct: the number of hours of uninterrupted darkness is key to determining which type of plant will flower.

The Detail Question

This type of question focuses on one specific piece of information drawn from the passage. It may ask you to locate a particular number from a table or graph or to pick a statement that accurately rephrases an idea found in the explanatory text.

Most Science Reasoning passages will be followed by one or two detail questions. There are two keys to answering them correctly:

(1) Read the question carefully. Students sometimes lose points through careless errors—thinking that the question asks about Experiment II when Experiment III is named, for example.

(2) Turn back to the passage and find the specific detail being asked about. Don't try to answer the detail question from memory. Instead, look up the answer. In most cases, if you used the three-step approach to reading the passage, you'll have a good sense of the overall organization of the passage, making particular details easy to find.

Here's a sample detail question based on Sample Passage I (beetles-in-the-flour):

3. According to the figure, if the initial population density is 16 beetles per 32 gm of flour, what will be the rate of population increase per female per day?

(A) 3
(B) 5
(C) 6
(D) 8

The answer, choice (C), can be read directly from the graph.

FYI

Distractors (wrong answers) to detail questions are often drawn from the wrong part of the passage. (In question 4, choice (G) is an example.) Don't pick an answer just because it "sounds familiar" or because you recognize it from the passage: the detail must be the right detail to answer the question posed.

Here's another detail question, this one based on Sample Passage III (salmon navigation):

4. According to the Chemoreception Theory, salmon are able to locate the particular river in which they were spawned by

  (F) following traces of particular chemicals found in the waters of that river.

  (G) sensing changes in the orientation of the earth's magnetic field.

  (H) following the track of other salmon returning to the same general region.

  (J) avoiding waters that contain chemical pollutants that may be harmful to the salmon.

If you understood the paragraph describing the Chemoreception Theory, this detail question won't be hard for you. The right answer is choice (F).

The Inference Question

The answer to a detail question will be stated directly in the passage. By contrast, inference questions require you to read between the lines or to draw connections between two or more details that are not explicitly stated in the passage. They're a little more sophisticated and challenging than either main idea or detail questions, and they're popular with the test-makers: most Science Reasoning passages will be followed by two, three, or four inference questions.

Here's an example, based on Sample Passage I (beetles-in-the-flour):

5. If a package of 320 grams of flour is infested with a population of 160 flour beetles, half male and half female, what will be the expected beetle population after the passage of one day?

  (A) 166
  (B) 320
  (C) 480
  (D) 640

A little computation is required to answer this one. The graph (refer back to the figure) shows initial population densities per 32 grams of flour; the question refers to 320 grams of flour. Obviously, the question has been set up to make figuring easy, multiplying the graph numbers by 10 (which is simple to do in your head).

If there are 160 beetles in 320 grams of flour, that's the equivalent of 16 beetles per 10 grams of flour. On the graph, this gives us an expected population increase of 6 beetles per female per day. Now, the question specifies that half the beetles in the batch are females. That means 80 females. Multiply 80 times 6, and we see that the population will grow by 480 beetles in one day. To get the total population on the second day, we have to add the original population back in: 480 + 160 = 640 total beetles.

Another example, based on Sample Passage II (flowering plants):

6. On the basis of the information in the figure, the long-day plants used in the study can be expected to flower when they are housed in conditions that include

   (F) a period of daylight at least 12 hours long.
   (G) no period of uninterrupted darkness longer than 11 hours.
   (H) no period of daylight shorter than 12 hours.
   (J) no period of uninterrupted darkness shorter than 10 hours.

The correct answer is choice (G). To answer this item correctly, you must not only understand the overall experimental setup and the special features of Experiment 3, but also note, in the figure, the dotted vertical line marking what's called "critical night length." You can infer that this represents the number of hours of darkness that separate long-day from short-day plants. The line is drawn so as to mark off 11 hours of darkness (or thirteen hours of daylight), which we see must be the maximum amount of uninterrupted darkness in which a long-day plant can flower.

The Application Question
As its name suggests, the application question requires you to apply the information in the passage to some context beyond what's in the passage itself. For instance, you might be asked to evaluate some new piece of evidence that could either strengthen or weaken one of the theories presented; you could be called upon to extrapolate from the information provided to some new situation that's literally "off the chart" (not included in the existing graph or table); or you might be asked how the ideas in the passage might affect some real-world problem.

Here's a typical application question based on Sample Passage II (flowering plants):

7. Scientists designing an experimental greenhouse aboard a space station are interested in minimizing the amount of electrical energy used for lighting while conducting studies of flowering plants. Which of the following methods of economizing on energy is suggested by the results of Experiment 3?

   (A) Substitution of short-day for long-day plants in experiments with flowering plants
   (B) Prolongation of the daily period of darkness in experiments with short-day flowering plants
   (C) Use of brief flashes of light in place of extra hours of light in experiments with long-day flowering plants
   (D) Use of brief periods of darkness in place of prolonged periods of darkness in experiments with short-day flowering plants

Like an inference question, an application question requires you to go beyond what is literally stated in the passage. Since the question asks about ways of economizing on energy, we can figure out that the answer must focus on somehow getting long-day plants to flower *without* paying for extended periods of lighting. Experiment 3 suggests how this could be done. A brief flash of light during the "night" has the same effect as two extra hours of daylight: it causes long-day plants to flower. Thus, one could substitute such flash for a longer daylight period, as stated in choice (C).

Finally, one more application question based on Passage III (salmon navigation):

8. The Magnetic Direction-Finding Theory would be most greatly strengthened by the discovery that

   (F) chemical-sensitive organs exist in the nasal cavities of coho salmon.
   (G) the earth's magnetic field is too weak to be detected by most species of salmon.
   (H) particles of magnetite exist in the skulls of Pacific salmon.
   (J) coho salmon are the only species of salmon with a highly sensitive sense of smell.

The passage suggests that one weakness of the magnetic theory is the absence of any obvious mechanism by which the magnetic sensing could work. Choice (H) would strengthen the theory by supplying this absence. Choice (G) would weaken the theory rather than strengthen it, and choices (F) and (J) relate only to the Chemoreception Theory rather than the magnetic theory.

THE INSIDER'S REPORT: THE MOST IMPORTANT WARNINGS

Beware of Irrelevant Information

Most Science Reasoning passages will include some information that's unrelated to any of the questions. It may appear in the introductory paragraphs or in the body of the passage, including any graphs, tables, or charts. Don't let this confuse you. Focus on the main ideas of the passage, skim the details, and then tackle the questions. If some—perhaps most!—of the details turn out to be unnecessary, so be it.

Keep Units of Measurement Straight

FYI

You don't need to memorize any difficult tables of equivalency—for example, between metric and English units (grams to ounces, meters to feet, and so on). The ACT test-makers consistently use metric units (as scientists do), and they will not expect you to translate between one system and another.

As we saw in the flour-beetles passage, math plays an important secondary role in interpreting Science Reasoning passages. It's important to pay attention to the units and of measurement used in the graphs or tables and in the questions; they may vary from one place to another, and you must be prepared to translate as necessary. For example, an application question might take a relationship described in liters (L) in the passage and ask you to apply it to a quantity in milliliters (ml). Pay attention, and perform the simple calculation necessary.

Don't Get Bogged Down in Technical Terminology

Some of the passages will deal with topics that are unfamiliar to you, and many will use terms, abbreviations, symbols, and phrases you haven't seen before. Don't worry about this. All the information you need to answer the questions is included in the passage, and you can safely ignore the unfamiliar terms.

Here's an illustration from a real ACT Science Reasoning Test. A particular passage dealt with bacterial reproduction, and described how twelve different types of bacteria grew in various kinds of "growth medium." The bacteria were listed using their Latin names: *Clostridium botulinum, Escherichia coli, Lactobacillus acidophilus,* and so on. Only one student in a hundred is likely to be familiar with these names. Even the list of growth media might be puzzling: glucose broth, lactose broth, milk. (Well, you probably know what milk is.)

What's the point? *None of those things mattered.* The questions following the passage did use the Latin names for the bacteria, but no interpretation or any real understanding was necessary to answer the questions. If you could read the table showing how the bacteria grew and recognize the right name when necessary ("Oh, the right answer is that *lacto* one—the one with the third-highest number on the chart"), you could answer all the questions fairly easily.

Don't be intimidated by scary-looking scientific verbiage. In almost every case, it's irrelevant to answering the questions correctly.

JUST THE FACTS

- Use the three-step methods—previewing, reading, reviewing—to master the information in the Science Reasoning passages.

- Learn the three formats for Science Reasoning passages and the kinds of main ideas each format focuses on.

- Look for main idea, detail, inference, and application questions; each requires a slightly different approach.

- Don't get bogged down in complex calculations or abstruse terminology.

PRACTICE, PRACTICE, PRACTICE: SCIENCE REASONING EXERCISES

Instructions

The following exercises will give you a chance to practice the skills and strategies you've just learned for tackling ACT Science Reasoning questions. As with all practice exercises, work under true testing conditions. Complete each exercise in a single sitting. Eliminate distractions (TV, music) and clear away notes and reference materials. Time yourself with a stopwatch or kitchen timer, or have someone else time you. If you run out of time before answering all the questions, stop and draw a line under the last question you finished. Then go ahead and tackle the remaining questions. When you are done, score yourself based only on the questions you finished in the allotted time.

Understanding Your Scores

0–3 correct: A poor performance. Study this chapter again, and (if you haven't already) read the Insider's Science Review for the ACT in Appendix D.

4–6 correct: A below-average score. Study this chapter again, focusing especially on the skills and strategies you've found newest and most challenging.

7–10 correct: An average score. You may want to study this chapter again. Also be sure you are managing your time wisely (as explained in Chapter 3) and avoiding errors due to haste or carelessness.

11–12 correct: An above-average score. Depending on your personal target score and your strength on other question types, you may or may not want to devote additional time to the Science Reasoning Test.

16–20 correct: An excellent score. You are probably ready to perform well on the ACT Reading Test.

EXERCISE 1

12 Questions

Time—10 Minutes

Directions: This test consists of two passages, each followed by several questions. Read each passage, select the correct answer for each question, and mark the oval representing the correct answer on your answer sheet. You may NOT use a calculator on this test.

Passage I

Phytoplankton are tiny aquatic plants that are an important food source for larger animals and may be an important source of carbon (the element that is a building block of all living organisms). Phytoplankton abundance is dependent on the presence of warm surface waters. Consequently, changes in phytoplankton abundance can be used as an indicator of changes in surface water temperature.

A system for documenting phytoplankton abundance has been developed using filtering silk towed by merchant ships. The organisms color the silk green, and the intensity of the color is correlated with their abundance. The first figure shows data on the average monthly phytoplankton abundance for four decades, as determined by the color index system. Data is given for two ocean areas in the Northern Atlantic just below the Arctic Circle. The boundaries of these areas are depicted in the second figure.

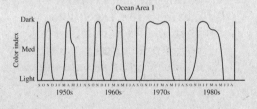

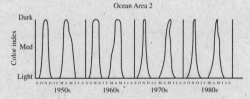

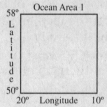
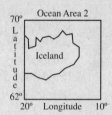

1. Based on the information in the first figure, which of the following statements concerning phytoplankton abundance in the four decades of the study is correct?

   (A) There was no discernible change in patterns of phytoplankton abundance in Ocean Area 1.

   (B) Annual phytoplankton abundance increased in Ocean Area 2.

   (C) Annual phytoplankton abundance increased in Ocean Area 1 and decreased in Ocean Area 2.

   (D) The season of high phytoplankton abundance increased in length in both Ocean Areas.

245

2. Assuming that the changes in phytoplankton abundance seen in the study occurred solely because of surface water temperature variations, the information in the figures indicates that which of the following statements is true?

(F) Surface ocean waters above latitude 62° North in the map areas cooled during the study.

(G) Surface ocean waters above latitude 50° North in the map areas cooled during the study.

(H) Surface ocean waters east of longitude 10° in the map areas warmed during the study.

(J) Surface ocean waters west of longitude 10° in the map areas cooled during the study.

3. Which of the following statements best describes typical phytoplankton abundance in Ocean Areas 1 and 2 in the 1950s?

(A) Abundance increased in October and remained at high levels until about June.

(B) Abundance increased slowly and fell off rapidly in two distinct periods.

(C) Abundance increased rapidly in two distinct periods and remained at peak levels for approximately three months during each of these periods.

(D) Abundance increased and fell off rapidly in two distinct periods.

4. The first figure indicates what about the changes in phytoplankton abundance?

(F) Changes occurred evenly over the course of the four decades.

(G) Changes occurred over the course of about a decade.

(H) Changes occurred over the course of about a year.

(J) Changes in area 1 were apparent earlier than changes in area 2.

5. Some researchers hypothesize that the changes in phytoplankton abundance reflect an increase in global temperature over the last century (global warming). Which of the following findings would support this hypothesis and fit the data seen in the first figure?

(A) A greater abundance of fresh water from melted ice and permafrost has begun flowing south to north from the Antarctic during the last century.

(B) A greater abundance of fresh water from melted ice and permafrost has begun flowing north to south from the Arctic during the last century.

(C) Warmer temperatures have been recorded in and around Iceland during the last century.

(D) Barring a few exceptions, phytoplankton numbers have begun to decrease dramatically in ocean areas around the globe during the last century.

6. Certain species of whales migrate annually in order to take advantage of abundant blooms of phytoplankton, one of their principal food sources. During which of the following months would a whale-watching tour in Ocean Area 1 be LEAST likely to encounter phytoplankton-eating whales?

(F)   January
(G)   April
(H)   May
(J)   August

Passage II

Airplane wings must be designed *aerodynamically* (with consideration to the airflow over the body of the plane) to ensure efficient flight. Aerodynamic design considers *lift* and *drag*.

Lift is the force acting upwards on the plane. It is generated because the top of a wing is curved, while the bottom is flat. The air moving over the top of the wings must move faster than the air moving over the bottom. This results in a lower pressure area above the wing.

Drag is the air resistance generated by the plane. This is a force acting in opposition to the plane's forward movement. The most efficient planes are those with the highest lift to drag ratio.

Researchers testing new wing designs conducted a series of experiments to measure their efficiency.

Experiment 1

Researchers tested aircraft with four wing designs (see the following figure) in a *wind tunnel* (a tunnel in which air is blown over a craft to simulate flight conditions). This test simulated flight at 400 mph. The lift and drag measured for each wing shape are recorded in Table 7.1.

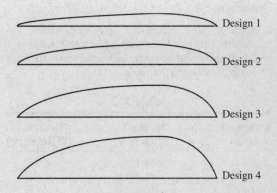

Table 7.1

Wing Design	Lift (neutrons)	Drag (neutrons)	Efficiency
1	3	.15	20:1
2	8	.2	40:1
3	10	1	10:1
4	18	2	9:1

Experiment 2

Aircraft with the four wing types depicted in the figure were tested under similar flight conditions to gauge fuel consumption. After reaching cruising altitude, the planes maintained a speed of 400 mph. The results appear in Table 7.2.

Table 7.2

Wing	Fuel consumption (gallons/hr)
1	40
2	20
3	80
4	88

Experiment 3

Lift, drag and efficiency are dependent on airspeed. The researchers tested wing designs 1 and 2 at different speeds. Efficiency (lift to drag ratio) was recorded (Table 7.3).

Table 7.3

Airspeed (mph)	Design 1 (Efficiency)	Design 2 (Efficiency)
200	22:1	43:1
300	21:1	42:1
400	20:1	40:1
500	18:1	12:1
600	10:1	8:1

7. The most efficient wing tested in Experiment 1 was

   (A) Design 1.
   (B) Design 2.
   (C) Design 3.
   (D) Design 4.

8. A passenger plane is able to carry a fixed weight, including passengers and fuel. Which wing design would be best for such a plane?

   (F) Design 1
   (G) Design 2
   (H) Design 3
   (J) Design 4

9. In cold, damp weather, the buildup of ice on airplane wings can pose significant aerodynamic problems. Which of the following effects would you expect?

   (A) As ice builds up on the top of the wing, drag increases.
   (B) As ice builds up on the top of the wing, lift increases.
   (C) As ice builds up on bottom of the wing, lift decreases.
   (D) All of the above.

10. Which of the following test pairs reflects consistent experimental data?

    (F) Experiment 1, wing design 2; Experiment 2, airspeed 200
    (G) Experiment 1, wing design 1; Experiment 2, wing design 2
    (H) Experiment 1, wing design 3; Experiment 3, airspeed 400
    (J) Experiment 1, wing design 1; Experiment 3, airspeed 400

11. Which of the following statements about airspeed is supported by the data in Experiment 3?

    (A) As airspeed increases, the lift to drag ratio increases.
    (B) As airspeed increases, lift and drag increase at about the same rate.
    (C) As airspeed increases, drag increases faster than lift.
    (D) As airspeed increases, lift increases faster than drag.

12. New fighter jets are being designed so that the wing is modifiable, depending on the speed at which the plane is going. Which of the following would be a logical adjustment of the wing for such jets?

    (F) At speeds above 500 mph, the top of the wing would become flatter.
    (G) At speeds above 500 mph, the top of the wing would become more curved.
    (H) At speeds above 500 mph, the bottom of the wing would become curved.
    (J) None of the above.

EXERCISE 2

Directions: This test consists of two passages, each followed by several questions. Read each passage, select the correct answer for each question, and mark the oval representing the correct answer on your answer sheet. You may NOT use a calculator on this test.

Passage I

A greenish, potato-sized meteorite discovered in Antarctica is believed to have originated on Mars. Investigations of the meteorite have revealed a number of unusual features. Some scientists believe that these features are evidence of primitive life on Mars, while other scientists believe that they are more probably the result of nonbiological (nonliving) processes, such as hydrothermal synthesis.

Hydrothermal Synthesis Hypothesis

The meteorite crystallized slowly from *magma* (molten rock) on Mars 4.5 million years ago. About half a million years later, the rock became fractured. This was a time when Mars was much warmer and had abundant water. Deep inside the planet, in a process called *hydrothermal synthesis*, hot water and carbon seeped into the fractured rock and formed new complex *organic* compounds called polycyclic aromatic hydrocarbons (PAHs). (Organic compounds, or those that contain carbon, are formed from life processes, such as bacterial decay, as well as processes that are not associated with life, including hydrothermal synthesis and star formation.)

As the chemical environment of the planet changed over time, crystals of magnetite, iron sulfides, and carbonate formed in the rock. The crystallization of the carbonate resulted in the formation of unusual elongated and egg-shaped structures within the crystals.

Primitive Life Hypothesis

The meteorite crystallized slowly from *magma* (molten rock) on Mars 4.5 million years ago. About half a million years later, the rock became fractured. This was a time when Mars was much warmer and had abundant water. The rock was immersed in water rich in carbon dioxide, which allowed carbon to collect inside the fractured rock, along with primitive bacteria.

The bacteria began to manufacture magnetite and iron sulfide crystals, just as bacteria on earth do. As generations of bacteria died and began to decay, they created PAHs inside of the meteorite's carbon molecules. Finally, some of bacteria themselves were preserved as elongated egg-shaped fossils inside of the rock.

1. About which of the following points do the two hypotheses differ?
   (A) The meteorite's age
   (B) The origin of the meteorite's organic molecules
   (C) The conditions on Mars when the meteorite formed
   (D) The origin of the fractures in the meteorite

2. Proponents of both theories would agree that which of the following statements is true?
   (F) The meteorite contains some type of fossil.
   (G) Water was important for the original entry of carbon into the meteorite.
   (H) The organic compounds seen in the rock were the result of decay.
   (J) Magnetite crystals from Antarctica seeped into the meteorite.

3. Which of the following represents a difference in opinion between proponents of the two theories?

(A) Proponents of the Primitive Life Hypothesis maintain that Mars has changed substantially since the meteorite was formed.

(B) Proponents of the Primitive Life Hypothesis dispute the notion that PAHs can occur from processes other than bacterial decay.

(C) Proponents of the Hydrothermal Synthesis Hypothesis believe that hot water and carbon formed organic compounds in the rock.

(D) Proponents of the Hydrothermal Synthesis Hypothesis believe that the fossils found inside the meteorite were probably the remains of an organism other than a bacteria.

4. Which of the following findings would help to bolster the case of proponents of the Hydrothermal Synthesis Hypothesis?

(F) The magnetite found in the meteorite sometimes occurred in chains, similar to those produced by bacteria on earth.

(G) Glass within the meteorite hints that it was probably fractured and launched toward earth when a meteoroid or comet hit Mars.

(H) Recent studies indicate that liquid water, one of life's most fundamental necessities, does not exist on Mars.

(J) Minerals can grow into shapes that are similar to the elongated egg-shaped structures seen in the meteorite.

5. Researchers analyzing glacial ice found very low concentrations of PAHs. Which of the following additional findings would help the case of proponents of the Primitive Life Hypothesis?

(A) The meteorite contained only a small number of the thousands of PAHs, and all of the ones found are known to be associated with bacterial decay.

(B) Organic molecules were also discovered in meteorites known to have originated in the *asteroid belt* (an area orbiting the sun that is rich in asteroids).

(C) Some of the carbonates in which the PAHs were found had element ratios that are similar to those found on earth.

(D) Experiments with the weathering of rocks have shown that under certain conditions, molecules in the environment can make their way deep within a rock.

6. Which of the following experiments might help to resolve the question of whether the PAHs in the meteorite actually originated on Mars?

(F) Examine the ratios of the PAHs found in glacial ice and see if these are similar to those seen in the meteorite.

(G) Test meteorites known to have come from the moon for PAHs.

(H) Test for PAHs in meteorites known to have formed on Mars after its era of abundant water ended.

(J) All of the above.

Passage II

Electrical circuits that allow electrical signals with some *frequencies* (number of waves per second) to pass while suppressing others are called *filters*. They are used in nearly every electronic device, from computers to VCRs. They may contain *resistors*, which resist the flow of current through a wire, *inductors,* which resist change in the current, and *capacitors,* which store electric charge. The following figure shows the design of three types of filters.

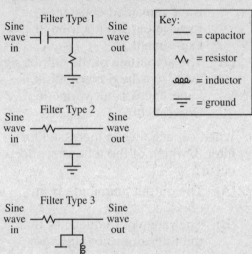

The effects of a filter can be demonstrated with a *frequency response curve.* Such a curve depicts the *amplitude* (wave height) of the output (vertical axis) as one varies the input frequency (horizontal axis), while keeping the input amplitude constant. Several experiments were conducted to test the effects of some filters.

Experiment 1

Researchers fed *sine waves* (oscillating voltage) into an electrical circuit containing the three filters depicted in the figure. The input amplitude was fixed at 2.0 volts. The amplitude of the resulting waves were measured, and the frequency response curves in the following figure were obtained.

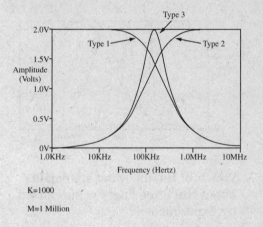

K=1000

M=1 Million

Experiment 2

A sine wave with an amplitude fixed at 2.0 volts was fed into a circuit with a type 3 filter, but in this experiment the researchers used four different values for the inductance (L). The resulting frequency response curves are shown in the following figure.

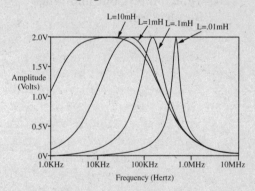

Experiment 3

Again, the researchers fed a sine wave with an amplitude fixed at 2.0 volts into a circuit with a type 3 filter. The inductance was held at .1 mH, while four different values of capacitance C were used. The resulting frequency response curves are shown in the following figure.

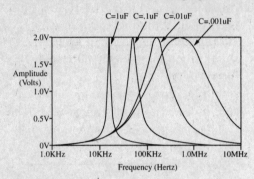

7. Which of the following statements about the three filters is supported by Experiment 1?

(A) Type 1 filters out high frequencies.

(B) Type 1 filters out low frequencies.

(C) Type 2 filters out high frequencies.

(D) Type 3 filters out mid-range frequencies.

8. Which of the following accurately described the difference between Experiments 1 and 2?

(F) The frequency of the input sign wave was varied in Experiment 1, but not in Experiment 2.

(G) The inductance of filter 3 was constant in Experiment 1 but varied in Experiment 2.

(H) The amplitude of the input sign wave remained constant in Experiment 1 but varied in Experiment 2.

(J) The amplitude of the output sign wave remained constant in Experiment 1 but varied in Experiment 2.

9. When capacitance is increased for filter 3, which of the following effects occur?

(A) The output amplitude is increased.

(B) The range of frequencies that the filter does not suppress increases.

(C) A smaller range of frequencies are accepted.

(D) The accepted frequencies are in a higher range.

10. In Experiment 2, the capacitance was most likely set at

(F) 1µF

(G) .1µF

(H) .01µF

(J) .001µF

11. The frequency response curves suggest possible applications for the three filters. Which of the following applications would be most logical?

    (A) Filter type 1 used by a radio receiver to screen out radio signals that are at a lower frequency than that of the desired station

    (B) Filter type 2 used in an audio circuit to eliminate high- frequency audio hum

    (C) Filter type 2 used in a radio receiver to tune in a particular radio station at a fixed frequency

    (D) Filter type 3 used in a radio receiver to tune in a particular radio station at a fixed frequency

12. It is often very important to design filters with *high Q* (a very narrow peak in the frequency response curve). An engineer discovers that the *tuned frequency* (the frequency at which the frequency response curve peaks) of a circuit with a type 3 filter is too low. Which of the following should he do in order to raise the tuned frequency and keep a high Q filter circuit?

    (F) Lower the capacitance

    (G) Lower the inductance

    (H) Raise the capacitance and the inductance

    (J) Raise the resistance

EXERCISE 3

Directions: This test consists of two passages, each followed by several questions. Read each passage, select the correct answer for each question, and mark the oval representing the correct answer on your answer sheet. You may NOT use a calculator on this test.

Passage I

Environmental levels of the *organic volatile chemical* benzene are of concern to public health officials because studies have shown that continual exposure to high concentrations of this compound can cause leukemia. Organic volatile chemicals are carbon-containing compounds that are easily vaporized and therefore are present in the air. Experiments to test for the presence of such chemicals were devised.

Experiment 1

Researchers outfitted individuals in urban, suburban, and rural areas with monitoring instruments that they could wear throughout the day. These instruments recorded the concentrations of benzene they were exposed to as they went about their normal activities. Other monitoring devices were used to record the benzene output of various known sources in the participants' environment. The average percentage of total benzene that participants were exposed to from various sources as well as the average percentage of total output from these sources are given in Table 7.4.

Table 7.4

Sources	% of Total Benzene Rmissions	% of Total Benzene Exposure
Automobiles	80%	20%
Industry	15%	4%
Household sources (e.g., stored paints and gasoline)	4.5%	35%
Cigarettes	0.5%	41%

Experiment 2

The researchers decided to look at whether other volatile organic compounds were found in greater concentrations indoors or outdoors. Residents from two areas wore monitoring devices that recorded the levels of a number of volatile organic compounds that they were exposed to during outdoor and indoor activities for several days. The first area was a highly industrial New Jersey city and the other was a rural township in Maine. The average exposure levels of residents in these areas are listed in Table 7.5.

Table 7.5

Volatile Chemical	NJ Industrial ($\mu g/m^3$)		Maine Rural Township ($\mu g/m^3$)	
	Indoor	Outdoor	Indoor	Outdoor
Trichloroethane	21	4	14	3
Tetrachloroethylene	9	3	8	1
Chloroform	5	0.2	2	0.1
O-oxylene	5	3	3	2
Styrene	5	0.5	1	0.2

Experiment 3

Fine particles in the air, particularly breathable particles (those that are 10 microns or smaller and are able to penetrate into the lungs), are another environmental concern. Large population studies have suggested that elevated outdoor concentrations of fine particles are associated with premature death. Most fine particles form through processes of combustion, such as cooking, burning candles, smoking, or burning firewood.

Researchers wanted to see what the total levels of such particles were indoors and outdoors and how these levels compared with an individual's exposure levels. Monitors that recorded levels of breathable particles were put inside and outside the homes of one individual from both of the communities in Experiment 2. These individuals were also asked to wear monitoring devices for one day and one night. The results from this experiment are shown in Table 7.6.

Table 7.6

	Day			Night		
	Personal Exposure $\mu g/m^3$	Indoor Levels $\mu g/m^3$	Outdoor Levels $\mu g/m^3$	Personal Exposure $\mu g/m^3$	Indoor Exposure $\mu g/m^3$	Outdoor Exposure $\mu g/m^3$
NJ Indust. City	152	98	100	75	65	95
Maine Rural Township	149	95	93	73	72	90

1. The results of Experiment 1 indicate that which of the following statements is true?

   (A) Automobiles and industrial pollution are not significant sources of benzene emissions.

   (B) The largest sources of benzene output were also the sources that caused the highest individual exposures.

   (C) Cigarettes caused more benzene emissions than any other source tested.

   (D) An individual's highest exposure to benzene was more likely to occur indoors than outdoors.

2. One of the differences between Experiment 1 and Experiment 2 is that:

   (F) Experiment 1 did not investigate a volatile compound.

   (G) Experiment 2 showed that people are exposed to higher levels of volatile organic compounds indoors, a finding that was contradicted by Experiment 1.

   (H) Experiment 1 looked at compound emission levels, while Experiment 2 looked only at compound exposure levels.

   (J) Experiment 2 looked at the average compound exposure levels from a pool of data, while Experiment 1 looked at individuals' compound exposure levels.

3. Which of the following hypotheses would best explain the results seen in Experiment 3?

 (A) Moving about stirs up a personal cloud of breathable particles.

 (B) Industrial sites tend to perform most combustion activities in the night hours, thus raising particle levels at night.

 (C) Particles formed during cooking and smoking tend to remain suspended for at least 24 hours, so that daytime levels generally do not drop off at night.

 (D) Exposure to breathable particles is largely attributable to automobile exhaust.

4. If the researchers conducting Experiment 3 added another study subject and found that he had a daytime indoor exposure level of 75 micrograms/meter^3, which of the following would be the most likely daytime personal exposure level for this individual?

 (F) 65 micrograms/meter^3
 (G) 75 micrograms/meter^3
 (H) 85 micrograms/meter^3
 (J) 125 micrograms/meter^3

5. Researchers hypothesized that volatile organic compounds follow the same pattern of personal exposure versus indoor exposure levels as that seen with breathable particles in Experiment 3. If this hypothesis is correct, which of the following is probably closest to the actual indoor level of trichloroethane in the rural Maine township?

 (A) 1 micrograms/meter^3
 (B) 6 micrograms/meter^3
 (C) 15 micrograms/meter^3
 (D) 19 micrograms/meter^3

6. To prove the hypothesis in Question 5, researchers would need to do which of the following?

 (F) Conduct Experiment 2 again, but ask the subjects to wear monitoring devices only during the day.

 (G) Conduct Experiment 3 again, this time asking all of the subjects from Experiment 2 to participate.

 (H) Conduct Experiment 2 again, but this time place monitors in the indoor settings in addition to those worn by individuals.

 (J) Conduct Experiment 2 again, but break down the individual exposure levels into those encountered during the day and during the night.

Passage II

In small communities, infectious organisms such as Varicella-zoster virus, which causes chickenpox, occasionally become extinct. The threshold at which such extinctions occur is known as the critical community size. Extinctions are followed by a period in which there are no infections until the virus is reintroduced from an outside source.

Researchers collected data on these extinctions or *fadeouts* in various communities before the development of the chickenpox vaccine. Fadeouts were defined as a period of three or more weeks in which there were no new reported cases of the infection. They then attempted to develop computer models of the patterns of fadeouts seen using information about the dynamics of the infection. The first of the following figures shows the real data on chickenpox versus the data generated by two different computer models. The second of the figures demonstrates the different assumptions made by the two models concerning the duration of the *infectious period* (the period in which an individual can transmit the infection to another individual). This was the only difference between the two models.

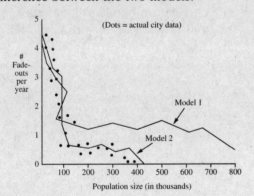

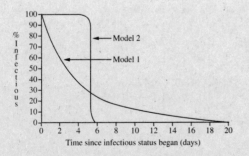

7. The critical community size for chickenpox is

   (A) over 1 million.
   (B) about 700,000.
   (C) about 400,000.
   (D) under 100,000.

8. The difference between models 1 and 2 is:

   (F) Model 1 predicts a more concentrated infectious period, compared with model 2.
   (G) Model 1 predicts more individuals will be infectious after six days, compared with model 2.
   (H) Model 2 predicts a greater number of individuals will be infectious in the early days of the infectious period, compared with model 1.
   (J) All of the above.

9. Which of the following statements is best supported by the first figure?

   (A) As the number of viruses climbs toward 1 million, the number of fadeouts per year declines.
   (B) As a community population increases, the discrepancy between the predictive abilities of the two models increases.
   (C) Model 1 is better at predicting annual fadeouts for communities under 300,000, while model 2 is better at predicting annual fadeouts for communities over 300,000.
   (D) Both models overestimate the number of annual fadeouts for chickenpox.

10. In a community with a population of 300,000, the number of fadeouts per year

    (F)   is below 1.
    (G)   is above 1.
    (H)   is more variable than in a population below 100,000.
    (J)   is lower than in a population of 500,000.

11. Which of the following statements might explain the difference in the abilities of models 1 and 2 to predict the actual number of annual fadeouts of chickenpox?

    (A)   Model 2 predicts that there will be more individuals spreading infection in the early infectious period, resulting in a lower number of predicted fadeouts, compared with model 1.
    (B)   Model 1 predicts that there will be some individuals spreading infection in the late infectious period, reducing the number of predicted fadeouts, compared with model 2.
    (C)   Model 2 predicts that there will be a longer infectious period in larger communities, increasing the number of predicted fadeouts, compared with model 1.
    (D)   Model 2 assumes a more constant rate of movement from an infectious to a noninfectious status.

12. If the researchers used another computer model for chickenpox using the assumption about the infectious period depicted below (see the following figure, model 3), what could you expect this model to predict?

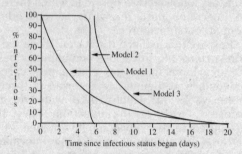

    (F)   Model 3 would predict more annual fadeouts than model 1.
    (G)   Model 3 would predict more annual fadeouts than model 2, but less than model 1.
    (H)   Model 3 would underestimate the number of annual fadeouts.
    (J)   Model 3 would predict a better correlation between fadeouts and population size than models 1 or 2.

EXERCISE 4

Passage I

Individuals usually have two copies of each *gene* (the basic unit of genetic material, found on the *chromosomes),* one from their mother and one from their father. Genetic or inherited diseases are those that can be passed down to the next generation through the genes. These diseases follow a number of patterns. Two of the basic ones are *dominant* and *recessive* inheritance.

In a genetic disease with a recessive inheritance pattern, an individual will not be affected by the disease unless he or she is passed two copies of the disease gene, one from each parent. An individual who is passed one copy of the disease gene is called a *healthy carrier.* He or she will not have the disease, but can still pass the gene on to an offspring. The first of the following figures shows a family with this type of genetic disease.

In a disease with a dominant inheritance pattern, any individual with a copy of the disease gene will have the disease. (Depending on the disease, individuals with two copies may have an accelerated or more severe disease course or may be unable to survive). There is no such thing as a healthy carrier with this type of disease. The second figure shows a family with this type of genetic disease.

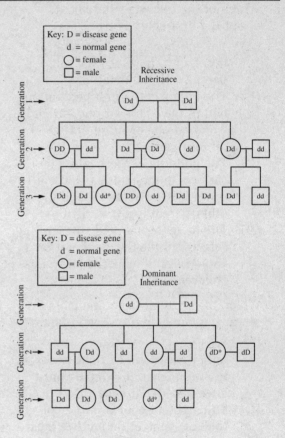

1. Which of the following is the correct number of healthy carriers in the third generation of the family depicted in the first figure?

(A) None
(B) 2
(C) 5
(D) 6

2. Which of the following is the correct number of family members with the disease in the first figure?

(F) 0
(G) 2
(H) 10
(J) 12

3. Which of the following statements about the first figure is true?

(A) The mother in the first generation had to have at least one parent with the disease.
(B) The father in the first generation had to have at least one parent who had one or more of the disease genes.
(C) The children of the healthy carriers in the family could end up with the disease even if the other parent is not a carrier.
(D) The daughter marked with an asterisk in the third generation could pass the disease on to her children.

4. Which of the following statements about the family in the second figure is true?

(F) Either the mother or father of the first generation father must have had the disease.
(G) Either the mother or father of the first generation mother must have been a carrier of the disease gene.
(H) There are three healthy carriers in the second generation.
(J) The couple marked with an asterisk in the second generation will be unable to have any healthy children.

5. What is the correct number of individuals with the disease in the second figure?

(A) 5
(B) 6
(C) 7
(D) There is not enough information to determine this.

6. If the generation 3 daughter marked with an asterisk in the family in the second figure was planning on having children, which of the following would be accurate advice for her regarding genetic testing?

(F) She should be tested to rule out the possibility that one or more of her children would be carriers of the disease gene, but she could be sure that none of them would develop the disease.
(G) Both she and her husband need to be tested to rule out the possibility that they are healthy carriers of the disease gene.
(H) Testing is unnecessary for the daughter; she is not carrying the disease gene.
(J) Testing one of the parents is sufficient to rule out the disease in their children.

7. The family in the following figure has a genetic disease that follows either the dominant or recessive pattern. Which of the following statements concerning this family is true?

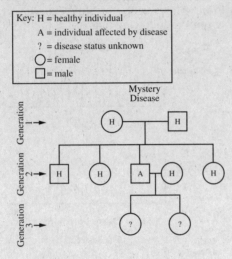

Key: H = healthy individual
A = individual affected by disease
? = disease status unknown
○ = female
□ = male

(A) Either the father or mother in the first generation is not carrying the disease gene.

(B) The family is definitely not suffering from a dominantly inherited genetic disorder.

(C) The healthy son in the second generation would have no reason to undergo genetic testing before having children.

(D) We can be sure that both of the affected son's daughters will have the disease.

Passage II

Interferometry is a highly sensitive method of measuring distances that are close to the wavelength of light. An interferometer (depicted in the following figure) uses a *partially reflecting mirror* (one that reflects half the light and allows the other half to continue through) to split a *coherent* light source, such as a laser beam.

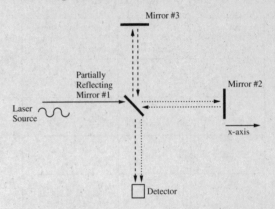

Coherent light consists of a single frequency. After the light is split, the two components will continue until they are reflected backwards by mirrors 2 and 3. After this reflection they proceed to the partially reflecting mirror again, and each path has a component (about a half) that proceeds to the light detector. The detector receives the sum of the two components of light, each with its own *phase* (shift of the wave with respect to a fixed spot).

Two experiments using an interferometer were conducted.

261

Experiment 1

In experiment 1, researchers moved mirror 2 backwards slowly, thereby lengthening the path that one component of the light travels and changing its phase. The light received by the detector was recorded at a number of positions. The following figure shows some of their findings along with the phase relationship of the waves that they deduced from these results.

Measured Light Intensity (milliwatts)	Mirror Position along x-axis (nanometers)	Phase relationship of the two different light components
1	0	
35	75	
57	150	
35	225	
1	300	

In Experiment 2, researchers used various light sources with different frequencies (number of waves per second). With each source, they moved mirror 2 backwards slowly, recording the light received by the light detector at each position.

Experiment 2

In Experiment 2, researchers used various light sources with different frequencies (number of waves per second). With each source, they moved mirror 2 backwards slowly, recording the light received by the light detector at each position. The results of this experiment are shown in the following figure.

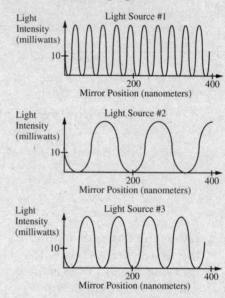

8.   The factor that was varied in Experiment 1 is

(F)   the angle of the partially reflecting mirror.

(G)   the wavelength (distance from one peak to the next) of one component of the light.

(H)   the frequency of one component of the light.

(J)   the phase of one component of the light.

9. Experiment 1 demonstrates that the lowest light intensity values occur in which situation?

   (A) Only when mirror 2 is at 0 nanometers.
   (B) When the two light components have different frequencies.
   (C) When the light component waves are 180% out of phase (troughs occur in one component where peaks occur in the other).
   (D) When the light component waves are in phase (troughs and peaks match).

10. In the figure, the asterisk on the graph 1 of light source 1 represents which of the following?

    (F) A mirror position at which the two light components are in phase
    (G) A mirror position where the light intensity is the same as at 300 nm in the figure
    (H) A mirror position at which the light source is at its highest frequency
    (J) A mirror position at which the entire light source is reflected by the partially reflecting mirror

11. Which of the following statements about the light sources in the figure is most accurate?

    (A) Light source 1 is always in phase.
    (B) Light source 2 has the longest wavelength.
    (C) Light source 3 has a shorter wavelength than light source 1.
    (D) The greatest light intensity was detected from light source 1.

12. In the figure, peak light detection should occur

    (F) when the distance from the laser to mirror 1 is the same as the distance from the laser to mirror 2.
    (G) when the distance from the laser to mirror 1 is the same as the distance from the laser to the light detector.
    (H) When the distance from mirror 1 to mirror 2 is the same as the distance from mirror 1 to mirror 3.
    (J) When the distance from the laser to mirror 3 is the same as the distance from mirror 1 to the light detector.

EXERCISE 5

> **Directions:** This test consists of two passages, each followed by several questions. Read each passage, select the correct answer for each question, and mark the oval representing the correct answer on your answer sheet. You may NOT use a calculator on this test.

Passage I

Scientists disagree over whether language is unique to humans. Part of the argument is what constitutes language as opposed to simple communication skills, which many animals are known to possess. However, most would agree that language is a system of words or symbols used in organized combinations and patterns to express thoughts and feelings.

In recent studies, Bonobo chimps have been taught to use a keyboard with symbols representing various words. The argument now is over whether the feats of these chimpanzees represent language.

Pro Argument

Researchers working with the chimpanzees argue that there is not an unbridgeable language divide between humans and the rest of the animals, but rather a gradation of linguistic skills in humans and some other animals. They point out that their chimpanzees have vocabularies of up to 200 words and that some have learned to understand and respond to complex sentences. Seventy percent of the time the animals can follow a command that they have not heard before as long as words they are familiar with are used.

Some chimpanzees have learned to string together two to three words, including noun and verb combinations. While the ability of the chimpanzees to string words together in complex ways does not compare to the ability in human children, the researchers argue that comprehension, where the chimpanzees' performance has been more impressive, is more difficult.

Con Argument

Some researchers feel that the Bonobo chimpanzees are simply well-trained or *conditioned* (taught to respond in a certain manner to a certain stimulus, for example, a dog taught to salivate at the sound of a bell because it associates the bell with food). They point out that most of the time the animals use the symbols in order to obtain food treats from the researchers.

Generally, opponents feel that language is uniquely human and developed after the family tree of chimpanzees and human ancestors split, several million years ago. They feel that the ability to acquire language is hard-wired into human brains. As proof, they point out the ease with which humans learn this task. Children move rapidly from two-word phrases to complex sentences with phrases embedded within phrases. Furthermore, there is evidence for universal rules of grammar that unite all human languages. Finally, they argue that the real test of language is not understanding strings of symbols but using such strings in complex ways.

1. The two arguments above differ in that
    (A) those in the pro group feel that the capacity for language is unique to humans and chimpanzees.
    (B) those in the con group feel that animals other than humans cannot communicate.
    (C) those in the pro group feel that the capacity for language exists in varying degrees in some other animals.
    (D) those in the pro group feel that all animals have the capacity to acquire language.

2. Scientists in the con group feel that the hallmark of language is

   (F) learning to comprehend complex sentences.
   (G) using symbols to obtain a reward.
   (H) learning to pair verbs with nouns.
   (J) generating complex sentences.

3. In early studies of chimpanzee language, claims were made that a type of chimp known as the common chimpanzee was taught to communicate with sign language. These studies were discredited when it was shown that the animals were simply moving their hands in complicated configurations to please their trainers and that the trainers were wishfully seeing words. How would proponents of the present studies defend themselves against similar attacks?

   (A) Point out that the keyboard symbol system eliminates the ambiguity of hand signals
   (B) Point out that different chimps were used in their experiments
   (C) Point out that it is controversial whether sign language is a true language
   (D) None of the above.

4. Most opponents of the chimpanzee language studies would agree that

   (F) the ability to acquire language developed in humans in the last few thousand years.
   (G) the ability to acquire language developed in human ancestors in the last few million years.
   (H) the ability to acquire language developed in human ancestors at least 5 million years ago.
   (J) the estimates of when human ancestors split from chimpanzees are too low.

5. In one experiment, one Bonobo chimp had access to a key that could be used to obtain a banana. Another chimp was shown where the key was hidden. This second chimp then used a keyboard to successfully communicate the whereabouts of the key to the first chimp. What objection might researchers in the con group raise against this experiment?

   (A) The monkey retrieving the key was acting in a conditioned manner.
   (B) The monkey retrieving the key was simply following a command, which is not as difficult as generating language.
   (C) The monkey who knew the whereabouts of the key had simply been trained to use the keyboard to indicate the key's whereabouts in order to obtain a food reward.
   (D) The first monkey may have been hitting the keyboard in a random manner in order to please its trainers.

6. Scientists in both the pro and the con group would agree that the Bonobo chimps described in the passage

   (F) are unable to produce complex combinations of symbols.

   (G) understand the meaning of a long sentence.

   (H) represent a middle point between animals and humans in linguistic ability.

   (J) are behaving in ways conditioned by food rewards.

Passage II

Seychelles warblers are insect-eating birds that usually lay one egg a year. Young warblers, particularly the females, often remain with their parents for several years helping them prepare and care for the next *hatchlings* (newly hatched birds), rather than mating themselves. A *breeding pair* (mating male and female) stays in the same territory from year to year.

Two experiments regarding the breeding behavior of the Seychelles warblers were performed.

Experiment 1

Biologists rated the territories of Seychelles warblers based on the density of insects available. They followed 100 breeding pairs in high- and low-quality territories over one breeding season, recording the breeding success (determined by the survival of a hatchling to leave the nest) for pairs with various numbers of helpers (previous offspring remaining with the mating pair). The results are seen in Table 7.7.

Table 7.7

Helper #	Reproductive Success (%)
High-Quality Territory	
0	86%
1	94%
2	95%
3	79%
Low-Quality Territory	
0	75%
1	65%
2	66%
3	64%

Experiment 2

The researchers hypothesized that Seychelles warblers might be able to adjust the *sex ratio* (number of males versus number of females) of their hatchlings depending on territory quality or number of helpers present. They again looked at 100 breeding pairs with various numbers of helpers in high- and low-quality territories and recorded the sex of their offspring for one breeding season. The results appear in Table 7.8.

Table 7.8

Helper #	Male Hatchlings (%)	Female Hatchlings (%)
High-Quality Territory		
0	15%	85%
1	13%	87%
2	78%	22%
3	76%	24%
Low-Quality Territory		
0	75%	25%
1	80%	20%
2	79%	21%
3	74%	26%

7. Which of the following statements about the design of Experiments 1 and 2 is most accurate?

   (A) Experiment 1 investigated breeding success, while Experiment 2 investigated sex ratios for hatchlings.

   (B) Experiment 1 followed warblers for several breeding seasons, while Experiment 2 followed them for only one season.

   (C) Experiment 1 looked at the effect of varying helper number, while Experiment 2 was concerned only with responses to variations in territory quality.

   (D) Experiment 1 followed breeding pairs, while Experiment 2 followed the helpers of breeding pairs.

8. Which of the following graphs best depicts the relationship between helper number and male hatchlings in a high-quality territory?

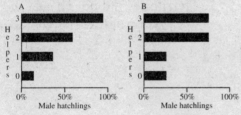

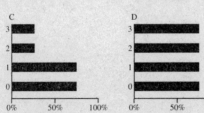

   (F) Graph A
   (G) Graph B
   (H) Graph C
   (J) Graph D

9. Based on the information in the passage, which of the following statements about reproductive success in Setchelles warblers is most accurate?

   (A) Reproductive success in low-quality territories goes up with helper number.

   (B) Reproductive success in high-quality territories goes down with helper number.

   (C) Reproductive success is dependent on helper number but not on territory quality.

   (D) Reproductive success in high-quality territories goes up if there are one or two helpers and down if there are more than two.

10. Which of the following statements about helper number is correct?

    (F) Helper number has no effect on the sex ratios of hatchlings.

    (G) Helper number has no effect on the sex ratio of hatchlings in low-quality territories.

    (H) Warblers with zero or one helper have a greater proportion of female hatchlings.

    (J) Warblers with zero or one helper have a greater proportion of male hatchlings.

11. Which of the following theories fits the data collected in Experiments 1 and 2?

(A) In high-quality areas, one or two helpers are useful, but more than two will put a drain on resources. Therefore breeding pairs with several helpers will adjust the sex-ratios of their hatchlings to favor males.

(B) Breeding pairs in low-quality territories need the most help in raising their hatchling and will adjust the sex-ratios of their hatchlings in an attempt to gain more males.

(C) All breeding pairs benefit from at least one helper and will adjust the sex ratios of their hatchlings to favor females if they have no helpers.

(D) Male hatchlings require more resources than female hatchlings, so only birds in high-quality territories with several helpers will adjust the sex ratios of their hatchlings to favor males.

12. Assuming that the hypothesis of the researchers conducting Experiment 2 is correct, which of the following results would you expect from experiments in which breeding pairs and their helpers were moved to different territories?

(F) Breeding pairs with several helpers moved from high-quality territories to low-quality territories switched to having more male hatchlings.

(G) Breeding pairs with one helper moved from high-quality territories to low-quality territories attempted to increase their helper number.

(H) Breeding pairs with one or two helpers moved from low- quality territories to high-quality territories switched to having mainly female hatchlings.

(J) Breeding pairs with two or more helpers moved from low-quality territories to high-quality territories did not change the sex ratios of their hatchlings.

Answer Key

Exercise 1	Exercise 2	Exercise 3	Exercise 4	Exercise 5
1. C	1. B	1. D	1. C	1. C
2. F	2. G	2. H	2. G	2. J
3. D	3. C	3. A	3. B	3. A
4. G	4. J	4. J	4. F	4. G
5. B	5. A	5. B	5. C	5. C
6. J	6. F	6. H	6. H	6. F
7. B	7. A	7. C	7. B	7. A
8. G	8. G	8. J	8. J	8. G
9. D	9. C	9. B	9. C	9. D
10. J	10. H	10. F	10. F	10. G
11. C	11. D	11. A	11. B	11. A
12. F	12. G	12. H	12. H	12. J

Explanatory Answers

EXERCISE 1

1. **The correct answer is (C).** You can literally "see" the answer to this question merely by glancing at the graphs in the figure. In Ocean Area 1, the two annual periods of phytoplankton abundance grew much longer as the decades passed until they merged into a single long period of abundance lasting half the year. By contrast, in Ocean Area 2, the two peaks got "thinner" as time passed, indicating a steady decrease in the phytoplankton population.

2. **The correct answer is (F).** Only choice (F) gives information consistent with the data in the graphs. Ocean Area 2 is north of latitude 62°; if the waters there got cooler, it would make sense that phytoplankton abundance would decrease (see the second sentence of the passage).

3. **The correct answer is (D).** Look at the shapes of the two peak periods in the graphs for the 1950s (roughly similar in both ocean areas). Both feature steep increases with equally steep declines, as described in choice (D).

4. **The correct answer is (G).** In both ocean areas, the most dramatic change by far appears between the 1960s and the 1970s.

5. **The correct answer is (B).** This answer would fit both the global warming hypothesis and the data shown in the graphs in several ways. First, the graphs for Ocean Area 1, showing an increase in phytoplankton, certainly fit the notion of global warming. Second, the idea that Arctic ice is melting would fit that idea as well. Finally, the abundance of fresh water newly-melted from ice appearing in the northern reaches of the Atlantic could help to explain why phytoplankton has actually declined around Iceland: the water temperature there has gone down slightly as a result of the melting ice.

6. **The correct answer is (J).** Of the months named, only August is a month with virtually no measurable phytoplankton in any of the four graphs for Ocean Area 1. Therefore, this is the least promising month for observing phytoplankton-eating whales.

7. **The correct answer is (B).** The answer can easily be found in the fourth column of Table 7.1: the efficiency of design 2 (in terms of lift to drag ratio) was 40:1, a higher ratio than any of the other wings.

8. **The correct answer is (G).** Since design 2 is most efficient according to all three experiments, it is the most desirable design.

9. **The correct answer is (D).** Ice building up on top of the wing would increase lift, since the higher the curved upper surface of the wing, the greater the difference between the speed of air moving under the wing and above it. It would also increase drag, as suggested by the third column of Table 7.1: notice how the wings with the higher upper surface also have greater drag. Finally, ice building up under the wing would decrease the speed of air moving under the wing and so reduce lift. Thus, all three effects would occur.

10. **The correct answer is (J).** In both experiments named here, conditions are the same: the same wing design is used, and the airspeed of 400 mph is the same. (Logically enough, the efficiency result is also the same: 40:1.)

11. **The correct answer is (C).** Remember that "efficiency" is the same as the lift to drag ratio. Since we note in Table 7.3 that efficiency decreases as speed increases, we can tell that drag must be increasing faster than lift.

12. **The correct answer is (F).** Consider again the results of Experiment 3 (Table 7.3). Wing design 2 is more efficient than design 1 at all of the lower speeds, but once a speed of 500 mph is reached, design 1 outperforms design 2. Thus, it appears that at high speeds a "flatter" wing design is more beneficial.

EXERCISE 2

1. **The correct answer is (B).** The Hydrothermal Synthesis Hypothesis states that the PAHs (the organic molecules in the meteorite) were formed by hydrothermal synthesis, while the Primitive Life Hypothesis says that they were formed by the decay of bacteria.

2. **The correct answer is (G).** See the fourth sentence of each of the sections describing the two hypothesis. In both cases, seeping water is described as the mechanism that allowed carbon to enter the rock.

3. **The correct answer is (C).** This is the only true statement that also names a difference between the proponents of the two theories. Choice (A) describes a belief that is actually shared by proponents of both theories, while choices (B) and (D) both make false statements about what the proponents of the theories state.

4. **The correct answer is (J).** If it's true that minerals can form "egg-shaped structures" like those found in the meteorite, this would strengthen the Hydrothermal Synthesis Hypothesis by providing an alternative explanation for these forms, which the Primitive Life proponents consider evidence of life on Mars.

5. **The correct answer is (A).** The fact that low concentrations of PAHs were found in glacial ice (mildly) strengthens the Primitive Life Hypothesis by tending to disprove the notion that the PAHs in the meteorite seeped in after the rock landed in Antarctica. The statement in choice (A) would further strengthen that hypothesis by suggesting that the PAHs in the meteorite were more probably produced by bacterial decay than by nonliving processes.

6. **The correct answer is (F).** This test would at least help to eliminate—or confirm—the possibility that the PAHs found in the meteorite actually appeared there as a result of contamination from glacial ice.

7. **The correct answer is (A).** Look at the line in the figure depicting the frequency response curve for filter type 1. It falls off dramatically in the middle of the graph, indicating that low frequencies (the left side of the graph) get through, while high frequencies (the right side of the graph) are suppressed.

8. **The correct answer is (G).** In both experiments, the input amplitude was fixed at 2.0 volts, and the frequency was varied (along the horizontal scale of each graph). However, the inductance was varied in Experiment 2 only.

9. **The correct answer is (C).** Look at the figure. As you go from right to left in the graph, the capacitance figures increase. And as you do so, the graphed lines form "steeper," "sharper," more "pointy" curves. This indicates that a narrower range of frequencies is being permitted through by the filter.

10. **The correct answer is (H).** To answer this question, you need to compare Experiments 2 and 3, along with the graphs showing the results. We're told that the inductance in Experiment 3 was held at .1 mH. This corresponds the third line from the left in the figure. Since that line most closely resembles the third line from the left in the figure—and since we're told that, for that line, the capacitance was set at .01μF—it makes sense to assume that the same capacitance must have been used to produce the matching line in Experiment 2.

11. **The correct answer is (D).** Look at the figure. Since filter type 3 "zeroes in" on waves of a very specific frequency, allowing only those waves to pass through, it makes sense that one might use this type of filter to tune in the fixed frequency of a particular radio station (while eliminating all other competing signals).

12. **The correct answer is (G).** As you can see from the figure, the lower the inductance, the higher the frequency at which the response curve attains its peak.

EXERCISE 3

1. **The correct answer is (D).** Since cigarettes and household sources produce the lion's share of individuals' benzene exposure (75% of the total), it seems clear that indoor rather than outdoor sources are responsible for the highest exposure levels.

2. **The correct answer is (H).** In Experiment 1, emission levels were compared to exposure levels; by contrast, in Experiment 2, only exposure levels were studied, while emission levels were ignored.

3. **The correct answer is (A).** The real anomaly in Table 7.6 is the high daytime "personal exposure" levels, which far exceed all the other numbers in the chart (which are all roughly comparable to one another, whether daytime or nighttime levels are considered). Of the four answer choices, (A) does the most to explain this result: if "moving about" stirs up a cloud of particles, this would explain why people have high personal exposure levels during the day, which subside at night (when they go to bed).

4. **The correct answer is (J).** Consider the second column of values in Table 7.6. The indoor exposure levels for the two experimental subjects shown there are quite close—98 and 95. If the third subject has an indoor exposure level of 75, that would be about 20% lower than either of the first two subjects. Now, if the personal exposure level varies by a similar amount, we'd expect the third subject to have a personal exposure level about 20% below 150—somewhere in the neighborhood of 120. Hence, choice (J).

5. **The correct answer is (B).** We see in Table 7.6 that the actual indoor levels of breathable particles are about $\frac{2}{3}$ the personal exposure levels as recorded by monitoring devices. If the same relationship holds true for trichloroethane, then the level of 14 would be reduced by the same amount, to about 9.

6. **The correct answer is (H).** Experiment 2 measured only personal exposure levels, while Experiment 3 monitored the indoor and outdoor environments as well. To test whether the results of Experiment 3 would be duplicated with the compounds tested in Experiment 2, indoor environmental monitors would have to be added to the experiment.

7. **The correct answer is (C).** The crucial data for answering this question are the dots in the figure, which show actual communities in which fadeouts occurred. Since all of the dots appear to the left of the 400,000 population mark, we can see that that represents the level at which fadeouts of the virus are no longer likely to occur.

8. **The correct answer is (J).** All of the statements given in choices (F), (G), and (H) are true, as seen in the figure. The infectious period predicts in model 1 is less concentrated than in model 2 (see how long it takes for the "tail" of Model 1 to disappear at the right end of the graph). Model 1 predicts that more people will be infected after 6 days than does model 2 (there's a severe drop-off in infected individuals just prior to day 6, according to model 2). And model 2 shows a much higher infection rate in the early days than does model 1 (its curve is at the very top of the scale).

9. **The correct answer is (B).** In the figure, notice how, at community sizes under 100,000 (the left end of the graph), the two curves of model 1 and model 2 track one another closely. (They are also both quite accurate as compared to the dots, which indicate actual experience of fadeouts.) Beyond the 100,000 population level, however, the curves gradually diverge more and more.

10. **The correct answer is (F).** Compare the height of the dots at the 300,000 population level with the vertical scale at the left hand side of the graph. The dots are below the one-per-year level; hence choice (F).

11. **The correct answer is (A).** To answer this question, you need to consider data from both graphs. Only choice (A) fits the information in both figures: model 2 does predict a larger number of infectious people early in the cycle, and it also predicts a smaller number of fadeouts than does model 1.

12. **The correct answer is (H).** Since the new model 3 predicts both a high number of infectious individuals in the early days (as does model 2), while also extending their recovery period over a long period of time (as does model 1), both factors would tend to reduce the number of predicted fadeouts. As a result, model 3 would probably be less accurate than model 2, erring on the side of predicting fewer fadeouts than would actually occur.

EXERCISE 4

1. **The correct answer is (C).** As the key explains, the disease gene is represented by a capital D, while the normal gene is represented by a lowercase d. Thus, a healthy carrier would be a person with one disease gene and one normal gene, or a Dd combination. There are five such people depicted in the third generation of the figure.

2. **The correct answer is (G).** Only people who have two disease genes—DD—will suffer from a disease transmitted as a recessive trait. In the figure, we see just two such people: a female (circle) in generation 2 and a female in generation 3.

3. **The correct answer is (B).** Since the father (the square) in generation 1 has one disease gene D, he must have had a parent from whom he inherited that gene.

4. **The correct answer is (F).** As with the father in generation 1 in the figure, we see that the disease gene D is present in the father of this family. And since this is a dominant trait, whichever parent of that individual transmitted the disease gene to him must also have suffered from the disease.

5. **The correct answer is (C).** Anyone in the figure with even a single disease gene D will suffer from the disease. There are seven such individuals in the chart: one in generation 1, three in generation 2, and three more in generation 3.

6. **The correct answer is (H).** Since the individual in question has genes labeled dd, she has two normal genes and does not need to worry about the possibility of transmitting a disease gene to her children.

7. **The correct answer is (B).** The disease cannot be a dominant trait. We can tell this because the male in generation 2 who is affected by the disease (center of chart) has two healthy parents. If he had inherited a dominant disease trait from one of his parents, one or both of them would be affected by the disease as well.

8. **The correct answer is (J).** By gradually moving mirror 2, the phase of the component of the light reflected by that mirror was gradually altered as well.

9. **The correct answer is (C).** Look at the first and last lines in the figure. In the last column, you can see that the phase relationship is 180° out of synch on both lines. And in the first column, the light intensity is at its lowest—just one milliwatt.

10. **The correct answer is (F).** Since, as the figure shows, light intensity is at its greatest when the two light components are in phase, then the "high points" in the figure (including the one marked with an asterisk) must represent such moments.

11. **The correct answer is (B).** In the graphs in the figure, wavelength is represented by the horizontal distance from peak to peak or from trough to trough of the wavy lines. Since this distance is greatest in the second graph, light source 2 must have the longest wavelength.

12. **The correct answer is (H).** As the figure suggests, maximum light intensity occurs when the two light components are perfectly in phase. The best way to ensure this happening would be for the distance traveled by the two light sources to be exactly equal, as is the case in the situation described in choice (H).

EXERCISE 5

1. **The correct answer is (C).** The first sentence of the Pro Argument section of the passage summarizes this point neatly.

2. **The correct answer is (J).** The last sentence of the Con Argument states this argument.

3. **The correct answer is (A).** As described in the question, the problem with the older studies was that the chimpanzees' trainers were interpreting hard-to-read hand movements as words out of a desire to believe that the animals were in fact using language. The best response to a similar charge against the current studies would be choice (A), since it would be difficult or impossible to misinterpret keyboarded messages.

4. **The correct answer is (G).** This can be inferred from the first sentence of the second paragraph of the Con Argument.

5. **The correct answer is (C).** The first paragraph of the Con Argument makes the point that animals conditioned through food rewards to use particular symbols are not really engaging in true language behavior. Choice (C) applies this argument to the example given in the question.

6. **The correct answer is (F).** Those who make the Pro Argument claim only that the chimps can use two- or three-word combinations; neither they nor their opponents say that chimps have learned to create complex strings of symbols.

7. **The correct answer is (A).** As the descriptions of the experiments make clear, Experiment 1 measured breeding success in relation to the quality of the birds' territory and the number of "helpers" the birds had, while Experiment 2 measured the ratio of male to female hatchlings against the same two variables.

8. **The correct answer is (G).** This graph accurately reflects the data found in the upper half of Table 7.8.

9. **The correct answer is (D).** As you can see in Table 7.7, the highest level of reproductive success in high-quality territories is found when one or two helpers are present (94 and 95% success); the rate falls off when a third helper appears (79%).

10. **The correct answer is (G).** Look at the lower half of Table 7.8. In low-quality territories, the percentage of male hatchlings varies in a narrow, seemingly random range (between 74 and 80%) as the number of helpers varies, suggesting that the number of helpers has no real effect on the sex ratio among hatchlings there.

11. **The correct answer is (A).** This is the only theory that even begins to explain the curious data in Table 7.8, in which all warbler pairs except low-helper pairs in high-quality territories produce more male offspring than female. If we assume that a shortage of resources favors male hatchlings (who perhaps have some different behavior from females; greater aggressiveness in pursuit of food, for example), then the pattern in Table 7.8 becomes at least understandable and consistent.

12. **The correct answer is (J).** Since all warbler pairs with two or more helpers have high male-to-female hatchling ratios—regardless of whether they are in high-quality or low-quality territories—one would expect no change in the ratio even with a change from one territory to another.

Part III

The Insider's ACT Sample Exam

Chapter 8

The Insider's ACT Sample Exam

INSTRUCTIONS

The following Insider's ACT Sample Exam will give you a chance to practice the skills and strategies you've learned throughout this book. As with all practice exercises, work under true testing conditions. Complete the entire exam in a single sitting. Eliminate distractions (TV, music) and clear away notes and reference materials. You may use a calculator only where indicated in the directions for a particular test.

Time each test separately with a stopwatch or kitchen timer, or have someone else time you. If you run out of time before answering all the questions, stop and draw a line under the last question you finished. Then go on to the next test. When you are done, score yourself based only on the questions you finished in the allotted time. Later, for practice purposes, you should answer the questions you were unable to complete in time.

Enter your responses on the answer sheets provided. The answer key and explanatory answers appear at the end of the test.

The Insider's ACT Sample Exam

Answer Sheet

Section 1

1. Ⓐ Ⓑ Ⓒ Ⓓ	16. Ⓕ Ⓖ Ⓗ Ⓙ	31. Ⓐ Ⓑ Ⓒ Ⓓ	46. Ⓕ Ⓖ Ⓗ Ⓙ	61. Ⓐ Ⓑ Ⓒ Ⓓ
2. Ⓕ Ⓖ Ⓗ Ⓙ	17. Ⓐ Ⓑ Ⓒ Ⓓ	32. Ⓕ Ⓖ Ⓗ Ⓙ	47. Ⓐ Ⓑ Ⓒ Ⓓ	62. Ⓕ Ⓖ Ⓗ Ⓙ
3. Ⓐ Ⓑ Ⓒ Ⓓ	18. Ⓕ Ⓖ Ⓗ Ⓙ	33. Ⓐ Ⓑ Ⓒ Ⓓ	48. Ⓕ Ⓖ Ⓗ Ⓙ	63. Ⓐ Ⓑ Ⓒ Ⓓ
4. Ⓕ Ⓖ Ⓗ Ⓙ	19. Ⓐ Ⓑ Ⓒ Ⓓ	34. Ⓕ Ⓖ Ⓗ Ⓙ	49. Ⓐ Ⓑ Ⓒ Ⓓ	64. Ⓕ Ⓖ Ⓗ Ⓙ
5. Ⓐ Ⓑ Ⓒ Ⓓ	20. Ⓕ Ⓖ Ⓗ Ⓙ	35. Ⓐ Ⓑ Ⓒ Ⓓ	50. Ⓕ Ⓖ Ⓗ Ⓙ	65. Ⓐ Ⓑ Ⓒ Ⓓ
6. Ⓕ Ⓖ Ⓗ Ⓙ	21. Ⓐ Ⓑ Ⓒ Ⓓ	36. Ⓕ Ⓖ Ⓗ Ⓙ	51. Ⓐ Ⓑ Ⓒ Ⓓ	66. Ⓕ Ⓖ Ⓗ Ⓙ
7. Ⓐ Ⓑ Ⓒ Ⓓ	22. Ⓕ Ⓖ Ⓗ Ⓙ	37. Ⓐ Ⓑ Ⓒ Ⓓ	52. Ⓕ Ⓖ Ⓗ Ⓙ	67. Ⓐ Ⓑ Ⓒ Ⓓ
8. Ⓕ Ⓖ Ⓗ Ⓙ	23. Ⓐ Ⓑ Ⓒ Ⓓ	38. Ⓕ Ⓖ Ⓗ Ⓙ	53. Ⓐ Ⓑ Ⓒ Ⓓ	68. Ⓕ Ⓖ Ⓗ Ⓙ
9. Ⓐ Ⓑ Ⓒ Ⓓ	24. Ⓕ Ⓖ Ⓗ Ⓙ	39. Ⓐ Ⓑ Ⓒ Ⓓ	54. Ⓕ Ⓖ Ⓗ Ⓙ	69. Ⓐ Ⓑ Ⓒ Ⓓ
10. Ⓕ Ⓖ Ⓗ Ⓙ	25. Ⓐ Ⓑ Ⓒ Ⓓ	40. Ⓕ Ⓖ Ⓗ Ⓙ	55. Ⓐ Ⓑ Ⓒ Ⓓ	70. Ⓕ Ⓖ Ⓗ Ⓙ
11. Ⓐ Ⓑ Ⓒ Ⓓ	26. Ⓕ Ⓖ Ⓗ Ⓙ	41. Ⓐ Ⓑ Ⓒ Ⓓ	56. Ⓕ Ⓖ Ⓗ Ⓙ	71. Ⓐ Ⓑ Ⓒ Ⓓ
12. Ⓕ Ⓖ Ⓗ Ⓙ	27. Ⓐ Ⓑ Ⓒ Ⓓ	42. Ⓕ Ⓖ Ⓗ Ⓙ	57. Ⓐ Ⓑ Ⓒ Ⓓ	72. Ⓕ Ⓖ Ⓗ Ⓙ
13. Ⓐ Ⓑ Ⓒ Ⓓ	28. Ⓕ Ⓖ Ⓗ Ⓙ	43. Ⓐ Ⓑ Ⓒ Ⓓ	58. Ⓕ Ⓖ Ⓗ Ⓙ	73. Ⓐ Ⓑ Ⓒ Ⓓ
14. Ⓕ Ⓖ Ⓗ Ⓙ	29. Ⓐ Ⓑ Ⓒ Ⓓ	44. Ⓕ Ⓖ Ⓗ Ⓙ	59. Ⓐ Ⓑ Ⓒ Ⓓ	74. Ⓕ Ⓖ Ⓗ Ⓙ
15. Ⓐ Ⓑ Ⓒ Ⓓ	30. Ⓕ Ⓖ Ⓗ Ⓙ	45. Ⓐ Ⓑ Ⓒ Ⓓ	60. Ⓕ Ⓖ Ⓗ Ⓙ	75. Ⓐ Ⓑ Ⓒ Ⓓ

Section 2

1. Ⓐ Ⓑ Ⓒ Ⓓ Ⓔ	16. Ⓕ Ⓖ Ⓗ Ⓙ Ⓚ	31. Ⓐ Ⓑ Ⓒ Ⓓ Ⓔ	46. Ⓕ Ⓖ Ⓗ Ⓙ Ⓚ
2. Ⓕ Ⓖ Ⓗ Ⓙ Ⓚ	17. Ⓐ Ⓑ Ⓒ Ⓓ Ⓔ	32. Ⓕ Ⓖ Ⓗ Ⓙ Ⓚ	47. Ⓐ Ⓑ Ⓒ Ⓓ Ⓔ
3. Ⓐ Ⓑ Ⓒ Ⓓ Ⓔ	18. Ⓕ Ⓖ Ⓗ Ⓙ Ⓚ	33. Ⓐ Ⓑ Ⓒ Ⓓ Ⓔ	48. Ⓕ Ⓖ Ⓗ Ⓙ Ⓚ
4. Ⓕ Ⓖ Ⓗ Ⓙ Ⓚ	19. Ⓐ Ⓑ Ⓒ Ⓓ Ⓔ	34. Ⓕ Ⓖ Ⓗ Ⓙ Ⓚ	49. Ⓐ Ⓑ Ⓒ Ⓓ Ⓔ
5. Ⓐ Ⓑ Ⓒ Ⓓ Ⓔ	20. Ⓕ Ⓖ Ⓗ Ⓙ Ⓚ	35. Ⓐ Ⓑ Ⓒ Ⓓ Ⓔ	50. Ⓕ Ⓖ Ⓗ Ⓙ Ⓚ
6. Ⓕ Ⓖ Ⓗ Ⓙ Ⓚ	21. Ⓐ Ⓑ Ⓒ Ⓓ Ⓔ	36. Ⓕ Ⓖ Ⓗ Ⓙ Ⓚ	51. Ⓐ Ⓑ Ⓒ Ⓓ Ⓔ
7. Ⓐ Ⓑ Ⓒ Ⓓ Ⓔ	22. Ⓕ Ⓖ Ⓗ Ⓙ Ⓚ	37. Ⓐ Ⓑ Ⓒ Ⓓ Ⓔ	52. Ⓕ Ⓖ Ⓗ Ⓙ Ⓚ
8. Ⓕ Ⓖ Ⓗ Ⓙ Ⓚ	23. Ⓐ Ⓑ Ⓒ Ⓓ Ⓔ	38. Ⓕ Ⓖ Ⓗ Ⓙ Ⓚ	53. Ⓐ Ⓑ Ⓒ Ⓓ Ⓔ
9. Ⓐ Ⓑ Ⓒ Ⓓ Ⓔ	24. Ⓕ Ⓖ Ⓗ Ⓙ Ⓚ	39. Ⓐ Ⓑ Ⓒ Ⓓ Ⓔ	54. Ⓕ Ⓖ Ⓗ Ⓙ Ⓚ
10. Ⓕ Ⓖ Ⓗ Ⓙ Ⓚ	25. Ⓐ Ⓑ Ⓒ Ⓓ Ⓔ	40. Ⓕ Ⓖ Ⓗ Ⓙ Ⓚ	55. Ⓐ Ⓑ Ⓒ Ⓓ Ⓔ
11. Ⓐ Ⓑ Ⓒ Ⓓ Ⓔ	26. Ⓕ Ⓖ Ⓗ Ⓙ Ⓚ	41. Ⓐ Ⓑ Ⓒ Ⓓ Ⓔ	56. Ⓕ Ⓖ Ⓗ Ⓙ Ⓚ
12. Ⓕ Ⓖ Ⓗ Ⓙ Ⓚ	27. Ⓐ Ⓑ Ⓒ Ⓓ Ⓔ	42. Ⓕ Ⓖ Ⓗ Ⓙ Ⓚ	57. Ⓐ Ⓑ Ⓒ Ⓓ Ⓔ
13. Ⓐ Ⓑ Ⓒ Ⓓ Ⓔ	28. Ⓕ Ⓖ Ⓗ Ⓙ Ⓚ	43. Ⓐ Ⓑ Ⓒ Ⓓ Ⓔ	58. Ⓕ Ⓖ Ⓗ Ⓙ Ⓚ
14. Ⓕ Ⓖ Ⓗ Ⓙ Ⓚ	29. Ⓐ Ⓑ Ⓒ Ⓓ Ⓔ	44. Ⓕ Ⓖ Ⓗ Ⓙ Ⓚ	59. Ⓐ Ⓑ Ⓒ Ⓓ Ⓔ
15. Ⓐ Ⓑ Ⓒ Ⓓ Ⓔ	30. Ⓕ Ⓖ Ⓗ Ⓙ Ⓚ	45. Ⓐ Ⓑ Ⓒ Ⓓ Ⓔ	60. Ⓕ Ⓖ Ⓗ Ⓙ Ⓚ

Section 3

1. Ⓐ Ⓑ Ⓒ Ⓓ	11. Ⓐ Ⓑ Ⓒ Ⓓ	21. Ⓐ Ⓑ Ⓒ Ⓓ	31. Ⓐ Ⓑ Ⓒ Ⓓ
2. Ⓕ Ⓖ Ⓗ Ⓙ	12. Ⓕ Ⓖ Ⓗ Ⓙ	22. Ⓕ Ⓖ Ⓗ Ⓙ	32. Ⓕ Ⓖ Ⓗ Ⓙ
3. Ⓐ Ⓑ Ⓒ Ⓓ	13. Ⓐ Ⓑ Ⓒ Ⓓ	23. Ⓐ Ⓑ Ⓒ Ⓓ	33. Ⓐ Ⓑ Ⓒ Ⓓ
4. Ⓕ Ⓖ Ⓗ Ⓙ	14. Ⓕ Ⓖ Ⓗ Ⓙ	24. Ⓕ Ⓖ Ⓗ Ⓙ	34. Ⓕ Ⓖ Ⓗ Ⓙ
5. Ⓐ Ⓑ Ⓒ Ⓓ	15. Ⓐ Ⓑ Ⓒ Ⓓ	25. Ⓐ Ⓑ Ⓒ Ⓓ	35. Ⓐ Ⓑ Ⓒ Ⓓ
6. Ⓕ Ⓖ Ⓗ Ⓙ	16. Ⓕ Ⓖ Ⓗ Ⓙ	26. Ⓕ Ⓖ Ⓗ Ⓙ	36. Ⓕ Ⓖ Ⓗ Ⓙ
7. Ⓐ Ⓑ Ⓒ Ⓓ	17. Ⓐ Ⓑ Ⓒ Ⓓ	27. Ⓐ Ⓑ Ⓒ Ⓓ	37. Ⓐ Ⓑ Ⓒ Ⓓ
8. Ⓕ Ⓖ Ⓗ Ⓙ	18. Ⓕ Ⓖ Ⓗ Ⓙ	28. Ⓕ Ⓖ Ⓗ Ⓙ	38. Ⓕ Ⓖ Ⓗ Ⓙ
9. Ⓐ Ⓑ Ⓒ Ⓓ	19. Ⓐ Ⓑ Ⓒ Ⓓ	29. Ⓐ Ⓑ Ⓒ Ⓓ	39. Ⓐ Ⓑ Ⓒ Ⓓ
10. Ⓕ Ⓖ Ⓗ Ⓙ	20. Ⓕ Ⓖ Ⓗ Ⓙ	30. Ⓕ Ⓖ Ⓗ Ⓙ	40. Ⓕ Ⓖ Ⓗ Ⓙ

Section 4

1. Ⓐ Ⓑ Ⓒ Ⓓ	11. Ⓐ Ⓑ Ⓒ Ⓓ	21. Ⓐ Ⓑ Ⓒ Ⓓ	31. Ⓐ Ⓑ Ⓒ Ⓓ
2. Ⓕ Ⓖ Ⓗ Ⓙ	12. Ⓕ Ⓖ Ⓗ Ⓙ	22. Ⓕ Ⓖ Ⓗ Ⓙ	32. Ⓕ Ⓖ Ⓗ Ⓙ
3. Ⓐ Ⓑ Ⓒ Ⓓ	13. Ⓐ Ⓑ Ⓒ Ⓓ	23. Ⓐ Ⓑ Ⓒ Ⓓ	33. Ⓐ Ⓑ Ⓒ Ⓓ
4. Ⓕ Ⓖ Ⓗ Ⓙ	14. Ⓕ Ⓖ Ⓗ Ⓙ	24. Ⓕ Ⓖ Ⓗ Ⓙ	34. Ⓕ Ⓖ Ⓗ Ⓙ
5. Ⓐ Ⓑ Ⓒ Ⓓ	15. Ⓐ Ⓑ Ⓒ Ⓓ	25. Ⓐ Ⓑ Ⓒ Ⓓ	35. Ⓐ Ⓑ Ⓒ Ⓓ
6. Ⓕ Ⓖ Ⓗ Ⓙ	16. Ⓕ Ⓖ Ⓗ Ⓙ	26. Ⓕ Ⓖ Ⓗ Ⓙ	36. Ⓕ Ⓖ Ⓗ Ⓙ
7. Ⓐ Ⓑ Ⓒ Ⓓ	17. Ⓐ Ⓑ Ⓒ Ⓓ	27. Ⓐ Ⓑ Ⓒ Ⓓ	37. Ⓐ Ⓑ Ⓒ Ⓓ
8. Ⓕ Ⓖ Ⓗ Ⓙ	18. Ⓕ Ⓖ Ⓗ Ⓙ	28. Ⓕ Ⓖ Ⓗ Ⓙ	38. Ⓕ Ⓖ Ⓗ Ⓙ
9. Ⓐ Ⓑ Ⓒ Ⓓ	19. Ⓐ Ⓑ Ⓒ Ⓓ	29. Ⓐ Ⓑ Ⓒ Ⓓ	39. Ⓐ Ⓑ Ⓒ Ⓓ
10. Ⓕ Ⓖ Ⓗ Ⓙ	20. Ⓕ Ⓖ Ⓗ Ⓙ	30. Ⓕ Ⓖ Ⓗ Ⓙ	40. Ⓕ Ⓖ Ⓗ Ⓙ

SECTION 1

ENGLISH

75 Questions

Time—45 Minutes

> **Directions:** This test consists of five passages in which particular words or phrases are underlined and numbered. Alongside the passage, you will see alternative words and phrases that could be substituted for the underlined part. You must select the alternative that expresses the idea most clearly and correctly or that best fits the style and tone of the entire passage. If the original version is best, select "No Change."
>
> The test also includes questions about entire paragraphs and the passage as a whole. These questions are identified by a number in a box.
>
> After you select the correct answer for each question, mark the oval representing the correct answer on your answer sheet.

Passage I

An Oboist's Quest

[1]

I started playing the oboe because I've heard it
                                                1
was a challenging instrument. That was

four years ago and, I've enjoyed learning to play
                       2
the oboe as much as I expected. However, it was

not until recently that I realized what an oboist's

real challenge is: finding good oboe reeds.

[2]

Though the reed is a small part of the

instrument, they largely determine the quality
                      3
of the oboe's sound. Professional oboists make

their own reeds, so students like me must buy
                   4

reeds either from their teachers or from

mail-order companies.

[3]

My troubles began when my teacher stopped

making reeds. Sending all of her students on a
                5
wild goose chase for the perfect reed. The

problem is that there is no such thing as a

perfect reed, though oboists like to daydream

about it. There is also no such thing as a perfect

reed supplier. Reed makers are much in de-

mand, and the reeds are often very expensive—

GO ON TO THE NEXT PAGE

$15 to $20 each for something which, in my
opinion, is only worth $7.
      6

[4]

Also, the reed makers tend to take their time in
sending reeds to you, I usually have to wait
           7
three to six weeks after they've received my
check in the mail. This wouldn't be a problem if
I always ordered my reeds in advance of the
time when I need them, but oboe reeds are
      8
temperamental and often crack or break without warning. Thus, I need to have several
back-up reeds available at all times.

[5]

I first tried buying reeds from a reed maker in
Massachusetts. They were pretty good at first,
but they became progressively worse
and lower and lower in quality the longer I
          9
bought them from him. It got to the point where
none of the reeds he supplied worked, so I had
to move on.

[6]

My next source was a company in California.
However, they sounded like ducks quacking, so I
    10
dropped them from my list. Desperate, an
oboist friend of my parents was the next
          11
person I called. She helped me fix a few
  11

salvageable reeds I owned, and soon I had
several that played in tune *and* had good tone. It
seemed my reed troubles were over.
However, within two weeks, those precious
         12
reeds were all played out, and I needed more.

[7]

Recently, a friend suggested a reed maker from
New York City whose reeds, she said, were
rather good. I called him up immediate, and he
        13
asked me questions about my playing so that he
could cater to my oboe needs. He promised to
send out a supply of reeds within a week.
Imagine my disappointment when the reeds he
sent turned out to be poorly made, with
unstable tones and a thin, unpleasant sound. My
search for the perfect reed continues. It may
never come to an end until I learn to make reeds
myself.

1. (A) NO CHANGE
   (B) I'd have heard
   (C) I've been hearing
   (D) I'd heard

2. (F) NO CHANGE
   (G) four years ago, and I've
   (H) four years ago; and I've
   (J) four years ago. And, I've

3. (A) NO CHANGE
   (B) they determine, in large part,
   (C) it largely determines
   (D) it determines largely

4. (F) NO CHANGE
   (G) reeds. So
   (H) reeds; although
   (J) reeds, but

5. (A) NO CHANGE
   (B) reeds. Thus sending
   (C) reeds, she sent
   (D) reeds, sending

6. At this point, the writer wants to provide readers with a specific detail to substantiate her claim about the expense of oboe reeds. Which alternative does that best?
   (F) NO CHANGE
   (G) something that I, a student with limited funds to spend, am highly concerned about.
   (H) with an additional $3 to $5 charged for shipping and handling on every order sent.
   (J) although professional oboe players could probably afford to pay a relatively high price for their reeds.

7. (A) NO CHANGE
   (B) you, usually I
   (C) you; I usually
   (D) one: I usually

8. (F) NO CHANGE
   (G) in advance of when I need them
   (H) before when they are needed
   (J) ahead of time

9. (A) NO CHANGE
   (B) and lower in quality
   (C) in quality
   (D) OMIT the underlined portion.

10. (F) NO CHANGE
    (G) their reeds
    (H) the reeds of this company
    (J) this company

11. (A) NO CHANGE
    (B) Desperate, my parents called an oboist friend of theirs.
    (C) Desperate, I called an oboist friend of my parents.
    (D) An oboist friend of my parents was the next person I called, desperate.

12. (F) NO CHANGE
    (G) However, within two weeks; those
    (H) Within two weeks however; those
    (J) However, within two weeks those

13. (A) NO CHANGE
    (B) (Place before *I*)
    (C) (Place after *I*)
    (D) (Leave where it is now) immediately

GO ON TO THE NEXT PAGE

Items 14 and 15 pose questions about the essay as a whole.

14. The writer wishes to include the following sentence in the essay:

    Oboe reeds are made from two pieces of cane tied together with string and supported by a cylindrical piece of metal with some cork wrapped around at the base.

    That sentence will fit most smoothly and logically into Paragraph

    (F)   2, before the first sentence.
    (G)   2, after the last sentence.
    (H)   3, after the last sentence.
    (J)   4, before the first sentence.

15. Suppose the writer were to eliminate Paragraph 4. This omission would cause the essay as a whole to lose primarily

    (A)   a relevant anecdote about the unreliability of many makers of oboe reeds.
    (B)   irrelevant details about the technicalities of ordering oboe reeds through the mail.
    (C)   relevant details about some of the difficulties oboists encounter in maintaining an adequate supply of reeds.
    (D)   an irrelevant anecdote about the slowness of mail-order oboe reed suppliers.

Passage II

The Viking Mission—In Search of Life

[1]

A major goal of the Viking spacecraft missions of the late 1980s were to determine whether the
_____
16
soil of Mars is dead, like the soil of the moon, or teeming with microscopic life, like the soils of Earth. Soil samples brought into the Viking lander were sent to three separate biological laboratories to be tested in different ways for the presence of living things indicating the
_____
17
existence of life.
_____
17

[2]

18 First, it was assumed that life on Mars would be like life on Earth; which is based on
_____
19
the element carbon and thrives by chemically transforming carbon compounds. Second, on Earth, where there are large lifeforms (like human beings and pine trees), there are also small ones (like bacteria), and the small ones are far more abundant, thousands or millions of
_____
20
them being in every gram of soil. To have the
_____
20
best possible chance of detecting life, an instrument should look for the most abundant kind of life.

[3]

21 Specifically, the three laboratories in the lander were designed to warm and nourish any life in the Martian soil and to detect with sensitive instruments the chemical activity of the organisms.
_____
22

[4]   .

One characteristic of earthly plants is transforming carbon dioxide in the air into the
_____
23
compounds that make them up. Accordingly,
_____
24
one Viking experiment, called the carbon assimilation test, added radioactive carbon dioxide to the atmosphere above the soil sample. The sample was then flooded with simulated Martian sunlight. 25 If any Martian lifeforms converted the carbon dioxide into other compounds, the compounds could be detected by their radioactivity.

[5]

(1) Living organisms on Earth give off gases. (2) A second experiment on each lander, the gas exchange test, was designed to detect this kind of activity. (3) Plants give off oxygen, animals give off carbon dioxide, and water is exhaled by
_____
26
both. (4) Nutrients and water were added to the
_____
26
soil, and the chemical composition of the gas above the soil was continuously analyzed for changes that might indicate life. 27

[6]

Finally, a third experiment on each lander was
_____
28
based on the fact that earthly animals consume organic compounds and give off carbon dioxide. The labeled release test added a variety of radioactive nutrients to the soil and then waited to see whether any radioactive carbon dioxide would be given off.

[7]

Much to the disappointment of scientists, the Viking experiments uncovered no clear indications of Martian lifeforms. However, the experience itself of designing and implementing the
_____
29
Viking experiments was useful. It has helped scientists to clarify their understanding of terrestrial life and formulate new ideas about life beyond Earth, which may be useful as further planetary explorations are conducted in the future.

GO ON TO THE NEXT PAGE

16. (F)   NO CHANGE
    (G)   was to determine
    (H)   were determining
    (J)   was the determination of

17. (A)   NO CHANGE
    (B)   beings that indicated the
          existence of life.
    (C)   creatures that contained life.
    (D)   life.

18. Which of the following sentences, if
    added here, would most clearly and
    accurately indicate the topic of
    Paragraph 2?
    (F)   This was a challenging scientific
          assignment.
    (G)   The tests were based on two
          assumptions.
    (H)   The Viking scientists were
          uncertain how to proceed.
    (J)   There were several main objec-
          tives being pursued in these
          experiments.

19. (A)   NO CHANGE
    (B)   Earth that is
    (C)   Earth, which is
    (D)   Earth—

20. (F)   NO CHANGE
    (G)   with thousands or millions of
          them
    (H)   containing thousands or millions
    (J)   numbering in thousands or
          millions

21. Which of the following sentences, if
    added here, would best provide a
    smooth transition between the
    previous paragraph and this one?
    (A)   The Viking instruments were
          designed, therefore, to detect
          carbon-based Martian microbes
          or similar creatures living in the
          soil.
    (B)   Thus, the Viking scientists had
          first to determine what kind of
          life they would seek before
          designing experiments to
          uncover it.
    (C)   The Viking mission, then, was as
          much a matter of biological
          experimentation as of interplan-
          etary exploration.
    (D)   The possibility of life on other
          planets has fascinated human-
          kind for as long as people have
          stared in wonder at the beauty
          and mystery of the nighttime
          sky.

22. (F)   NO CHANGE
    (G)   of the organism's.
    (H)   of the organisms'.
    (J)   the organisms engaged in.

23. (A)   NO CHANGE
    (B)   the transformation of
    (C)   to transform
    (D)   that they transform

24. At this point, the writer would like to
    provide specific details about the plant
    structures created out of carbon diox-
    ide. Which alternative does that best?
    (F)   NO CHANGE
    (G)   constitute the plants' physical
          substance.
    (H)   make up their roots, branches,
          and leaves.
    (J)   make up the various parts of the
          plants themselves.

25. At this point, the writer is considering the addition of the following sentence:

    The Martian day is 24.6 hours long, almost the same length as the day here on Earth.

    Would this be a logical and relevant addition to the essay?

    (A) Yes, because it provides an interesting fact about Mars, which is the planet being discussed in the essay.
    (B) Yes, because the length of the Martian day affects the amount of sunlight to which possible Martian lifeforms are exposed.
    (C) No, because the length of the Martian day is basically irrelevant to the topic of the Viking experiments.
    (D) No, because the sunlight mentioned in the previous sentence is simulated rather than real Martian sunlight.

26. (F) NO CHANGE
    (G) and both exhale water.
    (H) with both exhaling water.
    (J) from both water is exhaled.

27. Which of the following sequences of sentences makes this paragraph most logical?

    (A) NO CHANGE
    (B) 1, 3, 2, 4
    (C) 1, 4, 3, 2
    (D) 2, 4, 1, 3

28. (F) NO CHANGE
    (G) (Do NOT begin new paragraph) Finally, a
    (H) (Do NOT begin new paragraph) A
    (J) (Begin new paragraph) Nevertheless, a

29. (A) NO CHANGE
    (B) (Place after *implementing*)
    (C) (Place after *was*)
    (D) (Place after *useful*)

Item 30 poses a question about the essay as a whole.

30. Suppose the writer had been assigned to write a brief essay about the results of any single scientific research project of the last twenty years. Would this essay successfully fulfill the assignment?

    (F) Yes, because the essay explains that the Viking experiments failed to detect any life in the Martian soil.
    (G) Yes, because the essay describes in detail the nature of the experiments conducted by the Viking researchers.
    (H) No, because the Viking experiments could be considered a series of projects rather than a single project.
    (J) No, because almost the entire essay is devoted to the plans for the Viking missions rather than their results.

GO ON TO THE NEXT PAGE

Passage III

The Not-So-Good Old Days

[1]

Many of us look back at the turn of the century through a haze of nostalgia. Perhaps it's because we've begun to feel overwhelmed by
                              31
modern technology—computers, jets, fax machines—and long for an era we like to think of
                                           32
as having been a simpler time. Perhaps its
 32   33
images of glowing coal stoves, the gentle aura of gaslight, the sound of a horse and buggy on the pavement, the simple pleasures of the "good old summertime," that make that era seem so appealing.

[2]

34 Although in our imaginations we see the "Gilded Age" as a more genteel time, the reality was less pleasant. In many respects, things were really not as good as we imagine they were in "the good old days."

[3]

(1) Take, for example, those glowing coal stoves. (2) By the 1880s, those who could afford $2,000 to $4,000—a very considerable sum for
                                            35
the day—might install central heating. (3) But
 35
early radiators, though cleaner than coal, filled

their homes with the constant noises of "water hammer" and hissing. (4) While it provided
                                              36
relatively little heat, coal-burning stoves were
 36
all too powerful at using up the oxygen in a room and replacing it with enough soot and dust to make a house almost uninhabitable. 37

[4]

Then there were those horses in the street. We think nostalgically of the days before automobiles befouled our air, but horses and buggies
                      38
produced a different kind of pollution. The stench was overwhelming, and there was so much manure in the streets that some observers voiced fears that America's cities would disappear like ancient Pompeii—but buried under something other than volcanic ash. 39

[5]

Even worse, perhaps, were those "good old summertimes." There was, of course, no air conditioning, and in the cities, at least, summers were hotter than they are today, because of the
                                               40
shorter buildings then. Contemporary clothing,
 40
too, added to the problem—the garments worn
                                            41
by the average person during the 1890s were
 41
considerably more bulky than those worn
                            41
today.

[6]

Much worse could be cited—the condition of the poor, the status of women and children, <u>medical science was undeveloped; the list is</u> ₄₂ almost endless. <u>It's probably true that the pace</u> ₄₃ of life was slower <u>and, at least in that respect,</u> ₄₄ <u>perhaps more congenial to human sensibilities a</u> ₄₄ hundred years ago, the truth is that the "good old days" really weren't so good after all.

31. (A) NO CHANGE
    (B) we began
    (C) we've began
    (D) we begun

32. (F) NO CHANGE
    (G) what we think of as
    (H) a return to a period that we want to consider
    (J) a part of history that we regard as being

33. (A) NO CHANGE
    (B) it's
    (C) it may be
    (D) there are

34. Which of the alternatives best introduces the central theme of the essay and provides an appropriate transition between the first and second paragraphs?
    (F) Yet modern technology has been more of a boon than a bane.
    (G) None of us, however, have actually experienced life as it was at the turn of the century.
    (H) Admittedly, life in today's world has both positive and negative aspects.
    (J) But was that world really as idyllic as we think?

35. (A) NO CHANGE
    (B) —a huge chunk of change for those days—
    (C) —which would have been a lot of money then—
    (D) OMIT the underlined portion.

36. (F) NO CHANGE
    (G) Little heat though they gave,
    (H) Although they provided relatively little heat,
    (J) While relatively little heat was provided,

37. Which of the following provides the most logical ordering of the sentences in Paragraph 3?
    (A) NO CHANGE
    (B) 1, 3, 4, 2
    (C) 1, 4, 2, 3
    (D) 2, 3, 1, 4

38. (F) NO CHANGE
    (G) one's
    (H) their
    (J) this

GO ON TO THE NEXT PAGE

39. At this point, the writer is considering the addition of the following sentence:

> At the turn of the century in New York City, for example, there were 150,000 horses, each of which dropped between twenty and twenty-five pounds of manure every day, which was then spread around by the buggies' wheels.

Would this be a logical and relevant addition to the essay?

(A) Yes, because it provides details concerning the pollution created by horses at the turn of the century.

(B) Yes, because horses remain popular as pets and companions to this day.

(C) No, because it refers only to New York City, whereas the main theme of the essay is more widely applicable.

(D) No, because it fails to draw a detailed comparison to the pollution created today by automobiles.

40. (F) NO CHANGE

(G) because lower buildings did not shield the streets from the sun as well as today's skyscrapers.

(H) since the buildings in most cities at the time weren't as tall as they are now.

(J) due to the relatively low height of most buildings then.

41. Which of the alternatives most effectively supports the assertion made earlier in the sentence about the discomforts of summer clothing at the turn of the century?

(A) NO CHANGE

(B) most people at the time wore heavy clothes, even during the summer, despite the fact that it only made them feel hotter.

(C) heavy suits, long underwear, vests for men, and voluminous dresses with multiple undergarments and girdles for women.

(D) unlike today, when many people wear shorts, open-toed shoes, and thin, airy shirts or blouses on the hottest summer days.

42. (F) NO CHANGE

(G) the underdevelopment of the science of medicine,

(H) the undeveloped state of medical science;

(J) the fact that medical science had not been developed—

43. (A) NO CHANGE

(B) It may be

(C) Since it is

(D) While it's

44. (F) NO CHANGE

(G) and at least, in that respect perhaps

(H) and at least in that respect, perhaps

(J) and at least—in that respect— perhaps

Item 45 poses a question about the essay as a whole.

45. The writer wishes to include the following sentence in the essay:

> The heat waves were not just unpleasant, they could be deadly: during the summer of 1896, three thousand people and two thousand horses died of the heat in New York City alone.

That sentence will fit most smoothly and logically into Paragraph

(A)   3, after the last sentence.
(B)   5, after the first sentence.
(C)   5, after the last sentence.
(D)   6, before the first sentence.

Passage IV

Gloria Steinem, Feminist Heroine

[1]

Gloria Steinem is a political writer and activist, <u>mostly famous</u> for her work as a leading figure
46
in the women's rights movement. Growing up with the lasting effects of the Great Depression of the 1930s on her once-wealthy family, Steinem became an independent young woman, working her way through elite Smith College with minimal aid from the school or her family. While in college, she became engaged, but her fiancé called off the <u>wedding; because his</u>
47
parents felt that Steinem was not wealthy enough to marry into their family. It was one of Steinem's first encounters with the social and economic aspects of relations between the sexes.

[2]

After this upsetting breakup, Steinem decided to take refuge in India, making plans to attend the universities of Delhi and Calcutta. However, while on her way to India, she learned that she was pregnant with her fiancé's child. <u>This is the
48
fiancé who had previously left her.</u> Feeling that
48
becoming a mother was an impossible option at that time, Steinem had an abortion in England. <u>Where the procedure was considerably
49
easier and safer</u> than in the United States at that
50
time.

[3]

<u>Soon</u> Steinem was back in America, finding
51
steady work as a writer was quite difficult, especially for a young woman. However, she was given the opportunity to write one of her most enduring articles while freelancing for the now-defunct magazine *Show*. Steinem worked undercover as a scantily-clad "bunny" hostess

GO ON TO THE NEXT PAGE

in a Playboy club. And wrote a groundbreaking
   _____   _____
        52   53
first-person account of the joyless lives the

bunnies led.

[4]

54 She soon enjoyed regular assignments

writing for such magazines like *Vogue*. However,
         _____
                55
she was limited to writing about "women's

topics" such as hairstyles and weight loss.
       _____
                     56
Eventually, Steinem landed a job with *New York*

magazine, writing about politics. She also took

part in many liberal causes and joined the

Redstockings, a feminist group.

[5]

In 1963, Steinem attended a rally in support of

abortion rights, and this issue; she says, helped
_____
                     57
her make the transition to feminism. Abortion
                                      _____
                                         58
remains one of the most controversial topics in
_____
                     58
American politics. Steinem also supported causes
_____
        58
such as the unionization of Chicano farm

workers and peace in Vietnam. Steinem soon
                                _____
                                     59
stepped to the forefront of the women's rights
_____
                     59
movement, a tireless worker and advocate. In
_____
                     59
1972, she co-founded the most successful

feminist publication, *Ms*. Although the magazine

was popular and influential, it lost money due to

lack of advertising, and within fifteen years, the

magazine was sold.

[6]

Steinem was now able to concentrate on her

true love—writing. She wrote many famous

articles, the list of which included "Marilyn,"
         _____
                    60
about the actress Marilyn Monroe, and pub-

lished several books, including a psychological

memoir called *Revolution from Within*, a collec-

tion of essays titled *Beyond Words*, and, most

recently, her autobiography.

46. (F)   NO CHANGE
    (G)   most famous
    (H)   more famous
    (J)   famousest

47. (A)   NO CHANGE
    (B)   wedding because his
    (C)   wedding because, his
    (D)   wedding, because, his

48. (F)   NO CHANGE
    (G)   (Her fiance had already left her.)
    (H)   He had left Steinem, as previ-
          ously mentioned.
    (J)   OMIT the underlined portion.

49. (A)   NO CHANGE
    (B)   England, there
    (C)   England. In England,
    (D)   England, where

50. (F)   NO CHANGE
    (G)   than
    (H)   as in
    (J)   by comparison to

51. (A) NO CHANGE
    (B) (Do NOT begin new paragraph)
         Now that
    (C) (Begin new paragraph) Once
    (D) (Begin new paragraph) Being
         that

52. (F) NO CHANGE
    (G) club; and
    (H) club, and
    (J) club. And she

53. Which of the alternatives best
    emphasizes how unusual Steinem's
    article was?

    (A) NO CHANGE
    (B) fascinating
    (C) colorful
    (D) vivid

54. Which of the following sentences
    provides the best transition from the
    previous paragraph to this one?

    (F) Steinem was now thirty years
         old.
    (G) This famous story helped to
         boost Steinem's career.
    (H) Undercover reporting was not
         Steinem's major interest,
         however.
    (J) .The article has been widely
         reprinted and is still well-known
         to this day.

55. (A) NO CHANGE
    (B) magazines, that included
    (C) such magazines including
    (D) magazines like

56. (F) NO CHANGE
    (G) hairstyles and weight loss, for
         example
    (H) including topics like hairstyles
         and weight loss
    (J) OMIT the underlined portion.

57. (A) NO CHANGE
    (B) rights, and this issue, she says,
         helped
    (C) rights; and this issue she says
         helped
    (D) rights—and this issue, she
         says—helped

58. Which of the alternatives would most
    effectively support the assertion
    made in the previous sentence?

    (F) NO CHANGE
    (G) Abortion rights was only one of
         the many causes feminists
         espoused during the 1960s.
    (H) Many people, especially conser-
         vatives who oppose abortion,
         have been critical of her stand
         on this issue.
    (J) She wanted girls in situations
         like the one she'd faced to have
         the option of a safe and legal
         abortion.

59. (A) NO CHANGE
    (B) Steinem, tirelessly working and
         advocating, soon stepped to the
         forefront of the women's rights
         movement.
    (C) A tireless worker and advocate,
         Steinem soon stepped to the
         forefront of the women's rights
         movement.
    (D) Soon stepping to the forefront of
         the women's rights movement,
         Steinem was a tireless worker
         and advocate.

60. (F) NO CHANGE
    (G) they included
    (H) inclusive of
    (J) including

GO ON TO THE NEXT PAGE

Passage V

The following paragraphs may or may not be arranged in the best possible order. The last item will ask you to choose the most effective order for the paragraphs as numbered.

Movies: Economics and Artistry

[1]

The strength of the film as an art form has always derived from cinema's role of entertaining a large and avid public. As early as the 1920s, during the silent movie era, a generation of filmmakers grew up whose essential vision belonged to no other medium, than that of the
___
61
cinema, and whose public was a universal
___
62
audience spread across the world. Their movies
___
63
were watched by people around the world. Like
___
63
the first dramas of Shakespeare, their art was not a product of the *salon*, but of the common
___
64
playhouse. This is what gave such great moviemakers as Charles Chaplin, D. W. Griffith, and Sergei Eisenstein [65] their strength and freshness.

[2]

However, there has always been a price to be paid for the popular appeal of movies. The *salon* artist has only a known patron, or group of patrons, to satisfy, if he is strong enough he can,
___
66

like the painters of the Renaissance, mold their
___
67
taste to match his own. This may also be true of the greatest artists of the movies; from Chaplin
___
68
in the twenties to, say, Bergman or Antonioni in the sixties. Furthermore, the larger
___
69
and more numerous the public audience and
___
70
the more costly the movies to produce, equally great are the pressures brought to bear
___
71
on the less conventional creator to make your
___
72
work conform to the pattern of the more conventional artist. Today, the most expensive and popular movies—think of any film by Steven Speilberg as an example—are also the most thoroughly conventional, however skillfully crafted they may be.

[3]

As the twentieth century nears it's end, it is
___
73
clear that the greatest artistic innovation of the century has been the emergence of the movies. The worldwide popularity of film and its power to transmit culture and values are unprecedented in the history of art. But what makes the movies truly unique are the special relation-
___
74
ship between the moviemaker and his audience.

61. (A) NO CHANGE
    (B) medium than that of
    (C) medium, than
    (D) medium; than

62. (F) NO CHANGE
    (G) who's
    (H) for whom the
    (J) which had a

63. (A) NO CHANGE
    (B) People everywhere watched their movies.
    (C) They made movies that people from all over the world watched.
    (D) OMIT the underlined portion.

64. (F) NO CHANGE
    (G) a product not
    (H) in no way a product
    (J) not produced

65. The writer is considering adding the following phrase at this point in the essay:

    (three of the movie geniuses of the 1920s, two from America, one from Europe)

    Would this phrase be a relevant and appropriate addition to the essay, and why?

    (A) Yes, because it helps to clarify the role played by the three moviemakers named in the development of the art of film.
    (B) Yes, because it provides interesting details about the background of the three moviemakers mentioned.
    (C) No, because the only information it adds, that of the moviemakers' geographic origins, is irrelevant to the theme of the essay.
    (D) No, because it singles out these three moviemakers as though they were the only significant film artists of their era.

66. (F) NO CHANGE
    (G) satisfy—if
    (H) satisfy, and if
    (J) satisfy. For if

67. (A) NO CHANGE
    (B) as
    (C) similarly to
    (D) as with

68. (F) NO CHANGE
    (G) movies. From
    (H) movies. Consider
    (J) movies, from

69. (A) NO CHANGE
    (B) But
    (C) So
    (D) Therefore,

70. (F) NO CHANGE
    (G) and greater in number
    (H) in quantity
    (J) OMIT the underlined portion.

71. (A) NO CHANGE
    (B) the greater
    (C) so much greater
    (D) similarly great

72. (F) NO CHANGE
    (G) one's
    (H) his
    (J) their

73. (A) NO CHANGE
    (B) is nearing it's end
    (C) draws near to its end
    (D) nears its end

74. (F) NO CHANGE
    (G) is
    (H) will be
    (J) must be

GO ON TO THE NEXT PAGE

Item 75 poses a question about the essay as a whole.

75. For the sake of the unity and coherence of this essay, which of the following provides the most effective ordering of the paragraphs?

    (A) NO CHANGE

    (B) 1, 3, 2

    (C) 2, 3, 1

    (D) 3, 1, 2

S T O P   End of Section 1. If you have any time left, go over your work in this section only. Do not work in any other section of the test.

SECTION 2

MATHEMATICS

60 Questions

Time—60 Minutes

> **Directions:** Solve each problem below and mark the oval representing the correct answer on your answer sheet.
>
> Be careful not to spend too much time on any one question. Instead, solve as many questions as possible, and then use any remaining time to return to those questions you were unable to answer at first.
>
> You may use a calculator on any problem in this test; however, not every problem requires the use of a calculator.
>
> Diagrams that accompany problems may or may not be drawn to scale. Unless otherwise indicated, you may assume that all figures shown lie in a plane and that lines that appear straight are straight.

1. Of 42 horses in a stable, $\frac{1}{3}$ are black and $\frac{1}{6}$ are white. The rest are brown. What is the number of brown horses?

   (A) 7
   (B) 14
   (C) 21
   (D) 28
   (E) 35

2. A faucet is dripping at a constant rate. If at noon on Sunday 3 ounces of water have dripped from the faucet into a holding tank and if at 5 p.m. a total of 7 ounces have dripped into the tank, how many ounces will have dripped into the tank by 2:00 a.m. on Monday?

   (F) 10
   (G) $\frac{51}{5}$
   (H) 12
   (J) $\frac{71}{5}$
   (K) $\frac{81}{5}$

GO ON TO THE NEXT PAGE

3. $P = (-1,\underline{2})$; $Q = (3,5)$. What is the slope of $\overline{PQ}$?

   (A) $\dfrac{3}{4}$

   (B) $\dfrac{7}{4}$

   (C) $\dfrac{3}{2}$

   (D) $\dfrac{4}{3}$

   (E) $\dfrac{7}{2}$

4. $(2,6)$ is the midpoint of the line segment connecting $(-1,3)$ to $P(x,y)$. What is the value of $2x + y$?

   (F) 1
   (G) 9
   (H) 10
   (J) 12
   (K) 19

5. What is the value of $y^0 + y^{-1}$ when $y = \dfrac{1}{2}$?

   (A) 0.5
   (B) 1.50
   (C) 2.00
   (D) 4.00
   (E) 5.00

6. If the result of squaring a number n is greater than twice the number, then which of the following is true?

   (F) n is negative
   (G) n is any positive number
   (H) n is between -1 and $+1$
   (J) n is greater than 1
   (K) n is between 0 and 2

7. If the average of x and y is m, and $z = 2m$, what is the average of x, y, and z?

   (A) m

   (B) $\dfrac{2m}{3}$

   (C) $\dfrac{4m}{3}$

   (D) $\dfrac{3m}{4}$

   (E) $\dfrac{3}{4m}$

8. In the figure below, $\overline{AC}$ and $\overline{AD}$ trisect $\angle A$. What is the value of x?

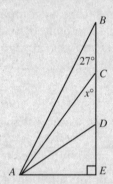

   (F) 21
   (G) 27
   (H) 42
   (J) 48
   (K) 60

Questions 9 and 10 refer to the following graphs.

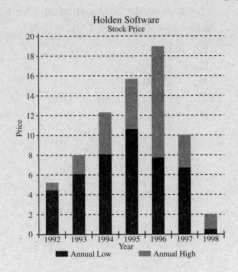

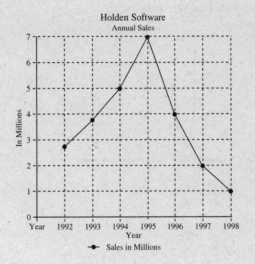

9. The lowest price of the stock in 1994 was what percent higher than the highest price in 1998?

    (A) 25
    (B) 50
    (C) 200
    (D) 300
    (E) 400

10. The median annual sales in millions for the seven years covered was

    (F) 2
    (G) 2.8
    (H) 3.4
    (J) 3.8
    (K) 5

11. What is the perimeter of a rectangle that is twice as long as it is wide and has the same area as a circle of diameter 8?

    (A) $8\sqrt{\pi}$
    (B) $8\sqrt{2\pi}$
    (C) 8π
    (D) $12\sqrt{2\pi}$
    (E) 12π

12. If the negative of the sum of two consecutive odd numbers is less than -35, which of the following may be one of the numbers?

    (F) 11
    (G) 13
    (H) 15
    (J) 16
    (K) 18

GO ON TO THE NEXT PAGE

13. In the figure below, what is the perimeter of triangle *OPQ*?

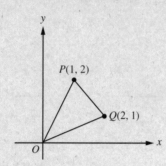

(A) $\sqrt{7}$

(B) 3

(C) $\sqrt{5} + \sqrt{2}$

(D) $\sqrt{5} + 2\sqrt{2}$

(E) $2\sqrt{5} + \sqrt{2}$

14. If $N = 3^P$ and $M = P - 1$, then, in terms of M, $\dfrac{3}{N} = ?$

(F) $\dfrac{1}{3^M}$

(G) 3^M

(H) $\dfrac{9}{3^M}$

(J) 3^{2M}

(K) 3^{1-M}

15. If A and B are positive integers, and $A^2 - B^2 = 36$, then $A = ?$

(A) 6

(B) 7

(C) 8

(D) 9

(E) 10

16. The price of a hat and scarf is $38. The hat costs $3 more than the scarf. What is the price of the scarf?

(F) $17.50

(G) $18.00

(H) $18.50

(J) $19.00

(K) $20.50

17. If $\sqrt{6} \times \sqrt{3x} = \sqrt{30}$, then $x = ?$

(A) $\dfrac{2}{5}$

(B) $\dfrac{3}{5}$

(C) $\dfrac{5}{3}$

(D) $\sqrt{3}$

(E) $\sqrt{5}$

18. If $2x - y + 4z = 7$ and $-4x + 2y - 3z = 1$, what is the value of z?

(F) -3

(G) 0

(H) 3

(J) 5

(K) It cannot be determined

19. If x and y are unequal positive integers and $xy = 36$, what is the smallest possible value of $x + y$?

(A) 12

(B) 13

(C) 15

(D) 20

(E) 37

20. If it costs c cents per minute plus
$5 per month for long distance calls,
what is the average price per minute
(in cents) in a month in which n calls
with an average length of 15 minutes
are made?

(F) $c + \dfrac{100}{3n}$

(G) $c + 15n$

(H) $15c + \dfrac{500}{n}$

(J) $\dfrac{15c + 500}{n}$

(K) $\dfrac{500 + nc}{15n}$

21. What is the area of a circle that has a
diameter of π?

(A) $\dfrac{1}{4}\pi^2$

(B) $\dfrac{1}{2}\pi^2$

(C) $\dfrac{1}{4}\pi^3$

(D) $\dfrac{1}{2}\pi^3$

(E) π^3

22. The altitude of a triangle is 20%
greater than the length of its base.
What is the area of the triangle in
terms of b, the length of the base?

(F) $\dfrac{6b^2}{5}$

(G) $\dfrac{3b^2}{5}$

(H) $\dfrac{20b^2}{3}$

(J) $\dfrac{3b}{5}$

(K) $\dfrac{6b}{5}$

23. A jar contains 6 numbered blocks.
Four of the blocks are numbered 0
and the other two are not. If two
blocks are drawn at random from the
jar, what is the probability that the
product of the two numbers is not
zero?

(A) $\dfrac{1}{15}$

(B) $\dfrac{1}{12}$

(C) $\dfrac{2}{15}$

(D) $\dfrac{1}{6}$

(E) $\dfrac{1}{3}$

GO ON TO THE NEXT PAGE

24. What is the value of $\dfrac{x^2 - 3x}{3x - 9}$ if $x = 3.03$?

   (F)   1.01
   (G)   1
   (H)   3
   (J)   101
   (K)   303

25. When the tires of a taxicab are underinflated, the cab odometer will read 10% over the true mileage driven. If the odometer of a cab with underinflated tires shows m miles, what is the actual distance driven?

   (A) $\dfrac{10m}{11}$

   (B) $1.1m$

   (C) $\dfrac{10}{11m}$

   (D) $0.9m$

   (E) $\dfrac{11}{10m}$

26. The ratio of Elaine's weekly salary to Carl's weekly salary was 3:2. If Elaine gets a 20% raise and Carl gets a $200 raise the ratio of their salaries will drop to 6:5. What is Elaine's salary?

   (F) $200
   (G) $400
   (H) $480
   (J) $600
   (K) $720

27. P percent of $20\sqrt{3}$ is 3. $P = ?$

   (A) $\sqrt{3}$

   (B)   3

   (C) $5\sqrt{3}$

   (D) $10\sqrt{3}$

   (E)   20

28. In triangle ABC, the measure of $\angle B$ is 50° more than the measure of $\angle A$, and the measure of $\angle C$ is three times the measure of $\angle A$. The measure of $\angle B - \angle C$ in degrees = ?

   (F) -6
   (G) -4
   (H) -2
   (J)   0
   (K)   2

29. If $2n - m = 6$, and $2n + m = 10$, $m = ?$

   (A)   1
   (B)   2
   (C)   3
   (D)   4
   (E)   5

30. In a group of 18 students taking Spanish or German, 12 are taking Spanish, and 4 are taking both languages. What is the number of students taking Spanish but not German?

   (F)   4
   (G)   6
   (H)   8
   (J)   10
   (K)   12

31. When $x = 2$, $3x^0 + x^{-4} = ?$

   (A) -8
   (B)   1.0625
   (C)   3.0625
   (D)   16
   (E)   19

32. If $x = \dfrac{1}{2}$ and $x^2 + 2y^2 = 1$, then which of the following values is closest to the value of $|y|$?

(F)   0.1
(G)   0.2
(H)   0.4
(J)   0.5
(K)   0.6

33. $S = \{1,2,2,2,3,5,6,7,8\}$. What is the mean minus the median of S?

(A)   −2
(B)   −1
(C)   0
(D)   1
(E)   2

34. In the figure below, if m$\angle ABC = 130°$, what is the area of triangle ABC?

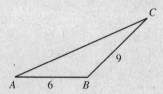

(F)   27sin50°
(G)   27cos50°
(H)   27
(J) $\dfrac{27}{\sin50°}$
(K)   54sin50°

35. The cost of 4 cookies, 6 doughnuts, and 3 boxes of doughnut holes is $8.15. The cost of 2 cookies, 3 doughnuts, and 4 boxes of doughnut holes is $7.20. What is the cost of a box of doughnut holes?

(A) $.85
(B) $.95
(C) $1.05
(D) $1.15
(E) $1.25

36. Which of the following is closest to the length of the hypotenuse of a triangle with legs 3 and 5?

(F)   4
(G)   5
(H)   6
(J)   7
(K)   8

37. If $x + 2y - 3z = 5$ and $2x + 2y + 3z = 8$, then $9x + 12y = ?$

(A)   15
(B)   23
(C)   31
(D)   39
(E)   It cannot be determined

38. What is the number of different 3-digit license plate numbers that can be formed if the first digit cannot be 0?

(F)   90
(G)   100
(H)   800
(J)   900
(K)   1,000

39. Three consecutive odd integers are written in increasing order. The sum of the first and second and twice the third is 46. What is the second number?

(A)   7
(B)   9
(C)   11
(D)   13
(E)   15

GO ON TO THE NEXT PAGE

40. In the figure below, the area of the shaded section of the circle is 33π. What is the diameter of the circle?

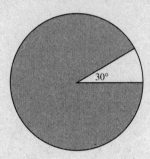

(F)   6
(G)   2π
(H)   9
(J)   12
(K)   4π

41. Jerome is 4 years older than Rodney. Two years ago, Rodney was $\frac{2}{3}$ of Jerome's age. How many years ago was Jerome twice as old as Rodney?

(A)   2
(B)   3
(C)   4
(D)   5
(E)   6

42. Point $Q(1,u)$ lies on a circle with a radius of 13 whose center is located at (6,9). Which of the following is a possible value of u?

(F)   −21
(G)   −3
(H)   3
(J)   6
(K)   12

43. John can vacuum a hotel room in 20 minutes. Armando needs 15 minutes to do the same job. How many hours does it take them working together to vacuum 30 rooms?

(A) $\frac{20}{7}$

(B)   3
(C)   4

(D) $\frac{30}{7}$

(E) $\frac{50}{7}$

44. If $x = \log 2$ and $y = \log 5$, then $2y - 3x = ?$

(F) $\log \frac{8}{25}$

(G) $\log \frac{25}{8}$

(H) $\log \frac{25}{4}$

(J) $\log 200$

(K) $\frac{25}{8}$

45. Simplified to simplest form, $\frac{(12x^2y - 4xy^2)}{(24xy^3 - 8y^4)} = ?$

(A) $\frac{x}{2y^2}$

(B) $\frac{x}{2y}$

(C) $\frac{3xy - 4}{2y^2}$

(D) $\frac{8xy}{24y^2 - 3y}$

(E) $\frac{x^2y}{3xy^3 - y^4}$

46. One x-intercept for the parabola $y = x^2 - 2x - 6$ is in which of the following intervals?
    (F) $[-3,-2]$
    (G) $[-2,-1]$
    (H) $[-1,0]$
    (J) $[0,1]$
    (K) $[1,2]$

47. If $f(x) = x^2$ and $f(g(x)) = \dfrac{1}{(x^2 + 1)}$, then $g(x)$ could be which of the following?

    (A) $\dfrac{1}{(x + 1)}$

    (B) $\sqrt{x} + 1$

    (C) $\dfrac{1}{(\sqrt{x^2 + 1})}$

    (D) $\dfrac{1}{x}$

    (E) $\dfrac{1}{x^2}$

48. The numbers -2, x, -8 are the first three terms in a geometric progression. Which of the following could be the sixth term in the progression?
    (F) -4096
    (G) -2048
    (H) -1024
    (J) 512
    (K) 1024

49. Given $A = \begin{bmatrix} 2 & -1 \\ 3 & -2 \end{bmatrix}$ and $B = \begin{bmatrix} 0 & 1 \\ 1 & 0 \end{bmatrix}$, then $2AB = ?$

    (A) $\begin{bmatrix} 3 & -3 \\ 2 & 6 \end{bmatrix}$

    (B) $\begin{bmatrix} 3 & 6 \\ 3 & 6 \end{bmatrix}$

    (C) $\begin{bmatrix} -1 & 2 \\ -2 & 3 \end{bmatrix}$

    (D) $\begin{bmatrix} 4 & -2 \\ 6 & -4 \end{bmatrix}$

    (E) $\begin{bmatrix} -2 & 4 \\ -4 & 6 \end{bmatrix}$

50. If points P and Q have coordinates $(-1,2)$ and $(1,6)$ respectively, which of the following is the equation of a line that is a perpendicular bisector of $\overline{PQ}$?

    (F) $y = -\dfrac{1}{2}x + 4$

    (G) $y = \dfrac{1}{2}x + 4$

    (H) $y = 2x + 4$
    (J) $y = -2x + 4$
    (K) $y = -2x - 4$

GO ON TO THE NEXT PAGE

51. A random survey of 50 computer users was taken to determine how many used a CD-drive and how many used a tape drive. The number who used both was 5 less than the number who used only a disc drive. In addition, there were 7 who used a tape drive but not a disc drive and 2 who used neither. How many used a tape drive?

   (A) 18
   (B) 20
   (C) 23
   (D) 25
   (E) 28

52. A surveyor standing at a point 50 meters from the base of a vertical cliff measures the angle of elevation to the top as 40°. She then walks another M meters directly away from the cliff until the angle of elevation to the top is 20°. M is equal to ?

   (F) $50\tan40° - 50\tan20°$

   (G) $\dfrac{50\tan40° - 50\tan20°}{\tan40°}$

   (H) $\dfrac{50\tan20°}{\tan40° - \tan20°}$

   (J) $\dfrac{50\tan40° - 50\tan20°}{\tan20°}$

   (K) $\dfrac{50\tan40°}{\tan40° - \tan20°}$

53. $3\sqrt{3} + 2\sqrt{8} = ?$

   (A) $5\sqrt{2}$

   (B) $7\sqrt{2}$

   (C) $5\sqrt{8}$

   (D) $5\sqrt{10}$

   (E) 20

54. When Caroline travels on business, she is reimbursed $16 more per day for meals than for lodging. If she were given 50% more for lodging and $\dfrac{2}{3}$ as much for meals, the difference would be reversed. What is the total daily amount that Caroline is reimbursed for food and lodging?

   (F) $32
   (G) $48
   (H) $64
   (J) $72
   (K) $80

55. If the numbers $-3 < M < N < 5$ are in arithmetic progression, then $M = ?$

   (A) $\dfrac{-1}{3}$

   (B) 0

   (C) $\dfrac{1}{3}$

   (D) $\dfrac{7}{3}$

   (E) 3

56. If $T = a^x$ and $S = a^y$, then $a^{x - 2y} = ?$

   (F) $\dfrac{T}{S^2}$

   (G) TS^2

   (H) $T - 2S$

   (J) $T - S^2$

   (K) $\dfrac{S}{T^2}$

57. Given $A = \begin{bmatrix} -2 & 1 \\ 1 & 3 \end{bmatrix}$ and $B \begin{bmatrix} x & 2 \\ 3 & y \end{bmatrix}$ and

$2A + B = \begin{bmatrix} -5 & 4 \\ 5 & 4 \end{bmatrix}$, then $xy = ?$

(A) -2
(B) -1
(C) 0
(D) 1
(E) 2

58. If $f(x) = x + 1$, then $\dfrac{1}{f(x)} f\left(\dfrac{1}{x}\right) = ?$

(F) 1

(G) $\dfrac{x + 1}{x}$

(H) $\dfrac{1}{x}$

(J) $\dfrac{x}{x + 1}$

(K) x

59. If the slope of the line from $(-1,0)$ to $P(x,y)$ is 1 and the slope of the line from $(-4,0)$ to $P(x,y)$ is $\dfrac{1}{2}$, what is the value of x?

(A) -1
(B) 0
(C) 1
(D) 2
(E) 3

60. In the diagram below, O_1 and O_2 are concentric circles and $\overline{AB}$ is tangent to O_1 at C. If the radius of O_1 is r and the radius of O_2 is twice as long, what is the area of the shaded region?

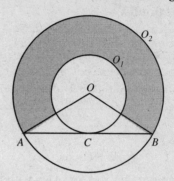

(F) $\dfrac{1}{2}\pi r^2$

(G) πr^2
(H) $1.5\pi r^2$
(J) $2\pi r^2$
(K) $3\pi r^2$

STOP   End of Section 1. If you have any time left, go over your work in this section only. Do not work in any other section of the test.

SECTION 3

READING

40 Questions

Time—35 Minutes

> **Directions:** This test consists of four passages, each followed by several questions. Read each passage, select the correct answer for each question, and mark the oval representing the correct answer on your answer sheet.

Passage I

Prose Fiction

Line Newland Archer was speaking with his
fiancée, May Welland. He had failed to
stop at his club on the way up from the
office where he exercised the profession
(5) of the law in the leisurely manner
common to well-to-do New Yorkers of his
class in the middle of the nineteenth
century. He was out of spirits and
slightly out of temper, and a haunting
(10) horror of doing the same thing every day
at the same hour besieged his brain.

"Sameness—sameness!" he muttered,
the word running through his head like a
persecuting tune as he saw the familiar
(15) tall-hatted figures lounging behind the
plate glass; and because he usually
dropped in at the club at that hour, he
had passed by instead. And now he
began to talk to May of their own plans,
(20) their future, and Mrs. Welland's insistence on a long engagement.

"If you call it long!" May cried. "Isabel
Chivers and Reggie were engaged for two
years, Grace and Thorley for nearly a
(25) year and a half. Why aren't we very well
off as we are?"

It was the traditional maidenly
interrogation, and Archer felt ashamed of
himself for finding it childish. No doubt
(30) she simply echoed what was said for her,
but she was nearing her twenty-second
birthday, and he wondered at what age
"nice" women like May began to speak
for themselves.

(35) "Never, if we won't let them, I suppose," he mused, and recalled his mad

outburst to his friend Jackson: "Women
ought to be as free as we are—!"

It would soon be his task to take the
(40) bandage from this young woman's eyes
and bid her look forth on the world. But
how many generations of women before
her had descended bandaged to the
family vault? He shivered a little, remem-
(45) bering some of the new ideas in his
scientific books and the much-cited
instance of the Kentucky cave-fish, which
had ceased to develop eyes because they
had no use for them. What if, when he
(50) had bidden May Welland to open hers,
they could only look out blankly at
blankness?

"We might be much better off. We
might be truly together—we might
(55) travel."

Her face lit up. "That would be lovely,"
she admitted; she would love to travel.
But her mother would not understand
their wanting to do things so differently.

(60) "As if the fact that it *is* different
doesn't account for it!" Archer insisted.

"Newland! You're so original!" she
exulted.

His heart sank. He saw that he was
(65) saying all the things that young men in
the same situation were expected to say,
and that she was making the answers
that instinct and tradition taught her to
make—even to the point of calling him
(70) original.

"Original! We're all as like each other
as those dolls cut out of the same folded
paper. We're like patterns stenciled on a

308

(75) wall. Can't you and I strike out for ourselves, May?"

He had stopped and faced her in the excitement of their discussion, and her eyes rested on him with a bright un-clouded admiration.

(80) "Goodness—shall we elope?" she laughed.

"If you would—"

"You *do* love me, Newland! I'm so happy."

(85) "But then—why not be happier?"

"We can't behave like people in novels, though, can we?"

"Why not—why not—why not?"

She looked a little bored by his

(90) insistence. She knew very well why they couldn't, but it was troublesome to have to produce a reason. "I'm not clever enough to argue with you. But that kind of thing is rather—vulgar, isn't it?" she

(95) suggested, relieved to have hit on a word that would certainly extinguish the whole subject.

"Are you so much afraid, then, of being vulgar?"

(100) She was evidently staggered by this. "Of course I should hate it—and so would you," she rejoined, a trifle irritably.

He stood silent, beating his walking-

(105) stick nervously against his shoe-top. Feeling that she had indeed found the right way of closing the discussion, she went on lightheartedly, "Oh, did I tell you that I showed cousin Ellen my engage-

(110) ment ring? She thinks it the most beautiful setting she ever saw. There's nothing like it in Paris, she said. I do love you, Newland, for being so artistic!"

1. What was Archer's reason for failing to stop at his club after leaving the office?

(A) He wanted to avoid talking with his friends there.

(B) He was afraid that his life was becoming overly routine.

(C) He disliked most of the other members of the club.

(D) He was eager to discuss the future with his fiancée.

2. The reference to "the Kentucky cave-fish" (line 47) underscores Archer's concern about May Welland's

(F) greed.

(G) timidity.

(H) immaturity.

(J) bossiness.

3. It can be inferred from the passage that Archer's engagement is expected to last

(A) two or three months.

(B) somewhat less than a year and a half.

(C) about two years.

(D) over two years.

4. The first paragraph suggests that Archer's work as a lawyer

(F) is not very demanding.

(G) has become tedious to him.

(H) is very lucrative.

(J) is a traditional family occupation.

GO ON TO THE NEXT PAGE

5. May Welland apparently considers the idea that she and Archer might elope

   (A) frightening.
   (B) romantic.
   (C) fascinating.
   (D) absurd.

6. The fifth paragraph (lines 35–39) suggests that Archer considers most women in the society of his time

   (F) unduly powerful.
   (G) indecisive and irresponsible.
   (H) unfairly dominated by men.
   (J) excessively demanding.

7. Archer's reaction to being called "original" by his fiancée is a feeling of

   (A) dismay.
   (B) pride.
   (C) bewilderment.
   (D) glee.

8. Which of the following conclusions about the relationship between Archer and May Welland is best supported by the details in the passage?

   (F) Archer's eagerness to accelerate their wedding is motivated by his passion for his fiancée.
   (G) Archer and May Welland both feel trapped in an unhappy relationship by social restrictions.
   (H) Archer feels stultified by his fiancée's conventionality, but feels unable to alter the situation.
   (J) May Welland is eager to do whatever she can to satisfy the emotional needs of her fiancé.

9. May Welland considers the discussion begun by Archer finished when she

   (A) dismisses his ideas as "vulgar."
   (B) appeals to the authority of her mother.
   (C) accedes to his request that their engagement be shortened.
   (D) realizes that Archer truly loves her.

10. Archer regards May Welland's attitudes as having been excessively influenced by which of the following?

   I.   The traditions of her sex and class
   II. Her mother
   III. The novels she has read
   IV. Her friends Isabel and Grace

   (F) I and II only
   (G) II and III only
   (H) I and IV only
   (J) II and IV only

Passage II
Social Science

Line   From the opening days of the Civil War, one of the Union's strategies in its efforts to defeat the rebelling Southern states was to blockade their ports. Compared
(5)   to the Union, relatively little was manufactured in the Confederacy—either consumer goods or, more important, war materiél—and it was believed that a blockade could strangle the South into
(10) submission. But the Confederacy had 3,500 miles of coastline and, at the start of the war, the Union had only 36 ships to patrol them.

     Even so, the Confederate government
(15) knew that the Union could and would construct additional warships and that in time all its ports could be sealed. To counter this, the Confederacy decided to take a radical step—to construct an
(20) ironclad vessel that would be impervious to Union gunfire. In so doing, the South was taking a gamble because, though the

British and French navies had already launched experimental armor-plated
(25) warships, none had yet been tested in battle.

Lacking time as well as true ship-building capabilities, rather than construct an entirely new ship, in July, 1861,
(30) the Confederacy began placing armor-plating on the hull of an abandoned U.S. Navy frigate, the steam-powered *U.S.S. Merrimack.* Rechristened the *C.S.S. Virginia,* the ship carried ten guns and an
(35) iron ram designed to stave in the wooden hulls of Union warships.

Until then, Union Secretary of the Navy Gideon Welles had considered ironclads too radical an idea and pre-
(40) ferred to concentrate on building standard wooden warships. But when news of the *Virginia* reached Washington, the fear it engendered forced him to rethink his decision. In October, 1861, the Union
(45) began construction of its own ironclad—the *U.S.S. Monitor*—which would revolutionize naval warfare.

Designed by John Ericson, a Swede who had already made substantial
(50) contributions to marine engineering, the *Monitor* looked like no other ship afloat. With a wooden hull covered with iron plating, the ship had a flat deck with perpendicular sides that went below the
(55) waterline and protected the propeller and other important machinery. Even more innovative, the ship had a round, revolving turret that carried two large guns. Begun three months after work
(60) started on the conversion of the *Virginia,* the *Monitor* was nevertheless launched in January, 1862, two weeks before the Confederacy launched its ironclad.

On March 8th, now completely fitted,
(65) the *Virginia* left the port of Norfolk, Virginia, on what was expected to be a test run. However, steaming into Hampton Roads, Virginia, the Confederate ship found no fewer than five Union ships at
(70) the mouth of the James River—the *St. Lawrence, Congress, Cumberland, Minnesota,* and *Roanoke.* The first three of these were already-obsolete sailing ships, but the others were new steam frigates,
(75) the pride of the Union navy.

Attacking the *Cumberland* first, the *Virginia* sent several shells into her side before ramming her hull and sinking her. Turning next to the *Congress,* the South-
(80) ern ironclad sent broadsides into her until fires started by the shots reached her powder magazine and she blew up. At last, after driving the *Minnesota* aground, the *Virginia* steamed off,
(85) planning to finish off the other ships the next day. In just a few hours, she had sunk two ships, disabled a third, and killed 240 Union sailors, including the captain of the *Congress*—more naval
(90) casualties than on any other day of the war. Although she had lost two of her crew, her ram, and two of her guns and sustained other damage, none of the nearly 100 shots that hit her had pierced
(95) her armor.

The *Monitor,* however, was already en route from the Brooklyn Navy Yard, and the next morning, March 9th, the two ironclads met each other for the first—
(100) and only—time. For nearly four hours the ships pounded at each other, but despite some damage done on both sides, neither ship could penetrate the armor-plating of its enemy. When a shot
(105) from the *Virginia* hit the *Monitor's* pilot house, wounding her captain and forcing her to withdraw temporarily, the Confederate ship steamed back to Norfolk.

Although both sides claimed victory,
(110) the battle was actually a draw. Its immediate significance was that, by forcing the withdrawal of the *Virginia,* it strengthened the Union blockade, enabling the North to continue its
(115) ultimately successful stranglehold on the South. Even more important, it was a turning point in the history of naval warfare. Although neither ship ever fought again, the brief engagement of the
(120) *Monitor* and *Virginia* made every navy in the world obsolete and, in time, spelled the end of wooden fighting ships forever.

GO ON TO THE NEXT PAGE

11. According to the passage, the Confederacy wanted an ironclad vessel for all the following reasons except

   (A) an ironclad vessel might be able to withstand Union attacks.

   (B) it needed open ports in order to receive supplies from overseas.

   (C) the British and French navies already had ironclads.

   (D) it knew that the Union would be building more warships.

12. The passage implies that the South was vulnerable to a naval blockade because of its

   (F) limited manufacturing capabilities.

   (G) relatively short coastline.

   (H) lack of access to natural resources.

   (J) paucity of skilled naval officers.

13. According to the passage, the Confederate government chose to refit the *Merrimack* rather than build an ironclad from scratch because

   (A) it lacked sufficient funds to construct a new vessel.

   (B) it had neither the time nor facilities to build a new ship.

   (C) the design of the *Merrimack* was especially suitable for armor plating.

   (D) it believed that converting a Union warship would damage Northern morale.

14. All of the following were unusual design features of the *Monitor* EXCEPT its

   (F) perpendicular sides.

   (G) revolving gun turret.

   (H) flat deck.

   (J) wooden hull.

15. As it is used in line 57, the word "innovative" most nearly means

   (A) dangerous.

   (B) unusual.

   (C) revolutionary.

   (D) clever.

16. It can be inferred from the passage that, by comparison with the design of the *Monitor,* that of the *Virginia* was more

   (F) offensively oriented.

   (G) costly.

   (H) versatile.

   (J) traditional.

17. It can be inferred from the passage that, although construction on the *Monitor* began three months after that of the *Virginia,* the *Monitor* was completed first because

   (A) the Union had more money to spend on building its ship.

   (B) the *Monitor* was less complicated to construct.

   (C) the Union had greater manufacturing abilities and resources.

   (D) the Confederacy did not feel compelled to hurry in completing its ship.

18. It can be inferred from the passage that the *Virginia* was able to sink or disable the *St. Lawrence, Congress* and *Cumberland* for which of the following reasons?

   (F) Its armor plating was virtually impervious to gunfire.

   (G) Its steam-powered engines made it highly maneuverable.

   (H) Its armor plating made it fireproof.

   (J) It was capable of greater speed than the Union warships.

19. As it is used in line 93, "sustained" most nearly means

   (A) survived.
   (B) inflicted.
   (C) suffered.
   (D) risked.

20. The author suggests that the most important long-term result of the battle between the *Virginia* and the *Monitor* was that it

   (F) enabled the Union to maintain its blockade of Southern ports.
   (G) demonstrated that ironclad ships represented the future of naval warfare.
   (H) saved the Union navy from destruction by the *Virginia*.
   (J) demonstrated the superior technological prowess of the North.

Passage III

Humanities

Line   On July 1, 1882, a brief notice appeared in the *Portsmouth* (England) *Evening News*. It read simply, "Dr. Doyle begs to notify that he has removed to 1, Bush
(5)   Villas, Elm Grove, next to the Bush Hotel." So was announced the newly formed medical practice of a 23-year-old graduate of Edinburgh University— Arthur Conan Doyle. But the town of
(10)   Southsea, the Portsmouth suburb in which Doyle had opened his office, already had several well-established physicians, and while he waited for patients, the young Dr. Doyle found
(15)   himself with a great deal of time on his hands.
        To fill it, he began writing—short stories, historical novels, whatever would keep him busy and, hopefully, bring
(20)   additional funds into his sparsely filled coffers. By the beginning of 1886, his practice had grown to the point of providing him with a respectable if not

munificent income, and he had managed
(25)   to have a few pieces published. Although literary success still eluded him, he had developed an idea for a new book, a detective story, and in March he began writing the tale that would give birth to
(30)   one of literature's most enduring figures.
        Although he was familiar with and impressed by the fictional detectives created by Edgar Allan Poe, Emile Gaboriau, and Wilkie Collins, Doyle
(35)   believed he could create a different kind of detective, one for whom detection was a science rather than an art. As a model, he used one of his medical school professors, Dr. Joseph Bell. As Bell's
(40)   assistant, Doyle had seen how, by exercising his powers of observation and deduction and asking a few questions, Bell had been able not only to diagnose his patients' complaints but also to
(45)   accurately determine their professions and backgrounds. A detective who applied similar intellectual powers to the solving of criminal mysteries could be a compelling figure, Doyle felt.
(50)   At first titled *A Tangled Skein,* the story was to be told by his detective's companion, a Dr. Ormand Sacker, and the detective himself was to be named Sherrinford Holmes. But by April, 1886,
(55)   when Doyle finished the manuscript, the title had become *A Study in Scarlet,* the narrator Dr. John H. Watson, and the detective Mr. Sherlock Holmes.
        A tale of revenge, in which Holmes is
(60)   able to determine that two Mormons visiting England from Utah have been killed by Jefferson Hope, an American working as a London hansom cab driver, *A Study in Scarlet* was rejected by several
(65)   publishers before being accepted that fall for publication by Ward, Lock & Company as part of *Beeton's Christmas Annual* in 1887. Although the author asked to be paid a royalty based on sale of the book,
(70)   his publisher offered instead only a flat fee of £25 for the copyright (the equivalent of approximately $50 today). Doyle reluctantly accepted.

GO ON TO THE NEXT PAGE

(75) A handful of reviewers commented kindly on the story, but the reading public as a whole was unimpressed. Ward, Lock published *A Study in Scarlet* in book form the following year, while the disappointed author returned to his

(80) historical novels, with which he had finally achieved some modest success. Fictional detection, Doyle thought, was behind him. In August, 1889, however, he was approached by the editor of the

(85) American *Lippincott's Monthly Magazine,* published in Philadelphia and London, to write another Sherlock Holmes story. Although he had little interest in continuing Holmes's adventures, Doyle was still

(90) in need of money and accepted the offer.

Published in *Lippincott's* in February, 1890, and in book form later that year, *The Sign of the Four* chronicled Holmes's investigation of the murder of Bartho-

(95) lomew Sholto and his search for Jonathan Small and a treasure stolen by British soldiers in India. It too, however, met with little enthusiasm from the public. In the meantime, however, Doyle's

(100) other small literary successes had enabled him to move to London, where he became a consulting physician. Fortunately, even this new London practice did not keep him very busy,

(105) leaving him time to concentrate on his writing.

In April, 1891, he submitted a short Sherlock Holmes story, "A Scandal in Bohemia," to a new magazine called *The*

(110) *Strand.* It was with the publication of this story, and the series of Holmes tales which followed, that the public finally took an interest in Dr. Doyle's detective, enabling him to give up his practice and

(115) turn to writing full time. Despite his own continuing lack of enthusiasm for his protagonist—he considered the Holmes stories insignificant compared to his "serious" historical novels—spurred by

(120) the public clamor for more Sherlock Holmes, Doyle eventually wrote fifty-six short stories and four novels in the series and in the process created what may be the best-known character in all of

(125) English literature.

21. According to the passage, Arthur Conan Doyle began writing for all the following reasons except

(A) his medical practice did not keep him very busy.
(B) he needed additional income.
(C) he was not interested in practicing medicine.
(D) he was fond of literary fiction.

22. As it is used in line 42, the word "deduction" most nearly means

(F) decreasing.
(G) discounting.
(H) reducing.
(J) reasoning.

23. It can be inferred from the passage that Sherlock Holmes differed from previous fictional detectives in that

(A) he conducted his investigations on a scientific basis.
(B) he used his own background in medicine as a source of detective methods.
(C) his cases were chronicled by a companion rather than by the detective himself.
(D) his exploits were based on the experiences of a real individual.

24. As it is used in line 49, "compelling" most nearly means

(F) inescapable.
(G) believable.
(H) fascinating.
(J) insistent.

25. In can be inferred from the passage that the first two Sherlock Holmes tales were similar in all the following respects except

   (A) both were based on historical events.

   (B) both were originally published in periodicals rather than as books.

   (C) neither received a strong initial reception from the public.

   (D) both were written more for financial than literary reasons.

26. The author implies that Doyle's move to London was primarily triggered by

   (F) Doyle's desire to move in literary circles.

   (G) the failure of his medical practice in Southsea.

   (H) an increase in Doyle's income from writing.

   (J) a growing demand for Doyle's medical services.

27. The author uses the word "Fortunately" in line 103 primarily to imply that

   (A) a medical practice in London can be especially demanding.

   (B) the popular demand for Doyle's writing had begun to grow at this time.

   (C) Doyle's literary career was more significant than his medical practice.

   (D) Doyle was strongly tempted at this time to abandon writing as a career.

28. It can be inferred from the passage that the public finally became interested in Doyle's Sherlock Holmes stories as a result of

   (F) their continued appearance in *The Strand* magazine.

   (G) the public's growing interest in detective stories.

   (H) the success of Doyle's other works.

   (J) the first publication of a Holmes story in the United States.

29. According to the passage, Doyle's reluctance to write further Holmes stories after 1891 was due primarily to

   (A) his belief that he was not fairly compensated for them.

   (B) his lack of interest in Holmes as a character.

   (C) his desire to be considered a serious author.

   (D) the significant income provided by his other literary efforts.

30. Which of the following titles best summarizes the content of the passage?

   (F) Arthur Conan Doyle and the Creation of the Modern Detective Story

   (G) A Detective's Reluctant Chronicler: The Birth of Sherlock Holmes

   (H) Physician and Author: How Arthur Conan Doyle Balanced Two Callings

   (J) The Many Strands in the Character of Sherlock Holmes

GO ON TO THE NEXT PAGE

Passage IV

Natural Science

Line If you've ever cupped your hand around
     a blinking firefly or noticed an eerie glow
     in the ocean at night, you are familiar
     with the phenomenon of biolumines-
(5) cence. The ability of certain plants and
     animals to emit light has long been a
     source of fascination to humans. Why do
     certain species of mushrooms glow? Why
     are midwater squids designed with
(10) ornate light-emitting organs underneath
     their eyes and ink glands? Why do
     certain particles and biological detritus
     floating in the depths of the ocean
     sparkle after a physical disturbance? Are
(15) these light displays simply an example of
     nature in its most flamboyant mode—a
     case of "if you've got it, flaunt it"—or do
     they serve any practical purposes?
         As it turns out, the manifestations of
(20) bioluminescence are as diverse as they
     are elegant. Yet virtually all of the known
     or proposed ways in which biolumines-
     cence functions may be classed under
     three major rubrics: assisting predation,
(25) helping escape from predators, and
     communicating.
         Many examples of the first two uses
     can be observed in the ocean's midwa-
     ters, a zone that extends from about 100
(30) meters deep to a few kilometers below
     the surface. Almost all of the animals
     that inhabit the murky depths where
     sunlight barely penetrates are capable of
     producing light in one way or another.
(35) Certain animals, when feeding, are
     attracted to a spot of light as a possible
     food source. Hence, other animals use
     their own luminescence to attract them.
     Just in front of the angler fish's mouth is
(40) a dangling luminescent ball suspended
     from a structure attached to its head.
     What unwitting marine creatures see as
     food is really a bait to lure them into the
     angler fish's gaping maw.
(45)   The uses of luminescence to elude
     prey are just as sophisticated and
     various. Some creatures take advantage
     of the scant sunlight in their realm by
     using bioluminescence as a form of
(50) camouflage. The glow generated by
     photophores, light producing organs, on

the undersides of some fishes and squids
acts to hide them through a phenomenon
known as countershading: the weak
(55) downward lighting created by the
photophores effectively erases the
animals' shadows when viewed from
below against the (relatively) lighted
waters above.
(60)   Some marine animals use bioluminescence more actively in their own defense,
turning their predators into prey. For
instance, there is the so-called "burglar
alarm effect," in which an animal coats
(65) an advancing predator with sticky
glowing tissue that makes the would-be
attacker vulnerable to visually cued
hunters—like bank robbers marked by
exploding dye packets hidden in stolen
(70) currency.
    Bioluminescence is used not only in
such interspecific feeding frays between
predators and prey, but also as an
intraspecific communication facilitator.
(75) The fireflies that seem to blink on and off
randomly in the summer woods are
actually male and female members
signaling each other during courtship.
Certain fish use their luminescence as a
(80) kind of Morse code in which the female
responds to the flashing of a male fish
with her own flash exactly two seconds
later, which the male recognizes by its
timing.
(85)   Bioluminescence clearly functions to
help certain species ensure their survival, whether it helps them to trick
predators or to mate and produce
offspring. Yet, when we look at the larger
(90) evolutionary picture, bioluminescence as
such is generally considered a "nonessential" characteristic. After all, closely
related species and even strains of the
same species may have both luminous
(95) and nonluminous members, and the
nonluminous ones appear just as viable
and vigorous as their glowing counter-
parts. For instance, while many of the
small marine organisms known as
(100) dinoflagellates are luminous, many are
not. Yet, on closer inspection, we find
that the nonluminous dinoflagellates may
benefit from the diversionary flashing
tactics of the luminous ones. When the
(105) sea is disturbed and light flashes create

phosphorescence, the species that flash
may provide enough light to serve the
entire population. Thus, selection
pressure for the development or mainte-
(110) nance of luminescence in additional
species is not great if light generated by
a part of the population serves the entire
community.

There are instances in which biolumi-
(115) nescence seems truly purposeless. What
does one make of a creature, such as a
newly discovered species of a tomopterid worm, that emits light for no
apparent purpose? This agile swimmer
(120) with a multitude of paired legs spews a
bright yellow bioluminescent fluid from
each of its leg pores. While other types
of spewers use this strategy to create a
visual distraction, this worm's display
(125) remains enigmatic, particularly since the
light produced is yellow, while most
midwater animals have eyes that are
sensitive only to blue-green. Perhaps
some animal species *are* simply exploit-
(130) ing their capacity for flamboyance in the
same way that some humans bring a
distinctively colorful flair to whatever
they do.

31. The passage focuses on all of the
following aspects of bioluminescence
EXCEPT

(A) its role in interactions between
predators and prey.
(B) its role in the evolution of
various animal species.
(C) whether bioluminescence is a
purely functional feature.
(D) how bioluminescent species may
serve nonluminous ones.

32. From the author's description of the
angler fish in lines 39–44, we can infer
that this fish

(F) is attracted to light as a possible
food source.
(G) uses its light-producing organ to
deter predators.
(H) dwells primarily in the ocean's
midwaters.
(J) uses countershading to elude
predators below.

33. The angler fish's use of bioluminescence in predation is most nearly
analogous to

(A) an exterminator's use of insecti-
cide to poison the insects that
have infested a home.
(B) a duck hunter's use of a reed-
shielded blind as a hiding place
from which to shoot at ducks.
(C) a trout fisherman's use of a lure
designed to resemble an insect
that trout love to eat.
(D) a police detective's use of a bright
lamp to blind and so intimidate a
suspect during questioning.

GO ON TO THE NEXT PAGE

34. Each of the following statements about the use of bioluminescence in countershading is true EXCEPT

(F) The light given off by photophores underneath certain fish and squid makes the animals appear to blend in with the sunlit waters above them.

(G) Bioluminescence allows the parts of an animal normally in shadow to appear lighter.

(H) Countershading is used most effectively in regions of relatively weak sunlight.

(J) Bioluminescent animals use countershading as a way to elude predators that lurk in the sunlit waters above them.

35. The reference to bank robbers in line 68 serves mainly to

(A) distinguish between two phenomena that appear similar but are fundamentally different.

(B) suggest a practical application for recent discoveries from natural science.

(C) point out the weaknesses in one proposed solution to a scientific conundrum.

(D) clarify a phenomenon of the animal world by comparing it to human behavior.

36. The author mentions the behavior of bioluminescent and nonluminous dionoflagellates (lines 98–104) primarily in order to illustrate

(F) why bioluminescence is generally considered an unnecessary function in dinoflagellates.

(G) one of the functions of bioluminescence in the ocean's midwaters.

(H) why more species have not evolved with bioluminescence.

(J) how nonluminous animals may benefit from proximity to luminous ones.

37. The passage implies that, if bioluminescence were NOT a nonessential characteristic, which of the following would be true?

(A) Luminous species would be seen to thrive more successfully than closely related nonluminous ones.

(B) Nonluminous species would enjoy a reproductive advantage by comparison to luminous ones.

(C) Luminous species would gradually die out and be replaced by closely related nonluminous ones.

(D) Luminous and nonluminous species would not be observed living in proximity to one another.

38. The phrase "selection pressure" in line 108–109 refers to

    (F) the potential extinction of an animal species due to the depletion of essential resources.

    (G) environmental factors that favor development of a particular biological characteristic.

    (H) competition among predators for a finite population of prey.

    (J) selective winnowing of an animal population based on the attractiveness of specific individuals.

39. By comparison with the other species mentioned in the passage, the phenomenon of bioluminescence in the tomopterid worm discussed in lines 116–125 might best be described as

    (A) extreme.
    (B) archetypal.
    (C) exceptional.
    (D) prototypical.

40. The author's comments about the tomopterid worm would be most seriously called into question by the discovery of which of the following?

    (F) A predator of the tomopterid worm that is sensitive to yellow light

    (G) Another species of tomopterid worm that produces bioluminescent blue-green fluid

    (H) A prey of the tomopterid worm that does not exhibit bioluminescence

    (J) Other species of midwater animals that produce bioluminescent yellow fluids

STOP End of Section 1. If you have any time left, go over your work in this section only. Do not work in any other section of the test.

SECTION 4

SCIENCE REASONING

40 Questions

Time—35 Minutes

Directions: This test consists of seven passages, each followed by several questions. Read each passage, select the correct answer for each question, and mark the oval representing the correct answer on your answer sheet. You may NOT use a calculator on this test.

Passage I

Tree age is important to researchers for understanding typical life cycles in the forest and developing sustainable forestry practices. Counting tree rings is the method that is usually used to determine the age of trees, but in tropical rain forests, such as the Amazon, tree rings may be irregular (not annual) or nonexistent.

Carbon-14 dating is another method of determining tree age. Trees take carbon dioxide, which contains some of the radioactive element carbon-14, into their tissues at a known rate. By measuring the levels of carbon-14 in a plant, scientists can determine its age. Table 8.1 lists the age and other data for trees that have emerged from the canopy in a small Amazon forest plot. The age of the trees was determined by carbon-14 dating.

Historical patterns of forest disturbance are also important to biologists for determining the extent to which the forest is affected and the forest's pattern of recovery. The following diagram (figure below) shows the catastrophic events that are known to have occurred in the area where the trees in Table 8.1 were growing.

Table 8.1

Tree #	Tree Species	Tree Diameter (cm)	Tree Age (Years)	Calculated Average Growth Rate (cm/yr)
1	Cariniana micrantha	140	200	0.7
2	Cariniana micrantha	100	400	0.25
3	Cariniana micrantha	140	1,400	0.1
4	Hymenolobium species	180	300	0.6
5	Hymenolobium species	90	900	0.1
6	Bagassa guianansis	120	400	0.3
7	Bagassa guianansis	150	300	0.5
8	Caryocar glabrum	130	200	0.65
9	Caryocar vilosum	120	200	0.6
10	Iryanthera grandis	160	800	0.2
11	Dipteryx odorata	120	1,200	0.1
12	Sclerolobium species	80	200	0.4

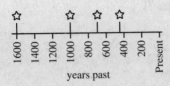

years past

Legend: ☆ = catastrophic event

1. Looking at trees in just the *Hymenolobium* species (trees 4 and 5) in Table 8.1, researchers might conclude that

   (A)   tree age is positively correlated with both tree diameter and growth rate.
   (B)   tree age is inversely correlated with tree diameter and positively correlated with growth rate.
   (C)   tree age is inversely correlated with tree diameter and growth rate.
   (D)   tree diameter is inversely correlated with growth rate.

2. Based on the data presented, which of the following statements is true?

   (F)   Trees 5 and 12 demonstrate that tree diameter is a relatively poor predictor of tree age.
   (G)   Trees 5 and 12 demonstrate that trees that survived a natural catastrophe will begin to grow at a faster rate because there is little competition for resources.
   (H)   Trees 5 and 12 demonstrate inconsistencies in the carbon-14 dating process.
   (J)   Trees 5 and 12 demonstrate that it is not always possible to calculate a tree's average growth rate even when the tree's diameter and age are known.

3. Looking at the catastrophe time line and the data in Table 8.1, it is clear that

   (A)   more than half of the canopy trees in the forest plot survived the most recent catastrophe.
   (B)   about half of the canopy trees in the forest plot survived at least two catastrophes.
   (C)   about one third of the canopy trees in the forest plot survived at least two catastrophes.
   (D)   some trees will always survive a natural catastrophe.

4. If a tree has an age of 1,100 years and a long-term average growth rate of 0.1 cm./year, what is the diameter of the tree?

   (F)   100 cm.
   (G)   110 cm.
   (H)   120 cm.
   (J)   It cannot be determined.

5. Which of the following conclusions do the growth rates of trees 1, 2, and 3 demonstrate?

   (A)   Canopy trees of a single species tend to be close in age.
   (B)   Canopy trees of different species may have widely divergent ages.
   (C)   Average growth rates generally remain constant for each species.
   (D)   Trees of the same species may have different average growth rates at different ages.

GO ON TO THE NEXT PAGE

6. Reaching the canopy, with its important resource of sunlight, is a critical goal for rain forest trees. The traditional view is that trees have a fast growth spurt to reach the canopy. The researchers in this study hypothesized that trees might reach the canopy using strategies of fast or slow growth and that both strategies might be used by trees in the same species. Which of the following findings would support their theory?

(F) It is discovered that tree #3 reached the canopy 1,200 years ago.

(G) Research on trees that have not reached the canopy show that they are all under 200 years of age.

(H) The growth rates of trees that have not reached the canopy are investigated and are found to be highly variable.

(J) The growth rates of trees that have not reached the canopy are investigated and are found to be relatively fast.

Passage II

Recently, flywheels with magnetic bearings have been designed (see figure below). These flywheels produce none of the friction associated with mechanical bearings, making them efficient energy storage devices. One application they may have is in alternative energy cars. In experimental designs, a flywheel is "spun-up" while the car is at rest with the electrical power supplied from a standard electrical outlet. After the flywheel has reached a high rate of rotation, the car can be disconnected from the socket and the energy can be extracted from the high-speed rotating flywheel.

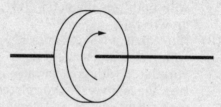

Experiment 1

Researchers looked at flywheels with different radii to gauge the effect of size on the total energy they could store. The wheels were all started at an initial frequency of 50 revolutions per second (rev/sec). All of the flywheels were *disk-type* (they had a uniform thickness along their entire radius), all were made of the same material, and all had the same thickness. After reaching the initial speed, a uniform resisting force was applied to determine how much energy it took to stop the wheel. The results of this experiment appear in Table 8.2.

Table 8.2

Radius (cm)	Energy Stored (joules)
10	100
20	1600
30	8100
40	25600

Experiment 2

Next, a disk-type flywheel with a radius of 30 cm was brought up to various initial speeds by an electric motor. The energy stored at each speed was measured. Results appear in Table 8.3.

Table 8.3

Frequency (rev/sec)	Energy Stored
40	5184
60	11664
80	20736
100	32400

Experiment 3

One of the limiting factors in the use of flywheels is the *centrifugal force* (the force pulling outward from the rim) that is generated as the wheel is turning. When this force becomes too great, it causes the wheel to fly apart or explode. The centrifugal force is determined by the frequency and the radius of the wheel. A doubling of the radius results in a doubling of the centrifugal force; a doubling of the frequency results in a quadrupling of the centrifugal force.

Researchers tested four wheel designs (see figure below). All of the wheels had a radius of 30 cm and the same mass; wheel thicknesses were changed to keep the mass constant. The frequency of each wheel was increased slowly until it exploded. The frequency at which this occurred as well as the energy stored in the wheel at the time was recorded. Results appear in Table 8.4.

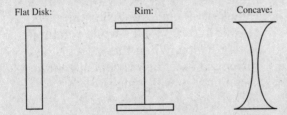

Flat Disk: Rim: Concave:

Table 8.4

Flywheel Type	Energy Stored (Joules)	Strength (Maximum Frequency) (rev/sec)
Flat Disk	17266	73
Rimmed	16231	42
Concave Disk	19627	72

7. The difference between Experiment 1 and Experiment 2 is

   (A) in Experiment 1, the flywheel radius is varied, while in Experiment 2, the initial speed of the flywheel is varied.

   (B) in Experiment 1 the flywheel type is varied, while in Experiment 2 the initial flywheel speed is varied.

   (C) in Experiment 2 the resisting force is varied, while in Experiment 1 it is uniform.

   (D) in Experiment 1 the centrifugal force was varied, while in Experiment 2 it remains constant.

8. Assuming that the researchers considered energy storage and wheel strength to be of equal importance, which of the wheel designs in Experiment 3 would they conclude was optimal?

   (F) Flat Disk
   (G) Rimmed
   (H) Concave disk
   (J) The best design would depend on the wheel radius.

9. The experimental data indicate that for optimal energy storage the flywheel should be a

   (A) concave wheel with a large radius.
   (B) rimmed wheel a small radius.
   (C) flat disk wheel with a large radius.
   (D) concave wheel with a small radius.

10. Which of the following statements about the centrifugal force on a flywheel is best supported by the data presented?

   (F) A graph of the force versus wheel radius would look similar to a graph of frequency versus energy stored.

   (G) A graph of the force versus wheel radius would look similar to a graph of energy stored versus wheel strength.

   (H) A graph of the force versus frequency would look similar to a graph of frequency versus energy stored.

   (J) A graph of the force versus frequency would look similar to a graph of energy stored versus wheel strength.

11. A car has a disk-type flywheel with a radius of 30 cm. The disk is initially storing 120,000 joules while rotating at 64 rev/sec. When the wheel is turning at half the original speed, how much energy will remain?

   (A) 10,000 joules
   (B) 30,000 joules
   (C) 50,000 joules
   (D) 70,000 joules

Table 8.5

	Sulphate Concentration (Mg/L)			
Lakes	1990–92	1992–94	1994–96	1996–98
1	0.65	0.60	0.60	0.59
2	0.60	0.59	0.58	0.50
3	0.82	0.82	0.80	0.69
4	0.89	0.69	0.66	0.66
5	0.68	0.65	0.67	0.69

12. Flywheels have been considered for the storage of energy that is collected using solar panels during the day. This stored energy could be used as a city power source at night. Such a flywheel would need to handle vast amounts of energy, perhaps 5 million Megajoules. In consideration of these energy storage needs and safety, which of the following would be the best design for such a system?

   I.   One very large flywheel that would turn at a relatively slow frequency

   II. Collections of small flywheels, each turning at high frequencies

   III. One large flywheel that would transfer its energy to many smaller flywheels as it slowed down

   (F) I only
   (G) II only
   (H) III only
   (J) I or III only

Passage III

Lake ecosystems are highly sensitive to changes in the acid-base balance. In the last few decades there has been concern about increases in lake sulphate concentrations and pH. This has led to an environmental campaign to reduce the amount of sulphates released into the atmosphere from industrial sources.

Experiment 1

Ecologists measured the *terrestrial deposition* (land deposits) of sulphate at five alpine stations located adjacent to lakes annually between 1990 and 1998. Sulphate was measured in soil and rock samples. The averages for two-year sampling periods appear in Table 8.5.

Experiment 2

In 1998, the researchers looked at the sulphate concentrations (in µ mequivalents/L) and pH in the lakes adjacent to the alpine stations and compared them to concentrations recorded in the same lakes in 1990. Results appear in the following figure.

GO ON TO THE NEXT PAGE

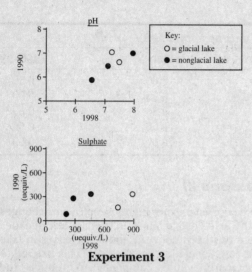

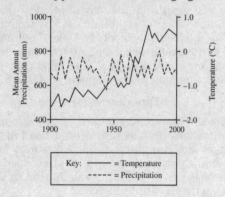

Experiment 3

In order to take into account changing climatic parameters in the study area, the researchers looked at rainfall and temperature since 1900. The results appear in the following figure.

13. The researchers discovered that during the study period

(A) the trend in sulphate lake concentration was neither up nor down, but tended to mirror terrestrial deposition trends.

(B) terrestrial deposition and lake concentrations of sulphate increased.

(C) terrestrial deposition and lake concentrations of sulphate decreased.

(D) terrestrial deposition of sulphate decreased, while lake concentrations increased.

14. One difference between Experiments 1 and 2 was

(F) Experiment 1 was conducted over a longer period of time.

(G) Experiment 2 looked at glacial and nonglacial lakes, while Experiment 1 looked at only glacial lakes.

(H) Experiment 2 measured pH and sulphate concentrations, while Experiment 1 measured only sulphate concentrations.

(J) in Experiment 1, data was collected by analyzing rocks and soil, while in Experiment 2, air samples were taken.

15. Experiment 2 demonstrated that

(A) lake pH did not increase in the study period.

(B) the increase in pH in the study period was more dramatic than the increase in sulphate.

(C) the increase in sulphate was more dramatic in glacial lakes than in nonglacial lakes.

(D) the increase in pH was more dramatic in glacial lakes than in alpine lakes.

Table 8.6

Terrestrial Bodies	Average Density (water = 1)	Average Distance From Sun (millions of miles)	Rotational Period (Earth days)	Orbital Period (Earth days)	Orbital Eccentricity	Mean Surface Temp. (°C)	Description
Mercury	5.4	36	59	.206	.206	179	Rocky, ferrous
Venus	5.2	67	243	.007	.007	480	Rocky, ferrous
Earth	5.5	93	24 hrs	.017	.017	22	Rocky, ferrous
Mars	3.9	142	25 hrs	.093	.093	−23	Rocky
Jupiter	1.3	484	9 hrs	.048	.048	−150	Gaseous
Saturn	0.7	887	10 hrs	.056	.056	−180	Gaseous
Uranus	1.2	1,783	11 hrs	.047	.047	−210	Icy, gaseous
Neptune	1.7	2,794	16 hrs	.009	.009	−220	Icy, gaseous
Pluto	1	3,600	6	.25	.25	−230	Icy, rocky, gaseous

16. Which of the following statements about the sulphate concentrations measured in Experiment 1 is best supported by the data presented?

(F) Concentrations dropped in all the study areas.

(G) Concentration drops were most profound for lake 4.

(H) Concentrations dropped by about 75% for most areas.

(J) Concentrations dropped by about 50% for most areas.

17. Which of the following hypotheses might explain the findings of Experiment 2 in a way that is consistent with the findings in the other two studies?

I. Warmer air temperatures in the lake areas may have resulted in less annual ice cover. This provided more time for the weathering, by light and wind, of sulphate-containing rocks, leading to sulphate runoff into the lakes.

II. Drought conditions in the lake areas may have led to lower water levels, which concentrated the sulphate present.

III. The environmental campaign failed to reduce sulphate emissions.

(A) I only

(B) III only

(C) I or II only

(D) II or III only

GO ON TO THE NEXT PAGE

Passage IV

In the 1970s, a spacecraft called the Mariner 10 flew by Mercury at close range three times. These *flybys* provided clues about an intriguing planet that we know less about than any other barring Pluto. Table 8.6 shows data on Mercury, compared with the other planets in our Solar System. Some of the numbers are approximations only. A planet's *rotational period* is the time it takes to turn once on its axis, completing one planetary day. A planet's *orbital period* is the time it takes to move once around the sun, completing one planetary year.

The following figure is a plot of the density versus the radius for the *terrestrial* (nongaseous) planets.

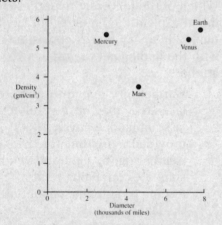

18. Looking at the rotational periods and orbital periods in Table 8.6, it is clear that
    - (F) a Mercury day is about two-thirds the length of a Mercury year.
    - (G) a Mercury year is about two-thirds the length of a Mercury day.
    - (H) a Mercury year is about half the length of a Mercury day.
    - (J) a Mercury year is about the same length as a Mercury day.

19. If the moon (a terrestrial body) has a diameter of about 4000 miles and a density of about 3.3 g/cm^3, which of the following statements is most probably correct?
    - (A) The density versus diameter of terrestrial bodies appears to have a linear relationship.
    - (B) The density versus diameter of terrestrial bodies appears to have a linear relationship for Mars, Venus, and Earth only.
    - (C) The density versus diameter for the moon follows the linear relationship seen with the other terrestrial bodies, with the exception of Mercury.
    - (D) The linear relationship of density versus diameter does not appear to apply to terrestrial bodies other than the planets.

20. Which of the following is the terrestrial planet with the most eccentric orbit?
    - (F) Mercury
    - (G) Earth
    - (H) Jupiter
    - (J) Pluto

21. Which planet has a density that is most similar to that of water?
    - (A) Jupiter
    - (B) Saturn
    - (C) Uranus
    - (D) Pluto

22. Mercury has the hottest peak daytime temperature of any planet (around 973 °C). Based on this information, which of the following statements is most probably correct?

   (F) Mean surface temperature is a good predictor of daytime temperature.
   (G) Mercury's temperature remains stable throughout its rotational period.
   (H) Temperatures plunge on Mercury at night.
   (J) Nighttime temperatures are warmer on Mercury than daytime temperatures.

23. It is thought that Mercury has the largest *core* (dense planet center) in relation to the planet's overall size of any of the terrestrial planets. If the Earth's core is approximately 3,000 miles in diameter, which of the following is a probable diameter for Mercury's core?

   (A) Greater than 3,000 miles
   (B) Around 2,000 miles
   (C) Around 1,000 miles
   (D) Around 500 miles

Passage V

Schizophrenia is a mental illness that involves the dissociation of reason and emotion, resulting in symptoms including hallucinations, hearing voices, intense withdrawal, delusions, and paranoia. The average age at which schizophrenia is diagnosed is 18 years for men and 23 years for women. It has been observed to run in families.

The cause remains a mystery, but there are several competing theories. These theories are based in part on findings from twin studies, which look at identical twins in which one or both have the disease. (Identical twins share 100% of their genetic material, while nonidentical twins share about 50%.) In 50% of the cases, when one identical twin is affected, the other will also suffer from schizophrenia. Identical twin pairs in which one individual is ill and the other is well are referred to as *discordant twins*.

Genetic Theory

One school of thought is that schizophrenia is a *genetic disorder* (one passed through the genes from parents to children). This theory gained support from the fact that schizophrenia runs in families. While it was originally believed that it was the family environment that caused this, a study has shown that children of schizophrenics adopted by families without the disease have the same risk of developing the illness as those raised by their birth parents. A final piece of evidence is the fact that the children of discordant identical twins all have the same chance of developing the illness: 17%. This indicates that even the healthy twin is somehow carrying the agent of the disease, presumably in the genes.

Infection Theory

Another school of thought is that schizophrenia arises because of a viral infection of the brain. Studies have shown that a class of viruses called "slow viruses" can linger in the brain for 20 years or longer before the infected person shows symptoms. Brain infections with viruses such as the common cold-sore virus and herpes simplex type 1 can cause symptoms that

GO ON TO THE NEXT PAGE

resemble schizophrenia. Schizophrenia is also more common in children born in the winter, the season when viral infections are more common. Also, one study looking at families with a history of schizophrenia showed a 70% increase in the rate of schizophrenia among children whose mothers had the flu during the second trimester of pregnancy.

24. The schizophrenia theories are similar in that

(F) both postulate that the foundation of the illness may be laid before birth.

(G) both postulate that the family environment plays some role.

(H) both predict that the children of schizophrenics are not at greater risk than other individuals.

(J) both show that identical twins are at greater risk for schizophrenia than other individuals.

25. Which of the following findings best supports the gene theory?

(A) Parents of discordant twins report that the behavior of the twins begins to diverge at about five years of age, on average.

(B) In discordant identical twin pairs, a brain structure called the basal ganglia is activated more often in the ill twin than in the healthy twin.

(C) An identical twin of a schizophrenia sufferer is four times as likely to have the illness as a nonidentical twin of a schizophrenia sufferer.

(D) Studies have shown that viral infections sometimes infect one identical twin in the uterus and not the other.

26. The infection theory is most effective at explaining the fact that

I. schizophrenic patients do poorly on some memory tests.

II. among identical twins discordant for schizophrenia, the healthy twin may have some borderline schizophrenic traits.

III. ill twins in discordant pairs have higher rates of finger abnormalities, which can be an indication of a viral infection that occurred in the womb.

(F) I only

(G) II only

(H) III only

(J) II and III only

27. Which of the following hypotheses might supporters of both theories agree with?

I. Individuals with schizophrenia have certain genes that predispose them to the disease but that require some kind of trigger to turn the disease on.

II. Individuals with schizophrenia have certain genes that predispose them to viral infections of the brain.

III. Schizophrenia is not one disease but a collection of diseases.

(A) I and II only

(B) I and III only

(C) II and III only

(D) I, II, and III

28. An identical pair of twins is found in which one was adopted at birth. Both received a diagnosis of schizophrenia as teenagers. An explanation that might be offered by supporters of the viral theory is

(F) children are most prone to viral infections when they are school age, long after the infant in this case was adopted.

(G) the stress of being an adopted child may have triggered schizophrenia in the predisposed twin.

(H) since 50% of identical twin pairs with schizophrenia are discordant for the disease, this case does not shed light on its origin.

(J) the brains of both twins may have been infected with a slow-acting virus when they were still in the womb.

29. Which of the following studies would be logical for supporters of the genetic theory to conduct next?

(A) One that looks for finger abnormalities in the parents and grandparents of schizophrenic children

(B) One that looks for differences in the chromosomes (which hold the genes) of schizophrenic individuals and healthy individuals

(C) One that looks for scarring in the brains of schizophrenic individuals, which might be a sign of an early injury or infection

(D) One that looks at the home environments of identical twins versus nonidentical twins.

Passage VI

Researchers are experimenting with chemical sensors that could act as artificial noses. These artificial noses are capable of detecting odors indicating that meats or produce are spoiling, making them useful in the food industry. The sensors detect volatile organic compounds (VOCs), which are indicators of food quality. In an experimental system, researchers created thick films of certain *semiconductors* (materials that are neither good electrical conductors nor insulators). Each film is sensitive to a small range of VOCs. When they come into contact with these VOCs, they are *oxidized*. In this process, oxygen molecules combine with the semiconductors to form new molecules, and free electrons are released. The addition of the free electrons alters the electrical properties of the semiconductor films, and this electrical change is detected.

Experiment 1

Researchers developed artificial noses by coupling a number of different VOC detectors, similar to those described above. They then tested the ability of the different artificial noses to detect these VOCs. Results appear in the following figure.

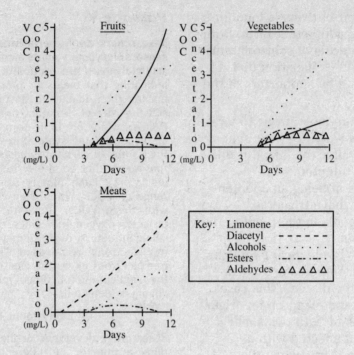

Experiment 2

The researchers sampled the air on a daily basis above a variety of stored fruits, vegetables, and meats. These air samples were injected into the column of a *chromatograph*. A chromatograph is a tool that separates mixtures into their component parts allowing researchers to identify the vapors. The results of the chromatograph experiment appear in the following figure. (Low-molecular weight alcohols, esters, and aldehydes appear grouped in the results.)

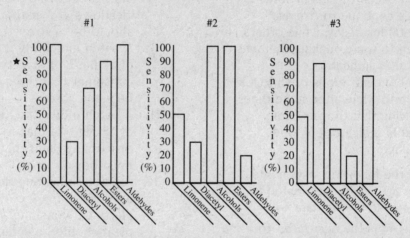

Artificial Noses

★ Sensitivity is the percentage of total VOC detected

30. Which of the following statements is best supported by the experimental data presented?

(F) Alcohols are the most important VOCs for the detection of fruit spoilage.

(G) Limonene is the most important VOC for the detection of fruit spoilage.

(H) Diacetyl is the most important VOC for the detection of vegetable spoilage.

(J) Esters are the most important VOCs for the detection of meat spoilage.

31. Which of the following is the most likely interpretation of the data on vegetable spoilage?

    (A) Vegetables start to spoil slightly earlier than fruits.
    (B) Vegetables start to spoil on about day 5, but show improvement by day 9.
    (C) The concentrations of some VOCs continue to rise as vegetables decay, while others begin to wane, making them less useful as indicators.
    (D) The concentrations of all VOCs begin to wane after some time, showing that they are not reliable indicators of food spoilage.

32. Which of the following statements about the artificial noses tested is best supported by the data?

    (F) Nose #1 is the best indicator of meat spoilage.
    (G) Nose #2 is the best indicator of vegetable spoilage.
    (H) Nose #2 is the best indicator of fruit spoilage.
    (J) Nose #3 is the best indicator of fruit spoilage.

33. If cost constraints limited a food processing company to one VOC detector for use in testing fruits, vegetables, and meats, which would be the best choice?

    (A) A limonene detector
    (B) An alcohol detector
    (C) An ester detector
    (D) A diacetyl detector

34. Diacetyl concentration accumulates slowly. Its first appearance signals the tenderization of the meat. If researchers were to create a patch that would appear on packaged meats indicating diacetyl presence, which of the following would be the best use of such a patch?

    (F) A patch sensitive to the presence of .05 mg/L of diacetyl, alerting a grocer that the meat should be destroyed
    (G) A patch indicating the presence of ≥2 mg/L of diacetyl, alerting a consumer that the meat should be eaten soon
    (H) A patch indicating the presence of ≥2 mg/L of diacetyl, alerting a processing plant that the meat must be sold soon
    (J) A patch indicating the appearance of 0.5 mg/L of diacetyl, alerting a consumer that the meat should be eaten soon

Passage VII

Interstellar objects (objects among the stars) in outer galaxies are often investigated using a method known as *spectroscopy*. Spectroscopy is a method of determining the atomic or molecular makeup of something by observing the object's *spectral lines*. Atoms and molecules have fixed energy levels. When an electron in an atom moves from one of its possible energy states to another, the atom releases light. This light has an energy equal to the difference in the two energy levels through which the electron moved. These energy transitions are observed as a sequence of spectral lines. Spectral lines that are close together indicate transitions in which the change in energy levels is similar.

The following figure depicts three hypothetical atoms. Energy levels are represented as horizontal segments. The distance between the segments is representative of the energy difference between the various levels. All possible transitions between energy levels are indicated by arrows.

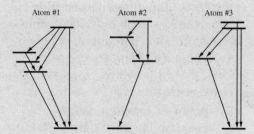

Scientists can observe the spectral lines of atoms that are dominant in far-away galaxies. Due to the speed at which these galaxies are traveling, these lines are shifted, but their pattern remains the same. This allows researchers to use the spectral pattern to determine which atoms they are seeing. Table 8.7 shows spectroscopic measurements made by researchers trying to determine the atomic makeup of a particular far-away galaxy. Light energy is not measured directly, but rather is determined from measuring the frequency of light, which is proportional to the energy.

Table 8.7

Frequencies Measured
2096400
2092790
2021140
1940200
1946260

35. Which of the following statements is correct, based on the information in the figure?

    (A) Atom #1 has five energy levels.
    (B) Atom #1 has seven energy levels.
    (C) Atom #3 has more energy levels than atom #2.
    (D) The greatest energy transition in atom #2 is larger than the greatest transition in atom #3.

36. Which of the following statements is most likely to be incorrect, based on the information in the figure?

    (F) Atom #1 would emit six spectral lines.
    (G) Atom #2 would emit four spectral lines.
    (H) Atom #3 would emit five spectral lines.
    (J) The number of spectral lines emitted by an atom does not necessarily match the number of energy levels.

37. Physicists using spectroscopy to investigate the atoms depicted in the figure would observe which of the following?

    (A) Atom #2 would have three spectral lines that are very close together.
    (B) Atom #3 would have two spectral lines that are very close together and three more spectral lines that are relatively far from each other.
    (C) Atom #3 would have three spectral lines that are very close together.
    (D) Atom #1 would have three spectral lines that were close together as well as another pair of spectral lines which are very close together.

38. The researchers making the measurements for Table 8.7 might reach which of the following conclusions?

    I. The atoms appear to have five energy levels, indicating that they could be the same as atom #1.
    II. The atoms appear to be emitting two sets of two closely spaced frequencies, indicating that they could be the same as atom #3.
    III. The observed atoms do not appear to be going through any transitions in energy levels.

    (F) I only
    (G) II only
    (H) III only
    (J) II and III only

39. Atoms have "forbidden" transitions. These are transitions between energy levels that are not allowed by the laws of conservation in atomic physics. Which of the following statements concerning the atoms in the figure are true?

    (A) Atom #1 has no forbidden transitions.
    (B) Atom #2 has one forbidden transition.
    (C) Atom #3 has no forbidden transitions.
    (D) Atom #3 has more than one forbidden transition.

40. The difference in the information represented in the figure and Table 8.7 is

    (F) the figure was arrived at with spectroscopic measurements, while the information in Table 8.7 was arrived at using only a mathematical formula.
    (G) the figure indicates the pattern of frequencies emitted by an atom, while Table 8.7 indicates the exact frequencies emitted by an atom.
    (H) the figure indicates the number of energy levels that an atom has, while in Table 8.7 this number can be determined only by identifying the atom being observed.
    (J) the figure gives an idea of the proximity of spectral lines associated with the atoms, while Table 8.7 indicates only the energy levels associated with the atoms observed.

STOP   End of Section 1. If you have any time left, go over your work in this section only. Do not work in any other section of the test.

Answer Key

	Section 1 English			Section 2 Mathematics		Section 3 Reading		Section 4 Reasoning	

Section 1 English			Section 2 Mathematics		Section 3 Reading		Section 4 Reasoning	
1. D	26. G	51. C	1. C	31. C	1. B	21. C	1. C	20. F
2. G	27. B	52. H	2. J	32. K	2. H	22. J	2. F	21. D
3. C	28. F	53. A	3. A	33. D	3. B	23. A	3. C	22. H
4. J	29. C	54. G	4. K	34. F	4. F	24. H	4. G	23. B
5. D	30. J	55. D	5. E	35. E	5. D	25. A	5. D	24. F
6. F	31. A	56. F	6. K	36. H	6. H	26. H	6. H	25. C
7. C	32. G	57. B	7. C	37. D	7. A	27. C	7. A	26. H
8. J	33. B	58. J	8. J	38. J	8. H	28. F	8. H	27. D
9. D	34. J	59. C	9. D	39. C	9. A	29. C	9. A	28. J
10. G	35. A	60. J	10. J	40. J	10. F	30. G	10. H	29. B
11. C	36. H	61. B	11. D	41. E	11. C	31. B	11. B	30. G
12. F	37. C	62. F	12. H	42. G	12. F	32. H	12. F	31. C
13. D	38. F	63. D	13. E	43. D	13. B	33. C	13. D	32. G
14. F	39. A	64. G	14. F	44. G	14. J	34. J	14. H	33. B
15. C	40. G	65. C	15. E	45. A	15. C	35. D	15. C	34. J
16. G	41. C	66. H	16. F	46. G	16. J	36. J	16. G	35. A
17. D	42. H	67. A	17. C	47. C	17. C	37. A	17. A	36. F
18. G	43. D	68. J	18. H	48. G	18. F	38. G	18. F	37. D
19. C	44. F	69. B	19. B	49. E	19. C	39. C	19. C	38. G
20. G	45. C	70. J	20. F	50. F	20. G	40. F		39. B
21. A	46. G	71. B	21. C	51. D				40. A
22. F	47. B	72. H	22. G	52. J				
23. D	48. J	73. D	23. A	53. B				
24. H	49. D	74. G	24. F	54. K				
25. C	50. F	75. D	25. A	55. A				
			26. J	56. F				
			27. C	57. E				
			28. H	58. H				
			29. B	59. D				
			30. H	60. J				

Scoring Guide

COMPUTING YOUR SCALED SCORES

Section 1—English: Count the number of correct answers you chose for the questions in Test 1. Write the total here: _____. This is your English Raw Score.

Look up your English Raw Score on the Score Conversion Table. Find the corresponding English Scaled Score and write it here: _____.

Section 2—Mathematics: Count the number of correct answers you chose for the questions in Test 2. Write the total here: _____. This is your Mathematics Raw Score.

Look up your Mathematics Raw Score on the Score Conversion Table. Find the corresponding Mathematics Scaled Score and write it here: _____.

Section 3—Reading: Count the number of correct answers you chose for the questions in Test 3. Write the total here: _____. This is your Reading Raw Score.

Look up your Reading Raw Score on the Score Conversion Table. Find the corresponding Reading Scaled Score and write it here: _____.

Section 4—Science Reasoning: Count the number of correct answers you chose for the questions in Test 4. Write the total here: _____. This is your Science Reasoning Raw Score.

Look up your Science Reasoning Raw Score on the Score Conversion Table. Find the corresponding Science Reasoning Scaled Score and write it here: _____.

Your Composite Score: Total your four scaled scores and divide the sum by 4. (Round a fraction to the nearest whole number; round up.) This is your Composite Score. Write it here: _____.

Score Conversion Table

Insider's ACT Sample Exam

Raw Score	English Scaled Score	Math Scaled Score	Reading Scaled Score	Science Scaled Score
75	36			
74	35			
73	34			
72	33			
71	32			
70	31			
69	30			
68	30			
67	29			
66	29			
65	28			
64	28			
63	27			
62	27			
61	26			
60	26	36		
59	25	35		
58	25	34		
57	24	34		
56	24	33		
55	23	32		
54	23	31		
53	23	30		
52	22	30		
51	22	29		
50	22	29		
49	21	28		
48	21	28		
47	21	27		
46	20	27		
45	20	26		
44	20	26		
43	19	25		
42	19	25		
41	19	24		
40	18	24	36	36
39	18	23	35	34

Raw Score	English Scaled Score	Math Scaled Score	Reading Scaled Score	Science Scaled Score
38	18	23	33	32
37	17	23	32	30
36	17	22	31	29
35	17	22	30	28
34	16	21	29	27
33	16	21	28	27
32	15	20	27	26
31	15	20	27	25
30	14	19	26	24
29	14	19	25	24
28	14	19	25	23
27	13	18	24	23
26	13	18	23	22
25	13	18	23	22
24	12	17	22	21
23	12	17	21	21
22	12	17	20	20
21	11	16	19	20
20	11	16	18	19
19	11	16	18	19
18	10	15	17	18
17	10	15	16	18
16	10	15	15	17
15	9	14	15	17
14	9	14	14	16
13	9	14	14	16
12	8	13	13	15
11	8	13	13	15
10	7	13	12	14
9	7	12	11	13
8	6	12	10	12
7	6	11	8	11
6	5	11	7	10
5	4	10	6	9
4	3	8	5	8
3	2	6	4	7
2	2	5	3	5
1	1	3	2	3
0	1	1	1	1

Explanatory Answers

SECTION 1: ENGLISH

1. **The correct answer is (D).** Since the event being described is a past event prior to another past event, the verb tense that's needed is the past perfect, not the present perfect: "I'd heard" rather than "I've heard."

2. **The correct answer is (G).** When two independent clauses are joined by the conjunction "and," a comma is normally inserted *before* the "and" (unless the clauses are very short). It's not necessary or particularly effective to use either a semicolon, as in choice (H), or a period, as in choice (J), to separate these two clauses; they naturally seem to belong together.

3. **The correct answer is (C).** Since the antecedent of the pronoun is "the reed" (singular), the pronoun should be the singular "it" rather than the plural "they."

4. **The correct answer is (J).** The logical connector here is "but" rather than "so," since a contrast rather than a cause-and-effect relationship is being described. The semicolon in choice (H) is wrong; with the conjunction "although," the second clause becomes a subordinate or dependent clause, which can't stand alone as a sentence and therefore can't properly follow a semicolon.

5. **The correct answer is (D).** In both the original wording and choice (B), what follows the period is a fragment rather than a complete sentence. In choice (C), the combined sentences form a run-on. Choice (D) avoids both errors.

6. **The correct answer is (F).** The original phrase substantiates the writer's complaint about the high price of oboe reeds. Choices (G), (H), and (J) introduce ideas that are either completely irrelevant or slightly off the point.

7. **The correct answer is (C).** Both the original wording and choice (B) create run-on sentences. The shift of pronoun to "one" in choice (D) sounds a little stilted, and the colon seems less appropriate than the semicolon. (Generally, the colon is best when it could be replaced with the phrase "that is," which isn't the case here.)

8. **The correct answer is (J).** All of the answer choices are grammatically correct, but choice (J) is the most concise.

9. **The correct answer is (D).** The underlined words can be omitted because they merely repeat the idea already stated in the words "progressively worse."

10. **The correct answer is (G).** The pronoun reference here is unclear: who or what is "they"? Choices (G) and (H) both clarify what is being referred to (the reeds, of course), but (G) does so more concisely.

11. **The correct answer is (C).** The modifier "desperate" must be next to "I," since that is the person whom the modifier describes.

12. **The correct answer is (F).** As in the original wording, the parenthetical phrase "within two weeks" should be set off from the rest of the sentence by a pair of commas.

13. **The correct answer is (D).** The placement of the modifying word is fine, but it should be changed from an adjective to an adverb ("immediately"), since it modifies the verb "called."

14. **The correct answer is (F).** This basic introductory information about what oboe reeds are needs to appear early in the essay.

15. **The correct answer is (C).** The information in Paragraph 4 is relevant to the overall contents and theme of the essay, since it contributes to the explanation of why oboists have so much difficulty in getting enough good reeds for their instruments.

16. **The correct answer is (G).** The subject of the verb is "goal," so the verb should be singular, "was" rather than "were." "To determine" is the idiomatic construction to use in this context.

17. **The correct answer is (D).** The original wording is verbose and repetitive; so, to a lesser extent, are choices (B) and (C). Choice (D) says the same thing concisely.

18. **The correct answer is (G).** The paragraph is devoted to explaining the two underlying ideas that guided the scientists who designed the Viking experiments. Choice (G) sets this up accurately and clearly.

19. **The correct answer is (C).** The semicolon in the original wording is wrong, since what follows the semicolon can't stand alone as a sentence. Changing the punctuation mark to a comma solves the problem.

20. **The correct answer is (G).** This is the most idiomatic (normal-sounding) and clear of the alternatives. Note that choice (H) is definitely wrong because it's unclear who or what "contains" the thousands or millions of lifeforms mentioned.

21. **The correct answer is (A).** Having explained in Paragraph 2 that the Viking scientists wanted to look for the most abundant forms of life and that these were expected to take the form of soil-dwelling microbes, this sentence makes a logical transition to Paragraph 3 by beginning the explanation of how the Viking experiments were designed to search for creatures of these kinds.

22. **The correct answer is (F).** The original wording is correct. The possessive form (using an apostrophe) isn't appropriate here, since "organisms" isn't followed by anything that is "possessed" by the organisms, nor is any such possession implied.

23. **The correct answer is (D).** The idiomatic way to phrase this is the one in choice (D): "one characteristic . . . is that they transform."

24. **The correct answer is (H).** This phrasing provides the most specific information about the plant structures that the writer is thinking about.

25. **The correct answer is (C).** The essay is about how the Viking experiments were designed to test for life on Mars. In that context, information about how long the Martian day lasts is basically irrelevant.

26. **The correct answer is (G).** The three clauses being strung together here should be in grammatically parallel form. Choice (G) carries out the parallelism.

27. **The correct answer is (B).** Sentences 1 and 3 belong together; both describe how living organisms on Earth give off gases. Sentence 2 follows naturally after these; it connects this phenomenon to one of the Viking tests. Sentence 4 provides detail about the test and makes a natural conclusion.

28. **The correct answer is (F).** It makes sense to start a new paragraph here; each of the three Viking experiments gets a paragraph of its own. And since this is the last of the experiments to be described, it's appropriate to start the paragraph with the adverb "Finally."

29. **The correct answer is (C).** This adverb sounds most natural immediately after the verb it modifies, "was."

30. **The correct answer is (J).** Only the last paragraph of the essay deals with the *results* of the Viking mission. The rest focuses on the theoretical concepts behind the Viking experiments and the design of the experiments themselves. Thus, the essay doesn't really fulfill the assignment given.

31. **The correct answer is (A).** The original wording is correct. The present perfect tense makes sense here, and the proper form of the verb, "begun," is used. ("Began" is the past tense and would never be used with a helping verb.)

32. **The correct answer is (G).** All of the answer choices say more or less the same thing. Choice (G) does so most succinctly and clearly.

33. **The correct answer is (B).** In this context, the contraction "its" is being used to mean "it is." Therefore, the word should contain an apostrophe: "it's."

34. **The correct answer is (J).** The main theme of the essay is that "the good old days" weren't really very good. The rhetorical question posed in choice (J) introduces this theme well and makes a good start to the second paragraph. Choice (F) is the best wrong answer, but it suggests that the essay will focus mainly on the advantages of modern technology, which is not true.

35. **The correct answer is (A).** This information is relevant to the theme of the essay because it underscores the fact that the average person at the turn of the century did not have access to many advantages that would make life more pleasant in later years. The original wording is best; choices (B) and (C) are both too informal (slangy) to fit comfortably into the overall tone of the essay.

36. **The correct answer is (H).** "It" is the wrong pronoun, of course, since what's being referred to is "coal-burning stoves," which is plural. Choice (H) corrects this error less awkwardly and more clearly than the alternatives.

37. **The correct answer is (C).** The second and third sentences describe the disadvantages of central heating, which came *after* coal stoves. Therefore, they should follow the sentences about coal stoves and appear last in the paragraph.

38. **The correct answer is (F).** The sentence begins with the first person pronoun "We," and "our" continues this construction in a logical and consistent way.

39. **The correct answer is (A).** The proposed addition is very appropriate: it contributes in a vivid way to our understanding of the problems created by the "romantic" horse and buggy in turn-of-the-century cities.

40. **The correct answer is (G).** The original wording is vague and fails to explain why the shorter buildings made the summers seem hotter. Choice (G) is the only alternative that provides the information needed to clarify the point.

41. **The correct answer is (C).** This choice provides specific details to support the writer's point. Choices (A) and (B) merely state the idea without providing evidence to support it, and choice (D) digresses into a discussion of *today's* summer fashions, which is basically irrelevant.

42. **The correct answer is (H).** This choice maintains the grammatical parallelism required to make the three items listed sound consistent.

43. **The correct answer is (D).** The original wording creates a run-on sentence, with two independent clauses merely jammed together. Choice (D) fixes this by adding the appropriate subordinating conjunction "While," which clarifies the logical relationship between the two ideas and also corrects the grammatical error.

44. **The correct answer is (F).** The phrase "at least in that respect" is a logical unit that should be kept together and set off from the rest of the sentence with a comma on either side.

45. **The correct answer is (C).** This fact clearly belongs in Paragraph 5, where the "bad old summers" are described; and since it offers a fact that is even worse than the facts already given in that paragraph, it seems appropriate to put it at the end of the paragraph, where it can serve as the climax of that portion of the essay.

46. **The correct answer is (G).** The correct superlative form of the adjective "famous" is "most famous"—the same kind of construction use with most adjectives that are two syllables long or longer.

47. **The correct answer is (B).** The semicolon is wrong because what follows the punctuation mark is not an independent clause. Choices (C) and (D) are wrong because they insert an intrusive comma after the word "because," which instead should flow directly into what follows.

48. **The correct answer is (J).** Omit this sentence as it merely repeats information stated a few sentences earlier. It's obvious that the fiancé being referred to is the same one mentioned previously.

49. **The correct answer is (D).** The two sentences should be joined into one, since the second is a mere fragment. Choice (C) is grammatically correct (it fixes the fragment), but it's repetitive and awkward to mention "England" twice within three words.

50. **The correct answer is (F).** The original wording is correct, since what's being compared is "abortion in England" to abortion "in the United States."

51. **The correct answer is (C).** "Once" makes a better introductory word for two reasons: it clarifies the logical relationship between the two clauses, and it makes the first clause into a subordinate clause, thus avoiding the grammatical problem of a run-on sentence.

52. **The correct answer is (H).** The best punctuation to use when two independent clauses are joined by "and" is a comma preceding the "and."

53. **The correct answer is (A).** Since the writer wants to stress the *unusual* nature of the article, "groundbreaking" seems to be the appropriate adjective.

54. **The correct answer is (G).** In Paragraph 3, Steinem was struggling to find work; in Paragraph 4, she is a successful writer. The sentence given in choice (G) explains the transition logically and gracefully.

55. **The correct answer is (D).** This choice is the most idiomatic, graceful, and concise.

56. **The correct answer is (F).** The details here are appropriate and help clarify the kind of writing Steinem was relegated to, so omitting them would be a poor choice. The original wording is the most graceful of the three alternatives.

57. **The correct answer is (B).** The semicolon isn't needed here; the independent clauses are joined by "and," which calls for a comma instead. Choice (B) appropriately sets off the parenthetical phrase "she says" with a pair of commas.

58. **The correct answer is (J).** This sentence is the only one that explains and demonstrates how concern over abortion rights motivated Steinem to become a committed feminist.

59. **The correct answer is (C).** The modifying phrase "a tireless worker and advocate" must be placed next to "Steinem," since that is what the phrase modifies. Choices (B) and (D) are grammatically correct, but they sound awkward and a little unclear.

60. **The correct answer is (J).** The simple "including" is the clearest and most concise choice for this context.

61. **The correct answer is (B).** The comparison being drawn here calls for the phrase to be uninterrupted by commas.

62. **The correct answer is (F).** The pronoun "whose" is perfectly correct; its antecedent is "filmmakers."

63. **The correct answer is (D).** This sentence should be omitted; it's redundant, since it merely repeats the idea stated in the clause immediately preceding it.

64. **The correct answer is (G).** It's better to put the word "not" after "product," to create the appropriate parallelism: "not of the salon but of the common playhouse." Now the words that follow the linked prepositions "not . . . but" are strictly parallel in form.

65. **The correct answer is (C).** We already know, from the rest of the paragraph, that the three persons named were geniuses of the early movies. Information about where they came from seems irrelevant, since the essay doesn't discuss national differences in cinema. This phrase can be left out without losing a thing.

66. **The correct answer is (H).** The original wording creates a run-on sentence. Choice (H) fixes the problem. So does choice (J), but "For" doesn't connect the two ideas logically; and the dash in choice (G) leaves the relationship between the two ideas vague and confusing.

67. **The correct answer is (A).** The preposition "like" is correct here, since what follows is a phrase rather than a clause.

68. **The correct answer is (J).** Since what follows the semicolon is not an independent clause, the mark should be changed to a comma.

69. **The correct answer is (B).** The idea in this sentence is in contrast to the idea of the previous sentence; therefore, "But" is a more logical word with which to start the sentence.

70. **The correct answer is (J).** The underlined phrase should be omitted; it merely repeats the idea contained in the word "larger" without adding any information.

71. **The correct answer is (B).** The idiomatic construction in English runs, "the larger . . . the greater." Once you've used the first half of a pair of phrases like these, you're committed to using the second half as well.

72. **The correct answer is (H).** The antecedent of the pronoun is "creator," so the third-person pronoun "his" (or the less-sexist "his or her") must be used here.

73. **The correct answer is (D).** Since this is the possessive "its" rather than the contraction meaning "it is," no apostrophe should be used.

74. **The correct answer is (G).** The subject of the verb is "what makes the movies truly unique," which is singular in form; therefore, the singular verb "is" must be used.

75. **The correct answer is (D).** The third paragraph should come first; it introduces the topic and places the movies in their context as the leading twentieth-century artistic innovation. The other two paragraphs, which discuss some specifics about the development of movies as an art form, follow logically after this.

SECTION 2: MATHEMATICS

1. **The correct answer is (C).** $\frac{1}{3}$ of 42 is 14, and $\frac{1}{6}$ of 42 is 7. Thus, 21 horses are black or white, leaving 21 horses that are brown.

2. **The correct answer is (J).** In 5 hours, 4 ounces $(7 - 3)$ of water have dripped. Therefore, the "drip rate" is $\frac{4}{5}$ of an ounce per hour. From 5:00 p.m. on Sunday until 2:00 a.m. on Monday is 9 hours, so the total that will have dripped is $7 + \left(\frac{4}{5} \times 9\right) = 7 + \frac{36}{5} = \frac{71}{5}$ ounces.

3. **The correct answer is (A).** $m_{PQ} = \dfrac{5 - 2}{3 - (-1)} = \dfrac{3}{4}$

4. **The correct answer is (K).** We know that the average of x and -1 must be 2. That is:

$$2 = \frac{x + (-1)}{2}$$

Thus, $4 = x - 1$, $x = 5$. Similarly, we know that the average of y and 3 must be 6. Thus: $6 = \dfrac{y + 3}{2}$; $12 = y + 3$; $y = 9$. So $2x + y = 19$.

5. **The correct answer is (E).** Substituting $y = \frac{1}{4}$, we have $\left(\frac{1}{4}\right)^{0} + \left(\frac{1}{4}\right)^{-1} = 1 + \left(\frac{1}{4}\right)^{-1} = 1 + 4 = 5$.

6. **The correct answer is (K).** If $n^2 > 2n$, that means that $n^2 - 2n > 0$, or $n(n - 2) > 0$. Clearly, if n is any positive number less than 2, then both n and $(n - 2)$ will be positive, making the result true.

7. **The correct answer is (C).** The arithmetic mean of x and y is $\dfrac{(x + y)}{2} = m$. This means that $x + y = 2m$, and $x + y + z = 4m$. Dividing by 3 to get the arithmetic mean of x, y, and z, we have $\dfrac{(x + y + z)}{3} = \dfrac{4m}{3}$.

8. **The correct answer is (J).** Looking first at triangle ABE, we have a right triangle with one angle of 90° and one angle of 27°. Thus, m$\angle A$ must be 63°. Hence, $\angle BAC$ is one-third of that, or 21°. So, looking at triangle ABC, m$\angle BCA$ must be $180° - 21° - 27° = 132°$. Since x is the supplement to that angle, $x = 48$.

9. **The correct answer is (D).** The low in 1994 was 8. The high in 1998 was 2. The ratio of these two numbers was 4:1 or 400%. Hence, the difference was 300%.

10. **The correct answer is (J).** The sales figures were 2.8, 3.8, 5, 7, 4, 2, and 1. Arranged in increasing order, they were 1, 2, 2.8, 3.8, 4, 5, and 7. Thus, the median—the middle number—was 3.8.

11. **The correct answer is (D).** The area of a circle with a diameter of 8 is $\pi 4^2 = 16\pi$, since its radius is 4. Let the width of the rectangle be w. Its length is $2w$ and its area is $2w^2$, which must be equal to 16π. Thus, $2w^2 = 16\pi$; $w^2 = 8\pi$, and $w = \sqrt{8\pi} = 2\sqrt{2\pi}$. Therefore, $L = 4\sqrt{2\pi}$. The perimeter is $2L + 2W = 8\sqrt{2\pi} + 4\sqrt{2\pi} = 12\sqrt{2\pi}$.

12. **The correct answer is (H).** Calling the numbers x and $(x + 2)$, the negative of the sum is $-[x + (x + 2)]$, and this should be less than -35. That is, $-[2x + 2] < -35$. Solving the inequality:

$$-2x - 2 < -35$$
$$-2x < -33$$

Dividing by -2 reverses the inequality:
$$x > 16.5$$

Of course, 18 and 16 are both even, and we need an odd number. $x = 15$ will work, because $(x + 2) = 17 > 16.5$.

13. **The correct answer is (E).** The length of $\overline{OQ}$ and $\overline{OP}$ are the same: $\sqrt{2^2 + 1^2} = \sqrt{5}$. The length of $\overline{PQ}$ is $\sqrt{1^2 + 1^2} = \sqrt{2}$. So the perimeter is $2\sqrt{5} + \sqrt{2}$.

14. **The correct answer is (F).** Since $P = M + 1$, $N = 3^P = 3^{M+1} = 3(3^M)$, and
$$\frac{3}{N} = \frac{3}{3(3^M)} = \frac{1}{3^M}.$$

15. **The correct answer is (E).** Since $A^2 - B^2 = (A - B)(A + B)$, $(A - B)$ and $(A + B)$ must be factors of 36. The possibilities are as follows:

$$A - B = 1 \qquad A + B = 36$$
$$A - B = 2 \qquad A + B = 18$$
$$A - B = 3 \qquad A + B = 12$$
$$A - B = 4 \qquad A + B = 9$$
$$A - B = 6 \qquad A + B = 6$$

Only the second and fifth possibilities yield integer solutions, and in the fifth case, $A = 6$ and $B = 0$, which is not positive. The only choice that works is $A = 10$, $B = 8$, for which $A + B = 18$ and $A - B = 2$.

16. **The correct answer is (F).** Letting h be the price of the hat and s be the price of the scarf, $h + s = 38$, and $h = s + 3$. Substituting:

$$s + s + 3 = 38$$
$$2s = 35$$
$$s = 17.5$$

17. **The correct answer is (C).** Multiplying radicals gives $\sqrt{18x} = \sqrt{30}$. Hence, $18x = 30$, and $x = \frac{5}{3}$.

18. **The correct answer is (H).** Doubling the first equation and adding it to the second gives us:

$$
\begin{aligned}
4x - 2y + 8z &= 14 \\
-4x + 2y - 3z &= 1 \\
\hline
5z &= 15 \\
z &= 3
\end{aligned}
$$

19. **The correct answer is (B).** The possible factors of 36 are (1,36), (2,18), (3,12), (4,9), and (6,6). The smallest possible sum is 12, but that is when x and y are equal. So we must take choice (B), 13, which we get with the factors (4,9).

20. **The correct answer is (F).** The total cost for the month is $500 + 15nc$ for $15n$ minutes of calling. Thus, the average is

$$
\frac{500 + 15nc}{15n} = c + \frac{100}{3n}
$$

21. **The correct answer is (C).** If the diameter is π, the radius is $\frac{1}{2}\pi$ and the area is $\pi r^2 = \pi\left(\frac{1}{2}\pi\right)^2 = \frac{1}{4}\pi^3$.

22. **The correct answer is (G).** If h is 20% longer than b, then $h = 1.2b = \frac{6b}{5}$. The area is $\frac{1}{2}bh = \frac{1}{2}(b)\left(\frac{6b}{5}\right) = \frac{3b^2}{5}$.

23. **The correct answer is (A).** Four out of 6 times, the first block drawn will be a zero. The remaining one third of the time, a non-zero number will be drawn, leaving one non-zero and four zero blocks. The chance of drawing a second non-zero block is $\frac{1}{5}$. Hence, the product will not be zero only $\frac{1}{5}$ of $\frac{1}{3}$ $= \frac{1}{5} \times \frac{1}{3} = \frac{1}{15}$ of the time.

24. **The correct answer is (F).** Factoring the numerator and denominator of the fraction, we see that we can divide out the common factor $(x - 3)$, thusly:

$$
\frac{x^2 - 3x}{3x - 9} = \frac{x(x - 3)}{3(x - 3)} = \frac{x}{3}
$$

Substituting $x = 3.03$ yields $\frac{3.03}{3} = 1.01$.

25. **The correct answer is (A).** If the true distance is T, then the odometer will show $m = T + 0.10T = 1.1T = \left(\frac{11}{10}\right)T$. That is, $T = \left(\frac{10}{11}\right)m$, which is the same as $\left(\frac{10m}{11}\right)$.

26. **The correct answer is (J).** Let Elaine's salary be $3k$, and Carl's will be $2k$. A 20% raise for Elaine will bring her salary to $(1.2)(3k) = 3.6k$, while a $200 raise for Carl will bring his salary to $2k + 200$. Thus, $3.6k:(2k + 200) = 6:5$, or, in fractional form:

$$\frac{3.6k}{2k + 200} = \frac{6}{5}$$

Cross-multiplying: $18k = 12k + 1200$; $6k = 1200$; $k = 200$. So Elaine's salary is $3k = 600$.

27. **The correct answer is (C).** P percent means $\frac{P}{100}$. Hence, $\frac{P}{100} \times 20\sqrt{3} = 3$ must be solved for P. Thus, $\frac{P\sqrt{3}}{5} = 3$. Multiplying by $\frac{5}{\sqrt{3}}$, and noticing that $\frac{3}{\sqrt{3}} = \sqrt{3}$ gives us $P = 5\sqrt{3}$.

28. **The correct answer is (H).** The sum of the angles in the triangle must be 180 degrees. Letting the degree measure of $\angle A$ be x, we have $x + 50$ for $\angle B$ and $3x$ for $\angle C$. Now:

$$x + (x + 50) + 3x = 180$$
$$5x + 50 = 180$$
$$x = 26$$

Hence, $m\angle B = 76°$ and $m\angle C = 78°$. Therefore, $m\angle B - m\angle C = -2°$.

29. **The correct answer is (B).** Adding the two equations gives us $4n = 16$, so $n = 4$. Knowing that $n = 4$, the second equation tells us that $8 + m = 10$, and $m = 2$.

30. **The correct answer is (H).** Of the 12 students taking Spanish, 4 are taking both languages, leaving 8 taking only Spanish.

31. **The correct answer is (C).** If $x = 2$, $x^0 = 2^0 = 1$; and $x^{-4} = 2^{-4} = \frac{1}{2^4} = \frac{1}{16} = 0.0625$. Hence, $3x^0 + x^{-4} = 3.0625$.

32. **The correct answer is (K).** If $x = \frac{1}{2}$, $x^2 + 2y^2 = \frac{1}{4} + 2y^2 = 1$ implies that $2y^2 = \frac{3}{4}$, and $y^2 = \frac{3}{8}$. Now $|y| = \sqrt{\frac{3}{8}} = \sqrt{0.375} = $ approximately 0.6.

33. **The correct answer is (D).** The median (middle number) is 3, and the mean is $(1 + 2 + 2 + 2 + 3 + 5 + 6 + 7 + 8) \div 9 = 4$. Thus, the mean minus the median is $4 - 3 = 1$.

34. **The correct answer is (F).** Dropping the perpendicular from C down to the extension of AB (see the diagram below), we see that m$\angle CBD = 50°$ and that the altitude of the triangle, h, given by $\frac{h}{9} = \sin 50°$. Thus, $h = 9\sin 50°$, and the area of triangle ABC is thus $\frac{1}{2}(6)(9)\sin 50° = 27\sin 50°$.

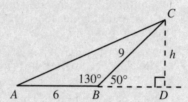

35. **The correct answer is (E).** Using the obvious notation, we have:

$$4c + 6d + 3h = 815$$
$$2c + 3d + 4h = 720$$

Multiplying the second equation by -2 and adding the equations together yields $-5h = -625$; $h = 125$.

36. **The correct answer is (H).** By the Pythagorean Theorem, $c^2 = \sqrt{3^2 + 5^2} = \sqrt{34}$ = about 5.83, which is closest to 6.

37. **The correct answer is (D).** Adding the two equations, we have $3x + 4y = 13$. Multiplying by 3 gives us $9x + 12y = 39$.

38. **The correct answer is (J).** We see that we have 9 choices for the first digit, 10 choices for the second digit, and 10 choices for the third digit. Thus, the total is $9 \times 10 \times 10 = 900$.

39. **The correct answer is (C).** Calling the smallest number x, the second is $(x + 2)$, and the third is $(x + 4)$. Therefore,

$$x + (x + 2) + 2(x + 4) = 46$$
$$x + x + 2 + 2x + 8 = 46$$
$$4x + 10 = 46$$
$$4x = 36$$
$$x = 9$$

Hence, the middle number is $9 + 2 = 11$.

40. **The correct answer is (J).** The unshaded region is a sector with a 30° angle, which is $\frac{1}{12}$ of the area of the circle. Hence, the shaded portion must be $\left(\frac{11}{12}\right)\pi r^2 = 33\pi$. Dividing by 11π and multiplying by 12, we have $r^2 = 36$. Hence, $r = 6$, and the diameter is 12.

41. **The correct answer is (E).** Using J and R to stand for their present ages, we have

$$J = R + 4$$
$$R - 2 = \frac{2}{3}(J - 2)$$

Multiplying the second equation by 3:

$$3R - 6 = 2(J - 2)$$

Substituting from equation one:

$$3R - 6 = 2(R + 4 - 2) = 2(R + 2)$$
$$3R - 6 = 2R + 4$$
$$R = 10$$

Hence, Rodney is 10 and Jerome is 14. x years ago, Rodney was $10 - x$ and Jerome was $14 - x$, giving us:

$$14 - x = 2(10 - x)$$
$$14 - x = 20 - 2x$$
$$x = 6$$

42. **The correct answer is (G).** The equation of the circle is $(x - 6)^2 + (y - 9)^2 = 13^2$. Substituting $x = 1$ and $y = u$, we have

$$25 + (u - 9)^2 = 169$$
$$(u - 9)^2 = 144$$
$$u - 9 = \pm 12$$

This gives us two possibilities: $u = -3$ or $u = 21$.

43. **The correct answer is (D).** Since John takes 20 minutes per room, he can do 3 rooms in one hour. Armando can do 4 rooms in an hour. Thus, together they do 7 rooms in one hour. To do 30 rooms will take them $\frac{30}{7}$ hours.

44. **The correct answer is (G).** Using the laws of logarithms, $2y - 3x = 2\log 5 - 3\log 2 = \log 5^2 - \log 2^3 = \log 25 - \log 8 = \log\left(\frac{25}{8}\right)$.

45. **The correct answer is (A).** Factoring $4xy$ in the numerator and $8y^3$ in the denominator, we have

$$\frac{4xy(3x - y)}{8y^3(3x - y)}$$

Now we can divide out the common factor $4y(3x - y)$, leaving

$$\frac{4xy^2(3x - y)}{8y^3(3x - y)} = \frac{x}{2y^2}.$$

46. **The correct answer is (G).** Setting $y = 0$ and solving by the quadratic formula with $a = 1$, $b = -2$, and $c = -6$:

$$x = \frac{-(-2) \pm \sqrt{(-2)^2 - 4(1)(-6)}}{2(1)} = \frac{2 \pm \sqrt{28}}{2} = \frac{2 \pm 2\sqrt{7}}{2} = 1 \pm \sqrt{7}$$

Since $\sqrt{7}$ is between 2 and 3, choosing the subtraction sign, $1 - \sqrt{7}$ is less than -1 and greater than -2.

47. **The correct answer is (C).** $f(g(x)) = (g(x))^2$. That is, $(g(x))^2 = \dfrac{1}{(x^2 + 1)}$, and

$g(x) = \pm\dfrac{1}{(\sqrt{x^2 + 1})}$. Choose the plus sign.

48. **The correct answer is (G).** Since the terms must have a common ratio, $\dfrac{-2}{x} = \dfrac{x}{-8}$. Cross multiplying, $x^2 = 16$, and $x = \pm 4$. For $+4$, the sixth term would be $(-2)(4)^5 = -2{,}048$, while for -4 it would be $2{,}048$.

49. **The correct answer is (E).** Each entry in the matrix you seek is 2 times the product of row i in A and row j in B. For example, in row 1, column 1, you have $2[2(0) + (-1)(1)] = 2(-1) = -2$.

50. **The correct answer is (F).** The slope of $\overline{PQ}$ is $m = \dfrac{(6 - 2)}{(1 - (-1))} = 2$.

Hence, any line perpendicular to it has slope $-\dfrac{1}{2}$. Averaging the coordinates of P and Q, we see that the midpoint of $\overline{PQ}$ is $(0,4)$, which must be the y-intercept of the line we seek. Thus, $y = -\dfrac{1}{2}x + 4$.

51. **The correct answer is (D).** We display the data in the Venn Diagram shown below, letting x be the number of users who have both a tape and disc drive.

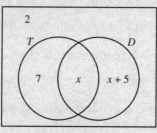

T = Tape Drive
D = Disc Drive

Totaling the numbers, we see that $2 + 7 + x + (x + 5) = 50$; $2x + 14 = 50$; $2x = 36$; $x = 18$. Knowing that $x = 18$, we can see from the diagram that the total number in T is 25.

52. **The correct answer is (J).** Calling the height of the cliff H and illustrating the situation with the diagram below, we see in triangle BCD that $\frac{H}{50} = \tan40°$, that is, $H = 50\tan40°$.

Then, in triangle ACD, we see that $\frac{H}{(50+M)} = \tan20°$, that is, $H = 50\tan20° + M\tan20°$.

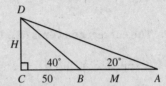

Equating the two expressions, since both are equal to H, we have

$$50\tan40° = 50\tan20° + M\tan20°$$

which we can solve for M by subtracting $50\tan20°$ from both sides and then dividing by $\tan20°$ to give us $M =$

$$\frac{50\tan40° - 50\tan20°}{\tan20°}$$

53. **The correct answer is (B).** Since $\sqrt{8} = \sqrt{(4)(2)} = 2\sqrt{2}$, $2\sqrt{8} = 4\sqrt{2}$, and $3\sqrt{2} + 4\sqrt{2} = 7\sqrt{2}$.

54. **The correct answer is (K).** Letting L be the amount reimbursed on lodging and M be the amount reimbursed on food, the first piece of information we have says: $M = L + 16$. The second one says that $\left(\frac{3}{2}\right)L = \left(\frac{2}{3}\right)M + 16$. Multiplying by 6, this equation becomes $9L = 4M + 96$.

Substituting $M = L + 16$, we have

$$9L = 4(L + 16) + 96$$
$$9L = 4L + 64 + 96$$
$$5L = 160$$
$$L = 32$$

Knowing $L = 32$, $M = 48$, and the total is 80.

55. **The correct answer is (A).** The numbers in an arithmetic progrssion have a common difference. Hence, $5 - (-3) = 3d$. That is, $8 = 3d$ and $d = \frac{8}{3}$. Thus, $M = -3 + d = -3 + \frac{8}{3} = \frac{-1}{3}$.

56. **The correct answer is (F).** $a^{x - 2y} = \frac{a^x}{a^{2y}} = \frac{a^x}{(a^y)^2} = \frac{T}{S^2}$.

57. **The correct answer is (E).** When adding the matrices, you add entries in corresponding locations. Remember to multiply each entry in A by 2 first. Thus, in the upper lefthand corner, you have $-4 + x = -5$, so $x = -1$. Similarly, in the lower righthand corner you have

$$6 + y = 4$$

so

$$y = -2.$$

Hence,

$$xy = 2.$$

58. **The correct answer is (H).** To calculate $f\left(\dfrac{1}{x}\right)$, you substitute $\dfrac{1}{x}$ for x wherever it appears, giving $f\left(\dfrac{1}{x}\right) = \dfrac{1}{x+1}$. Combining this into a single fraction, you have $f\left(\dfrac{1}{x}\right) = \dfrac{x+1}{x}$. Multiplying this by $\dfrac{1}{f(x)} = \dfrac{(x+1)}{x} \cdot \dfrac{1}{(x+1)} = \dfrac{1}{x}$.

59. **The correct answer is (D).** Since the slope is the change in y divided by the change in x, the line through $(-1,0)$ having slope 1 gives us the equation

$$1 = \frac{y-0}{(x-(-1))} = \frac{y}{x+1}$$

That is, $y = x + 1$.

The line through $(-4,0)$ having slope $\dfrac{1}{2}$ gives us the equation

$$\frac{1}{2} = \frac{y-0}{(x-(-4))} = \frac{y}{(x+4)}$$

That is, $2y = x + 4$.

We need to know x, so substitute $x + 1$ for y in the second equation:

$$2(x + 1) = x + 4;\ 2x + 2 = x + 4;\ x = 2.$$

60. **The correct answer is (J).** The entire area between the two circles is the area of the larger minus the area of the smaller. Call this value A. Now, $A = \pi(2r)^2 - \pi r^2 = 3\pi r^2$. Drawing the line segment from C to O forms two right triangles, each with a hypotenuse of length $2r$ and $OC = r$. Thus, angle A and angle B are each 30°, making m$\angle AOC = 120°$, or one third of the circle. Hence, the area of the shaded region is two thirds of the area A and must equal $2\pi r^2$.

SECTION 3: READING

1. **The correct answer is (B).** The first two paragraphs make this point, especially these words from the second paragraph: "because he usually dropped in at the club at that hour, he had passed by instead."

2. **The correct answer is (H).** Archer fears that May is becoming figuratively "blind," that is, unable to perceive reality because of the conventionality of her upbringing and her social surroundings. The cave-fish symbolizes his fear that May will never be grown-up enough to see and think for herself.

3. **The correct answer is (B).** Paragraph 3 makes it clear that the Archer–Welland engagement will be somewhat shorter than that of May's friends Grace and Thorley, which was "nearly a year and a half." However, it can't be *much* shorter than theirs; otherwise Archer would hardly be complaining about its length. Hence, choice (B) is correct.

4. **The correct answer is (F).** The first paragraphs refers to the "leisurely manner" in which men of Archer's class practiced the law.

5. **The correct answer is (D).** She laughs when she mentions the idea and considers it "boring" to have to explain to him why it would never do. Clearly, for May the idea of eloping is almost too silly to discuss.

6. **The correct answer is (H).** Archer recalls saying to his friend Jackson, "Women ought to be as free as we are—!" And earlier in the paragraph, he muses that "nice" women may begin "to speak for themselves" "Never, if we won't let them." The two statements in combination show that Archer feels that men ("we") are largely responsible for constraining women and taking away their freedom.

7. **The correct answer is (A).** As soon as May says this to Archer, the author comments, "His heart sank."

8. **The correct answer is (H).** Throughout the passage, Archer feels trapped by the "sameness" and conventionality of his relationship with May. Yet when she rejects his ideas about breaking out of this conventionality, he apparently is helpless to respond and is reduced to standing silently, "beating his walking-stick nervously against his shoe-top."

9. **The correct answer is (A).** The last three paragraphs state twice that May feels that calling the idea "vulgar" effectively dismisses the topic.

10. **The correct answer is (F).** The third, fifth, and tenth paragraphs refer to family, class, and gender traditions as the constraining forces that control May's attitudes. The second and eighth paragraphs refers to May's mother as the source of the idea that a long engagement is necessary. May mentions "novels" only as the kind of guide to behavior she would *never* follow, and her friends are mentioned merely for comparison's sake, not as sources of her beliefs.

11. **The correct answer is (C).** The fact that the British and French already had (experimental) ironclads is merely mentioned in the second paragraph, not cited as a reason for the South's eagerness to build one.

12. **The correct answer is (F).** This point is made in the second sentence of the passage.

13. **The correct answer is (B).** See the first sentence of the third paragraph.

14. **The correct answer is (J).** The last sentence of the third paragraph makes it obvious that wooden hulls were the rule, not the exception, among ships of the period.

15. **The correct answer is (C).** As used in the passage, "innovative" refers to the design choices made by John Ericson, which made the *Monitor* a remarkably new type of vessel.

16. **The correct answer is (J).** The *Virginia* was created simply by armor-plating a traditional wooden boat, whereas the *Monitor* had an entirely new design that "looked like no other ship afloat."

17. **The correct answer is (C).** As the third paragraph suggests, compared to the North, the South had fewer facilities for ship-building.

18. **The correct answer is (F).** See the last sentence of the seventh paragraph: "none of the nearly 100 shots that hit her had pierced her armor."

19. **The correct answer is (C).** To "sustain" damage, as the word is used in this sentence, means to receive or suffer it.

20. **The correct answer is (G).** Choice (B) restates the idea found in the last sentence of the passage.

21. **The correct answer is (C).** The first two paragraphs show that Doyle pursued both writing and medicine simultaneously, apparently eager to succeed in both fields; he abandoned medicine only much later, after his writing had attained great popularity.

22. **The correct answer is (J).** In this context, the word *deduction* is used to refer to the practice of drawing logical conclusions from evidence—reasoning, in other words.

23. **The correct answer is (A).** See the first sentence of the third paragraph, which explains what made Holmes "a different kind of detective" from his fictional predecessors.

24. **The correct answer is (H).** The word *compelling* is being used here to describe the effect of a character like Sherlock Holmes on readers; he compels the reader's interest because of his remarkable personal qualities.

25. **The correct answer is (A).** Although Doyle was writing historical novels at the same time as his mystery stories, neither of the Holmes tales mentioned here is described as "based on historical events."

26. **The correct answer is (H).** See the seventh paragraph: "Doyle's other small literary successes had enabled him to move to London."

27. **The correct answer is (C).** If the author considers it "fortunate" that Doyle was able to concentrate on his writing rather than on practicing medicine, clearly Doyle's literary career must have been more important or worthwhile in the author's eyes than his medical work.

28. **The correct answer is (F).** The second sentence of the last paragraph makes this point.

29. **The correct answer is (C).** According to the last paragraph, Doyle "considered the Holmes stories insignificant compared to his 'serious' historical novels."

30. **The correct answer is (G).** Choice (H) is too narrow, while choices (F) and (J) are too broad. The passage concentrates quite specifically on the origin of the Holmes character, which makes choice (G) the best choice.

31. **The correct answer is (B).** Each of the other answer choices is discussed in one or more paragraphs of the passage.

32. **The correct answer is (H).** The first sentence of the third paragraph of the passage, which is where the angler fish is discussed, makes it clear that the paragraph is entirely devoted to examples of bioluminescence found in the midwaters of the ocean.

33. **The correct answer is (C).** Just as the angler fish uses a fake piece of food as bait to capture a hungry prey, so does the trout fisherman when he lures a trout with a tasty-looking fake insect.

34. **The correct answer is (J).** Countershading is described in the fourth paragraph, where it is stated that this effect protects fish from predators *below* them, not above.

35. **The correct answer is (D).** The author mentions the "exploding dye packets" that help mark a bank robber in order to clarify how some animals coat predators with glowing tissue to mark them and make them vulnerable.

36. **The correct answer is (J).** This point is made in the first sentence of the eighth paragraph.

37. **The correct answer is (A).** The seventh paragraph says that bioluminescence is considered nonessential because nonluminous species seem to thrive as well as luminous ones. For this, we can conclude, that, if bioluminescence were essential, the opposite would be true—luminous species would do better than nonluminous ones.

38. **The correct answer is (G).** In the eighth paragraph, "selection pressure" is discussed specifically as an environmental force that helps promote "the development or maintenance of luminescence" among animal species. Choice (G) paraphrases this concept.

39. **The correct answer is (C).** The tomopterid worm is the only example in the passage of a kind of bioluminescence that seems to have no purpose at all; thus, it is "exceptional."

40. **The correct answer is (F).** This discovery would suggest that the tomopterid worm's bioluminescence is, in fact, useful, since it would mean that the yellow fluid it spews could help to distract dangerous predators.

SECTION 4: SCIENCE REASONING

1. **The correct answer is (C).** Considering only the two trees mentioned in the question, this would be a reasonable conclusion, since the younger of the trees (tree 4) has a much larger diameter and a much faster growth rate.

2. **The correct answer is (F).** The data in the table shows that these two trees, though they have almost the same diameter (90 cm versus 80 cm), are of vastly different ages (900 years versus 200 years). Thus, it seems clear that one cannot tell a tree's age by extrapolation from its diameter.

3. **The correct answer is (C).** Four of the twelve trees in the table—one third of the group—are 800 years old or older, which means that they survived at least the last two catastrophes charted on the timeline.

4. **The correct answer is (G).** This is a simple exercise in multiplication: 1,100 × 0.1 cm = 110 cm.

5. **The correct answer is (D).** The three trees listed, all of the same species, are widely different in age and have widely varying growth rates as well. This is consistent with the conclusion stated in choice (D)—that trees of the same species may have different growth rates at different ages.

6. **The correct answer is (H).** A hypothesis that trees might use more than one strategy for reaching the canopy and that varying growth rates might consequently be found, would certainly be supported by the finding that trees growing toward the canopy do in fact exhibit widely varying growth rates.

7. **The correct answer is (A).** The descriptions of the two experimental set-ups make it clear that the variable in Experiment 1 was the radius of the flywheel, while in Experiment 2 it was the initial speed of the flywheel.

8. **The correct answer is (H).** The concave disk design provides the best overall results in Experiment 3. As Table 8.4 shows, that design stores considerably more energy than either of the two alternatives, while its strength is almost equal to that of the flat disk, which is the strongest. If both criteria are equally important, then the concave disk design is the best.

9. **The correct answer is (A).** As the answer to question 8 indicates, the concave design is preferable to either the rimmed or flat disk. Experiment 1 shows that a flywheel with a larger radius is capable of storing more energy than a flywheel with a smaller radius. Thus, for optimal energy storage, a concave, large-radius wheel is best.

10. **The correct answer is (H).** As frequency increases, centrifugal force increases even more quickly; the same relationship exists between frequency and energy stored.

11. **The correct answer is (B).** Look at Table 8.3. By comparing the first and third lines of that table, we can see that when the speed of the flywheel is halved (from 80 to 40 revolutions per second), the amount of energy stored is quartered (from about 20,000 to about 5,000 joules). Applying this same relationship to the example in the question, we can estimate that the energy in the car flywheel will be quartered from 120,000 joules to about 30,000 joules.

12. **The correct answer is (F).** Since safety is mentioned in the question as a primary consideration, it seems logical to choose a system that uses size rather than frequency as the primary factor for storing a large amount of energy. As Experiment 3 shows, the flywheel's frequency has a far more powerful effect on centrifugal force than does the flywheel's radius.

13. **The correct answer is (D).** You can see in Table 8.5 that the average sulphate concentration in land deposits decreased between 1990 and 1998, while the figure shows that the amounts of sulphate in the five lakes increased during the same period. (To read the graph in the figure, compare the vertical axis—the 1990 reading—for each dot with the horizontal axis—the 1998 reading. In each case, the horizontal axis is greater.)

14. **The correct answer is (H).** The figure includes graphs for both sulphate and pH levels, while Table 8.5 shows only sulphate readings without pH numbers.

15. **The correct answer is (C).** You can see in the sulphate graph from the figure that the two dots furthest into the lower right-hand corner are "open" dots, representing glacial lakes. This indicates that these lakes experienced the greatest increase in sulphate levels between 1990 and 1998.

16. **The correct answer is (G).** The concentration for lake 4 was from 0.89 milligrams per liter to 0.66, a drop of almost 26%. This is a greater decline than experienced at any of the other lakes studied.

17. **The correct answer is (A).** The figure shows that precipitation varied within a steady range throughout the period, which isn't consistent with the idea of a serious drought, as suggested by hypothesis II. The notion that the overall level of sulphate emissions did not decrease during the period is weakened by the results of Experiment 1, which show a steady decline in terrestrial deposition of sulphates; this weakens hypothesis III. Hypothesis I, however, is not contradicted by any of the experimental findings and in fact may help to explain why the lakes might show increased sulphates while the adjacent land areas show lower levels.

18. **The correct answer is (F).** As you can see in the Mercury line on Table 8.6, a Mercury day is about 59 Earth days, while a Mercury year is about 88 Earth days. The former is about $\frac{2}{3}$ of the latter.

19. **The correct answer is (C).** Visualize where the moon would appear on the graph shown in the figure. It would be in very much the same line as Mars, Venus, and Earth. Only Mercury seems to have a different density/diameter relationship than the other terrestrial bodies.

20. **The correct answer is (F).** This figure can be read from Table 8.6. The only planet with a more eccentric orbit, Pluto, is not a terrestrial planet.

21. **The correct answer is (D).** The second column of Table 8.6 provides the answer. We're told at the top of the column that the density of water has been set to equal 1. Then we see that Pluto's density happens to be exactly 1; in other words, it is virtually the same as that of water.

22. **The correct answer is (H).** Since Mercury's mean (average) surface temperature is "only" 179°, the nighttime temperature must be very low in order to offset and reduce the very high daytime peak.

23. **The correct answer is (B).** If Earth's core has a diameter of about 3,000 miles, this represents about $\frac{3}{8}$ of the overall diameter of the planet. If Mercury's core represents a larger fraction of the planet's overall diameter and if Mercury's overall diameter is about 3,000 miles, then Mercury's core probably has a diameter that is around half the planet's overall diameter, or perhaps a little more. Any value in the 1,500- to 2,000-miles range would be appropriate, and only choice (B) fits.

24. **The correct answer is (F).** Both the genetic theory and the infection theory attribute schizophrenia to prenatal events: in one theory, to a genetic disorder; in the other, to a prenatal infection that affects the brain of a developing infant.

25. **The correct answer is (C).** The fact that the shared incidence of schizophrenia is four times as great between identical twins as between nonidentical twins supports the idea that shared genetic material is a major factor in the development of the disorder.

26. **The correct answer is (H).** The phenomenon described in option III would be consistent with the idea that an infection occurred during prenatal development, thus supporting the infection theory.

27. **The correct answer is (D).** All three hypotheses could be consistent with both theories, and, in fact, all three could help to explain how both genetic and disease factors could be involved in producing schizophrenia.

28. **The correct answer is (J).** Those who favor the viral theory would be apt to explain the shared incidence of schizophrenia in this case as having resulted from the shared experience of a viral infection when both infants were in the womb together.

29. **The correct answer is (B).** It would be natural for supporters of the genetic theory to want to study the genes themselves in the hope of substantiating their theory by pinpointing the actual genetic differences that cause (or help to cause) the illness.

30. **The correct answer is (G).** As the figure shows, limonene increases steadily and dramatically as fruit ages, making this the most relevant and useful VOC for the detection of fruit spoilage.

31. **The correct answer is (C).** You can see in the figure that the concentration of alcohols continues to rise steadily over time as vegetables decay, while some other VOCs, such as esters, rise for a time and then diminish. This state of affairs is succinctly described in choice (C).

32. **The correct answer is (G).** Since Nose #2 is highly sensitive to alcohols, which are the best indicator of vegetable spoilage, that nose would be the best choice for detecting vegetable decay.

33. **The correct answer is (B).** An alcohol detector would be the best single choice since that VOC is a fairly reliable indicator of spoilage for all three food groups.

34. **The correct answer is (J).** The figure shows that a concentration level of about half a milligram of diacetyl is reached some three days after the meat is fresh. Thus, it makes sense that this would be the level at which the consumer should be alerted that the meat should soon be consumed.

35. **The correct answer is (A).** Just count the number of horizontal lines shown in the illustration to determine the number of energy levels found in a given element. Atom #1 has five such lines; therefore, it has five energy levels.

36. **The correct answer is (F).** As explained in the passage, the spectral lines are emitted when an atom moves from one energy level to another. Thus, the number of spectral lines observed would correspond to the number of arrows seen in the figure (since each arrow represents an energy-level transition). Understanding this lets us pick choice (F) as incorrect; there are seven energy transitions possible for Atom #1, so seven spectral lines would be observed, not six.

37. **The correct answer is (D).** The passage says that the amount of space between spectral lines indicates the relative size of the change in energy levels. If two energy transitions are quite similar in size, then the spectral lines will be close; if the transitions are very different in size, the spectral lines will be far apart. Based on this, we can see that choice (D) is correct: the three transitions shown on the upper left-hand side of the diagram would be represented by three spectral lines that are close together, while the two transitions shown on the lower left-hand side would produce two more spectral lines that are close together.

38. **The correct answer is (G).** In Table 8.7, the first two frequencies measured are very close; so are the last two. These would correspond to spectral lines that are close to one another, and these would reflect two pairs of similar energy transitions—the situation found in Atom #3.

39. **The correct answer is (B).** A "forbidden" transition, as defined in the question, would be represented visually by a pair of horizontal lines that is *not* connected by an arrow. As you can see, Atoms #1 and #3 both have one or more pairs of horizontal lines that are not connected by arrows, making choices (A) and (C) wrong; Atom #3 has just one forbidden transition (between the two horizontal lines at the top), making choice (D) wrong. Choice (B) is correct because Atom #2 has one forbidden transition, between the highest and lowest energy levels, represented by the horizontal lines at the top and bottom of the diagram.

40. **The correct answer is (A).** As the explanation for Table 8.7 says, the information in that table does not reflect direct measurement of energy but rather "the frequency of light, which is proportional to the energy." Thus, whereas the figure is generated directly by spectroscopy, the information in Table 8.7 contains information that is analogous to that derived from spectroscopy but that is not the same.

Part IV

Making It Official

Chapter 9

Scheduling and Taking the Test

Get the Scoop On . . .

- Choosing the test date and location that's best for you
- Saving time and money when you register for the exam
- Obtaining any special test accommodations you may need to do your best
- Ensuring you'll feel good and perform well the day of the exam

DECIDING WHEN TO TAKE THE ACT

The ACT is usually administered five times per year: in late October, early December, early February, early April, and early June. So to begin, you have a fair amount of flexibility in picking your test date. But when you start factoring in college application deadlines and other considerations, your options rapidly begin to narrow. Here are some of the main points to consider in choosing a test date.

- **Check the application deadlines for your college(s) of choice.** Most schools set a single date by which they want to receive all the supporting data they need—not only test scores but also high school transcripts, your application essay, teacher recommendations, etc. Determine the *earliest* deadline of the colleges you are applying to, and then count back six weeks from that date. (This strategy allows a little extra time for your score report to be received; ACT aims to send reports out about four weeks after the test, but delays do happen.) The date you count back to should be your *latest* date for taking the ACT.

- **Allow yourself the option of retaking the ACT.** Suppose that, working backward from your earliest college deadline, you determine that you must take the ACT no later than October of your senior year. Don't simply apply for that test date. Instead, if you can, take the exam at least one test administration earlier—preferably two. This tactic means applying for a test in April or June of your junior year in high school.

Why the hurry? In the event your ACT scores don't hit the targets you've set, you'll want the opportunity to take the exam at least once more before your application deadline hits.

Most students find that their test scores rise the second time they take the ACT, and if you prepare in a focused and disciplined way before your second exam, you'll have the opportunity to achieve a significant score increase. (For more information about whether and how to plan to retake the exam, see chapter 10.) Raising your score by taking the test a second time will be impossible if you schedule your exam during the final pre- deadline window.

REGISTERING FOR THE EXAM

FYI

If you are interested in applying for early admission at a particular school, an earlier deadline will apply. Don't forget to take this fact into consideration.

ACT supplies high schools with plentiful stacks of bulletins and registration forms, so the easiest way to get the forms you need is to stop by the guidance office and ask for them. As an alternative, you can call ACT at 1-319-337-1270 and have them send you the materials.

When you register by mail, you'll fill in a fairly lengthy computerized paper folder that requires you to blacken in ovals using a #2 pencil. Surprise—it's the same technology used on the ACT answer sheets, so you might as well get used to it. Take your time filling out the form; it's easier than a tax return, but not much. Be especially careful when looking up and transferring the code numbers for the test center where you want to take the exam and the code numbers for the colleges you're listing to receive your test scores. Mistakes are easy to make.

If you have access to the Internet and the use of a Visa or Mastercard (to pay the fees), you can also register online. Log in at http://www.act.org.

Either way, you'll need to register well in advance of your chosen test date. Regular registration deadlines are about four weeks prior to the exam. You can register late for an extra fee (currently $15), but this only gives you a few more days. Late registration also makes it less likely you'll be assigned the test center of your choice. So don't put off registration.

After you've registered, you can use the phone to do things like register for subsequent tests, request a change in your test center, or add colleges to your score report list. The number for ACT customer service is 1-319-337-1270. Again, expect a fee for each service you request.

THE INSIDER'S REPORT: KNOW YOUR OPTIONS

Choosing the Best Location

Most high schools administer the ACT exams, but not every school serves as a test center on every test date. Carefully study the listing of test centers in the ACT bulletin. Your first choice, if it's available on the day you want to test, is probably your home high school; your second choice may be another nearby school.

At times, however, a different location may serve you better. Ask your guidance counselor, or, better still, classmates who've taken the ACT at your school, about the quality of the facilities on test days. (Remember, you'll probably be taking the exam on Saturday, a day when you're usually *not* in the building.) Are the testing rooms noisy? Are they adequately heated or cooled? Are the rooms too crowded, or poorly lit? If you hear a lot of complaints about a particular test center, it may be worthwhile to select a different one, even if it's slightly farther from home.

You may also want to consider a test center other than your home high school if you like the idea of taking the exam *away* from your classmates. Some students find it distracting to run into hordes of gossiping, nervous friends the morning of the test. If you're one such student, taking the test in the near anonymity of a "neutral site" may be better.

If you do pick a center away from home, make sure you know exactly how to get there and how long it will take. You don't want to arrive late or experience a long, anxiety-producing drive in search of the right street address on the morning of your exam. If necessary, make a preliminary visit the week before, just to be sure you can get there with a minimum of fuss.

Taking the Test for Free

Taking the ACT isn't cheap. Currently, the minimum fee to register for the exam is $23.00 in the United States. (For Florida residents only, the fee is $26.00; for students testing outside the United States, the fee is $38.00). And if you sign up for the Test Information Release service (which we recommend, as explained later in this chapter), request a few additional college score reports beyond the four you get "free," and throw in one or two other services, the cost can easily climb to $70 or more.

If your family finances make ACT fees a problem, visit your high school counselor and ask for information about getting the fees waived. She should have the ACT fee-waiver form, which must be enclosed with your registration form when you send it in. So be sure to check in with your counselor at least a week before the registration deadline, so there'll be plenty of time to get the necessary paperwork completed. You can only take the ACT on a fee-waiver basis once, and no special services are covered.

Untimed Testing

If you have a learning disability or any physical or psychological condition that would make it impossible or unfair for you to have to complete the ACT exam under the same time limits as other students, you may be able to take the test with special extended timing.

This option is available at regularly scheduled ACT test centers during October, December, and April only. Up to five hours of total testing time is provided. A special form, called the *ACT Assessment Application for Extended-Time National Testing,* must be completed; your high school guidance counselor should have a copy. Plan early so you'll have enough time to get all the necessary paperwork done.

Other Accommodations

FYI

If you take the ACT in a special untimed administration, your score reports will contain the notation "Special." Presumably, your disability will be known to the colleges you're applying to, so this notation should come as no surprise and have no negative impact on the evaluation of your scores.

Some students need other accommodations when they take the test. For example, a student in a wheelchair or a student whose sight or hearing is impaired may need special seating arrangements, the use of a large-print test booklet, or a sign-language interpreter for the proctor's spoken instructions.

If you fall into a similar category, speak to your high school counselor. You'll need a letter describing the accommodation needed, explaining the reason for it, confirming that a similar accommodation is provided for you when you take classroom tests, and verifying that no extra testing time is needed. You'll enclose this letter with your regular test registration form.

Non-Saturday Testing

If you can't take the ACT on Saturday because of your religion, you can apply for a non-Saturday administration. The official booklet *Registering for the ACT Assessment* contains a list of non-Saturday test dates and test centers. If none of these is convenient, contact the ACT Universal Testing office and ask for a copy of *Request for ACT Assessment Arranged Testing.* You should be able to arrange a special exam at a time and place appropriate for you. Write or call the following:

ACT Universal Testing
P.O. Box 4028
Iowa City, Iowa 52243-4028
319-337-1332

Score Reporting

When you register for the ACT, you'll be allowed to pick four colleges or universities to receive reports of your scores. Even if you're not yet completely sure which schools you'll be applying to, take advantage of this opportunity to name four of your most likely choices. Additional reports will cost you money (currently $6 per school).

You can add to the list of colleges that will receive your scores in several ways.

- Space for up to two additional reports is provided on the test registration form. The $6 fee will be charged for each college listed here, of course.

- You can fill out and mail an Additional Score Report request form, which you'll receive with your test result packet.

- You can request additional reports by phone using a credit card. Dial 1-319-337-1313. There is a $10.00 service fee plus the fees for the priority reports themselves. Additional score reports can also be ordered online using ACT's Online ASR Request Form. See www.act.org for more information.

See chapter 10 for more information about your score reports.

Other ACT Services

Besides the ACT Assessment, ACT provides other student services, some of which are optional. Here's a brief explanation of each.

- **ACT Interest Inventory, Student Profile, and Other Student Reports.** When you register for the ACT, you'll be asked to provide information about your high school coursework, your vocational interests, your college preferences and plans, and so on. This data is used by ACT to create personalized reports and profiles about you for the benefit of your high school and college guidance counselors. A version of this information will be included with the score report you receive after the exam; other versions will go to your high school and the colleges to which you're applying.

- **Test Information Release.** Depending on the date of your exam, you may be able to get detailed information about how you did on the ACT, which can be very useful if you retake the exam. (See chapter 10 for more details.) Our recommendation: Sign up. There is a fee (between $10 and $20, depending on what combination of information you request), but the cost is well worth the benefit. (In 2000–2001, these services are available only for U.S. administrations of the ACT on one of the following dates: Dec. 9, 2000, April 5–April 9, 2001, and June 9, 2001.)

- **Standby Testing.** If you miss both the regular and late registration deadlines, you can register for the exam on a standby basis. If space is available in the test center after all other students have been accommodated, you'll be permitted to take the exam. This service requires an extra $30 fee, so you'll want to take advantage of it only on an emergency basis.

WHEN TEST TIME COMES

The big weekend is here. You're about to face one of the important challenges of your young life, comparable to pitching in the county championship ball game or taking the leading role in the school musical. If you've used this book (and other resources) effectively, you can be confident that you're well prepared for the ACT exam. Here are some last-minute reminders and suggestions that will help you handle the stress of "game time" gracefully.

The Night Before

- **Don't cram.** Last-minute studying isn't likely to make much difference in your skills or knowledge, but it can elevate your levels of anxiety and fatigue needlessly.

- **Put out everything you'll want to bring with you to the test center.** This includes: your official admission ticket; a photo ID (or other ID with a physical description of you); two #2 pencils with erasers; a calculator; and a small snack, like a granola bar or a piece of fruit.

- **If the weather is cool, lay out a sweater or two.** Dressing in layers will let you adjust to conditions in the test room. If you're traveling to an unfamiliar test site, put out the map or directions you'll be following.

- **Set your clock, and, if possible, have a backup system in place to wake you if the clock fails.** (The best such system is called Mom or Dad.) You need to arrive at the test center by 8:15 a.m., so plan accordingly.

- **Get to sleep early.** Remember that the ACT—three and a half to four hours long—is a physical as well as a mental challenge.

The Morning of the Test

- **Wake up early and have your usual breakfast.** If you normally skip breakfast, consider having something light this day: cereal or fruit. You'll be needing more energy than usual.

- **Leave plenty of time for travel.** Your goal is to arrive early and relaxed, not late and frazzled.

- **Don't listen to the predictions and advice of the students around you.** If you've prepared with the help of this book, you know exactly what to expect—probably better than your fellow test-takers. Last-minute speculation can only fuel needless worry.

During the Test

- **Make sure your accommodations are appropriate and comfortable.** You should have a comfortable chair, an adequate writing surface, plenty of light, and a space that is reasonably quiet,

371

well-heated or cooled, and pollution-free. If you're left-handed, you should have a left-handed desk. You should be able to see and hear the proctor easily as he reads the test instructions. If any of these conditions is lacking, raise your hand and ask for help.

■ **Use your basic test-taking skills.** Preview each section before you begin working on it; save the hardest questions for last; keep track of the time; guess when in doubt; and mark your answer sheet neatly and accurately.

■ **If you find that you've mismarked your answer sheet, raise your hand and get the proctor's attention.** Explain the problem and ask for a few minutes after the test with your answer sheet only to make corrections. This request will probably be granted.

■ **You'll have a short break after each test, and a break of about 10 minutes after the second test.** Use these breaks to eat your snack and to relax. A three-minute relaxation routine (see the Bright Idea) will help you feel refreshed before you tackle the next test section.

After the Exam

■ If you encountered any problems with the tests or the testing procedures—a mistake by the proctor, incorrect timing, a disruptive environment, or a misprinted test booklet—make detailed notes about it immediately after the test. Fax a letter of complaint to ACT at 1-319-339-3039 no later than Wednesday of the following week.

■ If you're convinced that you bombed on the exam, consider canceling your scores. See chapter 10 for details on how this works and how to decide whether or not this option is right for you.

■ If you think you encountered an erroneous or flawed test question, consider mounting an official challenge to the item. Chapter 10 tells how.

■ Now go party. You've earned it.

JUST THE FACTS

■ Pick a testing date based on your college application deadlines, but leave yourself a chance to retake the test if needed.

■ Find a test center that's comfortable and close to home.

■ Be sure to request any test-taking accommodations you need and deserve.

■ Manage your energies the weekend of the exam to minimize anxiety and maximize performance.

Chapter 10

How to Interpret Your Scores

GET THE SCOOP ON . . .

- What your score report really means
- How colleges interpret your ACT scores
- How and when to consider canceling your scores
- What to do if you think your score is wrong or the test was flawed
- How to decide whether to retake the ACT

HOW TO INTERPRET YOUR SCORES

You've taken the ACT . . . congratulations! Getting this far hasn't been easy. We hope you found that your study-and-practice program prepared you well for the challenge of the exam, and that you're feeling reasonably confident about how you did.

While you await your scores, don't agonize over the test, and don't assume that the way you feel is any indication of your real performance. Students who think they did poorly often get surprisingly high scores. (This scenario happens more often than the reverse.) Here's why: When you took the exam, you spent more time puzzling over the hardest questions—the ones you may have gotten wrong—than over the easy ones, which you whizzed through. So when you think about the test later, your main memory is of struggling to figure out the toughest problems. That selective recall isn't necessarily an accurate gauge of how you did overall.

Even after you receive your scores, however, your "ACT work" may not be done. It's time now to analyze your scores and what they mean, which may be a little more complicated that you realize. And you may have some important decisions to make—especially about whether or not to try taking the exam again. In this chapter, we'll explain what you need to know to win this phase of the great ACT game.

YOUR ACT SCORE REPORT

Getting Your Scores

Despite the use of computers to score the ACT, students have always had to wait quite a while to receive score reports in the mail. Three weeks is the goal, but students say that four to five weeks is more common, and even longer delays aren't unusual. The wait can be nerve wracking.

Understanding Your Score Report

The printed score report you'll eventually receive in the mail offers more information than you can get by phone. However, even savvy test-takers don't always find it clear. Here's a point-by-point description and explanation of what your score report will tell you.

FYI

If a particular college's application deadline is fast approaching and you're worried that your ACT score may not arrive in time, you can request rush score reports to colleges starting three weeks after your test. Use the ACT phone number 1-319-337-1313 to request this service. Prices are currently between $7 and $15 for each college requested, depending on the delivery method you select.

- **Your ACT Test Scores.** These are your two-digit scaled scores on each of the four ACT tests, computed as explained in chapter 3. Possible scores range between 1 (low) and 36 (high). Average or mean scores vary from year to year and even from test to test, but means for current ACT test-takers are as follows:

English	20.3
Mathematics	20.6
Reading	21.3
Science Reasoning	21.2

- **Your Subscores.** On three of the tests, you'll also receive subscores, grading your performance in specific subject areas. Possible subscores range between 1 (low) and 18 (high). Here are current means for the seven subscores:

ENGLISH SUBSCORES
Usage/Mechanics	10.1
Rhetorical Skills	10.5

MATHEMATICS SUBSCORES
Pre-Algebra/Elementary Algebra	10.7
Algebra/Coordinate Geometry	10.1
Plane Geometry/Trigonometry	10.6

READING SUBSCORES
Social Science/Natural Sciences	10.6
Prose Fiction/Humanities	11.1

Your subscores can be a useful guide if you decide to retake the test—they'll help you locate the test areas where you need the most extra work and where you have the best chances of improving your scores next time.

- **Your Composite Score.** This is a single number, on the 1-to-36 scale, that represents your overall performance on the ACT Assessment. It's simply the average of your four test scores.

- **Score Ranges.** These are bands approximately 4 points wide—2 points on either side of your scaled score—that ACT provides because of the imprecision of ACT scores. Here's what we mean. If you scored, say, 22 on the Mathematics Test, does your score imply that your "true" math ability equals *exactly* 22 (whatever that would mean)? Obviously not; 22 is just ACT's best guesstimate as to how good you are at math, based on one morning's performance on one batch of questions. To reflect this imprecision, your score report will indicate a math score band of about 20 to 24, indicating (statistically) that it is ACT's opinion that your "true" math ability *probably* falls somewhere in that range. The band appears on your score report in the form of a broken line on either side of your percentile rank (explained next).

- **Your Percentile Ranks.** For every scale score you receive, you'll also receive a percentile score, called by ACT your "rank," which compares your performance to that of a large group of recent ACT test-takers. The rank indicates what percentage of these students scored *lower* than you on the test. So if you have an English rank of 70, then 70 percent of students did less well than you. Obviously, the higher your ranks, the better.

- **College Profile Data.** You'll also receive a printout with some information about the colleges to which you arranged to have your test scores sent. It includes some blindingly obvious facts that you surely already know—for example, does the college offer a four-year degree?—as well as some useful facts that you could probably uncover elsewhere—for example, how your ACT composite score compares to those of the college's typical entering class.

- **Educational and Occupational Planning Information.** Your ACT score packet will also include suggestions and ideas about your college and vocational interests based on the questionnaires you probably completed when you applied for the exam. You may find these interesting or a total waste of time. It would be rare for a students career decisions to be heavily influenced by a computer printout from Iowa City, but who knows? You may find that the ACT materials suggest an idea or two you might not have otherwise considered. (Maybe you *should* look into becoming a tree surgeon, rabbi, or helicopter pilot—three of the occupations charted on ACT's "Career Family List.")

Taking a Closer Look at Your Test

Thanks to Truth-in-Testing laws that require public disclosure of most standardized exams, ACT now offers—for a fee, of course!—to let you examine the ACT test you took more closely. This service, known as Test

Information Release, is invaluable for the student who wants to consider retaking the exam. It's available for most test administrations, depending on the date when you take the exam. (Check the current ACT bulletin for specifics.)

If you apply for this service, you'll receive a copy of the actual test questions from the ACT you took, an answer key, scoring instructions, and a printout of your own answers. Any questions used for experimental purposes (see chapter 2) aren't included. The current cost is $10. For an additional $10, you can also receive a copy of your actual answer sheet; you may want this if for some reason you think the machine may have misread your answer marks.

You can request this service at the time you register or after taking the exam. It's a good investment, for reasons we'll explain later in this chapter.

There are some test administrations from which ACT is not legally required to release the questions publicly. Therefore, ACT keeps them secret so that they can be used again on future test-takers, thereby saving the work and expense of writing a fresh exam. For these tests, the Test Information Release service isn't available.

HOW COLLEGES INTERPRET ACT SCORES

The colleges to which you ask ACT to send your scores will receive reports containing all the information from your own score report. The college reports also include your "personal profile" (high school grades, possible college major, and so on), based on the questionnaire you filled out at the time you registered for the exam.

What do colleges look for in reading your score report? Naturally, it varies from school to school. However, here are some general observations that apply to most colleges.

■ **Colleges look to ACT scores to amplify their picture of you.** In combination with your high school grades, ACT scores are supposed to help admissions officers measure your academic abilities and achievements. Did you pursue a challenging high school program and earn grades that were good but not great? Or were your classroom grades hampered by difficult personal circumstances—loss of a parent, for instance, or the need to work throughout high school? In cases such as these, good ACT scores could help confirm that you are brighter than your grades alone suggest.

FYI

ACT advises colleges not to use cutoff scores—rigid ACT requirements, below which applications are automatically rejected. Most colleges deny using them, but admissions officers report that a significant percentage of schools do use cutoff scores, either explicitly or implicitly. If you're applying to such a school, a few extra ACT points can be a make-or-break difference. Ask the admissions officer; you may not get a completely frank answer, but the nature of his response is likely to be revealing.

- **Colleges want to see a reasonable balance among your several test scores.** A composite score of 25 on the ACT is a good one—but it's best to achieve this score by earning scores between 23 and 28 on each test area rather than, say, 16 in English and Reading and 34 in Science and Math. The "balanced" student is likely to be considered more promising than the "unbalanced" one, who, in this example, might be a science whiz but might be weak in communication skills.

- **You control which scores are released.** If you take the exam twice or more, you can specify which set of scores should be sent to colleges by ACT. However, they must send all your scores from a particular test date; you can't pick and choose ("I'll take the English score from April, the Math score from June, the Science score from October . . .").

- **Colleges evaluate you against this year's pool of applicants.** Your college application—not only your test scores but all your credentials—will never be considered in a vacuum. You are always being measured against the hundreds or thousands of other students who've applied to a particular college. As the size and quality of this applicant pool rises and falls from one year to the next, a particular set of credentials may look better or worse by comparison.

Luck and fashion play a huge role in this process. For reasons that are often hard to fathom, some colleges get "hot" at particular times; everybody and her brother decides to apply to University *X*, and the happy admissions officers there get a chance, for a time, to skim off the very best students. An applicant who might have waltzed through the door two years earlier may not make the cut now. And the opposite happens when a college falls out of vogue. Bear this in mind if you're tempted to apply to this year's fashionable school: Although the education probably hasn't improved, getting in has gotten a lot harder.

THE INSIDER'S REPORT: KNOW YOUR OPTIONS

Now you know how colleges look at your ACT scores. What can you do about it? Are there ways of managing the post-test part of the ACT process to make it work better for you?

Absolutely. Let's look at some of the options you have *after* your exam to minimize the damage from a bad day in the testing arena and to maximize your chances of getting your best possible scores.

Canceling Your Scores

FYI

In recent years, so-called "early admission" (and its variants, such as "early decision") has become a more and more popular college application option. Many schools now fill half or more of their entering class from the ranks of those who apply early and promise to attend if accepted. If you're "in love" with a certain school, consider applying early: You'll compete in a somewhat smaller candidate pool and have a better chance of getting accepted.

Occasionally, a student knows on the day of the test that he has truly bombed. Most often, the problem is physical: People do get ill, sometimes unexpectedly, and the stress of a three-hour-plus exam can worsen the early symptoms of a flu bug or stomach virus. Once in a great while, a student simply freezes up and is psychologically or emotionally unable to finish the test. And sometimes an ill-prepared student realizes, in despair, that he really should have studied and practiced before sitting down on test day. (If you've read the previous chapters in the book you're holding, you're not a candidate for this problem.)

If any of these calamities befalls you, you have an option: score cancellation. At your request, ACT will wipe clear your score slate for a particular day; your test won't be graded, and neither you nor any school will know how well (or poorly) you did.

However, these caveats:

- **You must request score cancellation almost immediately.** You can ask the test proctor for a cancellation form and fill it out on the spot, or you can cancel by notifying ACT via mail or fax no later than the Thursday following your exam.

- **The request is irrevocable.** Once you cancel your scores, they can never be reinstated. And you can't cancel just your English or just your Math score: The whole day's testing must be wiped out.

- **You won't receive any refund of your testing fee.**

Obviously, canceling your scores is a fairly serious step. Probably most significantly, it will put you in a position where you must retake the exam a few months later, by which time college application deadlines may be looming. The sense of pressure you feel on this subsequent test date may be even greater than before.

Cancel your scores only if you really must, with illness being the most likely culprit.

If Your Scores Are Delayed

On rare occasions, a student's ACT scores are delayed. A simple glitch in mail delivery may be to blame. If you haven't received your scores by six weeks after the test date, call the admissions offices of the colleges to which you are applying and ask whether or not they have received your score report. If they have, the problem on your end is with the mail. Call ACT at 1-319-337-1313 to request a duplicate of your score report.

If neither you nor your colleges have received a report by six weeks after the test date, ask your high school guidance counselor whether or not other students are experiencing delays. Once in a while, computer or other problems at ACT cause general delays for all students who took a particular test. It's rare but frustrating, and there's not much you can do except sit tight.

Finally, if it appears that the score delay involves you alone (or only a handful of other students), ACT may be investigating an apparent testing irregularity or a test security problem.

A *testing irregularity* means a problem with the way the test was administered. It could be due to a proctor's error (test-takers were given too much or too little time to work), an ACT error (faulty test booklets were printed), or circumstances beyond anyone's control (a test center is disrupted by fire or flood).

A *test security problem* means, quite specifically, a suspicion that students had access to the test beforehand; used books, computers, or other forbidden aids during the exam; took the test under false names; passed answers to one another; or otherwise cheated.

If you fall under suspicion of cheating, you'll be in for an unpleasant experience, whether or not you are guilty. Although ACT makes an effort at "due process," the adjudication of such cases is basically an internal process controlled by the test-makers.

This doesn't mean, however, that you are helpless, much less that you should meekly accept a "guilty" verdict if you are really innocent. Here is some advice as to what to do if you find yourself accused of misconduct on the ACT.

> ■ **Insist on understanding the accusation and the process.** Make sure that the test-makers inform you as to exactly what misconduct is supposed to have occurred, so that you can marshal evidence in your defense.

> ■ **Enlist the help and advice of your parents and a college counselor, teacher, or other trusted advisor.** This is an important problem that can seriously affect your college prospects, and the bureaucracy at ACT can be intimidating. Don't try to handle it alone.

> ■ **Communicate with ACT clearly and in writing.** Use registered mail and keep copies of all your communications with the test-makers. Make sure you "admit" nothing that is not completely true.

> ■ **As soon as you can, make detailed notes of everything you remember about your test-preparation and test-taking experi-**

FYI

If you merely feel you may have done poorly on the exam, you should probably go ahead and allow the test to be graded. Then take advantage of the Test Information Release service to examine what you did right and what you did wrong. This will help you significantly in preparing to do better next time—and it's an option that's not available if you cancel your scores.

ence. In particular, if you remember anything "odd" that happened on the day of the exam, jot it down. (A mistake by a proctor, for example, may innocently explain some discrepancy ACT thinks is sinister.) Be sure to be as complete and accurate as possible. The sooner you make these notes, the clearer and more convincing your memory of events is likely to be.

■ **Provide the test-makers with any facts that could help to clear you.** If you know why you're suspected of wrongdoing, you may be able to resolve the dispute by responding with information. For example, if you're suspected of cheating because you left the test room several times during the exam, you may want to ask your doctor to provide a letter confirming that you were suffering from a stomach complaint on the day of the test (if, in fact, you were).

Sometimes, ACT will investigate a test-taker solely because of a dramatic score increase—10 points or more over a previous test. If you're in this category, be prepared to explain (and document, if possible) how you prepared for your second test. Describe your use of coaching, tutoring, books, software, and any other test-prep tools, and estimate the number of hours you devoted to study before the exam. A convincing account of your significant test-prep effort can go a long way toward showing that your score increase was produced not by trickery but by good old-fashioned hard work.

■ **Consider enlisting legal help.** ACT refers disputes over test scores to the American Arbitration Association, a non-governmental agency that provides experts to help resolve conflicts between private parties. You can accept arbitration by AAA if you wish. In America, however, final recourse in disputes between groups and individuals is to the law. Most wrangles with ACT don't require the help of a lawyer, but you may want to consider this option if you've been unjustly accused, if the test-makers refuse to resolve the dispute quickly and fairly, and if the cost is not a major problem for you and your family.

■ **If the dispute is not resolved within a reasonable time (say, four to six weeks), insist on your right to retake the exam as soon as possible, at no charge to you.** This alternative gives an innocent test-taker the chance to demonstrate his abilities again without penalty and free from any cloud of suspicion.

If You Think Your Scores Are Wrong

On rare occasions, a student who requests the Test Information Release service (as we recommend you do) becomes convinced, upon review of her test, that one or more of her test scores is inaccurate. Here's what to do if this happens to you.

FYI

Test-question challenges have been much more effective in regard to math questions than to questions in reading or English—not because the reading or English questions are "better," but because it's far easier to demonstrate actual errors on math questions. A degree of ambiguity and subjectivity is almost impossible to eliminate from non-math questions, making it almost impossible to prove that the test-maker's chosen answer is truly "wrong."

■ **Request hand scoring.** Sometimes, a student finds a discrepancy between the answer choices she is supposed to have made and the choices she remembers making. It's rare, but it happens. The machine that reads your answer grid could malfunction, for example, reading a choice (C) as a choice (D) or as no choice at all. If you strongly believe that the printout of your answer choices doesn't reflect your actual work on the day of the test, this may have happened to you.

Your best option in this case is to request hand scoring of your answer sheet. To do so, write to ACT giving your name, social security or ACT identification number, birth date, test date, and test center. (As you probably guessed, there's a fee for this service—currently $20.) You'll get a new score report within a few weeks. If it's found that your test *was* misgraded, ACT will send a notification letter to all of your colleges—and they'll refund your hand-scoring fee.

■ **Challenge a test question or procedure.** A more complicated problem arises if you become convinced that you were harmed either by some unfair procedure on the day of the test or by an inaccurate and flawed test question. There's a system for appealing such problems, but be prepared for a fairly lengthy process.

If you feel burned by a test procedure or question, write down all the details you can remember as soon as possible. Then send a registered letter to the test-makers at this address:

ACT Test Administration
PO Box 168
Iowa City, Iowa 52243-0168

Include your name, address, birth date and sex, social security number, and test registration number, and mention the name of the test you took, the date, and the name, number, and address of the test center you used. In your letter, explain what happened and why you think it was unfair.

ACT will investigate and respond. In most cases, it will defend its procedure or test question (and often they are right to do so). If you aren't satisfied, there are several further levels of appeal you can request. It's up to you to decide how significant your complaint is, how strongly you feel about it, and how much time and effort you want to invest in this process.

ACT is obviously not perfect. Over the years since Truth in Testing made challenges to test questions a genuine option, erroneous test questions have been discovered and corrected, resulting in score changes for many students.

So don't hesitate to challenge the test-makers if you're convinced it's appropriate. The only way powerful institutions like ACT can be kept responsive to human concerns is if individuals hold them accountable for their actions, right and wrong.

FairTest, the non-profit organization dedicated to fair and open testing, may be able to help you with information and referrals if you have a complaint or dispute about the ACT. Contact them at

> FairTest
> 342 Broadway
> Cambridge, Massachusetts 02139-1802
> Phone: 617-864-4810
> Fax: 617-497-2224
> fairtest@aol.com
> www.fairtest.org

The Decision To Retest

Should you retake the ACT if you're not satisfied with your scores? In many cases, the answer is Yes. Here are some questions to consider in making this decision:

- **How do the scores you've already received match the credentials wanted by the college(s) of your choice?** You need to establish target ACT scores based on the admission requirements of the schools you want to attend, as well as the other credentials you bring to the table, such as your high school grades. If the test scores you've already earned fall outside the range in which most freshmen at your target college score—or if they are at the lower end of the range—you should strongly consider retaking the test.

- **How often have you already been tested?** If you've taken the ACT twice or more previously—and especially if you prepared beforehand—you may have already tapped most of your potential for improvement. However, if you've been tested just once before—and especially if your preparation in the past was superficial—there's every reason to believe your score can go up—perhaps a lot.

- **Can you identify test areas with potential for improvement?** You're an especially strong candidate to retake the exam if your score report reveals specific areas of weakness. For example, if you performed well on all the math areas except plane geometry/trigonometry, where you got most of the items wrong, a targeted practice program focusing on those topics can boost your overall score significantly.

FYI

Most students who take the ACT a second time enjoy at least a modest score increase due to sheer familiarity with the exam. If you retake the test following a serious preparation program tailored to the weaknesses revealed by your first score report, the effects of that preparation, combined with the "familiarity effect," should give you a great shot at a significant score increase.

■ **Do you have time to invest in preparing for another test?** Look realistically at your plans for school and other activities. Before you schedule another exam, make sure you can block out hours during the prior weeks for study and practice. If you take the second test cold, without any real preparation or warm-up, you may wind up spinning your wheels, earning scores no higher than your first scores.

A final tip about retaking the exam: Don't forget to review *every* test area, at least briefly, before your second or later ACT. Although you may need to focus the bulk of your study on one area, such as algebra, it's important to keep your other skills sharp, too. You don't want to gain points on one end while losing them on the other.

JUST THE FACTS

■ Study your score report carefully, and make sure you understand what each number means.

■ Evaluate your performance as colleges will—against the credentials of their pool of applicants.

■ If you think you completely bombed on the exam, consider canceling your scores.

■ If you think your ACT was unfair for any reason, you have ways to complain and be heard.

■ Consider retaking the exam if your scores fall below the targets you need to achieve.

■ If you do retake the test, focus your preparation on areas where you need the most improvement.

Chapter 11

The Insider's Tip Sheet

GET THE SCOOP ON . . .

- Making the test work for you
- Why you don't need to answer every question
- What to do when the going gets tough
- How guessing can improve your score

It's the night before you'll be taking the ACT—or maybe the very morning of the exam. You've been studying, practicing, and preparing for days, weeks, even months, and you're about as ready to take the test as you'll ever be.

Trouble is, the strategies, techniques, and methods you've learned from this book feel as if they're lodged in dozens of separate compartments scattered throughout your overloaded brain. A few weeks may have passed since you last tried your hand at a particular question type; you've probably become a little fuzzy about exactly how to tackle it. But you don't have time now—hours before the test—to review hundreds of pages covering strategies for four separate question types. If you try, you'll just intensify that gnawing sense of anxiety in the pit of your stomach—and maybe even develop a full-blown case of panic.

That's where this chapter comes in. It's a concise recap of the most important tips, strategies, warnings, and techniques from the entire book, organized for easy study during the final day before your exam. You may want to tear these pages out of the book and carry them with you in the car, bus, or train that takes you to the test center for a truly last-minute review. It's even better to read them the night before—that way, if any one or two ideas don't ring a bell, you can look them up in the relevant chapters and refresh your memory.

OVERALL STRATEGIES FOR THE ACT

- Spend a few seconds previewing each test before you begin work on it. Check how many pages and questions there are so you can budget your time accordingly.

- Work at a steady pace. You don't need to rush madly through the tests, but you shouldn't dawdle, either. Remember, every question is worth the same amount, so rather than getting bogged down on an especially challenging question, move on to the next one—it may be more to your liking.

- Mark up the margins of the test booklet freely—to perform computations, outline reading passages, cross out answers as you eliminate them, and so on.

- Don't be afraid to guess. Use what you know to eliminate any answer that is clearly wrong, then pick the best answer from among those that remain. Chances are you'll gain points by following this method.

- Tackle the questions in order of difficulty, starting with those in a given test that you find the easiest. This will guarantee that you'll maximize the points you can gain from knocking off the questions you're the best at.

- Fill in the answer sheet carefully. Make sure you don't skip any spaces unintentionally, and don't mark two answers for the same question. Erase all stray pencil marks.

STRATEGIES FOR THE ENGLISH TEST

- Start by reading the sentence or paragraph carefully, "listening" for the error (if any). In most cases, the word or phrase that contains an error in grammar or usage will *sound* wrong.

- If no grammatical error is apparent, look for the four most common types of errors tested on the ACT: errors in the relationship between the verb and its subect; pronoun errors; sentence structure errors; and awkwardness, verbosity, and incorrect use of idioms.

- Once you spot the error, think of how you'd revise the sentence to correct it, and scan the answer choices, looking for the one(s) that fix the error. Then pick an answer that corrects the error without introducing any new error.

- Expect about one quarter of the items to be correct as originally written. For these, the first answer choice (A or F) is correct.

- If you can't decide which of two answer choices is best, prefer the shorter of the two.

- Every paragraph should be organized around a single idea; ideas should be connected by the use of logical and appropriate linking words.

STRATEGIES FOR THE MATHEMATICS TEST

- As soon as you've found the right answer, mark it and move on—there are no "degrees of rightness" to be considered.

- Use your pencil to mark up diagrams with additional information as you find it, or to sketch simple drawings when no diagram is provided. This can often help you "see" the answers to questions, with little or no figuring needed.

- The questions are designed to focus primarily on the underlying relationships among the numbers presented, not your ability to perform calculations—therefore, if you find yourself spending too much time doing figuring, you've probably overlooked a simple shortcut.

- Feel free to round off and guesstimate using approximate values.

- Don't over-use your calculator. Most questions can and should be answered using a few simple computations.

- When in doubt about how to get started on a problem, try something—anything! This will often lead you toward a solution.

- When stymied, try plugging in possible values for x or any other unknown—but remember to try zero, a fraction, and a negative number unless specifically ruled out.

STRATEGIES FOR THE READING TEST

- Use the three-stage method (previewing, reading, reviewing) to get the most out of each reading passage.

- Focus on the big ideas in each passage, not the small details.

- Look for the connections among the ideas in each passage.

- Use your pencil as you read to mark the main ideas and the connections among them. These notes will make it easier and faster to find the answers to the questions that follow.

- Review the passage as often as necessary to locate the answer for a specific question.

- Don't pick an answer just because it sounds familiar, seems to be true, or reflects information that actually appears in the passage— the answer must also accurately respond to the question being asked.

STRATEGIES FOR THE SCIENCE REASONING TEST

- Use the same three-stage method (previewing, reading, reviewing) to get the most out of each science reasoning passage.

- Focus on the big ideas in each passage, not the small details. This usually means ignoring such details as the specific numbers in the table or the values reflected in a graph; pay attention only to the overall trend exhibited, then move on.

- In data representation passages, focus on what is being measured, relationships among the variables, and trends in the data.

- In research summary passages, focus on the question asked, the variables being tested, and similarities and differences in the experimental results.

- In conflicting viewpoint passages, focus on what must be explained, similarities and differences in the theories presented, and the hidden assumptions that underlie each theory.

- Don't be confused by irrelevant information or technical terminology—most science reasoning passages have them, and they can almost always be ignored.

Part V

Appendices

The Insider's Word List for the ACT

VOCABULARY: DOES IT MATTER?

In a word: Yes.

Vocabulary *as such* is not tested on the ACT. It includes no test devoted to having you define difficult words.

However, these don't exclude *indirect* and *hidden* vocabulary questions—of which there are plenty.

1. **Reading comprehension passages sometimes include vocabulary-in-context questions.** These focus on particular words in the passage and ask you to determine their meaning *in the passage.* Sometimes, the words chosen are obviously "hard" words (like *inception,* a recent real example). More often, they are seemingly "easy" words that are tricky because they have several possible meanings (*gasps* and *engages,* for example). In both cases, the broader, more varied, and more accurate your vocabulary knowledge, the better your chances are of answering these questions quickly and correctly.

2. **The better your vocabulary knowledge, the easier you'll find it to understand the large amount of reading you must do on the ACT.** Three of the four tests—the Reading Test, the English Test, and the Science Reasoning Test—are built around extensive, often complicated passages you must read and accurately interpret. Even an occasional math item is made a little more complicated by the use of a challenging vocabulary word.

Therefore, vocabulary knowledge makes a clear and significant difference in your performance on the ACT. Fortunately, the kinds of words that regularly appear on the ACT—as with so much else on the exam—fall into definite patterns.

The ACT is basically a test of "book learning." It's written and edited by bookish people for the benefit of the other bookish people who run colleges and universities. It's designed to test your ability to handle the kinds of academic tasks college students usually have to master: reading textbooks, finding information in reference books, deciphering scholarly journals, studying research abstracts, writing impressive-sounding term papers, etc.

The hard words on the ACT are of a particular sort: scholastic words that deal, broadly speaking, with the manipulation and communication of *ideas*—words like *abstract, ambiguous, arbitrary,* and *astute.* The better you master this sort of vocabulary, the better you'll do on the exam.

Fortunately, you don't need to find these words on your own. We've done the spadework for you. By examining actual ACT exams from the last several years, we've been able to list the words most commonly used in the tests, including both the question stems and the answer choices. This list became the basis of the Insider's ACT Word List. It includes about 500 primary words that are most likely to appear in one form or another on your ACT exam. It also includes hundreds of related words—words that are either variants of the primary words (*ambiguity* as a variant of *ambiguous*, for example) or that share a common word root (like *acrid, acrimonious,* and *acerbity*).

If you make yourself acquainted with all the words in the Insider's ACT Word List, you will absolutely learn a number of new words that will appear on your ACT. You'll earn extra points as a result.

THE SIX BEST INSIDER'S VOCABULARY-BUILDING TIPS FOR THE ACT

Study Vocabulary Daily

There are some topics you can easily cram, vocabulary isn't one of them. Words generally stick in the mind not the first or second time you learn them but the fourth or fifth time. Try to begin your vocabulary study several weeks before the exam and take 15 or 20 minutes a day to learn new words. Periodically, review all the words you've previously studied, quiz yourself, or have a friend quiz you. This simple regimen can enable you to learn several hundred new words before you take the ACT.

Learn a Few Words at a Time

Don't try to gobble dozens of words in one sitting. They're likely to blur into an indistinguishable mass. Instead, pick a reasonable quantity—say, 10 to 15 words—and study them in some depth. Learn the definition of each word; examine the sample sentence provided in the word list; learn the related words; and try writing a couple of sentences of your own that include the word. Refer to your own dictionary for further information if you like.

Learn Words in Families

Language is a living thing. Words are used by humans, innately creative beings who constantly twist, reshape, invent, and recombine words. (Think of the jargon of your favorite sport or hobby, or the new language currently blossoming in cyberspace, for some examples.) As a result, most words belong to families in which related ideas are expressed through related words. This makes it possible to learn several words each time you learn one.

In the Insider's ACT Word List, we've provided some of the family linkages to help you. For example, you'll find the adjective *anachronistic* in the word list. It means "out of the proper time," as illustrated by the sample sentence: *The reference, in Shakespeare's* Julius Caesar, *to "the clock striking twelve" is anachronistic, since there were no striking timepieces in ancient Rome.*

When you meet this word, you should also get to know its close kinfolk. The noun anachronism means something that is out of its proper time. The clock in Julius Caesar, for example, is an anachronism; in another way, so are the knickers worn by modern baseball players, which reflect a style in men's fashions that went out of date generations ago. When you learn the adjective, learn the noun (and/or verb) that goes with it at the same time.

Become a Word Root Tracer

The two words we just discussed—*anachronistic* and *anachronism*—are like brother and sister. Slightly more distant relatives can be located and learned through the Word Origin feature that you'll find near many of the words in the list. The Word Origin for *anachronistic* connects this word to its origin in a source from another language: The Greek word *chronos* = time. Ultimately, this is the root from which the English word *anachronistic* grows.

As you explore the Word Origins, you'll find that many words—especially bookish ACT words—come from roots in Latin and Greek. There are complicated (and interesting) historical reasons for this, but the nub is that, for several centuries, educated people in England and America knew ancient Latin and Greek and deliberately translated words from those languages into English.

They rarely translated just one word from a given root. Thus, many word roots enable you to learn several English words at once. The Word Origin for *anachronistic* tells you that *chronos* is also the source of the English words *chronic, chronicle, chronograph, chronology, synchronize.* All have to do with the concept of time:

> *chronic* = lasting a long time
> *chronicle* = a record of events over a period of time
> *chronograph* = a clock or watch
> *chronology* = a timeline
> *synchronize* = to make two things happen at the same time

Learning the word root *chronos* can help you in several ways. It will make it easier to learn all the words in the *chronos* family, as opposed to trying to learn them one at a time. It will help you to remember the meanings of *chronos* words if they turn up on the exam, and it may even help you to guess the meaning of an entirely new *chronos* word when you encounter it.

Use the Words You Learn

Make a deliberate effort to include the new words you're learning in your daily speech and writing. It will impress people (teachers, bosses, friends, and enemies), and it will help solidify your memory of the words and their meanings. Maybe you've heard this tip about meeting new people: If you use a new acquaintance's name several times, you're unlikely to forget it. The same is true with new words: Use them, and you won't lose them.

Create Your Own Word List

Get into the habit of reading a little everyday with your dictionary nearby. When you encounter a new word in a newspaper, magazine, or book, look it up. Then jot down the new word, its definition, and the sentence in which you encountered it in a notebook set aside for this purpose. Review your vocabulary notebook periodically—say, once a week. It's a great way to supplement our Insider's ACT Word List, because it's personally tailored—your notebook will reflect the kinds of things you read and the words you find most difficult. And, the fact that you've taken the time and made the effort to write down the words and their meanings will help to fix them in your memory. Chances are good that you'll encounter a few words from your vocabulary notebook on the exam.

THE WORD LIST

Word Origin

Latin brevis = *short. Also found in English* brevity.

abbreviate (verb) to make briefer, to shorten. *Because time was running out, the speaker had to abbreviate his remarks.* abbreviation (noun).

abide (verb) to withstand. *It's extremely difficult to abide criticism when you feel that it is undeserved.*

abstain (verb) to refrain, to hold back. *After his heart attack, he was warned by the doctor to abstain from smoking, drinking, and over-eating.* abstinence (noun), abstemious (adjective).

abstract (adjective) intangible; apart from concrete existence. *The most difficult concepts for most students to learn are those which are most abstract.* abstraction (noun).

absurdly (adverb) in a meaningless or ridiculous manner. *Absurdly, the doctor asked the man with the broken arm if he was feeling well.* absurd (adjective).

accouterments (noun) accessories or equipment. *Other than his weapons, the equipment a soldier carries is considered accouterments.*

Word Origin

Latin acer = *sharp. Also found in English* acerbity, acrid, exacerbate.

acrimonious (adjective) biting, harsh, caustic. *The election campaign became acrimonious, as the candidates traded insults and accusations.* acrimony (noun).

adaptable (adjective) able to be changed to be suitable for a new purpose. *Some scientists say that the mammals outlived the dinosaurs because they were more adaptable to a changing climate.* adapt (verb), adaptation (noun).

adept (adjective) highly skilled or proficient. *Although with today's electronic calculators it's not absolutely essential, most accountants are nevertheless adept at arithmetic.*

admirable (noun) deserving the highest esteem. *Honesty has always been considered a particularly admirable trait.* admirably (adverb).

adulation (noun) extreme admiration. *Few young actors have received greater adulation than did Marlon Brando after his performance in A Streetcar Named Desire.* adulate (verb), adulatory (adjective).

adversary (noun) an enemy or opponent. *When the former Soviet Union became an American ally, the United States lost its last major adversary.*

adversity (noun) misfortune. *It's easy to be patient and generous when things are going well; a person's true character is revealed under adversity.* adverse (adjective).

aeons (noun) immeasurably long periods of time. *Although it hadn't actually been that long, it seemed to the two friends that it had been aeons since they'd seen each other.*

Word Origin

Latin levis = *light. Also found in English* levitate, levity.

allege (verb) to state without proof. *Some have alleged that Foster was murdered, but all the evidence points to suicide.* allegation (noun).

alleviate (verb) to make lighter or more bearable. *Although no cure for AIDS has been found, doctors are able to alleviate the sufferings of those with the disease.* alleviation (noun).

393

ambiguous (adjective)   having two or more possible meanings. *The phrase, "Let's table that discussion" is ambiguous; some think it means, "Let's discuss it now," while others think it means, "Let's save it for later."* ambiguity (noun).

ambivalent (adjective)   having two or more contradictory feelings or attitudes; uncertain. *She was ambivalent toward her impending marriage; at times she was eager to go ahead, while at other times she wanted to call it off.* ambivalence (noun).

anachronistic (adjective)   out of the proper time. *The reference, in Shakespeare's Julius Caesar, to "the clock striking twelve" is anachronistic, since there were no striking timepieces in ancient Rome.* anachronism (noun).

anomaly (noun)   something different or irregular. *The tiny planet Pluto, orbiting next to the giants Jupiter, Saturn, and Neptune, has long appeared to be an anomaly.* anomalous (adjective).

anonymity (noun)   the state or quality of being unidentified. *Fatigued by years in the public eye, the president had begun to long for anonymity.* anonymous (adjective).

anxiety (noun)   apprehension, worry. *For many people, a visit to the dentist is the cause of anxiety.* anxious (adjective).

apprenticeship (noun)   a period of time during which one learns an art or trade. *Before the advent of law schools, a young person interested in becoming an attorney generally enters into an apprenticeship with an already established lawyer.*

aptitude (noun)   natural ability or talent. *It was clear, even when he was a very young child, that Picasso had an extraordinary aptitude for art.*

arable (adjective)   able to be cultivated for growing crops. *Rocky New England has relatively little arable farmland.*

arbiter (noun)   someone able to settle a dispute; a judge or referee. *The public is the ultimate arbiter of commercial value: it decides what sells and what doesn't.*

arbitrary (adjective)   based on random or merely personal preference. *Both computers cost the same and had the same features, so in the end I made an arbitrary decision about which one to buy.*

aristocratic (adjective)   of the nobility. *Having been born a prince, and raised to succeed his father on the throne, the young man always had an aristocratic air about him.* aristocracy (noun).

artisans (noun)   skilled workers or craftsmen. *During the Middle Ages, hundreds of artisans were employed to build the great cathedrals.*

assiduous (verb)   working with care, attention, and diligence. *Although Karen is not a naturally gifted math student, by assiduous study she managed to earn an A in trigonometry.* assiduity (noun).

associate (verb)   to join or become connected. *After many years of working on her own, the attorney decided to associate herself with a large law firm.* associate (noun).

astute (adjective)   observant, intelligent, and shrewd. *Safire's years of experience in Washington and his personal acquaintance with many political insiders make him an astute commentator on politics.*

asymmetrical (adjective)   not balanced. *If one of the two equal-sized windows is enlarged, the room's design will become asymmetrical.* asymmetry (noun).

audible (adjective)   able to be heard. *Although she whispered, her voice was picked up by the microphone, and her words were audible throughout the theater.* audibility (noun).

Word Origin

Latin audire = *to hear. Also found in English* audition, auditorium, auditory.

auditory (adjective)   of, relating to, or experienced through hearing. *Attending a symphony concert is primarily an auditory rather than a visual experience.*

behavioral (adjective)   relating to how humans or animals act. *Psychology is considered a behavioral science because it concerns itself with human actions and reactions.* behavior (noun).

Word Origin

Latin bene = *well. Also found in English* benediction, benefactor, beneficent, beneficial, benefit, benign.

benevolent (adjective)   wishing or doing good. *In old age, Carnegie used his wealth for benevolent purposes, donating large sums to found libraries and schools.* benevolence (noun).

blithely (adverb)   in a gay or cheerful manner. *Much to everyone's surprise, the condemned man went blithely to the gallows, smiling broadly at the crowd.* blithe (adjective).

bombastic (adjective)   inflated or pompous in style. *Old-fashioned bombastic political speeches don't work on television, which demands a more intimate style of communication.* bombast (noun).

buttress (noun)   something that supports or strengthens. *The endorsement of the American Medical Association is a powerful buttress for the claims made about this new medicine.* buttress (verb).

candor (noun)   openness, honesty, frankness. *In his memoir about the Vietnam War, former defense secretary McNamara describes his mistakes with remarkable candor.* candid (adjective).

capitulate (verb)   to surrender or cease resisting. *After many proposals over a number of years, the young woman finally decided to capitulate and marry her suitor.* capitulation (noun).

Word Origin

Latin vorare = *to eat. Also found in English* devour, omnivorous, voracious.

carnivorous (adjective)   meat-eating. *The long, dagger-like teeth of the Tyrannosaurus make it obvious that this was a carnivorous dinosaur.* carnivore (noun).

cataloguing (verb)   creating a list or register. *The man was so busy cataloguing his library that he had no time to read.* catalogue (noun).

censure (noun)   blame, condemnation. *The news that Senator Packwood had harassed several women brought censure from many feminists.* censure (verb).

characterize (verb)   to describe the qualities of. *Although I am reluctant to characterize the man, I must say that he seems to me dishonest and untrustworthy.* characterization (noun).

chauvinism (noun)   a prejudiced belief in the superiority of one's own group. *The company president's refusal to hire any women for upper management was indicative of his male chauvinism.*

circuitous (adjective)   winding or indirect. *We drove to the cottage by a circuitous route, so we could see as much of the surrounding countryside as possible.*

Word Origin

Latin circus = *circle. Also found in English* circumference, circumnavigate, circumscribe, circumspect, circumvent.

circumlocution (noun)   speaking in a roundabout way; wordiness. *Legal documents often contain circumlocutions which make them difficult to understand.*

circumscribe (verb)   to define by a limit or boundary. *Originally, the role of the executive branch of government was clearly circumscribed, but that role has greatly expanded over time.* circumscription (noun).

circumvent (verb)   to get around. *When Jerry was caught speeding, he tried to circumvent the law by offering the police officer a bribe.*

cogent (adjective)   forceful and convincing. *The committee members were won over to the project by the cogent arguments of the chairman.* cogency (noun).

Word Origin

Latin cognoscere = *to know. Also found in English* cognition, cognitive, incognito, recognize.

cognizant (adjective)   aware, mindful. *Cognizant of the fact that it was getting late, the master of ceremonies cut short the last speech.* cognizance (noun).

cohesive (adjective)   sticking together, unified. *An effective military unit must be a cohesive team, all its members working together toward a common goal.* cohere (verb), cohesion (noun).

colloquial (adjective)   informal in language; conversational. *Some expressions from Shakespeare, such as the use of* thou *and* thee, *sound formal today but were colloquial English in Shakespeare's time.*

communal (adjective)   of or pertaining to a group. *Rather than have dinner separately, the members of the team chose to have a communal meal.*

conciliatory (adjective)   seeking agreement, compromise, or reconciliation. *As a conciliatory gesture, the union leaders agreed to postpone a strike and to continue negotiations with management.* conciliate (verb), conciliation (noun).

Word Origin

Latin caedere = *to cut. Also found in English* decide, excise, incision, precise.

concise (adjective)   expressed briefly and simply; succinct. *Less than a page long, the Bill of Rights is a concise statement of the freedoms enjoyed by all Americans.* concision (noun).

conditioned (adjective)   trained or prepared for a specific action or process. *In Pavlov's famous experiments, by ringing a bell when he was about to feed them, he conditioned his dogs to salivate at the sound of the bell.*

Word Origin

Latin dolere = *to feel pain. Also found in English* dolorous, indolent.

condolence (noun)   pity for someone else's sorrow or loss; sympathy. *After the sudden death of Princess Diana, thousands of messages of condolence were sent to her family.* condole (verb).

configuration (noun)   the arrangement of the parts or elements of something. *The configuration of players on a baseball field is governed both by tradition and by the rules of the game.* configure (verb).

conjure (verb)   to call to mind or evoke. *The scent of magnolia always conjures up images of the old South.*

connoisseur (noun)   an expert capable of acting as a critical judge. *There was no question that the woman's discriminating palate made her a connoisseur of vintage wines.*

constructive (adjective)   serving to advance a good purpose. *Although simply complaining about someone's behavior generally does no good, constructive criticism can sometimes bring about positive change.*

consummate (verb)   to complete, finish, or perfect. *The deal was consummated with a handshake and the payment of the agreed-upon fee.* consummate (adjective), consummation (noun).

contaminate (verb)   to make impure. *Chemicals dumped in a nearby forest had seeped into the soil and contaminated the local water supply.* contamination (noun).

Word Origin

Latin tempus = *time. Also found in English* temporal, temporary, temporize.*"*

contemporary (adjective)   modern, current; from the same time. *I prefer old-fashioned furniture rather than contemporary styles. The composer Vivaldi was roughly contemporary with Bach.* contemporary (noun).

contraband (noun)   goods or merchandise whose exportation, importation, or possession is illegal. *Illegal drugs smuggled across the border are considered contraband by U.S. legal authorities.*

convergence (noun)   the act of coming together in unity or similarity. *A remarkable example of evolutionary convergence can be seen in the shark and the dolphin, two sea creatures that developed from different origins to become very similar in form.* converge (verb).

converse (noun)   something which is contrary or opposite. *While women often wear clothes similar to those of men, the converse is generally not true.*

Word Origin

Latin volvere = *to roll. Also found in English* devolve, involve, revolution, revolve, voluble.

convoluted (adjective)   twisting, complicated, intricate. *Tax law has become so convoluted that it's easy for people to accidentally violate it.* convolute (verb), convolution (noun).

coveted (verb)   desired something belonging to another. *Although the law firm associate congratulated his co-worker on becoming a partner, in his heart he had coveted the position.* covetous (adjective), covetousness (noun).

credulity (noun)   willingness to believe, even with little evidence. *Con artists fool people by taking advantage of their credulity.* credulous (adjective).

Word Origin

Greek krinein = *to choose. Also found in English* criticize, critique.

criterion (noun)   a standard of measurement or judgment. (The plural is criteria.) *In choosing a design for the new taxicabs, reliability will be our main criterion.*

culpable (adjective)   deserving blame, guilty. *Although he committed the crime, because he was mentally ill he should not be considered culpable for his actions.* culpability (noun).

cultivate (verb)   to foster the growth of. *She was so impressed on first hearing Bach's* Brandenburg Concertos *that she decided to return to school to cultivate her knowledge of Baroque music.*

cumulative (adjective)   made up of successive additions. *Smallpox was eliminated only through the cumulative efforts of several generations of doctors and scientists.* accumulation (noun), accumulate (verb).

customary (adjective)   commonly practiced or used. *It is considered customary for a groom to give his best man a gift either immediately before or after the wedding.*

daunting (adjective)   intimidating. *Many recent college graduates consider the prospect of taking on a full-time job a daunting one.* daunt (verb), daunt-ingly (adverb).

debacle (noun)   a great disaster or failure. *The French considered Napoleon's defeat at the hands of the British at Waterloo a debacle of the first magnitude.*

decorous (adjective)   having good taste; proper, appropriate. *The once reserved and decorous style of the British monarchy began to change when the chic, flamboyant young Diana Spencer joined the family.* decorum (noun).

decry (verb)   to criticize or condemn. *Cigarette ads aimed at youngsters have led many to decry the marketing tactics of the tobacco industry.*

delegate (verb)   to give authority or responsibility. *The president delegated the vice-president to represent the administration at the peace talks.* delegate (noun).

Word Origin

Latin delere = *to destroy. Also found in English* delete."

deleterious (adjective)   harmful. *About thirty years ago, scientists proved that working with asbestos could be deleterious to one's health, producing cancer and other diseases.*

delineate (verb)   to outline or describe. *Naturalists had long suspected the fact of evolution, but Darwin was the first to delineate a process—natural selection—through which evolution could occur.*

demise (noun)   death. *The demise of Queen Victoria, after more than sixty years on the throne, was followed almost immediately by the coronation of her son Edward as king of England.*

denigrate (verb)   to criticize or belittle. *The firm's new president tried to explain his plans for improving the company without seeming to denigrate the work of his predecessor.* denigration (noun).

depicted (verb)   represented in a picture, sculpture or words. *In his novel* Lincoln, *Gore Vidal depicted the president not as the icon we had always known but rather as a shrewd and wily politician.* depiction (noun).

derivative (adjective)   taken from a particular source. *When a person first writes poetry, her poems are apt to be derivative of whatever poetry she most enjoys reading.* derivation (noun), derive (verb).

desolate (adjective)   empty, lifeless, and deserted; hopeless, gloomy. *Robinson Crusoe was shipwrecked and had to learn to survive alone on a desolate island. The murder of her husband left Mary Lincoln desolate.* desolation (noun).

despair (verb)   to lose all hope or confidence. *Having been unable to find a job for several months, the editor began to despair of ever securing a new position.* despair (noun), desperation (noun).

detached (verb)   free from involvement. *Because judges have no stake in the cases brought before them, they are able to take a detached view of the proceedings.* detachment (noun).

deter (verb)   to discourage from acting. *The best way to deter crime is to insure that criminals receive swift and certain punishment.* deterrence (noun), deterrent (adjective).

determined (verb)   decided conclusively. *After reviewing all the evidence, the jury determined that the defendant was not guilty of the crime.* determination (noun), determinedly (adverb).

deviate (verb)   to depart from a standard or norm. *Having agreed upon a spending budget for the company, we must not deviate from it; if we do, we may run out of money soon.* deviation (noun).

devious (adjective)   tricky, deceptive. *Milken's devious financial tactics were designed to enrich his firm while confusing or misleading government regulators.*

dictate (verb)   to speak or act domineeringly. *Whether we consider it fair or not, those whom we report to at work generally have the authority to dictate our actions.* dictator (noun), dictatorial (adjective).

diffident (adjective)   hesitant, reserved, shy. *Someone with a diffident personality should pursue a career that involves little public contact.* diffidence (noun).

diffuse (verb)   to spread out, to scatter. *The red dye quickly became diffused through the water, turning it a very pale pink.* diffusion (noun).

digress (verb)   to wander from the main path or the main topic. *My high school biology teacher loved to digress from science into personal anecdotes about his college adventures.* digression (noun), digressive (adjective).

diminish (verb)   to make less or to cause to appear to be less. *By a series of foolish decisions, the committee chairman substantially diminished his authority among the other members.* diminution (noun).

diminutive (adjective)   unusually small, tiny. *Children are fond of Shetland ponies because their diminutive size makes them easy to ride.* diminution (noun).

discern (verb)   to detect, notice, or observe. *I could discern the shape of a whale off the starboard bow, but it was too far away to determine its size or species.* discernment (noun).

discipline (noun)   control gained by enforcing obedience or order. *Those who work at home sometimes find it difficult to maintain the discipline they need to be productive.* discipline (verb), disciplinary (adjective).

disclose (verb)   to make known; to reveal. *Election laws require candidates to disclose the names of those who contribute money to their campaigns.* disclosure (noun).

Word Origin

Latin credere *= to believe. Also found in English* credential, credible, credit, credo, credulous, incredible.

discredit (verb)   to cause disbelief in the accuracy of some statement or the reliability of a person. *Although many people still believe in UFOs, among scientists the reports of "alien encounters" have been thoroughly discredited.*

discreet (adjective)   showing good judgment in speech and behavior. *Be discreet when discussing confidential business matters—don't talk among strangers on the elevator, for example.* discretion (noun).

discrepancy (noun)   a difference or variance between two or more things. *The discrepancies between the two witnesses' stories show that one of them must be lying.* discrepant (adjective).

disingenuous (adjective)   pretending to be candid, simple, and frank. *When Texas billionaire H. Ross Perot ran for president, many considered his "jest plain folks" style disingenuous.*

disparage (verb)   to speak disrespectfully about, to belittle. *Many political ads today both praise their own candidate and disparage his or her opponent.* disparagement (noun), disparaging (adjective).

disparity (noun)   difference in quality or kind. *There is often a disparity between the kind of high-quality television people say they want and the low-brow programs they actually watch.* disparate (adjective).

disproportionate (adjective)   imbalanced in regard to size, number, or degree. *Many people spend a disproportionate amount of their income on housing.* disproportion (noun).

dissemble (verb)   to pretend, to simulate. *When the police questioned her about the crime, she dissembled innocence.*

dissipate (verb)   to spread out or scatter. *The windows and doors were opened, allowing the smoke that had filled the room to dissipate.* dissipation (noun).

Word Origin

Latin sonare = *to sound. Also found in English* consonance, sonar, sonic, sonorous.

dissonance (noun)   lack of music harmony; lack of agreement between ideas. *Most modern music is characterized by dissonance, which many listeners find hard to enjoy. There is a noticeable dissonance between two common beliefs of most conservatives: their faith in unfettered free markets and their preference for traditional social values.* dissonant (adjective).

distinctive (adjective)   serving to identify or distinguish. *The teams in a football game can be easily distinguished by their distinctive uniforms.* distinctively (adverb).

divulge (verb)   to reveal. *The people who count the votes for the Oscar awards are under strict orders not to divulge the names of the winners.*

dogmatic (adjective)   holding firmly to a particular set of beliefs, often with little or no basis. *Believers in Marxist doctrine tend to be dogmatic, ignoring evidence that contradicts their beliefs.* dogmatism (noun).

durable (adjective)   long-lasting. *Denim is a popular material for work clothes because it is strong and durable.*

Word Origin

Latin durare = *to last. Also found in English* durance, duration, endure.

duress (noun)   compulsion or restraint. *Fearing that the police might beat him, he confessed to the crime, not willingly but under duress.*

eclectic (adjective)   drawn from many sources; varied, heterogeneous. *The Mellon family art collection is an eclectic one, including works ranging from ancient Greek sculptures to modern paintings.* eclecticism (noun).

ecumenical (adjective)   general or worldwide in influence, extent, or application. *With hundreds of millions of adherents on every continent, the Roman Catholic Church is truly ecumenical.*

eerie (adjective)   weird, strange. *The cobwebs hanging about its rooms gave the old mansion an eerie quality.*

efficacious (adjective)   able to produced a desired effect. *Though thousands of people today are taking herbal supplements to treat depression, researchers have not yet proven them efficacious.* efficacy (noun).

egalitarian (adjective)   asserting or promoting the belief in human equality. *Although the French Revolution was initially an egalitarian movement, during the infamous Reign of Terror human rights were widely violated.* egalitarianism (noun).

Word Origin

Latin grex = *herd. Also found in English* aggregate, congregate, gregarious.

egregious (adjective)   obvious, conspicuous, flagrant. *It's hard to imagine how the editor could allow such an egregious error to appear.*

elevate (verb)   to lift up. *When an individual successfully completes a difficult task, it generally tends to elevate his or her self-esteem.* elevation (noun).

elliptical (adjective)   very terse or concise in writing or speech; difficult to understand. *Rather than speak plainly, she hinted at her meaning through a series of nods, gestures, and elliptical half-sentences.*

elongate (verb)   lengthen, extend. *Because the family was having such a good time at the beach, they decided to elongate their stay for several more days.* elongation (noun).

Word Origin

Latin ludere = *to play. Also found in English* delude, illusion, interlude, ludicrous.

elusive (adjective)   hard to capture, grasp, or understand. *Though everyone thinks they know what "justice" is, when you try to define the concept precisely, it proves to be quite elusive.* elude (verb).

embodied (verb)   represented, personified. *Although his natural modesty would have led him to deny it, Mahatma Ghandi has been said to have embodied all the virtues of which man is capable.* embodiment (noun).

emend (verb)   to correct. *Before the letter is mailed, please emend the two spelling errors.* emendation (noun).

eminent (adjective)   noteworthy, famous. *Vaclav Havel was an eminent author before being elected president of the Czech Republic.* eminence (noun).

empathy (noun)   imaginative sharing of the feelings, thoughts, or experiences of another. *It's easy for a parent to have empathy for the sorrow of another parent whose child has died.* empathetic (adjective).

empirical (adjective)   based on experience or personal observation. *Although many people believe in ESP, scientists have found no empirical evidence of its existence.* empiricism (noun).

emulate (verb)   to imitate or copy. *The British band Oasis admitted their desire to emulate their idols, the Beatles.* emulation (noun).

encirclement (noun)   the act of surrounding or going around completely. *The greatest fear of the Soviet leadership was the encirclement of their nation by a collection of hostile countries.* encircle (verb).

enclave (noun)   a distinctly bounded area enclosed within a larger unit. *Since the late nineteenth century, New York City's Greenwich Village has been famous as an enclave for artists.*

encroach (verb)   to go beyond acceptable limits; to trespass. *By quietly seizing more and more authority, Robert Moses continually encroached on the powers of other government leaders.* encroachment (noun).

encumbered (verb)   burdened or weighed down. *Having never worked in the field before, the young architect was not encumbered by the traditions of the profession.* encumbrance (noun).

enervate (verb)   to reduce the energy or strength of someone or something. *The stress of the operation left her feeling enervated for about two weeks.*

engage (verb)   to hire or employ. *When the entrepreneur recognized that he was unable to handle the day-to-day responsibilities of his business, he engaged an assistant.* engagement (noun).

engender (verb)   to produce, to cause. *Disagreements over the proper use of national forests have engendered feelings of hostility between ranchers and environmentalists.*

enhance (verb)   to improve in value or quality. *New kitchen appliances will enhance your house and increase the amount of money you'll make when you sell it.* enhancement (noun).

enlighten (verb)   to furnish knowledge to. *Because the young woman knew her parents disliked her boyfriend, she neglected to enlighten them about her plans for marriage.* enlightenment (verb).

enmity (noun)   hatred, hostility, ill will. *Long-standing enmity, like that between the Protestants and Catholics in Northern Ireland, is difficult to overcome.*

enthrall (verb)   to enchant or charm. *When the Swedish singer Jenny Lind toured America in the nineteenth century, audiences were enthralled by her beauty and talent.*

entice (verb)   to lure or tempt. *Hoping to entice her husband into bed, the woman put on a provocative negligee.*

enviable (adjective)   extremely desirable. *After months without work, the job seeker suddenly found himself in the enviable position of having two offers from which to choose.*

envision (verb)   to picture in one's mind. *Despite her best efforts, the mother found it impossible to envision what her son would be like as an adult.*

ephemeral (adjective)   quickly disappearing; transient. *Stardom in pop music is ephemeral; most of the top acts of ten years ago are forgotten today.*

epistemological (adjective)   of the branch of philosophy that investigates the nature and origin of knowledge. *The question of how we come to learn things is an epistemological one.* epistemology (noun).

equanimity (noun)   calmness of mind, especially under stress. *Roosevelt had the gift of facing the great crises of his presidency—the Depression, the Second World War—with equanimity and even humor.*

equilibrium (noun)   a state of intellectual or emotional balance. *Due to the tragedies the man had endured, and their negative effect on his life, it took some time before he could regain his equilibrium.*

eradicate (verb)   to destroy completely. *American society has failed to eradicate racism, although some of its worst effects have been reduced.*

espouse (verb)   to take up as a cause; to adopt. *No politician in America today will openly espouse racism, although some behave and speak in racially prejudiced ways.*

ethic (noun)   a moral principle or value. *In recent years, many people have argued that the unwillingness of young people to work hard shows that the work ethic is disappearing.* ethical (adjective).

Word Origin

Latin anima = *mind, spirit. Also found in English* animate, magnanimous, pusillanimous, unanimous.

Word Origin

Latin radix = *root. Also found in English* radical.

evanescent (adjective)   vanishing like a vapor; fragile and transient. *As she walked by, the evanescent fragrance of her perfume reached me for just an instant.*

evident (adjective)   obvious, apparent. *Since the new assistant clearly had no idea of what her boss was talking about, it was evident that she had lied about her experience in the field.* evidence (noun).

evolving (verb)   developing or achieving gradually. *Although he had been a difficult child, it was clear that the young man was evolving into a very personable and pleasant adult.* evolution (noun).

exacerbate (verb)   to make worse or more severe. *The roads in our town already have too much traffic; building a new shopping mall will exacerbate the problem.*

exasperate (verb)   to irritate or annoy. *Because she was trying to study, Sharon was exasperated by the yelling of her neighbors' children.*

exculpate (verb)   to free from blame or guilt. *When someone else confessed to the crime, the previous suspect was exculpated.* exculpation (noun), exculpatory (adjective).

exert (verb)   to put forth or bring to bear. *Parents must often exert their power over children, although doing so too often can hurt the child's self-esteem.* exertion (noun).

exhilaration (noun)   the act of being made happy, refreshed or stimulated. *Diving into a swimming pool on a hot day generally provides people with a sense of exhilaration.* exhilarate (verb).

exonerate (verb)   to free from blame. *Although Jewell was suspected at first of being involved in the bombing, later evidence exonerated him.* exoneration (noun), exonerative (adjective).

expedite (verb)   to carry out promptly. *As the flood waters rose, the governor ordered state agencies to expedite their rescue efforts.*

exploitation (noun)   the act of making use of a person or thing selfishly or unethically. *The practice of slavery was a cruel case of human exploitation.* exploit (verb).

expropriate (verb)   to seize ownership of. *When the Communists came to power in China, they expropriated most businesses and turned them over to government-appointed managers.* expropriation (noun).

extant (adjective)   currently in existence. *Of the seven ancient "Wonders of the World," only the pyramids of Egypt are still extant.*

extenuate (verb)   to make less serious. *Karen's guilt is extenuated by the fact that she was only twelve when she committed the theft.* extenuating (adjective), extenuation (noun).

extol (verb)   to greatly praise. *At the party convention, speaker after speaker rose to extol their candidate for the presidency.*

extricate (verb)   to free from a difficult or complicated situation. *Much of the humor in the TV show "I Love Lucy" comes in watching Lucy try to extricate herself from the problems she creates by fibbing or trickery.* extricable (adjective).

extrinsic (adjective)   not an innate part or aspect of something; external. *The high price of old baseball cards is due to extrinsic factors, such as the nostalgia felt by baseball fans for the stars of their youth, rather than the inherent beauty or value of the cards themselves.*

exuberant (adjective)   wildly joyous and enthusiastic. *As the final seconds of the game ticked away, the fans of the winning team began an exuberant celebration.* exuberance (noun).

fabricate (verb)   to construct or manufacture. *Because the young man didn't want his parents to know where he'd spent the evening, he had to fabricate a story about studying in the library.* fabrication (noun).

Word Origin

Latin facere = *to do. Also found in English* facility, factor, facsimile, faculty.

facile (adjective)   easy; shallow or superficial. *The one-minute political commercial favors a candidate with facile opinions rather than serious, thoughtful solutions.* facilitate (verb), facility (noun).

fallacy (noun)   an error in fact or logic. *It's a fallacy to think that "natural" means "healthful"; after all, the deadly poison arsenic is completely natural.* fallacious (adjective).

felicitous (adjective)   pleasing, fortunate, apt. *The sudden blossoming of the dogwood trees on the morning of Matt's wedding seemed a felicitous sign of good luck.* felicity (noun).

fleshiness (noun)   fatness or corpulence. *Although he had been thin as a young man, as he aged he developed a certain amount of fleshiness that dieting never entirely eliminated.* fleshy (adjective).

flexibility (noun)   the state of being pliable or adaptable. *Because the job required someone who would be able to shift quickly from one task to another, the manager was most interested in candidates who showed flexibility.* flexible (adjective).

format (noun)   the shape and size of something. *The format of a book, i.e., its height, width, and length, is an essential factor in determining how much it will cost to produce.*

formidable (adjective)   awesome, impressive, or frightening. *According to his plaque in the Baseball Hall of Fame, pitcher Tom Seaver turned the New York Mets "from lovable losers into formidable foes."*

fortuitous (adjective)   lucky, fortunate. *Although the mayor claimed credit for the falling crime rate, it was really caused by several fortuitous trends.*

fractious (adjective)   troublesome, unruly. *Members of the British Parliament are often fractious, shouting insults and sarcastic questions during debates.*

fragment (verb)   a part broken off or detached. *Even though the girl overheard only a fragment of her parents' conversation, it was sufficient for her to understand that they had decided to get a divorce.* fragmentation (noun).

Word Origin

Latin frater = *brother. Also found in English* fraternal, fraternity, fratricide.

fraternize (verb)   to associate with on friendly terms. *Although baseball players aren't supposed to fraternize with their opponents, players from opposing teams often chat before games.* fraternization (noun).

frenetic (adjective)   chaotic, frantic. *The floor of the stock exchange, filled with traders shouting and gesturing, is a scene of frenetic activity.*

functionally (adverb)   in relation to a specific task or purpose. *Although the man knew the letters of the alphabet, since he could not read an entire sentence, he was considered functionally illiterate.* function (noun).

gargantuan (adjective)   huge, colossal. *The building of the Great Wall of China was one of the most gargantuan projects ever undertaken.*

genial (adjective)   friendly, gracious. *A good host welcomes all visitors in a warm and genial fashion.*

genre (noun)   kind or sort. *Surprisingly, romance novels constitute the literary genre that produces more book sales than any other.*

geometric (adjective)   increasing or decreasing through multiplication. *When two people give birth to two children, who marry two others and give birth to four children, who in turn marry two others and give birth to eight children, the population grows at a geometric rate.* geometrically (adverb).

graft (verb)   to unite or join two things. *When one uses a computer, it is possible to easily graft two existing documents together.*

grandiose (adjective)   overly large, pretentious, or showy. *Among Hitler's grandiose plans for Berlin was a gigantic building with a dome several times larger than any ever built.* grandiosity (noun).

gratuitous (adjective)   given freely or without cause. *Since her opinion was not requested, her harsh criticism of his singing seemed a gratuitous insult.*

gregarious (adjective)   enjoying the company of others; sociable. *Marty is naturally gregarious, a popular member of several clubs and a sought-after lunch companion.*

grotesque (adjective)   outlandish or bizarre. *The appearance of the aliens depicted in the film* Independence Day *is so different from that of human beings as to be grotesque.*

guileless (adjective)   without cunning; innocent. *Deborah's guileless personality and complete honesty make it hard for her to survive in the harsh world of politics.*

gullible (adjective)   easily fooled. *When the sweepstakes entry form arrived bearing the message, "You may be a winner!" my gullible neighbor tried to claim a prize.* gullibility (noun).

hackneyed (adjective)   without originality, trite. *When someone invented the phrase, "No pain, no gain," it was clever, but now it is so commonly heard that it seems hackneyed.*

hardheadedness (noun)   the quality of being stubborn or willful. *Hardheadedness is not a quality most people admire, because those who possess it can be extremely difficult to deal with.* hardheadedly (adverb).

harried (adjective)   harassed. *At the height of the Saturday dinner hour, the manager of a restaurant is likely to feel harried and overwhelmed.* harry (verb).

heinous (adjective)   very evil, hateful. *The massacre by Pol Pot of over a million Cambodians is one of the twentieth century's most heinous crimes.*

hierarchy (noun)   a ranking of people, things, or ideas from highest to lowest. *A cabinet secretary ranks just below the president and vice president in the hierarchy of the executive branch.* hierarchical (adjective).

humanistic (adjective)   concerned with human beings and their capacities, values, and achievements. *The humanistic philosophers of the Renaissance regarded humankind as the pinnacle of creation.* humanism (noun).

humility (noun)   the quality of being humble. *The president was an extremely powerful man, but his apparent humility made him seem to be very much like everyone else.*

iconoclast (noun)   someone who attacks traditional beliefs or institutions. *Comedian Dennis Miller enjoys his reputation as an iconoclast, though people in power often resent his satirical jabs.* iconoclasm (noun), iconoclastic (adjective).

idiosyncratic (adjective)   peculiar to an individual; eccentric. *Cyndi Lauper sings pop music in an idiosyncratic style, mingling high-pitched whoops and squeals with throaty gurgles.* idiosyncrasy (noun).

idolatry (noun)   the worship of a person, thing, or institution as a god. *In Communist China, Chairman Mao was the subject of idolatry; his picture was displayed everywhere, and millions of Chinese memorized his sayings.* idolatrous (adjective).

imminent (adjective)   about to incur, impending. *In preparation for his imminent death, the man called his attorney to draw up a last will and testament.* imminence (noun).

impartial (adjective)   fair, equal, unbiased. *If a judge is not impartial, then all of her rulings are questionable.* impartiality (noun).

impeccable (adjective)   flawless. *The crooks printed impeccable copies of the Super Bowl tickets making it impossible to distinguish them from the real things.*

impetuous (adjective)   acting hastily or impulsively. *Ben's resignation was an impetuous act; he did it without thinking, and he soon regretted it.* impetuosity (noun).

implicit (adjective)   understood without being openly expressed; implied. *Although most clubs had no written rules excluding blacks and Jews, many had an implicit understanding that no blacks or Jews would be allowed to join.*

imposing (adjective)   impressive because of bearing, size or dignity. *Because the man was well over six feet tall and weighed in excess of 300 pounds, most people found him an imposing figure.*

impunity (noun)   exemption from punishment or harm. *Since ambassadors are protected by their diplomatic status, they are generally able to break minor laws with impunity.*

Word Origin

Latin articulus = *joint, division. Also found in English* arthritis, articulate."

impute (verb)   to credit or give responsibility to; to attribute. *Although Sarah's comments embarrassed me, I don't impute any ill will to her; I think she didn't realize what she was saying.* imputation (noun).

inarticulate (adjective)   unable to speak or express oneself clearly and understandably. *A skilled athlete may be an inarticulate public speaker, as demonstrated by many post-game interviews.*

inception (noun)   the beginning of something. *After her divorce, the woman realized that there had been problems from the very inception of her marriage.*

incipient (adjective)   beginning to exist or appear. *The company's chief financial officer recognized the firm's incipient financial difficulties and immediately took steps to correct them.*

incisive (adjective)   expressed clearly and directly. *Franklin settled the debate with a few incisive remarks that summed up the issue perfectly.*

inclination (noun)   a disposition toward something. *The young woman had a strong inclination to have as many children as possible, mainly because she came from a large and happy family herself.* incline (verb).

incompatible (adjective)   unable to exist together; conflicting. *Many people hold seemingly incompatible beliefs: for example, supporting the death penalty while believing in the sacredness of human life.* incompatibility (noun).

inconsequential (adjective)   of little importance. *When the stereo was delivered, it was a different shade of gray than I expected, but the difference was inconsequential.*

inconsistency (noun)   the quality of being irregular or unpredictable. *The inconsistency of the student's work made it extremely difficult for his teachers to accurately gauge his abilities.* inconsistent (adjective).

incorrigible (adjective)   impossible to manage or reform. *Lou is an incorrigible trickster, constantly playing practical jokes no matter how much his friends complain.*

incremental (adjective)   increasing gradually by small amounts. *Although the initial cost of the Medicare program was small, the incremental expenses have grown to be very large.* increment (noun).

indelible (adjective)   permanent or lasting. *Meeting President Kennedy left an indelible desire in young Bill Clinton to someday live in the White House himself.*

indeterminate (adjective)   not definitely known. *The college plans to enroll an indeterminate number of students; the size of the class will depend on the number of applicants and how many accept offers of admission.* determine (verb).

indicative (adjective)   serving to point out or point to. *The fact that when the man got home he yelled at his children for no good reason was indicative of his bad day at the office.* indication (noun), indicate (verb).

indifferent (adjective)   unconcerned, apathetic. *The mayor's small proposed budget for education suggests that he is indifferent to the needs of our schools.* indifference (noun).

indistinct (adjective)   unclear, uncertain. *We could see boats on the water, but in the thick morning fog their shapes were indistinct.*

indomitable (adjective)   unable to be conquered or controlled. *The world admired the indomitable spirit of Nelson Mandela; he remained courageous despite years of imprisonment.*

induce (verb)   to cause. *The doctor prescribed a medicine that is supposed to induce a lowering of the blood pressure.* induction (noun).

indulgent (adjective)   lenient. *Abraham Lincoln was so indulgent of his children that while he was president he let them run freely through the Oval Office without reprimanding them.* indulgence (noun), indulge (verb).

inevitable (adjective)   unable to be avoided. *Once the Japanese attacked Pearl Harbor, American involvement in World War Two was inevitable.* inevitability (noun).

inexhaustible (adjective)   incapable of being entirely used up. *For many years we believed that the world's supply of fossil fuels was inexhaustible, but we now know that eventually it will be necessary to find other sources of energy.*

inexorable (adjective)   unable to be deterred; relentless. *It's difficult to imagine how the mythic character of Oedipus could have avoided his evil destiny; his fate appears inexorable.*

influential (adjective)   exerting or possessing the power to cause an effect in an indirect manner. *While the pope has direct authority only over Roman Catholics, he is also influential among members of other faiths.* influence (noun), influence (verb).

inherent (adjective)   naturally part of something. *Compromise is inherent in democracy, since everyone cannot get his way.* inhere (verb), inherence (noun).

initiative (noun)   the first step or opening move. *At those times when no one seems able to make a decision, someone must take the initiative to get things going.* initiation (noun), initiate (verb).

innate (adjective)   inborn, native. *Not everyone who takes piano lessons becomes a fine musician, which shows that music requires innate talent as well as training.*

innocuous (adjective)   harmless, inoffensive. *I was surprised that Andrea took offense at such an innocuous joke.*

innovative (adjective)   characterized by introducing or beginning something new. *The innovative design of its new computer gave the company an advantage over its competitors.* innovation (noun).

insecure (adjective)   not confident or sure. *The tenth-grade girl was very bright, but because she was not as attractive as some of her classmates she felt insecure about talking to boys.* insecurity (noun).

insipid (adjective)   flavorless, uninteresting. *Most TV shows are so insipid that you can watch them while reading without missing a thing.* insipidity (noun).

insistence (noun)   firm in stating a demand or opinion. *The man's insistence that Orson Welles—rather than Humphrey Bogart—had starred in* Casablanca *made it clear that he was quite ignorant about movies.* insistent (adjective), insist (verb).

inspiration (noun)   the action or power of moving the intellect or emotions. *The individual who is able to persevere, despite adversity, often serves as an inspiration to the rest of us.* inspire (verb).

instinct (noun)   a natural aptitude or ability. *The films for children produced by Walt Disney's studio were invariably successful because Disney had an instinct for what children would like to see.* instinctive (adjective).

insular (adjective) narrow or isolated in attitude or viewpoint. *New Yorkers are famous for their insular attitudes; they seem to think that nothing important has ever happened outside of their city.* insularity (noun).

integrity (noun) honesty, uprightness; soundness, completeness. *"Honest Abe" Lincoln is considered a model of political integrity. Inspectors examined the building's support beams and foundation and found no reason to doubt its structural integrity.*

intensity (noun) great concentration, force or power. *The intensity of the emotions evoked by the film* Gone With the Wind *have brought viewers to tears for mre than fifty years.* intense (adjective), intensify (verb).

interaction (noun) mutual or reciprocal influence. *It is the successful interaction of all the players on a football team that enables the team to win.* interact (verb).

Word Origin

Latin terminare = *to end. Also found in English* coterminous, exterminate, terminal, terminate.

interminable (adjective) endless or seemingly endless. *Addressing the UN, Castro announced, "We will be brief"—then delivered an interminable 4-hour speech.*

interrogation (noun) the act of formally and systematically questioning someone. *The results of the jewel thief's interrogation enabled the police to catch his accomplices before they could flee the country.* interrogate (verb).

intimidating (verb) frightening. *A boss who is particularly demanding can often be intimidating to members of his or her staff.* intimidation (noun).

intransigent (adjective) unwilling to compromise. *Despite the mediator's attempts to suggest a fair solution, the two parties were intransigent, forcing a showdown.* intransigence (noun).

Word Origin

Latin trepidus = *alarmed. Also found in English* trepidation.

intrepid (adjective) fearless and resolute. *Only an intrepid adventurer is willing to undertake the long and dangerous trip by sled to the South Pole.* intrepidity (noun).

intricate (adjective) complicated. *The plans for making the model airplane were so intricate that the boy was afraid he'd never be able to complete it.* intricacy (noun).

intrusive (adjective) forcing a way in without being welcome. *The legal requirement of a search warrant is supposed to protect Americans from intrusive searches by the police.* intrude (verb), intrusion (noun).

Word Origin

Latin unda = *wave. Also found in English* undulate.

intuitive (adjective) known directly, without apparent thought or effort. *An experienced chess player sometimes has an intuitive sense of the best move to make, even if she can't explain it.* intuit (verb), intuition (noun).

inundate (verb) to flood; to overwhelm. *As soon as playoff tickets went on sale, eager fans inundated the box office with orders.*

invariable (adjective) unchanging, constant. *When writing a book, it was her invariable habit to rise at 6 and work at her desk from 7 to 12.* invariability (noun).

Word Origin

Latin varius = *various. Also found in English* prevaricate, variable, variance, variegated, vary.

inversion (noun) a turning backwards, inside-out, or upside-down; a reversal. *Latin poetry often features inversion of word order; for example, the first line of Vergil's* Aeneid: *"Arms and the man I sing."* invert (verb), inverted (adjective).

inveterate (adjective) persistent, habitual. *It's very difficult for an inveterate gambler to give up the pastime.* inveteracy (noun).

invigorate (verb)   to give energy to, to stimulate. *As her car climbed the mountain road, Lucinda felt invigorated by the clear air and the cool breezes.*

Word Origin

Latin vertere = *to turn. Also found in English* adversary, adverse, reverse, vertical, vertigo."

invincible (adjective)   impossible to conquer or overcome. *For three years at the height of his career, boxer Mike Tyson seemed invincible.*

inviolable (adjective)   impossible to attack or trespass upon. *In the president's remote hideaway at Camp David, guarded by the Secret Service, his pri-vacy is, for once, inviolable.*

irresponsible (adjective)   lacking a sense of being accountable for one's actions. *The teenager was supposed to stay home to take care of her younger brother, so it was irresponsible for her to go out with her friends.*

irresolute (adjective)   uncertain how to act, indecisive. *When McGovern first said he supported his vice president candidate "one thousand percent," then dropped him from the ticket, it made McGovern appear irresolute.* irresolution (noun).

jeopardize (verb)   to put in danger. *Terrorist attacks jeopardize the fragile peace in the Middle East.* jeopardy (noun).

jettison (verb)   to discard. *In order to keep the boat from sinking, it was necessary to jettison all but the most essential gear.*

juxtapose (verb)   to put side by side. *It was strange to see the old-time actor Charlton Heston and rock icon Bob Dylan juxtaposed at the awards ceremony.* juxtaposition (noun).

laboriously (adverb)   in a manner marked by long, hard work. *The convicts laboriously carried the bricks from one side of the prison yard to the other.* laborious (adjective).

latent (adjective)   not currently obvious or active; hidden. *Although he had committed only a single act of violence, the psychiatrist said he had probably always had a latent tendency toward violence.* latency (noun).

Word Origin

Latin laus = *praise. Also found in English* applaud, laud, laudable, plaudit.

laudatory (adjective)   giving praise. *The ads for the movie are filled with laudatory comments from critics.*

lenient (adjective)   mild, soothing, or forgiving. *The judge was known for his lenient disposition; he rarely imposed long jail sentences on criminals.* leniency (noun).

lethargic (adjective)   lacking energy; sluggish. *Visitors to the zoo are surprised that the lions appear so lethargic, but in the wild lions sleep up to 18 hours a day.* lethargy (noun).

liability (noun)   an obligation or debt; a weakness or drawback. *The insurance company had a liability of millions of dollars after the town was destroyed by a tornado. Slowness afoot is a serious liability in an aspiring basketball player.* liable (adjective).

liberation (noun)   the act of freeing, as from oppression. *The liberation of the inmates of the Nazi concentration camps was an event long anticipated by the Jews of the world.* liberate (verb).

lucid (adjective)   clear and understandable. *Hawking's* A Short History of the Universe *is a lucid explanation of modern scientific theories about the origin of the universe.* lucidity (noun).

ludicrous (adjective)   laughable because of obvious absurdity. *The man with the lampshade on his head was a ludicrous sight to the others at the party.*

luminous (adjective)   emitting or reflecting light. *Because of their happiness, brides are often described as being luminous on their wedding days.*

Word Origin

Latin malus = *bad. Also found in English* malefactor, malevolence, malice, malicious.

malediction (noun)   curse. *In the fairy tale "Sleeping Beauty," the princess is trapped in a death-like sleep because of the malediction uttered by an angry witch.*

malevolence (noun)   hatred, ill will. *Critics say that Iago, the villain in Shakespeare's* Othello, *seems to exhibit malevolence with no real cause.* malevolent (noun).

malinger (verb)   to pretend illness to avoid work. *During the labor dispute, hundreds of employees malingered, forcing the company to slow production and costing it millions in profits.*

malleable (adjective)   able to be changed, shaped, or formed by outside pressures. *Gold is a very useful metal because it is so malleable. A child's personality is malleable and deeply influenced by the things her parents say and do.* malleability (noun).

Word Origin

Latin mandare = *entrust, order. Also found in English* command, demand, remand.

mandate (noun)   order, command. *The new policy on gays in the military went into effect as soon as the president issued his mandate about it.* mandate (verb), mandatory (adjective).

masquerading (verb)   disguising oneself. *In Mark Twain's classic novel* The Prince and the Pauper, *the prince was masquerading as a peasant boy while the peasant boy pretended to be the prince.*

mastery (noun)   possession of consummate skill. *The brilliance of William Butler Yeats' poetry exemplifies his mastery of the English language.*

Word Origin

Latin medius = *middle. Also found in English* intermediate, media, medium.

mediate (verb)   to reconcile differences between two parties. *During the baseball strike, both the players and the club owners were willing to have the president mediate the dispute.* mediation (noun).

mediocrity (noun)   the state of being middling or poor in quality. *The New York Mets, who'd finished in ninth place in 1968, won the world's championship in 1969, going from horrible to great in a single year and skipping mediocrity.* mediocre (adjective).

meditative (adjective)   characterized by reflection or contemplation. *His unusual quietness and the distant look in his eyes suggested that he was in an uncharacteristically meditative mood.* meditation (noun).

menacing (adjective)   threatening or endangering. *When their father gave the children a menacing look, they immediately quieted down and finished their dinner.* menace (noun), menace (verb).

mercurial (adjective)   changing quickly and unpredictably. *The mercurial personality of Robin Williams, with his many voices and styles, made him perfect for the role of the ever-changing genie in* Aladdin.

mete (verb)   to deal out or dole. *As late as the nineteenth-century, a leather whip called the "cat-o-nine-tails" was used to mete out punishment in the British navy.*

minuscule (adjective)   very small, tiny. *Compared to the compensation received by the people who head large corporations in the United States, the salary of the average American worker seems minuscule.*

misconception (noun)   a mistaken idea. *Columbus sailed west under the misconception that he would reach the shores of Asia that way.* misconceive (verb).

mitigate (verb)   to make less severe; to relieve. *Wallace certainly committed the assault, but the verbal abuse he'd received helps to explain his behavior and somewhat mitigates his guilt.* mitigation (noun).

modesty (noun)   a moderate estimation of one's own abilities. *It's unusual to find genuine modesty in politicians, as they must have healthy egos if they are to convince others of their abilities to lead.* modest (adjective).

Word Origin

Latin modus = measure. Also found in English immoderate, moderate, modest, modify, modulate.

modicum (noun)   a small amount. *The plan for your new business is well designed; with a modicum of luck, you should be successful.*

mollify (verb)   to soothe or calm; to appease. *Carla tried to mollify the angry customer by promising him a full refund.*

momentous (adjective)   important, consequential. *Standing at the altar and saying "I do" is a momentous event in anyone's life.*

monarchical (adjective)   of or relating to a ruler, such as a king. *Because he was raised with the knowledge that one day he would rule Russia, Czar Nicholas II perceived all that went on around him from a monarchical point of view.* monarch (noun).

mosaic (noun)   a picture or decorative design made by combining small colored pieces, or something resembling such a design. *The diversity of America's population makes it a mosaic of races, religions, and creeds.*

mundane (adjective)   everyday, ordinary, commonplace. *Moviegoers in the 1930s liked the glamorous films of Fred Astaire because they provided an escape from the mundane problems of life during the Great Depression.*

munificent (adjective)   very generous; lavish. *Ted Turner's billion-dollar donation to the United Nations is probably the most munificent act of charity in history.* munificence (noun).

Word Origin

Latin mutare = to change. Also found in English immutable, mutant, mutation.

mutable (adjective)   likely to change. *A politician's reputation can be highly mutable, as seen in the case of Harry Truman—mocked during his lifetime, revered afterward.*

mutually (adverb)   of or regarding something shared in common. *The terms of the contract were so generous to both parties that they considered the deal mutually beneficial.* mutual (adjective).

mythical (adjective)   of or relating to a traditional story not based on fact. *Although in the Middle Ages people believed in the existence of unicorns, they are mythical beasts.*

nocturnal (adjective)   of the night; active at night. *Travelers on the Underground Railroad escaped from slavery to the North by a series of nocturnal flights. The eyes of nocturnal animals must be sensitive in dim light.*

notorious (adjective)   famous, especially for evil actions or qualities. *Warner Brothers produced a series of movies about notorious gangsters such as John Dillinger and Al Capone.* notoriety (noun).

Word Origin

Latin novus =
*new. Also found
in English*
innovate, novelty,
renovate.

novice (noun)   beginner, tyro. *Lifting your head before you finish your swing is a typical mistake committed by the novice at golf.*

noxious (adjective)   harmful or injurious to health. *Because of the noxious fumes being emitted by the factory, the government forced the owners to shut it down.*

nuance (noun)   a subtle difference or quality. *At first glance, Monet's paintings of water lilies all look much alike, but the more you study them, the more you appreciate the nuances of color and shading that distinguish them.*

nurture (verb)   to nourish or help to grow. *The money given by the National Endowment for the Arts helps nurture local arts organizations throughout the country.* nurture (noun).

Word Origin

Latin durus =
*hard. Also found
in English*
durable, endure.

obdurate (adjective)   unwilling to change; stubborn, inflexible. *Despite the many pleas he received, the governor was obdurate in his refusal to grant clemency to the convicted murderer.* obduracy (noun).

objective (adjective)   dealing with observable facts rather than opinions or interpretations. *When a legal case involves a shocking crime, it may be hard for a judge to remain objective in her rulings.* objectivity (noun).

oblivious (adjective)   unaware, unconscious. *Karen practiced her oboe with complete concentration, oblivious to the noise and activity around her.* oblivion (noun), obliviousness (noun).

obscure (adjective)   little known; hard to understand. *Mendel was an obscure monk until decades after his death, when his scientific work was finally discovered. Most people find the writings of James Joyce obscure; hence the popularity of books that explain his works.* obscure (verb), obscurity (noun).

obstinate (adjective)   stubborn, unyielding. *Despite years of effort, the problem of drug abuse remains obstinate.* obstinacy (noun).

obtrusive (adjective)   overly prominent. *Philip should sing more softly; his bass is so obtrusive that the other singers can barely be heard.* obtrude (verb), obtrusion (noun).

officiate (verb)   to perform a function, ceremony, or duty. *Although weddings can be performed by judges, it is customary to have a clergyman officiate at such ceremonies.* official (noun).

oligarchy (noun)   government by a small faction of people or families. *Saudi Arabia, which is almost entirely controlled by one large family, is a good example of an oligarchy.* oligarchic (adjective).

onerous (adjective)   heavy, burdensome. *The hero Hercules was ordered to clean the Augean Stables, one of several onerous tasks known as "the labors of Hercules."* onus (noun).

opportunistic (adjective)   eagerly seizing chances as they arise. *When Princess Diana died suddenly, opportunistic publishers quickly released books about her life and death.* opportunism (noun).

opulent (adjective)   rich, lavish. *The mansion of newspaper tycoon Hearst is famous for its opulent decor.* opulence (noun).

ostentatious (adjective)   overly showy, pretentious. *To show off his wealth, the millionaire threw an ostentatious party featuring a full orchestra, a famous singer, and tens of thousands of dollars worth of food.*

ostracize (verb)   to exclude from a group. *In Biblical times, those who suffered from the disease of leprosy were ostracized and forced to live alone.* ostracism (noun).

overindulge (verb)   to yield to whims or desires to an excessive degree. *When offered tables laden with food at weddings and other such gatherings, many people overindulge and afterward find that they've eaten too much.* overindulgence (noun).

palatability (noun)   the state of being acceptable to the taste, the mind, or the sensibilities. *The woman had never eaten lobster before, so to test its palatability she took just a tiny bite.* palatable (adjective).

panacea (noun)   a remedy for all difficulties or illnesses, a cure-all. *Because the snake oil salesman promised that his product would cure everything from lumbago to an unhappy love life, it was considered a panacea by those foolish enough to buy it.*

pariah (noun)   outcast. *Accused of robbery, he became a pariah; his neighbors stopped talking to him, and people he'd considered friends no longer called.*

parochial (adjective)   narrowly limited in range or scope; provincial. *Those who grow up in small towns, as opposed to large cities, tend to be less worldly, and consequently often take a more parochial view of things.* parochialism (noun).

partisan (adjective)   reflecting strong allegiance to a particular party or cause. *The vote on the president's budget was strictly partisan: every member of the president's party voted yes, and all others voted no.* partisan (noun).

paternal (adjective)   fatherly. *In the past, people often devoted their entire lives to working for one company, which in turn rewarded them by treating them in a paternal manner.* paternity (noun).

pathology (noun)   disease or the study of disease; extreme abnormality. *Some people believe that high rates of crime are symptoms of an underlying social pathology.* pathological (adjective).

Word Origin

Greek pathos = suffering. Also found in English apathy, empathy, pathetic, pathos, sympathy.

patina (noun)   the surface appearance of something grown beautiful with use or age. *The patina that had grown over the bridge made it glow in the morning sunlight.*

pellucid (adjective)   very clear; transparent; easy to understand. *The water in the mountain stream was cold and pellucid. Thanks to the professor's pellucid explanation, I finally understand the relativity theory.*

Word Origin

Latin lux = light. Also found in English elucidate, lucid, translucent.

penitent (adjective)   feeling sorry for past crimes or sins. *Having grown penitent, he wrote a long letter of apology, asking forgiveness.*

permeate (verb)   to spread through or penetrate. *Little by little, the smell of gas from the broken pipe permeated the house.*

perceptive (adjective)   quick to notice, observant. *With his perceptive intelligence, Holmes was the first to notice the importance of this clue.* perceptible (adjective), perception (noun).

Word Origin

Latin fides =
faith. *Also found
in English*
confide, confi-
dence, fidelity,
infidel.

Word Origin

Latin specere =
*to look. Also
found in English*
circumspect,
conspicuous,
inspect, intro-
spective, spec-
tacle, spectator,
speculate.

perfidious (adjective)   disloyal, treacherous. *Although he was one of the most talented generals of the American Revolution, Benedict Arnold is remembered today as a perfidious betrayer of his country.* perfidy (noun).

persevere (adjective)   to continue despite difficulties. *Although several of her teammates dropped out of the marathon, Laura persevered.* perseverance (noun).

perspective (noun)   point of view. *Those politicians who are more disposed to change than to tradition are generally thought of as having a liberal rather than a conservative perspective.*

perspicacity (noun)   keenness of observation or understanding. *Journalist Murray Kempton was famous for the perspicacity of his comments on social and political issues.* perspicacious (adjective).

peruse (verb)   to examine or study. *Mary-Jo perused the contract carefully before she signed it.* perusal (noun).

pervasive (adjective)   spreading throughout. *As news of the disaster reached the town, a pervasive sense of gloom could be felt everywhere.* pervade (verb).

pigmented (verb)   colored. *The artist pigmented his landscape with such variety that the picture was a riot of color.* pigment (noun).

placate (verb)   to soothe or appease. *The waiter tried to placate the angry customer with the offer of a free dessert.* placatory (adjective).

plastic (adjective)   able to be molded or reshaped. *Because it is highly plastic, clay is an easy material for beginning sculptors to use.*

plausible (adjective)   apparently believable. *The idea that a widespread conspiracy to kill President Kennedy has been kept secret for over thirty years hardly seems plausible.* plausibility (noun).

pluralist (noun)   one who believes in the intrinsic value of all cultures and traditions. *Anyone who firmly believes in the advantages of multiculturalism can be said to be a pluralist.*

policing (verb)   regulating, controlling, or keeping in order. *The Federal Communications Commission is responsible for policing the television industry to see that it complies with government regulations.*

portability (noun)   the quality of being capable of being carried. *One of the great advantages of battery-powered radios is their portability.* portable (adjective).

pragmatism (noun)   a belief in approaching problems through practical rather than theoretical means. *Roosevelt's approach toward the Great Depression was based on pragmatism: "Try something," he said; "If it doesn't work, try something else."* pragmatic (adjective).

precision (noun)   exactness. *If all the parts of an engine aren't built with precision, it is unlikely that it will work properly.* precise (adjective).

predatory (adjective)   living by killing and eating other animals; exploiting others for personal gain. *The tiger is the largest predatory animal native to Asia. Microsoft has been accused of predatory business practices that prevent other software companies from competing with them.* predation (noun), predator (noun).

predilection (noun)   a liking or preference. *To relax from his presidential duties, Kennedy had a predilection for spy novels featuring James Bond.*

predominant (adjective)   greatest in numbers or influence. *Although hundreds of religions are practiced in India, the predominant faith is Hinduism.* predominance (noun), predominate (verb).

prepossessing (adjective)   attractive. *Smart, lovely, and talented, she has all the prepossessing qualities that mark a potential movie star.*

prerequisite (noun)   something that is required as a prior condition. *Generally speaking, a high school diploma is a prerequisite for matriculating at a university.*

presumptuous (adjective)   going beyond the limits of courtesy or appropriateness. *The senator winced when the presumptuous young staffer addressed him as "Chuck."* presume (verb), presumption (noun).

pretentious (adjective)   claiming excessive value or importance. *For an ordinary shoe salesman to call himself a "Personal Foot Apparel Consultant" seems awfully pretentious.* pretension (noun).

primarily (adverb)   at first, originally. *When people have children, their priorities change: they are no longer primarily individuals but, rather, primarily parents.* primary (adjective).

proficient (adjective)   skillful, adept. *A proficient artist, Louise quickly and accurately sketched the scene.* proficiency (noun).

proliferate (verb)   to increase or multiply. *Over the past fifteen years, high-tech companies have proliferated in northern California, Massachusetts, and other regions.* proliferation (noun).

prolific (adjective)   producing numerous offspring or abundant works. *With more than one hundred books to his credit, Isaac Asimov was one of our most prolific authors.*

promulgate (verb)   to make public, to declare. *Lincoln signed the proclamation that freed the slaves in 1862, but he waited several months to promulgate it.*

propagate (verb)   to cause to grow; to foster. *John Smithson's will left his fortune for the founding of an institution to propagate knowledge, without saying whether that meant a university, a library, or a museum.* propagation (noun).

propriety (noun)   appropriateness. *Some people had doubts about the propriety of Clinton's discussing his underwear on MTV.*

prosaic (adjective)   everyday, ordinary, dull. *"Paul's Case" tells the story of a boy who longs to escape from the prosaic life of a clerk into a world of wealth, glamour, and beauty.*

provocative (adjective)   likely to stimulate emotions, ideas, or controversy. *The demonstrators began chanting obscenities, a provocative act that they hoped would cause the police to lose control.* provoke (verb), provocation (noun).

proximity (noun)   closeness, nearness. *Neighborhood residents were angry over the proximity of the sewage plant to the local school.* proximate (adjective).

pseudonym (noun)   a fictitious name. *When an author does not want a book to carry his own name, he uses a pseudonym.* pseudonymous (adjective).

Word Origin

Latin dominare = *to rule. Also found in English* dominate, domineer, dominion, indomitable.

Word Origin

Latin vocare = *to call. Also found in English* evoke, invoke, revoke, vocal, vocation.

Word Origin

Latin pungere =
*to jab, to prick.
Also found in
English* pugilist,
punctuate,
puncture,
pungent."

pugnacious (adjective)   combative, bellicose, truculent; ready to fight. *Ty Cobb, the pugnacious outfielder for the Detroit Tigers, got into more than his fair share of brawls, both on and off the field.* pugnacity (noun).

punctilious (adjective)   very concerned about proper forms of behavior and manners. *A punctilious dresser like James would rather skip the party altogether than wear the wrong color tie.* punctilio (noun).

quell (verb)   to quiet, to suppress. *It took a huge number of police to quell the rioting.*

querulous (adjective)   complaining, whining. *The nursing home attendant needed a lot of patience to care for the three querulous, unpleasant residents on his floor.*

quintessential (adjective)   regarding the purest essence of something. *Tom Clancy, author of* The Hunt for Red October *and other bestsellers, is the quintessential writer of techno-thrillers.* quintessence (noun).

reciprocate (verb)   to make a return for something. *If you'll baby-sit for my kids tonight, I'll reciprocate by taking care of yours tomorrow.* reciprocity (noun).

reclusive (adjective)   withdrawn from society. *During the last years of her life, actress Greta Garbo led a reclusive existence, rarely appearing in public.* recluse (noun).

reconcile (verb)   to make consistent or harmonious. *Roosevelt's greatness as a leader can be seen in his ability to reconcile the demands and values of the varied groups that supported him.* reconciliation (noun).

reconstruct (verb)   to build or create again. *Because the South was so thoroughly destroyed during the Civil War, it was necessary to start from scratch and reconstruct the entire region.* reconstruction (noun).

refinement (noun)   polish, cultivation. *Although the man came from a humble background, by making an effort to educate himself, he managed over the years to develop a very high level of refinement.* refine (verb).

refute (adjective)   to prove false. *The company invited reporters to visit their plant in an effort to refute the charges of unsafe working conditions.* refutation (noun).

reincarnation (noun)   rebirth in a new body or form of life; a fresh embodiment. *Many of those who voted for Bill Clinton for president hoped that he would be a reincarnation of John F. Kennedy.* reincarnate (verb).

rejoinder (noun)   an answer or reply. *The man's rejoinder to the accusation that he had murdered his partner was that he had committed no crime.*

relevance (noun)   connection to the matter at hand; pertinence. *Testimony in a criminal trial may be admitted only if it has clear relevance to the question of guilt or innocence.* relevant (adjective).

relinquish (verb)   to surrender or give up something. *In order to run for Congress, the man had to relinquish his membership in the "restricted" country club.*

renovate (verb)   to renew by repairing or rebuilding. *The television program "This Old House" shows how skilled craftspeople renovate houses.* renovation (noun).

renunciation (noun)   the act of rejecting or refusing something. *King Edward VII's renunciation of the British throne was caused by his desire to marry an American divorcee, something he couldn't do as king.* renounce (verb).

replete (adjective)   filled abundantly. *Graham's book is replete with wonderful stories about the famous people she has known.*

reprehensible (adjective)   deserving criticism or censure. *Although Pete Rose's misdeeds were reprehensible, not all fans agree that he deserves to be excluded from the Baseball Hall of Fame.* reprehend (verb), reprehension (noun).

repudiate (verb)   to reject, to renounce. *After it became known that Duke had been a leader of the Ku Klux Klan, most Republican leaders repudiated him.* repudiation (noun).

Word Origin

Latin putare = *to reckon. Also found in English* compute, dispute, impute, putative.

reputable (adjective)   having a good reputation; respected. *Find a reputable auto mechanic by asking your friends for recommendations based on their own experiences.* reputation (noun), repute (noun).

resilient (adjective)   able to recover from difficulty. *A pro athlete must be resilient, able to lose a game one day and come back the next with confidence and enthusiasm.* resilience (adjective).

respectively (adverb)   in the order given. *On arriving home, the woman kissed her husband and son respectively.*

resurrect (verb)   to bring back to life, practice, or use. *When Rob's novel became a bestseller, he decided to resurrect one that he'd written years before to see if that book would sell as well.* resurrection (noun).

revitalize (verb)   give new life or vigor to. *Although he had been extremely popular at one time, Frank Sinatra had fallen from favor before his role in the film* From Here to Eternity *revitalized his career.* revitalization (noun).

rework (verb)   revise. *After playwrights create first drafts of their plays, they generally rework them until they feel they're strong enough to be performed.*

rigorous (adjective)   characterized by strictness or severity. *In order to make sure that they are tough enough, Marine recruits are put through rigorous training before they're allowed to join the Corps.* rigor (noun).

romanticize (verb)   to treat in an idealized manner. *Although World War II was one of the grimmest conflicts in history, most films about it romanticized it for propaganda reasons.* romantic (adjective).

Word Origin

Latin sanctus = *holy. Also found in English* sanctify, sanction, sanctity, sanctuary.

sanctimonious (adjective)   showing false or excessive piety. *The sanctimonious prayers of the TV preacher were interspersed with requests that the viewers send him money.* sanctimony (noun).

scrutinize (verb)   to study closely. *The lawyer scrutinized the contract, searching for any sentence that could pose a risk for her client.* scrutiny (noun).

secrete (verb)   to emit; to hide. *Glands in the mouth secrete saliva, a liquid that helps in digestion. The jewel thieves secreted the necklace in a tin box buried underground.*

sedate (verb)   to reduce stress or excitement by administering a drug for that purpose. *The woman was so upset by the events of the day that she had to be sedated to fall asleep.* sedative (adjective).

Word Origin

Latin sedere = *to sit. Also found in English* sedate, sedative, sediment.

sedentaryseb simulare (adjective)   requiring much sitting. *When Officer Samson was given a desk job, she had trouble getting used to sedentary work after years on the street.*

sermonizing (verb)   speaking in a didactic or dogmatic manner. *Because he was hardly in a position to give advice to anyone, the man's sermonizing only served to irritate his listeners.* sermon (noun).

shortcomings (noun)   deficiencies or flaws. *Although the woman believed her father had many outstanding qualities, it did not keep her from recognizing his shortcomings.*

simplification (noun)   the state of being less complex or intricate. *As a result of years of complaints by the public, the Internal Revenue Service has embarked on a simplification program designed to make tax forms more understandable to those responsible for filling them out.* simplify (verb).

Word Origin

Latin simulare = *to resemble. Also found in English* semblance, similarity, simulacrum, simultaneous, verisimilitude.

simulated (adjective)   imitating something else; artificial. *High-quality simulated gems must be examined under a magnifying glass to be distinguished from real ones.* simulate (verb), simulation (noun).

solace (verb)   to comfort or console. *There was little the rabbi could say to solace the husband after his wife's death.* solace (noun).

sophisticated (adjective)   worldly-wise or complex. *While many people enjoy drinking domestic beers, those with more sophisticated tastes often prefer imported brews.* sophistication (noun).

spurious (adjective)   false, fake. *The so-called Piltdown Man, supposed to be the fossil of a primitive human, turned out to be spurious, all though who created the hoax is still uncertain.*

squabble (verb)   to engage in trivial quarrels. *When he's had a bad day at the office, he often goes home and squabbles with his wife.*

stabilizing (adjective)   making reliable or dependable. *He was quite wild as a teenager, but since marriage his wife has had a stabilizing influence on him.* stability (noun), stabilize (verb).

stagnate (verb)   to become stale through lack of movement or change. *Having had no contact with the outside world for generations, Japan's culture gradually stagnated.* stagnant (adjective), stagnation (noun).

stimulus (noun)   something that excites a response or provokes an action. *The arrival of merchants and missionaries from the West provided a stimulus for change in Japanese society.* stimulate (verb).

stoic (adjective)   showing little feeling, even in response to pain or sorrow. *A soldier must respond to the death of his comrades in stoic fashion, since the fighting will not stop for his grief.* stoicism (noun).

strenuous (adjective)   requiring energy and strength. *Hiking in the foothills of the Rockies is fairly easy, but climbing the higher peaks can be strenuous.*

stylistically (adverb)   relating to the way something is said, done, or performed. *While Jim Croce's music was stylistically close to folk, it was usually categorized as rock.*

sublimate (verb)   to divert the expression of an instinctual desire or impulse into one that is socially acceptable. *He was so attracted to the woman when he first* *met her that he wanted to kiss her, but he knew he had to sublimate that desire if he didn't want to frighten her away.* sublimation (noun), subliminal (adjective).

subtle (adjective)   not immediately obvious. *Because the aroma of her perfume was so subtle, it took several moments before he even noticed it.* subtlety (noun).

succumb (verb)   to give in or give up. *Although he had serious reservations about joining the company, he knew that if they continued to pursue him he would eventually succumb to their blandishments.*

superficial (adjective)   on the surface only; without depth or substance. *Her wound was superficial and required only a light bandage. His superficial attractiveness hides the fact that his personality is lifeless and his mind is dull.* superficiality (noun).

superfluous (adjective)   more than is needed, excessive. *Once you've won the debate, don't keep talking; superfluous arguments will only bore and annoy the audience.* superfluity (noun).

suppress (verb)   to put down or restrain. *As soon as the unrest began, thousands of helmeted police were sent into the streets to suppress the riots.* suppression (noun).

surfeit (noun)   an excess. *Most American families have a surfeit of food and drink on Thanksgiving Day.* surfeit (verb).

surreptitious (adjective)   done in secret. *Because Iraq has avoided weapons inspections, many believe it has a surreptitious weapons development program.*

surrogate (noun)   a substitute. *When the congressman died in office, his wife was named to serve the rest of his term as a surrogate.* surrogate (adjective).

surveillance (noun)   close observation of someone or something. *The detective knew that, if she kept the suspect under surveillance long enough, he would eventually do something for which he could be arrested.*

suspend (verb)   to stop for a period, to interrupt. *When the young man was caught speeding for the third time, the judge suspended his license.*

symmetrical (adjective)   having balanced proportions. *Although the human face appears symmetrical, its component parts are never perfectly balanced.* symmetry (noun).

synchronize (verb)   to make to occur at the same time. *The generals planning the invasion wanted to synchronize the air, sea, and land attacks for maximum power.* synchronicity (noun).

tactile (adjective)   relating to the sense of touch. *The thick brush strokes and gobs of color give the paintings of Van Gogh a strongly tactile quality.* tactility (noun).

Word Origin

Latin tangere = *to touch. Also found in English* contact, contiguous, tangent, tangible.

tangential (adjective)   touching lightly; only slightly connected or related. *Having enrolled in a class on African-American history, the students found the teacher's stories about his travels in South America only of tangential interest.* tangent (noun).

tedium (noun)   boredom. *For most people, watching the Weather Channel for twenty-four hours would be sheer tedium.* tedious (adjective).

temerity (noun)   boldness, rashness, excessive daring. *Only someone who didn't understand the danger would have the temerity to try to climb Everest without a guide.* temerarious (adjective).

temperance (noun)   moderation or restraint in feelings and behavior. *Most professional athletes practice temperance in their personal habits; too much eating or drinking, they know, can harm their performance.* temperate (adjective).

temperament (noun)   the manner of behaving characteristic of a specific individual. *Her temperament was such that she was argumentative and generally difficult to deal with.* temperamental (adjective).

Word Origin

Latin tenere = *to hold. Also found in English* retain, tenable, tenant, tenet, tenure."

tenacious (adjective)   clinging, sticky, or persistent. *Tenacious in pursuit of her goal, she applied for the grant unsuccessfully four times before it was finally approved.* tenacity (noun).

tensile (adjective)   capable of being extended or stretched. *While ropes are not tensile, rubber bands are made to be so.*

terrestrial (adjective)   of the Earth. *The movie* Close Encounters *tells the story of the first contact between beings from outer space and terrestrial humans.*

titanic (adjective)   huge, colossal. *Because of the size of the armies arrayed against each other, the battle of Gettysburg was a titanic one.*

transcendent (verb)   rising above or going above the limits of. *Although she had been baptized as a child, when the young woman underwent a second baptism as an adult it was a transcendent emotional experience for her.* transcendence (noun).

transgress (verb)   to go past limits; to violate. *If Iraq has developed biological weapons, then it has transgressed the United Nation's rules against weapons of mass destruction.* transgression (noun).

transient (adjective)   passing quickly. *Long-term visitors to this hotel pay at a different rate than transient guests who stay for just a day or two.* transience (noun).

transition (noun)   a passage from one state to another. *In retrospect, the young man recognized that his joining the army had served as a transition from childhood to adulthood.*

transitory (adjective)   quickly passing. *Public moods tend to be transitory; people may be anxious and angry one month but relatively contented and optimistic the next.*

translucent (adjective)   letting some light pass through. *Blocks of translucent glass let daylight into the room while maintaining privacy.*

transmute (verb) to change in form or substance. *In the middle ages, the alchemists tried to discover ways to transmute metals such as iron into gold.* transmutation (noun).

trite (adjective) boring because of over-familiarity; hackneyed. *Her letters were filled with trite expressions, like "All's well that ends well," and "So far so good."*

triviality (noun) the condition or quality of being of little importance of significance. *Lacking anything of interest to talk about, the man's conversation was a study in triviality.* trivial (adjective).

truism (noun) something which is obvious or self-evident. *That one must be careful when driving a car is such a truism that it seems hardly worth mentioning.*

truncate (verb) to cut off. *The manuscript of the play appeared truncated; the last page ended in the middle of a scene, halfway through the second act.*

Word Origin

Latin turba *= confusion. Also found in English* disturb, perturb, turbid.

turbulent (adjective) agitated or disturbed. *The night before the championship match, Martina was unable to sleep, her mind turbulent with fears and hopes.* turbulence (noun).

tyrannical (adjective) despotic or oppressive. *The American colonists felt so oppressed by King George's tyrannical rule that they believed it necessary to rebel against him.* tyrant (noun), tyrannize (verb).

uncouth (adjective) crude, unrefined. *The man behaved in such an ill-mannered and obnoxious way that almost everyone who met him considered him to be uncouth.*

unctuous (adjective) characterized by false or affected earnestness. *The man's manner was so unctuous that people felt that he could not be trusted.*

undomesticated (adjective) not comfortable with or accustomed to a home environment. *Unlike dogs, which have lived with people for centuries, undomesticated animals like wolves do not make good pets.*

uneasiness (noun) the state of lacking comfort or a sense of security. *The prospective bride's uneasiness about the plans for the wedding led her to double-check everything that had to be done.* uneasy (adjective).

unimagined (adjective) not even conceived of. *The author's first book was so successful that it led not to unimagined wealth and fame.*

unnerving (verb) upsetting. *Being involved in even a minor automobile accident is invariably an unnerving experience.*

unpalatable (adjective) distasteful, unpleasant. *Although I agree with the candidate on many issues, I can't vote for her, because I find her position on capital punishment unpalatable.*

unparalleled (adjective) with no equal; unique. *Tiger Woods's victory in the Masters golf tournament by a full twelve strokes was an unparalleled accomplishment.*

unstinting (adjective) giving freely and generously. *Eleanor Roosevelt was much admired for her unstinting efforts on behalf of the poor.*

untenable (adjective)   impossible to defend. *The theory that this painting is a genuine Van Gogh became untenable when the artist who actually painted it came forth.*

untimely (adjective)   out of the natural or proper time. *The untimely death of a youthful Princess Diana seemed far more tragic than Mother Teresa's death of old age.*

unveiling (noun)   an act of uncovering or making public. *The culmination of the ceremony was the unveiling of the statue which had been commissioned to honor the late president.*

unyielding (adjective)   firm, resolute, obdurate. *Despite criticism, Cuomo was unyielding in his opposition to capital punishment; he vetoed several death penalty bills as governor.*

usurper (noun)   someone who takes a place or possession without the right to do so. *Kennedy's most devoted followers tended to regard later presidents as usurpers, holding the office they felt he or his brothers should have held.* usurp (verb), usurpation (noun).

utilitarian (adjective)   purely of practical benefit. *The design of the Model T car was simple and utilitarian, lacking the luxuries found in later models.*

utilize (verb)   to make use of. *When one does research for a book, it's not always possible to utilize all the information that's been gathered in the process.* utilization (noun).

utopian (adjective)   impractically idealistic. *Although there have been many utopian communities founded over the centuries, due to their impractical nature none has ever survived more than a few years.* utopia (noun).

vacillation (noun)   inability to take a stand. *The young man's vacillation over getting married made it impossible for him and his girlfriend to set a date for the wedding.* vacillate (verb).

validate (verb)   to officially approve or confirm. *The election of the president is validated when the members of the Electoral College meet to confirm the choice of the voters.* valid (adjective), validity (noun).

vanity (noun)   excessive pride in one's appearance or accomplishments. *The man's vanity was so extreme that, despite evidence to the contrary, he believed that everyone else thought as well of him as he did himself.* vain (adjective).

venerate (verb)   to admire or honor. *In Communist China, Chairman Mao Zedong was venerated as an almost god-like figure.* venerable (adjective), veneration (noun).

vestige (noun)   a trace or remainder. *Today's tiny Sherwood Forest is the last vestige of a woodland that once covered most of England.* vestigial (adjective).

vex (verb)   to irritate, annoy, or trouble. *Unproven for generations, Fermat's last theorem was one of the most famous, and most vexing, of all mathematical puzzles.* vexation (noun).

vindicate (verb)   to confirm, justify, or defend. *Lincoln's Gettysburg Address was intended to vindicate the objectives of the Union in the Civil War.* vindication (noun).

virtually (adverb)   almost entirely. *As a result of chemotherapy, he was virtually free of the cancer that had threatened his life.* virtual (adjective).

virtuoso (noun)   someone very skilled, especially in an art. *Vladimir Horowitz was one of the great piano virtuosos of the twentieth century.* virtuosity (noun).

vivacious (adjective)   lively, sprightly. *The role of Maria in "The Sound of Music" is usually played by a charming, vivacious young actress.* vivacity (noun).

volatile (adjective)   quickly changing; fleeting, transitory; prone to violence. *Public opinion is notoriously volatile; a politician who is very popular one month may be voted out of office the next.* volatility (noun).

vulnerable (adjective)   open to damage or attack. *In baring her soul to her friend, the woman recognized that she was making herself extremely vulnerable.*

wield (verb)   to exercise or exert (power or influence). *Because others tend to be afraid of him, when a dictator wants to wield his authority he only has to express his desires, and whatever he wants is done immediately.*

zealous (adjective)   filled with eagerness, fervor, or passion. *A crowd of the candidate's most zealous supporters greeted her at the airport with banners, signs, and a marching band.* zeal (noun), zealot (noun), zealotry (noun)

Appendix B

The Insider's Math Review for the ACT

Perhaps more than any other school subject, math creates a gulf between classes of students. Generally speaking, there are students who think of themselves as "good at math," who do well in all the usual math subjects and often take advanced classes in their junior and senior years of high school. Then there are the others, more numerous, who are a little afraid of math. They take only those math classes they are required to take, and breathe a sigh of relief when they pass.

Here's the good news. The test-makers know that the ACT will be taken by hundreds of thousands of students in both classes.

They've deliberately designed the exam to be fair to both. As a result, many of the math topics that high school students find most intimidating—such as calculus—do not appear on the test, while other difficult topics—such as trigonometry—make up only a small portion of the exam (less than 10 percent). Most of the ACT Mathematics Test is restricted to topics that virtually all high school students study in the ninth and tenth grades.

This doesn't mean that all of the ACT math questions are easy. But it does mean that it's unlikely that you'll be tested on any topic you never learned in high school.

In the Insider's ACT Math Review, we've selected the fifty math topics most frequently tested on the exam. For each, we've created a mini-lesson reviewing the basic facts, formulas, and concepts you need to know. We've also provided an example or two of how these concepts might be turned into test questions.

You'll probably find that you are comfortable with many of the topics included in the "Nifty Fifty" that follows. If so, great. Make a note of the other topics—the ones you find confusing, tricky, or difficult. Perhaps you never quite mastered those concepts when they were presented in class, or you've forgotten the details in the intervening months. In your study between now and the day of the ACT, concentrate on reviewing and practicing these topics. You can boost your ACT math score significantly by mastering as many of your personal "math demons" as possible.

ARITHMETIC

FYI

Remember: When comparing negative numbers, the one with the greater absolute value is the lesser *number!*

Topic 1: Numbers and the Number Line

We can think of the real numbers as points on a line. To represent this, we usually draw a horizontal line, with one point on the line chosen to represent zero. All the positive numbers are to the right of zero, and all the negative numbers are to the left of zero. Therefore, the numbers get greater as you go from left to right.

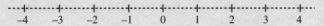

$$-4 \quad -3 \quad -2 \quad -1 \quad 0 \quad 1 \quad 2 \quad 3 \quad 4$$

The *absolute value* of any number N is symbolized by $|N|$ and is simply the positive distance a number is from zero. Thus, $|8| = 8$, $|-7| = 7$, and $|0| = 0$.

The further you get from zero, the greater the absolute value. So numbers far to the left are negative numbers with great absolute values.

When a number line is shown on the ACT, you can safely assume that the line is drawn to scale and that any numbers that fall between the markings are at appropriate locations. Thus, 2.5 is halfway between 2 and 3, and -0.4 is four-tenths of the way from 0 to -1. However, always check the scale, because the "tick marks" do not have to be at unit intervals!

Example 1

On the number line shown below, where is the number which is less than D and half as far from D as D is from G?

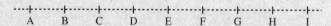

Solution

First, any number less than D must lie to the left of D. (Get it? Left = less!) The distance from D to G is 3 units. Thus, the point we want must be $1\frac{1}{2}$ units to the left of D—that is, halfway between B and C.

Example 2

On the number line shown below, which point corresponds to the number 2.27?

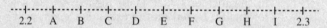

Solution

Since the labelled end points are 2.2 and 2.3, the ten intervals between must each be one-tenth of the difference. Hence the tick marks must represent hundredths. That is, A = 2.21, B = 2.22, and so on. Thus, we know that G = 2.27.

Topic 2: Laws of Arithmetic and Order of Operations

In carrying out arithmetic or algebraic operations, you should use the famous mnemonic (memory) device <u>P</u>lease <u>M</u>y <u>D</u>ear <u>A</u>unt <u>S</u>ally to recall the correct order of operations. The operations of <u>P</u>owers, <u>M</u>ultiplication, <u>D</u>ivision, <u>A</u>ddition, and <u>S</u>ubtraction should be carried out in that order reading from left to right.

If we want to indicate a change in order, we place the operation in parentheses, creating one number. Always calculate the number in parentheses first. Thus, 16 $- 3 \times 4 = 16 - 12 = 4$, because we multiply before adding. However, if we want the number $16 - 3$ to be multiplied by 4, we must write it this way: $(16 - 3) \times 4 = 13 \times 4 = 52$.

The basic laws of arithmetic were originally defined for whole numbers, but they carry over to all numbers. You should know all of them from past experience. They are:

- *The commutative law.* It doesn't matter in which order you add or multiply two numbers. That is:

  $$a + b = b + a$$
  $$ab = ba$$

- *The associative law,* also called *the regrouping law.* It doesn't matter how you group the numbers when you add or multiply more than two numbers. That is:

  $$a + (b + c) = (a + b) + c$$

  $$a(bc) = (ab)c$$

  Remember, enclosing the numbers in parentheses indicates that this operation should be done first.

- *The distributive law* for multiplication over addition. This law can be represented as follows:

  $$a(b + c) = ab + ac$$

  It means you can add first and then multiply, or multiply each term in the sum by the same amount and then add the two products. Either way the result is the same.

- *The properties of zero and one.* Zero times any number is zero. Zero added to any number leaves the number unchanged. One times any number leaves the number unchanged.

- *The additive opposite.* For every number n, there is a number $-n$ such that $n + (-n) = 0$. This number is the additive opposite.

- *The multiplicative inverse.* For every number n except 0, there is a number $\dfrac{1}{n}$ such that $\left(\dfrac{1}{n}\right)(n) = 1$. Division by n is the same as multiplication by $\dfrac{1}{n}$, and division by zero is never allowed.

Example

(a) What is the value of $\dfrac{3 + B}{4 \times 3 - 3B}$ if $B = 3$? (b) What value is impossible for B?

Solution

(a) The fraction bar in a fraction acts as a "grouping symbol," like parentheses, meaning we should calculate the numerator and denominator separately. That is, we should read this fraction as $(3 + B) \div (4 \times 3 - 3 \times B)$. When $B = 3$, the numerator is $3 + 3 = 6$, and the denominator is $12 - 3 \times 3 = 12 - 9 = 3$. Therefore, the fraction is $\dfrac{6}{3} = 2$.

(b) Since we cannot divide by zero, we cannot let $4 \times 3 - 3 \times B = 0$. But in order for this expression to equal zero, $4 \times 3 = 3 \times B$. By the commutative law, $B = 4$. Thus, the only value that B cannot have is 4.

427

Table B.1
Rules for Testing Divisibily

Number	Divides into a Number N if . . .
2	N is even; that is, its last digit is 2, 4, 6, 8, or 0.
3	The sum of the digits of N is divisible by 3.
4	The last two digits form a number divisible by 4.
5	The number's last digit is 5 or 0.
6	The number is divisible by 2 and 3.
8	The last three digits form a number divisible by 8.
9	The sum of the digits of N is divisible by 9.
0	The number's last digit is 0.

Topic 3: Divisibility Rules

A *factor* or *divisor* of a whole number is a number by which the whole number can be divided, leaving no remainder. For example, the divisors of 24 are 1, 2, 3, 4, 6, 8, 12, and 24 itself.

A *proper divisor* is any divisor except the number itself. Thus, the proper divisors of 24 are 1, 2, 3, 4, 6, 8, and 12. If you want to know whether k is a divisor of n, try to divide n by k and see whether there is any remainder. If the remainder is zero, then n is divisible by k.

There are several useful rules for testing for divisibility by certain small numbers. These are summarized in the table B.1

Example 1
Consider the number 7,380. How many numbers in the table above are not factors of 7,380?

Solution
7,380 is divisible by all the numbers in the table except 8. Do you see why? To start with, 7,380 is divisible by 10 and 5 because its last digit is 0. It is divisible by 2 because it is even, and by 4 because 80 is divisible by 4. However, it is not divisible by 8 because 380 isn't. In addition, the sum of its digits is 18, which is divisible both by 3 and by 9. Since it is divisible by both 2 and 3, it is also divisible by 6.

Example 2
Which numbers in the following list are divisible by 3, 4, and 5, but not by 9?

15,840
20,085
23,096
53,700
79,130

Solution
The easiest thing to look for is divisibility by 5. Just ask, is the last digit of the number 5 or 0? By inspection, we can eliminate 23,096, whose last digit is 6. We

want the number to be divisible by 4, which means it must be even and its last two digits must form a number divisible by 4. That knocks out the number ending in 5 (which is odd), as well as 79,130, because 30 is not divisible by 4.

This leaves 15,840 and 53,700. The digits of 15,840 add up to 18, while those of 53,700 total 15. Both are divisible by 3, but 15,840 is also divisible by 9. Therefore, only 53,700 meets all the conditions.

Topic 4: Divisibility in Addition, Subtraction, and Multiplication

If you add or subtract two numbers that are both divisible by some number k, then the new number formed will also be divisible by k. Thus, 28 and 16 are both divisible by 4. If you take their sum, 44, or their difference, 12, they too are divisible by 4.

If you multiply two numbers together, any number that divides either one also divides the product. Thus, if j divides M and k divides N, then jk divides MN.

If two numbers being multiplied have a common divisor, then the product is divisible by the square of that number. Thus, $21 \times 15 = 315$ is divisible by 7, because 7 divides 21, and by 5, because 5 divides 15. It is also divisible by $35 = 5 \times 7$ and by 9, because $9 = 3^2$ and three divides both 21 and 15.

Example 1

If a and b are whole numbers and $3a = 2b$, which of the following must be true?

(A) a is divisible by 2, and b is divisible by 3.
(B) a and b are both divisible by 2.
(C) a and b are both divisible by 3.
(D) a is divisible by 3, and b is divisible by 2.
(E) None of the above

Solution

The correct answer is (A). If $3a$ equals $2b$, then $3a$ must be divisible by 2, which means a must be divisible by 2, since 3 is not. Similarly, $2b$ must be divisible by 3, which means b must be divisible by 3, since 2 is not.

You should be especially aware of the divisibility properties of even and odd numbers.

- *Even numbers* are those that are divisible by 2: 0, 2, 4, 6, . . .

- *Odd numbers* are not divisible by 2: 1, 3, 5, 7, . . .

Certain simple but very useful results follow from these definitions:

- If you add or subtract two even numbers, the result is even.

- If you add or subtract two odd numbers, the result is even.

- Only when you add or subtract an odd and an even number is the result odd. Thus, $4 + 6$ is even, as is $7 - 3$. But $4 + 3$ is odd.

- When you multiply any whole number by an even number, the result is even.

- Only when you multiply two odd numbers will the result be odd. Thus, (4)(6) and (4)(7) are both even, but (3)(7) is odd.

Example 2

If $3x + 4y$ is an odd number, is x odd or even, or is it impossible to tell?

Solution

$4y$ must be even, so for the sum of $3x$ and $4y$ to be odd, $3x$ must be odd. Since 3 is odd, $3x$ will be odd only if x is odd. Hence, x is odd.

Example 3

If $121 - 5k$ is divisible by 3, may k be odd?

Solution

The fact that a number is divisible by 3 does not make it odd. (Think of 6 or 12.) Therefore, $121 - 5k$ could be odd or even. It will be odd when k is even and even when k is odd. (Do you see why?) Thus, k could be odd or even. For example, if $k = 2$, $121 - 5k = 111$, which is divisible by 3; and if $k = 5$, $121 - 5k = 96$, which is divisible by 3.

Topic 5: Comparing Fractions

Two fractions $\frac{a}{b}$ and $\frac{c}{d}$ are defined to be equal if $ad = bc$. For example, $\frac{3}{4} = \frac{9}{12}$ because $(3)(12) = (4)(9)$. This definition, using the process known as *cross-multiplication*, is very useful in solving algebraic equations involving fractions. However, for working with numbers, the most important thing to remember is that multiplying the numerator and denominator of a fraction by the same number (other than zero) results in a fraction equal in value to the original fraction. Thus, by multiplying the numerator and the denominator of $\frac{3}{4}$ by 3, we have $\frac{3}{4} = \frac{(3)(3)}{(3)(4)} = \frac{9}{12}$.

Similarly, dividing the numerator and denominator of a fraction by the same number (other than zero) results in a fraction equal in value to the original fraction. It is usual to divide through the numerator and the denominator of the fraction by the greatest common factor of both numerator and denominator to simplify the fraction to simplest form. Thus, by dividing the numerator and the denominator of $\frac{15}{25}$ by 5, we have $\frac{15}{25} = \frac{15 \div 5}{25 \div 5} = \frac{3}{5}$.

For all positive numbers, if two fractions have the same denominator, the one with the greater numerator is greater. If two fractions have the same numerator, the one with the lesser denominator is greater. For example, $\frac{5}{19}$ is less than $\frac{8}{19}$, but $\frac{8}{17}$ is greater than $\frac{8}{19}$.

Example 1

If b and c are both positive whole numbers greater than 1, and $\frac{5}{c} = \frac{b}{3}$, what are the values of b and c?

Solution

Using cross-multiplication, $bc = 15$. The only ways 15 can be the product of two positive integers is as $(1)(15)$ or $(3)(5)$. Since both b and c must be greater than

1, one must be 3 and the other 5. Trying both cases, it is easy to see that the only possibility is that $b = 3$ and $c = 5$, making both fractions equal to 1.

Example 2

Which is greater, $\dfrac{4}{7}$ or $\dfrac{3}{5}$?

Solution

The first fraction named has a greater numerator, but it also has a greater denominator. To compare the two fractions, rewrite both with the common denominator 35 by multiplying the numerator and denominator of $\dfrac{4}{7}$ by 5 and the numerator and denominator of $\dfrac{3}{5}$ by 7 to yield $\dfrac{20}{35}$ and $\dfrac{21}{35}$ respectively. Now, it is easy to see that $\dfrac{3}{5}$ is greater.

Example 3

Which is greater, $\dfrac{-6}{11}$ or $\dfrac{13}{-22}$?

Solution

First of all, it does not matter where you put the negative sign—numerator, denominator, or opposite the fraction bar; if there is one negative sign anywhere in a fraction, the fraction is negative.

Next, remember: In comparing negative numbers, the one with the greater absolute value is the lesser number. So start by ignoring the signs, and compare the absolute values of the fractions. If the two fractions had a common denominator or numerator, it would be easy. So, multiply the numerator and denominator of $\dfrac{6}{11}$ by 2 to yield $\dfrac{12}{22}$, and it is easy to see that $\dfrac{13}{22}$ is the greater. Hence, $\dfrac{13}{-22}$ has the greater absolute value, meaning that $\dfrac{-6}{11}$ is the greater number.

Of course, you could have solved either of these last two examples on a calculator. Dividing the numerator by the denominator will yield a decimal. Thus, in Example 2, as a decimal $\dfrac{4}{7} = 0.571 \ldots$ and $\dfrac{3}{5} = 0.6$. Try Example 3 this way for yourself.

FYI

When working with fractions, of can usually be interpreted to mean times.

Topic 6: Arithmetic with Fractions
Multiplication and Division

When multiplying two fractions, the result is the product of the numerators divided by the product of the denominators. In symbols, $\dfrac{a}{b} \times \dfrac{c}{d} = \dfrac{ac}{bd}$. Thus, $\dfrac{3}{7} \times \dfrac{2}{5} = \dfrac{6}{35}$.

Don't forget that the resulting fraction can be simplified to simplest form by dividing out common factors in numerator and denominator. Thus, $\frac{3}{5} \times \frac{10}{9} = \frac{2}{3}$.

Example 1

Jasmine earns $\frac{3}{4}$ of what Sidney earns, and Sidney earns $\frac{2}{3}$ of what Paul earns. What fraction of Paul's salary does Jasmine earn?

Using J, S, and P to stand for the people's earnings respectively, we have:

$$S = \frac{2}{3}P; J = \frac{3}{4}S$$

Thus:

$$J = \frac{3}{4} \times \frac{2}{3}P = \frac{1}{2}P$$

Hence, Jasmine's earnings are one-half Paul's.

When dividing fractions, simply multiply by the reciprocal of the divisor. (The *divisor* is the one you are dividing by, usually the second one named, or the denominator in a fraction.) In symbols:

$$\frac{a}{b} \div \frac{c}{d} = \frac{a}{b} \times \frac{d}{c} = \frac{ad}{bc}$$

or

$$\frac{\frac{a}{b}}{\frac{c}{d}} = \frac{a}{b} \times \frac{d}{c} = \frac{ad}{bc}$$

For Example:

$$\frac{3}{5} \div \frac{4}{11} = \frac{3}{5} \times \frac{11}{4} = \frac{33}{20}$$

Example 2

Pedro has half as many CDs as Andrea has, and Marcia has $\frac{3}{5}$ as many CDs as Andrea. What fraction of Marcia's number of CDs does Pedro have?

Solution

Using P, A, and M to stand for the number of CDs each owns respectively, we have:

$$P = \frac{1}{2}A; M = \frac{3}{5}A$$

Thus:

$$\frac{P}{M} = \frac{\frac{1}{2}A}{\frac{3}{5}A} = \frac{1}{2} \times \frac{5}{3} = \frac{5}{6}$$

So Pedro has $\frac{5}{6}$ as many CDs as Marcia.

Addition and Subtraction

To add or subtract fractions with the same denominator, simply add or subtract the numerators. For example, $\frac{5}{17} + \frac{3}{17} = \frac{8}{17}$, and $\frac{5}{17} - \frac{3}{17} = \frac{2}{17}$.

However, if the denominators are different, you must first rewrite the fractions so they will have the same denominator. That is, you must find a *common denominator*. Most books and teachers stress that you should use the *least common denominator (LCD)*, which is the least common multiple (LCM) of the original denominators. This will keep the numbers smaller. However, *any* common denominator will do!

If you are rushed, you can always find a common denominator by just taking the product of the two denominators. For example, to add $\frac{5}{12} + \frac{3}{8}$, you can multiply the denominators 12 and 8 to find the common denominator 96. Thus:

$$\frac{5}{12} + \frac{3}{8} = \frac{5 \times 8}{12 \times 8} + \frac{3 \times 12}{8 \times 12} = \frac{40}{96} + \frac{36}{96} = \frac{76}{96}$$

Now you can divide both the numerator and the denominator by 4 to simplify the fraction to its simplest form; that is: $\frac{76}{96} = \frac{19}{24}$.

To find the least common denominator, you must first understand what a least common multiple is. Given two numbers M and N, any number that is divisible by both is called a *common multiple* of M and N. The *least common multiple (LCM)* of the two numbers is the least number that is divisible by both. For example, 108 is divisible by both 9 and 12, so 108 is a common multiple; but the LCM is 36.

For small numbers, the easiest way to find the LCM is simply to list the multiples of each number (in writing or in your head) until you find the first common multiple. For example, for 9 and 12 we have the following multiples:

9 18 27 <u>36</u> 45 . . .

12 24 <u>36</u> 48 60 . . .

The first number that appears in both lists is 36.

The traditional method for finding the LCM, which is the method that translates most readily into algebra, requires that you find the *prime factorization* of the numbers.

Every whole number is either prime or composite. A *prime* is a whole number greater than 1 with exactly two factors, namely 1 and the number itself. Any whole number, except 1, that is not prime is *composite.*

All composite numbers can be factored into primes in an essentially unique way. To find an LCM, you must find the least number that contains all the factors of both numbers. Thus, 9 factors as (3)(3), and 12 factors as (2)(2)(3). The LCM is the least number that has all the same factors: that is, two 3s and two 2s. Since (3)(3)(2)(2) = 36, the LCM is 36.

This definition also extends to sets of more than two numbers. Thus, the LCM of 12, 15, and 20 must contain all the prime factors of all three numbers: (2)(2)(3);

(3)(5); (2)(2)(5). So the LCM is (2)(2)(3)(5) = 60. Now to add $\dfrac{5}{12} + \dfrac{3}{8}$ using the least possible numbers, we find the LCM of 12 and 8, which is 24. Then, we write $\dfrac{5}{12} = \dfrac{10}{24}$ and $\dfrac{3}{8} = \dfrac{9}{24}$. Thus:

$$\frac{5}{12} + \frac{3}{8} = \frac{10}{24} + \frac{9}{24} = \frac{19}{24}$$

Example 3
Find the LCM for 18 and 30.

Solution
Using prime factorization, 18 = (2)(3)(3), and 30 = (2)(3)(5). Since the factors 2 and 3 are common to both numbers, we need only multiply in one extra 3 to get the factors of 18 and a 5 to get the factors of 30. Thus, the LCM = (2)(3)(3)(5) = 90.

Example 4
Mario figures that he can finish a certain task in 20 days. Angelo figures that he can finish the same task in 25 days. What fraction of the task can they get done working together for seven days?

Solution

In seven days, Mario would do $\dfrac{7}{20}$ of the entire task. In the same week, Angelo would do $\dfrac{7}{25}$ of the entire task. Therefore, together they do $\dfrac{7}{20} + \dfrac{7}{25}$ of the whole job.

Now we have to add two fractions that have the same numerator. Can we add them directly by just summing the denominators? No! To add directly, it is the denominators that must be the same! Instead, we must find a common denominator. The LCD is 100. Thus:

$$\frac{7}{25} + \frac{7}{20} = \frac{28}{100} + \frac{35}{100} = \frac{63}{100}$$

$\dfrac{63}{100}$ may also be expressed as 0.63 or 63%. Do you know why? If not, read the next section carefully.

Topic 7: Fractions, Decimals, and Percents

Every fraction can be expressed as a *decimal*, which can be found by division. Those fractions for which the prime factorization of the denominator involves only 2's and 5's will have terminating decimal expansions. All others will have repeating decimal expansions. For example, $\dfrac{3}{20} = 0.15$, while $\dfrac{3}{11} = 0.272727. \ldots$

To rename a number given as a decimal as a fraction, you must know what the decimal means. In general, a decimal represents a fraction with a denominator of

10, or 100, or 1,000, . . . where the number of zeros is equal to the number of digits to the right of the decimal point. Thus, for example, 0.4 means $\frac{4}{10}$; 0.52 means $\frac{52}{100}$; and $0.103 = \frac{103}{1000}$.

Decimals of the form 3.25 are equivalent to *mixed numbers*; thus, $3.25 = 3 + \frac{25}{100}$. For purposes of addition and subtraction, mixed numbers can be useful, but for purposes of multiplication or division, it is usually better to rename a mixed number as an *improper fraction*. Thus:

$$3\frac{1}{4} = \frac{13}{4}$$

How did we do that? Formally, we realize that $3 = \frac{3}{1}$, and we add the two fractions $\frac{3}{1}$ and $\frac{1}{4}$, using the common denominator 4. In informal terms, we multiply the whole number part (3) by the common denominator (4), and add the numerator of the fraction (1) to get the numerator of the resulting improper fraction. That is, $(3)(4) + 1 = 13$.

Example 1

If $\frac{0.56}{1.26}$ simplified to simplest form is $\frac{a}{b}$, and a and b are positive whole numbers, what is b?

Solution

Rewriting both numerator and denominator as their fractional equivalents, $0.56 = \frac{56}{100} = \frac{14}{25}$, and $1.26 = 1 + \frac{26}{100} = 1 + \frac{13}{50} = \frac{63}{50}$.

We now accomplish the division by multiplying by the reciprocal the denominator of the fraction. Thus:

$$\left(\frac{14}{25}\right)\left(\frac{50}{63}\right) = \frac{4}{9}$$

As you can see, $b = 9$.

Of course, you could also solve this example by renaming the numerator and denominator of the original fraction as whole numbers. You would multiply both the numerator and the denominator by 100 to move both decimal points two places to the right; thus, $\frac{0.56}{1.26} = \frac{56}{126}$. Now you can divide out the common factor of 14 in the numerator and the denominator to simplify the fraction to $\frac{4}{9}$.

Per<u>cent</u> means per <u>hundred</u> (from the Latin word *centum* meaning "hundred"). So that, for example, 30% means 30 per hundred, or as a fraction $\frac{30}{100}$, or as a decimal 0.30.

FYI

If you divide on a calculator, you will find that 0.56 ÷ 1.26 = 0.4444444 . . . , which you might recognize as $\frac{4}{9}$ Here is a good trick to remember: Any repeating decimal can be written as the repeating portion divided by an equal number of 9's. Thus, 0.333 . . . $= \frac{3}{9} = \frac{1}{3}$. 0.279279279 . . . $= \frac{279}{999} = \frac{31}{111}$.

435

To rename a number given as a percent as decimal form, simply move the decimal point two places to the left. To rename a decimal as a percent, reverse the process—move the decimal point two places to the right.

To avoid confusion, keep in mind the fact that, when written as a percent, the number should look bigger. Thus, the "large" number 45% = 0.45, and the "small" number 0.73 = 73%.

Example 2
In a group of 20 English majors and 30 history majors, 50% of the English majors and 20% of the history majors have not taken a college math course. What percent of the entire group have taken a college math course?

Solution
Start with the English majors. Since 50% = 0.50, 50% of 20 = (0.50)(20) = 10. For the history majors, 20% = 0.20; 20% of 30 = (0.20)(30) = 6. Hence, a total of 16 out of 50 people in the group have not taken math, which means that 34 have. As a fraction, 34 out of 50 is $\frac{34}{50}$ = 0.68 = 68%.

Topic 8: Averages

There are three common measurements used to define the typical value of a collection of numbers. However, when you see the word *average* with no other explanation, it is assumed that what is meant is the *arithmetic mean*. The average in this sense is the sum of the numbers divided by the number of numbers in the collection. In symbols, $A = \frac{T}{n}$.

So, for example, if on four math exams you scored 82, 76, 87, and 89, your average at this point is (82 + 76 + 87 + 89) ÷ 4 = 334 ÷ 4 = 83.5.

Example 1
At an art show, Eleanor sold six of her paintings at an average price of $70. At the next show, she sold four paintings at an average price of $100. What was the overall average price of the 10 paintings?

Solution
You can't just say the answer is 85, the average of 70 and 100, because we do not have the same number of paintings in each group. We need to know the overall total. Since the first six average $70, the total received for the six was $420. Do you see why? ($70 = \frac{T}{6}$; therefore, $T = (6)(70) = 420$). In the same way, the next four paintings must have brought in $400 in order to average $100 apiece. Therefore, we have a total of 10 paintings selling for $420 + $400 = $820, and the average is $\frac{\$820}{10} = \$82$.

Example 2
Erica averaged 76 on her first four French exams. To get a B in the course, she must have an 80 average on her exams. What grade must she get on the next exam to bring her average to 80?

Solution

If her average is 76 on four exams, she must have a total of $(4)(76) = 304$. In order to average 80 on five exams, her total must be $(5)(80) = 400$. Therefore, she must score $400 - 304 = 96$ on her last exam. Study hard, Erica!

The other measurements used to define the typical value of a set of numbers are the *median*, which is the middle number when the numbers are arranged in increasing order, and the *mode*, which is the most common number.

Example 3

Which is greater for the set of nine integers {1,2,2,2,3,5,6,7,8}, the mean minus the median or the median minus the mode?

Solution

The median (middle number) is 3, the mode is 2 and the mean is $(1 + 2 + 2 + 2 + 3 + 5 + 6 + 7 + 8) \div 9 = 4$. Thus, the mean minus the median is $4 - 3 = 1$, and the median minus the mode is $3 - 2 = 1$. The two quantities are equal.

ALGEBRA

Topic 9: Signed Numbers

Addition and Subtraction

To add two numbers of the same sign, just add them and attach their common sign. So $7 + 9 = 16$, and $(-7) + (-9) = -16$. You could drop the parentheses and instead of $(-7) + (-9)$ write $-7 - 9$, which means the same thing. In other words, adding a negative number is the same as subtracting a positive number.

When adding numbers of opposite signs, temporarily ignore the signs, subtract the lesser from the greater, and attach to the result the sign of the number with the greater absolute value. Thus, $9 + (-3) = 6$, but $(-9) + 3 = -6$. Again, we could have written $9 + (-3) = 9 - 3 = 6$ and $(-9) + 3 = -9 + 3 = -6$.

When subtracting, change the sign of the second number (the *subtrahend*) and then use the rules for addition. Thus, $7 - (-3) = 7 + 3 = 10$ and $-7 - 3 = -7 + (-3) = -10$.

Example 1

Evaluate $-A - (-B)$ when A -5 and $B = -6$

Solution

All the negative signs can be confusing. However, if you remember that "subtracting a negative is adding a positive," you can do this in two ways. The first is to realize that if $B = -6$, then $-B = +6$, and if $A = -5$, then $-A = 5$ Thus, $-A - (-B) = 5 - 6 = -1$.

Alternatively, you can work with the letters first: $-A - (-B) = -A + B = -(-5) + (-6) = 5 - 6 = -1$.

Multiplication and Division

If you multiply two numbers with the same sign, the result is positive. If you multiply two numbers with opposite signs, the result is negative. The exact same rule holds for division. Thus $(-4)(-3) = +12$, and $(-4)(3) = -12$. For division, it doesn't matter which is negative and which positive; thus $(-6) \div (2) = -3$, and $(6) \div (-2) = -3$, but $(-6) \div (-2) = +3$.

If you have a string of multiplications and divisions to do, if the number of negative factors is even, the result will be positive; if the number of negative factors is odd, the result will be negative. Of course, if even one factor is zero, the result is zero, and if even one factor in the denominator (divisor) is zero, the result is undefined.

Example 2

If $A = (234,906 - 457,219)(35)(-618)$ and $B = (-2,356)(-89,021)(-3,125)$, which is larger, A or B?

Solution: Don't actually do the arithmetic! 457,219 is greater than 234,906, so the difference is a negative number. Now, A is the product of two negative numbers and a positive number, which makes the result positive. B is the product of three negative numbers and must be negative. Every positive number is greater than any negative number, so A is greater than B.

Example 3

If $\dfrac{AB}{MN}$ is a positive number, and N is negative, which of the following is possible?

(F) A is positive, and B and M are negative.
(G) A, B, and M are negative.
(H) A, B, and M are positive.
(J) B is positive, and A and M are negative.
(K) M is positive, and A and B are negative.

Solution

The correct answer is (G). To determine the sign of the fraction, we can just think of A, B, M, and N as four factors. Knowing that N is negative, the product of the other three must also be negative in order that the result be positive. The only possibilities are that all are negative, or one is negative and the other two are positive. This works only for case (G).

Topic 10: Laws of Exponents

In an expression of the form b^n, b is called the *base* and n is called the *exponent* or *power*. We say, "b is raised to the power of n." (Notice: $b^1 = b$; hence, the power 1 is usually omitted.) If n is any positive integer, then b^n is the product of n b's. For example, 4^3 is the product of three 4's, that is, $4 \times 4 \times 4 = 64$.

Certain rules for operations with exponents are forced upon us by this definition.

- $b^m \times b^n = b^{m+n}$. That is, when multiplying powers of the same base, keep the base and add the exponents. Thus, $3^2 \times 3^3 = 3^{2+3} = 3^5 = 243$.

- $(ab)^n = a^n b^n$ and $\left(\dfrac{a}{b}\right)^n = \dfrac{a^n}{b^n}$

  That is, to raise a product or quotient to a power, raise each factor to that power, whether that factor is in the numerator or denominator. Thus, $(2x)^3 = 2^3 x^3 = 8x^3$, and $\left(\dfrac{2}{x}\right)^3 = \dfrac{2^3}{x^3} = \dfrac{8}{x^3}$.

- $(b^m)^n = b^{nm}$. That is, to raise to a power to a power, retain the base and multiply exponents. Thus, $(2^3)^2 = 2^6 = 64$.

■ $\dfrac{b^n}{b^m} = b^{n-m}$ if $n > m$, and $\dfrac{b^n}{b^m} = \dfrac{1}{b^{m-n}}$ if $n < m$. That is, to divide powers of the same base, subtract exponents. For example, $\dfrac{4^5}{4^2} = 4^3 = 64$, and $\dfrac{4^2}{4^5} = \dfrac{1}{4^3} = \dfrac{1}{64}$.

For various technical reasons, $x^0 = 1$ for all x except $x = 0$, in which case it is undefined. With this definition, one can define b^{-n} in such a way that all the laws of exponents given above still work even for negative powers! This definition is $b^{-n} = \dfrac{1}{b^n}$.

Now you have the choice of writing $\dfrac{x^3}{x^5}$ as $\dfrac{1}{x^2}$ or as x^{-2}

Example 1
If $x = 2$, which is greater, 1.10 or $x^0 + x^{-4}$?

Solution

If $x = 2$, $x^0 = 2^0 = 1$, and $x^{-4} = 2^{-4} = \dfrac{1}{2^4} = \dfrac{1}{16} = 0.0625$. Hence, $x^0 + x^{-4} = 1.0625$, which is less than 1.10.

Example 2

Which of the following expressions is equivalent to $\dfrac{(2x)^3}{x^7}$?

(A) $\dfrac{1}{8x^4}$

(B) $\dfrac{8}{x^{-4}}$

(C) $(8x)^{-4}$

(D) $8x^{-4}$

(E) $\dfrac{x^4}{8}$

Solution
The correct answer is (D). Cubing the numerator, we cube each factor. Since $2^3 = 8$, we have $\dfrac{(2x)^3}{x^7} = \dfrac{8x^3}{x^7}$.

We now divide x^3 by x^7 by subtracting the exponents: $3 - 7 = -4$. Notice that we could have written $8x^{-4}$ as $\dfrac{8}{x^4}$.

Be alert to the properties of even and odd powers. Even powers of real numbers cannot be negative. This rule applies to both positive and negative integer powers. Thus, x^2 is positive, as is x^{-2} except for $x = 0$, when x^2 is zero and x^{-2} is undefined (because you cannot divide by zero).

Odd powers are positive or negative depending upon whether the base is positive or negative. Thus, $2^3 = 8$, but $(-2)^3 = -8$. Zero to any power is zero, except zero to the zero, which is undefined.

Example 3

If $x < 0$ and $y > 0$, what is the sign of $-4x^4y^3$?

Solution

x^4 is positive, because it has an even power. y^3 is positive because y is, and -4 is obviously negative. The product of two positives and a negative is negative. Thus,

$-4x^4y^3$ is negative.

Example 4

If $x^4 + 3y^2 = 0$, what is the sign of $2x - 6y + 1$?

Solution

Since neither x^4 nor $3y^2$ can be negative, the only way their sum can be zero is if both x and y are zero. Therefore, $2x - 6y + 1 = +1$, which is positive.

Topic 11: Ratio, Proportion, and Variation

A fractional relationship between two quantities is frequently expressed as a *ratio*. A ratio can be written as a fraction, $\dfrac{b}{a}$, or in the form $b{:}a$ (read "b is to a"). A *proportion* is a statement that two ratios are equal. To say, for example, that the ratio of passing to failing students in a class is 5:2 means that if we set up the fraction $\dfrac{P}{F}$ representing the relationship between the number of passing and failing students, it should simplify to $\dfrac{5}{2}$. If we write this statement as $P{:}F :: 5{:}2$, we read it "P is to F as 5 is to 2," and it means $\dfrac{P}{F} = \dfrac{5}{2}$.

Often, a good way to work with information given in ratio form is to represent the numbers as multiples of the same number.

Example 1

The ratio of Democrats to Republicans in a certain state legislature is 5:7. If the legislature has 156 members, all of whom are either Democrats or Republicans (but not both), what is the difference between the number of Republicans and the number of Democrats?

(A) 14
(B) 26
(C) 35
(D) 37
(E) 49

Solution

The correct answer is (B). Let the number of Democrats be $5m$ and the number of Republicans be $7m$, so that $D{:}R :: 5m{:}7m = 5{:}7$. The total number of legislators is $5m + 7m = 12m$, which must be 156. Therefore, $12m = 156$, and $m = 13$. Thus, the difference is $7m - 5m = 2m = 2(13) = 26$.

When you are told that one quantity, say y, *varies directly* with (or as) x, that means simply that $y = kx$, where k is some constant.

To say that y varies directly with x^2 or x^3 or any given power means that $y = kx^2$ or kx^3. If you are told that y varies inversely with x, it means that $y = \dfrac{k}{x}$. Similarly, if y varies inversely with x^n, it means that $y = \dfrac{k}{x^n}$.

Usually, the problem is to first determine k (the *constant of proportionality*) and then solve further.

Example 2

The time it takes to paint a wall is directly proportional to the area of the wall and inversely proportional to the number of painters. If 3 painters can paint 1000 square feet of wall in 6 hours, how many square feet can 8 painters paint in 15 hours?

Solution

The relationship must be $t = k\left(\dfrac{A}{p}\right)$, where t = time, A = area, and p = number of painters. Hence, when $A = 1000$ and $p = 3$, $6 = k\left(\dfrac{1000}{3}\right)$. That is, $6 = \dfrac{1000}{3}k$ and $k = \dfrac{9}{500}$. Now we substitute $p = 8$ and $t = 15$ into $t = \left(\dfrac{9}{500}\right)\left(\dfrac{A}{p}\right)$, yielding $15 = \left(\dfrac{9}{500}\right)\left(\dfrac{A}{8}\right) = \dfrac{9A}{1000}$. Multiplying by 4000 and dividing by 9, we have $A = 6666\dfrac{2}{3}$.

Topic 12: Solving Linear Equations

To solve a linear equation, remember these rules:

- If you add or subtract the same quantity from both sides of an equation, the equation will still be true and will still have the same roots (solutions).

- If you multiply or divide both sides of an equation by any number except zero, the equation will still be true and will still have the same roots.

Use these two properties to isolate the unknown quantity on one side of the equation, leaving only known quantities on the other side. This is known as *solving for the unknown*.

Example 1

If $14 = 3x - 1$ and $B = 6x + 4$, what is the value of B?

Solution

From the first equation, $3x - 1 = 14$. Add 1 to both sides:

$$
\begin{array}{rl}
3x - 1 & = 14 \\
1 & = 1 \\
\hline
3x & = 15
\end{array}
$$

Divide both sides by 3:

$$\frac{3x}{3} = \frac{15}{3}$$
$$x = 5$$

Of course, the question asked for B, not x. So we substitute $x = 5$ into $B = 6x + 4$ and get $B = 6(5) + 4 = 34$.

Example 2

If $\frac{2x}{3} + 2 = a$ and $y = 2x + 6$, what is the value of y in terms of a?

Solution

How do we do this? We realize that if we knew what x was in terms of a, then we could substitute that expression for x into $y = 2x + 6$ and have y in terms of a. In other words, we want to solve $\frac{2x}{3} + 2 = a$ for x.

Multiply through by 3 to clear the fractions. Be careful: use the distributive law and multiply every term on both sides by 3. You should now have:

$$2x + 6 = 3a$$

Now add -6 to both sides of the equation:

$$\begin{array}{r} 2x + 6 = 3a \\ -6 = -6 \\ \hline 2x \quad\;\; = 3a - 6 \end{array}$$

Now divide by 2:

$$\frac{2x}{2} = \frac{3a - 6}{2}; x = \frac{3a - 6}{2}$$

Substituting:

$$y = 2\left(\frac{3a - 6}{2}\right) + 6$$
$$y = 3a - 6 + 6$$
$$y = 3a$$

FYI

As a general rule, when an equation involves one or more fractional coefficients, it pays to multiply by a common denominator in order to clear the fractions.

Topic 13: Solving Linear Inequalities

The statement that a number M is less than another number N means that $N - M$ is positive. In other words, when you subtract a lesser number from a greater number, the result is positive. In symbols, this can be expressed:

$$M < N \text{ or } N > M.$$

On the number line, if $M < N$, we can infer that M lies to the left of N. This means, in particular, that any negative number is less than any positive number. It also implies that, for negative numbers, the one with the greater absolute value is the lesser number.

Inequalities (also called *inequations*) can be solved in the same way as equations are. When working with inequalities, remember these rules:

- If you add or subtract the same quantity from both sides of an inequality, it will still be true in the same sense. Thus, $14 > 7$ and $14 - 5 > 7 - 5$.

- If you multiply or divide both sides of an inequality by the same positive number, the inequality will still be true in the same sense. Thus, $3 < 8$ and $(6)(3) < (6)(8)$

- If you multiply or divide both sides of an inequality by the same negative number, the inequality will still be true, but with the sense *reversed*. Thus, $4 < 9$; but if you multiply by (-2), you get $-8 > -18$. (Remember, for negative numbers, the one with the greater absolute value is the lesser number.)

Notice that these rules hold whether you are working with $<$ (is less than) and $>$ (is greater than) or $\leq$ (is less than or equal to) and $\geq$ (is greater than or equal to). Use them to isolate the unknown quantity on one side of the inequality, leaving only known quantities on the other side. This is known as *solving for the unknown*. Solutions to inequalities can be given in algebraic form or displayed on the number line.

Example 1
For what values of x is $12 - x \geq 3x + 8$?

Solution
We solve this just like an equation. Start by adding the like quantity $(x - 8)$ to both sides in order to group the x terms on one side and the constants on the other; thus:

$$
\begin{array}{r}
12 - x \geq 3x + 8 \\
\underline{x - 8 = x - 8} \\
4 \geq 4x
\end{array}
$$

Now divide both sides by 4, which does not change the sense of the inequality, yielding:

$$1 \geq x$$

Hence, the inequality will be true for any number less than or equal to 1 and false for any number greater than 1. For example, if $x = 3$, $12 - x = 9$ and $3x + 8 = 17$, and the inequality is *not* satisfied. Graphically, this can be shown as in the figure below.

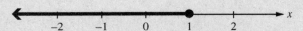

Notice that the darkened section is the set of solution values, and the solid dot at $x = 1$ indicates that the value 1 is included in the solution set. By contrast, see the figure below. It shows the solution set for $x < 2$, where the open circle shows that $x = 2$ is not included.

443

Example 2

If $A < 2 - 4B$, can you tell how great B is in terms of A? Can you tell how small B is?

Solution

We are really being asked to solve the inequality for B. To start, we add -2 to both sides, thus:

$$\begin{array}{rl} A & < 2 - 4B \\ -2 & = -2 \\ \hline A - 2 & < \quad -4B \end{array}$$

Next divide by -4, remembering to reverse the inequality, thus:

$$\frac{A - 2}{-4} > B; \frac{2 - A}{4} > B$$

Notice two things here. When we changed the denominator on the lefthand side from -4 to $+4$, we also changed the sign of the numerator, by changing $(A - 2)$ to $(2 - A)$. Of course, this is the equivalent of multiplying the numerator and the denominator by -1.

Also, this tells us what B is less than, nothing about what B is greater than. For example, if A were 6, then $B < -1$, but B could be -100 or -1000 or anything else "more negative" than -1.

Topic 14: Solving Two Linear Equations with Two Unknowns

Many word problems lead to equations in two unknowns. Usually, one needs as many equations as there are unknowns to solve for all or some of the unknowns: in other words, to solve for two unknowns, two independent equations are needed; to solve for three unknowns, three equations are needed, and so on. However, there are exceptions.

You should know two methods for solving two equations with two unknowns. They are the *method of substitution* and the *method of elimination by addition and subtraction*. We shall illustrate both methods by example. The first example uses the method of substitution.

Example 1

Mrs. Green and her three children went to the local movie. The total cost of their admission tickets was $14. Mr. and Mrs. Arkwright and their five children went to the same movie, and they had to pay $25. What was the cost of an adult ticket and what was the cost of a child's ticket?

Solution

Expressing all amounts in dollars, let x = cost of an adult ticket, and let y = cost of a child's ticket.

For the Greens:

$$x + 3y = 14$$

For the Arkwrights:

$$2x + 5y = 25$$

The idea of the method of substitution is to solve one equation for one variable in terms of the other and then substitute that solution into the second equation. Here, we solve the first equation for x, because that is the simplest one to isolate:

$$x = 14 - 3y$$

Substitute this value into the second equation:

$$2(14 - 3y) + 5y = 25$$

This gives us one equation with one unknown that we can solve:

$$28 - 6y + 5y = 25$$
$$-y = -3$$
$$y = 3$$

Now that we know $y = 3$, we put this into $x = 14 - 3y$ to get:

$$x = 14 - 3(3) = 5$$

Thus, the adult tickets were $5.00 each and the children's tickets were $3.00 each.

Here is an example using the method of elimination.

Example 2

Paula and Dennis both went to the bakery. Paula bought 3 rolls and 5 muffins for a total cost of $3.55. Dennis bought 6 rolls and 2 muffins for a total cost of $3.10. What was the price of one roll?

Solution

Let us express all amounts in cents. Let r = the cost of a roll; let m = the cost of a muffin. Paula paid:

$$3r + 5m = 355$$

Dennis paid:

$$6r + 2m = 310$$

The idea of the method of elimination is that adding equal quantities to equal quantities gives a true result. So we want to add some multiple of one equation to the other equation such that when the two equations are added together, one variable will be eliminated.

In this case, it is not hard to see that if we multiply the first equation by -2, the coefficient of r will become -6. Then, if we add the two equations, r will drop out. Here's how it works:

$$
\begin{array}{rr}
-2 \text{ times the first equation is:} & -6r - 10m = -710 \\
\text{The second equation is:} & 6r + 2m = 310 \\
\hline
\text{Adding:} & -8m = -400
\end{array}
$$

Dividing by -8, $m = 50$. We now substitute this into either of the two equations. Let's use the second:

$$6r + (2)(50) = 310$$
$$6r = 210$$
$$r = 35$$

Thus, muffins are 50¢ each and rolls are 35¢.

Topic 15: Word Problems with One or Two Unknowns

There are word problems of many different types. Many, like age or coin problems, involve only common sense. For others, there are specific formulas or pieces of factual knowledge that can be helpful.

For example, for *consecutive integer problems,* you need to know that consecutive integers differ by 1; therefore, a string of such numbers can be represented by $n, n + 1, n + 2, \ldots$

Consecutive even or odd integers differ by 2, so a string of such numbers can be represented as $n, n + 2, n + 4 \ldots$

Travel problems usually require you to use the formula $d = rt$; that is, Distance equals Rate times Time.

Example 1

Sally is 6 years older than Manuel; three years ago, Sally was twice as old as Manuel. How old is Sally today?

Solution

If you have trouble setting up the equations, try plugging in possible numbers. Suppose that Sally is 20 today. If Sally is 6 years older than Manuel, how old is Manuel? He is 14. You get from 14 to 20 by *adding* 6. So if S is Sally's age and M is Manuel's, $S = M + 6$.

Three years ago, Sally was $S - 3$, and Manuel was $M - 3$. So, from the second sentence, we know that $S - 3 = 2(M - 3)$ or $S - 3 = 2M - 6$. Thus, $S = 2M - 3$.

Now, substituting $S = M + 6$, into the second equation:

$$M + 6 = 2M - 3$$
$$M = 9$$

Which means that Sally is $9 + 6 = 15$.

Example 2

Three consecutive odd integers are written in increasing order. If the sum of the first and second and twice the third is 46, what is the second number?

Solution

Calling the least number x, the second is $x + 2$, and the third is $x + 4$. Therefore:

$$x + (x + 2) + 2(x + 4) = 46$$
$$x + x + 2 + 2x + 8 = 46$$
$$4x + 10 = 46$$
$$4x = 36$$
$$x = 9$$

Hence, the second number is $9 + 2 = 11$.

Example 3

It took Andrew $1\frac{1}{2}$ hours to drive from Aurora to Zalesville at an average speed of 50 miles per hour. How fast did he have to drive back in order to reach Aurora in 80 minutes?

Solution

The distance from Aurora to Zalesville must be given by $d = rt = (50)(1.5) = 75$ miles. Since 80 minutes is 1 hour and 20 minutes, or $1\frac{1}{3} = \frac{4}{3}$ hours, we must solve the equation $75 = \frac{4}{3}r$. Multiplying by 3, we have $225 = 4r$; then, dividing by 4, $r = 56.25$ mph.

Topic 16: Monomials and Polynomials

In any group of algebraic and arithmetic expressions, each expression is called a *term*. *Monomial* describes a single term; for example, we might say that $2x + 3y^2 + 7$ is the sum of three terms or three monomials.

Technically, if we enclose an algebraic expression in parentheses, it becomes one term, so that we could say that $(x + 2y) + (3x - 5y^2)$ is the sum of two monomials. But usually, when we talk about a monomial, we mean a term that is a single product of certain given constants and variables, possibly raised to various powers. Examples might be 7, $2x$, $-3y^2$, $4x^2z^5$. Each of these is a monomial.

In a monomial, the constant factor is called the *coefficient of the variable factor.* Thus, in $-3y^2$, -3 is the coefficient of y^2. If we restrict our attention to monomials of the form Ax^n, the sums of such terms are called *polynomials*. Polynomials with two terms are called *binomials,* and those with three terms are called *trinomials*. Expressions like $3x + 5$, $2x^2 - 5x + 8$, and $x^4 - 7x^5 - 11$ are all examples of polynomials.

In a polynomial, the highest power of the variable that appears is called the *degree of the polynomial*. The three examples just given are of degree 1, 2, and 5, respectively.

Example 1

Find the value of $3x - x^3 - x^2$ when $x = -2$.

Solution

Substitute -2 every place you see an x, thus:

$$3(-2) - (-2)^3 - (-2)^2 = -6 - (-8) - (+4) = -6 + 8 - 4 = -2$$

Monomials with identical variable factors can be added or subtracted by adding or subtracting their coefficients. Thus: $3x^2 + 4x^2 = 7x^2$, and $3x^4 - 9x^4 = -6x^4$.

To multiply monomials, take the product of their coefficients and take the product of the variable parts by adding exponents of factors with like bases. Thus:

$$(-4xy^2)(3x^2y^3) = -12x^3y^5$$

Monomial fractions can be simplified to simplest form by dividing out any common factors of the coefficients and then using the usual rules for subtraction of exponents in division. For example:

$$\frac{6x^3y^5}{2x^4y^3} = \frac{3y^2}{x}$$

Example 2

Combine into a single monomial $9y - \frac{6y^3}{2y^2}$.

Solution
The fraction simplifies to $3y$, and $9y - 3y = 6y$.

Topic 17: Combining Polynomials and Monomials

Polynomials are added or subtracted simply by combining like monomial terms in the appropriate manner. Thus, $(2x^2 + 5x - 3) + (3x^2 + 5x - 12)$ is summed by removing the parentheses and combining like terms, to yield $5x^2 + 10x - 15$.

Example 1
What is the sum of $(3a^2b^3 - 6ab^2 + 2a^3b^2)$ and $(5a^2b^3 - 2a^3b^2)$?

Solution
Removing the parentheses, we combine the terms with identical literal parts by adding their coefficients:

$$(3a^2b^3 - 6ab^2 + 2a^3b^2) + (5a^2b^3 - 2a^3b^2) = 3a^2b^3 - 6ab^2 + 2a^3b^2 + 5a^2b^3 - 2a^3b^2$$
$$= 8a^2b^3 - 6ab^2$$

Notice that the $2a^3b^2$ and $-2a^3b^2$ terms summed to zero.

To multiply a polynomial by a monomial, use the distributive law to multiply each term in the polynomial by the monomial factor. For example, $2x(2x^2 + 5x - 11) = 4x^3 + 10x^2 - 22x$.

When multiplying a polynomial by a polynomial, repeatedly apply the distributive law to form all possible products of the terms in the first polynomial with the terms in the second.

The most common use of this is in multiplying two binomials, such as $(x + 3)(x - 5)$. In this case, there are four terms in the result: $x \times x = x^2$; $x(-5) = -5x$; $3 \times x = 3x$; and $3(-5) = -15$; but the two middle terms are added together to give $-2x$. Thus, the product is $x^2 - 2x - 15$.

This process is usually remembered as the *FOIL method*. That is, form the products of the First, Outer, Inner, and Last terms, as shown below.

$$(x + 3)(x - 5) = x^2 + (-5x + 3x) - 15$$

$$= x^2 - 2x - 15$$

FYI

If there is a negative sign in front of a polynomial within parentheses, be careful to change the signs of all the terms within the parentheses when you remove the parentheses. Thus:

$(2x^2 + 5x - 3)$
$- (3x^2 + 5x - 12)$
$= 2x^2 + 5x - 3 -$
$3x^2 - 5x + 12 =$
$-x^2 + 9$

Be sure to remember these special cases:

- $(x + a)^2 = (x + a)(x + a) = x^2 + 2ax + a^2$
- $(x - a)^2 = (x - a)(x - a) = x^2 - 2ax + a^2$

Example 2

If m is an integer, and $(x - 6)(x - m) = x^2 + rx + 18$, what is the value of $m + r$?

Solution

The product of the last terms, $6m$, must be 18. Therefore, $m = 3$. If $m = 3$, then the sum of the outer and inner products becomes $-6x - 3x = -9x$, which equals rx. Hence, $r = -9$, and $m + r = 3 + (-9) = -6$.

Topic 18: Factoring Monomials and the Difference of Squares

FYI

The fact about the difference of two squares can be handy. For example, you can find $101^2 - 99^2$ as $(101 - 99)(101 + 99) = 2(200) = 400$.

Factoring a monomial from a polynomial simply involves reversing the distributive law. For example, if you are looking at $3x^2 - 6xy$, you should see that $3x$ is a factor of both terms. Hence, you could just as well write this expression as $3x(x - 2y)$. Multiplication using the distributive law will restore the original formulation.

Example 1

If $x - 5y = 12$, which is greater, $15y - 3x$ or -35?

Solution

We can see that $15y - 3x = -3(x - 5y)$. Hence, it must equal $-3(12) = -36$, which is less than -35.

When you multiply $(a - b)$ by $(a + b)$ using the FOIL method, the middle terms sum to zero, leaving just $a^2 - b^2$. Thus, the difference of two squares, $a^2 - b^2 = (a - b)(a + b)$.

For example, $x^2 - 16$ can be thought of as $x^2 - 4^2 = (x - 4)(x + 4)$. However, the sum of two squares—$b^2 + 16$, for example—cannot be factored.

Example 2

If x and y are positive integers, and $x - 2y = 5$, which of the following is the value of $x^2 - 4y^2$?

(A) 0
(B) 16
(C) 45

Solution

Since $x^2 - 4y^2 = (x - 2y)(x + 2y) = 5(x + 2y)$, $x^2 - 4y^2$ must be divisible by 5. Therefore, 16 is not possible. If the result is to be zero, $x + 2y = 0$, which means that $y = -2x$, so that both numbers cannot be positive. Hence, the expression must equal 45, which you get if $x = 7$ and $y = 1$. So the answer is (C).

Example 3

If x and y are positive integers, and $y^2 = x^2 + 7$, what is the value of y?

Solution

If we rewrite the equation as $y^2 - x^2 = 7$ and factor, we have $(y - x)(y + x) = 7$. Thus, 7 must be the product of the two whole numbers $(y - x)$ and $(y + x)$. But 7 is a prime number which can only be factored as 7 times 1. Of course, $(y + x)$ must be the greater of the two; hence, $y + x = 7$, and $y - x = 1$.

Adding the two equations gives us $2y = 8$; $y = 4$. (Of course, $x = 3$, but we weren't asked that.)

Topic 19: Operations with Square Roots

The square root of a number N, written $\sqrt{N}$, is a number that when squared produces N. Thus, $\sqrt{4} = 2$, $\sqrt{9} = 3$, $\sqrt{16} = 4$, and so on.

The symbol $\sqrt{}$ is called the *radical* sign, and many people refer to $\sqrt{N}$ as *radical N*. When we write $\sqrt{N}$, it is understood to be a positive number. So when you are faced with an algebraic equation like $x^2 = 4$, where you must allow for both positive and negative solutions, you must write $x = \pm\sqrt{4} = \pm 2$ (where $\pm$ is read as *positive or negative*).

You should be aware that $\sqrt{0} = 0$ and $\sqrt{1} = 1$. Square roots of negative numbers are not real numbers. All positive numbers have square roots, but most are *irrational numbers*. Only perfect squares like 4, 9, 16, 25, 36, . . . have integer square roots.

If you assume that you are working with non-negative numbers, you can use certain properties of the square root to simplify radical expressions. The most important of these rules is:

$$\sqrt{AB} = \sqrt{A} \times \sqrt{B}.$$

This can be used to advantage in either direction. Reading it from right to left, we may write $\sqrt{3} \times \sqrt{12} = \sqrt{36} = 6$. But you should also know how to use this rule to simplify radicals by extracting perfect squares from "under" the radical. Thus, $\sqrt{18} = \sqrt{9 \times 2} = 3\sqrt{2}$.

The key to using this technique is to recognize the perfect squares in order to factor in a sensible manner. Thus, it would do you little good to factor 18 as 3×6 in the preceding example, since neither 3 nor 6 is a perfect square.

Example

If $\sqrt{5} \times \sqrt{x} = 10$, which is larger, $\sqrt{x}$ or $2\sqrt{5}$?

Solution

Since $10 = \sqrt{100}$, and $\sqrt{5} \times \sqrt{x} = \sqrt{5x}$, we know that $5x = 100$, and $x = 20$. But $20 = 4 \times 5$, so $\sqrt{20} = 2\sqrt{5}$ Hence, the two quantities are equal.

Topic 20: Trinomial Factoring and Quadratic Equations

When you multiply two binomials $(x + r)(x + s)$ using the FOIL method, the result is a trinomial of the form $x^2 + bx + c$, where b, the coefficient of x, is the sum of the constants r and s, and the constant term c is their product.

Trinomial factoring is the process of reversing this multiplication. For example, to find the binomial factors of $x^2 - 2x - 8$, we need to find two numbers whose product is -8 and whose sum is -2. Since the product is negative, one of the numbers must be negative and the other positive. The possible factors of 8 are 1 and 8 and 2 and 4. In order for the sum to be -2, we must choose -4 and $+2$. Thus, $x^2 - 2x - 8 = (x - 4)(x + 2)$.

This technique can sometimes be used to solve quadratic equations. If you have an equation like $x^2 - 7x + 6 = 0$, you can factor the trinomial. To do this, you need two numbers whose product is $+6$ and whose sum is -7. Since the product is positive, both must be of the same sign, and since the sum is negative they must both be negative. It is not hard to see that -6 and -1 are the only correct options.

Once the trinomial is factored, the equation becomes $(x - 1)(x - 6) = 0$. Of course, the only way a product of two or more numbers can be zero is if one of the numbers is zero. Thus, either:

$$x - 1 = 0 \text{ or } x - 6 = 0$$
$$x = 1 \text{ or } x = 6$$

Example
The area of a rectangle is 60 and its perimeter is 32. What are its dimensions?

Solution
The area of a rectangle is determined by the formula $A = LW$, its perimeter by the formula $P = 2L + 2W$. (see topic 34) In this case, we have $LW = 60$ and $2L + 2W = 32$. Dividing by 2, $L + W = 16$. Therefore, $L = 16 - W$, which we substitute in $LW = 60$, giving:

$$(16 - W)W = 60$$
$$16W - W^2 = 60$$

Grouping everything on the righthand side, we have:

$$0 = W^2 - 16W + 60$$

Now, factoring:

$$0 = (W - 10)(W - 6)$$

This yields $W = 10$ or $W = 6$.

Of course, if $W = 6$, $L = 10$, and if $W = 10$, $L = 6$. Either way, the dimensions are 6×10.

Topic 21: The Quadratic Formula

FYI

Notice that you can move a term from one side of the equal sign to the other by simply changing its sign.

Some quadratic equations are not solvable by factoring using rational numbers. For example, because $x^2 + x + 1$ has no factors using whole numbers, $x^2 + x + 1 = 0$ has no rational roots (solutions).

In other cases, rational roots exist, but they are difficult to find. For example, $12x^2 + x - 6 = 0$ can be solved by factoring, but the solution is not easy to see:

$$12^2 + x - 6 = (3x - 2)(4x + 3)$$

Setting each factor equal to zero:

$$3x - 2 = 0 \text{ or } 4x + 3 = 0$$

yields $x = \dfrac{2}{3}$ or $x = -\dfrac{3}{4}$.

What can you do when faced with such a situation? You use the *quadratic formula*, which states that, for any equation of the form $ax^2 + bx + c = 0$, the roots are:

$$x = \frac{-b\sqrt{b^2 - 4ac}}{2a}$$

Example 1

If $6x^2 - x - 12 = 0$, what is the least integer greater than x?

Solution

Use the quadratic formula to solve for x. We identify a, b, and c as $a = 6$, $b = -1$, and $c = -12$. We substitute into the formula, yielding:

$$x = \frac{-(-1) \pm \sqrt{(-1)^2 - 4(6)(-12)}}{2(6)}$$

$$= \frac{1 \pm \sqrt{1 + 288}}{12}$$

$$= \frac{1 \pm \sqrt{289}}{12}$$

$$= \frac{1 \pm 17}{12}$$

Using the addition sign:

$$x = \frac{1 + 17}{12}$$

$$= \frac{18}{12}$$

$$= \frac{3}{2}$$

Using the subtraction sign:

$$x = \frac{1 - 17}{12}$$

$$= \frac{-16}{12}$$

$$= -\frac{4}{3}$$

Both possible values of x are less than 2.

Topic 22: Complex Numbers

Sometimes, when applying the quadratic formula, the *discriminant*, $d = b^2 - 4ac$, will be a negative number. In such a case, you have to deal with the square root of a negative number. Such a number is called *imaginary*. In general, if N is any positive number, then $\sqrt{-N}$ is written as $i\sqrt{N}$, where i is the square root of -1.

Numbers of the form bi, where b is a real number, are called *pure imaginary numbers*. For example, $\sqrt{-4} = i\sqrt{4} = 2i$ and $\sqrt{-3} = i\sqrt{3}$ are both pure imaginary numbers.

Numbers of the form $a + bi$, where a and b are both real numbers are called *complex numbers*. Thus, complex numbers have both a real and an imaginary part.

When doing arithmetic with complex numbers, just think of i as an unknown, like x, except whenever you get an i^2 in a computation, replace it by -1.

Example 1:

If $z = 4 + 3i$ and $w = 3 - 4i$, $zw - \dfrac{z}{w} = ?$

(A) $14 - i$
(B) $7 - 25i$
(C) $24 - 6i$
(D) $24 - 8i$
(E) $7 - i$

Solution

The correct answer is (D). Multiplying $(4 + 3i)(3 - 4i)$ by the FOIL method yields $12 - 7i - 12i^2$. Replacing i^2 by -1, we have $12 - 7i - 12(-1) = 12 - 7i + 12 = 24 - 7i$.

To find $\dfrac{z}{w}$ in the form $a + bi$ so that we can subtract it from zw, we need to rationalize the denominator of the fraction by multiplying the numerator and denominator of the fraction by the *complex conjugate* of w. (The complex conjugate of $a + bi = a - bi$.) When you multiply these two, the term involving i drops out, and you end up with just $a^2 + b^2$. Thus:

$$\frac{z}{w} = \left(\frac{4 + 3i}{3 - 4i}\right) \times \frac{3 + 4i}{3 + 4i} = \frac{12 + 25i + 12i^2}{3^2 + 4^2} = \frac{25i}{25} = i$$

Hence,

$$zw - \frac{z}{w} = (24 - 7i) - i = 24 - 8i.$$

Example 2

Which of the following is one root of $x^2 - 4x + 5 = 0$?

(F) $4 - i$
(G) $2 - i$
(H) $2 + 2i$
(J) $3i$
(K) $2 - 2i$

Solution

The correct answer is (G). Using the quadratic formula with $a = 1$, $b = -4$, and $c = 5$, we have:

$$x = \frac{-(-4) \pm \sqrt{(4)^2 - 4(1)(5)}}{2(1)} = \frac{4 \pm \sqrt{16 - 20}}{2} = \frac{4 \pm \sqrt{-4}}{2} = \frac{4 \pm 2i}{2}$$

Dividing each term in the numerator by the denominator 2 gives us $x = 2 \pm i$. Since we can choose either $+$ or $-$, we see that $2 - i$ is one root.

Topic 23: Higher Roots and Fractional Exponents

The symbol $\sqrt[n]{x}$ is used to represent the nth root of the number x. The nth root of x is that number which, when raised to the nth power, gives x as a result. For example, $\sqrt[3]{8} = 2$ because $2^3 = 8$.

Roots can also be represented by using fractional exponents. To be precise, we define $x^{\frac{1}{n}} = \sqrt[n]{x}$. In particular, the $\frac{1}{2}$ power of a number is its square root. So, for example:

$$16^{\frac{1}{2}} = \sqrt[2]{16} = 4$$

and

$$125^{\frac{1}{3}} = \sqrt[3]{125} = 5$$

In addition, other fractional powers can be defined by using the laws of exponents. That is, one can interpret an expression like $x^{\frac{3}{5}}$ to mean $(x^{\frac{1}{5}})^3$ because $\frac{3}{5} = \left(\frac{1}{5}\right)(3)$. Thus:

$$32^{\frac{3}{5}} = (\sqrt[5]{32})^3 = 2^3 = 8$$

Negative fractional powers can be similarly calculated by remembering that $x^{-n} = \frac{1}{x^n}$.

For example, to calculate $8^{-\frac{2}{3}}$, we first find $8^{\frac{2}{3}} = (\sqrt[3]{8})^2 = 2^2 = 4$.

Now, $8^{-\frac{2}{3}}$, is the reciprocal of $8^{\frac{2}{3}}$; that is, $\frac{1}{4}$.

Example 1

Find the value of $\dfrac{3x^0 + x^{\frac{1}{2}}}{2 + x^{-\frac{3}{4}}}$ if $x = 16$.

Solution

Let's calculate the numerator and denominator separately. In the numerator, $x^0 = 1$ for any x and, $x^{\frac{1}{2}} = \sqrt{x}$. Hence, $3(16^0) + 16^{\frac{1}{2}} = 3(1) + \sqrt{16} = 3 + 4 = 7$.

In the denominator, $16^{-\frac{3}{4}} = \frac{1}{8}$, which means that the denominator is $\frac{16}{8} + \frac{1}{8} = \frac{17}{8}$. So the original expression is equal to

$$\frac{7}{\frac{17}{8}} = 7\left(\frac{8}{17}\right) = \frac{56}{17}$$

Topic 24: Functions

Two variables, say x and y, may be related in a number of ways. In a *function* or *functional relationship*, one variable, usually x, is called the *independent variable*. The other, usually y, is the *dependent variable*. For every choice of x, precisely one y is defined. As x varies, y varies in an exactly predictable fashion.

In this situation, we say that "y is a function of x," meaning that the value of y is determined by the value of x. The function itself is denoted by f (or g, or h, . . .). The collection of possible values of the independent variable is called the *domain* of f. The y-value associated with a given x-value is denoted by $f(x)$ (read f of x). The collection of possible values of the dependent variable is called the *range* of f.

If an expression $f(x)$ defines a function, then the y corresponding to any specific x can be found by simply substituting that value for x in the expression $y = f(x)$.

Example 1
Suppose that the relation between x and y is given by $y = f(x)$, where $f(x) = x^2 + 3x - 4$. Find $f(1)$ and $f(2 + a)$.

Solution
To find the value of the function for any number, we substitute that number for x in the expression for $f(x)$. In essence, we think of this function as $f(\ ) = (\ )^2 + 3(\ ) - 4$, and then we fill in the blanks. So to find $f(1)$, we substitute 1 for x wherever it appears, thus:

$$f(1) = (1)^2 + 3(1) - 4 = 1 + 3 - 4 = 0$$

So $f(1) = 0$. In the same manner:

$$f(2 + a) = (2 + a)^2 + 3(2 + a) - 4$$
$$= 4 + 4a + a^2 + 6 + 3a - 4$$
$$= a^2 + 7a + 6$$

Example 2
Letting $f(x) = x^2$ and $g(x) = x + 3$, find each of the following:

    (A) $g(2)f(5)$
    (B) $f(g(1))$
    (C) $g(f(x))$

Solutions
(A) $g(2) = 2 + 3 = 5$; $f(5) = 5^2 = 25$; $g(2)f(5) = 5(25) = 125$.
(B) To find $f(g(1))$, first find $g(1) = 1 + 3 = 4$. Now $f(g(1)) = f(4) = 4^2 = 16$.
(C) To find $g(f(x))$, substitute $f(x)$ every place you see an x in $g(x) = x + 3$. In other words, $g(f(x)) = f(x) + 3$. But, since $f(x) = x^2$, $g(f(x)) = x^2 + 3$.

Two functions f and g for which $f(g(x)) = g(f(x)) = x$ are called *inverse functions*. When this occurs, $g(x)$ is called *f-inverse* and denoted $f^{-1}(x)$. The functions are called inverses because they "undo" one another. That is, for any value x, calculating $f(x)$ and substituting the result into $f^{-1}(x)$ brings you right back to the value x, where you started.

455

Example 3

Which of the following functions is $f^{-1}(x)$ for $f(x) = 3x + 2$?

(A) $-3x + 2$

(B) $\dfrac{x - 2}{3}$

(C) $\dfrac{1}{3x + 2}$

(D) $\dfrac{1}{3x} + 2$

(E) $\dfrac{1}{3}x + \dfrac{1}{2}$

Solution

The correct answer is (B). If you try calling each of these expressions in turn $g(x)$ and calculate $f(g(x)) = 3[g(x)] + 2$, you will see that only for (B) will the result be $f(g(x)) = x$. Thus, $f(g(x)) = 3\left(\dfrac{x - 2}{3}\right) + 2 = x - 2 + 2 = x$.

You may want to check for yourself that $g(f(x)) = x$.

Topic 25: Exponentials and Logarithms

Among the most important examples of inverse functions are the *exponential and logarithmic functions*. For any constant $b > 0$ and $\neq 1$, the exponential functions $f(x) = b^x$ and $g(x) = \log_b x$ are inverse functions. That is, $\log_b b^x = x$ and $b^{\log_b x} = x$. That is, the logarithm is the exponent. b is called the base of the logarithm.

The two most frequently encountered bases are 10, the base for *common logarithms*, and e, the base for *natural logarithms*. You should know that the symbol $\log x$ with no base shown is assumed to be the logarithm to the base 10. The symbol $\ln x$ is used as shorthand for the natural logarithm. That is, $\ln x = \log_e x$. Thus, $\log 10^x = x$; $10^{\log x} = x$; $\ln e^x = x$; and $e^{\ln x} = x$.

The main properties of the exponential functional are determined by the laws of exponents. It is important to recognize that the relationships $b^k = N$ and $\log_b N = k$ are equivalent. That is, any relationship between the variables written in logarithmic form may be rewritten in exponential form, and vice versa.

Example 1

If $\log_x 125 = 3$. what is x?

Solution

This statement is equivalent to $x^3 = 125$, for which we can see by inspection that $x = 5$.

There are certain properties of the logarithm that you should know that also follow from the laws of exponents.

- $\log_b M + \log_b N = \log_b MN$

- $\log_b M - \log_b N = \log_b \dfrac{M}{N}$

- $\log_b\dfrac{1}{M} = -\log_b M$
- $k\log_b M = \log_b M^k$

You should also know that $\log_b 1 = 0$, and that the $\log_b M$ is only defined for positive values of M; that is, the log is undefined for zero or negative values.

Example 2

If $f(x) = 6^x$ and $g(x) = \log_6 x$ what expression is equal to $f(2g(M))$?

(F) $2M$
(G) 6^M
(H) M^6
(J) M^2
(K) 6^{2M}

Solution

The correct answer is (J). $2g(M) = 2\log_6 M = \log_6 M^2$. Hence, $f(2g(x)) = M^2$

GEOMETRY

Topic 26: Angles, Complements, and Supplements

An *angle* is formed when two *rays* originate from the same point. Angles are usually measured in *degrees* or *radians*. As on the ACT exam, we shall use only degree measure.

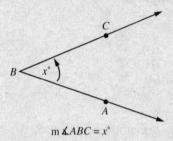

m∠ABC = x°

A *straight angle* has a measure of 180°. Any two angles that sum to a straight angle are called *supplementary*. Thus, two angles that measure 80° and 100° are supplementary.

Two equal supplementary angles are 90° each, and a 90° angle is called a *right angle*. Two angles that sum to a right angle are called *complementary*. Thus, 25° is the complement of 65°.

Angles less than 90° are called *acute,* and angles between 90° and 180° are called *obtuse*. The sum of all the angles around a given point must total to 360°.

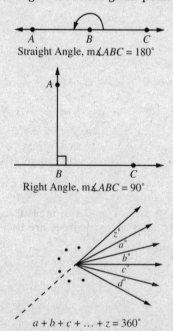

Straight Angle, m∠ABC = 180°

Right Angle, m∠ABC = 90°

$a + b + c + \ldots + z = 360°$

Example 1
Find x in the diagram below.

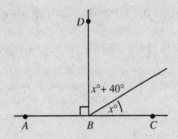

Solution
Since $\angle ABD$ is a right angle, so is $\angle DBC$. Thus, $x + (x + 40) = 90$. Removing parentheses: $x + x + 40 = 90$; $2x = 50$; $x = 25$.

Example 2
Find x in the diagram below.

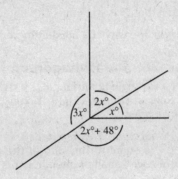

Solution
$8x + 48 = 360$; $8x = 312$; $x = 39$.

Topic 27: Properties of Triangles
The sum of the measures of the three angles in any triangle is 180°, which is the same as the measure of a straight angle. This fact is usually combined with other properties in the solution of geometric problems.

Example 1
In triangle ABC, the degree measure of $\angle B$ is 30° more than twice the degree measure of $\angle A$, and the measure of $\angle C$ is equal to the sum of the other two angles. How many degrees are there in the smallest angle of the triangle?

Solution
Calling the measure of $\angle A$ in degrees x, we have the following:

$$x = \text{number of degrees in } \angle A$$
$$2x + 30 = \text{number of degrees in } \angle B$$
$$x + (2x + 30) = \text{number of degrees in } \angle C$$

Summing, we have $x + 2x + 30 + 3x + 30 = 180$. Combining like terms:

$$6x + 60 = 180$$
$$6x = 120$$
$$x = 20.$$

Clearly, $2x + 30$ and $3x + 30$ are greater than x, so the smallest angle is $20°$.

In a triangle, the sum of the lengths of any two sides must exceed the length of the third. Thus, you cannot draw a triangle with sides of lengths 3, 6, 10, because $3 + 6 < 10$. In addition, in comparing any two sides, the longer side will be opposite the larger angle.

Example 2

A triangle has sides with lengths of 5, 12, and x. If x is an integer, what is the minimum possible perimeter of the triangle?

Solution

In any triangle, the sum of the lengths of any two sides must exceed the length of the third. Therefore, $x + 5 > 12$, which means that $x > 7$. The least integer greater than 7 is 8. Hence, the minimum possible perimeter is $5 + 12 + 8 = 25$.

Can you see why the maximum perimeter of this triangle is 33?

Topic 28: The Pythagorean Theorem

When one angle in a triangle is a right angle, the triangle is called a *right triangle*. The longest side of a right triangle, which is opposite the right angle, is called the *hypotenuse*.

The *Pythagorean Theorem* tells us that the square on the hypotenuse of a right triangle is equal to the sum of the squares on the other two sides (or *legs*). In symbols, we usually remember this as shown in the figure below.

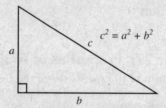

In practice, you should remember some well-known *Pythagorean Triples*, that is, sets of whole numbers such as 3-4-5 for which $a^2 + b^2 = c^2$. Right triangles whose sides correspond to the numbers that make up a Pythagorean Triple appear commonly on the ACT. Other less easily recognized Pythagorean Triples are 5-12-13, 8-15-17, and 7-24-25. In addition, look for multiples of the Triples, such as 6-8-10 or 15-20-25.

There are other important cases that yield non-integer solutions for the lengths of the sides of a right triangle. For example, the hypotenuse of a triangle with one leg of length 1 and the other of length 2 can be found by writing $c^2 = 1^2 + 2^2$. Thus, $c^2 = 5$ and $c = \sqrt{5}$.

Example 1
Find x in the diagram below.

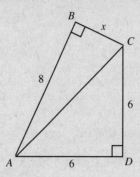

Solution
Using the Pythagorean Theorem in triangle ACD, the theorem tells us that $6^2 + 6^2 = c^2$. Hence $c^2 = 72$. In triangle ABC, letting x represent the length of BC, $72 = c^2 = x^2 + 8^2$. That is $x^2 = 72 - 64 = 8$. Thus, $x = \sqrt{8} = 2\sqrt{2}$.

Topic 29: The Area of a Triangle

FYI

For a right triangle, you can use the two legs as base and altitude. (By definition, they are always perpendicular to one another.) For example, the area of a 5-12-13 right triangle is $A = \frac{1}{2}(5)(12) = 30$ square units.

In any triangle, you can construct a line from one *vertex* (point) perpendicular to the opposite side. (Sometimes that side may have to be extended outside the triangle, as shown in the second case below.) This line is called the *altitude* or *height*. The area of a triangle is given by the formula $A = \frac{1}{2}bh$, where $b =$ the length of the base and $h =$ the length of the altitude.

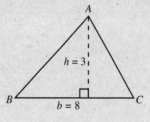

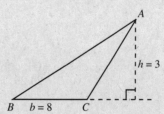

Both triangles shown in the diagram above have the same area: $A = \frac{1}{2}(8)(3) = 12$.

Example 1
In triangle ABC, $AB = 6$, $BC = 8$, and $AB = 10$. Find the altitude from vertex B to AC.

Solution

Since the sides are 6-8-10, the triangle is a disguised 3-4-5 right triangle with *AC* being the hypotenuse. Drawing the triangle as described produces the diagram below.

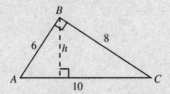

By using the two legs as base and height, the area of the triangle must be $A = \frac{1}{2}(6)(8) = 24$. By using the hypotenuse and the unknown altitude, the area must be $A = \frac{1}{2}(10)(h) = 5h$. Therefore, $5h = 24$, and $h = 4.8$.

Topic 30: Isosceles and Equilateral Triangles

A triangle with at least two sides of equal length is called an *isosceles triangle*. If all three sides are equal, it is called an *equilateral triangle*. The angles opposite the equal sides in an isosceles triangle (as shown in the diagram below) are equal in measure; thus, if two angles in a triangle are equal, the triangle is isosceles. If all three angles are equal, the triangle is equilateral. In particular, this tells us that for an equilateral triangle each angle has a degree measure of 60°.

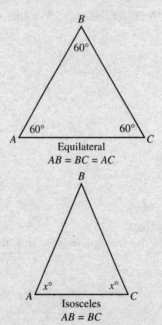

Here is a good example of how this fact can be used in a problem.

Example 1

If in triangle ABC, as shown in the figure below, $AC = BC$ and $x \leq 50$, what is the smallest possible value of y?

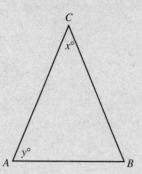

Solution

Since $\overline{AC}$ and $\overline{BC}$ are of equal length, the two base angles, m$\angle A$ and m$\angle B$ must be equal. As always, the three angles must total 180°. Hence, $x + 2y = 180$, which means that $y = \dfrac{180\text{-}x}{2} = 90 - \dfrac{1}{2}x$.

Now, the smallest possible value for y is achieved when x is as large as possible; that is, when $x = 50$, for which $y = 65$.

Example 2

In the triangle shown below, $AB = BC$. Which is longer, AC or AB?

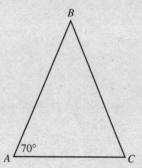

Note: Diagram not drawn to scale

Solution

Since the triangle is isosceles, the base angles are equal. Thus, m$\angle A$ = m$\angle C$ = 70°. This implies that m$\angle B$ = 40° (in order to reach the full 180° in the triangle). But that means that $AB > AC$, because it is the side opposite the larger angle.

Topic 31: Special Right Triangles

There are two special right triangles whose properties you should be familiar with. The first is the *isosceles right triangle*, also referred to as the *45°-45°-90° triangle*. By definition, its legs are of equal length, and its hypotenuse is $\sqrt{2}$ ·times as long as either leg.

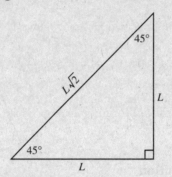

The other important right triangle is the *30°-60°-90° triangle*. You can see by dropping an altitude that this is half of an equilateral triangle. Hence, the shorter leg is half the hypotenuse, and the longer leg (the one opposite the 60° angle) is $\sqrt{3}$ times the shorter leg.

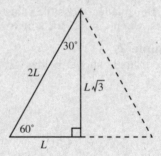

Example 1

Find the area of the region shown in the diagram below.

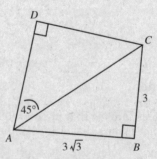

Solution

Since $BC = 3$ and $AB = 3\sqrt{3}$, we know that triangle ABC is a 30°-60°-90° right triangle. Hence, we know that $AC = 6$, and taking one-half the product of the legs, the triangle has an area of $\frac{1}{2}(3)(3\sqrt{3}) = \frac{9}{2}\sqrt{3}$.

Since triangle ADC is an isosceles right triangle with a hypotenuse of 6, each leg must be $\dfrac{6}{\sqrt{2}}$. Again, taking one-half the product of the legs, the triangle has an area of $\dfrac{1}{2}\left(\dfrac{6}{\sqrt{2}}\right)\left(\dfrac{6}{\sqrt{2}}\right) = \dfrac{36}{4} = 9$.

Adding the two areas, we have $9 + \dfrac{9}{2}\sqrt{3}$.

Topic 32: Vertical Angles Are Equal

When two lines intersect, two pairs of *vertical angles* are formed (as shown in the following diagram). The "facing" pairs are equal and, of course, the two angles that form a pair on one side of either line add up to $180°$.

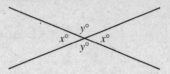

Example 1

In the diagram below, which is larger, $x + y$ or $w + z$?

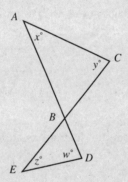

Solution

We know that the sum of the angles in any triangle is $180°$. Letting the measure of $\angle ABC$ be m, we have, in the upper triangle, $x + y = 180 - m$.

Similarly looking at the lower triangle, we know that $w + z = 180 - m$.

Therefore, $x + y = w + z$. The quantities named are equal.

Topic 33: Parallel Lines and Transversals

If you start with two lines parallel to one another and draw a line that crosses them, the crossing line is called a *transversal*. The intersection of the transversal with the parallel lines creates several sets of related angles. In particular, the *corresponding angles* (labelled *C* in the diagram below) and the *alternate interior angles* (labelled *A* in the diagram below) are always equal.

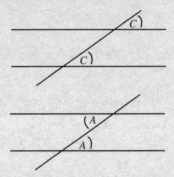

Combining these properties with your knowledge about vertical angles and the angles in a triangle can lead to interesting examples.

Example 1

In the diagram below, l_1 is parallel to l_2. Find x.

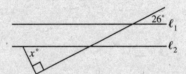

Solution

We'll label the diagram as shown below.

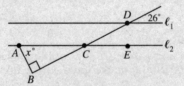

We see that m∠*DCE* = 26°, which makes m∠*ACB* = 26°. Since triangle *ABC* is a right triangle, x is the complement of 26°, or 64°.

Example 2

In the diagram below, l_1 is parallel to l_2. Find x.

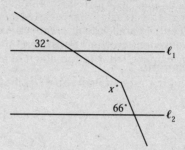

Solution

Extend $\overline{AB}$ as shown in the diagram below.

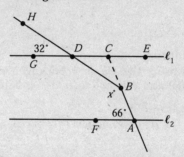

Look at the angles in triangle BCD. As alternate interior angles, m∠BCE = m∠BAF = 66°, so its supplement in the triangle, m∠C, must equal 114°. As vertical angles, m∠CDB = m∠HDG = 32°. Therefore, in the triangle, m∠D = 32°. Since the three angles in the triangle must sum to 180°, m∠B= 34°. x is the supplement to 34°—that is, 146°.

Topic 34: Rectangles, Parallelograms, and Other Polygons

Any geometric figure with straight line segments for sides is called a *polygon*. It is possible to draw a polygon with one or more interior angles greater than 180°, as illustrated in the figure below.

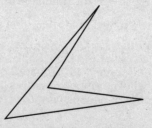

However, if all the interior angles in the polygon are less than 180°, we have a *convex polygon*. The sum of the angle measurements in any convex polygon is $180(n - 2)$, where n is the number of vertices. Thus, for a triangle, $n = 3$, and the sum is 180. For a *quadrilateral* (a four-sided figure), $n = 4$, and the sum is 360. For a *pentagon* (a five-sided figure), $n = 5$, and the angle sum is 540, and so on.

To find the *perimeter* of a polygon (the distance around the figure), simply add together the lengths of all the sides. Of course, it may require some thinking to determine each length.

To find its area, connect the vertices by line segments to divide the polygon into triangles; then sum the areas of these triangles.

Example 1

Find the area of figure *ABCDE* shown below.

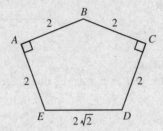

Solution

Drawing the $\overline{BE}$ and $\overline{BD}$ divides the region into three triangles as shown. Triangles *ABE* and *BCD* are both 45°-45°-90° right triangles, making $BE = BD = 2\sqrt{2}$.

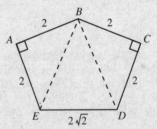

This makes the central triangle an equilateral triangle. The area of each of the two outer triangles is $\frac{1}{2}(2)(2) = 2$, so the two together have an area of 4. The center triangle has a base whose length is $2\sqrt{2}$. If you draw the altitude, you get a 30°-60°-90° right triangle with a shorter leg whose length is $\sqrt{2}$. This makes the height $\sqrt{3}$ times that, or $\sqrt{6}$. This gives an area of $\frac{1}{2}(2\sqrt{2})(\sqrt{6}) = \sqrt{12} = 2\sqrt{3}$. Hence, the total area of the polygon is $4 + 2\sqrt{3}$.

A *parallelogram* is a quadrilateral in which the pairs of opposite sides are parallel. The opposite angles in a parallelogram are equal, and the opposite sides are of equal length (see the figure below).

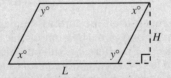

The area of a parallelogram is determined by its length times its height; that is, $A = LH$, as labelled in the diagram.

If the angles in the parallelogram are right angles, we have a *rectangle*. For a rectangle of length L and width W, the area is $A = LW$, and the perimeter is $P = 2L + 2W$.

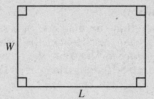

For example, the area of a rectangular garden that is 20 yards long and 10 yards deep is $(20)(10) = 200$ square yards. However, to put a fence around the same garden (that is, around its perimeter) requires $2(20) + 2(10) = 60$ running yards of fencing. These relatively easy formulas can lead to some tricky questions.

Example 2

If sod comes in 4×4 foot squares costing \$3.50 per square, how much will it cost to sod the lawn shown below (all distances indicated in feet)? You may assume that all angles that appear to be right angles are right angles.

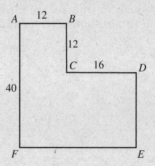

Solution

Completing the rectangle as shown in the figure below, we see that the large rectangle *AGEF* is $40 \times 28 = 1{,}120$ square feet.

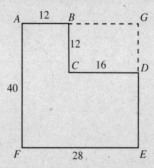

The smaller rectangle *BGDC* is $12 \times 16 = 192$ square feet. Hence, the area that must be sodded is $1{,}120 - 192 = 928$ square feet. Now, each 4×4 foot piece of sod is 16 square feet. Therefore, we need $928 \div 16 = 58$ squares of sod at \$3.50 each. The total cost is $(58)(3.50) = \$203$.

Example 3

A rectangle has one side whose length is 6 and a diagonal whose length is 10. What is its perimeter?

Solution

Notice that the diagonal of a rectangle divides the rectangle into two identical right triangles. Hence, the other side of this rectangle can be found by the Pythagorean Theorem. We recognize that side 6 and diagonal 10 implies that we have a 6-8-10 right triangle, so the unknown side is 8. The perimeter is, therefore, $2(6) + 2(8) = 28$.

Topic 35: Basic Properties of Circles

A line segment from the center of a circle to any point on the circle is called a *radius* (plural *radii*). All radii of the same circle are equal in length. A line segment that passes through the center of the circle and cuts completely across the circle is called a *diameter*. A diameter is, of course, twice as long as any radius. Thus, $d = 2r$.

Any line cutting across a circle is called a *chord,* and no chord can be longer than the diameter. A portion of a circle is called an *arc*. Any arc has a degree measure that equals the measure of the *central angle* (an angle whose vertex is the center of the circle) subtended by it, as shown in the figure below.

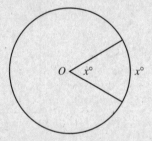

Example 1

If the arc PS in the diagram below has a degree measure of 62°, is the chord $\overline{PS}$ longer or shorter than the radius of the circle?

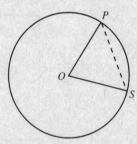

Solution

Since all radii are equal, triangle OPS is isosceles, and the angles at P and S must be equal. Suppose each is x. Now, $2x + 62 = 180$. Hence, $x = 59$. Therefore, PS is opposite the greatest angle in the triangle and must be the longest side. That is, PS is longer than a radius.

Topic 36: The Area and Circumference of a Circle

The distance around a circle (analogous to the perimeter of a polygon) is its *circumference*. For any circle of radius r, the circumference is given by the formula $C = 2\pi r$; that is, the circumference equals twice the radius times π (a constant, designated by the Greek letter pi, whose value is approximately 3.1415 or $\frac{22}{7}$).

The area of the same circle is given by the formula $A = \pi r^2$; that is, the area equals pi times the radius squared.

Example 1

Find the area of the shaded region shown in the diagram below. (The curved side is a *semicircle*; that is, an arc equal to half a complete circle.)

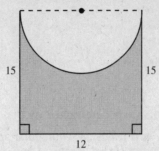

Solution

The dotted line completes the rectangle, whose area is $12 \times 15 = 180$ square units. The radius of the arc must be 6, since its diameter is 12. The area of the whole circle would be $\pi r^2 = \pi(6^2) = 36\pi$. Hence, the area of the semi-circle is half of that, or 18π. Subtracting, the area of the shaded region is $180 - 18\pi$.

Example 2

The larger circle shown in the diagram below has an area of 36π. Find the circumference of the smaller circle.

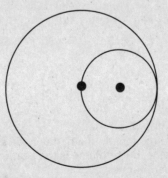

Solution

The larger circle has an area of $A_L = \pi(r)^2 = 36\pi$. This means that $r^2 = 36$, and $r = 6$. The diameter of the smaller circle equals the radius of the larger one, so its radius is $\frac{1}{2}(6) = 3$. Therefore, its circumference must be $2\pi(3) = 6\pi$.

Topic 37: Volumes

A solid (three-dimensional) figure with straight line edges and flat surfaces is called a *polyhedron*. The surfaces bounding the solid are called *faces*. The edges of a polyhedron have lengths; its faces have areas; and the entire figure has a *surface area*, which is the sum of the areas of all its faces.

A solid figure also has a *volume*. Volumes are expressed in cubic units. You should be familiar with the following formulas for volumes of polyhedrons:

- A *rectangular solid* is a polyhedron with rectangular faces at right angles to one another (think of a typical cardboard box, like a shoebox.)

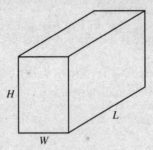

Its volume is determined by the formula $V = LWH =$ Lenghth $\times$ Width $\times$ Height.

- A *cube* is a rectangular solid with all edges of equal length; that is $L = W = H = s$. (Think of one die from a pair of dice.) Its volume is determined by the formula $V = s^3$

- A *right circular cylinder* is a solid with a circular base and a side perpendicular to that base (think of a soda can.) Its volume is the area of the base times the height, or $V = \pi r^2 h$.

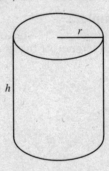

Example 1

Find the length of a rectangular solid with a height of 6 that is twice as long as it is wide, if its volume is the same as that of a cube with a total surface area of 864 square inches.

Solution

Let x = the width of the rectangular solid. Now, $2x$ = length. The volume of the rectangular solid is $V = 6(x)(2x) = 12x^2$.

Since the cube has six square faces, its total surface area is 6 times the area of one face. In symbols, $6s^2 = 864$, and $s = 12$. Hence, the volume of the cube is $12^3 = 1,728$. Since the two solids have the same volume:

$$12x^2 = 1728; \; x = 12$$

The length of the rectangular solid, which is twice the width, is thus 24.

Example 2
Which has the greater volume, a rectangular solid that is 6 feet long and has a square base with sides 4 feet long, or a cylinder with a length of 7 feet and a diameter of 4 feet?

Solution
The volume of the rectangular solid is $V = (4)(4)(6) = 96$ square feet. The radius of the cylinder is 2, so its volume is: $V_C = \pi(2)^2(7) = 28\pi$.

Since $\pi \approx \dfrac{22}{7}$, $28\pi \approx 88$. Therefore, the rectangular solid is larger.

Topic 38: Right Triangle Trigonometry
The usual convention is to label the angles of a right triangle A, B, and C, with C as the right angle. We then label the sides opposite the respective angles as a, b, and c, as shown in the figure below.

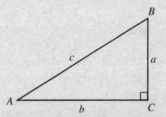

The *trigonometric functions* of the acute angles are then defined in terms of the ratios of the lengths of the sides. For angle A, we have:

$$\sin A = \frac{a}{c}$$

$$\cos A = \frac{b}{c}$$

$$\tan A = \frac{a}{b}$$

$$\cot A = \frac{b}{a}$$

$$\sec A = \frac{c}{b}$$

$$\csc A = \frac{c}{a}$$

The trigonometric functions for angle B are defined similarly. The important things to remember are:

$$\text{sine} = \frac{\text{opposite}}{\text{hypotenuse}}$$

$$\text{cosine} = \frac{\text{adjacent}}{\text{hypotenuse}}$$

$$\text{tangent} = \frac{\text{opposite}}{\text{adjacent}}$$

It is convenient to also know that for any angle x, $\tan x = \frac{\sin x}{\cos x}$.

The other trigonometric functions can be found by using the following simple identities:

$$\cot x = \frac{1}{\tan x}$$

$$\csc x = \frac{1}{\sin x}$$

$$\sec x = \frac{1}{\cos x}$$

These relationships between sides and angles make possible the solution of many interesting problems.

Example 1

A 60-foot-long guy wire is attached to the top of a 45-foot pole, as shown in the figure below. Using the table of values given below, which of the following is closest to the angle the wire makes with the ground?

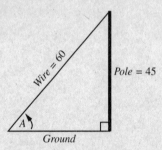

Angle	Sin	Cos	Tan
41	0.6561	0.7547	0.8693
42	0.6691	0.7431	0.9004
43	0.682	0.7314	0.9325
44	0.6947	0.7193	0.9657
45	0.7071	0.7071	1
46	0.7193	0.6947	1.0355
47	0.7314	0.682	1.0723
48	0.7431	0.6691	1.1106
49	0.7547	0.6561	1.1504
50	0.766	0.6428	1.1918

(A)　49°
(B)　47°
(C)　45°
(D)　43°
(E)　41°

Solution

The correct answer is (A). Using the relationship $\sin A = \dfrac{a}{c}$ with $a = 45$ and $c =$ 60, we have $\sin A = \dfrac{45}{60} = \dfrac{3}{4} = 0.75$. Referring to the table, we see that $\sin 49° = .7547$, which is the closest among the four choices. Hence, choice (A) is correct.

Example 2

A vertical pole casts a shadow 50 feet long when the sun is at an angle of elevation of 42°, as shown in the figure below. Using the table on the preceding page, what is the height of the pole to the nearest foot?

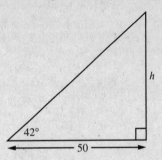

(F) 55
(G) 50
(H) 45
(J) 40
(K) 35

Solution

The correct answer is (H). Calling the unknown height h, we have $\tan A = \dfrac{h}{50}$.

From the table, we see that $\tan 42° = 0.9004$; multiplying by 50, we have $h = 50(0.9004) = 45.02$, or 45 feet to the nearest foot.

COORDINATE GEOMETRY

Topic 39: The Midpoint Formula

Given two points $P(x_1,y_1)$ and $Q(x_2,y_2)$, the *midpoint M* of the $\overline{PQ}$ has the following coordinates:

$$x_M = \frac{x_1 + x_2}{2}$$

$$y_M = \frac{y_1 + y_2}{2}$$

In words, to find the coordinates of the midpoint of a line segment, simply average the coordinates of the end points. For example, the midpoint between (3,4) and (2,−2) is

$$x_M = \frac{3 + 2}{2} = \frac{5}{2}$$

$$y_M = \frac{4 + (-2)}{2} = \frac{2}{2} = 1.$$

Hence, the midpoint is $\left(\frac{5}{2}, 1\right) = (2.5, 1)$.

Example 1

If (2,6) is the midpoint of the line segment connecting (−1,3) to $P(x,y)$, which is greater, $2x$ or y?

Solution

We know that the average of x and −1 must be 2. That is, $2 = \frac{x + (-1)}{2}$, or $4 = x - 1$; $x = 5$.

Similarly, we know that the average of y and 3 must be 6. Thus, $6 = \frac{y + 3}{2}$, or $12 = y + 3$; $y = 9$.

Since $2x = 10$, $2x > y$.

Example 2

If $b < 6$, is $(3,b)$ closer to $P(0,2)$ or $Q(6,10)$?

Solution

We see that (3,6) is the midpoint of $\overline{PQ}$. Therefore, in the x-direction, $(3,b)$ will be equidistant from both P and Q. However, if $b < 6$, then b must be closer to 2 than to 10. Therefore, $(3,b)$ is closer to (0,2) than to (6,10).

Topic 40: The Distance Formula and Equations for Circles

Given two points $P(x_1,y_1)$ and $Q(x_2,y_2)$ the distance from P to Q is given by the formula:

$$d = \sqrt{(x_1 - x_2)^2 + (y_1 - y_2)^2}$$

In words, the distance is the square root of the sum of the change in x squared plus the change in y squared. This can be symbolized as follows:

$$d = \sqrt{(\Delta x)^2 + (\Delta y)^2}$$

For example, the distance from $(6,3)$ to $(3,-1)$ is $d = \sqrt{(6-3)^2 + (3-(-1))^2}$ Thus:

$$d = \sqrt{3^2 + 4^2} = \sqrt{9 + 16} = \sqrt{25} = 5$$

Example 1

The point $(4,t)$ is equidistant from points $(1,1)$ and $(5,3)$. What is the value of t?

Solution

Since the distances from the two given points are the same, we use the distance formula twice and equate the results, thus:

$$\sqrt{(4-1)^2 + (t-1)^2} = \sqrt{(5-4)^2 + (3-t)^2}$$

$$\sqrt{9 + (t^2 - 2t + 1)} = \sqrt{1 + (9 - 6t + t^2)}$$

$$\sqrt{10 - 2t + t^2} = \sqrt{10 - 6t + t^2}$$

Squaring both sides:

$$10 - 2t + t^2 = 10 - 6t + t^2$$

Subtracting $t^2 + 10$ from both sides leaves:

$$-2t = -6t$$
$$4t = 0$$
$$t = 0$$

Since all points on a circle are equidistant from its center, you can use the distance formula to prove that the equation for a circle whose radius is r and whose center is at the origin is $x^2 + y^2 = r^2$.

Similarly, the equation for a circle whose radius is r and whose center is at (h,k) is $(x - h)^2 + (y - k)^2 = r^2$.

Example 2

The point $(t,-1)$ lies on a circle whose radius is 5 and whose center is at $(4,2)$. What are the possible values of t?

Solution

Since every point on the circle must be 5 units from the center, we know that $(t,-1)$ must be 5 units from $(4,2)$. Using the equation for the circle with $h = 4$ and $k = 2$, and $r = 5$, we have:

$$(x - 4)^2 + (y - 2)^2 = 25$$

Letting $x = t$ and $y = -1$:

$$(t - 4)^2 + (-1-2)^2 = 25$$

Expanding, we have:

$$t^2 - 8t + 16 + 9 = 25$$

We subtract 25 from both sides to yield:

$$t^2 - 8t = 0$$

This factors as $t(t - 8) = 0$, with two possible solutions, $t = 0$ or $t = 8$.

Topic 41: Slope of a Line

Given two points $P(x_1,y_1)$ and $Q(x_2,y_2)$, the *slope* of the line passing through P and Q is given by the formula:

$$M = \frac{y_1 - y_2}{x_1 - x_2}$$

In words, this says that the slope is the change in y divided by the change in x, or $M = \dfrac{\Delta y}{\Delta x}$.

For example, the slope of the line passing through (6,4) to (3,−1) is $\dfrac{4-(-1)}{6 - 3} = \dfrac{5}{3}$.

(Notice that it doesn't matter which point you consider the first point and which the second, as long as you are consistent in the numerator and denominator of the fraction. Try it!)

Example 1

The points $(-1,-1)$, $(3,11)$, and $(1,t)$ lie on the same line. What is the value of t?

Solution

Since the slope of a line is the same for any two points on the line, and since $M = \dfrac{y_1 - y_2}{x_1 - x_2}$ using $(-1,-1)$ and $(3,11)$, we must have:

$$M = \frac{11 - (-1)}{3 - (-1)} = \frac{12}{4} = 3.$$

Now, using the pair $(-1,-1)$ and $(1,t)$, $3 = \dfrac{t - (-1)}{1 - (-1)} = \dfrac{t + 1}{2}$.

Multiplying by 2, $6 = t + 1$; $t = 5$.

Topic 42: Equations of Lines

The equation that defines a straight line is usually remmbered as $y = mx + b$, where m is the slope and b is the y-intercept. When $m = 0$, we have the equation $y = b$, which has as its graph a horizontal straight line crossing the y-axis at $(0,b)$. The exceptional case is the vertical line, which is defined by the equation $x = a$, where a is the common x-value of all the points on the line. (Of course, $x = 0$ is the y-axis, and, naturally, $y = 0$ is the x-axis.)

Parallel lines have the same slope, and perpendicular lines (other than the vertical and horizontal case) have slopes that are negative reciprocals.

Example 1

Find the equation of a straight line parallel to the line with equation $y = 2x - 5$ that passes through the point $(-1,4)$.

Solution

By inspection, the given line has slope 2. Any line parallel to it must also have slope 2, and, therefore, must have equation $y = 2x + b$. To determine b, we use the fact that any point that lies on the line must satisfy the equation. Therefore, substituting the coordinates of the point $(-1,4)$ into the equation must yield a correct equation. Thus:

$$4 = 2(-1) + b; 4 = -2 + b; b = 6$$

The equation is $y = 2x + 6$.

Example 2

Find the equation of a straight line perpendicular to the line with equation $y = \frac{2}{3}x - 4$ that has y-intercept 9.

Solution

The given line has slope $\frac{2}{3}$. Any line perpendicular to it must have as its slope the negative reciprocal of $\frac{2}{3}$, that is, $-\frac{3}{2}$. Since the line we want has y-intercept 9, its equation must be $y = -\frac{3}{2}x + 9$. It is possible to multiply this equation by 2 to get $2y = -3x + 18$, which could also be written $3x + 2y = 18$.

Example 3

Find the equation of the line that is the perpendicular bisector of the line segment connecting points $P(-1,-1)$ and $Q(3,5)$.

Solution

$\overline{PQ}$ has a slope of $M = \dfrac{5 - (-1)}{3 - (-1)} = \dfrac{4}{4} = 1$.

Hence, the perpendicular bisector must have as its slope the negative reciprocal of 1, which is -1. Thus, its equation must be $y = -x + b$. Since the line bisects the segment, it must pass through the midpoint of $\overline{PQ}$, which we find by averaging the coordinates of the endpoints to get $(1,2)$. Substituting: $2 = -1 + b$; $b = 3$, and the equation is $y = -x + 3$.

Topic 43: Systems of Equations with Non-Unique Solutions

As we mentioned above, any equation of the form $Ax + By = C$ is the equation of a straight line because (unless $B = 0$), it can be rewritten in the form $y = mx + b$ by using algebra. Hence, when you try to solve two linear equations with two unknowns simultaneously, you could think of the process as trying to find the coordinates of the point of intersection of two lines.

Of course, a problem arises if the two lines have the same slope. In such a situation, there are two possibilities. The first is that the lines are parallel and have no point of intersection. In that case, the equations are called *inconsistent* (or *incompatible*) and there is *no* solution.

The other possibility is that the two equations are really two different forms of the same equation. In that case, you have only one line and there is an infinite number of solutions; any point (x,y) that lies on the line is at the "intersection" of the two (identical) lines.

Example 1

A certain store sells blouses and skirts at a fixed price regardless of style or size. Marla bought 4 blouses and 6 skirts and was charged $380 before taxes. Arlene went to the same store; she bought 2 blouses and 3 skirts and was charged $195 before taxes. What was the price of a blouse?

Solution

Letting b = the price of a blouse and s = the price of a skirt, we have for Marla $4b + 6s = 380$, and for Arlene $2b + 3s = 195$.

If we multiply the second equation by -2 and add it to the first, we have:

$$\begin{array}{r} 4b + 6s = 380 \\ -4b - 6s = -390 \\ \hline 0 = -10 \end{array}$$

But this is impossible! This means that the two equations represent parallel lines, and there is no solution. Someone must have made a mistake in calculating either Marla's or Arlene's bill, so there is no correct way to answer the question as posed.

Example 2

Juan has a package containing some 2¢ stamps and some 5¢ stamps with a total value of 62¢. If Juan had 3 more than twice as many 2¢ stamps as he now has, and twice as many 5¢ stamps, the assortment would be worth $1.30. What is the greatest number of 5¢ stamps Juan may have?

Solution

Let x be the number of 2's and y be the number of 5's. Expressing the given information in cents, we have $2x + 5y = 62$ and $2(2x + 3) + 5(2y) = 130$.

Expanding the second equation:

$$\begin{array}{r} 4x + 6 + 10y = 130 \\ 4x + 10y = 124 \end{array}$$

If we attempt to solve by elimination, we can multiply the first equation by -2 and add it to the second equation:

$$-4x - 10y = -124$$
$$\underline{4x + 10y = 124}$$
$$0 = 0$$

It is certainly true that $0 = 0$, but it is not much help! Actually, we see that the second equation is simply double the first. So really we have two equations—two definitions of the same line—yielding an infinite number of solutions.

However, the question posed can be answered. Since the nature of the given information implies that both x and y must be positive integers (there is no way to have a *negative* number of stamps), the greatest possible value of y is when $x = 1$, for which $y = 12$.

Topic 44: Parabolas and Quadratic Equations

The graph of the quadratic function $y = ax^2 + bx + c$ is a *parabola*. Visually, the graph of a parabola will "open up" if $a > 0$, and will "open down" if $a < 0$. In either case, the *vertex* or turning point of the parabola will be found at $x = \dfrac{-b}{2a}$, and the curve will be symmetrical with respect to the line $x = \dfrac{-b}{2a}$.

Naturally, there is a strong relationship between the graph and the solution to the equation $ax^2 + bx + c = 0$, which must be solved to find the x-intercepts of the graph.

If the equation has two real distinct roots, then the curve crosses the x-axis at two points. If there are two identical roots, then that value will be the x-coordinate of the vertex, and the curve will be tangent to the axis at that point. If the roots are both complex, then the curve will never cross the x-axis.

Example 1
Find the coordinates of the vertex of the parabola $y = x^2 - 4x + 3$.

Solution
The x-coordinate of the vertex is $x = -\dfrac{b}{2a} = -\dfrac{4}{2(1)} = 2$.

Substituting, the y-coodinate is $y = (2)^2 - 4(2) + 3 = -1$. Hence, the vertex is $(2, -1)$.

Just for the sake of completeness, you should see that the curve opens up (because $a = 1$) and that it has y-intercept $(0,3)$ and x-intercepts $(1,0)$ and $(3,0)$. The graph is shown below.

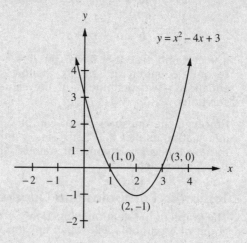

Example 2

Find the x-intercepts and coordinates of the vertex for the parabola $y = -2x^2 - 4x + 6$.

Solution

Finding the x-intercepts means finding the values of x for which $y = 0$; that is, the roots of the equation $-2x^2 - 4x + 6 = 0$.

Dividing by -2, we have $x^2 + 2x - 3 = 0$, which factors as $(x - 1)(x + 3) = 0$. Therefore, $x = 1$ and $x = -3$. The x-intercepts are $(1,0)$ and $(-3,0)$. The x-coordinate of the vertex is $x = -\dfrac{b}{2a} = -\dfrac{-4}{2(-2)} = -1$.

By substitution, the y-value is 8. Hence, the coordinates are $(-1,8)$. It is not an accident that the x-coordinate of the vertex falls halfway between the roots. That is a result of the symmetry of the curve. Again, for the sake of completeness, the graph is shown below. Notice that it opens down because $a = -2$.

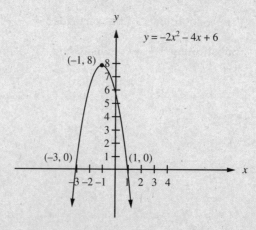

Topic 45: Trigonometric Graphs

FYI

You should recognize the following common angles: $30° = \dfrac{\pi}{6}$; $45° = \dfrac{\pi}{4}$; $60° = \dfrac{\pi}{3}$; $90° = \dfrac{\pi}{2}$; $180° = \pi$; $270° = \dfrac{3\pi}{2}$; and $360° = 2\pi$.

The trigonometric functions all have graphs. In particular, you should be comfortable with the sine and cosine curves. Remember that when you look at a function of the form:

$$y = A \sin kx \text{ or } y = A \cos kx$$

x should be expressed in *radian* measure.

To convert degrees to radians, divide by 180 and multiply by π.

The number A is called the *amplitude* of the curve, and $|A|$ is the maximum value that y reaches. ($-|A|$ is the minimum.) k is called the *frequency* and tells how many full cycles are completed in the interval $[0,2\pi]$.

The graphs below illustrate two possibilities.

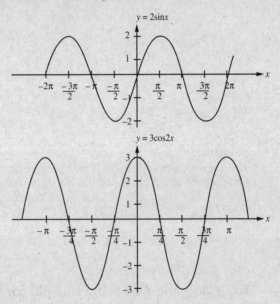

Example 1

What is the least possible positive value of x for which $4\cos 2x = 2$?

(A) $\dfrac{\pi}{12}$

(B) $\dfrac{\pi}{6}$

(C) $\dfrac{\pi}{4}$

(D) $\dfrac{\pi}{3}$

(E) $\dfrac{\pi}{2}$

Solution

The correct answer is (B). Referring to the graph, we know that the cosine curve starts at its maximum value at $x = 0$ and decreases thereafter until it reaches -1, when $x = \pi$. Since the amplitude of our curve is 4, we want to know when it reaches half its maximum; that is, we want to solve $\cos 2x = \frac{1}{2}$. Since $\cos 60° = \frac{1}{2}$ and $60° = \frac{\pi}{3}$, we want $2x = \frac{\pi}{3}$ or $x = \frac{\pi}{6}$.

Example 2

For which value of b will the graph of $y = \sin 4x$ complete 3 full cycles in the interval $[0, b]$?

(F) $\dfrac{\pi}{4}$

(G) $\dfrac{\pi}{2}$

(H) $\dfrac{3\pi}{4}$

(J) π

(K) $\dfrac{3\pi}{2}$

Solution

The correct answer is (K). The function has a frequency of 4. Therefore, it will complete four full cycles in the interval $[0, 2\pi]$. Hence, it will complete three full cycles in $\frac{3}{4}$ of that time, and $\frac{3}{4}(2\pi) = \frac{3\pi}{2}$.

OTHER TOPICS

Topic 46: The Addition Principle for Counting

If a set A has m elements, and a set B has n elements, and the two sets have no elements in common, then the total number of elements in the two sets combined is $m + n$. But if there are k elements common to the two sets, then the total in the combined set is $m + n - k$. In other words, when summing the two sets, you must take into account the double counting of elements common to both groups.

This kind of situation is usually handled most easily by displaying the given information in a Venn Diagram, as shown in the examples that follow.

Example 1

Helena applied to 12 colleges for admission. Sergei applied to 10. Between them they applied to 16 different colleges. How many colleges received applications from both students?

Solution

Let H be the set of colleges to which Helena applied, and let S be those to which Sergei applied. Letting x be the number that are common to both sets, the diagram shown below displays the data.

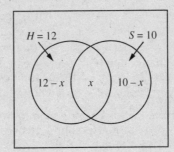

The central region is that common to both sets, and we can see that the total is $(12 - x) + x + (10 - x) = 16$. Removing parentheses and combining like terms, we have $22 - x = 16$; $x = 6$.

Example 2

A survey of voters shows that 43% listen to radio news reports, 45% listen to TV news reports, and 36% read a daily newspaper. What is the maximum possible percent that do all three?

Solution

If the three sets were totally disjointed, that is, had no overlap, the sum of the percentages would be 100%. The extent of various kinds of overlap will show up as an excess over 100%. Everyone in two of the three categories will be counted twice, and everyone in all three categories will be counted three times.

If we total $43 + 45 + 36$, we find that we have accounted for 124% of the voters, a 24% overcount. Therefore, the number common to all three cannot be greater than one-third of that, or 8%. This maximum of 8% is reached only if no one falls into two out of three categories, so that the entire overcount is the result of people in all three categories.

Topic 47: The Multiplication Principle for Counting

Suppose a process can be broken down into two steps. If the first step can be performed in m ways, and if, for each of those ways, the second step can be performed in n ways, then the total number of ways of performing the operation is $T = mn$. This is known as the *multiplication principle for counting*.

For example, suppose that a jar contains five blocks of different colors. We pick a block, record the color, and then pick a second block without replacing the first. The number of possible color combinations is $(5)(4) = 20$, since there are five possible colors to be drawn from in the first step and four possible colors in the second step. This process extends to more than two steps in the natural way.

Example 1

The diagram shown below is a road map from Abbottsville to Cartersburg.

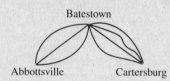

Batestown

Abbottsville   Cartersburg

How many different routes can you follow to drive from Abbottsville to Cartersburg if you go through Batestown only once?

Solution

You have 3 choices for a road from Abbottsville to Batestown and 4 roads from Batestown to Cartersburg. Hence, by the multiplication principle, the total number of routes is $3 \times 4 = 12$.

Example 2

How many different 3-digit license plate numbers can you form if the first digit cannot be 0?

Solution

By the natural extension of the multiplication principle to a three-step process, we see that you have 9 choices for the first digit (1, 2, 3 . . . 9), 10 choices for the second digit (0, 1, 2 . . . 9), and the same 10 choices for the third digit. Thus, the total is $9 \times 10 \times 10 = 900$.

As a natural extension of the multiplication principle, it is not hard to show that the number of distinct arrangements of n distinguishable objects in a row is n *factorial* calculated as follows:

$$n! = n(n-1)(n-2) \ldots (2)(1)$$

For example, there are $4! = 4 \times 3 \times 2 \times 1 = 24$ ways of arranging the four symbols, ♣, ♦, ♥, and ♠ in a straight line.

Example 1

If the five starting members of a basketball team are lined up randomly for a photograph, what is the chance that they will be in order of height from shortest to tallest, left to right?

Solution

There are 5 distinguishable people, who can be arranged in $5! = 5 \times 4 \times 3 \times 2 \times 1 = 120$ ways. In only one of these ways will they be in the correct order. Therefore, the chance is $\frac{1}{120}$.

Example 2

In how many ways can 3 men and 3 women be seated in theater seats if the seating must alternate men and women, starting with a woman?

Solution

The 3 women can be arranged in the first, third, and fifth seats in $3! = 6$ ways. However, for each of these possibilities, the 3 men can be seated in the remaining seats in $3! = 6$ ways. Hence, there are $6 \times 6 = 36$ ways altogether.

Topic 48: Probability

To find the probability of an event, divide the number of outcomes favorable to the event by the total number of possible outcomes. For example, if a bag contains 12 blue marbles and 9 red marbles, the probability that a marble selected at random is blue is the number of blue marbles divided by the total number of marbles, which is $\frac{12}{21} = \frac{4}{7}$.

Example: A box contains five blocks numbered 1, 2, 3, 4, and 5. Johnnie picks a block and replaces it. Lisa then picks a block. What is the probability that the sum of the numbers they picked is even?

Solution

Since each had 5 choices, there are 25 possible pairs of numbers. The only way the sum could be odd is if one person picked an odd number and the other picked an even number. Suppose that Johnnie chose the odd number and Lisa the even one. Johnnie had 3 possible even numbers to select from, and for each of these, Lisa had 2 possible choices, for a total of $(3)(2) = 6$ possibilities. However, you could also have had Johnnie pick an even number and Lisa pick an odd one, and there are also 6 ways to do that. Hence, out of 25 possibilities, 12 have an odd total and 13 have an even total. The probability of an even total, then, is $\frac{13}{25}$.

Topic 49: Arithmetic and Geometric Progressions

A sequence of numbers $a_1, a_2, a_3, \ldots, a_n$ is said to form an *arithmetic progression* if there is a constant (unchanging) difference between successive terms. That is, calling this difference d, we have $a_{k+1} = a_k + d$ for $k = 1, 2, 3, \ldots$ This means that we can write $a_k = a_1 + (k-1)d$. Usually, for simplicity, we write simply a for a_1 and write:

$$a_k = a + (k-1)d$$

The last (nth) term of the sequence is frequently abbreviated $L = a + (k-1)d$

The sum of the terms in the progression is then the average of the first and last terms times the number of terms. As a formula:

$$S = n\left(\frac{a+L}{2}\right)$$

or:

$$S = n\left(\frac{2a + (n-1)d}{2}\right)$$

Example 1

What is the sum of the first ten terms of the sequence $-5, -2, 1, 4, \ldots$?

(A) 17.5
(B) 22
(C) 40.5
(D) 85
(E) 135

Solution

The correct answer is (D). The first term is -5. The common difference, $d = 3$. Hence, the tenth (last) term is $-5 + 9(3) = 22$, and the first and last terms average 8.5. Therefore, the sum is $10(8.5) = 85$.

A sequence of numbers $a_1, a_2, a_3, \ldots, a_n$ is said to form a *geometric progression* if each term is a constant multiple of the preceding one. That is, the ratio of successive terms is a constant. Calling the common ratio r, we have $a_{k+1} = a_k r$ for $k = 1, 2, 3, \ldots$ which means that we can write $a_k = a_1 r^{k-1}$. *Usually, for simplicity, we use a for a_1 and write:*

$$a^k = ar^{k-1} \text{ for } k = 1, 2, 3, \ldots, n$$

The last (nth) term is $a^n = ar^{n-1}$. The sum of the terms in the progression is given by the formula:

$$S = a\left(\frac{1 - r^n}{1 - r}\right)$$

Example 2

If the fourth term of a geometric progression is 5 and the seventh term is -40, what is the sum of the first five terms?

(F) $\dfrac{-55}{8}$

(G) $\dfrac{19}{8}$

(H) 3

(J) $\dfrac{33}{8}$

(K) $\dfrac{55}{8}$

Solution

The correct answer is (F). If the fourth term is 5 and the seventh term is -40, we have two equations: $ar^3 = 5$ and $ar^6 = -40$.

Dividing the second by the first, we have:

$$\frac{ar^6}{ar^3} = \frac{-40}{5}; r^3 = -8.$$

This yields $r = -2$. Since $ar^3 = 5$ and $r^3 = -8$, $a = \dfrac{-5}{8}$. The sum of the first five terms, then, is:

$$S = -\frac{5}{8}\left[\frac{1 - (-2)^5}{1 - (-2)}\right] = -\frac{5}{8}\left(\frac{33}{3}\right) = -\frac{55}{8}.$$

Topic 50: Matrices

A *matrix* (plural *matrices*) is a rectangular array of numbers. The rows of the matrix are numbered from top to bottom, and the columns are numbered from left to right. Matrices with the same "shape," that is, having the same numbers of rows and columns, can be added and subtracted by adding or subtracting like entries in their positions.

Example 1
Find the sum of these two matrices:

$$A = \begin{pmatrix} 2 & 6 \\ 3 & -1 \end{pmatrix}$$

$$B = \begin{pmatrix} 4 & 0 \\ 2 & 1 \end{pmatrix}$$

Solution
The two matrices are both the same shape (2×2), and we can simply add the entries to get:

$$A + B = \begin{pmatrix} 6 & 6 \\ 5 & 0 \end{pmatrix}$$

To multiply a matrix A by a *scalar* (number) k, multiply every entry in A by k. For example:

$$3 \begin{pmatrix} 2 & 6 \\ 3 & -1 \end{pmatrix} = \begin{pmatrix} 6 & 18 \\ 9 & -3 \end{pmatrix}$$

To form the product of two matrices, you need to know how to form the product of a row matrix and a column matrix. The product, RC, of a row matrix R with a column matrix C can be defined only if the number of entries in each is the same. When this occurs, the product is a number which is the sum of the products of the respective entries.

For example, if $R = (1\ 2\ 3)$ and $C = \begin{pmatrix} 4 \\ 5 \\ 6 \end{pmatrix}$,

then

$$RC = (1\ 2\ 3) \begin{pmatrix} 4 \\ 5 \\ 6 \end{pmatrix} = (1)(4) + (2)(5) + (3)(6) = 32$$

Given two matrices A, which is $m \times n$, and B, which is $n \times p$, their product, AB, can be formed because the number of columns in the first matrix is equal to the number of rows in the second. The resulting matrix will be $m \times p$, and the entry in row number i, column number j in the product is the product of row i of A and column j of B.

Example 2

If $A = \begin{pmatrix} 2 & 6 \\ 3 & -1 \end{pmatrix}$ and $B = \begin{pmatrix} 4 & 3 & -2 \\ 2 & 1 & 5 \end{pmatrix}$ then the entry in the second row, third column of AB will be

(F) -11
(G) -1
(H) 1
(J) 11
(K) 20

Solution

The correct answer is (F). We need to find the product of the second row of A and the third column of B, that is:

$$(3 \;\; -2) \begin{pmatrix} -2 \\ 5 \end{pmatrix} = (3)(-2) + (-1)(5) = -11$$

The Insider's Writer's Manual for the ACT

Some find the study of the English language endlessly fascinating. Others, who have struggled through courses in grammar and composition, find it endlessly boring. Both agree, however, that the complications and subtleties of English make mastering it a genuine challenge—one on which serious writers may spend a lifetime.

Fortunately, preparing for the grammar and usage questions on the ACT won't take quite that long. In this area of the exam, as on all the others, the test-makers are creatures of habit. English may lend itself to endless complications, but you won't find them all on the ACT. Instead, the test-makers tend to focus on a handful of commonplace grammar and usage errors that the average writer typically makes. If you know the proper rules for this handful of writing situations, you'll do well on the ACT.

After examining many past ACT exams, we've determined that there are 40 key rules of grammar and usage that are most often tested on the exam. In this appendix, you'll learn those rules. Look for them when you practice for the ACT exam—and in your own writing as well. Chances are that you've stumbled over at least a few of these rules in the past.

RULES ABOUT VERBS

FYI

If you suspect that subject-verb agreement may be a problem in a sentence (it's a common error on the ACT), first find the verb—it's usually pretty easy to spot. Then look for the subject, by asking, "Who or what [insert verb]?" This process takes away the guesswork from locating the subject and verb in a sentence.

As you probably know, a *verb* is a word that tells what someone or something *does* or *is*. Every sentence has at least one verb, and it is a crucial word in the structure of the sentence. The "someone or something" that "does or is" the verb is called the *subject* of the verb. For example, in the sentence "George Bush was the forty-first president of the United States," *was* is the verb, and *George Bush* is the subject. Here are the rules you need to know that relate to the proper use of verbs.

Rule 1: A Verb Must Agree With Its Subject in Number

Number refers to whether the verb and its subject are *singular* or *plural*. A singular subject and verb refer to one person or thing; a plural subject and verb refer to more than one. Logically enough, the subject and verb have to match: If the subject is singular, the verb must be singular; if the subject is plural, the verb must be plural.

In most sentences, this rule is easy to follow. You can probably tell, just by the way the sentence sounds, that it would be wrong to write, "George Bush were the president" (singular subject + plural verb). It would also be wrong to write, "He and his wife was from Texas" (plural subject + singular verb). In these two examples, the error in subject-verb agreement is easy to spot.

In some sentences, however, it's not so easy:

Among those who played a crucial role in the Northern victory at Gettysburg were Joshua Chamberlain, a Union colonel from Maine who later enjoyed a distinguished career as an educator and politician.

In this case, the verb in the first, main clause of the sentence is *were*. Then find the subject: ask, "Who or what were?" In this case, the answer is *Joshua Chamberlain.* Is the subject singular or plural? Singular, of course; Joshua Chamberlain was one person. Therefore, a singular verb is needed: *were* should be changed to *was*.

Subject-verb agreement is a little tricky in this sentence because the subject *follows* the verb, rather than precedes it. And the sentence begins with the phrase *Among those who played a crucial role . . .* , which refers to a group of people. This structure could fool you into thinking the verb has a plural subject. Not so.

The next several rules deal with other cases in which subject-verb agreement can be tricky.

Rule 2: When Checking Agreement, Ignore Any Words Or Phrases That Separate A Verb From Its Subject

You can compare the subject and the verb easily when they are next to each other. It's much harder when they are separated by many other words. Watch out for this structure. In particular, watch out for *prepositional phrases* that come between the subject and the verb. A *preposition* is a word that links a noun (or a pronoun) to the rest of the sentence, usually by describing a logical or place relationship of some kind. Words like *of, by, for, with, in, on, to, through, from, against, near, under, beside,* and *above* are all prepositions. So are such phrases as *next to, along with, in place of,* and *as well as*.

A preposition is always followed by a noun or a pronoun. The preposition, together with the noun that follows, forms a prepositional phrase. *Of the people, by accident, for fun, with my sister, in a car, on fire, to the station,* and *through the tunnel* are all examples of prepositional phrases.

The key trick to remember is that *the subject of a verb never appears in a prepositional phrase.* So when you are checking a sentence for subject-verb agreement, and you want to find the subject, mentally "cross out" any prepositional phrase. The subject of the verb will *not* be there. Here's an example:

The purpose of such post-war international organizations as NATO, the World Bank, and the Organization of American States have been questioned since the demise of communism and the end of the cold war.

This sentence contains quite a few prepositional phrases. In looking for the subject of the verb *have been questioned*, you need to mentally cross out the prepositional phrases *of such post-war international organizations* and *as NATO, the World Bank, and the Organization of American States*. The subject will not appear within either of these phrases. What remains? *The purpose*, which is the subject of the verb: the thing that people are questioning is the purpose of all those organizations. Because it is singular, the verb should also be singular; to be grammatically correct, the verb should be changed to *has been questioned*.

Rule 3: Collective Nouns Are Usually Singular

Subject-verb agreement can be tricky when the subject is a *collective noun*—a noun that names a group of people or things rather than a single entity. Words like *team, group, club, class, family, collection, bunch, platoon,* and *organization* are all examples of collective nouns. Even names of institutions like *Harvard University, IBM,* and *the U.S. Senate* may be considered collective nouns because they refer to large numbers of individuals.

Although collective nouns refer to groups, in American English they are considered singular and take singular verbs. This may strike you as logical: these nouns do "look" singular (in other words, they don't end in the *s* that usually marks plural nouns). However, writers sometimes make mistakes with subject-verb agreement when collective nouns are involved, as in the following example:

> The League of Women Voters, boasting members from both major parties and all positions along the political spectrum, do not formally endorse candidates in national or local elections.

In this sentence, subject-verb agreement is complicated not only by the collective noun *League* but by the many prepositional and other phrases that divide the subject from the verb: *of Women Voters, boasting members, from both major parties and all positions,* and *along the political spectrum* all "interrupt" the sentence and separate the subject from the verb. Despite these distractions, the subject of the verb *do* is the singular collective noun *League*, and therefore the singular verb *does* should be used instead.

Rule 4: *The Number* Is Singular; *A Number* Is Plural

Distinguish these two phrases, which sound deceptively similar. Both are usually followed by prepositional phrases starting with *of*, but they play different roles in a sentence. In a sentence like the following, the word *number* is the subject of the verb, and the usual rule about ignoring the prepositional phrase applies:

> In the wake of the latest series of airline mergers, the number of carriers serving passengers in most mid-sized cities in the eastern United States have been reduced to just three.

It is the number of carriers that has been reduced to three, so the verb should be singular, as the word *number* itself is: "the number of carriers . . . *has* been reduced to just three" would be correct.

By contrast, when the phrase *a number* is used, it is generally the equivalent of a word like *several* or *many*. For example, consider:

> A number of scientists has testified before the Senate Armed Services Committee concerning the need for safer methods of handling nuclear wastes.

In this sentence, the entire phrase *a number of scientists* means much the same as *several scientists* or *a few scientists*. The meaning is plural, and the verb should be plural as well. The sentence should begin, "A number of scientists *have* testified . . ."

Rule 5: Pronouns Ending In *-One*, *-Body*, And *-Thing* Are Singular

Twelve indefinite pronouns belong in this group: *someone, anyone, no one, everyone, somebody, anybody, nobody, everybody, something, nothing, anything,* and *everything.* The rule to remember is simple: All 12 words are singular. This is true even when they refer to something that appears literally plural in meaning, as in this example:

> In the classic movie *Casablanca,* everybody seeking documents—forged or real—that will permit escape from Nazi-occupied northern Africa are forced to negotiate with black-market profiteers who make a living from others' desperation.

The subject of the verb *are forced* is *everybody seeking documents,* which clearly describes many people. Thus, it seems logical to use a plural verb. Unfortunately, logic doesn't always rule in English grammar, and this is a case in point. Because pronouns ending in *-body* are always considered singular, the singular verb *is forced* should be used instead.

Rule 6: The SANAM Pronouns—*Some, Any, None, All,* And *Most*—May Be Either Singular Or Plural

Grammar is a system, designed to be logical, that seeks to explain and codify language. However, language is a form of human behavior, and we humans are rarely completely logical. Thus, most rules of grammar have exceptions, twists, and complications that arise where the logic of the rule runs up against the illogic of human behavior.

Here's an example. We explained earlier that you should ignore prepositional phrases when looking for the subject of a verb. There are exceptions, however. The chief exception involves five pronouns—*some, any, none, all, most*—known by their initials as the SANAM pronouns. These may either be singular or plural, depending on how they are used in the sentence; and determining that generally requires you to look at the prepositional phrase beginning with *of* that usually follows the pronoun.

Consider this sentence:

> If any of the camera lenses produced by a particular worker is found to be defective, every other lens he or she produced during the same shift must be double-checked for quality before it is shipped.

In this sentence, the SANAM pronoun *any* is followed by the prepositional phrase *of the camera lenses.* To decide whether *any* is singular or plural, you have to look at the object of the preposition *of.* Because that object is the plural noun *lenses,* the pronoun *any* is plural; so the verb should be the plural *are found.*

By contrast:

> If any of the wreckage are recovered, forensic scientists will examine it for clues as to the cause of the accident.

In this case, the object of the preposition *of* is the singular word *wreckage.* Therefore, the pronoun *any* is singular, and the verb should also be singular: *is recovered.*

Rule 7: Verb Tenses Must Reflect The Sequence Of Events accurately

You may never have learned about verb tenses in an English class, but if you've studied Spanish or some other foreign language, you're probably familiar with the concept. The basic purpose of verb tenses is to indicate the *time sequence* of events. On the ACT, most questions related to verb tenses will involve the misuse of tenses in such a way as to confuse the order in which events happen.

There are six main tenses in English. In Table C.1, you'll find their names and their basic appearance, using the verb *to dance* for illustrative purposes.

The past, present, and future tenses obviously are used to describe events happening in the past, present, and future. The *perfect* tenses describe events occurring *prior to* the events in the other three tenses. For example, an event described in the past perfect tense is one that happened prior to an event in the past tense:

> Before she danced with her father, the bride had danced with her husband.

An event described in the present perfect tense is one that happens prior to or up until the present:

> As a ballet student, I have danced every day this month.

And an event in the future perfect tense is one that will happen prior to some anticipated future event:

> I will dance in a recital next Thursday; by then, I will have danced 30 recitals so far this year.

(The future perfect tense probably sounds less familiar to you than any of the others; it's the rarest tense in English.)

On the ACT, tense sequence is normally tested in a sentence or paragraph describing two or more events occurring in a particular, unmistakable order. Here's an example:

> Lincoln promulgated his controversial Emancipation Proclamation, which declared all slaves held in rebel territory free, only after the North would have won a significant military victory.

There are two events in this sentence: Lincoln's promulgation of the Emancipation Proclamation, and the North's winning a significant military

Table C.1
Six Main English Verb Tenses

Tense	Example
Past Perfect	had danced
Past	danced
Present Perfect	have danced
Present	dance
Future Perfect	will have danced
Future	will dance

Table C.2
Principal Parts of a Verb

Verb Part	Example
Infinitive	[to] dance
Past	danced
Past Participle	danced

victory. What is the time sequence of these two events? The sentence makes it obvious: Lincoln promulgated the Proclamation in the past (of course), and the North's victory occurred *prior to* that. Therefore, the promulgation should be in the past tense, and the victory should be in the past perfect tense: "Lincoln *promulgated* . . . only after the North *had won* . . ."

On the exam, watch for sentences in which two or more events are described. Make sure that the tenses used clearly and correctly match the sequence of events. If not, one of them needs to be corrected.

Rule 8: Always Use The Past Participle Form Of A Verb With The Helping Verb *To Have*

Take another look at Table C.1. Notice that the past perfect, present perfect, and future perfect tenses all contain forms of the verb *to have*. Used like this, to help create tenses of other verbs, the verb *to have* is called an *auxiliary verb*, or, more casually, a *helping verb*.

The rule to remember is that, when you are building a verb using the helping verb *to have*, you must be careful to use the proper form of the basic verb. The form *to use* is called *the past participle*. This is one of the three *principal parts* of any verb, as shown in Table C.2.

The infinitive is the basic, "root" form of the verb; the past is the same as the past tense; and the past participle, as we've said, is used with the helping verb *to have* in forming the perfect tenses.

Now, with most English verbs, forming verbs isn't tricky. As with *dance*, most verbs form the past and past participle exactly the same way: by adding *-d* or *-ed* to the infinitive. This is true of all *regular* verbs.

The problem arises with *irregular* verbs: verbs that form their past and past participle parts in nonstandard fashion. The verb *to fly* is an example, as shown in Table C.3.

Table C.3
Principal Parts of *Fly*

Part	Example
Infinitive	[to] fly
Past	flew
Past Participle	flown

It can be easy to confuse the past and past participle forms of an irregular verb. The most common mistake is to use the past tense form where the past participle is needed. Here's an example:

> By the time Lindbergh's little plane landed on an airfield outside Paris, thronged with astonished well-wishers, the exhausted pilot had flew single-handedly for over 30 hours without a break.

Because the past perfect tense is being used here, the past participle should be used; the verb should read *had flown* rather than *had flew*.

To avoid this kind of error, remember the rule: When a helping verb is involved, use the past participle form, not the past tense.

Rule 9: Use The Correct Past Tense And Part Participle Forms Of Irregular Verbs

FYI

Remember, the past tense form is used by itself; the past participle form is used with a helping verb, usually a form of the verb to have.

We've already explained that the past and past participle forms of irregular verbs can be tricky and confusing. In Table C.4, you'll find a list of some of the most commonly used, and commonly confused, irregular verbs, showing the correct forms for each of the three principle parts.

The list in Table C.4 doesn't show all irregular verbs in English, but it shows many of the most troublesome. Notice, in particular, the two verbs *lie* and *lay*. Not only is each irregular and confusing, but the two are quite easy to confuse with one another, leading to additional trouble. *To lie* is something one does oneself: You may *lie* on a sofa. *To lay* is something one does *to* something else: you may *lay* your coat on the back of a chair.

Take a look at this sample sentence:

> Although the state constitution was amended to provide the line-item veto to the governor over a year ago, the new provision has only took effect within the past two months.

Table C.4
Common English Irregular Verbs

Infinitive	Past	Past Participle
do	did	done
go	went	gone
take	took	taken
rise	rose	risen
begin	began	begun
swim	swam	swum
throw	threw	thrown
break	broke	broken
burst	burst	burst
bring	brought	brought
lie	lay	lain
lay	laid	laid
get	got	got *or* gotten

Can you spot the problem? It's the misuse of the irregular verb *to take*. The tense being used is the present perfect, which describes events happening in the past and up to the present (the new constitutional provision's taking effect is something happening just the past two months, up to and including today). In the present perfect tense, with the helping verb *has*, the past participle should be used, which is *taken*, rather than the past tense *took*.

Study the list of irregular verbs and their principle parts. Memorize it if necessary. And be on the lookout for other irregular verbs as they crop up in your reading and writing. Practice using them correctly, and you'll find it easy to recognize this type of error on the exam.

RULES ABOUT MODIFYING PHRASES

Rule 10: A Modifying Phrase Must Modify A Word Or Phrase Appearing In The Sentence

A *modifying phrase* is a group of words that works together as a unit to modify, or give more information about something else in the sentence. As you may recall from earlier grammar study, both adjectives and adverbs are considered modifiers; both of these parts of speech serve to modify, or give information about, other words in the sentence. Thus, modifying phrases are groups of words that act as adjectives or adverbs. Some modifying phrases work as adjectives; they modify nouns or pronouns. Others work as adverbs; they modify verbs, adjectives, or adverbs.

Got all that? If you're not sure, an example or two may help. In the sentence, "Waiting at the bus stop, Paula nervously glanced at her watch," the phrase *Waiting at the bus stop* works as an adjective; it modifies the noun *Paula*. On the other hand, in the sentence, "After six o'clock, buses stop here once an hour," the phrase *After six o'clock* acts as an adverb; it modifies the verb *stop* (by telling *when* the buses stop). So both phrases are modifying phrases, though of slightly different kinds.

So what? Well, all of this is important to you because of a grammar rule the test-makers like to challenge you on—a rule stating that a modifying phrase must refer to a specific word or phrase appearing elsewhere in the same sentence. If no such word or phrase appears, the modifying phrase is called a *dangling modifier*, and it's a definite no-no. Look at this example:

> Dismayed by the news that one of the firm's top executives had suddenly decided to accept a job with a rival company, the price of the company's stock fell sharply the following day.

This sentence contains a dangling modifier—and a long one at that. The entire opening phrase (technically a *clause*, since it contains a subject and a verb), beginning with the word *Dismayed* and ending with the word *company*, is designed as a modifying phrase, intended to modify or give more information about—whom? Who, exactly, was *dismayed by the news*? The problem with the sentence is that we can't tell. The modifying phrase "dangles"; there is no word or phrase to which it refers.

To be correct, the sentence would have to be rewritten to name the person or people who were dismayed—maybe something like this: "Dismayed by the news

. . . Wall Street traders drove the price of company's stock down sharply the following day." Now the modifying phrase has a clear referent—*Wall Street traders*—naming the people it modifies.

Rule 11: A Modifying Phrase Must Be Next To What It Modifies

FYI

On the ACT, modifying phrases often appear at the start of sentences, as in this example. When a sentence begins with a phrase like this, look closely to make sure that the person, thing, or idea being modified appears clearly somewhere in the sentence.

As you just learned, a dangling modifier lacks something clear to modify. A *misplaced modifier* has something in the sentence to modify, but the two things are separated. When the modifying phrase isn't next to what it is supposed to modify, the sentence becomes confusing—and sometimes unintentionally comic. Here's an example:

> A fabled center of monastic life during the Middle Ages, thousands of visitors travel to the island of Iona near the coast of Ireland each summer.

The phrase that begins this sentence, *A fabled center of monastic life during the Middle Ages,* is supposed to modify *the island of Iona*, since that's what it describes. However, the modifying phrase is misplaced. Rather than being next to what it modifies, it is next to the words *thousands of visitors*, almost as if the visitors were *a fabled center. . . .* Because this structure is ridiculous, we soon figure out what the writer really means to say. But the momentary confusion makes for slightly less pleasant reading, and causes this sentence to be erroneous.

The sentence could be corrected in several ways. The misplaced modifier could simply be moved to be next to what it modifies: "Thousands of visitors travel to the island of Iona, a fabled center of monastic life during the Middle Ages near the coast of Ireland, each summer." More gracefully, *the island of Iona* could be moved to a spot next to the modifier, with the sentence rewritten accordingly: "A fabled center of monastic life during the Middle Ages, the island of Iona, near the coast of Ireland is visited by thousands of travelers each summer." Either way, the misplaced modifier would be corrected.

RULES ABOUT GRAMMATICAL AND LOGICAL CONSISTENCY

Rule 12: Items In A List Must Be Grammatically Parallel

FYI

Remember, on the exam, you don't need to create a correct version of the sentence. You only need to recognize it when it appears: a much less burdensome challenge!

You know about parallel lines in geometry: They are lines that run in the same direction, never touching but never diverging either. In grammar, *parallelism* refers to words, phrases, or clauses that "run in the same direction": They have the same grammatical form and therefore sound and look similar—like matching bookends.

Deciding when and how to use parallelism is partly a matter of taste and judgment. But there are certain writing situations that clearly call for parallelism—situations in which phrases that *don't* match definitely sound wrong. One such situation is when two or more things or ideas are presented in the form of a list. Check out this example:

> Delegates to the conference on global climate were charged with pursuing several often contradictory goals: reducing pollution by automobiles and industry, slowing the deforestation of the third world, and the maintenance of high rates of economic growth in the developing nations.

The sentence lists three goals of the conference delegates. The first two are written in parallel grammatical form—technically speaking, in phrases that begin with *gerunds* (-*ing* verbs):

> *reducing* pollution by automobiles and industry

> *slowing* the deforestation of the third world

However, the third goal is written in a different grammatical form. Instead of a gerund, the phrase begins with a noun that describes the action:

> *the maintenance* of high rates of economic growth in the developing nations

Because of the lack of parallelism, the third item in the list sounds a bit "off," as though it doesn't match. To correct the sentence, the third item should be revised to match the other two by starting with a gerund: " . . . and *maintaining* high rates of economic growth in the developing nations."

Whenever a sentence contains a list of things that play the same logical role in the sentence, make sure they are also grammatically parallel. If not, one or more of the items should be rewritten to make them consistent.

Rule 13: Two Things Being Compared Must Be Grammatically Parallel

Like items in a list, items that are being compared to one another in a sentence generally need to be grammatically parallel. Otherwise, the sentence will sound disjointed. Here's an example:

> Because of the enormous expense of television advertising, to run for Congress today costs more than running for governor of a mid-sized state 20 years ago.

The costs of two kinds of political campaigns are being compared: a race for Congress today and a race for governor 20 years ago. Unfortunately, the sentence as written uses two different, unmatching grammatical constructions to describe the races:

> *to run* for Congress today

> *running* for governor of a mid-sized state 20 years ago

The first item is named in a phrase beginning with an infinitive verb (*to run*). The second is named in a phrase beginning with a gerund (*running*). It would be okay to use either an infinitive or a gerund in this sentence; the problem is with using both, inconsistently. The sentence should be corrected either by using an infinitive in both phrases ("*to run* for Congress today costs more than *to run* for governor") or by using a gerund in both phrases ("*running* for Congress today costs more than *running* for governor").

Rule 14: Two Things Being Compared Must Be Logically Similar

As the saying goes, you can't compare apples and oranges. When a sentence compares two (or more) things, it should be written so that the things being compared are logically, as well as grammatically, similar and consistent. Here's an illustration of how a comparison can go wrong:

Although the Disney Company and Murdoch's News Corporation have both built vast multi-media empires, the financial strategy being pursued by Disney is markedly different from Murdoch.

Actually, this sentence contains two comparisons. In the first half of the sentence, two companies are being compared: *the Disney Company* and *Murdoch's News Corporation*. The phrases that mention the two things being compared are logically similar: both simply name the companies.

In the second half of the sentence, however, an unclear and inconsistent comparison is made. *The financial strategy being pursued by Disney* is compared with *Murdoch*. A moment's thought reveals the problem. The first phrase mentions a company's financial strategy; the second phrase merely names the company (in the shorthand form of the name of the company's chief owner, Murdoch). You could logically compare one company's financial strategy with another company's financial strategy; you could also compare one company, as a whole, to another. But it makes no sense to compare a financial strategy to a company. They are two different types of things.

The second half of the sentence could be corrected in several ways. Here are three:

(1) . . . the financial strategy being pursued by Disney is markedly different from *that being pursued by Murdoch*.

(2) . . . the financial strategy being pursued by Disney is markedly different from *Murdoch's*.

(3) . . . Disney's financial strategy is markedly different from Murdoch's.

Each of these is correct.

Rule 15: A Subject And Its Complement Must Be Logically Consistent

FYI

The technical name for verbs of being is copulative verbs, *a term high school English teachers avoid because it sounds dirty. Congratulations— now you're old enough to use it!*

There are two kinds of verbs: verbs of *action* and verbs of *being*. Verbs of action tell what the subject does: *dance, type, dive, manage, eat*, and so on. Verbs of being tell what the subject is. The verb *to be* is the most obvious example, but there are many others: *seem, appear, feel, sound, look, remain, become*, and many others can all be used as verbs of being.

In general, what follows a verb of being is a *subject complement*: something that *complements* or completes the meaning of the subject. In other words, it tells us more about the subject. In the sentence "Harry seems tired," *tired* is a subject complement. In the sentence, "Renee became a firefighter," *firefighter* is a subject complement.

So far so simple. You've been constructing sentences like these all your life, with few mishaps. Problems arise with sentences like this—sentences built around verbs of being—when the subject and the subject complement are in some way mismatched. Logically, since the subject and the subject complement describe the same thing, they should be the same *kind* of thing. If they are not, then we have the same problem we saw a moment ago with unlike things being compared: what we might call the apples-and-oranges problem. Here's an example:

The antidemocratic bias of the Electoral College has long been criticized as an anachronistic institution that has outlived the role intended for it by the Founders.

The verb *to criticize* isn't always used as a verb of being, but in this case it is. What the sentence is saying is that, in the view of some people, the Electoral College *is* an anachronistic (that is, outmoded) institution. Since the sentence is telling what the subject *is* rather than what it *does*, the second half of the sentence—starting with the word *an*—is a subject complement.

The problem is that, in this sentence, the subject and the subject complement aren't logically matched. Look again at the first half of the sentence. The subject of the verb *has been criticized* isn't actually *the Electoral College*; it is actually *The antidemocratic bias*. (Remember, the subject of the verb isn't normally in a prepositional phrase—and *of the Electoral College* is a prepositional phrase.) It's now obvious that the subject and the subject complement don't go together clearly. The *bias* of the Electoral College isn't *an anachronistic institution*. It's not an institution at all. The author is trying to say that the Electoral College itself is anachronistic. However, by the time he got to the second half of the sentence, he forgot exactly what he'd written in the first half. Hence the confusion.

The sentence could be fixed by rewriting it to say what the author really intended: "Because of its antidemocratic bias, the Electoral College has long been criticized . . ." Now the connection between the subject and the subject complement is logical and clear.

RULES ABOUT ADJECTIVES AND ADVERBS

Rule 16: Use Adjectives To Modify Nouns Or Pronouns; Use Adverbs To Modify Verbs, Adjectives, Or Adverbs

Think hard and you may remember learning the rules about adjectives and adverbs (if you weren't lucky enough to be "home sick" the day they were covered in English class). An adjective is a word that modifies (gives more information about) a noun or a pronoun; it often answers such questions as *what kind? how many? which one?* By contrast, an adverb modifies a verb, an adjective, or another adverb; it often answers such questions as *how? when? where? in what way? how often? to what extent?* Adverbs often (not always) end in *-ly*.

Sometimes writers err by mistakenly using an adjective where an adverb is needed, or vice versa. Here's an example:

From 1964 through 1968, albums recorded by the Beatles appeared consistent on the charts of best-selling popular music not only in their native England but around the world.

The word *consistent* is an adjective; it could be used to modify a noun (*a consistent success*) or a pronoun (*she is consistent in her habits*). In this sentence, however, *consistent* is ill-chosen because the author is trying to modify the verb *appeared*. He wants to answer the question *how often did Beatles albums appear on the charts?* To answer this question, an adverb is needed.

The adverb form of the adjective *consistent* is formed like many adverbs: by adding *-ly* to the adjective. The sentence can easily be corrected by changing *consistent* to *consistently*.

Rule 17: Use A Comparative Adjective Or Adverb To Compare Two Things; Use A Superlative For Three Or More

Your basic form of an adjective is called the *positive* form. When you want to compare two things, you use the *comparative* form, which is usually formed in one of two ways: by adding *-er* to the positive form, or by putting the word *more* in front of the adjective. (Use the second method with an adjective that is three syllables long or longer.) When comparing more than two things, use the *superlative* form, which is formed by adding *-est* to the positive form or by using the word *most*. (Again, you can generally be guided by the length of the adjective.) Thus, you would write:

> I am *tall*.

> I am *taller* than my sister.

> My brother Stan is the *tallest* person in our whole family.

With a three-syllable adjective, the words would be formed this way:

> Suzy is *beautiful*.

> Sharon is more beautiful.

> Michelle Pfeiffer is the *most beautiful* woman in the galaxy.

Occasionally, errors arise when a writer gets confused about whether to use the comparative or superlative form of the adjective, as in this example:

> Of the many strange creatures that inhabit the continent of Australia, the wallabee is perhaps the more unusual.

Because the wallabee is being compared to more than one other creature, the superlative form of the adjective should be used: "the wallabee is perhaps the *most unusual*."

Comparative and superlative forms of adverbs are used in much the same way. The comparative form (made with the word *more*) is used when two things are being compared; the superlative form (made with *most*) is used when three or more things are being compared. Thus:

> Jerry swims *quickly*.

> Paula swims *more quickly* than Jerry.

> Karen swims *most quickly* of anyone on the swim team.

Rule 18: Distinguish Among The Adjective Good, The Adverb Well, And The Adjective Well

This trio of words can be a bit confusing, and since they are used quite often, it's important to get the differences straight. *Good* is an adjective with a very broadly positive meaning. *Well* is the adverb form of *good* (the equivalent of *goodly*, if there were such a word in modern English); it means, in effect, "in a good way." But *well* can also be an adjective meaning "healthy" or "the opposite of ill." Consider this example:

> Thanks to the improved acoustics in the newly renovated Carnegie Hall, the deepest notes of the bass violins sound as well as the highest tones of the piccolos.

The verb *sound* in this sentence is a verb of being; it is used here to tell us what the deepest notes of the bass violins *are* rather than what they *do*. So what follows should be a subjective complement, telling what those notes are (or, literally, what they sound like). In this situation, the adjective *good* is needed rather than either the adverb *well* or the adjective *well* (since the notes don't sound "healthy").

The adverb *well* would be correctly used in a sentence like this: "Carrie, the bass violinist in the Anderson Quartet, plays very *well*." (She plays "in a good way," in other words.) The adjective *well* would be correctly used in a sentence like this: "I just spoke to Carrie on the phone and she sounds *well*; I guess she has recovered from the flu." (She sounds "healthy," that is.) See the difference?

RULES ABOUT PRONOUNS

Rule 19: A Pronoun Must Have A Clear And Logical Antecedent

As you may recall, a *pronoun* refers to and takes the place of a noun. In a sentence like, "Laura said that Laura was planning to go with Laura's friends to Times Square on New Year's Eve," you'd want to use the pronouns *she* and *her* rather than repeating *Laura*; it sounds a little boring and awkward otherwise.

The noun that the pronoun refers to is called its *antecedent*. A problem arises when the reader can't easily tell who or what the antecedent is supposed to be—as in this example:

> Although the hospital administrators interviewed many staff members about the repeated cases of staph infections, they had no explanation for the puzzling pattern of outbreaks.

The second half of this sentence starts with the pronoun *they*. Unfortunately, we can't tell from the context who *they* are: logically, the antecedent could be *the hospital administrators* or the *staff members*, but the sentence doesn't help us figure out which group is intended. (Some grammarians say that, in an ambiguous case like this, the nearer antecedent applies, which would be the *staff members*; but really good writing wouldn't require the reader to puzzle over the intended meaning.)

The sentence ought to be revised. Here's one way: "Although *they* interviewed many staff members . . . *the hospital administrators* had no explanation . . ." Notice how flip-flopping the pronoun and its antecedent makes it unmistakable who *they* are. This strategy won't work in every sentence, but it works here. In other instances, you might have to repeat the noun (or some form of it) rather than using an ambiguous pronoun. Either way, the intended meaning would at least be clear.

Rule 20: The Antecedent Of A Pronoun Must Be A Noun (Or Another Pronoun)

Sometimes, rather than having two possible antecedents, a pronoun lacks an antecedent altogether. Here's an example:

> Corporate financial statements for the first three quarters of the year showed that the sales increases they had enjoyed each year of the previous decade had definitely stopped.

Who is the *they* referred to in the second half of this sentence? We can't tell. Presumably it refers to the corporation being discussed, but the words *the corporation* or their equivalent (*the company, the firm*) don't actually appear anywhere. (And in any case, *the company* would be an *it*, not a *they*.) The closest thing to an antecedent here is the adjective *Corporate*, which is no good. Remember, the antecedent of a pronoun has to be a noun or another pronoun; it can't be an adjective.

So the sentence would have to be revised, probably by replacing the pronoun *they* with a noun that makes the meaning clear: ". . . the sales increases *the company* had enjoyed . . ."

Rule 21: A Pronoun Must Agree With Its Antecedent In Number

Just like a subject and a verb, a pronoun and its antecedent must agree in number: If the antecedent is single, the pronoun must also be single; if the antecedent is plural, the pronoun must also be single.

Here's an example of how this can go wrong:

> A climber interested in scaling Everest must be prepared to invest a significant amount of their time and energy, as well as money, in preparing for the ordeal.

Notice the pronoun *their* in the second half of this sentence. Who does it refer to?—that is, what is the pronoun's antecedent? *A climber* is the answer; it is *a climber interested in scaling Everest* whose time and energy must be invested. Now you can see the problem with agreement: *A climber* is singular, but *their* is plural; it refers to two or more people only.

To correct the sentence, *their* must be changed to a singular pronoun. The choice of pronoun is a minor dilemma. One could use *his*, which, in a non-specific context like this one, is said by many writers and grammarians (especially conservative or old-fashioned ones) to embrace either a male or a female climber; or, to be more scrupulously gender-neutral, one could use the phrase *his or her*. The former option has come to sound a bit sexist; the latter is a little wordy. The truth is that there's no perfect solution.

Rule 22: Use Second- And Third-Person Pronouns Consistently

Grammarians refer to three "persons": first person (*I, me, we*, and so on), second person (*you*), and third person (*he, she, it, they*, and so on). In most contexts, it would be difficult to confuse these persons. In sentences where an indefinite person is being discussed, however, English allows either second-person or third-person constructions to be used; and this creates the possibility of inconsistency and error. Here's an example of what we mean:

FYI

People often use plural pronouns like they, them, *and* their *in a context like this precisely to avoid the dilemma of appearing sexist. However, that strategy is still considered grammatically incorrect. On the ACT, you'll need to pick a variant that maintains proper pronoun-antecedent agreement—despite the awkwardness of the only available options.*

If one lives in the northern hemisphere, on most clear winter nights you can easily see the three stars in a row that mark the belt of the hunter in the constellation Orion.

The sentence is describing how someone—anyone—can see Orion's belt in the winter sky. It starts by using the indefinite third-person pronoun *one*. (Other such words that could have been used include the pronouns *someone* and *anyone* and expressions like *a person* or *an observer*.) However, the sentence shifts in midstream to the second person: *you can easily see* . . . . This construction is a no-no.

The sentence could be corrected by maintaining the third person all the way through: *one can easily see* . . . Or you could change the entire sentence to second person: *If you live in the northern hemisphere, . . . you can easily see* . . . . Either way is consistent and correct. What's wrong is to mix and match inconsistently.

RULES ABOUT CONNECTING CLAUSES

Rule 23: Choose The Logical Conjunction

Conjunctions are connecting words: the screws and bolts of language, they clamp together words, phrases, and clauses, hopefully in ways that make both logical and grammatical sense.

Conjunctions can be classified in various ways. You only need to know two categories. *Coordinating conjunctions* connect words, phrases, and clauses that are equal in grammatical importance. There are six: *and, or, for, nor, but*, and *yet*. *Subordinating conjunctions* are used especially to connect clauses (that is, groups of words that contain a subject and a verb). The clause introduced by a subordinating conjunction is called a *dependent clause*; as its name implies, it is less important than a clause without such a conjunction, which is called an *independent clause*.

A dependent clause can't stand alone as a sentence. An independent clause can. Table C.5 shows a few examples of subordinating conjunctions, together with dependent clauses they might introduce.

Can you see that each of the dependent clauses in Table C.5 could *not* stand alone as a sentence? Each needs to be connected to another, independent clause. The conjunction helps to make the necessary connection.

So much for the basics of conjunctions. On the ACT, you'll have to recognize whether or not the proper, logical conjunction is being used to connect two

Table C.5
Sample Subordinating Conjunctions

Conjunction	Example
although	although it had begun to rain
when	when the plumber arrived
because	because the bicycle was broken
after	after she reached Paris

clauses. It depends, of course, on the meaning of the conjunction, which will either fit the context plausibly or not. Look at this example:

> Many theories as to how human beings first domesticated dogs have been proposed, and clear evidence to support any one of these theories has yet to surface.

Here, two independent clauses have been joined by the coordinating conjunction *and*. Grammatically, we're all right. The problem is with the logic of the sentence. The two clauses are actually somewhat opposed in meaning rather than complementary: *despite the fact that* many theories exist, *no evidence supporting them* has been found. This is surprising, no? One would think that a multiplicity of theories would go hand in hand with an abundance of evidence. But the sentence tells us, surprisingly, that this is not so.

Given this near-contradiction, the conjunction *and* doesn't seem the best choice. Instead, *but* should be used. This would logically fit the opposition in meaning between the two clauses.

Watch for similar disjunctions on the ACT. No matter what conjunction is used—*and, or, but, since, before, if, unless*—make sure it makes logical sense in the context. If not, look for a correction that better fits the meaning of the sentence.

Rule 24: Use A Semicolon (;) To Connect Two Independent Clauses

FYI

When in doubt as to whether a semicolon is being used correctly, look at what appears on either side. If it can't stand alone as a sentence, the semicolon is wrong.

We've explained that one of the six coordinating conjunctions can be used to connect two independent clauses. The other proper way to connect two independent clauses is with a semicolon (;).The main use of a semicolon is to connect two independent clauses. (The other uses are somewhat specialized; for example, you can use semicolons instead of commas to separate items in a list that themselves contain commas.) Ninety-five percent of the time, a semicolon is used between independent clauses.

Here's an example of a semicolon gone bad:

> Adams was initially drawn into the slavery question not by the controversy over slavery itself; but by the so-called "gag rule" used by the South to stifle debates in the Senate concerning slavery.

The semicolon in the middle of this sentence is wrong because it doesn't connect two independent clauses. The first part of the sentence (from *Adams* through *itself*) is an independent clause—it could stand alone as a sentence. However, the rest of the sentence couldn't stand alone as a sentence; it lacks a subject and verb (and therefore isn't even a proper clause). So the semicolon should be replaced by a comma.

Rule 25: Avoid Run-On Sentences

A run-on sentence isn't necessarily a particularly long sentence. It's simply a sentence in which two (or more) independent clauses have been shoved together without either a semicolon or a coordinating conjunction to join them properly. (When a comma is erroneously used to connect them, the result is a *comma splice*—one type of run-on sentence.) Here's an example:

Beside being a writer and lecturer, Mark Twain fancied himself an entrepreneur, he made and lost several fortunes backing various business ventures.

If this sentence were divided into two sentences after the word *entrepreneur*, either half could stand alone as a sentence. (Try it.) Therefore, it's a run-on sentence (specifically, a comma splice), which could be corrected in any of several ways:

- You could go ahead and break it into two sentences: Change the comma after *entrepreneur* into a period and capitalize *he*.

- You could change the comma into a semicolon, which is the proper punctuation mark to link two independent clauses.

- You could add a coordinating conjunction after the comma. *For* might do in this context.

- Finally, you could change one of the clauses into a dependent clause by adding a subordinating conjunction. It would require some rewriting—for example: "*Because* Mark Twain fancied himself an entrepreneur, beside being a writer and lecturer, he made and lost several fortunes . . ."

On the ACT, of course, you won't have to carry out all of these schemes for correcting the sentence; just recognize one of them when you see it among the answer choices.

Rule 26: Avoid Sentence Fragments

A *sentence fragment* is a collection of words punctuated as a sentence, but that cannot properly stand alone as a sentence. Some sentence fragments lack either a subject or a verb—two basic elements every sentence must have. In other cases, the sentence fragment has both a subject and a verb, but it is a dependent rather than an independent clause. This usually happens because the clause begins either with a subordinating conjunction or with a particular type of pronoun, called a *relative pronoun*, that makes the clause dependent on another clause.

Got all that? Here's an example that may help make it a bit clearer:

Carbon dating, which can be used in estimating the age of materials that are of organic origin only, since the method is based on the predictable decay of carbon-based organic compounds.

Although this collection of words is pretty long (31 words), it is a sentence fragment rather than a true sentence. Why? Not because it lacks a subject and a verb; actually, it contains *three* verbs, each with its own subject. But each of these clauses is a dependent rather than an independent clause, so none is enough to make a free-standing sentence.

The first clause here begins with the words *which can be used. Can be used* is the verb, and the pronoun *which* is the subject. Because *which* is a relative pronoun, it can't introduce an independent clause; instead, it connects the clause to the rest of the sentence (which, you hope, includes an independent clause). You can probably "hear" the fact that a clause whose subject is *which* sounds incomplete, and therefore dependent.

The second clause begins with *that are*. *Are* is the verb, and the relative pronoun *that* is the subject. Again, it's a dependent clause, which can't stand alone as a sentence.

The final clause begins with the words *since the method is based*. The verb is—*is based* and the subject is *the method*. This is a dependent clause because of the subordinating conjunction *since*. Any clause beginning with this word can't stand alone. Again, you can probably tell from the way it sounds that a clause starting with *since* needs another clause to complete the thought.

To turn this into a complete sentence, you would need to add something; most likely, a verb at the end, which would hook up with the words *Carbon dating* way back at the start of the sentence. Those words appear to be what the author originally intended for his subject, before he got distracted and lost in the midst of those three dependent clauses. A complete sentence might read something like this:

> Carbon dating, which can be used in estimating the age of materials that are of organic origin only, since the method is based on the predictable decay of carbon-based organic compounds, *is useless in studying materials that are completely non-organic.*

This new structure gives the sentence an independent clause, built around the subject and verb *Carbon dating . . . is*." Understand?

RULES ABOUT VERBOSITY

Rule 27: Avoid Needless Repetition

FYI

Notice that the length of the supposed sentence isn't at issue. A "frag-ment" can be quite big, yet still be a fragment. It all depends on whether the clauses are independent or dependent, and this in turn depends on the grammatical structure.

On the ACT exam, be on the lookout for sentences and paragraphs that are unnecessarily verbose—that is, wordy and too long. Good writing is economical and concise. The test-makers will usually make their examples of verbosity fairly obvious. One form of verbosity to watch out for is sheer, needless repetition of a fact or an idea—also called *redundancy*. Here's an example:

> As much as 125 years ago, the science fiction writer Jules Verne wrote predictions that foretold the future existence of such modern mechanical devices as the airplane, the submarine, and even the fax machine.

This sentence isn't grammatically "wrong"; it breaks no rules of sentence structure or usage. But it's poorly written because of the needless repetition it contains. We're told that Jules Verne wrote "predictions that foretold" something—a clear example of repetition, since a prediction *by definition* foretells something. Then we learn that his predictions foretold "the future existence" of certain things. Obviously, if Verne was foretelling something, what he was foretelling *had to be* in the future.

Each of these redundancies should be eliminated, saving words and making the revised sentence much crisper in style. Other words can also be eliminated with no loss of meaning. Like this: "As much as 125 years ago, the science fiction writer Jules Verne predicted such devices as the airplane, the submarine, and even the fax machine." Compare this sentence, 25 words long, with the original version, 34 words long. Isn't the shorter version better? Apply the same kind of thinking on the exam.

Rule 28: Eliminate Words If Removing Them Doesn't Sacrifice Grace, Clarity, or Meaning

FYI

On the ACT, when you have a choice between two or more answer choices, all of which are grammatically correct and say the same thing, choose the shortest version. It is usually the best.

Redundancy isn't the only form of wordiness. Sometimes sentences are just plain "flabby," sagging under the weight of extra words that add nothing to the meaning and can easily be eliminated. Here's an example:

> Spielberg's *Amistad* is the filmmaker's second attempt to show that someone who is an unexcelled creator of funny, fast-paced action movies can also be a producer of films that try to deal in a serious fashion with weighty historical and moral themes.

This sentence can be significantly shortened without changing or obscuring its meaning. One way is by eliminating the "empty" clause *someone who is*. Clauses like this are often injected into sentences without any real purpose; they are mere verbal tics, like the "ers" and "ahs" that people sometimes interject when they speak. Similarly, the convoluted clause *can also be a producer of films* can be radically simplified into *can also produce films*.

The improved sentence might read like this:

> Spielberg's *Amistad* is the filmmaker's second attempt to show that an unexcelled creator of funny, fast-paced action movies can also produce films dealing seriously with weighty historical and moral themes.

(Note the other changes we've made here.) The sentence has been reduced from 42 words to just 30, a 29% "weight loss." More important, it now sounds more lively and vigorous, a direct result of the elimination of "verbal flab."

Rule 29: Avoid Needless Use Of The Passive Construction

Another way to avoid verbosity is by using active rather than passive verbs wherever possible. You remember the difference: "Sharon built the birdhouse" is active; "The birdhouse was built by Sharon" is passive. In an active construction, the subject of the verb (in this case, *Sharon*) *does* the action named. In a passive construction, the subject (*The birdhouse*) *receives* the action. The one doing the action is named, if at all, in a prepositional phrase (*by Sharon*) after the verb.

At times, passive construction is useful and appropriate; for example, when it isn't important who did the action, or when it is unknown ("We found that our summer cottage had been vandalized while we were away"). But in most sentences, the active construction sounds more vigorous and is also more concise. Consider this example:

> When the basic elements of the theory of natural selection were conceived by Darwin, it was unknown to him that most of the same ideas had already been developed by a rival naturalist, Charles Russel Wallace.

If this sentence sounds clumsy and stilted, it's largely because of the needless use of the passive construction. On reflection, it seems strange to de-emphasize the roles of Darwin and Wallace (the "doers" of the deeds being described) by relegating them to mere "by" phrases, rather than making them the subjects of the sentence. And it also makes the sentence unnecessarily wordy.

Here's how the improved sentence reads when active verbs are used instead: "When Darwin conceived the basic elements of the theory of natural selection, he didn't know that Charles Russel Wallace, a rival naturalist, had already developed most of the same ideas." The sentence is shorter, crisper, and a trifle easier to understand.

Unless there is some good reason to prefer a passive verb in a particular sentence, choose active constructions instead.

RULES ABOUT IDIOMATIC USAGE

Rule 30: When Idiomatic Paired Phrases Are Used, Always Complete The Idiom

An *idiom* is a phrase that is peculiar to a particular language. Often there is no special "logic" or "rule" behind the use of a given idiom; we explain idioms (when a child or a non-native speaker asks for an explanation) by saying, "That's just the way you say it," and let it go at that.

If you grew up speaking English, you've been surrounded by thousands of English idioms all your life, and you've learned to use most of them flawlessly by osmosis—by hearing them used and imitating what you've heard, often unconsciously. But some idioms are tricky even for native speakers. Here's one instance.

Certain idiomatic pairs of phrases must always be used together. When they aren't, the resulting sentence "sounds wrong," as if something is missing. (As the saying goes, we're left waiting "for the other shoe to drop.") Look at this example:

> Many historians now contend that the American Revolution was caused as much by economic factors than by political ones.

This sentence sounds slightly "off" because the idiom demands that the phrase *as much by X* be followed inexorably by *as by Y*. It seems odd to hear the word *than* where the second *as* should be.

Another illustration:

> Demographers have long recognized an inverse relationship between family size and income: that is, the more a family earns, greater will be their likelihood of practicing family planning and birth control.

The proper idiom for describing this kind of cause-and-effect relationship is *the more X, the more Y*, or some close variation on that. The sentence sounds wrong because our expectation that the pair of phrases will be completed is not met. The second half of the sentence should be rewritten this way: "the more a family earns, *the greater* will be their likelihood . . ."

Keep your ear cocked for paired idioms like these, and make sure that your sentences complete the construction by using both phrases correctly.

Rule 31: Distinguish Gerunds From Infinitives

These two peculiar word types combine some of the qualities of a verb with some of the qualities of a noun. Unless you're a grammarian, you don't normally need to think about these terms and the subtleties of their usage, with one

511

exception: You need to know the difference between a gerund and an infinitive and to be sensitive to which one "sounds" right in a particular sentence.

A *gerund* is a noun formed by adding *-ing* to a verb. It looks the same as the present participle form of the verb—*swimming, working, enjoying*—but it's used in all the ways a noun is used: as the subject or object of a verb, as the object of a preposition, and so on. For example, in the sentence, "Swimming is my favorite exercise," *Swimming* is the subject of the verb.

An *infinitive* is the basic form of a verb, usually with *to* in front of it: *to swim, to work, to enjoy.* Like a gerund, it can also be used as a noun, either by itself or in a phrase called an *infinitive phrase.* For example, in the sentence, "To know him is to love him," the infinitive phrase *To know him* is the subject of the sentence (and *to love him* is the subject complement).

Problems arise when writers get confused as to whether a gerund or an infinitive is needed in a particular type of sentence. Here's an example:

> The sensitive nature of the negotiations required the company president's traveling halfway around the globe to participate personally in the final phase of the discussion.

According to idiomatic usage, the word *required* should be followed by an infinitive rather than a gerund, so the sentence should say, "required the company president *to travel* halfway around the globe . . ."

By contrast, look at this example:

> The president assured the senator that his administration had no intention to encroach on congressional prerogatives in this matter.

Here, the infinitive sounds wrong; the sentence should read, "the administration had no intention *of encroaching* on congressional prerogatives . . ."

Unfortunately, there are no logical rules to be followed (as is usually true with idioms). Similar meanings sometimes require opposite structures: A person *promises to do* something, but she is *committed to doing* it; she may *hesitate to do* something, but she *objects to doing* it, and so on.

Rule 32: Distinguish Likely From Liable

In casual speech, many people confuse these two words. In careful writing, however, they should be distinguished. *Likely* means "probably destined to happen"; a likely event is one you think will occur. *Liable* means "legally responsible"; if you run into another car when you're driving, you will be liable for the damages. Don't use *liable* to mean "likely," as in this example:

> Recent history suggests that many American voters are liable to deliberately split their votes, choosing a President and a member of Congress from different parties as if to limit the power of both.

The author of this sentence wants to say that vote-splitting is a common practice among American voters; legal liability is not being referred to. Therefore, the word *liable* should be changed to *likely* in this sentence.

Rule 33: Distinguish *Like* From *As*

The words *like* and *as* are used in similar ways, mainly in sentences where a similarity between two things is being described. However, they should be distinguished grammatically. Here's how.

In careful writing, *like* is used as a connecting word only as a preposition, never as a conjunction. In other words, *like* should be followed by a noun or pronoun, not by a clause. By contrast, *as* is used as a subordinating conjunction; it may be followed by a clause. Look at this example:

> As the famous North Atlantic clipper ships of the nineteenth century, today's jumbo jets have revolutionized trans-Atlantic commerce by making travel between Europe and America far faster than ever before.

What follows the word *As* in this sentence is not a clause but the noun *ships* (along with various modifying words that give more information about what kind of ships the author is talking about). Therefore, the preposition *Like* should be used instead.

As would be correct if a clause followed it—in other words, if a subject and verb appeared. You might start the same sentence this way: "*As* the famous North Atlantic clipper ships of the nineteenth century *did*, . . ." Adding the word *did* turns the phrase into a clause, and makes *As* the proper connecting word.

Rule 34: Distinguish Countable Quantities From Quantities That Cannot Be Counted

The word *much* is used correctly to describe quantities that cannot be counted, whereas *many* is used for quantities that can be counted. For example, you might refer to the beach as having "so *much* sand," since *sand* is a noncountable substance—you don't refer to "a hundred sands," for example. By contrast, you could say that your shoe contains "so *many* grains of sand," since *grains of sand* are countable—you might count "a hundred grains of sand," for instance.

Here's another example:

> Apparently, the university administration short-sightedly overlooked the fact that an influx of much more students would naturally require much more room for housing, classrooms, and other facilities.

Much more room is fine construction, since "room" is a noncountable substance of which more is required on this particular campus. But *much more students* should be *many more students*, since students are, obviously, countable.

Distinguish *fewer* (countable) and *less* (noncountable) in much the same way.

Rule 35: Use The Idiomatic Preposition

Prepositions are among the most ornery and troublesome words in English. There are dozens of expressions in which specific prepositions are paired with other words (often verbs) to convey a particular meaning. If the wrong preposition is used, the meaning may be obscured; but even if it isn't, the resulting sentence sounds non-idiomatic—that is, wrong. Here are a couple examples:

> Paradoxically, city planners have found that building new highways in the intention for reducing traffic congestion often increases it.

The continuing skirmishes between Microsoft and the U.S. Justice Department suggest that antitrust law has not yet been successfully adapted regarding such new fields as the software industry.

In the first sentence, the preposition *for* should be changed to *of*, since one normally speaks of an "intention *of* doing something," not *for* doing it (or anything else). In the second sentence, the offending preposition is *regarding;* it should be *to*, which is the idiomatic preposition to pair with the verb *adapt*.

Occasionally, choosing the idiomatic preposition seems illogical and arbitrary. For example, you *agree to* do something, but you *agree with* someone; two things *differ from* each other, but two people with opposite opinions *differ with* each other. Non-native speakers find these constructions difficult to distinguish and remember.

RULES ABOUT PUNCTUATION

We've already considered one of the most common punctuation errors tested on the ACT: misuse of the semicolon (Rule 24). Although there are dozens of ways that the various punctuation marks in English can be used and misused, we'll focus on just a few, which happen to turn up repeatedly on the exam.

Rule 36: Use A Colon (:) To Introduce A List Or A Restatement

FYI

Here's a handy rule of thumb for testing whether a colon is appropriate in a given sentence. If the word that is or namely could be inserted at the same spot, then a colon is probably correct.

Many students (and many graduates, for that matter) are uncertain as to how the colon and semicolon differ. Consequently, they use both interchangeably, often treating them as if they were merely "extra-strength commas" representing longer or more emphatic pauses.

Actually, each has its distinct use. As we discussed earlier, the semicolon is used primarily to separate two independent clauses. In such a role, the colon would usually be incorrect. Instead, use the colon to introduce a list or a restatement. Here's an example of each:

> For my term paper, I decided to write about the Beatles' last three albums: *The White Album, Abbey Road,* and *Let It Be.*

The colon is used correctly here. It alerts the reader that a list, which specifies the "last three albums" referred to, is about to be presented.

One warning: Usually, if an introductory *word* precedes the list and leads directly into it, you should omit the colon. Thus, if the sentence reads like the following, you do not need a colon:

> For my term paper, I decided to write about several of the Beatles' albums, including: *The White Album, Abbey Road,* and *Let It Be.*

The colon here seems intrusive, separating the introductory word "included" from the list it introduces. Better have no punctuation in that spot.

Here's an example of using a colon to introduce a restatement:

> Barbara was named valedictorian for one reason: her exceptional academic achievement.

What follows the colon "restates" what precedes it; the words "her exceptional academic achievement" name the "one reason" mentioned before the colon.

Rule 37: Use Commas To Separate Items In A List Of Three Or more

When three or more words, phrases, or clauses are presented in sequence, they should be separated by commas. Here are examples of each. First, words:

> The Galapagos Islands boast some of the world's most unusual plants, birds, mammals, reptiles, and fish.

Next, phrases:

> We looked for the missing gloves under the sofa, in the closet, and behind the dresser, but we never found them.

Finally, clauses:

> The plot of the movie was a familiar one: boy meets girl, boy loses girl, mutant from outer space devours both.

Notice two things about how these lists are crafted. First, you normally insert the word *and* before the final item in the series ("plants, birds, mammals, reptiles, *and* fish"). Second, the last comma (the one after *reptiles* in this example) is optional. Sometimes called *the serial comma,* it may be included or omitted according to taste. (The ACT test-makers have no special preference, and there's no "right" or "wrong" about it on the exam.) The other commas, however, are not optional; they *must* be used.

Rule 38: Use A Pair Of Commas To Set Off A Parenthetical Phrase

Think of a parenthetical phrase as an "interrupter"; it breaks into the flow of the main idea of the sentence, adding one or a few words in the most convenient spot, and then returning you to the main idea. Although parenthetical phrases may literally be set off by parentheses (as this one is), they may also be set off from the rest of the sentence by a pair of commas. Obviously, if the parenthetical phrase appears at the beginning or end of the sentence, only one comma is needed.

Some parenthetical phrases are frequently used. Examples include *for example, as you can see, that is, as I said before,* and so on. Whenever a similar phrase is used, it should be separated from the rest of the sentence by commas:

> Not all men like cars; my uncle, for example, never learned to drive and can't tell a Porsche from a Volkswagen.

Another type of parenthetical phrase is an *appositive,* which names or describes a noun. It, too, should be set off by commas. In this example, "the great left-handed Dodger pitcher" is an appositive:

> Sandy Koufax, the great left-handed Dodger pitcher, was the guest of honor at this year's sports club banquet.

Sometimes a parenthetical phrase may be quite long:

> I was surprised to learn that Paula, my cousin Frank's former girlfriend and a well-known local artist, had decided to move to Santa Fe.

You can probably see how the ten words enclosed by commas interrupt the main flow of the sentence. If you're unsure, try this test: Read the sentence without the phrase. If it still makes grammatical sense and the meaning is basically the same, then the phrase is parenthetical and should be set off by commas. This example passes the test:

> I was surprised to learn that Paula had decided to move to Santa Fe.

The interrupting words ("my cousin Frank's former girlfriend and a well-known local artist") should be surrounded by commas.

Rule 39: Don't Needlessly Separate Sentence Elements That Naturally Belong Together

Some writers overuse commas. Perhaps they do so because they think of a comma as a pause—even as a "pause for breath"—and therefore insert one whenever they fear that their own energy, or that of the reader, may be flagging.

A comma is indeed a pause, but it should correspond to a pause in the logic of the sentence. That is why commas are used to set off parenthetical phrases, as we just saw; in such a case, the commas make it clear to the reader that the logic of the sentence is being (temporarily) interrupted.

One sign of a comma-happy writer is when commas needlessly separate parts of the sentence that want to be together. For example, the subject and verb:

> Former secretary of state Henry Kissinger, is the author of several books on the history of diplomacy.

The verb *is* should not be separated by a comma from its subject *Henry Kissinger* (unless a parenthetical phrase intervenes between them—not the case here).

Similarly, avoid placing a comma between the verb and a subject complement that may follow it:

> The nineteenth-century explorers Lewis and Clark may be, two of America's most-admired historical figures.

In the same way, a preposition should not be separated from its object by a comma:

> As the storm continued, pieces of driftwood as well as, large quantities of sand were blown up onto the front porch.

The preposition *as well as* needs to remain connected to its object, the phrase *large quantities of sand.*

When commas are overused on the ACT, it will usually be in sentences like these examples, where the commas jarringly separate parts of the sentence that seem to "want" to be together.

Rule 40: Use The Apostrophe (') Correctly When Forming A Possessive Or A Contraction

The apostrophe is used for two purposes in English, both frequently tested on the ACT. Fortunately, the rules for both are pretty simple. Here they are.

A *possessive* is used to indicate ownership or some other close connection between a noun or pronoun and what follows it ("Susan's car," "the company's employees"). Form the possessive as follows:

- For a singular noun, add *'s*:

  the dog's paw
  James's necktie

- For a plural noun ending in *s*, just add an apostrophe:

  the Wangs' apartment
  the birds' feathers

- For a plural noun that does not end in *s*, add *'s*:

  the children's teacher
  the cattle's hooves

- The possessive pronouns *his, hers, its, ours, yours,* and *theirs* contain no apostrophes.

The other use of an apostrophe is in a *contraction,* a word made up of two or more words from which letters have been omitted for easier pronunciation. (By the way, contractions are *not* generally considered "incorrect" or "slangy"; they are perfectly acceptable in all but the most formal writing.) The apostrophe is usually (not always!) inserted in place of the letters omitted. If in doubt, mentally "expand" the contraction to determine which letters have been left out; this is often a useful guide to where the apostrophe belongs.

> we've got to go = we have got to go
> I'd rather not = I would rather not
> she won't mind = she will not mind
> it's your turn = it is your turn
> you're welcome = you are welcome

Proper use of the apostrophe in a contraction is basically a matter of correct spelling. If you've had problems with this in your writing, get into the habit of noticing how contractions are spelled in good writing. Then go and do likewise.

The Insider's Science Review for the ACT

THINKING IN SCIENCE

The purpose of the ACT Science Reasoning Test, say the test-makers, is to "measure the interpretation, analysis, evaluation, reasoning, and problem-solving skills associated with science." That's quite a mouthful. But what it comes down to, in the end, is a test of your ability to *think like a scientist*. The exam tries to measure this ability through a variety of specific tasks: interpreting the numbers on a graph; reading about an experiment and trying to figure out what it does and doesn't prove; and comparing two or more explanations of some natural phenomenon and analyzing how the explanations are similar and how they are different. By throwing these kinds of tasks at you and then having you answer questions about them, the ACT people hope to measure your skill at "thinking in science."

For some people, scientific thinking may come naturally, but for most people it is often difficult and frustrating. Those who find scientific reasoning easy and effortless usually don't realize that their thought processes follow a set pattern, and they often can't explain how they "know" something is true or teach others how to arrive at the same conclusion. (You may have had a classmate or teacher who was like this; his helpful "explanations" usually needed explanations of their own.)

Fortunately, however, the thinking processes employed by scientists do follow a specific, limited set of rules, making scientific reasoning a skill that can be taught and learned. In this appendix, you'll learn some basic strategies for "thinking in science." On the ACT, these strategies will help you to quickly decide what's important in the information provided on the test and will help you answer more questions quickly and correctly.

A Test of Facts or a Test of Skills?

The ACT Science Reasoning Test is made up of forty multiple-choice questions in seven test units, each covering a topic selected from the science courses most high school students take: biology, chemistry, earth/space sciences, and physics. Officially, you have been told that you do not need any "advanced knowledge" of these subjects to do well on the test.

That's true; all the specific information you'll need is provided either in the informational reading or in the question itself. However, you will need some broad background knowledge. For example, the exam might include a test unit that presents data about how well different kinds of solutions are able to permeate (that is, seep through) the membrane (the outer wall) of a certain kind of cell. All the data about these various levels of permeability will be given in the test unit. But if you don't know what the word *solution* means, or if you don't know what a *cell* is, you'll probably have trouble understanding the information and the questions about it.

However, if you don't have a thorough background in science, don't worry, and *don't* try to learn it all now. It would be very difficult to do, and the effort would probably prove to be more of a waste of time than a help. Instead, concentrate on learning the science thinking strategies in this chapter, and practice them as much as you can before taking the test. Ultimately, the ACT Science Reasoning Test is more a test of skills than of facts. You'll be better off honing those skills rather than trying to memorize a horde of facts.

Each of the test units is written in one of three different formats: Data Representation, Research Summaries, and Conflicting Viewpoints. Each format is designed to test a different set of skills. The next three sections of this chapter focus on the science thinking skills that are specifically emphasized in each of the three test formats.

MAKING SENSE OF DATA: READING GRAPHS, CHARTS, AND TABLES

One key to the advancement of scientific knowledge is the public presentation and sharing of experimental data. The sharing of the results of scientific work, and the idea that such results are the property of the scientific community as a whole and humanity in general, has been an integral part of science since its formal beginnings in ancient Greece. Not only does it encourage the sharing of ideas and information, often leading to further innovation, but it also fosters a feeling of goodwill among scientists. It also means that any scientific result must pass the scrutiny of many other scientists before it is generally accepted into the body of scientific knowledge.

The desire to share data brings with it the problem of how to present it. Today scientific papers are the primary medium for the sharing of data and other experimental results. These papers are printed in journals, most of which specialize in particular fields (*Cell*, for example, prints papers only in the field of cell biology) and are read almost exclusively by the scientists who specialize in those fields. Journals have strict guidelines regarding the format of papers, including rules about how data may be presented. Today, graphs and tables are an integral part of almost any scientific paper, for reasons that we will soon see.

The data recorded by scientists describe the phenomenon being observed in unambiguous, concrete terms, usually involving numbers: How many? How large? How hot? How fast? How bright? etc. The *data* derived from well-designed, properly-performed experiments cannot be disputed; only the *conclusions* drawn from the data can be. The publication of data makes it possible for experiments to be duplicated exactly (an important criterion for the acceptance of any new discovery or theory) and for variations or discrepancies to be quantified.

Furthermore, data can presumably be understood by anyone familiar with the experiment from which they derive and the science behind the experiment. Finally, data constitute a kind of world-wide language. A scientist in Japan, for example, can read a paper written in German, and even if he can only understand a few words in German he will be able to understand the data presented. For these reasons scientists frequently discuss their work in terms of the data they collect.

Ways of Presenting Data

There are many ways to present and share data. One way is to simply describe the data within a paragraph in a list-like fashion. Take, for example, the following passage from a scientific paper submitted by Professor H. I. Brau to the (fictitious) *New England Journal of Cola Science (NEJCS)*:

> The plants were each watered with different solutions of Jolt Cola, three times a day. Each solution had a different concentration of Jolt syrup in carbonated water. For Plant 1, the concentration was 0.0%; for Plant 2, 0.5%; for Plant 3, 1.0%; for Plant 4, 1.5%; for Plant 5, 2.0%; and for Plant 6, 2.5%. At the end of the month, the plants were measured. Plant 1 had grown 10 inches; Plant 2, 8 inches; Plant 3, 6 inches; Plant 4, 4 inches; and Plant 5, 2 inches. Plant 6 died before growing at all.

As you can probably tell, the purpose of Dr. Brau's experiment is to determine the effects of different concentrations of Jolt Cola on the growth of plants. However, although the data presented here are useful, they are difficult to grasp. If you want to look up the growth of a plant fed with a particular concentration of Jolt (such as Plant 4—1.5%), you may have to read through a great deal of undesired data before you can find it. Patterns and trends are difficult to observe. You may even find it somewhat confusing. These disadvantages are why a simple listing in paragraph form is a very poor way to present data.

Value-Value Sets

A better method of presenting data is in *value-value sets*. In Dr. Brau's experiment, the two values measured are Jolt concentration (measured as a percentage of Jolt syrup in carbonated water) and plant growth (measured in inches). Thus, the value-value set for each experimental concentration would be (concentration, growth in inches). The same data presented in this way would look like this:

$$(0.0\%, 10), (0.5\%, 8), (1.0\%, 6), (1.5\%, 4), (2.0\%, 2), (2.5\%, 0)$$

This is a distinct improvement. The data are condensed, and individual values are more easily accessible. However, some of the disadvantages of the simple listing are still present. Trends and patterns in the data are still very difficult to observe. (You may find this even more difficult in the value-value set format.) Furthermore, this format also omits much needed information. It is impossible to know what the numbers represent without some further explanation.

Tables

Fortunately, at the insistence of *NEJCS*, Professor Brau created a table of his data for inclusion in the published paper. (See Table D.1.)

This is a truly useful data format. Rather than being forced to read through a paragraph to find one particular set of data, we can now find the value we are interested in with a glance at the table. Because it is important that scientific data be clear and easy to understand, tables have become a very common feature in scientific papers and texts.

Dependent and Independent Variables

Tables are generally divided into horizontal rows and vertical columns. The values for the independent variable usually appear in the leftmost column. The

**Table D.1
The Effect on Plant Growth of Watering with
Varying Concentrations of Jolt Cola Solution**

Jolt Concentration (%)	Growth in Inches
0.0	10
0.5	8
1.0	6
1.5	4
2.0	2
2.5	0

independent variable is the experimental condition that is changed (or varied) in order to test its effect on the phenomenon being studied. In Dr. Brau's experiment, the independent variable is the concentration of Jolt.

The other variable being measured is called the *dependent variable*, because it is supposed to vary as a result of the effect of the independent variable. The dependent variable in Dr. Brau's experiment is the growth of the plants. The dependent variable generally appears in the second column (and other columns, if needed). In this simple table, the value-value pairs are next to each other, in the same row.

To find the plant growth after one month for the plant given a 1.0% concentration of Jolt, just look for this concentration in the leftmost column. You then move along the row to the column containing the corresponding growth measurement (6 inches).

In this table, there are only two columns because there is only one set of data points. If a second set of data points had been collected for the same independent variable, these values could have been entered in a third column. Possible reasons why there would be more than one set of data points are, for example, if Dr. Brau had repeated his experiment for another month, or if he had also tested to see the effect of Jolt concentration on another variable, such as budding. (See Table D.2.)

Notice that in both tables each column is clearly labeled at the top to tell the viewer what data is in the column. Aside from the number of rows and columns, tables come in many styles, but the differences between them are largely cosmetic.

**Table D.2
The Effect on Plant Growth and Budding of Watering with Varying
Concentrations of Jolt Cola Solution**

Jolt Concentration (%)	Growth in Inches	Buds Observed
0.0	10	32
0.5	8	16
1.0	6	8
1.5	4	4
2.0	2	2
2.5	0	0

Trends and Relationships

When using tables, trends in the data may become apparent. You probably noticed how, as the Jolt concentration increased, the monthly plant growth decreased. When one variable increases and the other decreases, we say that the relationship between the two variables is an *inverse relationship*. The opposite of this is a *direct relationship*, in which the variables increase or decrease together. Dr. Brau's experiment seems to suggest that an inverse relationship exists between the amount of Jolt in the water and the growth of the plant.

The table makes it easy to see the inverse relationship, but it may not be easy to see that the decrease in growth is proportional to the increase in concentration. A *proportional relationship* is one in which the ratio between two variables is constant (i.e., always the same). In Dr. Brau's experiment, every time the Jolt concentration increases by 0.5%, the plant growth decreases by 2 inches. Thus, the ratio between these two values is always the same, -4 (it is *minus* 4 because growth is *decreasing*; if the relationship were direct rather than inverse, the ratio would be a positive number).

Combining the two facts we've discovered allows us to say that the relationship between Jolt concentration and plant growth is *inversely proportional*. Because the numbers in Dr. Brau's experiment are nice, round numbers, the calculation is easy. If they were not—if the plants had grown by amounts like 2.12 inches and 3.97 inches—the calculation would be a little more difficult and the pattern would be less obvious.

The Birth of the Graph

The invention of the graph is commonly attributed to Rene Descartes, a French philosopher and mathematician who lived from 1596 to 1650. Although the first true graphs did not appear for nearly 150 years after Descartes, his crucial observation that a series of numbers can be represented by a line is the basis for all graphs. In the case of Dr. Brau's epoch-making work on Jolt, the ratio we uncovered above can also be thought of as the *slope* of the line that describes the data—a concept you should remember from your study of coordinate geometry.

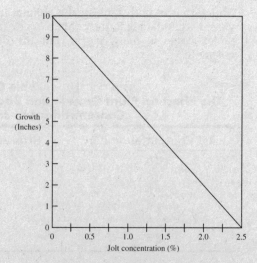

In the preceding figure, the data from Dr. Brau's experiment have been represented by a line. Like any other line, this one can be described by an equation. The equation for this line is:

$$y = 10 - 4x$$

where y is the value representing growth (measured in inches), and x is the value for the Jolt concentration (as a percentage of the solution). The value at which the line crosses the y axis is 10. This, is called the y-intercept, and can also be thought of as the value of y when the value of x is zero. The slope of the line is the same as the ratio above, -4. Thus the line is straight, the ratio is always the same, and we know that the proportionality discussed above is true.

Try plugging values into the equation and you will see that this equation describes the data accurately. For example, if Jolt concentration equals 2, by substituting 2 for x we get the equation $y = 10 - 4(2) = 2$.

For a curved line, the slope is constantly changing and the relationship the line describes is not proportional. By using a graph, we can avoid having to make any calculations to know this. Because graphs put numerical data into visual form, such patterns are easily spotted.

There are many different types of graphs. Scientists generally only use two: *bar graphs* and *line graphs*.

Bar Graphs

Bar graphs are good for making simple comparisons, such as comparing a single set of statistics (birth rates, for example) for different countries or different years. Dr. Brau's data could have been easily presented using a bar graph.

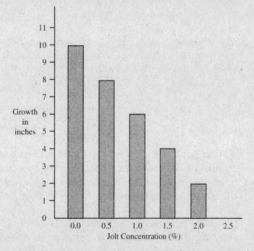

In the preceding figure, each bar represents the growth of a different plant fed with a different concentration of Jolt. The height of each bar represents the amount each plant grew.

This type of graph makes the differences in growth caused by varying the concentration of Jolt very clear. However, if the data were more complex, this graph would be more difficult to look at and understand. Imagine how the graph would look if Dr. Brau had used 100 different concentrations! A bar graph also has limitations when it comes to spotting trends. The proportionality mentioned above cannot be easily recognized in this graph.

Line Graphs

FYI

By convention, the independent variable in an experiment is usually placed on the horizontal axis, and the dependent variable on the vertical axis.

By contrast, line graphs can be both precise and intricate. For this reason, line graphs are the kind of graph most often used by scientists.

Both bar and line graphs have certain features in common:

All graphs have two *axes*, the *horizontal* (or *x*) *axis* and the *vertical* (or *y*) *axis*.

If chemist Vera Brainee were studying the effect of temperature on the solubility of a substance, the independent variable would be temperature, and the dependent variable would be solubility. The chemist would design the experiment so as to keep all other factors (such as the volume of the solvent, the pressure, etc.) constant, so that any changes in the solubility could clearly and unambiguously be attributed to the temperature. When the experiment was documented later, a graph of her data would have temperature along the horizontal axis and solubility on the vertical axis.

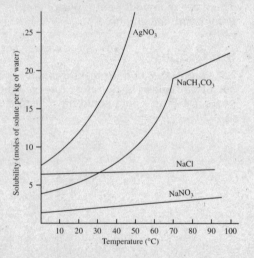

Notice that the preceding figure has more than one line. Each line shows the solubility of a different solute, with the name of the solute next to the line. The lines could also have been drawn differently, using different colors or styles, to differentiate them more clearly. In that case, the grapher could have identified each line separately in the key (see below). Because the independent and dependent variables are the same for each solute—temperature and solubility—they can be placed on the same axes. Presenting all the lines on the same graph allows comparisons to be made easily.

All properly-designed graphs have axes clearly labeled with the names of the variables being studied and the units of measurement (degrees, centimeters, percent, etc.). The divisions along the axes should be clearly numbered. All graphs should also have a title. Many graphs have a *key* providing additional information about the graph or the data. The key is usually found in one corner of the graph, or outside the limits of the graph altogether. A key is most often used when more than one line (or bar, or set of points) is plotted on one graph (see the following figure).

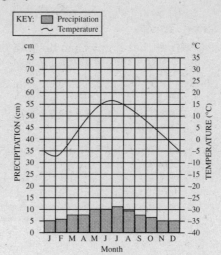

Because it would be otherwise impossible for the viewer to know what is meant by the data in such a case, different sets of data are distinguished from each other by using different colors or patterns for each line, bar, or set of points. The key explains to the viewer what each of the colors or patterns represents. You should always be sure to examine all of these features carefully whenever you encounter a graph.

By noting the independent and dependent variables in Dr. Brainee's graph, we can tell that the question her graph is designed to answer is, "How does temperature affect the solubility of these substances?" Once you know this, the specific details provided by the data—the answers to the questions, in effect—are easy to look up if you need them.

Scatter Graphs

As we've seen, a line graph is created by plotting data points (value-value sets) on graph paper (or, nowadays, most often by entering these points into a computer which is programmed to create the graph automatically). These points are then connected to create a line. If these points are not connected, the graph is called a *scatter graph*. This style of graph is often used when the points cannot be connected into a smooth line, perhaps because the relationship between the independent and dependent variables is complex or influenced by other, secondary factors.

For example, we know that, in a general way, a person's height and weight tend to vary together: NBA basketball players, who are usually very tall, usually weigh a lot as well, while professional jockeys are usually both short and light. But other factors (like diet) play a role in determining height and weight, and there are certainly exceptions to the general relationship: there are some people who are quite tall but very thin, and there are some people who are short and fat. Thus, a graph depicting the height and weight data sets for twenty randomly-chosen people (say, the first twenty men to sign up for a college gym class) would yield, not a neat line, but a scattering of points that reflects a direct relationship between the two variables only roughly (see the following figure).

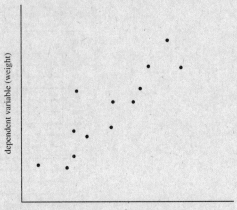

It is sometimes difficult to elucidate trends from a scatter graph. To help, a *best fit* line can be drawn in (see the following figure). The best fit line is designed to lie as close as possible to each of the data point. Some points may lie right on the line, others may lie on either side of it, but in general all the points should come close to the line.

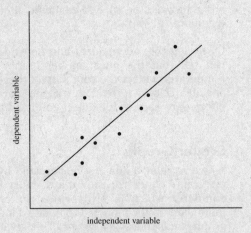

Scatter graph c̄ best fit line

Interpolation and Extrapolation

If the data form a continuous line (that is, a smooth line, either straight or curved), it can be represented by an equation. When this is the case, you can "work backward" by using the equation to determine specific values. When the relationship is clear, you can also use such a line (or its equation) to get values for points beyond those that have been determined experimentally. From Dr. Brau's data we can assume that if he had fed a seventh plant with a concentration of 0.25% Jolt, this plant would have grown nine inches. Although Dr. Brau did not test for this concentration, the graph and its equation can be used to infer this result. This is called *interpolation* (see the following figure).

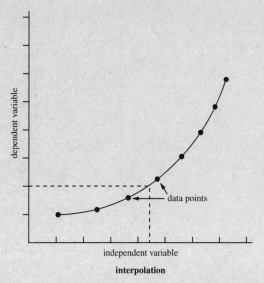

interpolation

Similarly, the lines on graphs can be extended beyond the limits of the experimentally tested values. This allows the observer to imagine what the results might have been for even higher concentrations of Jolt. (Actually, that's not a good example, since the highest concentration tested by Dr. Brau resulted in the *death* of the plant, and it's hard to imagine a more extreme effect than that. But you can imagine how this could work in a different case.) Extending the line in this way is called *extrapolation* (see the following figure). This is part of the power of graphs.

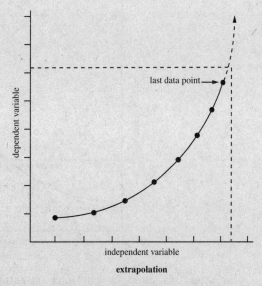

extrapolation

Population growth is a classic example of the limitations of extrapolation. As long as resources (food, water, living space) are plentiful, a human, animal, or plant population may continue to grow over time in accordance with predictable ratios, based on the number of offspring generated by each individual (see the following figure).

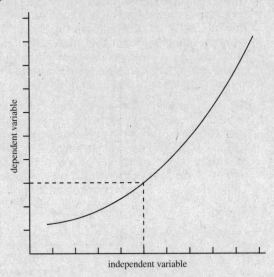

But the same line can't be extended forever. At some point, resources will begin to be scarce; food, water, even clear air may run out. Famine, disease, and perhaps warfare (among humans) will take their toll. (Among humans, artificial contraception—birth control—may have an important, somewhat unpredictable effect, too.) Eventually, the trend line will take a dramatic turn south, as in the following figure.

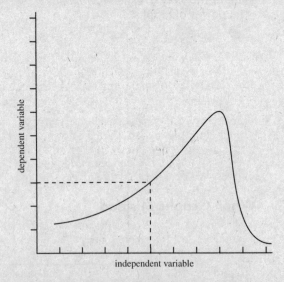

So scientists must be cautious in extrapolating trend lines. An intelligent assessment of limiting factors that may influence the trend must be part of any analysis that goes beyond what has been directly observed in nature or demonstrated in a laboratory.

Advantages and Disadvantages of Graphs

Graphs and tables share the advantage of making data points easily accessible. As we've seen, values can be found on one axis and, by tracing from the axis to the line and from this point on the line to the other axis, we can determine the corresponding value on the other axis. The superiority of the graph over the table lies in its clear visual representation of a trend, tendency, or underlying relationship. When there is no such trend or relationship, then a table of values is probably more useful and appropriate than a graph.

See the following figure, for example; here, the experimental results are "all over the map"; no clear relationship exists between the independent and dependent variables. Perhaps the independent variable is height, while the dependent variable is ACT scores. Since there's no tendency for taller (or shorter) people to score higher (or lower) on the ACT, there's no true trend line here—just a bunch of random points which, when connected, produce no coherent shape. This data would be more meaningfully presented in table form.

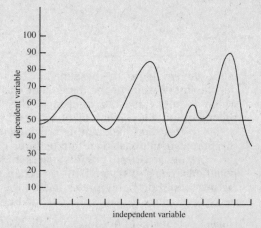

Graphs do have other basic advantages over tables. Lines and patterns are easier to remember than numbers, and are capable of catching the eye and stimulating the imagination. Many people do not respond to numbers but have a very intense response to pictures. Graphs exploit this.

Graphs can also condense a large amount of information into a small space. If Dr. Brau's experiment had been performed using hundreds of different concentrations, the table needed to contain all those values would have to be hundreds of lines long. But all the concentrations could be represented on a graph no larger than any of those we've already looked at.

When Graphs Mislead

A major disadvantage of graphs is that they can be less accurate than the numbers they represent. One reason is that values are sometimes rounded, either to make plotting easier or (a little less honestly) to better fit the pattern that the scientist has found—or hoped to find. The condensation of data, just described as an advantage, can also lead to imprecision. When a single graph is used to illustrate hundreds of thousands of individual pieces of data, any one case, or handful of cases, will be hard to pick out.

Graphs are also subject to subtle manipulation. One way of doing this is by adjusting the scale of values or the baseline of the graph. The *baseline* is the line from which any increase or decrease in a variable is measured. Usually the baseline value is zero, and it appears at the origin on the vertical axis, as in the following figure. (It forms, literally, the "bottom line" of the graph.) However, sometimes the baseline is set at a different value, as shown in the second of the following figures.

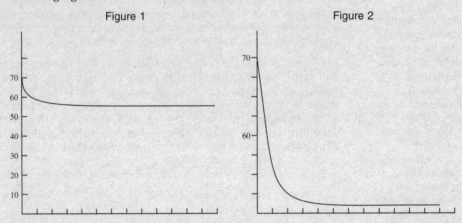

Figure 1   Figure 2

In the second figure, the baseline has been shifted up in order to emphasize the decline in the value of the dependent variable. The drop from 70 to around 52, which is noticeable but modest in the first graph, appears dramatic in the second graph. Such manipulation can be completely innocent, making the data easier to read and highlighting crucial variations. However, an adjustment like this can also emphasize certain features of the data, sometimes misleadingly. If the variable in these graphs represented, for example, the quantity of air pollutants being produced by a certain factory, the company managing the factory would probably prefer having the second graph published in the local newspaper, since it makes the decline in emissions appear so much greater.

Honest scientists do not intentionally present data in a false or misleading way. Sometimes, though, because they have such a good idea of the effect they hope to demonstrate even *before* they examine the data, scientists will emphasize certain portions of the data or certain trends without fully realizing what they are doing. (And journalists, social and political activists, and others with an "ax to grind" have often been known to deliberately manipulate graphic presentations to force a particular conclusion.)

Exercise 1

> **Directions:** Read the passage below, including the table and graph. Then answer the questions that follow.

Johannes Kepler (1571–1630) was a German philosopher and scientist who developed three laws of planetary motion, known today as Kepler's Laws. One of these laws states that the ratio of the cube of a planet's distance from the sun and the square of the planet's orbital period is the same for all planets. (*Orbital period* is the length of time it takes for a planet to complete one orbit around the Sun. It is determined by the ratio between the length of the planet's orbit and

Table D.3
Mean Distance from the Sun, Orbital Period, and Orbital Speed for the Nine Planets in Earth's Solar System

Planet	Mean Distance from the Sun (miles)	Orbital Period	Orbital Speed (miles per second)
Mercury	36,000,000	88 days	29.75
Venus	67,000,000	225 days	21.76
Earth	93,000,000	1 year	18.51
Mars	141,000,000	1 yr, 323 days	14.99
Jupiter	480,000,000	12 years	8.12
Saturn	900,000,000	29.5 years	5.99
Uranus	1,800,000,000	84 years	4.23
Neptune	2,800,000,000	164 years	3.38
Pluto	3,600,000,000	247.7 years	2.95

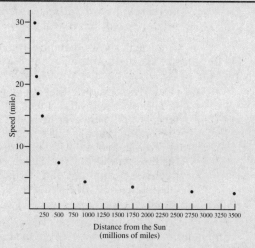

Distance from the Sun
(millions of miles)

the speed at which it travels in its orbit.) Another of Kepler's Laws states that the further a planet is from the Sun, the slower its orbital speed will be. We can deduce that the further a planet is from the sun, the longer the planet's orbit will be.

Table D.3 lists the planets in our solar system, their mean distance from the Sun, and their orbital speed. The figure following the table displays a part of this data graphically.

Questions

1. What term(s) are defined in the passage?

2. What relationship(s) between variables are described in the passage?

3. According to the data in the passage, how are the variables related to one another?

4. What variable appears on the horizontal (x) axis in the figure? What units of measurement are used on this axis?

5. What variable appears on the vertical (y) axis in the figure? What units of measurement are used on this axis?

6. What is the relationship between the variables shown in in the figure?

Answers

1. *Orbital period* is defined as the time it takes for a planet to orbit the Sun, as determined by the ratio between the length of the planet's orbit and the speed at which it travels in its orbit.

2. Two relationships are described in the passage. One is the relationship between a planet's mean (that is, average) distance from the Sun and the planet's orbital period. The other is the relationship between the planet's mean distance from the Sun and the planet's orbital speed.

3. By studying the three columns of data in Table D.3, we can see three clear relationships among variables. First, we can see that as a planet's mean distance from the Sun increases, its orbital period also increases. Second, we can see that as a planet's mean distance from the Sun increases, its orbital speed *decreases*. Finally, we can see that as the orbital speed decreases, the orbital period *increases*.

4. The x axis shows distance from the Sun, measured in millions of miles.

5. The y axis shows orbital speed, measured in miles per second.

6. The graph shows that as a planet's mean distance from the Sun increases, its orbital speed *decreases*. Thus, the relationship is an *inverse* one. However, it is not a proportional relationship, since the line on the graph is not straight. Instead, the rate of decrease in orbital speed diminishes with distance from the Sun. In other words, the further away from the Sun a planet is, the less its orbital speed is decreased from that of its neighbor nearer the Sun. Hence, the gradual "flattening out" of the curve as it moves toward the right side of the graph.

FROM HYPOTHESIS TO THEORY: BASIC METHODS OF SCIENTIFIC RESEARCH

Inductive and Deductive Reasoning

Scientists employ two types of logic to explain the natural and physical world, known as inductive and deductive reasoning.

Inductive reasoning moves from the specific to the general. Scientists do this when they use data from experiments or observations as the basis for a more general theory. Gregor Mendel (1822–1884) developed his theory of genetics based on his observations in growing many generations of pea plants. Mendel collected extensive data regarding the characteristics of over 28,000 of these plants and the ways in which those characteristics were transmitted from one generation to the next, with particular traits emerging as dominant and others receding in importance over time.

Needing a way to explain what he saw, Mendel was able to find certain statistical relationships among the data he collected, from which he determined, correctly, that independent units of heredity, now called *genes*, formed the basis by which traits were continually recombined from one generation to the next. Mendel's mental leap from specific observation to a general theory that explained those observations was a classic example of inductive reasoning.

Deductive reasoning, on the other hand, involves applying general laws to specific cases. Scientists do this when they use existing theories to explain experimental results or observations. Suppose a scientist observed that a particular characteristic in humans—for example, the hereditary condition known as sickle-cell anemia—was transmitted from one generation to the next following the same statistical relationships that Mendel observed in his pea plants. This scientist could use deduction to determine that Mendel's Laws of heredity apply to the inheritance of the sickle-cell trait, and on this basis make predictions about who is or is not likely to develop the disease.

Induction and deduction, in combination, form the underpinnings of the scientific method. As you'll see, both processes are involved in the development of a scientific theory.

Starting With a Hypothesis

The scientific method, in simple terms, involves first forming a hypothesis and then testing that hypothesis through observation, experimentation, and/or prediction.

A *hypothesis* is a tentative explanation for some natural phenomenon, one which has not been tested or verified in any way. Think of a hypothesis as an educated guess about why something happens or about the nature of the relationship between two or more variables. Nearly all scientific research starts with a hypothesis.

On reflection, you might think it is odd to *start* with a proposed explanation. Why not simply gather data at random first, and wait until later to develop a hypothesis? Forming a hypothesis first sets out a clear direction and goal for the subsequent observations and experiments. It also forces the scientist to think at length about what factors are likely to be influential and what scientific elements are involved (remember, it should be an *educated* guess).

Starting with a poor hypothesis usually leads to time-wasting, dead-end experiments. A good hypothesis must pass certain tests. In general, it must fit into the totality of the existing scientific framework. A hypothesis that runs contrary to the current body of scientific thinking is unlikely to gain favor in the scientific community, even to the extent of being widely examined, debated, or tested. This is because the theorems and laws in all the branches of science are highly interdependent. If a new hypothesis is based on the assumption that some major element in the dominant world-view of science is wrong, it's likely that many other elements must be assumed to be wrong as well. Most scientists would consider this both unlikely and too difficult to be worth testing.

Since much of what we believe today about the natural world has been demonstrated over time by extensive experimentation and a generally consistent body of observations, scientists are reluctant to accept a hypothesis that would require either a drastic rethinking of basic scientific principles or a wholesale junking of previously observed results. This helps to explain, for example, why few serious scientists are interested in experiments to test the existence of psychic phenomena (ESP, telekinesis, clairvoyance, etc.). Such a vast weight of evidence, experience, and theory exists that suggests the physical impossibility of these phenomena that it seems likely to be a waste of precious and limited resources to invest much time and effort in studying them.

FYI

"Entities are not to be multiplied without necessity"— William of Ockham (1285–1349), English philosopher. As applied to science, the significance of this principle— often called Ockham's Razor—*is that, when choosing between possible explanations for phenomena, it is generally better,* all other things being equal, *to choose the simpler one. Only if this fails would you resort to the more complex hypothesis.*

Nonetheless, it is true that hypotheses that dramatically diverge from the common body of knowledge will occasionally be proven true through experimentation or observation. Darwin's Theory of Evolution and Einstein's Theory of Relativity are two examples. Both were revolutionary in that they forced scientists to rethink certain basic assumptions they had previously taken for granted—the immutability of species in the case of Darwin, and traditional notions about the nature of gravity, matter, and energy in the case of Einstein. Such theories are rare, but they are integral to scientific advancement.

Another requirement for a good hypothesis is that it may not disagree with any observed phenomena. Furthermore, anything that can be deduced logically from the hypothesis also may not disagree with any observable phenomena. This test can often be used to rule out an incorrect hypothesis before any experimentation is done. Galileo (1564–1642), the Italian physicist and astronomer, used this test when attempting to form a hypothesis regarding the motion of falling bodies. He had initially hypothesized that the speed of a falling body would be proportional to the distance the body traveled: in other words, the greater the height from which an object fell, the faster it would fall. However, a logical deduction from this hypothesis was that the time required for two objects to fall different distances would be the same, which is contradicted by actual observation of falling objects. Thus, Galileo was able to eliminate this as a working hypothesis.

Testing a Hypothesis

Once a good hypothesis has been chosen, the next step is to test the hypothesis through experiment, observation, and/or prediction. The method(s) to be used will depend on the nature of the hypothesis. Mendel was able to perform genetic experiments using pea plants because of their short life cycle, which made it possible to study many generations of plants in just a few years. Similar experiments in human genetics are impossible, both because human generations are so long and because ethical and moral considerations forbid tinkering with human beings "just to see what happens."

In some fields of science, prediction is the crucial test of a hypothesis. The Copernican model of the solar system (with the Sun at its center) was largely confirmed because of its success in predicting such phenomena as eclipses. Similarly, Einstein's General Theory of Relativity was strongly supported in 1919 when, during a solar eclipse, starlight was observed to bend in the vicinity of the Sun in a manner predicted by Einstein.

Experimental Design

Scientific observation and experimentation today are generally very rigorous, strictly ordered, and highly accurate. In order to achieve this it is important that experiments are well designed and carefully executed and documented. The experimental methods and techniques must be consistent and clear. The crucial objectives in the design of all scientific experimentation are objectivity and reproducibility.

Objectivity refers to the need to design an experiment so as to eliminate the effects of personal bias on the part of any experimenter or of anyone who participates in analyzing the resulting data. Bias need not be conscious; in fact, the most insidious and difficult-to-eliminate forms of bias are so subtle that the experimenter is unaware they exist. For example, even if the experimenter has no "preference" for a particular outcome of an experiment, he or she may unconsciously hope merely that the experiment will yield results that are clear and "interesting." A bias as slight as this may influence how an experimenter "reads" the results, producing slight errors in the observation or recording of data that, cumulatively, may have a major impact on the accuracy of the research.

To reduce or eliminate such bias, experiments are often designed to be *blind*. In a blind experiment, the experimenter is prevented from knowing which test subjects represent the variable and which represent the control. For example, suppose an experiment is being performed to test the effect of a new drug on laboratory rats. The new drug will be placed in the food of the test group, but not in the food of the control group. If this experiment were blind then the experimenter would have no knowledge about which rat is being fed the drug until after all the data has been collected. By doing this, the experimenter will have no way of knowing what results to expect from each individual rat.

Blind experiments are especially common in research involving human subjects. Such experiments are often designed to be *double blind*, meaning that neither the experimenter nor the subjects know who represents the control group. If the new drug was tested on people, the test group would receive a pill containing the drug, and the control group would receive a pill containing no active ingredient (known as a *placebo*), but all subjects would believe that they were receiving the new drug.

In addition, the experimental protocol (that is, the written procedure to be followed in conducting the experiment) must be carefully planned so as to remove any opportunity for experimental bias to affect the results. For example, decisions as to the timing of steps in the experiment, the selection of subjects, and other methodologies must not be left to the discretion of the experimenter but must be deliberately predetermined. If practicalities dictate that a selection process must occur in choosing experimental subjects, a truly random procedure must be developed (for example, selecting every tenth seedling in a nursery rather than a "representative sampling" arbitrarily chosen by the experimenter).

Reproducibility means that it must be possible to duplicate the procedures in the experiment so as to test the validity of the results. One hallmark of scientific knowledge is that, within specified parameters, it is broadly and generally applicable. Subject to specified conditions, such as air pressure, pure water will boil at exactly the same temperature everywhere in the world. A sound experiment is equally reproducible by any competent scientist.

Maybe you recall the furor several years ago when some scientists claimed to have successfully produced the phenomenon known as "cold fusion." If true, this would have been an epochal scientific discovery with enormous practical implications; fusion is a powerful energy source, and cold fusion (i.e. fusion at a temperature close to normal room temperature) would have the potential of being an incredibly cheap, virtually unlimited form of energy. The excitement quickly turned to disappointment and anger when, the scientists' description of their experiments proved to be too vague to be reproducible, and the attempts to duplicate their work failed to yield any noteworthy amount of energy. It was widely understood that *reproducibility* was the crucial test on which the significance of these remarkable claims would rise and fall.

Degrees of reproducibility may differ from one field of science to another, however. In a field like physics, the precision and reproducibility of a particular experiment may be almost unbelievably high. Physics experiments generally occur under conditions that are precisely controlled, and the phenomena being observed are often very fleeting and frequently involve very tiny particles. Small errors can therefore make a huge difference (units like "a second" or "a centimeter" would be laughably vague in this context). The conditions, then, are specified with enormous precision, and the experiments are usually reproducible provided that the same equipment is used and the same procedure is followed.

In other fields, experimental design is less precise. Experiments in chemistry and biology may only have marginal reproducibility. This is, in part, because variables other than those being tested may affect the results, including such basic and largely unavoidable variables as the source of supplies (are the vials of hydrochloric acid sold by Chemical Company A as pure as those sold by Chemical Company B?) and the climate and altitude in which the experiments are performed.

Generally speaking, the more reproducible the experiment, the more likely the results are to be accepted by the scientific community at large, and, in time, integrated into the scientific canon. However, each branch of science has its own acceptable level of reproducibility. In the social and psychological sciences, "human factors" are so pervasive—indeed, they are the very *subject matter* of these sciences—that true reproducibility and universality of results is almost never achieved.

Variables

Nearly all experiments are designed with certain elements in common. Two of these basic elements are the *independent* and *dependent variables*.

The independent variable is named so because it is adjusted independently of other factors. Usually the independent variable is controlled by the experimenter, although there are many instances in which it is not under any control and may only be observed. (Consider weather, a possible variable in an earth science or biology experiment, as one obvious example.) In any case, it's desirable to have one and only one independent variable in a given experiment. Experiments with two or more variables are harder to reproduce, and it's difficult to draw reliable conclusions from them since it's usually impossible to determine with certainty the relative importance of each variable—or the unpredictable ways that two or more variables may affect each other. Ideally, scientists need to be able to account for all the phenomena they observe, or else they cannot say for sure why changes occur.

The Control

Another element used in nearly all experiments is the *control*. The control is an experimental subject for which all the relevant variables, including the independent variable, are held constant. Because the independent variable is held constant, any changes observed in the control must be caused by other factors. These changes can then be accounted for throughout the rest of the experiment.

For example, in testing a new experimental therapy for AIDS, researchers might study two groups of patients: a group receiving the new treatment and a control group that is not receiving the new treatment. It would be important to match the two groups as closely as possible in every other way: the average age, the severity of AIDS symptoms, and the nature of any other health problems suffered, among other characteristics, ought to be quite similar in both groups. If this is done, and if the experimental group shows a markedly better rate of recovery than the control group, it would be reasonably good evidence that the improvement is due to the new therapy rather than any other factor.

FYI

If an experiment lacks a control group, it severely limits the conclusions that can be drawn from it. Thus, the health cures claimed by medical charlatans can often be discounted because no control group is tested.

Exercise 2

Directions: Read the passage below, including the accompanying graphs. Then answer the questions that follow.

Enzymes are special proteins that act as catalysts to speed up chemical reactions in cells. Enzymes catalyze reactions by first having their active site bind to its *substrate*, usually the molecule that is undergoing reaction. The ability of an enzyme to bind substrate is called its *activity*. Thus, activity is also a measure of how well an enzyme catalyzes a reaction. The active site of an enzyme is very specific for its substrate. This specificity is created by the three-dimensional shape of the enzyme. However, this three-dimensional shape is dependent upon environmental factors, such as temperature and pH, a measure of acidity.

If the shape of the enzyme is changed, the enzyme may no longer be able to bind to its substrate. In this case, the enzyme is said to be *denatured*. Extremes of either temperature or pH can cause enzymes to denature.

A scientist isolated three enzymes from a mamalian cell. These enzymes will be denoted Enzyme A, Enzyme B, and Enzyme C.

Experiment 1

A scientist placed samples of Enzyme A into twelve different tubes. Each tube contained a buffer solution at a different pH such that the first tube was at pH = 1, the second tube at pH = 2, the third tube at pH = 3, and so on up to the twelfth tube, which was at pH = 12. The scientist then added an indicator that would turn the solution yellow if bound by the enzyme. Thus, the solution would turn more yellow when more indicator was bound. The temperature for all the tubes was 25°C. This procedure was repeated for Enzyme B and Enzyme C. The scientist was then able to create the graph shown in the following figure.

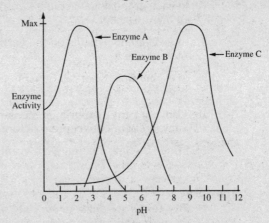

Experiment 2

A sample of Enzyme A was placed into a single tube containing a buffer solution at the pH that gave the greatest activity in Experiment 1. The tube was then brought to near freezing, and a sample was taken and tested for activity by addition of the same indicator above. The tube was then gradually warmed, with samples taken every five degrees and tested for activity. The process was repeated for Enzyme B and Enzyme C. The scientist was then able to make the graph shown in the following figure.

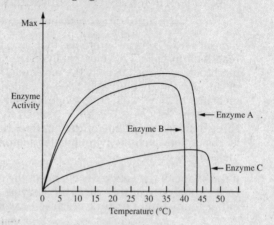

Questions

1. What terms are defined in the passage?

2. What relationships are described in the first paragraph of the passage?

3. What is the independent variable in Experiment 1? In Experiment 2?

4.   What is the dependent variable (i.e., what is being observed) in Experiment 1? In Experiment 2?

5. What factor(s) are kept stable in Experiment 1? In Experiment 2?

6. In each experiment, what is the hypothesis that is being tested?

7. In each graph, what is on the horizontal (x) axis, and what are the units of measurement?

8. In each graph, what is on the vertical (y) axis, and what are the units of measurement?

9. In each graph, what relationship is shown between the variables on the axes for each of the three enzymes (A, B, and C)?

10.   How are the two graphs similar and different? What relationship, if any, is there between the data in the two graphs?

11.   Does the information each graph presents support the other?

Answers

1. Five terms are defined: *enzyme, substrate, activity, denature* and *pH*. We learn that an enzyme catalyzes reactions—that is, it speeds them up. The reactant the enzyme catalyzes is the substrate. We learn that activity, in the special sense in which the word is used here, is the ability of an enzyme to bind substrate. We learn that to denature is to change the three-dimensional shape of an enzyme in such a way that it

is no longer able to bind to its substrate. Finally, we learn that pH is a measure of the acidity of a substance.

2. We learn that there are certain relationships among all the terms defined in the first paragraph of the passage. If the three-dimensional shape of the enzyme is changed, then the ability of the enzyme to bind the substrate is lessened. If the enzyme's ability to bind the substrate is lessened, then its ability to catalyze the reaction (i.e. activity) is lessened. Therefore, there is a relationship between the three-dimensional shape of the enzyme and its activity. Furthermore, we learn that, in certain circumstances, there is a relationship between the three-dimensional shape and temperature and between the three-dimensional shape and pH.

3. In Experiment 1, the independent variable is pH. In Experiment 2, the independent variable is temperature.

4. For both experiments, the scientist is observing the enzyme's activity. We know this by combining the information in the first paragraph of the passage with the description of the two experimental protocols. *Activity*, we've seen, is defined as the ability to bind substrate. In both experiments, the degree of yellow in the solution is used to measure how much enzyme binds the indicator; thus, the degree of yellow indicates the enzyme's activity. The activity, then, is the dependent variable.

5. In Experiment 1, temperature is kept stable (so as to highlight the effects of varying pH levels in the twelve tubes). In Experiment 2, pH is kept stable (to highlight the effects of varying temperatures).

6. In Experiment 1, since the scientist is measuring the effect of varying levels of pH on enzyme activity, we can infer that the hypothesis being tested is the following: *The activity of Enzymes A, B, and C is dependent to a greater or lesser extent upon the pH level of the surrounding solution.*

   In Experiment 2, the scientist is hypothesizing as follows: *The activity of Enzymes A, B, and C is dependent to a greater or lesser extent upon the temperature of the surrounding solution.*

7. In the first figure, pH appears on the horizontal axis; the unit of measurement is pH units. In the second figure, temperature appears on the horizontal axis; the unit of measurement is degrees Celsius.

8. In both graphs, enzyme activity appears on the vertical axis; the unit of measurement is not specified, but we are told that maximum activity is at the top of the y-axis. Thus, eznyme activity increases as you travel up the y-axis.

9. In the first figure, each enzyme shows the tendency first to increase in activity as pH rises, then to decrease in activity as pH rises further. Thus, each enzyme has a pH at which it displays maximum activity. This differs for each enzyme. For Enzyme A, the pH at which maximum activity occurs is around 2; for Enzyme B, it is around 6; for Enzyme C, it is around 10.

   In the second figure, each enzyme shows the tendency to slowly increase in activity as temperature rises. This increase eventually levels out, and the enzyme activity is stable over a range of temperatures. Then, it suddenly drops off, quickly falling to no activity. The temperatures at which the enzyme activity rises and (suddenly) falls differ from enzyme to enzyme. In addition, Enzymes A and B attain a markedly higher level of activity that Enzyme C.

10. The graphs are similar in that they both present data regarding the activity levels of the same three enzymes (A, B, and C). However, the independent variable is different in each. Therefore, there is no direct relationship between the two graphs; each shows the effect on enzyme activity of a different key variable.

11. In this case, the graphs do not support or contradict each other because each shows activity as a function of a different variable.

FROM DATA TO CONCLUSION: UNDERSTANDING AND COMPARING DIFFERENT VIEWPOINTS

Earlier, we said that *data*, if compiled and recorded accurately, cannot be disputed, but the *conclusions* drawn from data can be. Scientists often disagree with the conclusions of their peers. The level of disagreement varies from time to time, and sometimes even between the different branches of science.

Currently, for example, the field of paleontology (the study of ancient life, as recorded in fossil remains) is one in which disagreement even about fairly fundamental matters is frequent. The origins of the human species are still hotly debated, and each new discovery seems to create a new controversy. In this case, one cause of the debate lies in the fact that the data (the fossils) can be interpreted in a variety of ways. And because of the random destruction wrought by time, and the inaccessibility of many fossils, there are also many gaps in the fossil record which can be filled at present only by speculation and educated guesses.

By contrast, there is currently relatively little debate about fundamental principles among chemists. This is because the field of chemistry as presently conceived appears to be fairly complete. Almost every new discovery can be explained in a way which agrees nicely with the current body of knowledge. Only on the rare occasion when a new discovery seems to disagree with previous theories or ideas do chemists sometimes argue.

Complex Systems

Sometimes different conclusions are possible when scientists are examining a complex system in which there are several interrelated variables. Because of the complexity of living systems—referring not only to individual creatures but to the interconnected webs of life that make up an ecological system—there is often disagreement among biologists concerning cause and effect, the forces behind ecological change, and so on. Biological complexity is difficult to eliminate even under experimental conditions; it is hard to eliminate variables without upsetting the equilibrium of the system. As a result, ecologists often argue. The different conclusions they draw about the systems they study may all be logically correct and consistent with the data. The differences are due to the fact that different ecologists will give different weights to the same complexly-interconnected variables.

Identifying Significant Factors

FYI

Occasionally a particular scientific field which appears to be a more or less settled body of knowledge is revolutionized by a new theory or a dramatic series of discoveries. The field of earth science was basically uncontentious in the late 19th and early 20th centuries until the new theory of plate tectonics exploded onto the scene. By the 1960s, earth science had become a hotbed of scientific controversy.

When you think like a scientist in an effort to form a conclusion about the cause of some observed phenomenon, you must first decide what factors are important in the situation under scrutiny. When there are many different factors to consider, this may be difficult. The process of isolating the most significant factors is often best managed through gradual elimination of the unimportant or irrelevant factors. Consider the following situation:

> Jane was walking to school one day in November when she noticed that about two dozen small orange fish, which she had previously seen swimming in the pond next to the school, were floating on top of the water, dead. Looking more closely, Jane could find no other sign of animal life in the pond, but she did observe that there were dozens of frogs on the lawn next to the pond. (She couldn't recall noticing frogs near the pond before.)
>
> The day was sunny and mild, but Jane knew that the previous night there had been a severe storm of rain mixed with sleet; the local temperature had plummeted below freezing for the first time that autumn. Jane also noticed that the Squmb River emptied into the pond. She knew that the Squmb River flowed past an operational nuclear power plant about two miles upstream. Jane went to school. Later that morning, when she happened to glance outside during history class, she saw the school's custodian emptying yesterday's lunch leftovers into the pond.

Here is a mystery. What caused the death of the fish in the pond? Let's consider each element in the situation, beginning by eliminating all the factors that are unlikely to be relevant. Could the frogs somehow be responsible for the death of the fish? This seems implausible. Frogs are obviously not predators of fish. And although it is possible that the frogs and the fish might compete for some resources—they might both eat some of the same insects, for example—it seems unlikely that dozens of fish would die suddenly because the frogs managed to eat up all of their food. We can probably eliminate the frogs as a relevant factor in this case.

Next, consider the role that the weather could have played. It is possible that the sudden cold killed the fish. However, two factors make this unlikely. First, we know that water usually acts as an insulator; water temperatures change much more slowly than air temperatures, which is why the pond did not freeze overnight, despite the cold weather. (Remember, Jane saw the dead fish *floating* on the liquid surface of the pond.) The fact that the frogs are alive also tends to weaken this hypothesis. If the cold had killed the fish, it probably would have killed the frogs, too.

That leaves us with two other pieces of evidence: the existence of the nuclear power plant upstream and the dumping of cafeteria wastes in the water. It's possible that either cause might have killed the fish, since either could have introduced some unhealthful chemicals into the pond. How could Jane determine which factor was responsible?

It would be pretty tough to set up experimental conditions, controlling for all but a single variable, in the real world, as in Jane's pond. Thus, Jane would probably need to make an educated guess about the cause of the dead fish. Additional data could certainly be gathered. Jane could ask the custodian about the nature of the food he had dumped into the pond. His answer, if accurate, could help clarify whether any toxic substances were involved.

Jane could also conduct some research into the activities of the nuclear power plant. How recently did it begin operating? (If the plant had been on line for several years, with the fish thriving until now, it would tend to weaken the argument that the plant is the cause of the fish's demise.) What pollutants, if any, are known to be emitted into the stream by the plant? (Government records are likely to exist that may shed light on this question.) Did any substantive change in the plant's operations occur just prior to the death of the fish? If so, it could be relevant to an explanation.

As you can see, the mystery of the fish pond is unlikely to have an easy-to-find solution. Real-life scientific issues like this one generally lead to disagreements among researchers. However, disagreement is not necessarily a bad thing. Very often, disagreement spurs on research, as scientists in the different camps search for the proof that their theory is correct.

Exercise 3

Directions: Read the passage below. Then answer the questions that follow.

The origin of modern humans and the evolutionary path by which our ancestors first emerged has long been the subject of heated debate. Of particular interest is exactly where and when modern humans (*Homo sapiens*) evolved, and the relationship between modern humans and so-called Neanderthal man (generally considered to be a primitive form of *Homo sapiens*). Three varying theories concerning these issues are presented below.

Theory 1

Homo erectus (a primitive ancestor of *Homo sapiens*- modern humans) evolved in Africa about 1.6 million years ago and soon after spread to all parts of the Old World. The Neanderthals and all other primitive forms of *Homo sapiens* then evolved from *Homo erectus*. In time, these primitive forms evolved into modern humans. This was the first proposed theory, based originally on fossil dating that suggested a continuous time line leading, one by one, from *Homo erectus* to the various primitve forms (including Neanderthal) and, from these, on to modern humans. Since then, new fossil discoveries have been accounted for (with varying success) by using this theory.

Theory 2

Homo erectus evolved in Africa about 1.6 million years ago and soon spread to all parts of the Old World. Neanderthals are evolutionarily decended from those *Homo erectus* individuals that migrated to the Old World. However, the Neanderthals did not evolve into modern humans. Rather they represent a now-extinct side branch on the evolutionary tree of the genus *Homo*. *Homo sapiens* evolved independently of Neanderthals in the Old World, eventually supplanted the Neanderthal population, and later evolved into modern humans. This is based on fossil evidence, which suggests that the Neanderthals were too primitive (based primarily upon cranial measurements taken of fossilized skulls) to possibly have been ancestors of modern humans. However, the skulls of other early *Homo sapiens* show traits that seem to follow the evolutionary line to modern humans.

Theory 3

Homo erectus evolved in Africa about 1.6 million years ago and soon spread to all parts of the Old World. The Neanderthals are evolutionarily decended from those *Homo erectus* individuals that migrated to the Old World, as are the other primitive *Homo* forms, which were determined to be direct ancestors of *Homo sapiens* according to the evidence in Theory 2. However, according to this theory, modern humans actually evolved separately in Africa, and did not spread to the rest of the world until about 90,000 years ago. This is based on evidence taken from mitochondrial DNA (DNA that resides in the mitochondria and that passes undisturbed from mother to child), which suggests that all modern humans can trace their lineage to a single group of individuals living in southern Africa about 90,000 years ago.

Questions

1. What assumptions are at the core of each theory?

2. How does the evidence cited differ in each case?

Answers

1. Theory 1 assumes that *Homo sapiens* evolution must have been a continuous event, stemming from the first *Homo erectus* to enter the Old World.

   Theory 2 also assumes that *Homo sapiens* evolved from the *Homo erectus* population in the Old World. However, it assumes that the Neanderthals were too primitive to have been an ancestor of modern humans. Thus, there were two branches on the evolutionary tree.

   Theory 3 assumes that modern humans evolved in Africa and are not related to primitive *Homo sapiens* in the Old World, including Neanderthal. This assumes that there are three or more branches on the human evolutionary tree, and that these evolutionary changes took place in drastically different places.

2. Theory 1: The evidence is fossils. Weight is given to dating techniques.

   Theory 2: The evidence is fossils, but this time weight is being given to features (mainly of skulls), not dating.

   Theory 3: The evidence is mitochondrial DNA.

THE INSIDER'S ACT SCIENCE GLOSSARY: 180 TERMS AND CONCEPTS MOST LIKELY TO APPEAR ON THE EXAM

Introduction

The following terms and concepts have been chosen as among the most significant in the fields tested on the ACT Science Reasoning test—that is, biology, chemistry, earth/space sciences, and physics.

This list is by no means a complete list of all the terms and concepts you should have encountered in high school science. Furthermore, to fully grasp the meaning of some of these terms may require an understanding of other concepts that are not listed. So this is not intended as a thorough review of high school science. However, you'll find that studying this list is a helpful way to refresh your memory of crucial science topics you've studied throughout your high school years. It'll also highlight for you the topics or areas in which your background is strongest and weakest. If you find that some of these terms are unfamiliar to you, you may wish to review the relevant topics, using your favorite science textbook or study guide.

Chemistry

I.   Basic Definitions

matter—anything that exhibits the property of *inertia* (see below).

energy—a property of matter, which describes the ability to do work. Energy takes many forms, including *potential energy* and *kinetic energy* (see below).

mass—the measure of the amount of matter.

atom—the smallest unit of an element, composed of electrons, protons, and neutrons, that still has all the properties of that element.

atomic mass—the average mass of the atoms of a given element. Atomic mass is measured in atomic mass units. One atomic mass unit has been set at one-twelfth the mass of the carbon-12 atom.

molecular mass—the mass of a molecule, found by summing the atomic masses of each of the atoms within the molecule.

Avogadro's number—the number of atoms in 12 grams of carbon-12, equal to 6.022×10^{23}. This constant is used in various chemical and physical calculations and formulas.

mole—The amount of a substance consisting of Avogadro's number of elementary particles (atoms or molecules). Therefore, one mole of any substance contains 6.022×10^{23} elementary particles.

empirical formula—the chemical formula of a compound that shows the relative number of atoms of each element in terms of the smallest integers. Thus, the empirical formula shows the ratio of elements within a compound.

molecular formula—the chemical formula of a compound that specifies the actual number of atoms of each element in a compound.

conservation of mass—the law that states that in every chemical reaction there must be an equal quantity of matter before and after the reaction.

II.   Atomic Structure

electron—a negatively charged subatomic particle.

proton—a positively charged subatomic partcle.

neutron—a neutrally charged subatomic particle

nucleus—the small, positively charged center of an atom, composed of protons and neutrons.

orbital—one of several spaces around the nucleus of an atom, each of which can be occupied by up to two electrons. All the electrons in a given orbital must have the same energy level, energy sublevel, and spatial orientation.

III. Molecular Bonding

lone-pair electrons—an unshared pair of electrons in the outermost orbital of an atom.

ion—an atom or group of atoms that has gained or lost one or more electrons. This causes the atom or group of atoms to become either negatively or positively charged.

compound—a substance containing two or more elements.

ionic bond—a bond formed through the attraction of two ions of opposite charge.

covalent bond—a bond formed between two atoms by the sharing of electrons.

isomers—two forms of a chemical compound that have the same chemical formula but a different spatial configuration.

polarity—asymmetrical charge distribution over a molecule. Such a molecule is called a *dipole*.

hydrogen bond—the strong dipole-dipole interaction that forms between a hydrogen atom bonded to a strongly electronegative atom (such as oxygen) and a lone-pair electron on a nearby electronegative atom. Hydrogen bonds are very weak. (Millions of hydrogen bonds are constantly forming and unforming in a glass of water. These bonds are responsible for the special properties of water, such as its elevated boiling point.)

van der Waals forces—weak forces of attraction between two molecules. These forces do not result in a bond. Rather, they represent the attraction of the electrons of one atom for the protons of another, in much the same way opposite pole of a magnet attract each other.

IV. States of Matter

solid—a phase of matter in which a substance has definite shape and volume. The atoms in a solid have the lowest kinetic energy of the three phases, because their molecules are relatively fixed in space.

liquid—a phase of matter in which a substance has no definite shape but has a definite volume. Matter in the liquid phase has a kinetic energy intermediate between that of mass in solid phase and mass in the gaseous phase.

gas—a phase of matter having no definite shape and a volume that is defined only by the size of the container. The gaseous phase is the most energetic phase for a given substance.

crystal—a solid in which the particles are arranged in a repeating geometrical pattern.

V. Methods of Separation

fractionation—the separation of a mixture into its parts.

chromatography—a method of fractionation in which a mobile phase containing the mixture to be separated is passed over a stationary phase, which displays some affinity for the materials in the mobile phase. This affinity may be based upon polarity, size, or some form of reversible binding ability (such as between an enzyme and its substrate). The stationary phase must be carefully chosen so as to maximize the differences in affinity for the various substances in the mobile phase.

fractional distillation—the separation of two or more components of a liquid solution on the basis of their different boiling points. This is done by repeated evaporation and recondensation of the components.

VI. Kinetics and Thermodynamics

pressure—the force exerted by moving particles on a specified unit area. Thus, pressure may be expressed as pounds (the force) per square inch (the unit area).

temperature—a measure of the average kinetic energy of molecules.

heat—the means by which energy is transferred from a hot body to a colder body.

calorie—the amount of heat required to raise one gram of water 1°C.

melting point—the temperature at which the liquid and solid phases of a substance are in equilibrium.

boiling point—the temperature at which the liquid and gas phases of a substance are in equilibrium.

enthalpy—a measurement of the energy of a system due to the movement of its particles. At constant pressure, the enthalpy change of a system is equal to the heat absorbed.

entropy—a measurement of the disorder of a system. A fundamental law is that the enthalpy of the universe is constantly increasing. However, in many reactions the enthalpy is decreased (i.e., the system is more ordered after the reaction than before). (Biological systems tend to employ reactions which increase the order of the system. In order to do this, they must create more disorder in the surrounding environment. This is one of the reasons many reactions in biological systems require a great input of energy.)

free energy—the chemical potential energy of a chemical substance or system.

VII. Solutions and Reactions

solution—a homogeneous mixture of a solute and sovent. The solute is that which is dissolved in the sovent.

concentration—the ratio between solute and sovent in a solution.

molarity—the number of moles of solute present per liter of solute.

molality—the number of moles of solute present per kilogram of solvent. Because one kilogram of water has a volume of one liter, molality is also the number of moles of solute present per liter of water, and the molality and molarity of such solutions are equal.

acid—a substance capable of donating hydrogen ions. This is called the Bronsted-Lowry definition. Alternately, the Lewis definition says that an acid is any species that accepts electron pairs. This definition is more general. Acids have a sharp, sour taste; vinegar is an example

base—a substance capable of accepting hydrogen ions. This is known as the Bronsted-Lowry definition. (By corollary, bases dissolved in water increase the amount of hydroxide ion [OH].) Alternately, the Lewis definition says that a base is any species that donates lone-pair electrons. This definition is more general. Bases are slippery.

salt—a compound consisting of the positive ion of a base and the negative ion of an acid.

pH—a measure of the hydronium ion concentration in a solution. $pH = -\log[H_3O^+]$.

titration—a technique in which small ammounts of an acid or base of known concentration and pH are added to a solution in order to determine the pH of the solution. By using an indicator or a pH meter, the experimenter can observe the change in pH caused by these additions, and from this data and from the known pH and volume of acid or base added, the pH of the solution can be determined.

buffer—a solution that maintains a constant pH despite the addition of small amounts of acid or base. A buffer is usually made by mixing a weak acid with its conjugate weak base.

activation energy—the minimum collision energy required between two molecules for a reaction to occur.

catalyst—a substance that takes part in a chemical reaction and causes it to go faster. The catalyst itself is not a reactant and undergoes no chemical change.

inhibitor—a substance that slows the rate of a reaction. There are three main types of inhibitors: competitive, uncompetitive, and mixed inhibitors.

reaction rate—the rate of formation of product in a reaction.

oxidation—the loss of electrons.

reduction—the gain of electrons.

functional group—a group of atoms in a molecule (usually organic) that exhibit charateristic properties. Examples of functional groups commonly encountered are alcohols ($-OH$), aldehydes and ketones ($-C=O$; in ketones this group is internal), carboxylic acid ($-COOH$), and amines ($-NH_2$).

Biology

I. The Building Blocks of Life

amino acid—a compound made up of carbon, hydrogen, nitrogen, oxygen, and contain one of more than 20 different possible side groups. The general formula for amino acids is $H_2N-CHR-COOH$, where R is the side group.

protein—a compound made up of many amino acids linked together end to end. Proteins are integral to building many structural features in the cell. Enzymes are also proteins.

carbohydrate—a compound made up of carbon, hydrogen, and oxygen with the general formula $C_n(H_2O)_m$. Carbohydrates are commonly known as *sugars* and are the primary sources of cellular energy. Examples of carbohydrates are starch and cellulose.

lipid—a large, oily organic molecule. Examples are fats, oils, and steroids. Lipids can be converted into twice the cellular energy of carbohydrates, and are therefore used to store energy in the body.

vitamin—a compound, which the body cannot synthesize for itself, that is necessary in small quantities for life functions. Vitamins come in a variety of structurally unrelated forms. Many vitamins work as co-enzymes (i.e., they are necessary to make certain enzymes active).

enzyme—a protein which acts as a catalyst in chemical reactions. Enzymes have binding sites on their surface, which is generally where the reaction occurs.

II. The Cell

cell—the basic unit of organization in all living things. Any cell is surrounded by a plasma membrane, which separates the interior environment from the exterior and regulates the passage of materials into and out of the cell. All cells also must contain the hereditary material of the cell and some structures capable of processing energy. There are two distinct types of cells *prokaryotic cells* and *eukaryotic cells.*

prokaryote—an organism whose genetic material is not contained within a nucleus, but rather free in the cytoplasm. This is the simplest form of cell. Bacteria and viruses are prokaryotes.

eukaryote—an organism whose genetic material is contained within a nucleus. All life forms other than the viruses and bacteria are eukaryotes.

nucleus—The centrally located chamber in eukaryotic cells, which contains the chromosomes. It is bounded by a double membrane and is the information center of the cell.

diffusion—the process by which molecules pass across a porous membrane. Diffusion may be *passive*, in which case the molecules cross from the region of highest concentration to the region of lowest concentration, or either *facilitated* or *active*, in which cases the passage is helped in some way so as to not be entirely dependent upon the concentration.

osmosis—the process by which water passes across a porous membrane. In osmosis, water will flow from a region with a low concentration of dissolved molecules to a region with a high concentration of dissolved molecules.

tissue—a group of similar cells which are organized into a single unit and perform the same function. Tissue types in animals include epithelial, (such as skin, the linings of the lungs, the digestive tract, and blood vessels), muscle, nerve, connective/supportive, blood, and reproductive tissue. Tissues in animals group together to form organs. Tissue types in plants incude conducting (xylem and phloem), growing, supporting, storage, and reproductive tissue.

III. Life Functions

homeostasis—the maintenance of a steady state.

nutrition—all the activities by which an organism obtains and processes materials necessary for energy, growth, reproduction, and regulation.

transport—the process by which materials are absorbed and circulated throughout an organism.

respiration—the conversion of chemical energy in food by oxidation into forms which can be used to drive the chemical reactions essential to life. The two types of respiration are *aerobic* and *anaerobic respiration.*

circulation—the process by which materials are transported throughout the body. The circulatory system in humans consists of the blood vessels (arteries, veins, and capillaries) and the heart. This system is a closed circulatory system. Some lower animals, such as the hydra, have an open circulatory system.

excretion—the removal of cellular waste products from an organism.

synthesis—the process by which materials necessary for energy, growth, reproduction, and regulation are made by an organism from energy sources obtained from the environment.

reproduction—there are two types of reproduction, asexual and sexual. *Asexual reproduction* involves only one parent. There are three main types of asexual reproduction; fission, budding, and spore formation. *Sexual reproduction* involves two parent cells. If these cells are the same, then the joining of these cells is called *conjugation*. If these cells are different, then the joining of these cells is called *fertilization*.

metabolism—the process by which complex, high-energy componds are broken down by organisms into usable forms of energy.

regulation—the coordination and control of life activities. In all animals, regulation involves chemical control. In higher animals, regulation also involves nerve control.

IV. Types and Phases of Nutrition

autotroph—an organism that manufactures organic food from inorganic sources. Plants are autotrophs.

photosynthesis—the process by which visible light is trapped and converted into usable forms of energy. Plants and green algae do this. Photosynthesis occurs in two reactions, the light and dark reactions. A byproduct of the light reaction is oxygen. Photosynthesis occurs in the chlorophyll of plants.

chemosynthesis—the process by which chemical energy is trapped and converted into usable forms of energy. Nitrogen-fixing bacteria do this.

heterotroph—an organism that obtains premade organic food from other sources. These organisms are unable to make organic food from inorganic sources. Animals are heterotrophs.

ingestion—the process of taking in food.

digestion—the process by which large, insoluble molecules are broken down into small, soluble molecules. Digestion may be intracellular or extracellular.

egestion—the removal of undigested material.

V. Methods of Reproduction

asexual reproduction—reproduction involving the cells of only one parent. As such, there is no fusion of nuclei and no transfer of genetic material. Thus, the offspring is genetically identical to the parent. There are five types of asexual reproduction: binary fission, budding, sporulation, regeneration, and vegetative reproduction.

sexual reproduction—reproduction in which the cells of two parents combine through the process of fertilization to produce a fertilized egg cell, which develops into a new, genetically unique organism. During the process of fertilization, there is an exchange of genetic material that allows for genetic variation.

gene—a unit of a chromosome that contains all the gentic information to create a single polypeptide.

chromosome—a structure composed of DNA and sometimes protein that contains some or all of the genetic material of a cell.

mitosis—the process of cell division in which the chromosomes replicate so that there are two exactly similar sets of genetic material in the cell. The cell then divides into two cells, with each cell taking one set of chromosomes. The result is two cells that are genetically identical.

meiosis—The process by which specialized reproductive cells in sexually reproducing organisms are created. These reproductive cells are called *gametes*, and they are special in that they are *haploid* (having only one set of chromosomes). Because normal cells are usually *diploid* (having two sets of chromosomes) meiosis involves the halving of the number of chromosomes. Meiosis occurs in two phases and results in four haploid cells.

alternation of generations—The succession of haploid and diploid phases in a sexually reproducing organism. In most animals, only the gametes are in the haploid phase. In fungi, algae, and plants, the haploid phase may be the dominant phase, although in vascular plants the diploid is dominant.

VI. Genetics and Evolution

DNA—the fundamental herditary material of all living organisms. George Watson and Francis Crick elucidated the double-stranded nature of the DNA molecule and the helix structure it assumes. DNA molecules make up the gene. DNA molecules are composed of nucleotides, which consist of a 5-carbon sugar (deoxyribose), a phosphate, and a nitrogen base. The nitrogen base determines the nucleic acid. In DNA, there are four types of nitrogen bases (adenine, thymine, guanine, cytosine), and therefore four types of nucleic acids. These four bases also are the basis for the gentic code. Key to the continuation of life is the fact that DNA can reproduce with a high degree of accuracy.

RNA—the material through which the genetic information in DNA is converted into the proteins for which it codes. RNA has a different 5-carbon sugar (ribose) and instead of the nitrogen base thymine it has uracil. RNA is single stranded. There are two main types of RNA: *messenger RNA* (mRNA), and *transfer RNA* (tRNA).

genetics—the study of heredity, founded by Gregor Mendel. There are three main laws in genetics that Mendel developed. The first is the *Law of Dominance*, which states that when organisms containing pure contrasting traits are crossed, only one of the traits will be expressed in the offspring. The trait that is expressed is the *dominant* trait; the trait not expressed is the *recessive* trait. The second law is the *Law of Segregation,* which states that alleles segregate during gamete formation and then recombine. The third law is the *Law of Independent Assortment,* which states that alleles on different genes assort independently during gamete formation.

genotype—the exact description of the genetic makeup of an organism.

phenotype—the description of the traits observable in an organism. These traits are the result of the genetic makeup of the organism as well as environmental factors.

evolution—the process by which organisms change from generation to generation. Evolution is a gradual change involving random genetic mutations. Charles Darwin suggested that genetic mutations resulting in physiological changes will sometimes confer an advantage to the organism over its competitors. This advantage leads to *natural selection,* which is the driving force behind all evolutionary change.

VII. Ecology

See Earth/Space Sciences section below.

I. Mechanics

scalar—a quantity that has magnitude but no direction. Examples of scalars are mass, length, time density, energy, and temperature.

vector—a quantity that has both magnitude and direction. Examples of vectors are velocity, force, acceleration, momentum, electric field strength, and magnetic field strength. It is very important when describing vector quantities that both the magnitude and strength be described. The magnitude of force, for example, is important, but without knowing the direction of the force we cannot know how the force acts on the body. Because vectors have direction, we must be able to quantify the directional qualities of a vector. This is done by breaking a vector into two components (see the following fiugre.) These components are given by the formula $A_x = A\cos\rho$ and $A_y = A\sin\rho$, where ρ is the angle at which the vector is traveling relative to its origin or the body on which it acts.

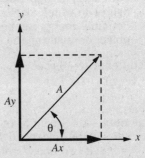

speed—the distance traveled by a body over a given period of time.

$$S\,(\text{speed}) = \frac{d}{t}\left(\frac{\text{distance}}{\text{time}}\right).$$

velocity—the combinination of the magnitude of speed with its direction. Thus, the equation for the magnitude of velocity is the same as that for speed, $\frac{d}{t}$. However, some direction must also be specified using the components found above (see *vector*).

acceleration—the rate of velocity change over a given period of time. This is given by the equation $a = \frac{\Delta v}{\Delta t}$. Because velocity is a component of acceleration, acceleration is a vector quantity (see *vector*).

centripetal acceleration—acceleration towards a central point. When bodies move in a circular motion, their velocity at any one time is tangential to the circle. Thus, for the body to continue to move circularly, the velocity must constantly be moving towards the center. Thus, it is accelerating towards the center. This acceleration is what accounts for *centripetal force*.

angular velocity—velocity around a circular path.

angular acceleration—the change in angular velocity.

force—any phenomena that pulls or pushes a mass. Force is a vector quantity, described by the formula $F = ma$.

gravity—the force that pulls masses toward the Earth. Gravity accelerates all masses at $\frac{9.8m}{s^2}$ and is always perpendicular to the surface of the earth.

inertia—the characteristic of mass that dictates that the motion of a mass will not change unless an outside force is applied to it.

torque—the force that causes the rotation of a mass about a fixed point.

work—done on an object whenever a force moves the object some distance. Work is the product of the force causing the motion and the distance the object moves, or $W = F\Delta d$.

potential energy—energy dependent upon relative position as opposed to motion. Potential energy is caused by gravity or elasticity. Thus, an object's potential energy is dependent upon either its distance from the earth or the degree to which a coiled sping attached to the object has been stretched. Potential energy can be changed into kinetic energy either by dropping the object or releasing the spring.

kinetic energy—the energy of a body associated with its motion, defined as $k = \frac{1}{2}mv^2$.

momentum—the quantity of motion an object possesses, dependent upon the mass of the object and the velocity at which it travels. Thus, p (momentum) $= mv$. If two objects of unequal size are traveling at the same speed, the object with the greater mass has more momentum. Likewise, if two objects of equal size are traveling at different speeds, then the object with the greater speed has more momentum. Momentum is dependent upon velocity (a vector quantity), and is thus a vector quantity.

II. Electricity and Magnetism

The Law of Electrostatics—states that like charges repel each other, while opposite charges attract each other.

electric charge—a fundamental measure based upon the idea that the electron represents a negative charge. Charge is measured in coulombs, where one coulomb equals 6.25×10^{18} electrons. Charge can either be negative or positive, depending upon whether it is likely to repel or attract electrons.

electric force—the force generated between charges as a result of the repulsive or attractive characteristics described in the Law of Electrostatics.

electric field—that region in space in which a charge can experience an electric force. Electric fields can act to move charges from one point to another.

electric current—in a circuit, the amount of charge flowing past a certain point per unit of time. Current is represented by the letter I and is measured in amperes or coulombs per unit time. Thus, $I = \dfrac{Q}{t}$, where Q is charge.

conductor—something through which electric charge may move. Conductors, however, vary in terms of how easily they allow charge to move through. This is because of *resistance*.

resistance—the opposition of current flow. When resistance occurs in a conductor, some of the kinetic energy from the moving particles is converted into heat.

magnetism—the property of a charge in motion, caused by the revolution of atoms around the nucleus of an atom. The direction of the magnetic effect is determined by the direction in which the electron spins around its axis.

magnetic field—the region in space in which a charge can experience a magnetic force. Magnetic fields flow out of the north pole and into the south pole.

electromagnetic induction—the creation of a magnetic field as a result of the flow of an electric current.

III. Optics

wave—any disturbance that propagates through a material medium (mechanical waves) or space (electromagnetic waves).

wavelength—the distance between a point on a wave to the same point on the next wave.

frequency—the number of cycles of a wave that pass a particular point per unit time.

period—the time it takes for one complete wave to pass a certain point.

amplitude—the distance from the crest or the trough to the center of a wave.

reflection—the bouncing of a wave off a surface. Reflection of light is responsible for the formation of images in mirrors.

refraction—the bending of light as it passes from one medium to a second medium. Because different media will allow light to pass through at different speeds (i.e., different *optical densities*), there will be a change in velocity when light makes such a transition. This velocity change is responsible for refraction.

interference—what happens when two waves come together. Interference results in a change in amplitude. If the change is additive (i.e., the amplitudes of the two waves are added) then the interference is *constructive*. If the opposite occurs, it is *destructive interference*.

diffraction—the bending of waves caused when a wave encounters an opening that is the same size as its wavelength.

polarization—the selective passage of waves that only vibrate in a particular plane.

IV. Kinetics and Thermodynamics

Also see "Kinetics and Thermodynamics" in the Chemistry section above.

efficiency—as applied to an engine, the ratio of the net work done by the system to the heat added to the system at the higher temperature.

thermodynamic efficiency—the ideal efficiency an engine would have if it could be operated in a purely reversible fashion.

Earth/Space Sciences

I. Space and Celestial Bodies

geocentric model—the model of the solar system, which sets the earth at the center of the solar system and has all of the celestial bodies rotating around the earth. This model is unnecessarily complicated and was eventually abandoned in favor of the heliocentric model.

heliocentric model—the model of the solar system, which has the sun at the center with the planets rotating around it. In this model, the apparent motion of the stars is explained by the rotation of the earth.

orbit—the path an object takes when travelling around a large body due to its gravitational force.

satellite—any object that travels around a large body (such as a planet or a sun) due to the gravitational forces exerted by that body upon the object.

planet—a large celestial body travelling in orbit around a star. There is currently much debate as to what exactly differentiates a planet from other large bodies in space, such as asteroids.

moon—a large celestial body travelling in orbit around a planet.

star—a large celestial body composed of incandescent gases, largely hydrogen and helium. A star radiates energy created by internal nuclear fusion reactions, in which two lighter atoms are fused to create a single heavier atom and a release of energy. Thus, hydrogen nuclei are fused to create helium (a process called *hydrogen burning*), and then helium nucleii are fused to eventually create carbon (*helium burning*). As a result of these reactions, the density of a star is constantly increasing as it ages, and its increasingly powerful gravitational field constantly causes it to contract.

sun—a star, which has planets orbiting within its gravitational field.

asteroid—a large celestial body composed mostly of rock. Asteroids usually are under the influence of a star's gravitational field, but have larger, more eccentric orbits than planets.

system—a grouping of planets, all rotating around a star (sun) due to the gravitational forces exerted by it.

galaxy—a grouping of hundreds of millions of stars. All these stars interact gravitationally and orbit around a common center. The galaxy in which the earth exists is called the Milky Way galaxy.

II. The Earth

atmosphere—the gaseous layer that envelopes the earth. The thickness of the earth's atmosphere is about 1,100 km. It consists of three layers: the *troposphere*, the *stratosphere,* and the *mesosphere*. The earth's atmosphere is important in that it shields the earth from harmful radiation and excessive heat. It also prevents the earth from cooling too rapidly at night.

hydrosphere—the layer of water on the surface of the earth. This includes all the oceans, as well as the rivers, lakes, etc. It is estimated to cover about 70.8 percent of the earth's surface.

lithosphere—the layer of the earth's crust composed of rock and extending for about 100 km below the surface. The lithosphere is composed of two shells, known as the *crust* and the *upper mantle*. These are in turn divided into *tectonic plates*. See *Tectonic Plate Theory*.

mantle and core—the heavy interior of the earth, which constitutes most of the earth's mass. The core is composed of a molten layer surrounding a solid center. It is the source of much of the earth's heat. The mantle, on the other hand, is solid and rigid.

Tectonic Plate Theory—the theory, which states that the tectonic plates of the earth's crust and upper mantle move about, collide, and separate over time. Tectonic Plate Theory explains the relative positions of the continents and the formation of large mountain ranges such as the Himalayas, as well as natural phenomena such as earthquakes.

earthquake—a shifting of the rock layers of the earth's crust, most commonly caused by either the movement of tectonic plates or the eruption of volcanoes. Earthquakes emit two kinds of shockwaves: *P-waves* and *S-waves*. P-waves travel through both liquids and solids, while S-waves travel only through solids.

III.   Atmospheric Changes and the Movement of Water

meteorology—the study of the earth's atmosphere, specifically the day-to-day variations of weather conditions.

weather—the state of the atmosphere at a particular time and place. Elements of weather include temperature, humidity, cloudiness, precipitation, wind, and pressure.

climate—all the characteristics of weather, including precipitation, temperature, and humidity, which a particular region experiences over a long period of time. The averages of all these factors constitute the climate for a particular place.

depression—an area of low atmospheric pressure around which winds travel anticlockwise in the Northern Hemisphere and clockwise in the Southern Hemisphere. Depressions tend to occur when warm air meets cold air. Because the cold air is heavier than the warm air, the warm air rises above the cold, causing winds as well as cloud formation.

hydrological cycle—(water cycle) the cycle whose primary components are (1) the evaporation of moisture from the surface of the earth, due to the warming of the sun's rays, (2) the carrying of this moisture into higher levels of the atmosphere, (3) the condensation of water vapor into clouds, and (4) the return of water to the surface as precipitation.

evaporation—the changing of water from a liquid to a gas. Heat must be added to the water in this process. (This is why your skin feels cooler when water evaporates from it.)

transpiration—the process by which plants release moisture to the atmosphere.

condensation—the changing of water from a gas to a liquid, involving the removal of heat from the water. The heat is then released into the atmosphere in the form of *latent heat*, called so because the temperature remains the same during this process.

sublimation—the change from a solid to a gas without passing through the liquid phase.

precipitation—the moisture that falls to the earth's surface. Examples are rain, snow, sleet, and hail.

infiltration—the process by which water passes into the earth through the soil.

runoff—the water that is unable to infiltrate the surface of the earth, and thus runs down into streams, rivers, lakes, etc.

permeability—a measure of the rate at which water passes through particles. Permeability is dependant upon *porosity*, which is a measure of the amount of space between particles. Larger particles have a greater porosity and therefore a greater permeability.

IV. Energy and the Earth

electromagnetic energy—the energy exhibited by the earth due to its magnetic field.

geomagnetism—the magnetic phenomena exhibited by the earth and its atmosphere. The study of geomagnetism often centers on the study of the earth's gravitational field and the changes that occur in it.

solar energy—the energy released by the sun, in the form of light, heat, and other types of radiation.

radiation—energy absorbed by the earth's atmosphere from space. Most of the radiation we are subjected to comes from the sun, called *insolation* (short for incoming solar radiation).

terrestrial radiation—the radiation of energy from the earth's surface into space. This generally occurs at night when temperatures are cooler.

conduction—the transfer of heat through solids. This occurs because, when a solid is heated, its atoms will move faster. Random collisions between these atoms and those neighboring will cause the neighboring atoms to also move faster. This process repeats until the heat has tranferred across the solid.

convection—the transfer of heat through the air.

V. The Rock Cycle

igneous rock—rock formed during the cooling and crystallization of a hot, molten fluid from the earth's core called *magma*. Igneous rock makes up over 95 percent of the earth's crust.

sedimentary rock—rock formed from the products of weathering on other rocks. This happens when water and carbon dioxide break up and dissolve small pieces of rock.

metamorphism—a process of structural change in rocks induced by heat and pressure.

metamorphic rock—rock formed by the process of metamorphism, which involves partial melting and recrystallization of sedimentary or igneous rock. An example is marble, which is caused by the metamorphosis of limestone.

erosion—the physical process by which rocks are corroded and coverted into other forms by the action of heat, cold, gases, water, wind, gravity, and plant life. The process of erosion is key to the formation of sedimentary rock and soil.

compression cementation—the process by which sediment is cemented together into sedimentary rock due to the large compression forces exerted by heavy layers of overlying material.

crystallization—the process by which igneous rock is formed from molten magma.

VI. Ecology

population—all the members of a species inhabiting a given location.

community—all the microorganisms, plants, and animals inhabiting a given location, which interact and are ecologically integrated.

environment—all of an organism's surroundings. This includes all of the species that influence the organism as well as temperature, humidity, light, etc.

ecosystem—all of the organisms of a particular habitat together with the environment in which they live.

biosphere—the portion of the earth, which supports life, including most of the hydrosphere, the lower portions of the atmosphere, and nearly all of the earth's surface.

greenhouse effect—the effect of atmospheric carbon dioxide, water, and other trace gases at the average temperature of the surface. This effect is caused by the absorption by these substances of energy radiated from the earth.

pollutant—any substance found in the environment in levels above that normally found and that may cause harm.

The Insider's Stress-Buster's Guide

by Mary-Jo D. Weber, M.S.
Psychiatric Nurse Practitioner

THE ROLE OF STRESS IN PEAK TEST PERFORMANCE

Let's face it—if you're like most people, you're not really looking forward to taking the ACT. In fact, the very thought of the test might make your stomach queasy and your neck and shoulders tight. You might become aware of your heart beating, and your hands might get clammy. You might even feel restless and be tempted to close this book right now and get a snack!

All these physical responses to the stress of test-taking can work for you or against you. Conditioned by millions of years of evolution, your body has developed a complex natural reaction, sometimes called the *fight or flight* response, which comes into play whenever you feel physically or psychologically threatened. This reaction has a very real value in getting you ready to meet whatever challenge you face, whether it's a menacing stranger on a dark street, an auditorium full of people waiting to hear you deliver a speech, or a standardized exam.

The adrenaline and other hormones that are released when you are under stress can get you ready for peak performance. They arouse your senses to increased sensitivity, alert your brain cells to pay attention, sharpen your mental focus, increase the amounts of energizing oxygen delivered to all parts of your body, and raise the levels of glucose available to fuel your brain. These chemical processes account for the sense of excitement you feel when you're under stress. Some people—artists who thrill to public applause, for example, or world-class athletes—actually relish this state of physical and mental arousal, and even the average person finds it exhilarating, though perhaps scary, too.

The problem comes when these responses get out of control, freezing your thoughts and leaving you feeling uncomfortably tense or anxious. When that happens, you may develop "tunnel vision," a narrowing of perception that hampers your awareness of what's around you; you may even feel that your mind is "going blank," as if your brain is on overload and is starting to shut down.

Fortunately, you *can* manage your stress so that the natural stress response will sharpen your focus without limiting your perspective or closing off your options, making you more creative and imaginative and helping you to retrieve more of the useful information stored in your memory.

This appendix will give you specific, scientifically-tested techniques to use in the weeks before the exam, while you are studying, and on the very day you take the ACT. If you practice these methods, you may find yourself almost looking forward to the opportunity to tackle the test—and beat it!

PREPARING FOR PEAK PERFORMANCE

Top athletes find that mental preparation is as important to their success in competition as practicing their specific athletic skills. The field of sports psychology has taught us a lot about how you can best prepare for your test. Practicing your academic skills is something like a basketball player working on his foul shot or a swimmer perfecting her stroke; It's essential, but it's not enough. The best performers don't stop there. They also use relaxation and visualization techniques to ensure that they'll be able to apply their skills and to respond effectively and creatively to the challenges that game day will bring their way.

Similar relaxation and visualization techniques can help keep you from freezing up and allow you to efficiently handle whatever comes your way in the test-taking situation. They can also help you experience the test as a positive challenge, not a looming source of terror. You will maintain a degree of comfort and be able to manage the unpleasant symptoms of anxiety without letting them overwhelm you.

Learning to Relax

First, you'll need to learn to be able to relax whenever you decide you want to. Yes—for most people, it's a skill that must be learned. If you're like most people, you probably tend to keep going—with work, play, or just hanging around—until you're physically exhausted, and then you crash. It's not the most efficient way to harness the energy in your body and mind. Instead, if you learn to relax whenever you want to, you'll be able to control your stress responses so that you'll feel only the amount of anxiety you need to wake up your brain cells and perform your best.

The following exercise is a good way to start. If you're feeling any sense of tiredness or anxiety—after a couple of hours of studying, for example—this is a better way to refresh yourself than napping or taking a TV break. It takes only a few minutes and will leave you feeling energized and alert. You can either read through this suggested exercise and then try it, or, even better, get a friend with a pleasant voice to read it aloud to you while you try it. (Later, you can return the favor.) As you go through the exercise, feel free to alter it in any way that seems pertinent to your individual situation.

Relaxation Exercise

Start by sitting comfortably with both feet flat on the floor. Take some time to notice how the floor is supporting your feet. Allow the surface on which you are resting to support you completely. Take all the time you need to notice the comfort and security of this.

Next, turn your mind toward your breathing. Don't try to change it; just observe it. Observe how effortless your breathing is, realizing that, with every exhalation, the tension of the day is flowing out, and, with every inhalation, revitalizing oxygen is flowing in to nourish all parts of your body.

Turn your attention again to your feet. Notice that they are comfortably resting on the floor. Notice that feeling of comfort spreading up to your ankles, calves, and knees. Feel how securely the chair is supporting your thighs, your buttocks, your lower back, and your upper back.

Your hands may be in your lap or at your sides. Allow them to open, and as you continue to breathe comfortably and naturally, experience any tension flowing down from your shoulders to your arms and out your finger tips. You will notice that, the more relaxed you can keep your hands, the more relaxed and alert you will be.

Notice whether your eyes are open or closed. Either way is fine. Take some time now to notice the muscles around your eyes, in your cheeks, and around your mouth. Notice whatever expression you naturally have on your face, whether it's frowning, neutral, or smiling. Don't feel you need to change it. Allow these muscles to soften. Close your eyes if you wish. Feel the heaviness of your jaw, and don't try to hold it up.

As you continue to notice the comfort in your body, pay attention to your neck and scalp. If you perceive any tension there, allow it to flow out with your next breath. Scan your body now, and if you notice any areas of discomfort or tension, notice that, as you breathe, any tension or discomfort flows out with each exhalation, while energy flows in with each inhalation.

Now, as you continue to enjoy the comfort of your body securely supported by the chair and energized by your breathing, imagine that you are in a special, favorite place. It may be the beach, or the mountains, or your room, or just inside yourself. Notice how comfortable and alert you are to all the things that make that place pleasurable for you. Notice the sights, sounds, smells, and feelings that make the place so nice.

Take your time enjoying your special place. When you are ready to return to the room in which you are sitting, gently reorient yourself, experiencing your calm alertness and renewed enthusiasm for all your endeavors.

Now that you're back from your special place, notice how revitalized you feel.

With practice, this process of relaxation will become easier and quicker, but you already have noticed that, from the very first attempt, you can recharge your batteries in a way that is even better than a nap because your alertness will be increased and your focus will be sharpened. Try using this method of relaxation whenever the pressure of studying is making you feel exhausted or tense. You'll find yourself learning more—and enjoying it more, too.

Visualizing Success

The next step is to add visualization of the test-taking situation and your desired successful outcome. It's a favorite preparation strategy of many successful athletes and entertainers; they find that visualizing themselves hitting the perfect tennis stroke or playing a difficult piano concerto with fluency and ease makes it much easier to actually perform that way.

It works for test-takers, too. Here's how to use it in preparing for the ACT.

Visualization Exercise

Repeat the relaxation exercise. This time, however, after you've imagined your special place and while you're alertly and attentively noting the sights, sounds, and feelings that you experience there, imagine that you are entering the room in which you'll take the ACT. Notice the rows of desks and chairs, the other students sitting and waiting for the exam to begin, and the proctor at the front of the room, with a stack of sealed test booklets on the desk before her.

Take your seat, noting how comfortably your feet are supported by the floor, how your body is supported by the chair, and how your breathing is energizing your body and mind. The proctor walks up and down the rows of desks, handing out the ACT booklets and giving you instructions for the exam. When the proctor says, "Begin work," you tear open the seal on the booklet in front of you and turn to the first page of questions. You begin your work, knowing that you have prepared for this test and that you will correctly answer all the questions you need to in order to achieve your desired goal.

You experience just the right amount of anxiety you need to feel in order to achieve your peak performance. As you work, the questions appear familiar and interesting to you. You look forward to reading each question because you know you will find it to be an interesting challenge to the skills you've been learning and practicing. You work efficiently, and, when you come to the end of the test, you experience the sense of a job well done. At this time, reorient to the room.

You may also use this exercise before going to sleep, perhaps after a strenuous study session. If you do the exercise in bed, when it's completed, simply allow yourself to drift into a refreshing sleep.

During the weeks while you are studying for your exam, you can ensure peak performance by practicing relaxation and visualization every day. The best time for many people is at night, just before sleep. This will help your learning because your mind is working even while you sleep. Thus, if you practice visualizing test-taking success before you go to sleep, your brain will probably continue to process that information while you sleep, reinforcing the positive message.

Some people find it very effective to make an audiotape of of the relaxation and visualization exercises, to be played while they fall asleep.

TECHNIQUES OF POWER STUDYING

If you're an athlete, a musician, or an actor, you know how important your physical condition is to your training. What you eat or drink before practice will influence how effective your training will be. The same is true of test preparation.

Physical Conditioning for Effective Study

Everyone knows his or her own best time of the day for studying. For some people, it's early in the morning, before class or work; for others, it's late at night. Whatever time you favor, make sure you're in peak condition before you hit the books. It should go without saying, but remember that if you drink alcohol or use mood-altering chemicals in the days preceding your exam, your performance will definitely be impaired. You're using this book, so you have an obvious interest in doing your best. Avoid these performance-killers.

Nutrition is just as important for studying as it is for athletic training, because thinking and learning are physical functions of your body, carried out by the cells of your brain. It so happens that your brain cells work on glucose (sugar) only. That said, it would be incorrect to deduce that your diet while studying should consist of candy bars and sodas. But you do learn and think best when your brain has a steady stream of glucose.

The best way to ensure this is to eat high-protein and so-called "complex carbohydrate" foods before studying and about every 3 hours during studying. Fruit, lean meat and fish, vegetables, pasta with low-fat sauce, cereal, crackers, bread, and legumes (such as peas and beans) are the foods associated with high mental performance. These foods will keep your blood sugar steady at an optimal level.

Avoid greasy or fatty foods; the work of digesting them actually pulls oxygen-rich blood away from your brain and toward your digestive system. (So, pizza, although you may love it, is really not the best study food. Wait until after the exam, and then treat yourself to a pie with your favorite toppings—as a reward for the high score you've earned.)

Rest is often neglected when people are studying very hard, but this is a mistake. Research has shown that people who are in a state of chronic sleep deprivation just don't think or perform very well. When hospitals shorten the working shifts of their medical residents, the doctors suffer fewer mental lapses and make better treatment decisions. The same applies to anyone working with his or her brain. The optimal amount of sleep varies from one person to another, but few people do well on less than 6 hours a night over any extended period of time, and most people thrive on 7 or 8 hours a night. Don't pull an all-nighter; get the sleep you need, and you'll find yourself learning more, and more easily, the next morning.

Reducing Stress When You Study

When you sit down to study, you can improve your memory and creativity by practicing the relaxation and visualization exercises earlier in this chapter. If you don't want to spend that much time, there is a brief technique that can be used just before studying or as needed during breaks in your study sessions. It takes only a few minutes. It works best if you have already experienced the longer exercise, and the more familiar you become with the long exercise the better this short one will work.

The Three-Minute Relaxation Technique

Sit comfortably wherever you like, with your feet flat on the floor. Rest your hands on your lap or desk. Place the thumbs and index fingers of each hand together.

Close your eyes. Take a moment to notice your breathing. After a few seconds, turn your attention to the pressure of your thumbs on your index fingers. The pressure can be light or firm. Notice that pressure as you inhale and exhale several times; really notice how your fingers feel.

Then, as you exhale, release the pressure, relaxing your hands, feeling your tension and fatigue flowing out with your exhalation and melting down your arms and out your fingertips.

Continue to focus on your breathing for a few minutes. When you are ready, open your eyes and reorient yourself to your surroundings.

This quick exercise will allow you to capture a sense of calm alertness whenever you need it.

Music to Learn By

Many people enjoy listening to music while they are studying. There is nothing wrong with music as long as you like it and don't find it distracting, but there are some things to consider when you choose music for your study sessions.

Music can help you to concentrate by filtering out extraneous sounds or thoughts. For this purpose, it is helpful if the music is familiar, so listening to a selection of favorite CDs would help you to study more efficiently than listening to the radio (which will probably play both familiar and unfamiliar selections, as well as interjecting a stream of chatter and commercials that may well be distracting).

Music can also set a helpful mood while you're studying. It's a very personal choice, but in certain recent studies, when research subjects listened to classical music, particularly the works of Mozart, just before and during cognitive (mental) tasks, their performance on those tasks improved. You might want to experiment with different kinds of music to see which help you to concentrate best.

STRESS-BUSTING STRATEGIES FOR TEST DAY AND TEST DAY MINUS ONE

Hopefully you're not reading these suggestions for peak performance for the first time the day before your test. Ideally, you'll have used the ideas we've presented for developing your personal test-preparation plan and you will be following it, more or less closely, in the weeks leading up to the exam. In particular, repeatedly visualizing success in the weeks before the test will motivate you to study and to view the test as a challenge you can meet, not a disaster in the making.

The Night Before

On the day before the test, make sure you have your admission form, your identification, a pen and pencil, and your directions to the test site, all ready and available for the morning. Make sure you know how to get to the test center and how long it will take you to get there given the expected weather conditions and traffic patterns. If you control these "petty" details, they won't inject an unecessary note of anxiety or uncertainty on the morning of the exam.

It's really helpful if you can do something pleasant and relaxing the night before the test. Make sure you go to bed early enough to get the amount of sleep you need to do your best. If you've made a tape of your relaxation and visualization exercises, have it playing as you drift off into a refreshing sleep.

However, if you're going to be worrying about that one last math rule or grammar principle while you're watching that movie—or if you're feeling that you haven't suffered enough yet to appease the testing gods so they'll allow you to get your highest score—here are some tips for last-minute studying.

Don't try to reread this book or do any kind of comprehensive review. At this point, that will only increase your anxiety and convince you, incorrectly, that all the studying you have already done was inadequate and futile. Instead, decide how long you can study while still getting a good night's sleep. If you need 9 hours to feel rested, your score will be boosted more by getting the full 9 hours than by another few hours of studying.

Then pick a few topics you can comfortably cover in the amount of time you have left. Choose topics you are good at but feel can use a little more polishing, keeping in mind that you don't need a "perfect" score or to get every question correct.

Always remember that it is really all the previous study you've done that will determine your score; you're only reviewing the night before to appease the testing gods. When it's time to go to sleep, set your alarm clock to give you plenty of time to get ready, eat breakfast, and get to the testing site without rushing. Then practice your relaxation and visualization exercises, and have pleasant dreams of test-taking victory.

The Morning of the Exam

In the morning, eat something, even if you normally don't eat breakfast. Study after study has demonstrated that people perform better on tests when they have eaten about 30–60 minutes beforehand. The foods you should eat are the same as those recommended during studying—high protein, low fat, and complex carbohydrates. Bring a piece of fruit or a nutrition bar to the test center to eat during the brief mid-exam break.

During the exam itself—especially during the short breaks provided between test sections—you might try using the Three-Minute Relaxation technique if you feel fatigued or stressed.

All these tips, if practiced along with the study outlined in this book, will ensure your optimal performance on the ACT. They'll also help you attain an even higher goal: to feel balanced and sane before and after the test.

Appendix F

College Admissions Calendar and Checklist*

11TH GRADE

This year the college search process begins in earnest. Exploration and testing should help you start developing a list of target schools by spring. Poor grades will not be as easily forgiven as those from previous years, and colleges will look for commitment and accomplishment outside of the classroom.

September

❏ Make sure that PSAT/NMSQT registration is handled by your guidance counselor staff (except in regions where ACT test is prevalent). Ascertain and save the date.

❏ Ask your guidance department about college fairs in your area and college admission-representative visits to the school. Attend fairs and sessions with reps at school.

❏ Familiarize yourself with guidance-office resources.

October

❏ Make sure PSAT/NMSQT date is on your calendar. Read the student bulletin and try the practice questions.

❏ Schedule a day trip to visit nearby colleges. Don't worry if these are places where you won't apply. The goal is to explore different types of schools. Aim for variety. Discuss which characteristics are attractive and which aren't.

December

❏ Questions about PSAT scores? Contact your guidance counselor. If necessary, discuss strategies for improving weak areas. Evaluate different SAT prep options, as needed.

❏ Take advantage of college students home for vacation. Ask them questions.

❏ Take an introductory look at financial-aid forms, just to see what you'll need by this time next year.

---

* Reprinted from Arco's *College Admissions/A Crash Course for Panicked Parents* (Sally Rubenstone & Sidonia Dalby).

January

❑ Evaluate academic progress so far. Are grades up to par? Are course levels on target? Do study habits need improvement?

❑ Begin thinking about worthwhile summer plans (job, study, camp, volunteer work, travel, etc.)

❑ Mark projected SAT I & II or ACT test dates on your calendar. Also mark registration deadlines.

February

❑ Look ahead to SAT or ACT registration deadlines for the tests you plan to take. Are you about to miss one? Mark appropriate dates on your calendar. (A few juniors have reason to take the SAT I in March. If you will do so, heed February registration deadline).

❑ Buy a general guidebook to U.S. colleges and universities. (For ideas, see www.petersons.com)

March

❑ Consider and plan spring-vacation college visits.

❑ Begin listing target colleges in a notebook ("The College Bible").

❑ Begin calling, writing, or e-mailing target colleges to request publications.

❑ Set aside an area for college propaganda. Invest in folders for materials from front-runner schools.

❑ Look ahead to SAT or ACT registration deadlines for the tests you plan to take. Are you about to miss one? Mark appropriate test and registration dates on your calendar.

❑ Make sure you discuss plans to take Advanced Placement exams with teachers and/or guidance counselor as needed.

April

❑ Look ahead to SAT or ACT registration deadlines for the tests you plan to take. Are you about to miss one? Mark appropriate test and registration dates on your calendar.

❑ Decide on senior-year classes. Include at least one math course or lab science, as well as the most challenging courses possible. Recognize that colleges weigh senior classes and grades as heavily as the junior record.

❑ Update activities record.

May

❑ Look ahead to SAT or ACT registration deadlines for the tests you plan to take. Are you about to miss one? Mark the appropriate test and registration dates on your calendar.

❑ Assess the need for and affordability of special services such as standardized test-prep courses, independent college counselors, and private group-tour programs.

❑ Do you need to take the TOEFL (Test of English as a Foreign Language)? Select date and oversee registration.

June

❑ Look ahead to SAT or ACT registration deadlines for the tests you plan to take. Are you about to miss one? Mark the appropriate test and registration dates on your calendar.

Summer

❑ Make sure you have a job or constructive activities throughout most of the summer. Study, jobs, and volunteer work always rate high with admission officials.

❑ Consider and plan summer and fall college visits.

❑ Request publications from additional target colleges.

❑ Plan and execute supplemental submissions such as audition tapes and art slides/portfolio, if required and/or appropriate.

❑ Review and update target college list. Include pros and cons. Make tentative plans for fall visits.

12TH GRADE

This is the year when the college search can feel like a full-time job—with all of the toil, tedium, and triumphs that that implies.

September

❑ Discuss plans and goals for the months ahead; pros and cons of target schools.

❑ Look ahead to SAT or ACT registration for the tests you plan to take. Are you about to miss one? Mark the appropriate test and registration dates on your calendar.

❑ Ask your guidance counselor about college fairs in your area and college admission-representative visits to the school. Make certain that you attend fairs and sessions with reps at schools.

❑ Finalize fall college-visit plans. Include campus overnights, where possible. Visit!

❑ Request additional publications and applications from target colleges.

October

❑ Look ahead to SAT or ACT registration for the tests you plan to take. Are you about to miss one? Mark the appropriate test and registration dates on your calendar.

❑ Draw up a master schedule of application and financial-aid due dates, and then put them on your calendar.

❑ Begin considering essay topics and requesting teacher recommendations.

❑ Visit colleges. Include interviews on campus (or with local alumni representatives).

❑ Attend college fairs.

❑ For another look at college life, rent a movie like *Animal House* or *School Daze*.

❑ Look at "Early Decision" and "Early Action" options.

November

❑ Look ahead to SAT or ACT registration for the tests you plan to take. Are you about to miss one? Mark the appropriate test and registration dates on your calendar.

❑ Reduce target college "long list" to a "short list," where applications will be made.

❑ Plan a Thanksgiving break that includes college visits (to almost-empty campuses).

❑ What is the status of your applications? Get someone to proofread your applications and essay(s).

December

❑ Look ahead to SAT or ACT registration for the tests you plan to take. Are you about to miss one? Mark the appropriate test and registration dates on your calendar.

❑ Pick up financial-aid material from guidance office and attend planning workshops, if available.

❑ Make sure that teachers and guidance counselors are up to date with reference forms and that transcripts are being sent to all short-list colleges.

January

❑ Begin filling out financial-aid forms. Finish and mail these forms as soon as possible and *never LATE*.

❑ Complete all applications, including those with later deadlines. Don't forget to photocopy everything and save in accordion files.

❑ If SAT's are being taken this month, are "Rush" scores required? Ask target colleges, if you're not certain.

February

❑ Unless confirmations have been received, call colleges to check on completion of applications. Record the name of the person you spoke with. Track down missing records.

March

❑ WAIT!

April

❑ Keep in mind that "thin " letters aren't always rejections. Some schools send out enrollment forms later.

❑ Rejoice in acceptances; keep rejections in perspective.

❑ Plan "crunch-time" visits to campuses, as needed, to help prompt final decisions.

❑ Compare financial-aid decisions, where applicable. Contact financial-aid offices with questions.

❑ Make sure your return "Wait-List" cards, as needed. Contact admission offices to check on Wait-List status. Send updated records and other information, if available. Write an upbeat "Please take me, and this is why you should" letter.

❑ Is the verdict final? Have your parents send the required deposit. Don't dawdle and miss the May 1 deadline or colleges can give away your place. Also notify those schools you won't be attending, especially if an aid offer was made.

May

❑ Take AP exams, if appropriate.

❑ Stay abreast of housing choices, etc. When will forms be mailed? Should you be investigating living-situations options? When is a freshman orientation? (Some schools have spring and summer programs.) When is course registration?

June

❑ Write a thank-you note to anyone who may have been especially helpful. Guidance counselors are often unsung heroes. Don't forget teachers who wrote recommendations, admission counselors or secretaries, tour guides, or other students.

❑ Consider summer school if you want to accelerate or place out of requirements. ALWAYS check with colleges first to make sure credits will count. Get permission in writing when it's questionable.

❑ Make sure that a final high-school transcript is sent to the college you will attend. (Most schools should do this automatically.)

Appendix G

College Application Log

Use this log for every school you apply to in order to track the application process:

School Name: _____

_____

School Telephone Number: _____

_____

School Address: _____

_____

School Web site: _____

_____

Catalog/Application Request Date: _____

_____

Catalog/Application Receipt Date: _____

_____

Application Deadline: _____

_____

Application Fee: _____

_____

Rolling Admissions, Standard or Early: _____

_____

Date Application Mailed: _____

_____

Financial Aid Material Request Date: _____

_____

Financial Aid Material Receipt Date: _____

_____

Financial Aid Deadline: _____

_____

Letter of Recommendation 1

Name: _____

_____

Telephone Number: _____

_____

Date Requested: _____

_____

Verified Sent: _____

_____

Date School Received: _____

_____

Letter of Recommendation 2

Name: _____

_____

Telephone Number: _____

_____

Date Requested: _____

_____

Verified Sent: _____

_____

Date School Received: _____

_____

Letter of Recommendation 3

Name: _____

_____

Telephone Number: _____

_____

Date Requested: _____

_____

Verified Sent: _____

_____

Date School Received: _____

_____

ACT Scores Request Date: _____

_____

Date School Received ACT Scores: _____

_____

Personal Statement Due Date: _____

_____

Personal Statement Completion Date: _____

_____

Financial Aid Glossary*

Assistantships Financial aid provided for performing work (usually on a part-time basis). Types of assistantships include teaching, research, administrative, and residence. Assistantships are usually awarded according to merit.

Campus-Based Programs Federal aid programs administered by a school's financial aid administrator. For graduate study, these programs include Federal Work-Study (FWS) and Perkins Loans.

Consolidated Loan Program Federal loan consolidation program enabling students to combine different types of federal loans to simplify repayment after graduation. The lender pays off the existing loans; the borrower then repays the consolidation loan. Borrowers have from ten to thirty years to repay it.

Cooperative Education Work-study arrangements in which the student receives academic credit for work outside the school. Students work full- or part-time as salaried employees for participating companies.

Cost of Attendance (COA) Also called Student Budget. The total amount it will cost a student to go to school, usually expressed in a yearly figure. The COA covers tuition and fees; housing; food; and allowances for books, supplies, transportation, loan fees, dependent care, costs related to a disability, and miscellaneous expenses. For part-time students, the COA does not include room and board.

Default Borrower's failure to repay a loan according to the terms agreed upon. Default may also result from failure to submit requests for deferment or cancellation on time. Borrowers in default may be subject to garnishment of wages, credit difficulties, and other penalties.

Endowments As pertaining to financial aid, the portion of private donations to schools that is administered by the financial aid office in the form of loans, grants, scholarships, and other awards.

Expected Family Contribution (EFC) For graduate students, the amount you and your spouse are expected to contribute to your educational costs. This figure is subtracted from the Cost of Attendance to determine your financial need. Factors such as taxable and nontaxable income, assets (such as savings and checking accounts), and benefits (such as unemployment and social security) are all considered in this calculation. If you're married, your spouse's contribution is also calculated. No student contribution is calculated for eligibility of unsubsidized Stafford Loans.

Federal Work-Study (FWS) Federal subsidy program that provides jobs for students with financial need, allowing them to earn money to pay educational expenses. The program encourages community service work and work related to student's course of study.

Fellowship An outright stipend usually awarded on a merit basis.

Financial Aid Financial assistance from government, institutional, and private sources given to supplement the student's family contribution.

Financial Aid Package The total amount of financial aid a student receives. Federal and nonfederal aid, such as scholarships, loans, or work-study, are

---

* Reprinted from Arco's *10 Minute Guide to Paying for Grad School* (Ellen Liichtenstein).

combined to help the student. One of the major responsibilities of a school's financial aid administrator is to use available resources to give each student the best possible package.

Financial Aid PROFILE Form from the College Scholarship Service (CSS). This form has replaced the CSS Financial Aid Form. Many schools use this needs-analysis form along with the Free Application for Financial Aid.

Forbearance Regarding the repayment of loans, forbearance means that the lender has agreed to let the borrower defer payments for a period of time. During this period of time, interest accrues on the loan. The act of forbearance is solely at the discretion of the lender.

Free Application for Federal Student Aid (FAFSA) Needs-analysis form required for obtaining all federal aid as well as state aid. Many schools use it as their only financial aid application form.

Grant Outright award usually awarded to students in particular fields of study.

Institution A postsecondary educational institution. The terms "institution" and "school" are used interchangeably.

Internship Work-study arrangement allowing students to gain practical experience through off-campus work with participating companies. In some instances, stipends are paid to the student by the outside organization.

Merit-Based Aid Outright awards, such as fellowships, grants, and scholarships, that may or may not have a work-related component. Much merit-based aid is determined by GRE scores.

Need Analysis Process of analyzing the financial information on the student's financial aid application and calculating the amount the family (student) can contribute to his or her educational costs.

Need-Based Aid Aid awarded on the basis of financial need usually determined by the government need formula: Cost of Attendance (COA) minus expected family contribution equals Student's Financial Need.

Origination Fee Loan process fee charged to borrower by lender, usually calculated as a percentage of the loan amount. On federal loans, this fee is deducted from the loan amount before the borrower receives the loan.

Outright Award Financial aid that does not have to be repaid. Loans are not outright awards.

Perkins Loan Federal low-interest loan to students with exceptional financial need. Federal Perkins Loans are administered through a school's financial aid office; the school is the lender and the loan is made with government funds. Borrowers must repay this loan.

Professional Judgment Authority of the financial aid administrator to make individual adjustments in determining financial need. For graduate students, the administrator is allowed to adjust the components of the student's Cost of Attendance (budget) and adjust the data elements used to calculate the Expected Family Contribution (EFC). These adjustments must be made on a case-by-case basis, and the adjustment reasons must be documented in the student's file.

Promissory Note The binding legal document a borrower signs to get a student loan. It lists both borrowing and repayment terms. It includes information about the loan's interest rate and about deferment and cancellation provisions.

State Guaranty Agency The state agency responsible for administering student loans. Telephone numbers of state agencies can be found by calling the Federal Student Aid Information Center at 800-433-3243.

Statement of Educational Purpose/Certification Statement on Refunds and Default Statement that must be signed by the borrowers to receive federal student aid. It signifies that the borrower does not owe a refund on a federal grant, is not in default on a federal loan, and that the amount borrowed does not exceed the allowable limits. Borrowers also agree to use their student aid only for education-related purposes.

Student Aid Report (SAR) Document received from the FAFSA processor about four weeks after submitting the original FAFSA form. The SAR must be carefully read and verified to ensure accuracy of all data.

Subsidized Stafford Loan (formerly Guaranteed Student Loan—GSL) Federally subsidized low-interest loans available to students who demonstrate financial need. The federal government pays interest on the loan until the borrower begins repayment and during authorized periods of loan deferment. Students do not begin repayment until after graduation.

Targeted Aid Both outright awards and loans from government, institutional, and private sources earmarked for specific groups of students. These special aid programs often aid minorities and women.

Unmet Need Portion of the financial aid package that the student is eligible to receive but that the school is unable to fund.

Unsubsidized Stafford Loan Federal loan not awarded on the basis of need. Interest is charged on the loan from the time the loan is disbursed until it's paid in full. Payment of interest and principal can be deferred while student is in school.

Verification Procedure used by the school financial aid office for verifying accuracy of the financial aid data filled out on the FAFSA and other financial aid applications. Students may be asked to fill out additional forms or submit additional documentation, such as tax returns and earnings statements. Some schools verify 100 percent of all financial aid applications; others do not.

Appendix I

State Student Financial Aid Offices*

Following are current addresses and phone numbers for each state's student financial aid office. (Puerto Rico and the Virgin Islands are also included.) Call the agency to find out about state financial aid programs, requirements for resident and nonresident students, and to obtain all application forms, deadline information, and the phone number of your state's Guaranty Agency (the entity responsible for student loans). Information on your state's Guaranty Agency can also be obtained from the Federal Student Aid Information Center at (800) 433-3243.

Alabama
Commission on Higher Education
100 North Union Street
P.O. Box 302000
Montgomery, AL 36130–2000
334-242-1998

Alaska
Commission on Postsecondary Education
3030 Vintage Boulevard
Juneau, AK 99801-7109
907-465-2962

Arizona
Commission for Postsecondary Education
2020 North Central Avenue, Suite 275
Phoenix, AZ 85004-4503
602-229-2591

Arkansas
Department of Higher Education
114 East Capitol Street
Little Rock, AR 72201
501-371-2000

California
Student Aid Commission
P.O. Box 419026
Rancho Cordova, CA 95741-9026
916-526-7590

Colorado
Commission on Higher Education
1300 Broadway, Second Floor
Denver, CO 80203
303-866-2723

---

* Reprinted from Arco's *10 Minute Guide to Paying for Grad School* (Ellen Liichtenstein).

Connecticut
Department of Education
61 Woodland Street
Hartford, CT 06105-2326
860-947-1855

Delaware
Commission on Higher Education
820 North French Street
Wilmington, DE 19801
302-577-6765

District of Columbia
Office of Postsecondary Education
2100 Martin Luther King, Jr. Avenue SE, Suite 401
Washington, DC 20020
202-727-3688

Florida
Office of Student Financial Aid Assistance
1344 Florida Education Center
325 West Gaines Street
Tallahassee, FL 32399
888-827-2004

Georgia
Student Finance Authority
2082 East Exchange Place, Suite 100
Tucker, GA 30084
770-724-9030

Hawaii
Postsecondary Education Commission
2444 Dole Street. Room 209
Honolulu, HI 96822-2394
808-956-8207

Idaho
State Board of Education
P.O. Box 83720
Boise, ID 83720-0037
208-334-2270

Illinois
Student Assistance Commission
1755 Lake Cook Road
Deerfield, IL 60015
800-899-4722

Indiana
State Student Assistance Commission
150 West Market Street, Suite 500
Indianapolis, IN 46204
317-232-2350

Iowa
College Student Aid Commission
200 10th Street, 4th Floor
Des Moines, IA 50309-3609
515-281-3501

Kansas
Board of Regents
700 SW Harrison, Suite 1410
Topeka, KS 66603-3760
785-296-3517

Kentucky
Higher Education Assistance Authority
1050 U.S. 127 South
Frankfort, KY 40601-4323
800-928-8926

Louisiana
Office of Student Financial Assistance
P.O. Box 91202
Baton Rouge, LA 70821-9202
800-259-5626 ext. 1012

Maine
Finance Authority of Maine
P.O. Box 949
Augusta, ME 04332-0949
207-288-3734

Maryland
Maryland Higher Education Commission
Jeffrey Building
16 Francis Street
Annapolis, MD 21401-1781
410-974-5370

Massachusetts
Board of Higher Education
Office of Student Financial Assistance
330 Stuart Street, 3rd Floor
Boston, MA 02116
617-727-1205

Michigan
Michigan Higher Education Assistance Authority
Office of Scholarships and Grants
P.O. Box 30462
Lansing, MI 48909-7962
517-373-3394

Minnesota
Higher Education Services Office
1450 Energy Park Drive, Suite 350
St. Paul, MN 55108-5227
651-642-0567

Mississippi
Postsecondary Education Financial Assistance Board
3825 Ridgewood Road
Jackson, MS 39211-6453
601-982-6663

Missouri
Student Assistance Resource Services
3515 Amazonas Drive
Jefferson City, MO 65109-5717
573-751-3940

Montana
Office of Commissioner of Higher Education
Montana Guaranteed Student Loan Program
P.O. Box 203101
Helena, MT 59620-3101
800-537-7508

Nebraska
Coordinating Commission for Postsecondary Education
P.O. Box 95005
Lincoln, NE 68509-5005
402-471-2847

Nevada
Department of Education
700 East Fifth Street
Carson City, NV 89701-5096
402-687-9200

New Hampshire
Postsecondary Education Commission
Two Industrial Park Drive
Concord, NH 03301-8512
603-271-2555

New Jersey
Higher Education Student Assistance Authority
P.O. Box 340
Trenton, NJ 08625
609-588-3316

New Mexico
Commission on Higher Education
1608 Cerrillos Road
Santa Fe, NM 87501
800-279-9777

New York
Higher Education Services Corporation
One Commerce Plaza
Albany, NY 12255
888-697-4372

North Carolina
Education Assistance Authority
P.O. Box 13663
Research Triangle Park, NC 27709-3663
800-700-1775

North Dakota
Student Financial Assistance Program
600 East Boulevard Avenue, Dept. 215
Bismarck, ND 58505-0230
701-328-4114

Ohio
Board of Regents
P.O. Box 182452
Columbus, OH 43218-2452
888-833-1133

Oklahoma
State Regents for Higher Education
500 Education Boulevard
Oklahoma City, OK 73105-4503
405-858-4356

Oregon
State Scholarship Commission
1500 Valley River Drive
Eugene, OR 97401-2130
800-452-8807

Pennsylvania
Higher Education Assistance Authority
1200 North Seventh Street
Harrisburg, PA 17102-1444
800-692-7435

Puerto Rico
Council on Higher Education
Fernandez Juncos Station
P.O. Box 19900
San Juan, PR 00910-1900
787-724-7100

Rhode Island
Higher Education Assistance Authority
560 Jefferson Boulevard
Warwick, RI 02886
401-736-1170

South Carolina
Higher Education Tuition Grants Commission
1310 Lady Street, Suite 801
Columbia, SC 29211
803-734-1200

South Dakota
Department of Education and Cultural Affairs
Office of the Secretary
700 Governors Drive
Pierre, SD 57501-2291
605-773-3134

Tennessee
Student Assistance Corporation
404 James Robertson Parkway, Suite 1950
Nashville, TN 37243
615-741-1346

Texas
Texas Higher Education Coordinating Board
P.O. Box 12788, Capitol Station
Austin, TX 78711
800-242-3062

Utah
State Board of Regents
355 West North Temple
3 Triad Center, Suite 550
Salt Lake City, UT 84180-1205
801-321-7200

Vermont
Student Assistance Corporation
P.O. Box 2000
Winooski, VT 05404-2601
800-642-3177

Virginia
State Council of Higher Education
101 North 14th Street
Richmond, VA 23219-3684
804-786-1690

Virgin Islands
Joint Boards of Education
Charlotte Amelie
P.O. Box 11900
St. Thomas, VI 00801
340-774-4546

Washington
Higher Education Coordinating Board
917 Lakeridge Way
Olympia, WA 98501-3430
360-753-7850

West Virginia
State College and University Systems Central Office
1018 Lanawha Boulevard East, Suite 700
Charleston, WV 25301-2827
304-558-4016

Wisconsin
Higher Education Aids Board
P.O. Box 7885
Madison, WI 53707-7885
608-267-2944

Wyoming
Wyoming Community College Commission
2020 Carey Avenue, 8th Floor
Cheyenne, WY 82002
307-777-7763

NOTES

NOTES

NOTES

NOTES

NOTES

NOTES

NOTES

NOTES

NOTES

NOTES

NOTES